# Brief Contents

**Note:** This custom edition of *The Bedford Book of Genres* for Middle Tennessee State University includes issues from *Understanding Rhetoric*. As a result, pagination is not sequential.

## GUIDE

# the Bedford Book of Genres

## for Middle Tennessee State University

with issues from *Understanding Rhetoric*

**Amy Braziller**
Red Rocks Community College

**Elizabeth Kleinfeld**
Metropolitan State College of Denver

macmillan learning
curriculum solutions

bedford/st.martin's ▪ hayden-mcneil ▪ w.h. freeman ▪ worth publishers

Manufactured in the United States of America.

2   1   0   9   8   7
f    e    d    c

*For information, write:* Macmillan Learning Curriculum Solutions, 14903 Pilot Drive, Plymouth, MI 48170   (macmillanlearning.com)

ISBN 978-1-319-14823-2 (Middle Tennessee State University edition)

**Acknowledgments**

Acknowledgments and copyrights appear on the same page as the text and art selections they cover; these acknowledgments and copyrights constitute an extension of the copyright page. It is a violation of the law to reproduce these selections by any means whatsoever without the written permission of the copyright holder.

# Preface for Middle Tennessee State University

On behalf of the English Department at Middle Tennessee State University, welcome to Composition! This two-semester, first-year composition sequence is part of the required general education study at the university. Maybe in the past, you've had that wonderful feeling of the perfect words coming to you at the right time as you wrote the perfect paper. Maybe you've watched a paper develop through different stages and had the satisfaction of revision. But maybe in the past, you've been told that you're a poor writer. Maybe you have struggled with developing the right response to a writing situation. Who hasn't? The key is how we allow these experiences to teach us something about writing so we can transfer that knowledge to other academic, professional, and personal writing situations. In the broadest sense, learning how to approach writing situations effectively and how to make the most of our writing experiences is the purpose of the general education writing courses.

The composition sequence is particularly important in predicting student achievement at MTSU. According to Dr. Rick Sluder, Vice Provost for Student Success at MTSU, "Seventy-eight per-cent of students who earn an A in the course graduate." One of the most important keys for success in these courses—and thus for your development as a writer outside of the classroom—is to adopt a growth mindset by embracing areas of difficulty instead of turning away from challenges. English studies scholar Kelly Gallagher believes that confusion leads to learning. Ultimately, what sets successful readers and writers apart is not some innate ability, but rather the willingness to acknowledge confusion and then persevere until they understand.

As you begin the sequence, consider: What matters to you as a student? What do you want to take away from these courses? We look forward to supporting you in meeting your goals.

Wishing you a successful year.

*Julie M. Barger*

**Dr. Julie Myatt Barger**
Associate Professor of English
Co-Director of General Education
English

*Kate Pantelides*

**Dr. Kate Pantelides**
Assistant Professor of English
Co-Director of General Education
English

# Composition Learning Objectives

The learning objectives found on pages vi–viii are the foundation for the composition sequence. Composition I, Literacy For Life, (the ENGL 1010 course) focuses on writing processes, ensuring that students are flexible, rhetorical writers. Students practice primary research and writing in different **genres**, or types of writing situations. They are invited to consider each **rhetorical situation**, or the context in which writing develops. Instead of preparing students for all of the writing they will encounter in their academic and professional lives (which unfortunately isn't possible!), the course draws attention to the questions we should ask when composing and the conventions of different genres. Composition II, Research and Argumentative Writing, (the ENGL 1020 course) builds on the Composition I foundation, extending attention to *genre*, *rhetoric*, and *convention* specifically into the realm of secondary research. In this course, students are invited to ask unique, critical questions, find answers to those questions, and compose projects that share these findings with an audience. The learning objectives outlined on pages vii–viii demonstrate the differences between the two courses, as well as their relationship to each other.

## LEARNING OBJECTIVES First-Year Writing

| ENGL 1010 Objectives | Program Outcomes | ENGL 1020 OBJECTIVES |
|---|---|---|
| conduct primary research; make appropriate decisions about content, form, and presentation | *Composing Processes* | conduct secondary research; demonstrate recursive relationships between reading, writing, research, and reflection |
| examine literacies across contexts; read and analyze various types of text—print, digital, and audio | *Reading* | interpret and respond to complex ideas in sources; identify and contribute to critical conversations |
| develop genre awareness and practice genre analysis; complete writing tasks that require understanding of the rhetorical situation | *Rhetorical Knowledge* | identify and address appropriate audiences and contexts; demonstrate flexibility and awareness of effective delivery within different genres |
| reflect on literacy in student lives; develop a writing theory that can transfer to writing situations in other classes and professions | *Integrative Thinking* | identify connections between coursework and other academic and external contexts |
| learn about discourse communities; demonstrate understanding of ethical primary research practices | *Information Literacy* | locate sources and analyze their relevance and credibility; demonstrate rhetorical understanding of source attribution |

*First-Year Writing learning objectives map to TBR course outcomes.

| Program Outcomes | ENGL 1010 Objectives | ENGL 1010 Key Concepts |
| --- | --- | --- |
| *Composing Processes* | conduct primary research; make appropriate decisions about content, form, and presentation | genre analysis, primary research, multimodality |
| *Reading* | examine literacies across contexts; read and analyze various types of text—print, digital, and audio | recursive/reflexive reading, reading strategies, annotation |
| *Rhetorical Knowledge* | develop genre awareness and practice genre analysis; complete writing tasks that require understanding of the rhetorical situation | rhetorical situation, genre convention and deviation, genre affordances and constraints |
| *Integrative Thinking* | reflect on literacy in student lives; develop a writing theory that can transfer to writing situations in other classes and professions | habits of mind, metacognition, backward-reaching transfer |
| *Information Literacy* | learn about discourse communities; demonstrate understanding of ethical primary research practices | research ethics, discourse community, campus resources |

## Cultivating Habits of the Mind

Informed by current writing-studies research as well as by concerns that the writing experiences of today's students are limited by widespread emphasis on standardized testing, the "Framework for Success in Postsecondary Writing," developed by the Council of Writing Program Administrators, the National Council of Teachers of English, and the National Writing Project, identifies the orientation toward education that students need to embrace in order to succeed in college and beyond. This document calls on educators, parents, policymakers, and students to recognize the benefits of assignments that demand rhetorical (rather than formulaic) approaches to writing. The document's authors contend that "[s]tudents who come to college writing with these habits of mind and these experiences will be well positioned to meet the writing challenges in the full spectrum of academic courses and later in their careers" (Council of Writing Program 2). Refer to the habits of mind on pages viii–ix to identify specific behaviors you might cultivate this academic year.

| Program Outcomes | ENGL 1020 Objectives | ENGL 1020 Key Concepts |
| --- | --- | --- |
| *Composing Processes* | conduct secondary research; demonstrate recursive relationships between reading, writing, research, and reflection | rhetorical analysis, secondary research, writing across genres |
| *Reading* | interpret and respond to complex ideas in sources; identify and contribute to critical conversations | self-directed reading, critical reading, source analysis |
| *Rhetorical Knowledge* | identify and address appropriate audiences and contexts; demonstrate flexibility and awareness of effective delivery within different genres | rhetorical appeals, *kairos*, delivery |
| *Integrative Thinking* | identify connections between coursework and other academic and external contexts | experimentation, metalanguage, forward-reaching transfer |
| *Information Literacy* | locate sources and analyze their relevance and credibility; demonstrate rhetorical understanding of source attribution | ethical source use, public audiences, research integration |

When combined with the learning experiences in your first-year composition class, your attention to these habits of mind will help you leave the first-year composition course equipped to address the kinds of writing you will encounter as a student and professional.

**Habits of mind** refers to ways of approaching learning that are both intellectual and practical and that will support students' success in a variety of fields and disciplines. The Framework identifies eight habits of mind essential for success in college writing:

» *Curiosity*—the desire to know more about the world.

» *Openness*—the willingness to consider new ways of being and thinking about the world.

» *Engagement*—a sense of investment and involvement in learning.

» *Creativity*—the ability to use novel approaches for generating, investigating, and representing ideas.

» *Persistence*—the ability to sustain interest in and attention to short- and long-term projects.

» *Responsibility*—the ability to take ownership of one's actions and understand the consequences of those actions for oneself and others.

» *Flexibility*—the ability to adapt to situations, expectations, or demands.

» *Metacognition*—the ability to reflect on one's own thinking as well as on the individual and cultural processes used to structure knowledge.

## How to Succeed in Composition and Beyond

Whether you have been in college for a few semesters or whether this is your first semester, revisiting patterns reflected in the habits of successful students often serves as a helpful reminder of specific behaviors that lead to positive learning experiences. We consider the following list of recommendations to be generally consistent with habits we have observed among successful students in first-year composition and in the university more generally.

### Know What to Expect

Your first-year composition instructor will:

» allow you to write often, in a variety of forms, and for diverse purposes;

» value your ideas and allow you to pursue issues you consider worthwhile;

» foster a classroom community of writers;

» help you recognize the value of writing, whether only for yourself or for an audience;

» motivate you to write by offering constructive feedback;

» challenge you to try your hardest and offer support for these efforts; and

» help you learn to think like a writer, remember your readers, and recognize the resources available to you so that you can approach communication strategically, both now and in the future.

### Read Your Syllabus

No, *really*, read it. Read it on the first day of class. Read it a second time carefully and completely by the end of the first week of class. Why should you read it more than once? The syllabus is the primary framing document for the entire semester. In fact, we would even go so far as to encourage you to read the syllabus thoroughly again at the end of the fourth week of classes and yet another time around the middle of the semester. Get to know the syllabus well. Office hours, contact information, important due dates, and specific policies are all outlined within a course syllabus. When in doubt, consult the syllabus. When you have questions about the syllabus, ask your instructor.

### Attend Class

Consistent, on-time attendance is essential to your success in first-year writing and in college. Those who show up and who show up on time are far more likely to have a grasp on pacing and workload related to a project, on the expectations of the instructor, and on the activities that reinforce key approaches to the gradual build-up of the class. In-class time cannot be reconstructed or made up. And, above all, learning in discourse communities requires more than just your physical presence; it demands active engagement. That is, communities cease to work in quite the same way when you are away or when you are completing tasks independently of the classroom interactions with your peers and your instructor.

### E-mail with Care

Frequent access to your MTMail account matters for your prospective success at MTSU. Please check your e-mail account daily throughout the semester. Course changes, updates and announcements, and other campus information will reach you primarily via e-mail. It is fine if you have another e-mail account, but, in such cases, you should either have your e-mail forwarded to the personal account or check MTMail frequently. Be mindful when you send e-mails, and consider your audience. Compose concise, formal messages when sending e-mail to instructors.

Your instructor considers your e-mail message important and will respond to e-mails within a reasonable and appropriate amount of time, but make sure you've composed responsible, complete e-mails. As a general rule, allow 24–48 hours for a response, not including weekends. If more than four days pass without a response, consider following up with a second message to reiterate your question, or seek your instructor out during office hours.

## Bring Your Books

Bring your books to class daily. They are cornerstones of the curriculum, and as such, successful students will interact with them frequently, both in and out of class. *The Bedford Book of Genres* is a book that provides practical guidelines for many aspects of writing. We believe it to be a resource that will serve you well in *all* of your college classes.

## Check Your Electronic Devices

Mobile technologies, such as smartphones, laptops, and tablets, are easy to carry in and out of classes. When used *responsibly*, they can be powerful complements to annotation and Web-based look-ups (e.g., of definitions or reference materials), and they can provide ready access to supplemental readings available as PDFs or on the Web. But these technologies can oftentimes distract you. With this in mind, we urge you to heed your own habits of interacting with electronic devices as well as to know and honor the specific policies set in place by your instructor. Most classes include a managed-use policy in the syllabus. If you have any doubts about whether you are using a mobile technology responsibly, ask your instructor. All of this is to say that successful students pause and check their use of devices in classes. You should, too. One digital tool to consider using is the MTSU Mobile app, which enables you to access Pipeline, check D2L, and search Walker Library's databases from your mobile device.

## Keep All of Your Work

Reflecting on your continued development as a writer depends upon your keeping all copies of your work throughout the semester. Keep drafts, annotated copies, daily homework, and in-class writing. Keep everything. Gather your work in a folder, and keep it organized. Keeping track of your writing in this way applies to digital copies, too. It is a good idea to back up your work, and there are several free and easy ways to do so using cloud-based services, such as D2L ePortfolio, Google Drive, or Dropbox. There are also inexpensive alternatives to the cloud, such as a USB drive. Lost or misplaced work can be a serious setback, one we hope you don't experience. Taking a few steps to gather and back up your work systematically will prove exceedingly helpful when major projects are due and again at the end of the semester.

## Manage Your Time

Time is slippery, especially during your first year of college. Although it is easy to overlook a due date, it is never acceptable, and missing a deadline for one draft can make it difficult to get an entire project back on track. Plan accordingly. Successful students keep calendars or planners. They enter reminders into scheduling systems, such as Google Calendar. They plan ahead. They reread the assignment sheet and schedule so they know what is expected of them and when an assignment is due. College is challenging enough without discovering deadlines at the last minute and scrambling to meet them. Because we want you to be successful, we want you to understand that time management is vital to your success.

## Sleep

The first year of college can be exciting, especially in the Boro with so many fun goings-on. Activity and noise might seem a constant, and it is easy to make trade-offs, such as staying up late for a Netflix marathon (because it is fun!). But you need rest. Your success in college this year and beyond depends upon sufficient rest. The importance of getting enough rest may seem obvious, but *seriously*, sleep. Yawning frequently or putting your head down in class is never okay. Writing can be challenging, but all coursework can seem insurmountable without sleep. Make sure to take at least 6–8 hours every night to recharge. Your well-being requires this much rest. And your success in college and in the first-year composition sequence is nearly impossible without it.

## Know Your Peers

Many of your peers are making the same adjustments to college that you are. Peer interaction is a substantial part of any writing class. Learning and writing are social acts, and small classes make it all the more likely that you will interact with and learn the names of several of your classmates. We encourage you to actively get to know your peers because we think you have a lot to learn from each other.

Consider exchanging contact information with a few of your classmates so that if you happen to miss a class or if you think some conversation about how to approach a project would be useful to you, you have a way of connecting. Writing is a thoroughly social process. Setting up study sessions or writing days with your peers helps, especially if you are feeling unsure or tentative about a project or how to approach it.

## Visit the Margaret H. Ordoubadian University Writing Center

Do you ever sit, staring at a blank page or screen, willing your draft to write itself and wishing you could just talk to someone about what you are working on? Well, that is where the University Writing Center comes in. *All* writers, whether struggling with compositions or sailing through them with apparent ease, benefit from having constructive conversations about a work-in-progress. University Writing Center consultants are trained, thoughtful, careful readers and listeners. They don't judge your work; they simply respond to your text as a reader would and provide supportive and appropriate recommendations. They can also meet your multiliteracy and digital media needs, so don't hesitate to take that class presentation project to the UWC. Writing Center sessions are most helpful when they happen well in advance of a due date, so don't wait until your deadline is looming to visit. For more information about the University Writing Center, visit **mtsu.edu/writing-center**. Appointments can be made online, and walk-in appointments are available only if a tutor is available.

## Talk to Your Instructor

Because composition classes are small, not only do instructors know your name, but they also care if you're in class, if you're feeling unsure about course material, and if you write something sophisticated and challenging. Instructors are your *primary* resource in composition courses, so take them up on their office hours, visit them, and ask questions. Getting individual feedback is one of the best ways to improve your writing, so ask your instructor specific, focused questions about your work, and make sure that you fully understand what is required for success on each course project.

## Have Academic Integrity

It should go without saying (but here it is *said*) that academic integrity is a central, shared value across our university community. And in your classroom community, trust is central to the success of the course. All composition classes will include a statement about academic integrity in the course syllabus, and the department stands behind the university's policy on academic integrity. If you feel confused or overwhelmed by work in the classroom, talk with your instructors and peers, and make use of the numerous student resources available on campus. Plagiarizing work or disregarding the university's Student Conduct Code is never an effective answer, and frequently, violating the code can result in serious consequences. Take late points. Visit the counseling center. Ask for help before you feel stuck.

## Be Mindful of the Importance of Self-Care

It can be very easy to get wrapped up in the busyness of college and coursework and forget to take care of yourself. Make sure to exercise self-care throughout the semester. What self-care looks like can vary from person to person: You can take a walk, enjoy a nice meal, spend time with friends, practice yoga or play sports, or even do something creative. The goal of self-care is to take a break and de-stress when necessary. By taking time to rest, you are enabling yourself to recharge, re-group, and reengage with your coursework and your studies. Taking breaks and allowing your mind to rest will set you up to be a more successful student and help prevent burnout.

# What Happens in a Composition Class?

## Discussion and Participation

Writing is a social process. Learning to write is underpinned by discussion and participation. By interacting with your classmates and your instructor this way, you are learning how to respond constructively to writing done by others as well as how to accept feedback on your own ideas and your own writing. Each instructor will have different policies regarding discussion and participation, but you can expect that all sections of composition will feature discussion and participation as a component of the in-class experience.

## Feedback and Interaction

Writing improves through a process of sharing your work with other readers and taking their genuine responses into consideration. Throughout the semester, you will receive numerous comments, suggestions, and questions from your classmates, your instructor, and if you visit the University Writing Center, writing consultants. All of this feedback is invaluable to you, and you will have decisions to make as a result. Should I rearrange a section, moving it closer to the beginning? Should I cut this paragraph? How can I rewrite this sentence so it is clearer? Is my title both descriptive and attention-getting? Revising according to responses from invested readers is a tremendously important factor in effective communication practices.

## Peer Review

Peer review goes hand in hand with feedback and interaction. Such review is a structured interaction, either in class or online, and it is one in which readers respond to a draft according to a series of specific questions or prompts. You will receive valuable feedback from the peer review process in first-year composition, and you will gain experience as a reviewer first by reading and then by writing responses to your classmates. By reading another's project draft, you can also gain insights about the decisions you have made. Remember, good peer review feels like an engaged, energetic conversation about your ideas. And, like any conversation about ideas, there are elements that you will agree with and want to incorporate into your work and elements that won't be as helpful for your project. So, filter. In the end, you're the author, so you have to feel comfortable with and have ownership of the final product.

## Reading

At first, you may be surprised by the amount of reading you will complete for your first-year composition courses. You should expect to frequently read and respond to readings both in and out of class. Learning more about how you—and others—read and respond to texts will help you become a more informed and engaging writer. Your instructor will provide you the opportunity to:

» experiment with a variety of reading strategies, including rereading;

» discuss your reactions to readings with others—and hear others' reactions to those same readings;

» reflect on your reading experiences;

» consider the relationship between reading and writing;

» analyze real-world informational texts serving as models for your own writing;

» practice performing different reader/writer identities; and

» share your writing with audiences beyond the classroom.

These practices are essential in helping you apply your developing *rhetorical awareness* of your own writing. Each occasion for writing is unique, and because there's no one-size-fits-all approach, you need to learn the kinds of questions you should ask of the diverse writing situations you will encounter beyond the first-year composition classroom. Writing scholar Irene Clark explains that a writing assignment—and, we would add, any impetus for writing—serves as "an invitation, not a set of specific instructions. Understanding what is involved in responding to that invitation appropriately will enable you to participate in the performance more successfully" (Clark). Remember that all writing, including your own, is the product of informed choices. You, too, can craft effective writings, and critical, rhetorical reading is central to being able to accurately interpret the context of and adopt a role appropriate for that particular performance.

## Reflection

Reflection names the conscious effort to look back at what has happened and to think about your approach, how you have done what you have done, and how you think and feel about that approach. In composition classes, you will be asked frequently to reflect on your writing. The primary purpose of such reflections is to encourage conscious, deliberate decision-making in your compositions, particularly as they relate to audience, purpose, and context. Writing about your choices makes you more fully aware of the decisions you seem to make unconsciously. In the long term, reflection helps you become a writer who notices subtleties and nuances—the small differences that make writing effective in a specific situation. Reflective-writing practice helps you become a more flexible, adaptable, successful writer in other classes and outside of the classroom.

# University Resources

## The Library

The James E. Walker Library is located on the southeast side of campus, across from the Business and Aerospace Building. There, you can check out books and periodicals, reserve group-study rooms, complete class assignments on one of the many computers, print documents for class, utilize study spaces, and get research help from the reference librarians. Around thirty thousand people visit the library every week to make use of available resources, including the newly renovated Research Commons and the Digital Media Studio. Visit the library's Web site for a complete list of services: **library.mtsu.edu**.

## Counseling Services

Handling the stresses of college life and dealing with personal problems can be difficult, and talking to a trained professional can sometimes be beneficial to your academic success and overall well-being. MTSU's Counseling Services, located in KUC 326-S, provides confidential counseling sessions and can help with a variety of issues, including grief, post-traumatic stress disorder, and personal crises. Counseling services are free to students, and you can make an appointment by either stopping by the office or calling (615) 808–2670. For more information, and to find free mental health self-assessments, you can visit the center's Web site at **mtsu.edu/countest**.

## Disability and Access Center

If physical, mental, or emotional difficulties are interfering with your ability to be an effective and confident student, you might want to consider registering with the Disability and Access Center, located in KUC 107. If you had student accommodations as a high school student, you should consider registering with DAC as well, insofar as these accommodations do not automatically transfer to college. There is no shame in registering with DAC—receiving the accommodations you need is simply a way to help level the academic playing field and help you be a successful student.

To register:

» First, you will need to complete and submit an application. (You can find and submit an application online at **mtsu.edu/dac**.)

» Next, you will need to submit medical documentation verifying your diagnosis(es). This submission must be formal documentation that is typed on letterhead and signed by a medical professional. You cannot submit school records (such as an Individualized Education Plan [IEP] or a 504 plan) as proof of diagnosis(es). You can fax documents to (615) 898-4893, e-mail them to **dacemail@mtsu.edu**, or mail or hand-deliver the medical documentation to the DAC office.

» Wait to be contacted by the DAC office for an appointment. If you have not been contacted within a week, the DAC office invites you to call.

» Attend the appointment, during which you and a representative from the office will talk about the kinds of accommodations you can receive to help your growth as a student.

Once you receive accommodations from the DAC, you *must* provide your instructors with a copy as soon as possible. Accommodations only go into effect once the instructor is notified; they cannot be applied retroactively. You and your instructor should have a conversation about how to best implement your accommodations in your course.

## MTSU Veterans and Military Family Center

If you are a current military member, a veteran, or a military family member, the MTSU Veterans and Military Family Center can assist you in transitioning to college life and from college to a career. Located in KUC 124, MTSU's Veterans' Center can help student veterans apply for GI Bill benefits, can provide academic advising, and can even serve as a study space. For more information, you can contact the center's director, Dr. Hilary Miller, at hilary.miller@mtsu.edu or the senior advisor, Lt. Gen. Keith M. Huber, at keith.huber@mtsu.edu. You can also contact the office directly by visiting in person or by e-mailing **mtsuveterans@mtsu.edu**.

## TRiO Student Support Services

If you are a first-generation college student, are registered with the Disability and Access Center, or meet federal income guidelines, you are eligible for TRiO Student Support Services. The TRiO Student Support Services office is located in KUC 308, and you can either call the center at (615) 898–5443 or e-mail **ssupport @mtsu.edu**. By registering with the TRiO office, you can receive financial advising, free tutoring, mentoring and career counseling, and other services. For more information and to find an application form, you can visit the center at **mtsu.edu /ssupport**.

## June Anderson Center for Women and Nontraditional Students

Located in SUB 330, the June Anderson Center provides services such as legal clinics, professional development, networking opportunities, and scholarships for women and adult learners. The June Anderson Center also serves to connect adult learners and women to existing campus resources, such as research coaching, that they might not otherwise know about. To find more information about the June Anderson Center, stop by the office, call (615) 898–5812, e-mail jacwns@mtsu .edu, or visit the Web site at **mtsu.edu/jac**.

## Intercultural and Diversity Affairs

If you are interested in promoting cultural awareness and a greater sense of community and understanding, you should contact the Office of Intercultural and Diversity Affairs. Located in SUB 330, Intercultural and Diversity Affairs provides a variety of services for ethnic minority students, including tutoring, scholarships, career planning, financial advice, personal counseling, and housing. The Intercultural and Diversity Affairs office can also provide information on a wide variety of student interest groups, and this information showcases the ethnic, religious, and cultural diversity present here at MTSU. Throughout the semester, Intercultural and Diversity Affairs hosts a variety of cultural and social events that are open to all students regardless of background. You can find more information by calling (615) 898–5812, e-mailing ida@mtsu.edu, or visiting the Web site at **mtsu.edu/idac**.

## English Department Faculty

If you have questions or concerns, or if you would like additional information about your instructor, please see his or her profile page on the English department Web site: **mtsu.edu/english**. Click on your instructor's name to access information such as office hours, office location, and current courses. Additionally, your instructor has a mailbox located in Peck Hall 303.

If you have would like additional information about MTSU's First-Year Composition sequence, please contact:

**Dr. Julie Myatt Barger and Dr. Kate Pantelides**
Peck Hall 324 (on the blue hallway)
julie.barger@mtsu.edu, kate.pantelides@mtsu.edu

## Debunking Myths about Majoring in English

It's no secret that majoring in English has gotten a bad rap as of late. Telling someone that you're majoring in English and planning to get a great job after graduation has become the equivalent of planning to be a professional athlete or a pop star. But wait. Data show that this just isn't true. If you enjoy your composition courses and think that you might want more, there are lots of reasons to pursue a major in English, and there

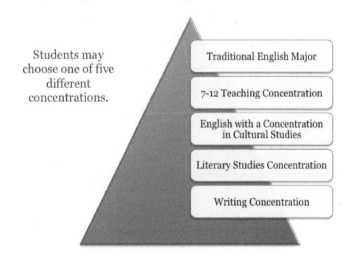

**The English Program at MTSU**

Students may choose one of five different concentrations.

- Traditional English Major
- 7-12 Teaching Concentration
- English with a Concentration in Cultural Studies
- Literary Studies Concentration
- Writing Concentration

## ENGLISH MAJOR EXPERIENCE

### What It's Like to Be an English Major

» The major consists of 32–39 hours out of the 120 required for the BA. Students have more than 100 courses in the English major to choose from.

» Upon declaring English their major, students are matched with a faculty advisor with whom they work closely throughout their tenure as MTSU students.

» English classes are small (15–25 students, typically), so students and teachers get to know each other and work collaboratively.

» Students have the opportunity to participate in seminars, lecture-discussion classes, internships, study abroad offerings, and online classes.

» Students study more than words on a page. English majors are invited to read and respond to diverse texts, films, images, and audio recordings.

» Peck Hall is located on the historic side of campus, and students often carry conversations from the classroom out into the shade of Walnut Grove.

are lots of empirical studies that prove that a major in the liberal arts paves the way for success after graduation.

Although most students who graduate with degrees in the liberal arts initially make lower salaries, most retire with salaries $2,000 above their peers from professional and preprofessional majors. Furthermore, fewer liberal arts majors are unemployed, and many go into so-called helping or service careers that may not have traditionally high salaries; but employees in these fields report being happier than peers in other fields noted for high salaries.

Locally, employers are less concerned with specific majors and more interested in an individual's ability to make independent decisions, communicate effectively, and be a leader. A recent study of businesses that have hired MTSU graduates demonstrates that having these intangibles—namely, the critical thinking and communication skills that majoring in English teaches—is the difference between getting a job or not, and then, being successful at that job or not. By exploring avenues of inquiry that support their growth as readers, writers, and thinkers, English majors develop their abilities to compete in a market that is, as scholars such as Deborah Brandt remind us, characterized by changing workplace literacies.

WORKS CITED

Clark, Irene. "A Genre Approach to Writing Assignments." *Composition Forum*, vol. 1, no. 2, Fall 2005, compositionforum.com/issue/14.2/clark-genre-writing.php.

"Framework for Success in Postsecondary Writing." *Council of Writing Program Administrators*, Jan. 2011, wpacouncil.org/files/framework-for-success-postsecondary-writing.pdf.

# Brief Contents

**Note:** This custom edition of *The Bedford Book of Genres* for Middle Tennessee State University includes issues from *Understanding Rhetoric*. As a result, pagination is not sequential.

# Contents

## 2   Narrative Genres   38

## 3 Informative Genres  87

e For e-Pages content, visit **bedfordstmartins.com/bookofgenres**.

# 7   Integrating & Documenting Sources   366

## 10   Assembling a Multigenre Project   501

# Guide

Issue 1 • Why Rhetoric?

# IS THAT A RHETORICAL QUESTION?!!

HMF.

SOME PEOPLE CALL A QUESTION **"RHETORICAL"** BECAUSE NO ANSWER IS ACTUALLY EXPECTED.

DO I LOOK **STUPID** TO YOU?

ACCORDING TO THEM, RHETORIC AND RHETORICAL ARE ALL ABOUT **SHUTTING DOWN** CONVERSATION AND DEBATE!

BUT I--

ACTUALLY, THE ANCIENTS DEVELOPED THE CONCEPT OF **RHETORIC** TO **FACILITATE** DISCUSSION.

THEY THOUGHT THAT RHETORIC PROVIDED A SET OF SKILLS THAT HELPED PEOPLE FOREGROUND IDEAS --

-- DISCUSS AND DEBATE THEIR THOUGHTS WITH OTHERS --

-- AND POTENTIALLY REACH COMMON GOALS OR MAKE DIFFICULT DECISIONS.

## REANIMATING ANCIENT VIEWS OF RHETORIC

MANY COMMONLY HELD NEGATIVE IDEAS ABOUT RHETORIC CAN BE TRACED TO THE ANCIENT GREEK PHILOSOPHER **PLATO.**

HE BELIEVED THAT TEACHERS LIKE US WHO TAUGHT RHETORIC WERE INSTRUCTING THEIR STUDENTS TO DECEIVE OTHERS RATHER THAN TO BETTER THEMSELVES.

IF SERIOUS DISCUSSION IS LIKE GYMNASTICS, THEN RHETORIC IS LIKE **COSMETICS.**

RHETORIC IS INTENDED ONLY TO HIDE FLAWS, NOT ENCOURAGE SELF-IMPROVEMENT.

**PLATO** (427–347 BCE)
ANCIENT GREEK PHILOSOPHER, STUDENT OF SOCRATES, AND FOUNDER OF THE ATHENIAN ACADEMY, AN IMPORTANT EARLY SCHOOL OF THOUGHT.

AS FAR AS PLATO WAS CONCERNED, RHETORIC WAS AN EMPTY, UNWHOLESOME DISTRACTION THAT TOOK ATTENTION AWAY FROM IMPORTANT PHILOSOPHICAL AND CIVIC MATTERS.

INDULGING THE POPULATION'S APPETITE FOR RHETORIC IS AS BAD AS SELLING **PASTRIES** INSTEAD OF DISPENSING **MEDICINE.**

PLATO ALSO THOUGHT THAT VIVID MEDIA EXPERIENCES, SUCH AS ANCIENT GREEK TRAGEDIES THAT SHOWED EXPLICIT SEX AND VIOLENCE, WOULD HAVE A BAD INFLUENCE ON YOUNG PEOPLE.

ALL POETS AND PLAYWRIGHTS SHOULD BE **BANISHED!**

PLATO FELT THAT THE YOUNG SHOULD BE PROTECTED FROM AMBIGUOUS MORAL MESSAGES.

PRETENDING TO BE CRIMINALS CAUSES CHILDREN TO GROW UP TO BE CRIMINALS IN REAL LIFE. EVERYONE KNOWS THAT.

PLATO WASN'T JUST WORRIED ABOUT CHILDREN. HE BELIEVED THAT THE INVENTION OF WRITING IN THE ANCIENT WORLD ALLOWED ADULTS TO LIE ABOUT THE TRUTH, PRETEND TO BE SOMEONE THEY WERE NOT, OR FORGET THE PAST AND TRADITION.

JUST AS PEOPLE WORRY TODAY ABOUT MANY OF THE EFFECTS OF TECHNOLOGY ON WRITING, PLATO WORRIED ABOUT THE EFFECT OF WRITING ON OUR ABILITY TO SPEAK THE TRUTH.

eHarmonium

Please Describe Yourself:
(Be ACCURATE!)
NAME: STUDICUS MAXIMUS
HAIR: FLOWING
HYGIENE: IMPECCABLE
DENTAL ISSUES: NONE
OCCUPATION: MODEL

THINGS WERE SURE A LOT BETTER BEFORE WE HAD WRITING!

PLATO'S STUDENT **ARISTOTLE** HAD A VERY DIFFERENT VIEW ABOUT WRITING AND RHETORIC.

PLATO

ARISTOTLE

**ARISTOTLE** WAS A PROPONENT OF THE USE OF RHETORIC TO PUT ACROSS A BROAD RANGE OF IDEAS.

ARISTOTLE (384–322 BCE)
ANCIENT GREEK PHILOSOPHER (AND STUDENT OF PLATO) WHOSE THINKING CONTRIBUTED MUCH TO THE DEVELOPMENT OF WESTERN EMPIRICAL AND SCIENTIFIC THOUGHT.

ARISTOTLE THOUGHT THAT PLAYS COULD SERVE AN **EDUCATIONAL** PURPOSE BY ENCOURAGING GREEK CITIZENS TO DEVELOP THEIR CAPACITIES FOR PITY AND FEAR.

BY SEEING THE CONSEQUENCES OF SEXUAL AND VIOLENT CRIMES THAT WERE COMMITTED BY ACTORS ON STAGE, SPECTATORS COULD LEARN **NOT** TO IMITATE **BAD ACTIONS.**

ARISTOTLE **DISAGREED** WITH HIS TEACHER ABOUT RHETORIC.

WHILE PLATO THOUGHT THAT RHETORIC WAS PART OF A FALSE WORLD OF APPEARANCES, ARISTOTLE CONSIDERED RHETORIC TO BE ONE OF THE FOUNDATIONS OF EDUCATION.

THIS DEVELOPMENT OF RHETORIC COINCIDES WITH THE BIRTH OF **DEMOCRACY** IN ANCIENT GREECE.

IF A SOCIETY IS TO THRIVE **DEMOCRATICALLY**, A NUMBER OF VIEWPOINTS AND OPINIONS NEED TO BE AIRED, DISCUSSED, DEBATED, AND EVENTUALLY **VOTED ON.**

EVEN NOW, UNDERSTANDING RHETORIC --

-- BOTH AS A **CONCEPT** AND AS AN **ACTIVITY**, LIKE TALKING AND VOTING --

-- IS CENTRAL TO PARTICIPATION IN THE DEMOCRATIC PROCESS.

IN *THE ART OF RHETORIC,*

# ETHOS

IS THE CREDIBILITY THAT A SPEAKER OR WRITER BRINGS TO THE SUBJECT THAT HE OR SHE IS COMMUNICATING ABOUT.

WE TRUST CERTAIN KINDS OF PEOPLE MORE THAN OTHERS -- BECAUSE THEY HAVE EXPERTISE, OR BECAUSE THEY ARE WELL INFORMED ABOUT THE SUBJECT AT HAND.

# PATHOS

IS THE USE OF EMOTION IN DEBATE OR ARGUMENT.

APPEALS TO PATHOS SURROUND US, PARTICULARLY IN VISUAL ARGUMENTS SUCH AS ADVERTISEMENTS AND MANY ONLINE VIDEOS.

# LOGOS

IS THE APPEAL TO REASON, TO THE FORCEFULNESS OF A WELL-THOUGHT-OUT AND WELL-STRUCTURED POSITION.

SOME ARGUMENTS MAKE MORE **LOGICAL** SENSE THAN OTHERS, AND MANY CONSIDER LOGOS TO BE CRITICAL IN THE DEVELOPMENT AND DISSEMINATION OF IDEAS AND VALUES.

LEARNING TO RECOGNIZE THESE CONCEPTS WILL HELP YOU UNDERSTAND OTHER PEOPLE'S ARGUMENTS.

YOU'LL ALSO STRENGTHEN YOUR OWN POSITION AND THE WAY OTHERS SEE YOU.

ETHOS PATHOS LOGOS

ETHOS PATHOS LOGOS

FOR EXAMPLE, AN ONLINE PROFILE IS A RHETORICAL SPACE IN WHICH ETHOS, PATHOS, AND LOGOS ARE VERY IMPORTANT.

ONLINE PROFILES ALLOW USERS TO CREATE RICH, ENGAGING, AND SOMETIMES SATIRIC SELF-PORTRAITS.

Social Network

Jonathan is thinking about getting a new computer.

Plato: Pff! It would just be the shadow of the CONCEPT of a computer, anyway.

Aristotle: Ooh, but the new X432g's are so AWESOME! 1 DISLIKE

Jonathan wonders if he should eat some breakfast.

Aristotle: 1) Consider the pros and cons, 2) ask an expert, and 3) do it if you're hungry.

Jonathan likes:

Douglass  Aristotle  Jet-Skis

Lincoln  Funny Hats  The US Constitution

Asian Food  Monkeys

THE MIX OF PICTURES, VIDEO, AND TEXT CAN ESTABLISH -- OR **DESTROY** -- YOUR CREDIBILITY, OR **ETHOS**.

FOR INSTANCE, IF JONATHAN, AS A PROFESSOR OF ENGLISH, HAS A PROFILE RIDDLED WITH TYPOS AND IMAGES OF HIM GETTING DRUNK WITH HIS STUDENTS...

HIS CREDIBILITY MIGHT **RISE WITH SOME**, BUT FALL WITH MOST OTHERS.

Social Network

Jonathan: Oh HAI I am Drunk with studentz !!!1!!

IMAGES AND WORDS CAN ALSO CONTRIBUTE TO THE PATHOS OF A PAGE...

ONE DAY:

Liz: is fine, keeping busy with work.

BUT THE NEXT:

Liz: is mourning the loss of a beloved cat.

"SNOOKUMS"

1999    2012

CERTAINLY, **PATHOS** IS BEING USED HERE TO PROMOTE SYMPATHY FOR LIZ...

...AND PERHAPS GENERATE A FEW KIND WORDS FOR HER **PAGE**.

WE GENERALLY DON'T THINK OF SOCIAL NETWORK PROFILES AS MAKING "LOGICAL ARGUMENTS," BUT IN A WAY, THEY **ARE** MAKING ARGUMENTS --

-- ARGUMENTS ABOUT WHO WE ARE, WHAT WE ARE INTERESTED IN, AND WHY SOMEONE MIGHT WANT TO "FRIEND" US.

@JONATHAN: Are you trying to seem cool by having a social network homepage?

BUT RHETORIC ISN'T JUST ABOUT **SPACE**. IT IS ALSO ABOUT **TIME**.

# BENDING TIME through KAIROS

ALL OF US HAVE HAD EXPERIENCES THAT WERE EMBARRASSING, INSULTING, HUMILIATING, OR DEMORALIZING.

OFTEN WE WISH THAT WE COULD HAVE TRAVELED BACK IN TIME TO SAY JUST THE RIGHT THING AT THAT PARTICULAR MOMENT.

WE MAY COME UP WITH THE PERFECT THING TO HAVE SAID MUCH LATER, BUT IT IS ALREADY TOO LATE.

TONGUE TIED

LUMP IN THROAT

SHORT OF BREATH

RACING HEART

BUTTERFLIES IN STOMACH

RUBBER KNEES

today: AUDITIONS 5-9 pm

I-I KNOW YOU ARE, BUT WHAT AM I...?

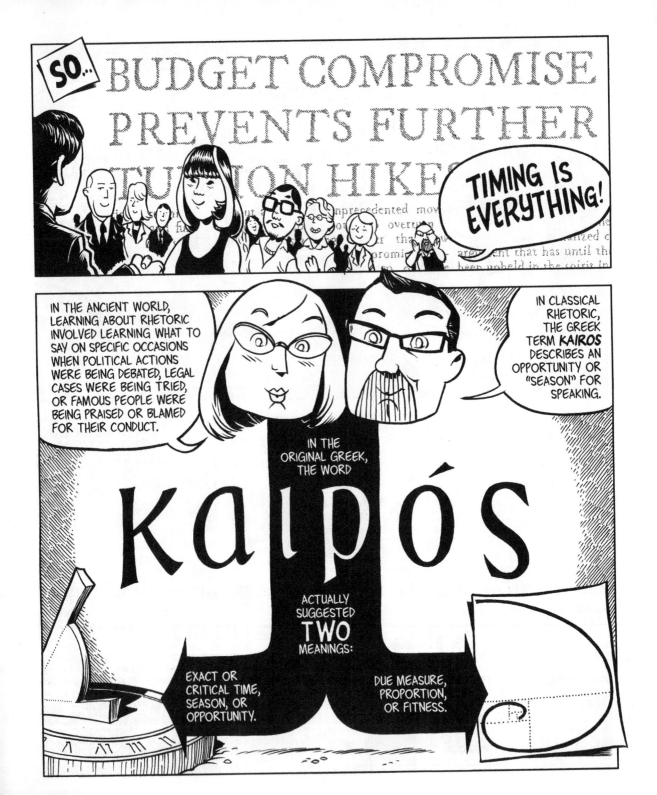

KAIROS WORKS IN MANY WAYS, ESPECIALLY TODAY.

DIGITAL WRITERS WHO COMMUNICATE USING THEIR COMPUTERS OR MOBILE PHONES OFTEN FEEL COMPELLED TO HIT "SEND" OR "ENTER" AS RAPIDLY AS POSSIBLE TO KEEP UP WITH A FAST-MOVING ONLINE CONVERSATION.

I NEED TO SEND THIS EMAIL RIGHT AWAY TO THE PRESIDENT OF THE UNIVERSITY.

BUT IT'S USUALLY BETTER FIRST TO CONSIDER BOTH THE APPROPRIATENESS OF YOUR MESSAGE **AND** THE TIMING OF YOUR REPLY.

DING!

&%$#@!

I HIT "SEND" BEFORE I MEANT TO!

WRITERS OFTEN MISS THE LONG-TERM **APPROPRIATENESS** OF KAIROS WHEN THEY FOCUS ON THE IN-THE-MOMENT **RESPONSIVENESS** OF KAIROS.

IF YOU THINK ABOUT A RHETORICAL OCCASION **ONLY** IN TERMS OF REACTING QUICKLY, YOU COULD EASILY END UP WITH AN EMBARRASSING DISASTER.

TENURE

THE ROMAN RHETORICIAN **MARCUS TULLIUS CICERO** REALLY UNDERSTOOD THE IMPORTANCE OF KAIROS.

FOR EXAMPLE, WHEN HE WAS ABOUT TO BE EXECUTED ON ARBITRARY POLITICAL GROUNDS HE SAW A MOMENT FOR GRACIOUS WIT:

"There is nothing proper about what you are doing, soldier...

"...but at least make sure you cut off my head properly."

AFTER ALL, ARISTOTLE WASN'T THE **ONLY** FAMOUS RHETORICIAN IN THE ANCIENT WORLD.

CICERO, WHO LIKE MANY CULTURED ROMANS **ADMIRED** THE ANCIENT GREEKS, TRAINED ORATORS FOR THE ROMAN **SENATE**.

"No one can speak well, unless he thoroughly understands his subject."

CICERO (106–43 BCE)
ANCIENT ROMAN PHILOSOPHER, LAWYER, AND STATESMAN

CICERO THOUGHT ABOUT THE "TEXTS" OF RHETORIC VERY BROADLY AND REALIZED THAT SPEECHES AND WRITING ARE NOT THE ONLY WAYS PEOPLE COMMUNICATE.

THE ROMANS DEVELOPED AN ELABORATE SYSTEM OF LAWS AND PUBLIC ENGINEERING PROJECTS TO REGULATE AN INCREASINGLY COMPLEX SOCIETY.

THESE **RES PUBLICA**, OR "PUBLIC THINGS," ARE WORTH CONSIDERING AS RHETORICAL ACTS AND SPACES.

AS ARCHEOLOGISTS KNOW, EVEN GOVERNMENT BUILDINGS AND TRIUMPHAL ARCHES CONVEYED MESSAGES TO CITIZENS IN THE ANCIENT ROMAN WORLD AND PRESENTED IMPLICIT ARGUMENTS ABOUT AUTHORITY, PARTICIPATION, AND SHARED VALUES.

THE ROMANS UNDERSTOOD THAT ARCHITECTURAL SPACES COULD BE RHETORICALLY IMPORTANT IN ESTABLISHING THE CULTURE ASSOCIATED WITH THE ROMAN WAY OF LIFE, MUCH AS ADVERTISERS TODAY TALK ABOUT "BRANDING" PRODUCTS.

WE STILL NEED SPACES TO DEBATE IMPORTANT ISSUES IN PUBLIC.

AND KNOWING SPECIAL LANGUAGE FROM THE FIELD OF RHETORIC CAN BE HELPFUL TO IDENTIFY EFFECTIVE -- AND INEFFECTIVE -- TECHNIQUES.

GREEK TERMS LIKE **ETHOS, LOGOS, PATHOS,** AND **KAIROS** MIGHT NOT BE WORDS THAT YOU ADD TO YOUR EVERYDAY VOCABULARY.

BUT YOU USE THE GENERAL CONCEPTS ALL THE TIME...

...IN PERSON AND ONLINE.

and Jonathan

**Aristotle:** haha nice hairstyle LOL

**Plato:** If you saw where the rain came from, you could never go back to your happy ignorance !!!!

**Cicero:** As the mature

# REFRAME

with

## Luis & Cindy

What does ARISTOTLE have to do with ME?

LUIS! WHAT'S UP?

NOT MUCH. HEY, HERE'S A QUESTION. I HAVE TO BE OUT OF TOWN FOR MY BIG BROTHER'S GOING-AWAY PARTY, SO I WROTE AN EMAIL TO MY WRITING TEACHER SAYING I'D MISS CLASS.

WHAT DO YOU THINK?

TO: l.losh@univ.edu
SUBJECT: HEY

Hey Mrs. Losh: I'm super busy on Friday. Please let me know if we do anything important. TTYL.

Luis

UH, WELL...

...MAYBE YOU'D BETTER START FROM SCRATCH.

WHAT? WHAT'S WRONG?

WELL, I DUNNO. I THINK THAT IF I WAS YOUR TEACHER, I MIGHT BE KIND OF INSULTED.

INSULTED? I'M LETTING HER KNOW AHEAD OF TIME THAT I'M NOT GOING TO BE IN CLASS!

WELL, THAT'S TRUE. BUT YOU AREN'T TELLING HER **WHY** YOU HAVE TO BE GONE...AND YOU'RE ACTUALLY IMPLYING THAT HER CLASS TIME MIGHT **NOT** BE IMPORTANT!

TO: l.losh@univ.edu
SUBJECT: Upcoming Absence

Dear Dr. Losh,

My older brother is on active duty in the military and is being deployed this month. My extended family will have his going-away party on Friday. I'd very much like to be there, given the circumstances. May I be excused from class? I'll be happy to make up any work, and I will ask my classmates for notes.

Sincerely,

Luis

TO: luis@univ.edu
SUBJECT: RE: Upcoming Absence

Dear Luis,

Thanks for the heads-up. We'll be starting brainstorming and process work on your first assignment, an analysis of the design of a print advertisement for an on-campus organization, service, or cause.

You should analyze the rhetorical strategies of the advertisement by commenting on its logos, pathos, ethos, and kairos. You should study details in the wording, images, typography, organization, and visual design on the. Let me know if you have any questions, and I'll see you in class on Monday.

Best,
Liz

Calling all PROSPECTIVE PLEDGES!

JOIN US AT AN **INFORMATIONAL LUNCHEON** TO

★ Get a HEAD START on building your RÉSUMÉ!

★ Learn new SKILLS!

★ NETWORK with potential COLLEAGUES and EMPLOYERS!

SPONSORED BY

BETA BETA BETA

Monday, November 2nd
11 am – 1 pm

[ No shorts or jeans, please! ]

I SEE WHAT YOU MEAN—THEY ARE TOTALLY DIFFERENT.

WE CAN START WITH THESE QUESTIONS:

**Questions for RHETORICAL ANALYSIS**

1. Who is the intended **AUDIENCE** for the text?

2. What is the **PURPOSE** of the text?

3. Does the author seem **CREDIBLE**? Why, or why not?

4. What is your gut **REACTION** to the text? What **EMOTIONS** does it evoke?

5. How are the elements arranged or **ORGANIZED**? Why? Does the arrangement seem **LOGICAL**?

6. When and where was the text **WRITTEN**? Was it timely given this context? Why, or why not?

**QUICK REVIEW:**

**ETHOS**
The credibility that a speaker/writer brings to a subject.

**PATHOS**
Use of emotion in debate/argument.

**LOGOS**
Appeal to reason, to the forcefulness of a well-thought-out and well-argued position.

I-25

COMING UP IN THE NEXT EXCITING EPISODE OF **REFRAME**

" How do I **READ** this? "

# WALK the TALK

## "ETHOS, LOGOS, PATHOS"

**1 What's the RHETORICAL SITUATION?**

AN ACADEMIC ARTICLE OFTEN NEEDS AN ABSTRACT LIKE THIS ONE.

I WROTE THIS FOR AN ESSAY ABOUT PRESIDENT OBAMA'S USE OF SOCIAL MEDIA.

AN ACADEMIC ABSTRACT NEEDS TO SUMMARIZE THE MAIN POINT OF THE ARTICLE AND SHOW WHY THE ARTICLE IS IMPORTANT.

---

COMPARATIVE AMERICAN STUDIES · ELIZABETH LOSH

# ABSTRACT

" The persuasive power of social network sites, blogs, Twitter, and SMS messages was obviously important for the Obama campaign and subsequent presidency in associating him with youth, technology, volunteerism, and user-generated content. The conventional wisdom is that Obama has been a user of social media who models to other heads of state ways to disseminate political messages successfully without notable incidents of stalled reception or public disgrace. However, since taking office, Obama's abandonment of YouTube public diplomacy efforts and White House online town halls might represent him as imitating pre-digital presidents like Kennedy and Reagan. "

Comparative American Studies

**4 How does the WRITER USE PATHOS?**

NOTING THAT OBAMA'S USE OF SOCIAL MEDIA ASSOCIATES HIM "WITH YOUTH, TECHNOLOGY, VOLUNTEERISM" MAY APPEAL TO READERS' EMOTIONS. IN OUR CULTURE, THOSE ATTRIBUTES ARE USUALLY SEEN AS POSITIVE.

SOME RHETORICAL SITUATIONS CALL FOR PATHOS -- BUT AN ABSTRACT MAY NOT DEVOTE MUCH SPACE TO SUCH APPEALS. AFTER ALL, THE GOAL HERE IS TO SUMMARIZE.

# DRAWING CONCLUSIONS

The following assignments ask you to practice thinking about the rhetorical strategies of **ETHOS**, **LOGOS**, **PATHOS**, and **KAIROS**.

**1** Keep your eye out for published texts around campus: newspapers, flyers, posters, zines, etc. When you find an interesting one, grab a copy or take a picture of it.

Who is producing the text, and for whom? What does the text aim to do, how does it do it, and how effectively does it do it? Why might this text exist on your college campus? (Luis and Cindy perform a similar analysis in the Reframe; how does the text you've found compare to the ones they've found?)

**2** Jot down some ideas about the rhetorical characteristics of informal and formal writing. In what ways are they similar? In what key ways are they different?

Then, pick a kind of formal writing that you either are working on now or have encountered in the past.

Think about how a consideration of logos, ethos, pathos, and kairos could help you compose a formal piece better.

**3**

The Internet brings together diverse groups of people and invites them to share their ideas and opinions, so conflicts, disagreements, and arguments are common online.

Find a contentious or polemical exchange on one of your favorite Internet haunts. Dissect the appeals used by the various parties in the exchange. Look specifically for places where people lean on their reputation or expertise (ethos), where the participants solicit specific emotional responses from one another or from their audiences (pathos), and where logic, facts, or evidence are used (logos). What are the effects of using the appeals? Whose arguments are most convincing in this exchange, and why?

**4**

Your classmate has just heard that your instructor plans to test students on this chapter by requiring in-class essays summarizing the content, closed book.

In whatever text you see fit -- an email, a text message, an open letter, a social media rant, a formal letter to your instructor or someone else -- try to stop this in-class essay from happening!

Consider the rhetorical occasion and the context, and compose -- alone or with your classmates -- an effective rhetorical response. What appeals will be most effective for your audience? What genre feels most kairotic?

PART 1
# EXPERIMENTING WITH GENRES
## FROM ANALYSIS TO DRAFT

# UNDERSTANDING GENRES

## CONTENTS

MEMOIR ▶
**Marjane Satrapi,**
***Persepolis.*** *Everett Collection.*

What is a *genre*, anyway? A *genre* is a composition's kind, category, or sort. Genres give us a way to categorize or describe types of compositions. For example, a song is a musical composition—but individual songs fall into specific genre categories, including punk, rap, R&B, soul, indie, and death metal.

Why bother thinking about genres? Because they represent possibilities. We wrote this book to acknowledge that in college and beyond there are *way* more genres available to us besides the five-paragraph essay or the traditional term paper. As respectable and time-honored as those genres are, there are a whole lot of other options out there. We wrote this book to help you understand and create in a variety of genres—and we invite you to produce works that matter to you and enjoy doing so. As an added bonus, paying attention to genre will make you a better writer and artist. Why? Because you'll be focused on the needs of your audiences and your own purposes as a composer. ▶

What do you need to know about genres? First, genres change according to the ways people use them. Before digital composing, writers who wanted to record their thoughts wrote with a pen in a journal or diary, in a physical notebook. Then blogs were created.

Second, genres are flexible: They overlap and don't fall neatly into the categories and primary purposes we've outlined in this book. For example, we present graphic memoirs in Chapter 2, "Narrative Genres," but this genre could also work in Chapter 4, "Persuasive Genres." That's because while memoirists tell the stories of their own lives, they also persuade readers to empathize with them and to see the world in a certain way. Remember that as a writer, you define your use of a genre based on your purposes and audiences, and you can do more than one thing at a time. Your ad can do more than persuade; your literacy narrative can do more than tell a story.

What do you already know about genres? Think for a minute about the different genres you compose in each day. As a student, you write research papers and presentations; these are two examples of academic genres. In each case, you know what is expected of you as a writer, because you understand certain features of the genre. You know that to write a research

What kinds of composing have you done so far as a student? What are some of the features that define the works you've composed?

▼ BLOG
*The Dragonfly Woman* Blog. *Christine L. Goforth.*

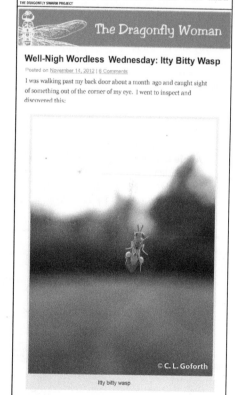

HOME   GALLERY   EDUCATIONAL MATERIALS   GLOSSARY   SCIENTIFIC NAMES   DW ARCHIVE   ABOUT DW   CONTACT ME
THE DRAGONFLY SWARM PROJECT

The Dragonfly Woman

**Well-Nigh Wordless Wednesday: Itty Bitty Wasp**
Posted on November 14, 2012 | 6 Comments

I was walking past my back door about a month ago and caught sight of something out of the corner of my eye. I went to inspect and discovered this:

© C. L. Goforth

Itty bitty wasp

A very tiny wasp! I'm betting it's one of the parasitic wasps based on the diminutive size and enormous hind legs. I grabbed my iPhone and my "macro" lens and snapped a few photos because it was simply too adorable to pass up. Apparently my glass could do with a bit of cleaning though...

For an Index of Sources & Contexts for material referenced in this chapter, see the e-Pages at **bedfordstmartins.com /bookofgenres.**

**What do you already know about advertising? What qualities make an ad successful?**

paper, you must gather and interpret a variety of reliable sources and cite them in a specific way.

In other situations, you choose your own genre to compose in, depending on what you want to say, who you want to say it to, and how you want to say it. Your choice of genre also depends on your own skills and interests, as well as the materials available to you. For example, your band is playing next week and you need to advertise the event. Your purpose is to persuade your potential audience to come to your show. You might choose to present your ad as a poster. Depending on your supplies and desired effect, you could create a hand-made poster to tape up at school or design one on your computer to post on Facebook. Alternatively, you might choose to advertise by creating and posting a short music video.

One of the best ways to become a better writer/composer is to read like one—to pay attention to what other writers/composers do, how and why they work in a particular genre, and how they make that genre work for them.

Let's look at an example from history. Annie L. Burton (ca. 1858–unknown) was born a slave and as an adult decided

PHOTO ▶
**Annie L. Burton**
author of the memoir *Memories of Childhood's Slavery Days* (1909). Images courtesy of Documenting the American South, Wilson Special Collections Library, The University of North Carolina at Chapel Hill Libraries.

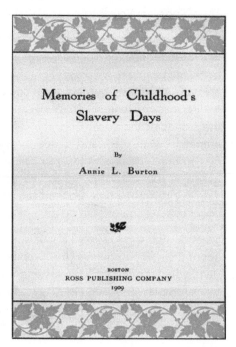

Memories of Childhood's Slavery Days

By

Annie L. Burton

BOSTON
ROSS PUBLISHING COMPANY
1909

to write about her experiences; her 1909 memoir is titled *Memories of Childhood's Slavery Days*. Why did she choose to write a memoir instead of poetry or editorials or technical manuals? Most likely, Burton chose the memoir because it was a popular genre in her day that allowed her to tell the story she wanted to tell, suited her interests and skills, and reached the audience she wanted to reach. Maybe if she had been trained in music, she would have written operas, or if she had been born a little later, she would have told her story as a documentary film.

> Our clothes were little homespun cotton slips, with short sleeves. I never knew what shoes were until I got big enough to earn them myself. If a slave man and woman wished to marry, a party would be arranged some Saturday night among the slaves. The marriage ceremony consisted of the pair jumping over a stick. If no children were born within a year or so, the wife was sold. At New Year's, if there was any debt or mortgage on the plantation, the extra slaves were taken to Clayton and sold at the court house. In this way families were separated.
> —**Annie L. Burton**

What we do know is that Burton wrote a memoir (a genre), specifically one that detailed her life as a slave. In her memoir, Burton wrote in the first person, portrayed real people, described settings, conveyed conflict, and told stories from her own life. These elements are features of the memoir genre and of any autobiography. Burton's purpose as a memoirist would have been to inform readers about what life as a slave—and later as a free person—was like; another purpose might have been to connect with women readers about what it was like to be a woman and a slave; yet another might have been to engage the imagination of readers. Her audience would have been literate former slaves and white readers, most likely in the North because her book was published in Boston. Her current readers might include students, scholars, and historians who want to read a firsthand account of slave life.

Do you read memoirs? What other observations can you make about the memoir as a genre?

## The Rhetorical Situation

What is *rhetoric*? *Rhetoric* refers to the ability to communicate effectively and with a purpose. So what is a *rhetorical situation*? It's the context in which you create a composition. To put it simply, as a writer, you have a specific purpose and an audi-

For examples of **literacy narratives** and **memoirs,** see the Index of Genres on page G-1.

ence. You need to know what you want to say; you also need to know your readers' expectations and accommodate them in some way. For example, when you write a review of a restaurant on yelp.com, you know that Yelp readers want to know your opinion of the meal; they also expect specific details about the individual dishes, service, and ambience you experienced.

## Purpose: Why are you composing?

Every time you write—or compose anything, in any genre—you do so for a reason. In this book, we've identified three main purposes for composing:

» To present a narrative / to tell a story (Chapter 2)

» To inform (Chapter 3)

» To persuade (Chapter 4)

There are many reasons to write and sometimes these reasons overlap. As writers, we often have several purposes for creating a single text. Let's look at a possible example. Let's assume that you love farmers' markets and want to establish one in your town.

**Your purpose** You want to start up a weekly local farmers' market. To make this happen, you need to (1) present your idea to others and (2) persuade them that it's worth acting upon. You expect that some people will object.

**Your rhetorical situation** In this context, you have more than one purpose. In order to persuade others, you need to explain your idea, say what's great about it, provide supporting statistics, and tell a persuasive story about how a similar plan succeeded in a neighboring town. You also have more than one audience. Some people will agree with you 100 per-

---

## CHECKLIST Composing with a Purpose

As you begin to compose, ask yourself:

☐ Why am I writing? What do I want to communicate? And to whom?

☐ What do I want my audience to believe or do after reading my composition?

☐ Is what I'm communicating objectionable or controversial to anyone? If so, how will I address this?

☐ If I'm telling a story, why is it significant, and how will I make it compelling?

☐ If I'm sharing information, why is it important, and how will I communicate its authority?

☐ If I'm trying to persuade others, what are the best ways to do so, for my particular readers?

cent; others won't be so sure; still others, maybe grocery store owners or city planners, will reject your idea altogether.

**Your plan and genre choice**   After considering your purpose and audience, you decide to write an editorial on your local newspaper's blog. You also plan to present your idea in person at the next town meeting.

As you begin writing your editorial, you may shift your purpose slightly—away from simply proposing and arguing for your plan—and toward focusing on the success of neighboring towns' farmers' markets and how they benefited local grocery stores. This will boost your persuasiveness with your resistant grocery store owners.

However, you may decide that rather than an editorial or a presentation, some other genre might better serve your purpose. For example, you may find that the best way to establish a farmers' market is to take a more personal approach by writing a letter to the mayor. You might also survey local citizens to see whether they'd like the opportunity to buy produce from local farmers. The point here is to see how your purpose affects your choice of genre, and how you can work in your genre to impact your audience.

## Audience: Who are you composing for?

Every time you compose, you do so for an audience. Audiences are made up of people—and people can be easily bored, pressed for time, or generally disinterested. You need to grab their attention and keep it.

Let's look at an example: Imagine you are traveling across the country and want to tell stories of your adventures (your purpose) to your friends, family, and even strangers interested in travel (your audience). You decide that the best way to reach your audience is to create a blog where you can write about your experiences, show maps and photos, and connect to other social media sites. That is what the world-traveling blogger who calls himself Giladhiz decided to do (see p. 10).

Giladhiz clearly understands his audience and wants them to stick with him. To this end, he:

» Provides a photo of himself and an "About the Author" section so that readers can make a personal connection with him.

What genres have you written in today? Why? And who were your audiences?

CHECKLIST **Composing for an Audience**

As you begin to compose, ask yourself:

☐ Who is my audience in terms of demographics? Are they mostly male or mostly female? What is their age range? Where do they live? What do they like? Do they have particular religious beliefs? Are they from a particular social class? Are they of a particular race or ethnic background?

☐ What is my audience's stake in the issue I'm presenting? Do they care? Why or why not?

☐ What does my audience value? Will my message be in line with—or contradictory to—their values? How can I present my message so that my audience will consider it? And perhaps even be persuaded by it?

☐ What level of education does my audience have? What kind of language will best reach them?

- » Addresses his readers directly: "So, dear friends and accidental surfers, allow me to begin with the reasons that brought me to plan and go on that trip."
- » Writes in a casual, readable, and humorous style, meant to hook his readers and keep them interested in his ongoing adventures.

When you write, do you think of who will read your writing? When you compose a song, a video, or even a status update, do you think of who will experience what you've created?

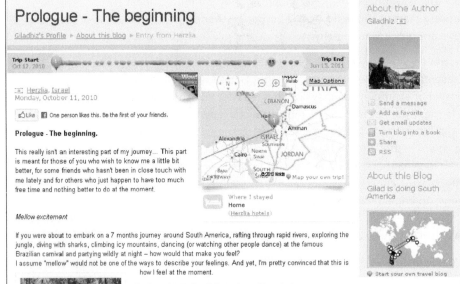

# Prologue - The beginning

Giladhiz's Profile ▸ About this blog ▸ Entry from Herzlia

**Trip Start** Oct 12, 2010 — — — — — — — — 65 ● ● ● **Trip End** Jun 15, 2011

Herzlia, Israel
Monday, October 11, 2010

👍Like  One person likes this. Be the first of your friends.

**Prologue - The beginning.**

This really isn't an interesting part of my journey... This part is meant for those of you who wish to know me a little bit better, for some friends who hasn't been in close touch with me lately and for others who just happen to have too much free time and nothing better to do at the moment.

*Mellow excitement*

If you were about to embark on a 7 months journey around South America, rafting through rapid rivers, exploring the jungle, diving with sharks, climbing icy mountains, dancing (or watching other people dance) at the famous Brazilian carnival and partying wildly at night – how would that make you feel?
I assume "mellow" would not be one of the ways to describe your feelings. And yet, I'm pretty convinced that this is how I feel at the moment.

But I jump ahead... first of all – thank you all for navigating your browsers to my Blog. If you've read all the way down to this line – I assume you're the "reader" kind of person rather than the "browser" type who's looking for anchor words or just looking at the pretty pictures... so from now on I'll consider my writing as a kind of a monologue, knowing that there's someone out there who actually listens to me babble.

So, dear friends and accidental surfers, allow me to begin with the reasons that brought me to plan and go on that trip.

**Reason #1**
*Coincidence*

I still have no idea how it happened. One day I was in a middle of a long term relationship (3 year), living in a rented apartment in Ramat Gan, working at a place I'd rather not mention – while studying for my MBA degree.
The next day I found myself alone, mourning the loss of a dead-end relationship (which ended like a train crash – unexpected derailing and crashing into the mountain side instead of going through a dark tunnel). And on the next day – I graduated my MBA, giving me even more free time for myself, alone. Lo and behold – at the very next day I decided to dump my promising career and quit, surprising many of my colleagues who were convinced I would reach a high position in my organization, as I was a highly valued (and well rewarded) employee.
Hmm...

*Just chilling...*

Where I stayed
Home
(Herzlia hotels)

About the Author
Giladhiz 

Send a message
Add as favorite
Get email updates
Turn blog into a book
Share
RSS

About this Blog
Gilad is doing South America

Start your own travel blog

» Structures his post with subheadings to guide readers, and provides options for navigating content and for e-mailing or connecting by social media.

For examples of **blogs** and **blog posts**, see the Index of Genres on page G-1.

## Rhetorical Appeals: Ethos, pathos, and logos

Whether your purpose is to tell a story, report information, or persuade, you need to get your audience on board. Even when persuasion is not your primary goal, it is always part of what you're doing, no matter what. We persuade our audiences by using what are called rhetorical appeals. There are three types of these, and they are often used in combination:

» *Ethos* is the credibility, authority, and trustworthiness the writer/composer conveys to the audience.

» *Pathos* is an appeal to an audience's emotions or values.

» *Logos* is the logic and connection of facts and evidence to the point being made.

As a writer/composer, you get to decide which appeals to use, depending on your audience, purposes, and choice of genre. For example:

» You're creating a memoir or an encyclopedia entry; you need to get readers to see you as an expert and accept your information as credible. In this case, you rely on *ethos*.

» You're creating an ad to persuade your audience to buy a product (especially something without tangible benefits, such as potato chips or a vacation package). In this case, you might appeal to their emotions and desires, relying on *pathos*.

» You're writing an editorial or an argumentative essay; you need to get your readers to agree with your conclusions. In this case, you might take them logically through the different elements of the arguments you're analyzing, relying on *logos*.

## Modes & Media

What is a *mode*? What does it have to do with *media*? *Mode* is how a composition is experienced by readers/viewers/listeners.

For the purposes of this book, we work with three modes: writer or text-based, visual, and audio.

Media is the delivery mechanism of the composition, including the following:

» Print

» Digital

» Face-to-face

A particular mode can be delivered in multiple media; for example, an audio essay could be recorded either on an old-fashioned tape recorder or digitally. We've broken out the modes and media of some of the genres in this chapter.

For examples of **graphic works,** see the Index of Genres on page G-1.

| NARRATIVE GENRES | Mode | Medium |
|---|---|---|
| **MEMOIR** Marjane Satrapi, *Persepolis* (p. 4) | **WRITTEN AND VISUAL** | **PRINT AND FILM** |
| **MEMOIR** Annie L. Burton, *Memories of Childhood's Slavery Days* (p. 6) | **WRITTEN** | **PRINT** |
| **TRAVEL BLOG** Giladhiz, *Gilad Is Doing South America* (p. 10) | **WRITTEN AND VISUAL** | **DIGITAL** |
| **ARTIST'S STATEMENT** Kristen LaCroix, *Prescription for Change* (p. 33) | **WRITTEN (BUT ACCOMPANIES A COLLAGE/SCULPTURE** | **DIGITAL** |

## Genre Conventions

Do you want to be a great writer or composer? If so, you need to know something about the genre you're composing in; you need to know its basic qualities and agreed-upon rules, and you need to be familiar with some examples. As Scott McCloud shows in his book *Understanding Comics*, writers ▶ and artists who work on comics use visual images and text to convey ideas, balloons to indicate dialogue, and simple but dynamic drawings and design to hold the reader's attention. Let's say you want to tell a story and you want to convey it graphically. You don't need to be McCloud or Picasso or Art Spiegelman, but you do need to understand how artists, graphic novelists, and memoirists work with visuals and text to tell stories. It helps to have some familiarity with the genre (read a few examples!) and perhaps have one example in mind as a model (see p. G-1 for some ideas). Or let's say you want to draw an annotated map of your neighborhood. It would help to know some of the established conventions of map-makers, such as using color to represent specific geography, or symbols to identify features or places. If your blog posts give your opinions on the editorials published on *Slate* or *The Huffington Post*, for example, you will have more author-ity if you link directly to the material you're responding to. Hyperlinking is a convention of the blog genre.

How much do you need to know? Keep an open mind as you choose genres to compose in. Consider collaborating with classmates who have more detailed knowledge of the gen-res that you're less familiar with. Often students in our writing

◀ COMIC
**Scott McCloud,**
from his book
*Understanding Comics: The Invisible Art.*
Excerpt from p. 66;
Copyright © 1993,
1994, Scott McCloud.
Reprinted by permission of HarperCollins Publishers.

classes will discuss and figure out together the conventions of specific genres and media (e.g., video or PowerPoint) and go from there. Other times they keep it simple but thoughtful, creating scrapbooks, print-based texts, or audio essays.

## Elements of the Genre

In this book, we ask you to pay attention to the main features of a given genre: the specific elements that are common to most examples of the genre. For instance, most press release writers try to be as brief and objective as possible, and aim at answering the questions who, what, why, where, and when. For those reasons, we consider brevity, objectivity, and thoroughness to be elements of the press release genre. (For an example, see Paul Henderson's press release on p. 18 about the Wall Arch collapse.)

## Style

*Style* refers to the particular ways we communicate. In this book, we pay attention to the techniques that individual writers use—and to what extent these techniques reflect the style of others composing in the same genre. We look at how much detail writers include, and how precise that detail is. We listen for tone (seriousness, humor, etc.) and voice (the presence of the author) and analyze how these qualities affect the overall composition. How a writer uses sources is part of style, as well. A writer who has cultivated a serious, academic style will probably use serious, academic sources as evidence. On the other hand, a writer with a more casual, chatty style might depend more on conversations with friends for evidence.

As a writer, you use style when you compose. The trick is to make sure that the style you're using is appropriate to your purpose and accessible and persuasive to your audience. For example, the writer and traveler Giladhiz uses a particular style on his blog. Because he is interested in attracting "accidental surfers" to his blog—that is, people who stumble upon his blog accidentally—he takes a casual and funny approach to his travels rather than a serious, scholarly tone. A serious, scholarly tone would probably appeal to an audience interested in the economics or politics of his travels, but because Giladhiz's purpose is to share his quirky, funny adventures, his casual, humorous style makes more sense.

## Design

*Design* describes the visual features of a composition, including the use of headings, format, color, and illustration. Design is aesthetic but also functional. As we discuss throughout the book, the design features you and other writers choose can play an important role in the level of success in achieving purposes and reaching audiences. Take a look at how Giladhiz uses images in his blog. Maps show readers exactly where this traveler is, and the photos of Giladhiz help readers connect with him personally. Giladhiz's photos documenting his travels let readers see what he saw. Because one of his purposes is to allow others to share in his travels vicariously, the photos are particularly important.

## Sources

*Sources* are the people, conversations, documents, books, journal articles, movies, and other works that we refer to for facts, perspectives, and models as we compose. For example, sources Giladhiz drew on for his travel blog (see p. 10) include Google Maps, the people he meets, and tourist information, such as brochures from historical sites. In this book, we consider sources because sources shape what writers create.

When you compose in certain genres, such as academic and research essays, you need to document the sources you refer to. In other cases, such as novels, comics, and music lyrics, while you've read and used sources, you're not required to document them formally. Whether or not sources need to be documented depends on the rhetorical situation. Sources referred to in a research essay aimed at academic readers should be documented because readers will want to know where ideas and information came from; the purposes of song lyrics are different, though. Listeners of a song aren't listening for information, so the sources of information are less important. Throughout the book we look at the conventions of specific genres in this regard, and in Chapter 7, we provide specific guidelines for using documentation styles.

In order to compose in different genres, you first should be able to identify them, see how other writers use them to achieve purposes and reach audiences, and learn some of the basic features so you can experiment.

How might the use of sources help boost—or undermine—your ethos as a composer?

# CHECKLIST: Identifying Genres

Are you looking at a particular composition and wondering what genre it is? Keep the following questions in mind.

## THE RHETORICAL SITUATION

☐ **Purpose.** Is the author telling a story? (See Chapter 2, "Narrative Genres.") Is the author reporting information? (See Chapter 3, "Informative Genres.") Is the author persuading? (See Chapter 4, "Persuasive Genres.") Is the writer telling a story, reporting, writing creatively, and persuading all at the same time? Don't worry. Sometimes purposes for writing/composing—and the genres we use—overlap.

☐ **Audience.** Who seems to be the author's primary audience? Secondary audience? How do you know? Why do you think someone would read (view, listen to, etc.) the text? How does the author capture and sustain audience attention?

☐ **Rhetorical appeals.** How does the author use the rhetorical appeals—ethos, pathos, and logos—to reach his or her audience? How does the author convey credibility? What kinds of evidence does the author offer to support the point of the piece?

☐ **Modes & media.** What choices has the writer made about mode? If multiple modes are used, how do they interact with each other? For example, if the piece includes both visuals and writing, is meaning conveyed by both the visuals and the writing, or does one mode convey more meaning than the other? What choices has the writer made about media? How do the writer's choices about modes and media reflect his or her purposes and audiences?

## THE GENRE'S CONVENTIONS

☐ **Elements of the genre.** What do you know about this genre already? What are some of the typical features of this genre? How is the content organized? How does the author use words, images, or other media to convey a purpose and reach an audience?

☐ **Style.** What is the author's tone? How would you describe the language of the piece? How much detail does the author use?

☐ **Design.** What does the composition look (sound, feel, smell, etc.) like? How do words and visuals and other media work together in the genre, physically? How would you describe the format of the composition? Would the format change if the mode were changed? For example, if a newspaper editorial moves from a print medium to an online medium, what changes occur in the genre?

☐ **Sources.** What sources does the author draw on for research? How do you know? How does the author incorporate and give credit to sources? Is there documentation? Hyperlinking?

# CASE STUDY:
## ONE EVENT, TWO GENRES

## Arch Collapse at a National Park

In this case study, two writers report on a single event. One writes a press release, the other a blog post.

**The event:** In August 2008, a rock formation in Utah's famous Arches National Park collapses.

**The writers:**

» **Paul Henderson**, a ranger at the park who also wrote press releases

» **Shaan Hurley**, a blogger and fan of the park who had hiked and photographed it

**The compositions:**

» "Wall Arch Collapses," a press release by Paul Henderson

» "The Wall Arch Collapses in Arches National Park," a blog post by Shaan Hurley

As you'll see, Henderson and Hurley provide much of the same information about the arch collapse, but they write in different genres, and with different purposes and audiences in mind. The notes in the margins of each piece explain their rhetorical situations and how they work within the conventions of the press release and the blog post.

Think of a current issue. How is the issue covered in different genres— for example, in a news report, an editorial, documentary footage, and a comic strip?

## Guided Reading: Press Release

## Paul Henderson

### *Wall Arch Collapses*

At the time of the collapse, Paul Henderson was chief of Interpretation and Visitor Services for Arches National Park, which is managed by the National Park Service, part of the U.S. Department of the Interior. When the arch collapsed, Henderson was interviewed by news outlets, including MSNBC, which also quoted from the press release on page 18.

*(Image on page 18 courtesy of National Park Service.)*

## What is the composer, **Paul Henderson,** doing?

### THE RHETORICAL SITUATION

Purpose
Audience
Rhetorical appeals
Modes & media

see page 19

## How do I know this is a **press release?**

### THE GENRE'S CONVENTIONS

Elements of the genre
Style
Design
Sources

see page 19

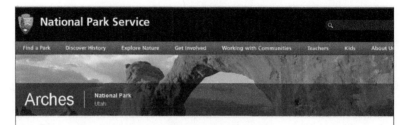

**National Park Service**

Find a Park    Discover History    Explore Nature    Get Involved    Working with Communities    Teachers    Kids    About Us

Arches | National Park
Utah

# Wall Arch Collapses

**Date:** August 8, 2008
**Contact:** Paul Henderson, 435-719-2140

Subscribe 🔊 | What is RSS

Wall Arch, located along the popular Devils Garden Trail at Arches National Park collapsed sometime during the night of August 4, 2008. Rock has continued to fall from the arms of the remaining portion of the arch necessitating the closure of the Devils Garden Trail just beyond Landscape Arch.

On August 7, 2008, representatives from both the National Park Service Geologic Resources Division and the Utah Geological Survey visited the site and noted obvious stress fractures in the remaining formation. Rock debris has completely blocked this section of the trail. The closure will remain in effect until visitor safety issues can be resolved.

First reported and named by Lewis T. McKinney in 1948, Wall Arch was a free standing arch in the Slickrock member of the Entrada sandstone. The opening beneath the span was 71-feet wide and 33-1/2 feet high. It ranked 12th in size among the over 2,000 known arches in the park.

All arches are but temporary features and all will eventually succumb to the forces of gravity and erosion. While the geologic forces that created the arches are still very much underway, in human terms it's rare to observe such dramatic changes.

No one has reported observing the arch collapse and there were no visitor injuries.

## THE RHETORICAL SITUATION

### Purpose

Henderson, who works for the National Park Service, a government agency, writes **to inform** readers about the collapse. He reports that there were no injuries and that the area is temporarily closed. He reassures readers that the event is normal, that arches are temporary and "eventually succumb to the forces of gravity and erosion."

### Audience

Henderson's readers want an **official statement** from park management, rather than one by an outside observer. Readers are mainly members of news organizations—but also park patrons, including hikers and nature photographers, looking for details.

### Rhetorical appeals

For Henderson and other press release writers, **ethos** is crucial. Readers need to trust the authority of the writer and his information, especially because Henderson represents a government agency.

Henderson establishes **logos** by presenting information in a sensible order, beginning with the event and ending with its effects.

### Modes & media

Henderson **uses text to inform and visuals to show the effect** of the collapse. His press release was posted digitally on the National Park Service's site and was probably also distributed by e-mail to various news organizations.

## THE GENRE'S CONVENTIONS

### Elements of the genre

**Addresses who, what, when, where, why, and how.** Henderson does so as follows:
*Who* = readers who care about the environment and park
*What* = the arch collapse
*When* = 8/4/08
*Where* = specific location of the collapse
*Why* = gravity and erosion
*How* = falling debris

**Is brief and timely.** Like most press releases, this is concisely worded, just a few paragraphs long. Henderson wrote it just four days after the event.

**Begins with most important content.** Henderson begins with the most crucial information and follows it with significant details.

**Includes contact info for media.** Henderson wants readers, especially the news media (the target audience for press releases), to be able to get in touch.

### Style

**Conveys an objective tone.** Henderson doesn't give his opinion; he also writes in the neutral third person.

**Is clear, direct writing.** Henderson provides facts simply and details concisely (e.g., "Rock debris has completely blocked this section of the trail").

### Design

**Presents a simple, clean layout.** Henderson uses a standard press release design, with a headline to summarize and get attention, a dateline, and contact information. There are just two images to support the text. The Web page itself includes the name of the park, an image, and a menu bar for easy navigation.

### Sources

**Draws on official information.** Henderson uses facts from the National Park Service and from the Utah Geological Survey, which he credits in the body of his press release.

## Shaan Hurley

### *The Wall Arch Collapses in Arches National Park*

Blogger Shaan Hurley has a background in mechanical design and works in the field of technology. *All Things Autodesk & Technology* is Hurley's personal blog; he also posts on Twitter. He posted the following entry in August 2008. *(Image courtesy of Shaan Hurley at Autodesk.)*

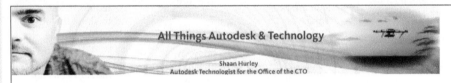

**All Things Autodesk & Technology**

Shaan Hurley
Autodesk Technologist for the Office of the CTO

**The Wall Arch Collapses in Arches National Park**

Almost one year ago to the week I was in the beautiful and world famous Arches National Park which is little more than 4 hours drive from my home in Utah. Just this week perhaps Tuesday one of the famous sandstone arches fell, Wall Arch is now Wall Pile. While Wall Arch was not the most spectacular or stunning, it was a beautiful arch.

Arches are formed by an ever changing nature and erosion and leave us with only a small window of geological time in which to marvel at the arches before they succumb to gravity. Who knows, perhaps another arch was born that we have not seen in the past year as well. Last year while I was photographing many of the arches and absolutely enjoying the natural beauty and silence in between the tourist buses,

I hiked back to Landscape arch which itself had suffered a partial collapse in 1991. Since it was so hot that day and I figured I would get back there again soon I did not hike the remaining quarter mile to photograph Wall Arch by the Devils Garden. Now I will not have the opportunity to photograph Wall Arch except the remnants on the ground. It is another example of how things you take for granted may disappear.

If you ever have the chance to Visit the Moab Utah region or Southern Utah you should do so as it is beyond words and one of the reasons I know call this state home. This is photography heaven for color and so many varied landscape and rare geography. One of the other things I love about the area is the history of the Fremont people from thousands of years ago leaving their art on the rock walls and then last but not least Green River Utah having the worlds best watermelon when hiking in 100+ deg F. weather. If you are ever in Utah let me know as I am always happy to get an excuse to head to Moab and love showing the hidden gems beyond the tourist trails.

Here are a couple of my photos from the hike back on August 4th 2007 in Arches National Park. I still have hundreds of photos yet to publish, It may sound odd for someone to see some sense of loss in what to some may just be a sandstone structure born of erosion but if you have ever been there in the silence and the vibrant glow of red at twilight you would understand the magic of the area. This is natures art and landscape at it's finest.

http://www.flickr.com/photos/btl/

Never take for granted who or what you can see today, you may not have the opportunity tomorrow.

Have a great weekend,

Shaan

**What is the composer, Shaan Hurley, doing?**

THE RHETORICAL SITUATION

Purpose
Audience
Rhetorical appeals
Modes & media

*see page 21*

**How do I know this is a blog post?**

THE GENRE'S CONVENTIONS

Elements of the genre
Style
Design
Sources

*see page 21*

## Purpose

Hurley has a few reasons for writing: **to inform** readers about the collapse, **to share** his own experiences and photos of the park, and **to persuade** readers to enjoy nature now, rather than later, when the opportunity may not exist. He writes: "Now I will not have the opportunity to photograph Wall Arch except the remnants on the ground. It is another example of how things you take for granted may disappear."

## Audience

His readers are fans of the park, other hikers and photographers, and even potential park visitors. His readers are looking for a **personal take** (rather than an official statement) on the arch collapse.

## Rhetorical appeals

Because Hurley's main goal is to urge readers to seize an opportunity, he relies largely on **pathos** to appeal to emotion. Notice how he describes the beauty and "magic" of the park.

He also establishes **ethos**, or his authority to write on this topic, by sharing his firsthand experiences and photos of the park.

## Modes & media

Hurley **uses text and visuals to inform**. His blog is digital and embedded with hyperlinks that bring readers to additional information. Readers can also share the link so others can read Hurley's post.

## Elements of the genre

**Presents brief, visual, hyperlinked content.** Like most effective blog posts, Hurley's is just a few paragraphs long, visually interesting, and embedded with links that offer more information without adding length.

**Written in short paragraphs.** Hurley's concise, chunked text keeps digital readers interested.

**Includes relevant photos.** Hurley's images provide context, attract readers, and offer his perspective on the event.

**Provides an "about" page and a comments area (not shown here).** Hurley gives biographical information and a space for readers to offer feedback and share their own views on the park.

## Style

**Conveys a conversational voice/tone.** Hurley, like many bloggers, offers his own reflections and is present in his writing. He writes in the first person, addressing readers directly.

## Design

**Clear layout; user-friendly navigation.** Like other blogs, Hurley's is designed so users can easily find additional content; they can also access his page on flickr.com.

## Sources

**Draws on official and firsthand information.** Hurley credits the National Park Service for some of the photos; he also draws on his own experience (his trip of 2007) and external sources such as *Wikipedia*.

## Questions: Analyzing Paul Henderson's press release and Shaan Hurley's blog post

**1. Purpose.** Reread Henderson's press release and Hurley's blog post. What are the writers' purposes? How can you tell? How do these purposes differ? How might they overlap?

**2. Audience.** Who do you imagine is the primary reader for Henderson's press release? For Hurley's blog post? Explain.

**3. Rhetorical appeals.** How effective are Henderson and Hurley in using ethos, pathos, or logos to reach their audiences? Which appeals do they rely on most effectively, and why?

**4. Rhetorical appeals.** Consider how hyperlinks, photos, and other information can contribute to a composer's ethos. Why do you think Hurley used the National Park Service as a source for information and images? How did this choice affect his ethos?

**5. Modes & media.** Both Henderson and Hurley use a combination of text and visuals. If you were to add audio or video to either piece, what would you add? What meaning or information would the audio or video add?

**6. Elements of the genre.** As a reader interested in the arch collapse, would you be likely to consult a press release? A blog? Both? Neither? Explain. To what extent is genre important? And in what contexts? When might it not matter?

**7. Elements of the genre.** What are the most significant differences between the press release and blog post as genres? Based on these examples, what conventions of these genres can you identify? How do these conventions affect what the writers say and how they convey it?

**8. Style.** Analyze the language Henderson and Hurley use. What do their words and tone suggest about their different purposes and audiences?

**9. Design.** How does the design of each piece enable readers to quickly find information they want or need?

**10. Design.** Look again at the photos included in the blog post and press release. What purposes do they serve in each? How effectively do the authors use them?

**11. Sources.** How does Hurley use the National Park Service's press release as a source? How does that source contribute to his success in achieving his purpose and reaching his audience?

For examples of **informative genres,** see Chapter 2 and the Index of Genres on page G-1.

# STUDENT CASE STUDY:
## ONE TOPIC, MULTIPLE GENRES

## Kristen LaCroix's Project on Drug Advertising

Let's look at a project by student writer Kristen LaCroix. Kristen is a former student of Liz Kleinfeld (coauthor of this textbook); Kristen was enrolled in Liz's composition class at Red Rocks Community College.

Kristen reflects on what she's doing now:

> Following my time at Red Rocks, I attended Colorado State University and graduated in the summer of 2010 with a degree in biological sciences. I am an intern with the Rocky Mountain Raptor Program and volunteering at the Denver Aquarium to pursue a career working with exotic wildlife. I hope to end up working as a medical director of a sanctuary or rehabilitation clinic for exotic animals.

Kristen reflects on her project:

> Looking back at this project, I remember wanting to choose a topic that I could find a lot of information on—I also wanted to be able to conduct interviews with experts. My grandfather worked in the pharmaceutical industry, and it's an area that has always interested me. It's a topic I care about and could easily take a stance on, largely because of my grandfather's experience. I found that the most challenging portion of this project was connecting all of the information together and getting it to flow. This project ultimately got me to see that there are lots of ways to present information and to persuade other people about your ideas.

For more examples of **student projects,** see Chapters 8, 9, and 10.

Kristen created her project in response to an assignment Liz gave the class. Liz asked students to:

» Research a specific issue or topic of interest to them.

» Present an argument about that topic to their audience (their primary audience would be Liz and the rest of the class).

◀ STUDENT AUTHOR PHOTO
**Kristen LaCroix.**
*Kristen LaCroix.*

» Choose three genres to compose in, being sure to pick those that would work well for their topics and arguments.

» Persuade their audience to agree with their perspective—and/or to take action on the issue.

Students were also asked to submit the following with their genre pieces:

» An Author's/Artist's Statement for each piece, in which they explain their rhetorical choices and include an MLA-style Works Cited list

» An Introduction to the project that states the overall objective and unifies the genre pieces into a whole

## Researching a Topic

Kristen thought she'd like to write about the pharmaceutical industry because her grandfather had spent his career in that field and his stories about it fascinated her. She had no idea how she would focus her topic, so she started by doing some research. In addition to interviewing her grandfather, she also began her research

**What issues are most important to you? How do you figure out which issues make the best topics for research and writing projects?**

PEER-REVIEWED ▶
JOURNAL ARTICLE
**Julie M. Donohue, PhD, et al.,**
from *The New England Journal of Medicine (NEJM).*
*Courtesy of the New England Journal of Medicine.*

The NEW ENGLAND JOURNAL of MEDICINE

| HOME | ARTICLES & MULTIMEDIA ▾ | ISSUES ▾ | SPECIALTIES & TOPICS ▾ | FOR AUTHORS ▾ | CME ▸ |

SPECIAL ARTICLE

### A Decade of Direct-to-Consumer Advertising of Prescription Drugs

Julie M. Donohue, Ph.D., Marisa Cevasco, B.A., and Meredith B. Rosenthal, Ph.D.
N Engl J Med 2007; 357:673-681 | August 16, 2007 | DOI: 10.1056/NEJMsa070502

Share:

| Abstract | Article | References | Citing Articles (89) |

It has been 10 years since a change in a policy of the Food and Drug Administration (FDA) allowed direct-to-consumer advertising of prescription drugs on television. Such advertising has been criticized for encouraging inappropriate use of medications and driving up drug spending.[1,2] Concern that such advertising may lead to increased use of expensive medications was amplified by the introduction of a prescription-drug benefit in Medicare in 2006 (Part D). Studies of the effect of advertising on prescribing practices have shown that such advertising increases classwide sales, helps to avert underuse of medicines to treat chronic conditions, and leads to some overuse of prescription drugs.[3-5]

with some copies of *Health* magazine and *Good Housekeeping,* which contained ads and articles related to the drug industry, geared toward a general audience. As her research deepened, she looked into more scholarly professional resources, too, such as an article (by Julie M. Donohue, PhD, et al.) on advertising prescription drugs from *The New England Journal of Medicine* (*NEJM*). (For complete guidelines on research and working with sources, see Chapter 5, "Exploring Topics & Creating a Research Proposal," Chapter 6, "Evaluating & Choosing Sources," and Chapter 7, "Integrating & Documenting Sources.")

## Choosing a Topic

Kristen reflected on the conversations she'd had with her grandfather and the articles she'd read in *Health, NEJM*, and other periodicals. She was particularly struck by the number of direct-to-consumer drug ads she'd found in *Health* magazine and at the Food and Drug Administration Web site. She did more research and found that this type of advertising by drug companies is pervasive in popular magazines and media. Kristen felt these ads might also be dangerous and decided to explore further.

## Determining a Purpose

As she focused her topic and conducted more research, Kristen was further persuaded that direct-to-consumer drug ads could be harmful. She decided that she would use her project to persuade others as well. With this purpose in mind, she thought about her audience of classmates. They might not be aware of the extent of direct-to-consumer drug ads; she realized that she would first need to inform her readers of the ads' pervasiveness before she could build her main argument about their possible impact on consumers.

## Considering Audience

In order to connect with her audience, Kristen knew she needed to first consider what her potential readers might already know and think about pharmaceutical companies and the ads they produced. She figured her classmates were probably a lot like her: interested in staying healthy and somewhat ignorant about how drug companies market their products and spend their money. She knew they would not want to read a dry report about advertising trends, so she began thinking about genres that might grab and hold their attention.

Who are the main audiences for the compositions you create as a student? Your classmates? Instructor? Anyone with an Internet connection? How do you negotiate and appeal to your audiences?

## Using Rhetorical Appeals

Kristen knew that she would need to use ethos, pathos, and logos to her advantage in order to persuade her audience. She could establish her ethos as an author by taking her subject seriously and by drawing upon authoritative sources. She could appeal to her readers' pathos by including sad stories of consumers who suffered or even died as the result of the aggressive marketing of a drug. And while she didn't want to bog down her audience with excessive detail, she did want to provide major facts about how drug companies advertise—and the figures related to the money they make as a result. This information, presented in an order that made sense and accompanied by an Author's Statement explaining her choices, would appeal to her readers' sense of logos.

## Choosing a Genre(s)

Taking into account her purpose, audience, and the ways she planned to persuade her audience, Kristen decided to create a series of compositions:

**A collage/sculpture**   Kristen created a giant capsule and covered it with a collage of prescription drug ads pulled from *Health* magazine and *Good Housekeeping*. She thought this creative and visual genre would get her classmates' attention and give them a sense of the hefty volume of direct-to-consumer ads created by drug companies. Kristen hoped that once readers saw in a visually graphic way exactly how many direct-to-consumer ads by drug companies appeared in two mainstream magazines, they would be persuaded that there was a problem. Kristen chose drug ads for her collage that appeal to the emotions (pathos) of her readers through scary stories of untreated illness; the ads also feature statistics, which appeal to readers'

ARTIFACT ▶
**Kristen LaCroix,**
pill capsule collage/
sculpture. *This and all
images on pages 27–31
courtesy of Kristen
LaCroix.*

sense of logic (logos) and draw on the authority (ethos) of doctors. She also used the capsule in a creative and functional way—as a container for her other genre pieces, described below.

**A biographical profile**   Kristen wrote a profile of her grandfather, Charles, who worked in the pharmaceutical industry. She used this genre as a way to convey facts and information about the drug industry. She thought that this information, coming through her grandfather's perspective, would be more interesting to her audience than if she presented it in a different genre, such as a report. She hoped that because her grandfather worked in the pharmaceutical industry, his observations about how it had changed over time would help persuade readers to question some industry practices. Kristen used her profile of her grandfather—which is based on her own primary research and his recollections—to appeal to readers' sense of logic (logos) and draw on her grandfather's authority (ethos) as a professional in the field.

LaCroix 7

Charles

He appeared weathered with thousands of memories and emotions; consequently, he sat serenely in his chair inhaling the calm air around him. This skillful man, Charles Fortin, had cared for and supported three beautiful daughters and an amazing wife. Charles presented himself with pride due mainly to his great success during his younger years. However, after retiring from a lifetime spent traveling while working for growing companies, he had suffered greatly through many medical tribulations. His outfit this day, a gray sweat suit, illustrated his need for comfortable settings and less movement. His bulbous glasses encompassed his face, demanding attention. A man of eighty-five years, his movements were gradual and his responses defined tranquility.

Gently, Charles began, "After finishing college, I paid a visit to my student advisor in hopes that I would be able to find a suitable career to support my wife and three-month-old daughter." His statement, coupled with perfect presentation, depicted Charles as the man who worked relentlessly to accomplish his goals. His advisor organized an interview with Lederle Laboratories where Charles was first introduced to the pros and cons of the drug industry. Slightly tipping back his frail head, Charles explained, "I worked for Lederle for fifteen years, promoting their products to doctors and pharmacies around the globe before I switched companies and gained the title of Sales Manager of Pharmaceuticals for all countries except the U.S." Charles paused shortly to collect his thoughts, illustrating his irrefutable abilities as a well-spoken gentleman.

Charles's pale complexion began to glow as he described the fulfillment he gained during his career. His grin spread across his face as he explained that through his profession he was able to help people because he assisted in the distribution of life-saving products to individuals all over the world. Charles's smile defended his achievements as he slowly leaned back in the black chair, reminiscing about his past. Inhaling deeply, he continued, "Back in those days, prescriptions were so successful in healing people, they were only used when they were needed."

His face bloomed with frustration as he considered the different advertising campaigns utilized throughout the pharmaceutical industry today. Pausing for a short break, Charles went into the kitchen. He came back with several pills of different colors and sizes, explaining, "Each of these medications I take for many reasons, whether for my heart, arthritis, or my cold, each of these came from my doctor and are the only things stopping the pain that I would be forced to deal with on an everyday basis." His assorted prescriptions all seemed necessary. Charles inhaled deeply while looking down at his medications, revealing the different purposes each pill served. None of the pills, he divulged, were medications he'd asked for after seeing them in advertisements; they'd all been prescribed by his physician. "I wouldn't know what I wanted if I needed medication, that is a decision best left in the hands of a trained professional," he explained.

▲ BIOGRAPHICAL PROFILE
**Kristen LaCroix,** the first page of her biographical profile of her grandfather, Charles.

▲ PHOTO
Kristen LaCroix's grandmother and grandfather.

▲ OBITUARY
**Kristen LaCroix,** remembrance
of Robert C. Ernst.

**An obituary**   Kristen also created an obituary for a man named Robert C. Ernst, who died from a prescription drug–induced heart attack. She drew on an article that she'd read about Ernst's death, and also listed it in her Works Cited list. Kristen created the obit to help bring home to her audience the life-and-death seriousness of the topic; here she was able to convey facts to inform her readers, and also appeal to her readers' pathos. She thought that once readers learned that prescription drugs themselves can be lethal, they would be persuaded to take the issue seriously. Kristen uses the genre of the obituary to appeal to readers' emotions (pathos) by building sympathy for the man who died and the family left behind.

**An Artist's Statement and Introduction**   To accompany each of her three compositions (her capsule, profile, and obituary), Kristen also wrote an Artist's Statement in which she explained her rhetorical choices. Kristen's primary audience for these Statements is her instructor, Liz, but she also knew some of her classmates would be interested in knowing more about the decisions she made as she worked on her project. Kristen used a serious tone to convey to Liz that she approached the entire project in a scholarly, serious way (ethos). She also talked methodically about the choices she made, to show that she had thought through her decisions and their consequences (logos). Kristen composed an Introduction that addressed her project as a whole; in it, she discussed how her genre compositions work together to form a unified argument about direct-to-consumer drug advertising—and also prepared her audience to experience her project in a coherent way.

## Working with Modes & Media

Kristen was comfortable working in written modes, but she also wanted to use visuals to stimulate her readers' imaginations and keep their attention. Her pill capsule collage/sculpture is the most visual composition she created and the only one that is three-dimensional; Kristen assumed her readers would be seeing it face-to-face (you are seeing it in print because the collage has been photographed and reprinted in this book). She wrote the biographical profile and it appears in print. She also wrote the obituary and included visuals; this piece also appears in print. However, if she'd had more time, she might have included these pieces on a blog or Web site. When considering her audience—her classmates and instructor—Kristen decided to create print pieces that could be passed around and read in class. Kristen composed her Artist's Statements as print documents; however, if she had decided to present her genre pieces digitally on a Web site or blog, she

Have you ever created a project that you wish you'd had more time to complete? Reflecting on that experience, what would you have done differently or better to make your point? What would you revise, and why?

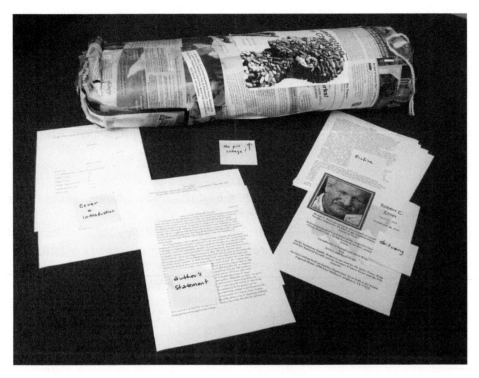

might have chosen to incorporate different media into her Statements, or recorded them as audio or video essays, for example.

## Working with Style

Kristen observed the conventions of the genres she chose: She also chose to compose in a style that would be very accessible to her readers. She did not want to bore her readers with technical language, or alienate readers she hoped to persuade. She anticipated that many of her readers might not see direct-to-consumer advertising by pharmaceutical companies as a serious enough problem for them to spend time and energy worrying about. Kristen knew that she had to provide enough details to convince readers to take her argument seriously, but not so many that readers would feel overwhelmed.

## Working with Design

To catch her readers' attention, Kristen included visuals (see the obituary) and color (see her collage). Further, while a collage is normally flat and two-dimensional,

Kristen decided to present hers in sculpture form. She also hoped that by composing her collage out of prescription drug ads, she'd spark her audience's curiosity so that they'd want to know more about her project and main point.

## Drawing from Sources

Kristen used a variety of sources for her project, including interviews with her grandfather, the advertisements she found in *Good Housekeeping* and *Health* magazine, and several articles from peer-reviewed journals. When she selected her sources, she thought about how her choices would reflect upon her ethos. She wanted to come across as authoritative, thoughtful, and intelligent, so she chose sources that struck her as authoritative, thoughtful, and intelligent. She found articles in journals she knew were respected, such as *The New England Journal of Medicine*. She wrote an Artist's Statement for each genre piece she created, and in those Statements she spoke directly about how the sources she used affected her thinking about her subject. She also provided a Works Cited list with each Statement.

## Guided Reading: Collage/Sculpture

### Kristen LaCroix (Student)

*Prescription for Change:*
*The Impact of Direct-to-Consumer*
*Drug Advertising*

Following is a photo of Kristen's collage capsule. The annotations on page 32 show how she addressed her rhetorical situation and connected with her audience through the genre she chose.

What is the composer, **Kristen LaCroix,** doing?

THE RHETORICAL SITUATION

Purpose
Audience
Rhetorical appeals
Modes & media

*see page 32*

How do I know this is a **collage/ sculpture**?

THE GENRE'S CONVENTIONS

Elements of the genre
Style
Design
Sources

*see page 32*

Kristen LaCroix, *Prescription for Change*

**LaCroix,** *Collage/Sculpture, Continued*

## THE RHETORICAL SITUATION

### Purpose

Kristen's main purpose—for her project as a whole—is **to persuade** her audience that direct-to-consumer ads are potentially dangerous; she must also first inform her audience about the pervasiveness of these ads, which she does by creating this capsule.

### Audience

Kristen's instructor and classmates are her primary readers.

### Rhetorical appeals

Kristen appeals to **pathos** by presenting viewers with an imaginative object, and to **logos** and **ethos** by providing her sources as part of that sculpture.

### Modes & media

Mode = visual
Medium = face-to-face

## THE GENRE'S CONVENTIONS

### Elements of the genre

As a piece of sculpture, it is **three-dimensional,** and in this case, handmade out of everyday materials.

As a collage, it features **layered texts and images,** which convey a main theme. Color directs attention to different content. **A DIY feel** invites viewers to interact with and explore the object.

### Style

Kristen conveys a **playful tone, but also makes an argument** with this piece. The numerous ads from two mainstream magazines reinforce her argument that they are pervasive and potentially dangerous. Her title, "Prescription for Change," and the image of the pill-covered face on the cover sheet further telegraph her argument.

### Design

While most collages are two-dimensional, Kristen's piece is a **3-D sculpture** made from plastic bottles and **covered with a collage.** The two halves fit together in the middle and open up, capsule-like, to reveal not medicine, but her individual genre pieces.

### Sources

Kristen draws on ads from *Good Housekeeping* and *Health* magazine.

Kristen submitted her project with an Author's/Artist's Statement for each genre piece in which she explains and supports the rhetorical choices she made as she created her project. On page 33 is her Statement for the capsule collage/sculpture part of her project. Sometimes an instructor will specify that students write one Author's/Artist's Statement that encompasses an entire project instead of individual Statements for each piece. For this particular class, Liz asked students to provide individual Statements for each genre piece, as well as an Introduction to provide a kind of project-wide Statement.

# Guided Reading: Artist's Statement

## Kristen LaCroix (Student)

### Artist's Statement

What is the composer, **Kristen LaCroix**, doing?

LaCroix 4

Artist's Statement:

How and Why I Created My Collage/Sculpture

It is necessary for all individuals to realize the amount of drug advertisements in all forms of media, to recognize the problem with our current drug industry. I created a collage to allow people to see the immense amount of marketing found merely throughout common magazines. Using only two magazines, I created a collage that couldn't even hold all the full-page advertisements that I found. Furthermore, oddly enough, the two magazines that included such an intense amount of advertising were *Health* and *Good Housekeeping*. The drug advertisements throughout these magazines included anything from sleeping pills to medication to ease the aftereffects of chemotherapy.

My collage, which I shaped as a capsule, displays a few examples of the marketing campaigns for prescription drugs and is in turn the best genre to present the obvious problem. The collage represents a message to simply acknowledge the ways companies advertise in an attempt to gain consumers' trust while marketing a product. A massive amount of pharmaceutical companies' income is turned around to be used for advertising. One CBS News article I found listed the top twenty drugs advertised in 2000. The drug with the largest advertising campaign, Vioxx, had approximately $161 million spent on advertising that year (Lee). Soon thereafter, in 2004, the drug Vioxx was pulled off the market after causing the death of many patients using it. Many prescriptions that are on the collage, such as Flonase and Celebrex, were listed in this article as well. The company that produced the nasal spray Flonase spent $78 million advertising their product in 2000 (Lee). There have been no adverse implications for this drug thus far; nevertheless, similar to several other drugs that are heavily advertised, there are other products available for consumers that are not as pricey and work as well if not even better.

Drug companies create their advertisements to be directed at specific target audiences in an effort to gain the most profit during their campaigns. However, my collage capsule is not intended for a specific audience. Instead it is meant to heighten the awareness of anyone who sees it because we will all at some point be manipulated by drug advertising. My collage capsule functions as the packaging for the other pieces of my project including the introduction. It highlights the overwhelming number of advertisements for prescription medications the average person is exposed to on a regular basis. Another way I incorporated information throughout the entire project was by displaying different facts scattered around my collage as well. I believe this helps describe the information being portrayed throughout the collage.

*Continues next page*

---

**THE RHETORICAL SITUATION**

Purpose
Audience
Rhetorical appeals
Modes & media

*see page 34*

How do I know this is an **Artist's Statement?**

**THE GENRE'S CONVENTIONS**

Elements of the genre
Style
Design
Sources

*see page 35*

## THE RHETORICAL SITUATION

### Purpose

In her Statement, Kristen **describes the rhetorical choices** she made while creating the collage/sculpture piece of her project. She also **discusses the sources** she drew on.

### Audience

Kristen's audience for her collage and Statement is the same as that for the rest of her project: her instructor and classmates.

### Rhetorical appeals

Kristen clearly articulates her intentions and shows her credibility (**ethos**) by noting and documenting her sources. She supports her argument logically (**logos**) by drawing on research and providing her sources in her Statement. She informs readers about drug ads, and supports her claims with specific ads.

### Modes & media

Mode = written
Medium = print

---

LaCroix, *Artist's Statement,* Continued

LaCroix 5

As a result of my research, I believe that the next step to fighting drug advertising is to look at how ads impact a drug's current usage. The drug industry defends their promotional advertising, suggesting that it "helps educate consumers of potential conditions and encourages them to see their doctor for diagnosis and treatment" ("Direct-to-Consumer"). However, critics argue that this advertising is primarily emotional and commonly understates the side effects, causing misleading information to be fed to consumers. According to SourceWatch, a report conducted by the U.S. Government Accountability Office in November 2006 explained:

> "Studies we reviewed found that increases in [direct-to-consumer] advertising have contributed to overall increases in spending on both the advertised drug itself and on other drugs that treat the same condition . . . one study of 64 drugs found a median increase in sales of $2.20 for every $1 spent on [direct-to-consumer] advertising" ("Direct-to-Consumer").
>
> Moreover, it was also found that 86% of consumers who had seen promotional advertisements for prescription drugs requested and ultimately received a prescription for the drug they wanted (Graham).

Although this genre piece doesn't directly convey information gathered from the advertisements themselves, different sources pointed out the common characteristics throughout each advertisement. Almost all of the advertisements use the same techniques to persuade the consumer to relate health, well-being, and happiness with the use of the prescription medication. In one analysis, it was found that 67% of advertisements collected used emotional appeals to gain the reader's attention. Of the 60% of advertisements that were using emotion to promote their product, the most commonly portrayed emotion was the aspiration to get back to normal (Woloshin). This is evident in advertisements on the collage in which individuals with allergies run through fields with flowers because they're "Claritin clear" and elderly arthritis sufferers can convey their happiness hugging a child because of Celebrex. Overall, this genre shows the common characteristics of drug advertisements presenting the ways they induce a reader to believe that the answer to their problem lies within being prescribed the medication.

---

**LaCroix, *Artist's Statement*, *Continued***

LaCroix 6

Works Cited

"Direct-to-Consumer Advertising." *SourceWatch*, The Center for Media and Democracy, www.sourcewatch.org/index.php/Direct-to-consumer_advertising. Accessed 19 Apr. 2007.

Graham, John R. "Direct-to-Consumer Pharmaceutical Advertising: What Does the Literature (Not) Say?" *Health Policy Prescriptions*, vol. 3, no. 4, 2005, www.pacificresearch.org/pub/hpp/2005/hpp_11-5.html. Accessed 25 Apr. 2007.

Lee, Kent. "Drug Advertising Skyrockets." *CBS News*, www.cbsnews.com/2100 -204_162-329293.html. Accessed 25 Apr. 2007.

Woloshin, Steven, et al. "The Value of Benefit Data in Direct-to-Consumer Drug Ads." *Health Affairs*, Project HOPE, 28 Apr. 2004, content.healthaffairs.org/content/ suppl/2004/04/28/ hlthaff.w4.234v1.DC1.

## THE GENRE'S CONVENTIONS

### Elements of the genre

Composers use Statements to **explain how and why they created a work.** Kristen explains why she created her collage: to give viewers a sense of the quantity of drug ads in mainstream magazines.

### Style

A Statement can be written in different styles: Kristen chose an **academic style and tone.** She makes a case for how she reached her audience through appeals and discusses how she used sources.

### Design

Kristen designed this document using **MLA format.** (For more on MLA guidelines, see pp. 395–414.)

### Sources

Kristen documents her sources using MLA in-text parenthetical citations that are, in turn, listed in her Works Cited page. (See also MLA, Chapter 7.)

## Questions: Analyzing Kristen LaCroix's project

**1. Purpose.** Kristen's overall purpose is to persuade her audience that direct-to-consumer drug ads are dangerous. How persuasive are her individual genre compositions (capsule, profile, obituary, and Artist's Statement)? Explain.

**2. Audience.** Kristen, who was writing for her instructor and classmates, made some assumptions during her composing process about how to reach them. What are some of her assumptions? And how accurately do you think she assessed her audience?

**3. Audience.** As a student, do you feel you are included in the audience for these pieces? Why or why not?

**4. Rhetorical appeals.** How effectively does Kristen work with the appeals of logos, pathos, and ethos? Does she seem to favor one over the others? Explain.

**5. Modes & media.** Kristen created her biographical profile and obituary in print form; do you think they would be more effective in digital form? Why or why not? How might her pill capsule collage/sculpture be conveyed digitally? How might she make her compositions more interactive?

**6. Elements of the genre.** How does Kristen use the conventions of each genre to help her make her point? For example, how does the image of the deceased man make the obituary more powerful? How does the overlapping of images in the collage help to make her point?

**7. Style.** Kristen wanted to write the biographical profile in a tone that would appeal to her classmates. Did the tone she used appeal to you? Why or why not? And how effective is her use of detail in the obituary? Explain.

**8. Design.** How does the shape of the collage contribute to its appeal and persuasiveness? Look again at the obituary and think of some related genres. For example, at some memorial services, small brochure-type documents that include memories about the deceased are distributed. How might Kristen's obituary message have changed (or not) if she had chosen a different genre?

**9. Sources.** After reviewing Kristen's Artist's Statement for her collage/sculpture, are you surprised to see how her sources informed her work? Why or why not?

## CHECKLIST: Choosing a Genre
Do you need to decide on a genre to compose in? Ask yourself the following questions.

### WHAT'S YOUR RHETORICAL SITUATION?

☐ **Purpose.** Is my purpose to tell a story, inform, or persuade? Do I have several purposes, and if so, which is my primary purpose?

☐ **Audience.** How would I describe my primary audience? Whose attention do I want most? Who are the people I want to persuade? Do I have another, secondary audience? How will I entice this audience?

☐ **Rhetorical appeals.** How will I establish my credibility (ethos)? Will appealing to my audience's emotions help me persuade them (pathos)? How might logic (logos) help me convince others?

☐ **Modes & media.** Do I want to work with written words? Will I present my ideas in person, orally? Will I use visuals? How about audio? Does my idea lend itself to video? Do I want my piece to be available digitally or in print? Will I use some combination of these modes and media?

### WHAT GENRE CONVENTIONS MATTER?

☐ **Elements of the genre.** How will I structure my composition? What is the best way to combine elements to convey my purpose—and make my case to my audience?

☐ **Style.** Whatever form my composition takes (visual, verbal, etc.), what is the best tone to use to reach my audience? What voice will I use? How present will I be in my composition? What kind of language will I use? What level of detail will I need to convey my purpose?

☐ **Design.** How do I want my composition to look? How will the layout help me achieve my purpose?

☐ **Sources.** What sources will I draw on for my composition? Do I need to conduct interviews? Do I need to research online or in the library? How will I attribute my sources?

# 2

# NARRATIVE GENRES

## CONTENTS

FAIRY TALE ▶
**Gustave Doré**
illustration from "Le Petit Chaperon Rouge."

**e** For e-Pages content, visit **bedfordstmartins**
**.com/bookofgenres.**

We share stories every day: on the bus, in the checkout line, at home. We experience them through social media, memoirs (p. 57), history books, comics, movies, and the evening news. We remember them from the fairy tales of childhood. Constructing narratives is a universal impulse; stories help us make sense of our lives and connect with others. Regardless of the specific genres our stories take—and whether they're fact or fiction, comedies or tragedies, or something in between—they generally include real people or made-up characters, a setting, a conflict, and action.

In your composition course, you may be asked to write a literacy narrative: a story about how you learned to read and write. But there are other, less formal ways to share stories. For example, even a single page from a photo album or scrapbook, such as the one below, suggests part of the story of someone's life. Enikö DeLisle, a blogger in Edgartown, Massachusetts, created an online scrapbook page dedicated to the story of Peter Farkas and Edith Nanay. ▼

**ᴇ** For an Index of Sources & Contexts for material referenced in this chapter, see the e-Pages at **bedfordstmartins.com /bookofgenres.**

◀ SCRAPBOOK PAGE **Enikö DeLisle,** "Peter and Edith." The caption for this couple, Peter Farkas, and Edith Nanay, reads: "Like the story of the country mouse and the city mouse, Peter and Edith were from very different worlds, brought together by fate and circumstance—Or was it destiny? They met at a photographer friend's studio on the day this photo was taken of Edith at age 20—it was love at 1st sight." Above the photos of Peter and Edith are images of their parents. *Heritage Scrapbook, Design by Enikö DeLisle.*

Creating narratives goes back to ancient times: Early aboriginal people painted cave walls with symbols and pictures of animals to convey meaning. Ancient Greeks told stories of gods and heroes, and Native Americans created and passed down legends to warn about tricksters and celebrate heroes. Today's oral histories function similarly, preserving stories that might otherwise be forgotten. For example, the StoryCorps project, archived at the Library of Congress, records the life stories of everyday people. ▼

ORAL HISTORY ▶
**StoryCorps project**.
*StoryCorps.*

**StoryCorps**

## tell your story. pass it on.

▼ OBITUARY
**Elizabeth A. Niles,**
from the National Archives and Records Administration.
*Old Records Division Reference File, Record Group 94, Records of the Adjutant General's Office, National Archives.*

### Woman Who Fought In Civil War Beside Hubby Dies, Aged Ninety-Two

RARITAN, N.J., Oct. 4.—Mrs. Elizabeth A. Niles, 92, who, with close-cropped hair and a uniform, concealed her sex and is said to have fought beside her husband through the civil war is dead here today, aged ninety-two.

The war call found the couple on their honeymoon. The husband, Martin Niles, joined the ranks of the Fourth New Jersey Infantry, and when the regiment left Elizabeth Niles marched beside him. She fought through many engagements, it is said, and was mustered out, her sex undiscovered. Her husband died several years after the war.

Another narrative genre is the obituary. Sound morbid? Check ◀ out the obituaries shown here for Elizabeth A. Niles and Harvey Phillips (on p. 47). Don't these sound like people you wish you'd met? Writers of obituaries, sometimes the deceased himself or herself (some people write them well in advance), sometimes a friend or family member, tell the story of the deceased through key biographical details. A related genre, the eulogy, is a speech delivered at the funeral or memorial, usually written by friends or family members. Through eulogies, writers share stories about the deceased's life, character, and accomplishments. Even an epitaph, the inscription on a gravestone, can tell a story about a life.

## The Rhetorical Situation

There are a lot of ways to tell a story—and countless genres for telling them. However, as a composer you always make specific rhetorical choices. These choices have to do with your purpose and audience, the strategies you use to reach your readers, the media you create in, the style and design of your story, and the sources you draw on to create it.

## Purpose: Why tell stories?

As we worked on this book, we always began our sessions with an exchange of stories about what happened during the course of the day. It helped us reconnect. Our students do this before class, talking about what happened in other classes or at their jobs; no doubt, they do the same at home.

We also use narrative genres to chronicle events. A story may be just a few sentences or it may be epically long, such as *The Odyssey* or *War and Peace*. A story can be true (such as an autobiography) or it can be made up (such as a short story, novel, or other work of fiction). Some stories change history, such as the *Narrative of the Life of Frederick Douglass, an American Slave, Written by Himself*. Douglass's autobiography, which he published in 1845 while living in the North as an escaped slave, helped spark the abolitionist movement in ▼ the United States.

**e** For coverage of **fairy tales** and a sample tale, see e-Pages at **bedfordstmartins.com /bookofgenres**.

◀ MEMOIR
**Frederick Douglass (1818–95).**
*Narrative* frontispiece and title page. *Newberry Library, Chicago, Illinois, USA / Bridgeman Images.*

We also use stories to entertain—and instruct. For example, while most well-known fairy tales are pretty good reads, they were actually created to teach children some kind of lesson. Following is the text of "The Shepherd's Boy and the Wolf," commonly known as "The Boy Who Cried Wolf." This fable is attributed to Aesop (ca. 620–564 BCE), a (possibly mythical) storyteller who lived in Ancient Greece. Note the final line, which explicitly states the moral of the story.

FABLE ▶
**Aesop,**
"The Shepherd's Boy and the Wolf," from the digital collections of the University of Virginia Library.

# UNIVERSITY *of* VIRGINIA LIBRARY

### The Shepherd's Boy and the Wolf

A SHEPHERD-BOY, who watched a flock of sheep near a village, brought out the villagers three or four times by crying out, "Wolf! Wolf!" and when his neighbors came to help him, laughed at them for their pains. The Wolf, however, did truly come at last. The Shepherd-boy, now really alarmed, shouted in an agony of terror: "Pray, do come and help me; the Wolf is killing the sheep"; but no one paid any heed to his cries, nor rendered any assistance. The Wolf, having no cause of fear, at his leisure lacerated or destroyed the whole flock.

There is no believing a liar, even when he speaks the truth.

Why else do we tell stories? To persuade others—or even to sell something. For example, in a job interview, you might tell relevant stories about your previous experience that show you're qualified for the position you're discussing. In terms of selling, think of the many TV ads that use a narrative to make a case about a product, such as car commercials that go something like this: A well-dressed young couple walks through the woods with their kids and golden retriever and then they all pile into their shiny new SUV. The creators of the ad, hired by the SUV manufacturer, are selling you not only the shiny vehicle, but an entire conceptual package including luxury, romance, the American dream, and even environmentalism. In this case, the brief story (couple, kids, dog, woods, car) is used to convince you to buy a large automobile.

## Audience: How do we get others to connect with our stories?

We write stories in order to explore our experiences and share them with others. For a story to resonate, readers must be able to connect with it personally. As writers, we strive for ways to make that happen. For example, in his memoir, *Dreams from My Father*, Barack Obama shares his experiences growing up

Have you ever read a story and wondered about its authenticity? How much does a story's validity have to do with its author? Can you think of examples of an author (or speaker) who seems unreliable?

as a black American and the struggles he faced as he traced his origins, something many readers can relate to. He tells his story through a series of anecdotes that read like a conversation, beginning with how he heard of his father's death. By beginning with such a universal situation and using an informal tone, Obama gets readers invested in his story. Alison Bechdel's *Fun Home* (p. 70) is a graphic memoir about her family's sometimes comedic, sometimes tragic, dysfunction. To reach her audience, she tells a series of stories through images and text written in the first person. She uses humor and her strong writer's voice to invite readers into her story.

There are many reasons for sharing stories—and many ways of reaching readers or listeners. For example, Erna Anolik tells of her experience at Auschwitz through the University of Southern California's Shoah Foundation. Anolik appeals directly to her audience by appearing on video. (To view her testimony, select "Camps" from the topics menu at Shoah.) ▼

What are the stories that make up your life? What are your earliest memories? How did you learn to read and write?

◄ ORAL HISTORY/ TESTIMONIAL **Erna Anolik,** "On Surviving a Concentration Camp," from the Shoah Foundation. *Image of Erna Anolik, "On the Topic of Camps," provided by the USC Shoah Foundation— The Institute for Visual History and Education, http://sfi.usc.edu/.*

## Rhetorical Appeals: How do we use ethos, logos, and pathos to tell stories?

Whether your favorite narrative genre is the Facebook status line or the memoir, you'll be most effective if you tap into the rhetorical appeals: ethos, logos, and pathos.

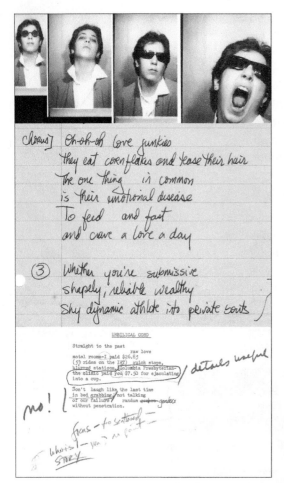

▲ VIDEO MEMOIR
**Amy Braziller,**
from *Writing the
Music Train.*

**Ethos**—How you, as an author or composer, are perceived by your audience is crucial when you tell a story. For example, if you write an autobiography, deliver a eulogy, or share an oral history, your readers and listeners assume that what you are telling them is true, that the stories have actually taken place. If you create a photo essay, such as the one included in this chapter (p. 81), your viewers assume that you have accurately depicted real events. If you create a work of fiction (a short story, a novel, etc.), your ethos as an author is also important. Readers want to trust that you're going to tell them an interesting, worthwhile story, perhaps with a solid, interesting plot and relatable characters they can care about.

◀ In her video memoir, *Writing the Music Train*, Amy documents her days as a punk rocker. She presents herself as a writer who was stunted by a teacher's comments on her early writing; she tells how she succeeded as a writer by composing songs and lyrics in a punk rock band. Here, Amy establishes her ethos as a memoirist by presenting original lyrics, a piece of writing "corrected" by her teacher, and a series of punk-inspired self-portraits.

**Logos**—The logic you use as an author or composer is also significant when you tell a story. For example, a short story, even if it is not told chronologically, usually follows a pattern in which the plot and characters unfold in a logical manner to the reader.

**Pathos**—Your appeal to readers' emotions can go a long way in bringing your story home. For example, when you write a memoir, you identify a moment in your life that has emotional significance, and convey it in a way that gets readers to identify emotionally with that experience.

The Tyler Clementi Foundation was created in memory of Tyler Clementi, a Rutgers University student who was bullied for being gay and who ultimately committed suicide in 2010. The language on the page titled "Tyler's Story" reflects love, pride, and grief. The foundation briefly described at the bottom of the screen was created in Tyler's honor and to provide anti-bullying resources for gay teens.

◄ WEB SITE
**The Tyler Clementi Foundation,** "Tyler's Story." *The Tyler Clementi Foundation.*

## Modes & Media: What are the best choices? How will they affect your story?

A story's *mode* is how the story is communicated—text, audio, video, or a combination of these modes. A story's *medium* can be print, digital, or face-to-face.

| NARRATIVE GENRES | Mode | Medium |
|---|---|---|
| **MEMOIR** Frederick Douglass, *Narrative of the Life of Frederick Douglass* (p. 41) | **WRITTEN** | **PRINT** |
| **FABLE** Aesop, "The Shepherd's Boy and the Wolf" (p. 42) | **WRITTEN** | **DIGITAL** |
| **ORAL HISTORY/TESTIMONIAL** Erna Anolik, "On Surviving a Concentration Camp" (p. 43) | **VISUAL AND AUDIO** | **DIGITAL** |

# The Genre's Conventions

## Elements of the Genre: What do all stories have in common?

Writers rely on certain techniques and conventions to tell a story. You might start with a premise and think about how to convey the story in terms of exposition (the basic information you need to share), tension, rising action, conflict, climax, and resolution (also known as plot, if you're writing creatively). You need to think about your viewpoint, tone, and voice as a storyteller, and how that will affect your reader or listener. You also need to make sure the people involved (or characters, if you're writing creatively) are as interesting and dynamic as possible. Use every sentence to move your story forward to its resolution.

## Style: How does it contribute to your story?

What is your individual style? Individual writers use different styles, have different voices, and include different kinds of details. The following paragraph is by the fiction author Junot Díaz. This is his character Yunior speaking in a short story called "Fiesta, 1980." Pay attention to how he works with the short story genre.

### EXCERPT FROM A SHORT STORY

Mami's youngest sister—my Tia Yrma—finally made it to the United States that year. She and Tio Miguel got themselves an apartment in the Bronx, off the Grand Concourse, and everybody decided that we should have a party. Actually, my dad decided, but everybody—meaning Mami, Tia Yrma, Tio Miguel, and their neighbors—thought it a dope idea. On the Friday of the party Papi got back from work around six. Right on time. We were all dressed by then, which was a smart move on our part. If Papi had walked in and caught us lounging around in our underwear, man, he would have kicked our asses something serious.

—**Junot Díaz,** from "Fiesta, 1980" (*Drown*)

Díaz uses style and voice to convey a narrator who is young and hip within the context of 1980. His narrator, Yunior—who Díaz has acknowledged in interviews is an alter ego—uses language such as "dope idea" and "man, he would have kicked our asses something serious." He creates a narrator who is observant, who has an eye for detail. Díaz writes from the first-person (I) point of view, inviting readers to identify with his main character/narrator. He hints at a conflict between the narrator and his father; Díaz uses the technique of foreshadowing to suggest a future struggle, telling readers that the father's response to laziness ("lounging around in our underwear") would have been to "have kicked our asses." Díaz assures us, as readers, that we'll get the whole story: His choices contribute to his ethos as an author, and to the ethos of his narrator as a central character and storyteller.

---

What stories (or other kind of writing) have you read that have a strong, memorable "voice"—whether in terms of the author or a character? How does voice affect your experience as a reader?

---

For more on **short stories**, see the e-Pages for this chapter at **bedfordstmartins.com /bookofgenres.**

## Design: What is the best format for your story?

How we design a narrative contributes to our readers' experience. The obituary shown here for Harvey Phillips, for example, was designed by editors and designers at *The New York Times,* who made careful decisions about what to emphasize through images, typeface, and interactive features. The photo of Harvey Phillips playing the tuba reinforces his career as "Titan ▶ of the Tuba." The large font size used for the title and the second color used for the hyperlinks add emphasis, making essential information clear to the reader. Hyperlinks in the obituary connect readers to related content. For example, the phrase "to play carols and other festive fare" links to a YouTube video of Harvey Phillips playing at Rockefeller Center's skating rink in 2008. Clearly, the editors and designers anticipated that readers might want to see and hear one of Phillips's performances, and so they added that link and presented it in the first paragraph.

## Sources: What information should you draw on to tell stories?

When we tell or write stories, we often draw on our own experiences. For example, Liz may tell a story about something funny that happened to her this morning, in which case her own life is the source. In other situations, we draw on other sources. Take, for example, the obituary of Elizabeth A. Niles (p. 40). The author interviewed Niles's family to learn details about her life and death. Another example is Amy's video memoir (p. 44); sources she used include photographs, video recordings of her musical performances, and a poster from the club where she performed. Other works, such as fairy tales (see "The Shepherd's Boy and the Wolf," p. 42, and "Little Red Riding Hood," in the e-Pages for this chapter), movies such as *Star Wars,* and books such as *The Lord of the Rings,* draw on tales and legends of the past, including Greek mythology, European folklore, and Icelandic epic poetry.

---

### Music

#### Harvey Phillips, a Titan of the Tuba, Dies at 80
By DANIEL J. WAKIN
Published: October 24, 2010

The tuba players mass by the hundreds every year on the Rockefeller Center ice-skating rink to play carols and other festive fare, a holiday ritual now ingrained in the consciousness of New York.

The tradition began in 1974, the brainchild of Harvey Phillips, a musician called the Heifetz of the tuba. In his time he was the instrument's chief evangelist, the inspirer of a vast solo repertory, a mentor to generations of players and, more simply, Mr. Tuba.

Most tuba players agree that if their unwieldy instrument has shed any of the bad associations that have clung to it — orchestral clown, herald of grim news, poorly respected back-bencher best when not noticed, good for little more than the "oom" in the oom-pah-pah — it is largely thanks to Mr. Phillips's efforts. He waged a lifelong campaign to improve the tuba's image.

▲ OBITUARY
**Daniel J. Wakin,** "Harvey Phillips, a Titan of the Tuba, Dies at 80." *From The New York Times, October 24, 2010 © 2010 The New York Times. All rights reserved.*

# LITERACY NARRATIVES

A literacy narrative tells a story of remembering. In this sense, it is similar to the memoir (p. 57) and the graphic memoir (p. 67). Like memoirists, when the writers of literacy narratives tell their own stories, they relate events and also analyze how these events have shaped their identities. However, there is an important difference between the memoir and the literacy narrative: The writers of literacy narratives tell a story specifically about how they learned to read and/or write.

**What was the first book (or sentence or word) you read? What was the context? Where were you, and who was present? What was the experience like for you?**

You may be familiar with literacy narratives already; many memoirs include sections about how the author learned to read or write or important moments in the development of their literacy. Examples include Jimmy Santiago Baca's *Working in the Dark* and Eudora Welty's *One Writer's Beginnings*. Other memoirs focus more on the development of the author's literacy, such as Stephen King's *On Writing* and Anne Lamott's *Bird by Bird*. Sometimes memoirists will use the story of the development of their reading and writing as a context in which other stories are woven, as Azar Nafisi does in *Reading Lolita in Tehran: A Memoir in Books*, in which she tells the story of a secret women's book group in Iran and how the books they read reflected and affected the lives of the women in the group.

## Analyzing Literacy Narratives: What to Look For

THE RHETORICAL SITUATION

**Purpose**   People write literacy narratives because their formative experiences with reading and writing are important to them; they want to share their stories with others, especially if their literacy histories involve obstacles or challenges. Some may also want to make an argument about the importance of literacy.

**Audience**   Literacy narratives are often written in composition classes and other college courses. Instructors assign this genre to help students understand what influences their speaking, reading, and writing. In this case, a writer's main audience is his or her instructor and classmates. Outside of the classroom, writers create literacy narratives to help educators, librarians, and other people involved in literacy fields better understand how literacy practices and histories manifest themselves in people's lives. (For examples of narratives in various media—text, audio, and video—see the Digital Archive of Literacy Narratives at Ohio State University.)

Literacy narratives are often published for a wider, popular audience; they may appear in a magazine or journal, or as part of a larger collection of essays, as is the case for the narrative that appears later in this section (the excerpt from Richard Rodriguez's *Hunger of Memory* on p. 51).

**Rhetorical appeals**   Writers of literacy narratives use direct language and real details from their lives to establish credibility (ethos). They also make logical connections (logos) between their narratives and the larger issues of literacy; oftentimes, these authors write to emphasize and argue about the importance of literacy, which makes the use of logos especially important.

**Modes & media**   Many writers of literacy narratives use the traditional essay or book form; for example, Helen Keller includes her memoir of learning to understand Braille in her autobiography, *The Story of My Life*. Other literacy narratives appear on the Internet as blog entries or YouTube videos, or are presented in online archives.

### THE GENRE'S CONVENTIONS

**Elements of the genre**   Literacy narratives can take the form of memoirs, in which writers reflect on moments in their lives that show how reading and writing have affected their experiences and sense of self. Authors of literacy narratives convey their experiences, framing their interactions with the world in terms of reading and writing. They also use personal anecdotes and autobiographical details to re-create their experiences for the reader.

Like memoirs, most literacy narratives are written in the first person. Authors of literacy narratives tell stories not just for the sake of recounting events; rather, their goal is for the narrative to culminate in a larger idea or theme that drives the essay. Writers also use literary elements such as setting, character development, dialogue, vivid descriptions and details, symbols, and metaphors.

**Style**   Authors use detail to re-create their literacy experiences for readers. For example, in her literacy narrative, Helen Keller shows readers, through specific examples, what it was like to be a blind and deaf child:

EXCERPT FROM A LITERACY NARRATIVE
My aunt made me a big doll out of towels. It was the most comical, shapeless thing, this improvised doll, with no nose, mouth, ears or eyes—nothing that even the imagination of a child could convert into a face. Curiously enough, the absence of eyes struck me more than all the other defects put together. I pointed this out to everybody with provoking

Think of the stories, memoirs, and other narratives you've read, viewed, or listened to in your life. What details stand out from these stories? How do they affect the ways you think about and remember each story?

persistency, but no one seemed equal to the task of providing the doll with eyes. A bright idea, however, shot into my mind, and the problem was solved. I tumbled off the seat and searched under it until I found my aunt's cape, which was trimmed with large beads. I pulled two beads off and indicated to her that I wanted her to sew them on my doll. She raised my hand to her eyes in a questioning way, and I nodded energetically. The beads were sewed in the right place and I could not contain myself for joy.

—**Helen Keller,** from *The Story of My Life*

Most authors of this genre take literacy seriously, which is why they want to write about it and share their experiences with readers; however, each author of a literacy narrative conveys his or her story in a unique voice. Keller's voice emphasizes that in many ways, she was just like any other child, playing with dolls, for example. Her matter-of-fact tone helps readers identify with and understand her childhood experiences.

**Design**    The literacy narrative usually takes an essay format: It has an introduction, body paragraphs, and a conclusion. However, literacy narratives can take different forms, including audio essay and documentary. In their written form, literacy narratives use typography to emphasize certain points or language.

**Sources**    Like print and graphic memoirs, literacy narratives seldom cite outside sources, because the source of information is almost always just the writer's memories of his or her own life.

## Richard Rodriguez

### *From* Hunger of Memory: The Education of Richard Rodriguez

Richard Rodriguez's *Hunger of Memory* is a collection of autobiographical essays. In the following excerpt, which he calls a memoir, and which is also a literacy narrative (see how genres overlap!), Rodriguez focuses on the power of language as he explores his childhood experiences in a bilingual world. Rodriguez relates the struggles he faced living in between a Spanish-speaking world and an English-speaking world.

The notes in the margins point out Rodriguez's goals as a writer and his strategies for connecting with his readers. They also show how he works with the genre's conventions to tell a compelling story about literacy. *(Excerpt on pp. 52-53 reprinted by permission of David R. Godine, Publisher, Inc. Copyright © 1982 by Richard Rodriguez.)*

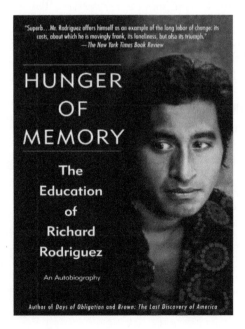

What is the composer, **Richard Rodriguez**, doing?

THE RHETORICAL SITUATION

Purpose
Audience
Rhetorical appeals
Modes & media

*see page 53*

How do I know this is a **literacy narrative**?

THE GENRE'S CONVENTIONS

Elements of the genre
Style
Design
Sources

*see page 54*

# Richard Rodriguez
# From *Hunger of Memory*

Three months. Five. Half a year passed. Unsmiling, ever watchful, my teachers noted my silence. They began to connect my behavior with the difficult progress my older sister and brother were making. Until one Saturday morning three nuns arrived at the house to talk to our parents. Stiffly, they sat on the blue living room sofa. From the doorway of another room, spying the visitors, I noted the incongruity—the clash of two worlds, the faces and voices of school intruding upon the familiar setting of home. I overheard one voice gently wondering, "Do your children speak only Spanish at home, Mrs. Rodriguez?" While another voice added, "That Richard especially seems so timid and shy."

*That Rich-heard!*

With great tact the visitors continued, "Is it possible for you and your husband to encourage your children to practice their English when they are home?" Of course, my parents complied. What would they not do for their children's well-being? And how could they have questioned the Church's authority which those women represented? In an instant, they agreed to give up the language (the sounds) that had revealed and accentuated our family's closeness. The moment after the visitors left, the change was observed. "*Ahora,* speak to us *en inglés,*" my father and mother united to tell us.

At first, it seemed a kind of game. After dinner each night, the family gathered to practice "our" English. (It was still then *inglés,* a language foreign to us, so we felt drawn as strangers to it.) Laughing, we would try to define words we could not pronounce. We played with strange English sounds, often over-anglicizing our pronunciations. And we filled the smiling gaps of our sentences with familiar

**Rodriguez, From *Hunger of Memory*, Continued**

Spanish sounds. But that was cheating, somebody shouted. Everyone laughed. In school, meanwhile, like my brother and sister, I was required to attend a daily tutoring session. I needed a full year of special attention. I also needed my teachers to keep my attention from straying in class by calling out, Rich-heard—their English voices slowly prying loose my ties to my other name, its three notes, Ri-car-do. Most of all I needed to hear my mother and father speak to me in a moment of seriousness in broken—suddenly heartbreaking—English. The scene was inevitable: One Saturday morning I entered the kitchen where my parents were talking in Spanish. I did not realize that they were talking in Spanish, however, until at the moment they saw me, I heard their voices change to speak English. Those gringo sounds they uttered startled me. Pushed me away. In that moment of trivial misunderstanding and profound insight, I felt my throat twisted by unsounded grief. I turned quickly and left the room. But I had no place to escape to with Spanish. (The spell was broken.) My brother and sisters were speaking English in another part of the house.

Again and again in the days following, increasingly angry, I was obliged to hear my mother and father: "*Speak to us en inglés*" (*Speak*). Only then did I determine to learn classroom English. Weeks afterward, it happened: One day in school I raised my hand to volunteer an answer. I spoke out in a loud voice. And I did not think it remarkable when the entire class understood. That day, I moved very far from the disadvantaged child I had been only days earlier. The belief, the calming assurance that I belonged in public, had at last taken hold.

---

**THE RHETORICAL SITUATION**

**Purpose**
Rodriguez aims to share the story of how he came to speak both English and Spanish.

**Audience**
The author knows his primary readers care about language and identity. They are bilingual or native English speakers interested in themes of education, family, and coming-of-age.

**Rhetorical appeals**
Rodriguez begins with a brief story about his parents being willing to do anything for their children, an appeal to **pathos**. The teachers' connecting of Rodriguez's behavior to his lack of English is an example of **logos**.

**Rodriguez, From *Hunger of Memory*, *Continued***

### THE RHETORICAL SITUATION

#### Modes & media

**Mode = written** This literacy narrative is written. Because Rodriguez's topic is language, his choice to convey his story in written words makes sense. If he were to adapt this narrative using digital technology, he might embed audio so his readers could hear what he experienced.

**Medium = print** Rodriguez's book is intended to be read in hard-copy format or as an e-book. In either case, it's intended to be read from beginning to end, one page at a time, unlike online literacy narratives, which can be read in a non-linear fashion.

### THE GENRE'S CONVENTIONS

#### Elements of the genre

This is an **autobiographical account about literacy.** Rodriguez shares childhood experiences of learning to speak, read, and write.

He uses **anecdotes** to advance a central idea; e.g., with the brief, personal story in paragraph 1, Rodriguez prepares readers for his ideas about language and identity, and his argument about bilingual education.

He writes in the **first person** and **describes settings** to connect readers with his experience. He contrasts his home setting with his classroom (where he is an outsider) to emphasize the difference in his private and public encounters with literacy.

#### Style

Rodriguez **uses rich detail** to re-create his experience for readers. Because his essay centers on how he hears language, he focuses on bringing the dialogue alive and uses **phonetic spelling** so that readers hear exactly what he hears.

His **tone and voice reflect his personality and speech.** He quotes the nuns to emphasize how they enunciate and "Americanize" words.

#### Design

Rodriguez uses italics to highlight Spanish and English words, and also to emphasize certain passages and sounds (*"That Rich-heard!"*).

#### Sources

Rodriguez does not cite outside sources because he is the source of his story.

## Questions: Analyzing Rodriguez's literacy narrative

**1. Purpose.** Rodriguez not only tells a story about his experiences with language, but also makes an argument regarding bilingual education. What is his argument? How persuasive is he?

**2. Purpose.** Reread the final paragraph of the essay. Why do you think Rodriguez chose to conclude this way?

**3. Audience.** What techniques does Rodriguez use to connect with his audience? Is an audience that has experienced bilingual education his target audience? Why or why not?

**4. Rhetorical appeals.** How does Rodriguez develop his ethos as someone who speaks about education with authority? How does his phonetic spelling of "Rich-heard" contribute to the pathos of the piece?

**5. Modes & media.** Imagine Rodriguez's literacy narrative as a digital text online. Which words of the excerpt could be linked to other Web sites? For example, perhaps the word "Rich-heard" could be linked to a YouTube video in which someone says the name as Rodriguez's family would say it; this might emphasize how strange the Americanized pronunciation sounded to Rodriguez.

**6. Elements of the genre.** What are some similarities between Rodriguez's literacy narrative and memoirs that you may be familiar with (e.g., see Dave Eggers's memoir on p. 61)?

**7. Style.** Given that writers of literacy narratives tell stories about how they learned to speak, read, or write, why might many of them include dialogue? What role does dialogue play in Rodriguez's literacy narrative?

**8. Style.** Rodriguez includes some Spanish words in his narrative. How do the Spanish words contribute to the essay's effect?

**9. Design.** Rodriguez italicizes bits of dialogue. What do you think is his purpose for doing so?

**10. Sources.** The source for this literacy narrative excerpt is Rodriguez's own memory. Do you think a narrative written by one of the nuns would differ significantly from Rodriguez's? Why or why not?

# Drafting a Literacy Narrative

---

## CHECKLIST: Drafting a Literacy Narrative
Thinking of writing about how you learned to speak, read, and write? Ask yourself the following questions.

### WHAT'S MY RHETORICAL SITUATION?

- ☐ **Purpose.** What specific moment in my life as a reader or writer do I want to write about? Why? What questions do I have about that moment? How might I interpret that moment? What insights do I want to share with others? How did that moment shape me as a reader or writer?

- ☐ **Audience.** How would I describe my readers? Why will my experience with reading or writing matter to my readers? What do I want them to get out of my story? And how will I reach them?

- ☐ **Rhetorical appeals.** How will I establish my authority as a writer? How reliable will I be as a narrator? To what extent will I appeal to my readers' emotions? To what extent will I rely on logic to support my interpretations of my experiences?

- ☐ **Modes & media.** Do I want readers to experience my story in written, audio, or visual form? Do I want my literacy narrative to be print, electronic, or presented face-to-face?

### WHAT GENRE CONVENTIONS MATTER?

- ☐ **Elements of the genre.** I'm writing about my own life: How will I keep my writing true and accurate? How much will I disclose about myself (and others) in my literacy memoir? Will I write in the first person? What anecdotes will I use to tell the story of myself as a reader or writer, and why? Also, what literary elements might I use? For example, will I use dialogue (as Rodriguez does) or a metaphor to help readers compare my experience to something else?

- ☐ **Style.** What tone will I take in my writing? Will my literacy narrative be serious or funny? Academic or down-to-earth? What kind of language will I use? How much detail will I include?

- ☐ **Design.** What format will my literacy narrative take? Do I want to compose a standard literacy narrative, focusing on words, or do I want to create a graphic literacy narrative that includes illustrations?

- ☐ **Sources.** What memories will I draw on? Will I need to check my story with others from my life, or will I rely on my own recollections and interpretations?

---

## PRACTICE  Want to experiment? Draft your own literacy narrative.

Do some freewriting about an early memory of reading or speaking and how that early event shaped your attitudes and experiences with language. Draft a narrative in which you tell the story of your early experience; be sure to make specific points about how that experience shaped you as a reader, writer, and/or speaker. Include anecdotes, details, and quotations from conversations, as Rodriguez does.

# MEMOIRS

The word *memoir* comes from the Old French *memoire* and Latin *memoria*, both meaning "memory." A memoir is a written (or graphic, film-based, etc.) and true account about one's own life and experience. Often, memoirists' works focus on a specific and significant moment in their lives—one that has specific meaning and importance.

A memoir is like a personal essay, except that memoirists tend to focus on looking at their past, asking questions, analyzing, and attempting to make sense of their lives. Memoirists also tend to use literary techniques, including dialogue. Some memoirs are funny, like David Sedaris's *Me Talk Pretty One Day*, which includes essays about his life as an American in France. Other memoirs are more serious, such as Joan Didion's *The Year of Magical Thinking*, about her loss of her husband and daughter, and Frank McCourt's *Angela's Ashes*, about his impoverished childhood in Ireland.

Some memoirists are famous; some are infamous. For example, former president Bill Clinton, in his memoir, *My Life*, discusses his two presidential terms with a focus on his successes and failures, as well as the life that brought him to the White House, and even his intimate life, including his affair with an intern. In the category of infamous, French art thief Stéphane Breitwieser wrote a memoir, *Confessions of an Art Thief*, about how he stole a billion dollars' worth of art. Another infamous example is author James Frey, who came under fire for fabricating his struggles with addiction in *A Million Little Pieces,* a book that he and his publisher originally presented as a memoir.

> What moment(s) in your life would you most want to write about in a memoir? Why?

## Analyzing Memoirs: What to Look For

THE RHETORICAL SITUATION

**Purpose** Memoirists share their stories because they believe they can offer insights to others, as does Mitch Albom in his memoir, *Tuesdays with Morrie*, in which he writes about how people develop values. Memoirists write because they want to share lessons learned in difficult times, as Isabel Allende does in *Paula*, her memoir of watching her adult daughter die. Sometimes they write because they want to explain themselves, or "tell their side of the story," as rapper Eminem's mother, Debbie Nelson, does in her memoir, *My Son Marshall, My Son Eminem*. Many memoirists (like Sedaris) also aim to entertain their readers, but for most, the goal is to share their experiences.

**Audience**  Memoirists (such as Albom and Allende, mentioned above) often write for a wide readership and publish their works in books and magazines such as *The New Yorker* and *O: The Oprah Magazine*. Some write for popular audiences (such as Nelson, especially). However, some write for narrower audiences, such as fans of poetry: Donald Hall, in his memoir *The Best Day the Worst Day*, writes about his life with poet Jane Kenyon. This book appeals to Liz, for example, because she is a fan of both of these poets, and is interested in learning about them as writers and partners too. Memoirists can offer insights and information about what they are most famous for (in Hall's case, poetry).

**Rhetorical appeals**  To earn their readers' trust, memoirists must be reliable narrators of their own stories. They develop their ethos through the anecdotes they share, but also through the language and tone they use. Isabel Allende, in another memoir, entitled *Aphrodite: A Memoir of the Senses*, uses sophisticated yet playful language to establish herself as—you guessed it—sophisticated and playful: "I repent of my diets, the delicious dishes rejected out of vanity, as much as I lament the opportunities for making love that I let go by because of pressing tasks or puritanical virtue." Sensationalist or overly dramatic language, such as the use of many superlatives (*biggest, grandest, smartest*), or an overreliance on exclamation points (*I was so scared!!*) could compromise the ethos of the memoirist.

**Modes & media**  Traditionally, memoirs are written in book or essay form. A memoir will sometimes include photos of the memoirist to supplement the text, giving the reader a visual image to associate with an anecdote or bit of personal history. Memoirs are occasionally adapted into films or television movies, as in the case of *Persepolis*, Marjane Satrapi's graphic memoir, which was made into an animated film in 2007.

How would you describe your life—in six words? *SMITH* magazine invites you to publish your mini-memoir at their site.

THE GENRE'S CONVENTIONS

**Elements of the genre**  Because memoirs are based on writers' memories, most are naturally written in the first person. Memoirs feel intimate not only because of their first-person perspective, but because their authors reveal personal thoughts and feelings to the reader. Self-disclosure, the sharing of emotion, personal ideas, facts, and other information, invites readers into a bond with the author, drawing them into a shared sense of trust.

Memoirists use many of the same techniques fiction writers use, such as dialogue, vivid descriptions of settings, imagery, and metaphor. Instead of inventing *characters*, memoirists include other real people in their work. For example, in David Sedaris's memoirs, his boyfriend Hugh is a frequent presence, as are members of Sedaris's family.

Memoirists present anecdotes to illustrate specific moments or points. An anecdote is usually just a few sentences long and is usually amusing rather than sad, such as this anecdote from Donald Hall's *The Best Day the Worst Day*:

> One morning when I tried to start the Plymouth, it barely turned over and wouldn't catch. I was puzzled until I checked the thermometer on the porch. It was minus twenty-one degrees—and I had not noticed: New Hampshire's cold is drier than Michigan's and less painful.*

Memoirs are true, or at least represent the truth as the author honestly remembers it. Sometimes others who have a stake in the stories in someone else's memoir challenge the accuracy of those stories. For example, some of Frank McCourt's neighbors from his hometown in Ireland have different memories of the degree of misery McCourt suffered. McCourt writes in his memoir *Angela's Ashes*:

> People everywhere brag and whimper about the woes of their early years, but nothing can compare with the Irish version: the poverty; the shiftless loquacious alcoholic father; the pious defeated mother moaning by the fire; pompous priests; bullying schoolmasters; the English and the terrible things they did to us for 800 long years.
>
> Above all—we were wet.

But is *Angela's Ashes* a totally factual story? asks *Los Angeles Times* writer Tim Rutten, upon McCourt's death. Rutten explores the answer:

> [S]ome outraged Limerick residents insisted not, and the local newspaper dredged up old photos of Frank and [McCourt's brother] Malachy well dressed and their long-suffering mother sleek and fed. Still, if the McCourt family misery was neither as unrelieved nor as perfect as the author recalled it, his account "was no less true for all of that."

How "true" or accurate a memoir is has to do with the nature of memory; memory is subjective and imperfect. Memory, and how we write about it, also has to do with our personalities, our sense of others—and of justice and injustice, our hopes and wishes. As readers and writers, we need to take these factors into account when we approach the memoir. However, there is a big difference between lapses and

*Excerpt from *The Best Day, The Worst Day*, by Donald Hall: © 2006 Houghton Mifflin Harcourt.

other imperfections of the memory—and the purposeful invention of things that never happened. In extreme cases, when an author's work is more fiction than truth, the memoirist loses all credibility (see the discussion of James Frey on p. 57).

**Style** Memoirists use a lot of detail to tell their stories. In fact, Bill Clinton's memoir was criticized for being too richly detailed. (One Amazon.com review asks, "Do we really need to know the name of his childhood barber?")

For more **memoirs** and other biographical genres, see the Index of Genres on page G-1.

Memoirists also use a great range of tones to tell a story. For example, even Frank McCourt's memoir about misery is not without wit and charm ("Above all—we were wet"). The style of a memoir can vary considerably depending on who the author is. Bill Clinton, known as charismatic and talkative as governor of Arkansas and president of the United States, comes across as charming and garrulous in his memoir. His vocabulary reflects his worldliness and education, and his sentences are often long and detailed. Consider the first sentence in Clinton's *My Life*:

> Early on the morning of August 19, 1946, I was born under a clear sky after a violent summer storm to a widowed mother in the Julia Chester Hospital in Hope, a town of about six thousand in southwest Arkansas, thirty-three miles east of the Texas border at Texarkana.

At forty-nine words long, this sentence is three times the length of the average written sentence. A much shorter but very powerful sentence begins Isabel Allende's memoir *Paula*:

> Listen, Paula.

These words instantly indicate that the memoir is part letter to Paula, Allende's dying daughter.

**Design** Most memoirs are print texts published in book form (however, see also "Graphic Memoirs," p. 67). Although the text-based memoir focuses on words (not images), some memoirs feature a gallery of photos and documents from the writer's life. The book cover usually presents a flattering photo of the writer. For example, on the cover of his memoir, Bill Clinton does not look beleaguered (as he may have felt during the Whitewater hearings or impeachment proceedings of his second term); rather, he is smiling and looks healthy and at ease.

**Sources** Most memoirs are based on personal observation and experience. For this reason, memoirists seldom cite outside sources. However, if someone were to write a memoir of a group or an organization, that person would, no doubt, draw on historical documents, interviews, and other sources of information.

## Dave Eggers

### *From* A Heartbreaking Work of Staggering Genius

The following excerpt is from Dave Eggers's memoir, *A Heartbreaking Work of Staggering Genius*. In it, Eggers tells the true story of how, at the age of twenty-two, he became the guardian fully responsible for raising his younger brother after both his parents died within a few weeks of each other. This excerpt is from the beginning of the book, when his mother is dying. Eggers has since made a name for himself as an author and editor, writing several highly praised novels and running McSweeney's, an independent publisher. Eggers also cofounded 826 Valencia, a literacy tutoring center for kids.

Annotations in the margins of the excerpt on pages 62–63 show the choices Eggers made in terms of his purpose, sense of audience, and use of rhetorical appeals. You'll also see notes on how this work reflects the conventions of the memoir genre—in terms of its real-life content and specific techniques. *(Excerpt on pp. 62–63 reprinted with the permission of Simon & Schuster, Inc., from* A Heartbreaking Work of Staggering Genius, *by David ("Dave") K. Eggers. All rights reserved.)*

PHOTO ▶
**Dave Eggers.**
*Courtesy of McSweeney's Publishing.*

**What is the composer, Dave Eggers, doing?**

THE RHETORICAL SITUATION

Purpose
Audience
Rhetorical appeals
Modes & media

*see page 63*

**How do I know this is a memoir?**

THE GENRE'S CONVENTIONS

Elements of the genre
Style
Design
Sources

*see page 63*

# Dave Eggers
# From *A Heartbreaking Work of Staggering Genius*

I am holding the nose. As the nose bleeds and we try to stop it, we watch TV. On the TV an accountant from Denver is trying to climb up a wall before a bodybuilder named Striker catches him and pulls him off the wall. The other segments of the show can be tense—there is an obstacle course segment, where the contestants are racing against each other and also the clock, and another segment where they hit each other with sponge-ended paddles, both of which can be extremely exciting, especially if the contest is a close one, evenly matched and with much at stake—but this part, with the wall climbing, is too disturbing. The idea of the accountant being chased while climbing a wall . . . no one wants to be chased while climbing a wall, chased by anything, by people, hands grabbing at their ankles as they reach for the bell at the top. Striker wants to grab and pull the accountant down—he lunges every so often at the accountant's legs—all he needs is a good grip, a lunge and a grip and a good yank—and if Striker and his hands do that before the accountant gets to ring the bell . . . it's a horrible part of the show. The accountant climbs quickly, feverishly, nailing foothold after foothold, and for a second it looks like he'll make it, because Striker is so far below, two people-lengths easily, but then the accountant pauses. He cannot see his next move. The next grip is too far to reach from where he is. So then he actually *backs up*, goes down a notch to set out on a different path and when he steps down it is unbearable, the suspense. The accountant steps down and then starts up the left side of the wall, but suddenly Striker is there, out of nowhere—*he wasn't even in the screen!*—and he has the accountant's leg, at the calf, and he yanks and it's over. The accountant flies from the wall (attached by rope of course)

**Eggers, From *A Heartbreaking Work of Staggering Genius,* Continued**

and descends slowly to the floor. It's terrible. I won't watch this show again.

Mom prefers the show where three young women sit on a pastel-colored couch and recount blind dates that they have all enjoyed or suffered through with the same man. For months, Beth and Mom have watched the show, every night. Sometimes the show's participants have had sex with one another, but use funny words to describe it. And there is the funny host with the big nose and the black curly hair. He is a funny man, and has fun with the show, keeps everything buoyant. At the end of the show, the bachelor picks one of the three with whom he wants to go on another date. The host then does something pretty incredible: even though he's already paid for the three dates previously described, and even though he has nothing to gain from doing anything more, *he still gives the bachelor and bachelorette money for their next date.*

Mom watches it every night; it's the only thing she can watch without falling asleep, which she does a lot, dozing on and off during the day. But she does not sleep at night.

"Of course you sleep at night," I say.

"I don't," she says.

## THE RHETORICAL SITUATION

### Purpose

As a memoirist, Eggers's overall purpose is to tell a story about his life. In this case, the story is also about the lives of his family members.

### Audience

Eggers's audience is adults who appreciate creative, innovative, and literary memoirs.

### Rhetorical appeals

Eggers establishes his **ethos** as an author, writing directly to readers and setting up the story of his mother's illness. He details the chase scene on TV, building tension and appealing to the **pathos** (emotions) of his readers, inviting us to identify with his experience.

## THE GENRE'S CONVENTIONS

**Elements of the genre**

**Is written in first person** ("I am holding . . .").

**Is a true story** about the writer's real life. The narrative represents Eggers's memory of this time in his life; however, his sister Beth objected to this account because Dave did not portray her as an equal parent to their brother Toph, though she claims to have been.

**Mentions actual people in the writer's life.** Here Eggers writes about his mother and mentions his sister Beth; elsewhere he writes about his younger brother, Toph; other siblings; friends; and acquaintances.

Eggers, From *A Heartbreaking Work of Staggering Genius,* Continued

## THE RHETORICAL SITUATION

### Modes & media

**Mode = written**
Author Dave Eggers probably assumed that his readers would be adults reading his memoir alone to themselves because that is the conventional way that books are read. Although some memoirs include photographs of the author, Eggers did not include any images beyond artwork for the cover.

**Medium = print** *A Heartbreaking Work of Staggering Genius* is available in print and as an audiobook. It is presented here in print, and the assumption is that you will read it linearly, that is, from beginning to end. (Though in this case, you might be noticing the annotations in the margins as well.)

## THE GENRE'S CONVENTIONS

**Includes a personal anecdote.** In this case, it's a serious one about his mother's illness, and how it shows itself one night in front of the TV.

**Is written using literary techniques, including dialogue** ("Of course you sleep at night.").

### Style

**Eggers's style and tone convey his personality.**
"There is an obstacle course segment, where the contestants are racing against each other and also the clock, and another segment where they hit each other with sponge-ended paddles, both of which can be extremely exciting," for example, indicates his wry wit.

**The writing is rich in details.**
Instead of simply saying he is watching a physical contest on TV, he specifies, "On the TV an accountant from Denver is trying to climb up a wall before a bodybuilder named Striker catches him and pulls him off the wall."

### Design
Text with little white space between paragraphs.

### Sources
No footnotes or Works Cited list. The main source for the memoir is Eggers's life.

## Questions: Analyzing Eggers's memoir

**1. Purpose.** Why might Eggers give so much detail about the shows he is watching on television?

**2. Audience.** Why would someone want to read Eggers's story, which is, in part, about his mother dying of cancer?

**3. Audience.** In this excerpt from his memoir, how does Eggers develop a sense of intimacy with his readers?

**4. Rhetorical appeals.** Most memoirists are themselves their main source of information. Based on this excerpt, are you convinced that Eggers has established his ethos? Is he a reliable narrator? Why or why not?

**5. Modes & media.** If you were in charge of selecting an actor to read the audio version of this book, whom would you select, and why?

**6. Elements of the genre.** Considering how fallible human memory is, how much accuracy do you expect in a memoir? Do you have higher or lower expectations of accuracy for autobiographies or histories? Why? And how does creativity figure into the memoir as a genre?

**7. Style.** Eggers wrote his memoir in the first person. Imagine that he rewrote this excerpt in the third person ("*Dave is holding his mother's nose. As the nose bleeds and they try to stop it, they watch TV.*"). How would you read the memoir differently?

**8. Style.** Based on the excerpt from *A Heartbreaking Work of Staggering Genius*, what is your impression of Eggers's personality? Which details in the excerpt lead you to feel this way?

**9. Design.** In this brief excerpt, Eggers uses a long, unbroken paragraph: What do you think this text style indicates about the tone and style of the book?

**10. Sources.** Because Eggers himself is the main source of the book, the story he tells is told from his perspective. His sister, Beth, claimed that he inflated his role in raising their little brother, Toph. Is there anything in this excerpt that you think might be seen differently by someone who was there?

# Drafting a Memoir

---

## CHECKLIST: Drafting a Memoir
Thinking of composing a memoir? Ask yourself the following questions.

### WHAT'S MY RHETORICAL SITUATION?

☐ **Purpose.** What specific moment in my life do I want to write about? Why? What questions do I have about that moment? How might I interpret that moment? What insights do I want to share with others?

☐ **Audience.** How would I describe my potential readers? Why will my memoir matter to them? What do I want them to get out of it? And how will I reach them?

☐ **Rhetorical appeals.** How will I establish my authority as a writer? How reliable will I be as a narrator? To what extent will I appeal to readers' emotions? How will I use logic to support my interpretations?

☐ **Modes & media.** Do I want readers to experience my story in written, audio, or visual form? Do I want my memoir to be print, electronic, or presented face-to-face?

### WHAT GENRE CONVENTIONS MATTER?

☐ **Elements of the genre.** As a person writing about my own life, how will I keep my writing true and accurate? How much will I disclose about myself (and others) in my memoir? Will I write in the first person? What anecdotes will I use, and why? Also, what literary elements might I use? For example, will I use dialogue?

☐ **Style.** What tone will I take in my writing? Will my memoir be funny? Serious? Tragic? What kind of language will I use? How much detail will I provide?

☐ **Design.** What format will my memoir take? Will I compose a print memoir—and if so, will I include photographs and other images? Or will I compose a graphic memoir or other type of memoir?

☐ **Sources.** What memories will I draw on? Will I need to check my story with others from my life, or will I rely on my own recollections and interpretations?

---

## PRACTICE Want to experiment? Draft your own memoir.

Think about a key event in your life. Draft a few paragraphs in which you begin telling the story of the event in the first person. Use specific details and language so that your readers will feel like they were there. Consider how you want your readers to feel as they read your draft: Do you want them to laugh, cry, be outraged, or something else?

# GRAPHIC MEMOIRS

The graphic memoir is a memoir told through text and images, usually drawings. Sometimes there are more words than images, but usually it's the other way around. If you are interested in composing any kind of memoir (whether it's in graphic or comic book form, or a film, for example), we suggest that you read the "Memoirs" section of this chapter (p. 57).

The graphic memoirist Alison Bechdel (p. 70) has described her process in interviews: First she writes her text; then she inks the images. Other graphic memoirists use different techniques, foregrounding the images in the panels and writing the text in later. You may already be familiar with graphic memoirs, a genre first made popular by Art Spiegelman's *Maus*, a graphic memoir about surviving the Holocaust. Graphic narratives now have a place as respected literary texts: They're the focus of college courses; they've won Pulitzer Prizes; and they've inspired successful movies including *A History of Violence* and *Sin City*.

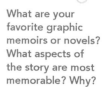

What are your favorite graphic memoirs or novels? What aspects of the story are most memorable? Why?

## Analyzing Graphic Memoirs: What to Look For

THE RHETORICAL SITUATION

**Purpose**   Like other memoirists, graphic memoirists tell the story of (or a story from) a writer's life. Using such literary devices as character (in this case, real people rather than fictional ones), dialogue, and setting, graphic memoirists connect their readers with their work. Graphic memoirs, which look something like extended comic strips, focus on transporting the reader to a world that is very different from everyday reality. Sometimes a graphic narrative, such as Marjane Satrapi's *Persepolis*, discloses elements of a culture—Satrapi's life growing up in Iran and later as an expatriate— showing readers a world that may be outside their own experience.

**Audience**   Graphic memoirists know that their audiences want a look into someone else's life, as told by that person. Graphic memoirists know their audiences are particularly drawn toward the visual, and perhaps grew up reading comic books, or really like illustrated texts or alternative narrative forms.

As graphic memoirs are becoming more popular in academic settings, with instructors assigning them as part of their reading lists—or as an alternative to the print memoir in composition classes—more students are creating and reading them.

**Rhetorical appeals**   The play between visuals and text helps graphic memoirists emphasize certain aspects of the narrative to readers. Because memoirists want their readers to empathize with their experiences, they often use appeals to emotion to draw readers into their world. For example, when a story is meant to elicit shock, the shape of the letters and the use of bold graphics, along with the expressions on the character's face, can guide the reader's emotional response, emphasizing pathos. In a graphic memoir, ethos is a central concern, because the audience must trust that the writer is accurately representing experience and events.

**Modes & media**   Graphic memoirs usually take print form but are sometimes digitized for the Web. Graphic memoirs and novels are often adapted for film, reimagined as animated stories, as is the case with *Persepolis*.

Consider Art Spiegelman's graphic memoir *Maus*, which is a Holocaust narrative (the story of Spiegelman's father). To what extent is the graphic memoir an appropriate genre for dealing with traumatic experiences?

THE GENRE'S CONVENTIONS

**Elements of the genre**   Like all memoirs, the graphic memoir has a real-life plot that revolves around a series of events, or a storyline. The storyline hinges on a central conflict driven by real people who function as characters do in fiction. The central conflict of Marjane Satrapi's *Persepolis*, for example, is her (and her family's) struggle to survive the Iranian Revolution (of 1979, also known as the Islamic Revolution); at that time, the country's monarchy was overthrown and Iran became an Islamic republic with an increasingly repressive government.

To tell their stories, graphic memoirists use words—usually organized into short, simple sentences—that provide dialogue and move the plot along toward the conflict and its resolution. The visuals (usually inked drawings) move the plot, too, but also assist in creating the setting, atmosphere, and emotion of the memoir.

The written content of the graphic memoir often appears in boxes or in sentences interspersed among the visuals. Dialogue is usually placed in a bubble or box linked to the character's mouth. Most graphic composers do not present words and sentences in traditional paragraphs. The advantage is that by isolating a sentence in a box, the author creates a snapshot of a moment, or of a series of moments, adding to the power of the story. Further, though the graphic narrative may not provide traditional transitions between ideas and scenes, there are some transitional expressions that help the visual memoirist move from one idea to the next. For example, the words "only four months earlier" show a jump back in time.

Just as in comic strips, the visuals of a graphic memoir do a lot to relate the story and reinforce aspects of the written narrative. The visuals, which can focus in on a detail and pan out like a movie camera, for example, emphasize certain moments and allow readers to see what is happening. See the "Design" section below for more on how drawings function in a graphic memoir.

**Style**    The reader's experience depends on the written and visual style of the graphic memoirist—how much (and what kind of) detail and specific techniques he or she uses, and the quality of the visual story's voice and tone.

*Tone and voice.* Graphic memoirists communicate the tone of their stories and their voices as storytellers through word choice, diction, visuals, and the choice of typeface and other graphics. For example, if a character is feeling exasperated, the writer might choose a font (such as **Impact**) to illustrate that mood.

*Detail.* Depending on their target audience, graphic memoirists may use intricate, almost lifelike detail, as in Bechdel's *Fun Home* (p. 70). Other times, graphic memoirists might take a more cartoon/superhero approach, such as that of DC Comics' *Watchmen*. Typically, graphic memoirists limit their reliance on text, using it primarily to keep the plot moving. Sentences in a given panel tend to be short, without much embellishment. In Satrapi's *Persepolis*, the narrative detail is written in a journalistic style, giving readers a sense of watching a revolution unfold.

**Design**    Like comic strips, graphic memoirs are organized into visual panels, usually squares or rectangles that essentially freeze a moment in its own individual space. Like all graphic composers, graphic memoirists make choices about where to place panels, how large to make them, and what words from the written narrative to emphasize. They also decide how and where to place figures and objects within a panel, in order to direct the reader. The size of one object next to another (scale), the direction an object is facing in relation to the page, and the cutting off of part of an object in a frame are all careful choices that create meaning for readers.

For more **graphic memoirs** and other biographical genres, see the Index of Genres on page G-1.

Other design choices include whether to use a font, real handwriting or lettering, or a font that mimics handwriting. Many graphic composers use block lettering, boldface, and italics when they want to show emphasis, and use different graphical styles when needed (such as `Courier` or other distinctive fonts). Graphic memoirists also need to make decisions about the style, shape, and size of boxes, balloons, or other word-framing devices. Sometimes they assign specific shapes for specific speakers in the story. They also make choices about white space from panel to panel, and within a frame of text. White space is used for aesthetic reasons, but also to call attention to certain parts of the text, to provide a visual pause, or to represent the absence of something or someone.

**Sources**    See "Memoirs" (p. 57).

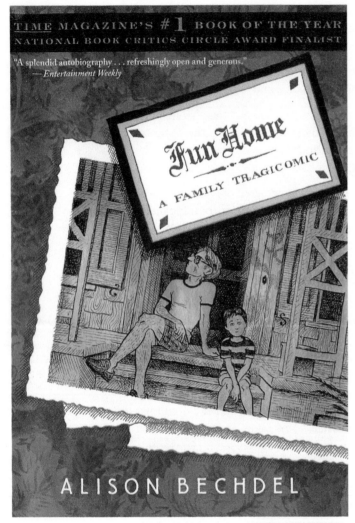

▲ BOOK COVER
& AUTHOR PHOTO ▶
**Alison Bechdel,**
*Fun Home: A Family
Tragicomic.* Author
photo: Liza Cowan.

## Alison Bechdel

## *From* Fun Home: A Family Tragicomic

Alison Bechdel gained notoriety in the comics scene in 1983 with her syndicated strip *Dykes to Watch Out For.* In her comic strip, Bechdel combined political commentary with the daily lives of mostly lesbian characters, narrating their love affairs, breakups, and adventures as attendees at such lesbian festivals as the Michigan Womyn's Music Festival.

After years of working on this comic strip, Bechdel wrote a graphic memoir, *Fun Home: A Family Tragicomic,* published in 2006. In *Fun Home,* she tells the story of growing up with a closeted father who ran a funeral parlor and taught English. In this work, Bechdel conveys the importance of her father in her life. The section that we've excerpted is from the book's first chapter. In it, Bechdel's own coming-out story is overshadowed by the death of her father.

As a graphic memoirist, Bechdel makes plenty of decisions about her purposes and how she will draw in her readers. She also works with many of the conventions of the graphic narrative, while using a style that is all her own. The annotations in the margins of the work draw your attention to these choices, inviting you to think critically about their impact on you as a reader and composer.

**Bechdel, From *Fun Home*,** *Continued*

*Continues next page*

**What is the composer, Alison Bechdel, doing?**

THE RHETORICAL SITUATION

Purpose
Audience
Rhetorical appeals
Modes & media

*see page 72*

**How do I know this is a graphic memoir?**

THE GENRE'S CONVENTIONS

Elements of the genre
Style
Design
Sources

*see page 73*

Alison Bechdel, From *Fun Home*

## Purpose

Bechdel's goal is to tell a story about her life, which includes childhood, coming out, and coming to terms with her father's identity and death.

## Audience

Bechdel knows her readers enjoy memoirs and are especially drawn to comics and graphic novels. They are also interested in the coming-of-age and sexual identity themes in *Fun Home*.

## Rhetorical appeals

Bechdel appeals to readers' emotions (**pathos**) by showing how her father's "queer death" caused her to feel "qualmish, faint, and, on occasion, drunk." The author uses events from her life to establish her **ethos**. Announcing "I am a lesbian" helps establish her ethos in what is partly a coming-out story.

*(Continued on p. 74)*

**Bechdel, From *Fun Home*,** *Continued*

**Bechdel, From *Fun Home*,** *Continued*

### Elements of the genre

Bechdel **tells a real-life story** in a form that **looks like a comic strip.**

The author **focuses on a central conflict**: her attempt to understand a childhood surrounded in secrets. (Elsewhere in the work, she moves back and forth between her own coming-out story and her father's inability to come out as a gay man.)

**Her plot and conflict are driven by real people**: Bechdel, the narrator; her mother; and her father. Sometimes she presents characters visually (narrator and father), other times through dialogue (mother).

(Continued on p. 74.)

Alison Bechdel, From *Fun Home*

**Bechdel, From *Fun Home*,** *Continued*

## Modes & media

**Mode = written and visual** Bechdel uses both the written and visual texts to communicate her story about coming out. Bechdel's use of visuals—such as when she mails a letter to her parents or talks on the phone with her mother—shows readers how Bechdel wants us to view her at that moment.

**Medium = print** Just like traditional memoirs, graphic memoirs are available in both print and digital media. Bookstores, these days, have sections devoted to graphic novels, where you can also find graphic memoirs such as Bechdel's. There are, however, digital graphic novels and memoirs that are often created online. Web sites such as Comic Master allow you to create your own short graphic novel/memoir online using their free software.

**The visuals don't just represent the text**—they highlight specific aspects and create emphasis. E.g., Bechdel presents the dictionary definition of the word *queer*. By blowing up the dictionary page, she shows her narrator-self coming to grips with ways to read her father's identity and death. **The visuals move the action along** by showing it. E.g., we know Bechdel mails the letter not because the text says so, but because she shows herself licking the envelope and putting it in the mailbox.

Bechdel's **drawings take up more space than her words**; her words convey the weight of the narrative while the images convey emotion. **Text is not presented in paragraphs.** E.g., the isolated sentences in the top frame create a snapshot of moments. Combined, they would create a traditional paragraph but would have a very different effect.

## Style

Bechdel uses **diction and word choice** to portray an educated, articulate character. E.g., she says she "imagined my confession as an emancipation. . . ." **The distance Bechdel's narrative voice has from her story** gives the reader a lens through which she sees her past from an adult perspective. E.g., when she tells how others responded to her coming-out letter, she states, "The news was not received as well as I had hoped."

## Design

Bechdel's text font mimics handwriting and she uses bold, italics, and other type effects to convey emotion.

She also **varies her layout**; e.g., some panels are parallel to each other, while others are not aligned evenly. The **shapes of frames** around the text indicate what is thought, spoken, or narrated. Different shapes indicate who is speaking. In the bottom right frame, the mother's dialogue appears in a jagged box that comes out of the phone. Bechdel uses **graphical style** to approximate reality. E.g., when the narrator types out, "I am a lesbian," Bechdel switches to Courier to approximate typing. On the third page shown here, Bechdel uses a lot of **white space** to call attention to the text and to represent the absence of her father.

## Sources

Bechdel's source is her own memory, so there are no citations to outside materials.

## Questions: Analyzing Bechdel's graphic memoir

**1. Purpose.** What parallels does Bechdel draw between her father's homosexuality and her own coming out?

**2. Audience.** Based on the short excerpt, who would you say is the audience for this graphic memoir? Why?

**3. Rhetorical appeals.** How do the visuals emphasize the main character's emotional state?

**4. Modes & media.** What different elements of the plot do the text and visuals emphasize?

**5. Elements of the genre.** Are there any places where the visuals and words seem to contradict each other or seem to be in tension with each other? If so, why do you think there is a contradiction or tension?

**6. Elements of the genre.** How much time is covered in the pages shown? How does Bechdel show the passage of time?

**7. Elements of the genre.** Only three pages of the graphic memoir are represented here. Even though it is a small snapshot of the book, what sense do you get of Bechdel as the narrator of her own story? How do the different graphic elements, combined with words, give you that sense of her?

**8. Style.** How would you describe the level of detail Bechdel uses in her visuals? In her text? Does the level of detail serve different purposes? If so, how?

**9. Design.** Sometimes Bechdel chooses to sandwich the narrative text between the visual panels. Other times, she places the narrative text within its own box. What reasons might she have for this? Are the narrative pieces that are in a box more significant? Why?

**10. Sources.** The main source for the graphic memoir is Alison Bechdel's life and experience. How does this influence your reading of the work?

# Drafting a Graphic Memoir

---

**CHECKLIST: Drafting a Graphic Memoir** Thinking of composing a graphic memoir? Ask yourself the following questions.

## WHAT'S MY RHETORICAL SITUATION?

☐ **Purpose.** What specific moment in my life do I want to write about? Why? What questions do I have about that moment? How might I interpret that moment? What insights do I want to share with others? How would visuals illustrate the moment and make my experience more tangible for my reader?

☐ **Audience.** Who are my potential readers? Why will my memoir matter to them? What do I want them to get out of it? How old are they and how will I reach them? How will I use visuals to do that?

☐ **Rhetorical appeals.** How will I establish my authority as a writer? How reliable will I be as a narrator? To what extent will I appeal to my readers' emotions? How might I use logic?

☐ **Modes & media.** Do I want to create my story first with graphics or text? What aspects will I represent visually, and what aspects will I represent in written form? Would my graphic memoir be appropriate to translate into a film? Do I want to create my story using ink on paper or using a digital program?

## WHAT GENRE CONVENTIONS MATTER?

☐ **Elements of the genre.** How will I keep my writing true and accurate? How much will I disclose about myself (and others) in my graphic memoir? Will I write in the first person? What anecdotes will I use to tell my story, and why? How will I visually represent my characters? Will they be true to life or exaggerated? How will I balance the narrative with dialogue?

☐ **Style.** What tone will I take in my writing? Will my graphic memoir be funny? Serious? Tragic? What kind of language will I use? How much detail will I provide? How will I use the visuals to convey my tone?

☐ **Design.** What fonts will I use? How might I use shapes of boxes to indicate specific character voices? Will I vary the shapes of my panels?

☐ **Sources.** What specific memories will I draw on? Will I need to check my story with others from my life, or will I rely on my own recollections and interpretations? Will I need to research historical and cultural events related to the time period of my story?

---

**PRACTICE** Want to experiment? Draft and sketch out your own graphic memoir.

Identify a pivotal moment in your life. Sketch out a few panels of a graphic memoir that convey the moment and its importance. Think about how you want the key people who participated in the event to come across to readers and how you can convey those characteristics with visual details. Think about what you want to convey through dialogue and what you want to convey through internal reflection.

# PHOTO ESSAYS

A photo essay is a group of photos that tells a unified story or makes a unified argument. Some photo essayists provide supplementary text or brief captions for their images; others choose to present the images without words. Some photo essayists are journalists whose purpose is to convey a news or human interest story or offer commentary on an event. The photo essays published by *Mother Jones* about the aftermath of the 2010 earthquake in Haiti and a piece on how Ikea has partnered with UNICEF in a program to encourage reading in Albania are examples of works by photo essayists using images and text to provide information and even make an argument.

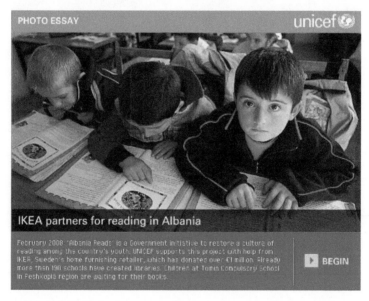

◀ PHOTO ESSAY STILL
**UNICEF,**
"Ikea Partners for
Reading in Albania."
© UNICEF/NYHQ2008-
0133/Giacomo Pirozzi.

Photo essays can also be viewed as works of art that express ideas and evoke emotional responses in the viewer. You can find them online, in galleries and museums, and also in magazines such as *Life*, *Time*, and *National Geographic*. Photo essayists generally aim to make a particular point or argument; some make specific social commentaries. For example, photographer Walker Evans (1903–75) and writer James Agee (1909–55) collaborated on a book-length photo essay about the hardships of tenant farmers in the American South in the 1930s. *Let Us Now Praise Famous Men* is a very word-heavy photo essay.

TEXT FROM PHOTO ESSAY

During July and August 1936 Walker Evans and I were traveling in the middle south of this nation, and were engaged in what, even from the first, has seemed to me rather a curious piece of work. It was our business to prepare, for a New York magazine, an article on cotton tenancy in the United States, in the form of a photographic and verbal record

PHOTO FROM ▶
PHOTO ESSAY
**Walker Evans,** "Lily Rogers Fields." This photo appeared in *Let Us Now Praise Famous Men.* Shown here is Lily Rogers Fields, the wife of sharecropper Bud Fields, and their two children. Evans took this photo in 1936 in Hale County, Alabama. *Library of Congress.*

of the daily living and environment of an average white family of tenant farmers. We had first to find and to live with such a family; and that was the object of our traveling.

—**James Agee,** from *Let Us Now Praise Famous Men*

Other photo essays involve fewer words, such as many of the photo essays available online at the *Time* magazine site. See, for example, the photo essay titled "Famous Couples."

## Analyzing Photo Essays: What to Look For

THE RHETORICAL SITUATION

**Purpose**  Photo essayists have two main goals: to tell a story and/or to make a point. Usually their work is focused on a specific theme. For example, the Agee and Evans photo essay collaboration (p. 77) focuses on the experiences of sharecroppers in the South, and in doing so, asks the viewer to look at the relationship of those who are privileged (those who read the book) and those who are less fortunate (the subjects of the book). Photo essayists usually seek to evoke an emotional response in the viewer. For example, the creators of the *Time* essay on famous couples emphasize the endurance of love in relationships by showing celebrity couples enjoying a happy moment.

**Audience**   Photo essayists know that their audiences are drawn to visual storytelling—and to the issues and themes of their works, which may be social and cultural, journalistic, and/or artistic. For example, photo essayist and documentarian Brenda Ann Kenneally, creator of an ongoing project called "Upstate Girls," aims her work at those interested in her intimate look at working-class women and their families. Norbert Wu targets his essay "Life beneath Antarctic Ice" at an audience interested in nature.

**Rhetorical appeals**   Depending on their subject matter and composition, photo essayists may emphasize logos, pathos, or ethos to make their point. For instance, Andrew Testa's disturbing photo essays of Bangladeshi women who were scarred by acid for refusing to accept marriage proposals emphasize pathos by showing the women's scars close up; ethos is also important because viewers must trust that Testa has not used lighting or perspective to distort reality.

**Modes & media**   While photo essayists usually combine visuals with some written text, some also incorporate bits of audio, such as in *The New York Times* photo essay "One in 8 Million," which highlights the lives of ordinary New Yorkers. Photo essays can be print based, but also offered digitally, as is *Let Us Now Praise Famous Men;* or they can be created mainly for online publication, such as *Time* magazine's photo essays.

When might it be more appropriate to create a photo essay rather than a written essay? To what extent do your purpose, audience, and subject affect your choice of whether to create in a visual mode?

THE GENRE'S CONVENTIONS

**Elements of the genre**   A photo essay can be used to tell a simple story, but the genre is often used to persuade viewers to sympathize with a point of view or to take a specific action. For example, through "Upstate Girls," Brenda Ann Kenneally, hopes that viewers connect with the subjects' struggles and triumphs.

Some photo essayists include captions to provide context; others include more text, with a 50:50 text-to-image ratio, such as in Suzanne Merkelson's "Keeping Up with the Qaddafis," published online in March 2011 in *Foreign Policy*. In this piece, Merkelson accompanies each photo with at least one paragraph of text.

Photo essayists make rhetorical choices about their purpose and audience, and they choose images carefully, in the same way a writer chooses words, paragraphs, and structure. The photo essayist chooses each image with the viewer's intellectual, emotional, or other responses in mind. Similarly, a photo essay can be structured much like any persuasive essay. For example, the introductory images, which function like a written essay's introduction, need to establish the subject matter and further the purposes of the piece—to push the narrative or argument forward.

Photo essayists use some techniques that narrative essayists, storytellers, and persuasive writers do (pp. 45–46 and 183). That is, they select and sequence their content in a way that will spark their readers' interest, keep them reading/viewing, and ultimately convince them of a particular point of view. Initial images may serve as an introduction, while those that follow may build in terms of intensity to support the argument the photo essayist wants to make. (See "Design," below.)

### Style

*Detail.* Most photo essayists do not provide much detail in the text of their essays. For example, most captions give just enough information for readers to understand the story behind (and location of) the related photo. The photos themselves can show varying degrees of detail—in some cases, capturing one element up close, such as a person's face; in others, showing a panoramic view of a landscape.

*Tone.* Photo essayists choose images that reflect the mood they want to convey. For example, a photo essayist who wants to stir readers to take action in response to an environmental disaster such as an oil spill might feature an image of someone rescuing and rehabilitating an oil-soaked bird.

For more **visual genres**, see the Index of Genres on page G-1.

**Design**   A good photo essayist usually presents a variety of images (from different perspectives) and arranges the images in an order that builds emotion, furthers an argument, or advances a story. For example, a photo essayist who wants to tell a story might sequence the images from one event to the next, much like a narrative essayist would. In other cases, the photo essayist might not choose a linear progression, but might instead order images for maximum impact, especially when presenting an argument.

**Sources**   Photo essays always involve primary research, as the photographer is always witnessing the subject of the photos firsthand. Brenda Ann Kenneally's photo essay on working-class women, for example, is entirely informed by Kenneally's interviews with the women she photographed. Sometimes secondary research must be conducted as well, to fill in historical details or other information.

# Eros Hoagland

## From "Life in the Googleplex"

*Time*, a weekly news and current events magazine, often features photo essays related to world events. The magazine commissioned and published in February 2006 an online photo essay titled "Life in the Googleplex." Presented as a slide show, the essay was created by photojournalist Eros Hoagland of Redux Pictures. Hoagland, who began his career reporting on the fallout of El Salvador's civil war, is also interested in showing the subtleties of place, something he clearly brought to the Googleplex project. Given the range of his subject matter, the quality of his work, and the publications he calls his clients (including *The New York Times* and *Newsweek*), Hoagland, like *Time* magazine, has some good ethos.

His purpose in creating "Life in the Googleplex" was to give readers an inside look at what it's like to work at Google. By highlighting gadgets and leisure opportunities, Hoagland suggests that employees do serious work but also have plenty of time to play. Further, by showing the human side (and human faces) of Google, Hoagland establishes that the company is more than a search engine.

The annotations in the margins point out the decisions that Hoagland made, perhaps with the input of editors at *Time*, including the purpose of the piece, the perceived audience, and the genre conventions applied. *(All images on pp. 81–84: Eros Hoagland/Redux Pictures.)*

▲ AUTHOR PHOTO &
▼ PHOTO ESSAY
**Eros Hoagland,** from his profile at Redux, and the "Life in the Googleplex" slide show online at *Time*.

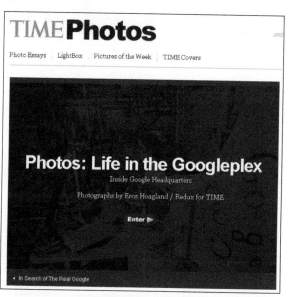

Hoagland, *From "Life in the Googleplex,"* Continued

What is the composer, **Eros Hoagland**, doing?

**THE RHETORICAL SITUATION**

Purpose
Audience
Rhetorical appeals
Modes & media

*see page 83*

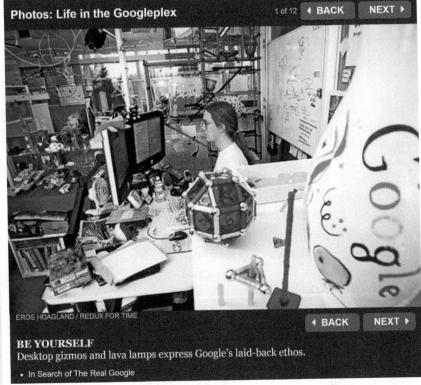

Photos: Life in the Googleplex          1 of 12   ◀ BACK   NEXT ▶

EROS HOAGLAND / REDUX FOR TIME          ◀ BACK   NEXT ▶

**BE YOURSELF**
Desktop gizmos and lava lamps express Google's laid-back ethos.

• In Search of The Real Google

*Continues next page*

How do I know this is a **photo essay**?

**THE GENRE'S CONVENTIONS**

Elements of the genre
Style
Design
Sources

*see page 83*

**Hoagland, *From "Life in the Googleplex,"* Continued**

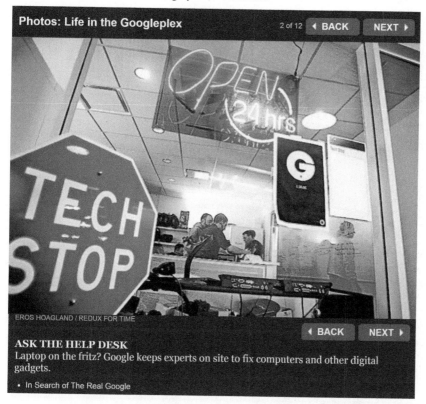

Photos: Life in the Googleplex    2 of 12  ◀ BACK   NEXT ▶

OPEN 24 hrs

TECH STOP

◀ BACK   NEXT ▶

EROS HOAGLAND / REDUX FOR TIME

**ASK THE HELP DESK**
Laptop on the fritz? Google keeps experts on site to fix computers and other digital gadgets.

• In Search of The Real Google

*Continues next page*

## THE RHETORICAL SITUATION

### Purpose
Hoagland (perhaps with the help of *Time* editors) set out to illustrate how a high-tech work environment, such as Google, can be filled with creativity and fun.

### Audience
The audience for the photo essay is *Time* magazine readers, Google fans, and people interested in cultural trends related to technology and the workplace.

### Rhetorical appeals
Hoagland uses **logos** to appeal to readers by building a logical case about how a creative work environment inspires workers' creativity. He establishes the essay's **ethos** by using photos of Google workers.

### Modes & media
**Mode = written and visual**
Hoagland's primary goal was to visually portray a typical workday at Google.

*(Continued on p. 84.)*

## THE GENRE'S CONVENTIONS

### Elements of the genre
**Is comprised mainly of photos,** with some text.

**Is focused on a topic,** in this case, specifically workers' play and leisure time at Google's offices.

**Tells a story,** in this case, about a typical workday at Google.

**Makes an argument,** in this case that Google's workers are productive and inspired by creativity and recreation.

**Includes captions that explain the photos.** For example, the caption with the first image reads, "Be Yourself." Without it, viewers could assume the message is that the office is crowded and cluttered rather than supportive of individuality and expression.

### Style
**Use of the present tense** reinforces the "this is happening now" feel of the piece.

Hoagland, *From "Life in the Googleplex,"* Continued

Adding written details tells a more complete story; it also provides a commentary about what is taking place, to persuade viewers that the workplace atmosphere is pleasant.

**Medium = digital**

Although *Time* publishes photo essays in their print edition, "Life in the Googleplex" was published digitally at *Time*'s Web site. Publishing this essay online is especially appropriate because Google is a digital company; further, the advantages of publishing online are obvious. As long as viewers have an Internet connection, they can see and share the essay; if it were only in print form, they would need to locate a copy of that edition of the magazine.

**Photos: Life in the Googleplex** 3 of 12 ◄ BACK | NEXT ►

EROS HOAGLAND / REDUX FOR TIME

◄ BACK | NEXT ►

**GOOGLER WITH GOGGLES**
A lifeguard sits on duty as an employee works out in one of two swim-in-place pools at Google's headquarters.

- In Search of The Real Google

## THE GENRE'S CONVENTIONS

A **playful tone** emphasizes that Google is a fun place to work. For example, the swimmer is referred to as a "Googler with Goggles."

**Design**

The variety of the photos suggests the breadth of activities that can take place in the Googleplex. Elements of the text are highlighted by typeface choice and color.

Captions consistently appear below the photos and each caption has a pithy heading.

**Sources**

Hoagland conducted primary research—spending time at Google, following around employees, trying to capture the elements of a typical day and different aspects of work and play.

## Questions: Analyzing Hoagland's photo essay

**1. Purpose.** What is the unifying message of the three photos shown? Explain in one sentence.

**2. Purpose.** Do the photos tend to focus more on people or objects? Why do you think Hoagland chose that emphasis?

**3. Audience.** What techniques did Hoagland use so that viewers would see the playful nature of working at Google?

**4. Rhetorical appeals.** Based on the three photos shown, what is your impression of the ethos of Hoagland and the *Time* editors he most likely worked with?

**5. Modes & media.** If there were no captions, what assumptions might you make about life at Google? Are there places where the image is able to fully convey its message without the text? Where and how? Why is this essay best viewed digitally, rather than in print?

**6. Elements of the genre.** In "Life in the Googleplex," do the photos illustrate the captions or do the captions describe the photos? Explain your answer.

**7. Elements of the genre.** View the entire "Googleplex" slide show. Now that you've seen the whole thing, would you say that this essay is primarily telling a story or making an argument? Why?

**8. Style.** How does the tone and voice of the writing emphasize the working environment at Google? How does the selection and presentation of photographs contribute to that tone? Use specific examples to illustrate your answer.

**9. Design.** View the entire "Googleplex" slide show again. Pay attention to how Hoagland and *Time* ordered the images. How might a different ordering of images impact the narrative? How do Hoagland and *Time* use organization of the images to build logic?

**10. Sources.** The photos were taken by Eros Hoagland, a professional photographer commissioned by *Time* magazine (Hoagland is the source of the images). Do you think someone working at Google would choose to highlight different aspects of working there? How?

# Sketching Out a Photo Essay

---

## CHECKLIST: Sketching Out a Photo Essay Thinking of composing a photo essay? Ask yourself the following questions.

### WHAT'S MY RHETORICAL SITUATION?

☐ **Purpose.** What is my story, and why do I want to tell it? Or do I want to do more than tell a story? If so, what main point or argument do I want to make, and why?

☐ **Audience.** Who are my readers/viewers that I want to attract to my photo essay? Why will my photo essay matter to them? What do I want them to get out of it? And how will I reach them?

☐ **Rhetorical appeals.** How will I use ethos, pathos, and logos to reach my audience? How will I establish my authority as a photographer and writer? Will I rely more on pathos or logos? How will my photos and text work together to appeal to my readers' sense of ethos, pathos, and/or logos?

☐ **Modes & media.** Do I want to present my photo essay in hard-copy format, as in a photo album; or electronically, as on a Web site; or in some other way? How will these choices impact how my viewers experience my photo essay? For example, would it be better to present it online or as a collection of large photos matted and framed on the wall?

### WHAT GENRE CONVENTIONS MATTER?

☐ **Elements of the genre.** I know that the best photo essays tell a story but also put forth some type of argument. For example, in his "Googleplex" essay, Eros Hoagland asks viewers to see Google as a successful company in part because the workplace itself encourages creativity. How does this compare to what I want to do? What argument will I make in my photo essay—and how will I do it?

☐ **Style.** What tone do I want to strike? Playful, like in "Life in the Googleplex"? Or more serious, like in Kenneally's photo essay?

☐ **Design.** What order will I arrange the photos in, and how will the order affect how my viewers understand my story?

☐ **Sources.** Where will I need to go to take my photos? Will I want to photograph individuals and their possessions? Or perhaps historical sites? Will I need to request special permission to do so?

---

## PRACTICE Want to experiment? Draft your own photo essay.

Just as Hoagland and *Time* convey a sense of work life at Google in their photo essay, you might want to do something similar. What do you have to say about your own workplace, campus, or residence? Brainstorm about how people at one or more of those locations feel about that place; then take three to five photos of the place that convey that feeling. Your draft photo essay should offer some kind of commentary on the place you've chosen as your subject; it should not simply show it. Add brief captions similar to the ones in the "Google-plex" essay that help tell a story and offer perspective.

# INFORMATIVE GENRES

## CONTENTS

◀ CHART/INFOGRAPHIC
See p. 117.

For e-Pages content, visit **bedfordstmartins.com/bookofgenres**.

For an Index of Sources & Contexts for material referenced in this chapter, see the e-Pages at **bedfordstmartins.com /bookofgenres.**

Information is everywhere, all the time: online, on your phone, in e-mail, on social networking sites, on TV, and on radio. It's on billboards, road signs, and menus. But not all information is equal: Some is reliable; some is not. How do we make sense of it all? The trick is to (1) figure out which *sources* of information are the best, and (2) analyze, use, and share that information according to your needs as a reader or writer.

In daily life, you draw on a variety of sources for information. When you don't know the meaning of a word, you might go to *Dictionary.com.*

DICTIONARY ENTRY ▶
**Dictionary.com,**
"Vertiginous."
© *Dictionary.com, LLC vertiginous. Dictionary .com. Collins English Dictionary—Complete & Unabridged 10th Edition. HarperCollins Publishers, dictionary .reference.com/browse /vertiginous. Accessed: November 28, 2012.*

How else do you use sources? A few more scenarios:

» You're curious about Prohibition after watching a movie set in the 1920s, so you check out the History Channel site, a trusted encyclopedia, or a PBS documentary for a better sense of that period.

» You want to plant tomatoes on your back porch, so you consult a reference book or online guide by the American Horticultural Society on varieties that grow best in your region.

» You want to avoid the flu, so you read the U.S. Department of Health and Human Services' latest recommendations online or stop in at your pharmacy for information about the flu vaccine.

» You need to create a presentation using software you don't know how to use, so you refer to a Microsoft PowerPoint tutorial or ask an experienced colleague for a quick lesson.

How do you deal with the information you encounter online every day? How do you know what's fact and what's not?

» There's something wrong with your car and you don't know what the flashing light on your dashboard means, so you flip through your owner's manual or call a knowledgeable mechanic.

In each of these cases, you've found convenient but also authoritative sources.

**Authoritative sources of information**  Here's another scenario. Let's say you want to prepare for a disaster. You do a quick search on YouTube, and turn up a video by a guy in a gas mask who is part of a survivalist fringe group living in a desert bunker. His instructions in the video are rambling, confusing, and possibly paranoid (to take the example to an extreme). Though the video may be riveting, this is a poor source of information because the author lacks credibility (or ethos) and logic (logos). A better, if less colorful, source would be a government organization such as Homeland Security, FEMA (Federal Emergency Management Agency), or the American Red Cross. These are considered excellent sources of information because these organizations are long established and made up of experts. The material they publish is researched, written, and reviewed by authorities in the field of emergency preparation; approved by the government; and tested out in actual emergencies. For example, Homeland Security's "Preventing Terrorism" advice has been vetted by a major government organization (see p. 90).

**Author bias**  No author is purely objective, including Homeland Security. Personal viewpoints, inclinations, and prejudices can creep into any communication, whether it's a recipe or a government document. Bias can show up in the language that writers use. For example, Homeland Security's use of the terms *Counterterrorism* and *Border Security* indicate a specific point of view. No matter its source, information is never 100 percent unbiased.

Bias can also be apparent in the tone a writer uses. Let's say an article appears in your local newspaper about a family lost during a snowmobiling trip. You might expect the reporter to simply present the facts of what happened. However, after reading closely, you see the reporter's opinion has subtly found its way onto the page: The family's lack of preparation and

▼ PHOTO
**John W. Gertz,**
"Man Wearing Gas Mask Using Cell Phone." Beware of information from unreliable sources. *John W. Gertz/Corbis.*

# Homeland Security

Home　Topics　How Do I?　Get Involved　News　About DHS

## Preventing Terrorism

### Preventing Terrorism Overview
Protecting the American people from terrorist threats is the reason the Department of Homeland Security was created, and remains our highest priority.

### Biological Security
We protect the nation's health security by providing early detection and early warning of bioterrorist attacks.

### Chemical Security
Some chemical facilities possess materials that could be stolen and used to make weapons. A successful attack on certain high-risk facilities could cause a significant number of deaths and injuries.

### Countering Violent Extremism
The threat posed by violent extremism is neither constrained by international borders nor limited to any single ideology.

### Critical Infrastructure Security
Critical infrastructure is the physical and cyber systems and assets so vital to the United States that their incapacity or destruction would have a debilitating impact on our physical or economic security or public health or safety.

### Explosives
DHS works to enhance the nation's counter-IED capabilities and reduce the threat of explosive attack against critical infrastructure, the private sector, and federal, state, local, tribal, and territorial entities.

if you SEE something SAY something

### If You See Something, Say Something
A program to raise public awareness of indicators of terrorism and terrorism-related crime, and to emphasize the importance of reporting suspicious activity to the proper state and local law enforcement authorities.

NTAS
National Terrorism Advisory System

### National Terrorism Advisory System
NTAS alerts communicate information about terrorist threats by providing timely, detailed information to the public, government agencies, first responders, public sector organizations, airports and other transportation hubs.

When was the last time you noticed a sign in an airport, train station, or bus stop? Make a point to examine one and ask yourself: Who created the sign? Whose point of view does it convey? What assumptions does it convey about travelers?

ignorance about avalanche safety influenced the writer and affected his or her tone and the use (or omission) of details. On the other hand, imagine that the reporter thinks the family did the best they could have—they were as prepared as possible, but no one could have survived that avalanche. In that case, the writer would use a more sympathetic tone.

Even a nutritional label reflects the biases, assumptions, and values of its authors. For example, the creators of the label here ▶ assume that calories and fat are more important than other nutritional information, and so calories, calories from fat, and total fat grams are presented first. Protein, vitamins, and minerals appear toward the bottom of the chart. The author, in this case, is a government organization, the National Heart, Lung, and Blood Institute (NHLBI) at the National Institutes of Health.

Presenting information is not a neutral activity. All writing has a persuasive quality, and informative writing is no exception. This is not a bad thing, just something to keep in mind as you read and compose.

**Nutrition Facts**
Serving Size 1/2 cup (67g)
Servings Per Container 16

**Amount Per Serving**

Calories 100     Calories from Fat 0
                    % Daily Value

| | |
|---|---|
| Total Fat 0g | 0% |
| Saturated Fat 0g | 0% |
| Cholesterol 0g | 0% |
| Sodium 60mg | 3% |
| Total Carbohydrate 22g | 7% |
|   Dietary Fiber 0g | 0% |
|   Sugars 15g | |
| Protein 3g | |

| | | | |
|---|---|---|---|
| Vitamin A | 2% | Vitamin C* | 0% |
| Calcium | 45% | Iron* | 0% |

*Percent Daily Values are based on a 2,000 calorie diet.

◀ LABEL
**National Institutes of Health,**
standard U.S. food label.

# The Rhetorical Situation

## Purpose: Why share information?

When we write to inform, we share facts and details with our readers. One type of informative writing is instructions. If you've ever purchased a piece of furniture that required assembly, you've probably worked with a set of instructions. The instructions were likely designed by an engineer or technical writer with two goals: (1) to help you put together parts of an object, and (2) to persuade and assure you that through simple language and design that the task would be easy.

Sharing information, according to *Merriam-Webster*, is sharing "knowledge obtained from investigation, study, or instruction." A set of instructions certainly gives information "obtained from investigation": Most instructions undergo usability testing and are revised for clarity and accuracy before publication.

Another example of informative writing is the informational brochure. You've probably seen these at your doctor's or dentist's office—brochures about how to control asthma or whiten your teeth. Consider the teeth whitening brochure: It may provide facts about various methods; however, it might also offer reasons for whitening, pricing information, and a photo of an attractive model with sparkling-white teeth. Is the material in the brochure presented *only* to inform, or is there another motive at work? Could the brochure creators also be trying to convince you to whiten your teeth?

What instructions have you referred to lately? How helpful were they? Were they written for someone like you? How could you tell?

INFOGRAPHIC ▶
**Joe Palca,**
"Explainer: What Are
Spent Fuel Rods?"
Palca knows his
audience. He gives a
clear explanation of a
complex problem and
uses plain language
to break down what
happens during a
nuclear meltdown.
See also p. 94. © 2001
National Public Radio,
Inc. Illustrations from
NPR news report titled
"Explainer: What Are
Spent Fuel Rods?" was
originally published on
NPR.org and is used
with the permission of
NPR. Any unauthorized
duplication is strictly
prohibited.

## SPECIAL SERIES

# the science of japan's nuclear crisis

## Explainer: What Are Spent Fuel Rods?

by JOE PALCA

March 15, 2011   2:28 PM

### Inside The Nuclear Reactors

| Latest Problems | Normal Functioning Reactor |
| --- | --- |

**Reactor Core**

**Spent Fuel Pools**

At the **No. 4 reactor**, fires broke out Tuesday and Wednesday near where spent fuel rods are stored in pools of water. Workers at the plant have been having trouble maintaining water levels in these pools, and experts are concerned about the status of the rods. If the pools drain and the spent rods are exposed, they too can melt, releasing radiation and potentially starting a fire.

**Suppression Pool**

Officials say the March 15 blast at the No. 2 reactor affected a section known as the **suppression pool.** The suppression pool is used in emergencies to absorb excess heat and steam from the reactor. After the explosion, officials reported a drop in pressure in the No. 2 reactor's suppression pool, indicating a failure of some kind -- potentially a crack or leak. In five of the reactors at the Fukushima Daiichi plant, the suppression pool is located in a large ring-shaped tank surrounding the reactor core.

Source: General Electric via U.S. Nuclear Regulatory Commission

Credit: Adam Cole, Andrew Prince, Maria Godoy, Stephanie d'Otreppe, Nelson Hsu/NPR

When you read informative genres, keep an eye out for what *else* is going on. An author of a scientific report, for example, may present facts, but as a way to influence you to share an opinion or take an action.

stations    donate    🛒 shop    sign in/register

| Latest Problems | Normal Functioning Reactor |

**POWER GENERATION**

REACTOR
Steam
Fuel Rods
Core
Control Rods
Feed-water Pump
Water
Turbine
Generator
Condenser
Cold Water Pump
Sea Water
**COOLING SYSTEM**

**PRIMARY CONTAINMENT STRUCTURE**

**Normally Functioning Boiling Water Reactor (BWR)**
The Fukushima Daiichi reactors are boiling-water reactors. Nuclear reactions driven by radioactive uranium inside the **fuel rods** generate heat, boiling water in the **reactor**. The resulting steam turns a **turbine**, which powers a **generator**. When hot steam flows over pipes in the **condenser**, it cools to become water and re-enters the reactor via the **feed-water pump**. A cold-water pump draws in **seawater** that keeps the condenser pipes cool. Under normal operation, this water does not enter the reactor.

## Audience: How do we inform others?

As writers, we need to know our audiences—who they are and what they want. For example, in the piece above an "Explainer" feature created for National Public Radio, writer

The Rhetorical Situation    93

For more examples of **news articles** and **charts/infographics,** see the Index of Genres on page G-1.

Joe Palca, along with the illustrators listed below the images, provides the facts of a recent news event (Japan's nuclear reactor problems following the March 2011 tsunami) and visuals that show the differences between a normally functioning reactor and a damaged one. The NPR writer and illustrators know that most of their readers are not nuclear experts and do not want tons of text or technical jargon; general readers want clear information (in "layman's terms") so they can understand the basics of a complex system.

## Rhetorical Appeals: How do we use ethos, logos, and pathos to inform?

When we write to inform, how do we get our audiences invested? Whether you're composing a research paper, fact sheet, or flowchart, you will use the rhetorical appeals: ethos, logos, and pathos.

**Ethos**—how you, as an author, are perceived by your audience—is extremely important when reporting information. That's why it's essential to draw on reliable sources of information in your research, and to convey that knowledge with authority, and as neutrally as possible. If your audience thinks you are unreliable, or that you have some unstated motive, then you will not have established your ethos.

The article on page 95 was written by Mireya Navarro, an environmental reporter for *The New York Times*. In her article, "E.P.A. Rejects City Timeline on PCBs," she covers the facts of how the Environmental Protection Agency is putting pressure on New York City public schools to speed up their plan to replace toxic and potentially hazardous fluorescent light fixtures. Navarro establishes her ethos by stating facts, quoting from authoritative sources, and keeping her tone neutral and her writing as free of her own opinion as possible. Further, her position as a writer for a renowned newspaper contributes to her ethos, as does her profile, which notes her experience and links to her other articles about the environment.

**Logos**—or your use of logic as an author—is also significant. "How to" or instructional genres, such as recipes, make heavy use of logos. When cooks create recipes, they direct the reader in what to do, in a specific order. Chopping ingredients, mixing them, and cooking them must be presented to readers as logical steps. In the example on page 96, the chef, Lora Guillotte of *Saucie.com*, presents her recipe for Louisiana Pork Chops in a logical manner, listing the ingredients and measures clearly, outlining the steps, and illustrating them with helpful images.

**Pathos**—your appeal to your readers' emotions—is generally not a priority when you're writing to inform. On the other hand, if you want to inform but also persuade your readers, you can appeal to their emotions. For example, in the *Saucie .com* recipe for Louisiana Pork Chops, the author appeals to readers' pathos by suggesting that like her, they are busy preparing for holidays, and therefore want an uncomplicated

RECIPE ▶
**Lora Guillotte,**
"Louisiana Pork Chops," *Saucie.com.* Guillotte's instructions are clear and logical.
*Lora Guillotte.*

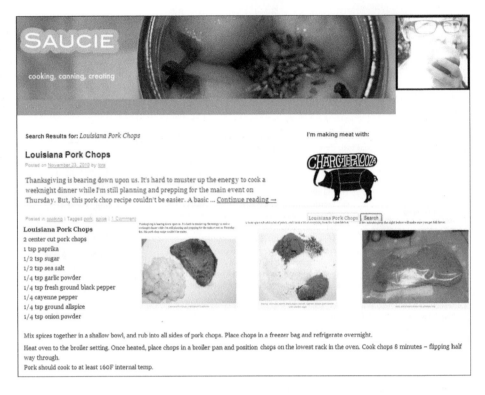

recipe. Lora also posts two final images under her recipe that reflect her sense of humor and show that she enjoyed her own "fine" creation. Use your judgment about when to use humor when writing to inform; generally it is appropriate for less formal informational genres, but you also have to consider this in terms of your specific purposes and audiences.

RECIPE PHOTOS ▶
**Lora Guillotte,**
"Louisiana Pork Chops." These images show the final steps in cooking: the pleasures of plating and eating. They reflect the chef's sense of humor, which she uses as a rhetorical strategy to draw readers in.
*Lora Guillotte.*

## Modes & Media: How can they help you inform?

A composition's *mode* is how the content itself is communicated—whether in writing, by voice, through images, through sounds, or in some combination. A composition's *medium* is the final form or mechanism that it's delivered in, such as print, digital, or face-to-face. Following is a breakdown of the modes and media of some of the compositions presented in this chapter:

| INFORMATIVE GENRES | Mode | Medium |
|---|---|---|
| **ILLUSTRATION, ONLINE**<br>Harvard School of Public Health, "Food Pyramid" (p. 117) | VISUAL | DIGITAL |
| **INSTRUCTIONS, ONLINE**<br>Homeland Security, "Preventing Terrorism" (p. 90) | WRITTEN | DIGITAL |
| **DICTIONARY ENTRY, ONLINE**<br>*Dictionary.com*, "vertiginous" (p. 88) | WRITTEN AND AUDIO | DIGITAL |
| **RECIPE, ONLINE**<br>Lora Guillotte, "Louisiana Pork Chops" (p. 96) | WRITTEN AND VISUAL | DIGITAL |
| **INSTRUCTIONS, ONLINE**<br>Ann Pizer, "Downward Facing Dog" (p. 99) | WRITTEN, VISUAL, AND VIDEO | DIGITAL |

## A Word about Modes

Visuals are crucial when we're learning something new, such as the pork chop recipe (p. 96) and the yoga pose (p. 99), which is provided in three modes—through text, an image, and video. For the yoga pose, without the visual, readers would need much more text to understand what they should be doing. Even better is the video, which shows viewers all the steps required to achieve the pose.

The pork chop recipe also benefits from accompanying visuals. When people are cooking, they usually want text that describes the ingredients they need and steps they need to follow—as well as images of what the food should look like as they prepare it, and when it's done. Still images might be best in this case. While a video might show a reader how the actual steps are performed, it's difficult to cook and watch a video at the same time.

Think about your favorite ads or commercials (or even the ones you find most annoying). Do you find yourself identifying with the people featured in them? Why or why not?

Audio is also useful in certain situations. For example, *Dictionary.com* presents information about the word *vertiginous* in two modes—as text (for readers and writers), and as an audio file (for speakers) so users of the site can learn the correct pronunciation of the word.

What informative texts have you read today? Think of street signs, recipes, product labels, news articles, and course assignments. What traits do they share? How do these texts function to inform you?

## The Genre's Conventions

### Elements of the Genre: What does all informative writing have in common?

Two essential qualities of the best informative writing are accuracy and clarity. Whether you are writing a news report in which you provide straight facts, or are creating a set of instructions in which you detail the steps for performing a certain task, you need to be accurate, clear, and direct. Informative writing should also be presented in an order that will make sense to readers. For example, when providing instructions, it's a good idea to present information in small, digestible units—and to move from simple to complex.

Let's examine the choices Ann Pizer makes in her instructions for doing a yoga pose, shown on page 99. In this example, Pizer starts with basic information about a yoga pose known as "downward facing dog," including the benefits of the pose. She then breaks it down into a series of numbered tasks; each step represents a single move, so that viewers can take their time. The order of the steps is very important too. While an experienced yogi may go into the pose in what appears to be one fluid motion, a new practitioner needs to consciously move each body part into place and do so in a particular order to avoid injury. Because alignment is important in yoga, Pizer carefully specifies how body parts should line up, as in step 1, where she notes that the wrists should be "underneath the shoulders" and the knees should be "underneath the hips." Barry Stone's photo of a woman in the pose shows readers how wrists and knees should be aligned. Pizer follows her directions with notes tailored for beginners and more advanced practitioners to allow for some customization of the directions.

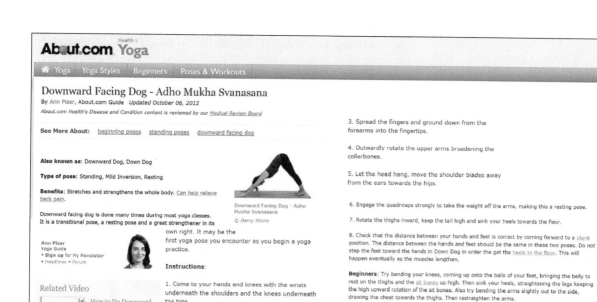

## Style: How does it help you inform?

When you're writing to inform, it's important to present content in a style that's accessible to your audience. You'll also want to consider the voice and tone you will use. Is a strong writer's presence appropriate for your composition, or should you be more neutral? And how much detail will you need to provide to get your ideas across? For most informative genres, you will probably use a neutral tone to convey information. Because your primary goal is to inform your readers about something, you'll probably want to avoid wild flourishes of language. For example, in the pork chop recipe, the writer instructs readers to "mix spices together"; she does not say "merge all the aromatic flavors of world cuisines." Attention to detail is also crucial in genres that inform. For example, in step 8 of Ann Pizer's yoga pose instructions, she gives enough detail so beginners understand how the pose will change for them over time as they become more practiced.

For more examples of **instructions**, see the Index of Genres on page G-1.

## Design: What is the best format for informing?

Design helps readers (and viewers, listeners, etc.) navigate information. In the instructions below, the designers at Tieknots.org show readers where to begin, what steps to follow, and where to end. The number next to each step shows readers where they are in the process. The simple design and limited detail allow readers to focus in on each move. Further, the design is scaled so that it can fit on a business card, making the instructions both concise and portable.

INSTRUCTIONS ▶
"How to Tie a Tie." Who needs words when a clear "how to" diagram can do the trick? *Shutterstock.*

What colors grab your attention? Do these colors change depending on what you're looking at? For example, what colors might attract your attention in a textbook design, or an advertisement, or online instructions?

## Sources: What research should you draw on to inform your readers?

When you write to inform, you need to be informed yourself: You need to draw on the best sources possible (see "Authoritative sources of information," p. 89). For example, journalist Mireya Navarro, author of "E.P.A. Rejects City Timeline on PCBs" (p. 95), interviews EPA administrator Judith Enck for her article. We can assume that Enck is an expert in her field and a reliable source. To take another example, imagine that it's an election year, and you're creating a chart about voting trends. You might use information from the U.S. Census Bureau.

# ENCYCLOPEDIA ENTRIES

Collecting facts has been a human pursuit for a long time. In the first century CE, a Roman author, naturalist, and military man named Pliny the Elder tried to record everything known about the natural world in his thirty-seven-volume *Naturalis Historia*, the world's first encyclopedia-like document. (You can read it at the Perseus Digital Library, in English or the original Latin.)

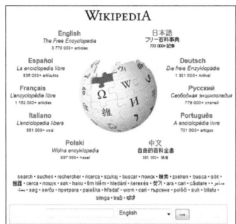

Pliny, like all encyclopedists, aimed to provide what was known about a specific or general topic in a way that worked best for his target audience. The *Encyclopaedia Britannica* is a source of general information on many topics; it's geared toward readers who want to gain a broad understanding of a given subject. More specialized encyclopedias, such as *The Encyclopedia of Women's History in America* by Kathryn Cullen-DuPont, may cover topics in more depth, assuming readers already have some understanding of the topic.

Encyclopedias share several characteristics:

» They serve as a general (or sometimes specialized) reference.

» They provide information that is considered true (meaning it is agreed upon by experts on the topic).

» They are compilations and syntheses of what others have said, rather than original research (that is, they are tertiary sources).

» They are organized into individual articles that are well researched and written by content experts, typically people with an academic degree related to the subject they're writing about.

How often do you refer to encyclopedias? What are the benefits—and limitations—of using an encyclopedia as a source?

# Analyzing Encyclopedia Entries: What to Look For

## THE RHETORICAL SITUATION

**Purpose** Encyclopedists provide an overview of a subject so that readers can gain a general understanding of it. For example, here is how editors of *The Columbia Encyclopedia* describe their reference book (accessed at *Encyclopedia.com*):

> **Encyclopedias available in our online research library**
>
> The Columbia Encyclopedia (Sixth Edition): An authoritative, English-language dictionary containing more than 51,000 topics, The Columbia Encyclopedia provides trusted facts and information you can count on. Because more than 200 editors and academic advisors strive for depth and accuracy in each edition of the oldest, most venerable English-language encyclopedia in the world, this encyclopedia's topics are thorough and clear.

Other encyclopedias are more specialized; they tend to be aimed at readers interested in a particular field. The *Gale Encyclopedia of Medicine* is an example of a specialized resource. Below is the entry for "Psychosis," written by Paula Ford-Martin and Rebecca Frey.

| International Encyclopedia... | Gale Encyclopedia of... | The Oxford Companion to the... | Gale Encyclopedia of Psychology | Further reading |
| --- | --- | --- | --- | --- |

**Psychosis**

Gale Encyclopedia of Medicine, 3rd ed. | 2006 | Ford-Martin, Paula; Frey, Rebecca | Copyright

Psychosis
Definition
Psychosis is a symptom or feature of mental illness typically characterized by radical changes in personality, impaired functioning, and a distorted or nonexistent sense of objective reality.

Description
Patients suffering from psychosis have impaired reality testing; that is, they are unable to distinguish personal subjective experience from the reality of the external world. They experience **hallucinations** and/or **delusions** that they believe are real, and may behave and communicate in an inappropriate and incoherent fashion. Psychosis may appear as a symptom of a number of mental disorders, including mood and **personality disorders.** It is also the defining feature of **schizophrenia,** schizophreniform disorder, **schizoaffective disorder,** delusional disorder, and the psychotic disorders (i.e., brief psychotic disorder, shared psychotic disorder, psychotic disorder due to a general medical condition, and substance-induced psychotic disorder).

Causes and symptoms
Psychosis may be caused by the interaction of biological and psychosocial factors depending on the disorder in which it presents; psychosis can also be caused by purely social factors, with no biological component.

Biological factors that are regarded as contributing to the development of psychosis include genetic abnormalities and substance use. With regard to chromosomal abnormalities, studies indicate that 30% of patients diagnosed with a psychotic disorder have a microdeletion at chromosome 22q11. Another group of researchers has identified the gene G72/G30 at chromosome 13q33.2 as a susceptibility gene for child-hood-onset schizophrenia and psychosis not otherwise specified.

With regard to **substance abuse,** several different research groups reported in 2004 that cannabis (**marijuana** ) use is a risk factor for the onset of psychosis.

Migration is a social factor that influences people's susceptibility to psychotic disorders. Psychiatrists in Europe have noted the increasing rate of schizophrenia and other psychotic disorders among immigrants to almost all Western European countries. Black immigrants from Africa or the Caribbean appear to be especially vulnerable. The stresses involved in migration include family breakup, the need to adjust to living in large urban areas, and social inequalities in the new country.

**Audience** Encyclopedists know that their primary audience is general readers looking for a reliable but quick snapshot of a topic. For example, writers for the online encyclopedia *MedlinePlus* know their readers are mainly nonprofessionals consulting *Medline* for basic information about symptoms, causes, and treatment. The writers know they must be accurate and fairly brief; they can link to additional resources with more in-depth information. On the other hand, encyclopedists who write for more specialized reference works aimed at specific professional audiences, such as *Medpedia*—an open resource geared toward doctors and associated with major medical schools including Harvard and Stanford—provide a deeper level of information in their entries.

## A Word about *Wikipedia*

*Wikipedia* is the most popular reference site on the Internet. As an encyclopedia, *Wikipedia* has all the features of that genre, with one important exception: Instead of entries being written by scholars, entries can be written by anyone. Indeed, that's what the *wiki* part of the name means: A wiki is a Web site that can be edited by users. *Wikipedia* is open-access, meaning almost all of its entries can be edited by anyone who registers with the site.

Because anyone can edit an entry, many people have concerns about the reliability of the information found on *Wikipedia*. However, others argue that because anyone who finds an error can correct it, *Wikipedia* is actually as reliable as any other reference source. In fact, a 2005 study by the science journal *Nature* found that *Wikipedia* entries had no more errors than entries in *Encyclopaedia Britannica*.

**Tip:** Most entries on *Wikipedia* include a list of (often linked) sources drawn on by the entry authors. These sources are often worth checking out, so even if you (or your instructor) decide that *Wikipedia* is not an appropriate source for your research, you might find an entry's reference list useful.

**Rhetorical appeals**   Encyclopedists appeal to readers through ethos—as content experts presenting accurate information. In turn, readers can assume that an encyclopedia entry is authoritative and trustworthy. Encyclopedists also appeal through logos, presenting content in a logical manner, often moving from general to more specific information. Writers begin an entry by defining the topic and often then break it out into subtopics, bringing up associated terms, people, and places. You can see this at work in the "Psychosis" entry from the *Gale Encyclopedia of Medicine* (p. 102). Further, in an online encyclopedia, keywords and subtopics are hyperlinked, which contributes to the logos of the entry.

What are your thoughts on digital encyclopedias— specifically on open-source reference works such as *Wikipedia*? How do you use these sources? And to what extent do you consider them trustworthy?

**Modes & media**   Encyclopedia entries are written texts that can appear in print or digital formats. Before the digital age, a family would purchase an entire set of print encyclopedias; it's now more common to purchase an encyclopedia on DVD, or to use free online resources such as *Encyclopedia.com* or *Wikipedia*.

## Elements of the genre

*Well researched and accurate.* Entries are completely fact based. Encyclopedists gather, scrutinize, and synthesize information from many reliable sources to create an entry on a given topic. They convey proven information as objectively as possible (without the interference of opinion).

*Written by experts.* Most encyclopedias enlist professionals who have a deep level of knowledge on the topic of the entry to be written. This can also be true of wiki-platform encyclopedias that have a peer-review policy.

*Clear.* Encyclopedists provide basic information in a direct and straightforward manner.

*Brief.* Entries are not exhaustive; rather, they are intended as jumping-off points for further research. While some entries can be relatively long—for example, the complete entry on "Global Warming" from *Encyclopaedia Britannica* (p. 108) prints out at thirty-four pages long—they are still extremely short compared with the length of a book on the subject. The top three books on global warming at this moment—*Climate of Extremes* by Patrick J. Michaels and Robert Balling Jr., *Climate of Corruption* by Larry Bell, and *Climate Change* by Edmond A. Mathez—average 303 pages long.

## Style

*Just enough detail.* Encyclopedists provide just enough detail to inform general readers. However, in a given entry, they mention related topics, concepts, and keywords that readers may want to pursue with further research. For example, *Wikipedia*'s "Motivation" entry (approximately seven printed pages) includes a one-paragraph summary of self-determination theory as well as links to a separate entry on that topic, one of the developers of the theory, and the topic of intrinsic motivation (see p. 105).

In contrast, Daniel H. Pink's book on motivation, *Drive: The Surprising Truth about What Motivates Us*, offers a deeper level of information on the theory, devoting five pages to who originally posed it, how it's been applied, and how it's held up through cultural and societal changes.

*Precise language/word choice.* Encyclopedists are specific and exact writers. For example, the *Wikipedia* entry on "Motivation" refers not just to "researchers" but

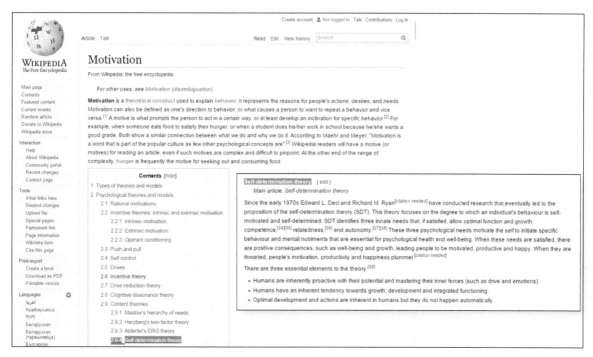

to specific researchers, including Edward L. Deci and Richard M. Ryan. Imagine how you might question the authority of a reference work if the writers used ambiguous terms and generalizations, rather than specifics.

Encyclopedists often use formal, academic language to bolster their authority and emphasize their seriousness. That means they avoid contractions, slang, and abbreviated forms such as "info" for "information."

*Use of the third person and a serious tone.* Encyclopedists write in the third person, which reinforces their ethos and reminds readers that the entries are based on shared knowledge amongst an expert group, not just the perspective of one person. They use a serious tone to project credibility (ethos) to readers. If you were creating an encyclopedia entry, you probably wouldn't write it in the sarcastic tone of Jon Stewart, for example. Although the information in an entry might be informative *and* funny, using humor as a rhetorical strategy in an encyclopedia entry might undermine your authority and trustworthiness as an encyclopedist.

## Design

*Accessible.* Encyclopedia entries need to be designed so that readers can quickly identify and use information on a particular page. Hard-copy reference works often use descriptive headers or footers so readers can navigate easily.

▲ WIKIPEDIA ENTRY
**Wikipedia,**
"Motivation and "Self Determination Theory." The "Motivation" entry includes a section on "self-determination theory" (shown here as a detail). The writers of this entry use clear language and specifically name the researchers who developed self-determination theory. *The Wikipedia trademark is licensed under CC BY-SA 3.0. (Author User: Paul Stansifer, User: Nohat, Philip Metschan.)*

*Consistent.* Encyclopedias and other reference works follow a consistent format. In a dictionary, for example, each entry might begin with the name of the entry, followed by the part of speech, followed by a phonetic spelling. Every entry in the dictionary would follow that format.

When you refer to an encyclopedia entry, do you think about the people who composed it? About their expertise? Their biases? To what extent do these factors affect your trust in the source itself?

*Clearly titled.* The name or title of the entry is in large, bold letters at the top of the entry, in order to clearly indicate the topic. In the case of a longer entry, the repetition of the title words orients the reader back to the original search term.

*Hyperlinked to other entries (in online editions).* The use of hyperlinks in an entry allows encyclopedists to provide more information without lengthening the entry itself. These links identify terminology (see "Just enough detail" above) and provide additional search terms to assist readers in narrowing their investigation of a broad subject. For example, the *Gale Encyclopedia of Medicine* entry on "Psychosis" (p. 102) connects that topic with schizophrenia and other specific disorders, helping narrow the broad initial term. As a researcher, you might then go to *EBSCOhost* or another rich database to explore the connection between psychosis and schizophrenia.

### Sources

*Variation in attribution of sources.* Encyclopedia entries may not contain any documentation attributing the information to particular sources. While this might appear to be plagiarism, it is not. Encyclopedia entries are usually composed by experts in the field; therefore, the encyclopedists have firsthand knowledge of the information through their extensive research background.

*Encyclopaedia Britannica* entries, for example, are written and overseen by an editorial board of advisors. Board members often include Nobel Prize winners, scholars, and scientists who are well-known in their respective fields.

For coverage and more examples of **reference works entries,** see the Index of Genres on page G-1.

On the other hand, *Wikipedia* entries and many other encyclopedia entries do include footnotes as well as extensive reference lists. For example, here is the bibliography section of the entry for "Psychosis" by Paula Ford-Martin and Rebecca Frey, from the *Gale Encyclopedia of Medicine*:

| International Encyclopedia... | Gale Encyclopedia of... | The Oxford Companion to the... | Gale Encyclopedia of Psychology | Further reading |

## Psychosis

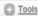 Tools

Gale Encyclopedia of Medicine, 3rd ed. | 2006 | Ford-Martin, Paula; Frey, Rebecca | Copyright

Resources
### BOOKS

American Psychiatric Association. *Diagnostic and Statistical Manual of Mental Disorders.*4th ed., revised. Washington, D.C.: American Psychiatric Association, 2000.

Beers, Mark H., MD, and Robert Berkow, MD., editors. "Psychiatric Emergencies." In *The Merck Manual of Diagnosis and Therapy.* Whitehouse Station, NJ: Merck Research Laboratories, 2004.

Beers, Mark H., MD, and Robert Berkow, MD., editors. "Schizophrenia and Related Disorders." In *The Merck Manual of Diagnosis and Therapy.* Whitehouse Station, NJ: Merck Research Laboratories, 2004.

### PERIODICALS

Addington, A. M., M. Gornick, A. L. Sporn, et al. "Polymorphisms in the 13q33.2 Gene G72/G30 Are Associated with Childhood-Onset Schizophrenia and Psychosis Not Otherwise Specified." *Biological Psychiatry* 55 (May 15, 2004): 976-980.

Hutchinson, G., and C. Haasen. "Migration and Schizophrenia: The Challenges for European Psychiatry and Implications for the Future." *Social Psychiatry and Psychiatric Epidemiology* 39 (May 2004): 350-357.

Sharon, Idan, MD, and Roni Sharon. "Shared Psychotic Disorder." *eMedicine* June 4, 2004. ⬚http://www.emedicine.com/med/topic3352.htm⬚.

Sim, M. G., E. Khong, and G. Hulse. "Cannabis and Psychosis." *Australian Family Physician* 33 (April 2004): 229-232.

Tolmac, J., and M. Hodes. "Ethnic Variation among Adolescent Psychiatric In-Patients with Psychotic Disorders." *British Journal of Psychiatry* 184 (May 2004): 428-431.

Verdoux, H., and M. Tournier. "Cannabis Use and Risk of Psychosis: An Etiological Link?" *Epidemiologia e psichiatria sociale* 13 (April-June 2004): 113-119.

Williams, N. M., and M. J. Owen. "Genetic Abnormalities of Chromosome 22 and the Development of Psychosis." *Current Psychiatry Reports* 6 (June 2004): 176-182.

◀ ENCYCLOPEDIA ENTRY *Gale Encyclopedia of Medicine,* via *Encyclopedia.com,* "Psychosis." The bibliography for the "Psychosis" entry by Paula Ford-Martin and Rebecca Frey lists solid sources, such as the American Psychiatric Association's diagnostic manual and *The Merck Manual of Diagnosis and Therapy.* Both are considered to be authoritative texts. From Gale Encyclopedia of Medicine *V4, 3E.* © *2006 Gale, a part of Cengage Learning, Inc. Reproduced by permission.* www.cengage.com/ permissions.

## Guided Reading: Encyclopedia Entry

# Michael E. Mann, Henrik Selin, et al., for *Encyclopaedia Britannica*

## *Global Warming*

Visit the *Britannica* site to see the presentation of advertising in the entry. How does the presence of ads affect your reading of this entry? To what extent do ads affect *Britannica's* ethos?

*Encyclopaedia Britannica* has been publishing for nearly 250 years, giving it a level of credibility and authority that other, newer encyclopedia brands can't compete with. This status is further bolstered by the fame of some of its recent contributors, who include Albert Einstein, Marie Curie, Sigmund Freud, and Carl Sagan.

The primary contributors for the entry below on "Global Warming" are Michael E. Mann and Henrik Selin. Mann is a professor of meteorology at Pennsylvania State University and the director of the Earth System Science Center. He has published many journal articles and received numerous awards for his research. Selin is a professor in the international relations department at Boston University and an affiliated researcher at the Center for Climate Science and Policy Research at Linköping University in Sweden. He has authored books, book chapters, and articles on energy and climate. These authors and *Encyclopaedia Britannica* have some serious ethos.

The following example from the online edition of *Britannica* is typical of an entry in a general encyclopedia. Note: Reprinted here are short excerpts from the much longer entry for "Global Warming." *(Illustrations on pages 108–113: Reprinted with permission from Encyclopaedia Britannica, © 2012 by Encyclopaedia Britannica Inc.)*

ENCYCLOPEDIA ▶
PAGE *Encyclopaedia Britannica,* Editorial Board of Advisors. An encyclopedia entry is only as good as its writers and editors. *Britannica* has bragging rights to some authoritative contributors, including Albert Einstein and Marie Curie. *Reprinted with permission from Encyclopaedia Britannica, © 2012 by Encyclopaedia Britannica, Inc.*

**The Encyclopædia Britannica Editorial Board of Advisors**

About the Editorial Board

*Current Members*
Wendy Doniger
Richard Fishman
Benjamin M. Friedman
Leslie H. Gelb
David Gelernter
Murray Gell-Mann
Vartan Gregorian
Lord Sutherland of Houndwood
Lord Weidenfeld of Chelsea

*Recent Members*
Rosalia Artaega
David Baltimore
Nicholas Carr
Zaha Hadid

For any organization that aspires to take all human knowledge, organize it, summarize it, and publish it in a form that people find useful, the challenges and opportunities have never been greater than they are today. The volume of information is exploding, the world is shrinking, and digital media are changing the way we read, think, and learn.

To meet these challenges and opportunities, Britannica has done what we have always done throughout our 240-year history: sought the very best minds in the world to help us.

In the past, they had names like Albert Einstein, Sigmund Freud, Marie Curie, Bertrand Russell, T.H. Huxley, and George Bernard Shaw, all of whom were Britannica contributors in their day.

Today they are the men and women of Britannica's Editorial Board of Advisors—the Nobel laureates and Pulitzer Prize winners, the leading scholars, writers, artists, public servants, and activists who are at the top of their fields. They meet regularly to share ideas, to debate, and to argue, in a unique collegium whose purpose is to understand today's world so that the resulting encyclopedia can be the best there is. We are proud to be associated with these exceptional people, and we are deeply grateful for their contributions, not only to our own publishing objectives but to the larger cause of promoting knowledge in the world today.

**Search Articles**

# global warming

Contributors

## Primary Contributors

Michael E. Mann

Henrik Selin

## Other Contributors

The Editors of *Encyclopaedia Britannica*

Heather Campbell

Swati Chopra

Darshana Das

John Higgins

Gloria Lotha

J. E. Luebering

Richard Pallardy

Dutta Promeet

John P. Rafferty

Marco Sampaolo

Veenu Setia

Gaurav Shukla

Shiveta Singh

---

What are the composers, **Mann, Selin, et al.**, doing?

**THE RHETORICAL SITUATION**

Purpose
Audience
Rhetorical appeals
Modes & media

*see page 110*

How do I know this is an **encyclopedia entry**?

**THE GENRE'S CONVENTIONS**

Elements of the genre
Style
Design
Sources

*see page 110*

Michael E. Mann, Henrik Selin, et al., for *Encyclopaedia Britannica, Global Warming*

## THE RHETORICAL SITUATION

### Purpose

Authors Mann and Selin (and other contributors) write to inform readers with facts and uncontested ideas. While they acknowledge that there is debate around the term ("A vigorous debate is in progress. . . . "), their purpose is not to express opinions or persuade. Their writing is businesslike and factual.

## THE GENRE'S CONVENTIONS

### Elements of the genre

**Gives an overview** of the topic, providing established facts (e.g., facts about temperature and gases).

**Serves as a starting point** for further research; introduces related concepts (e.g., the political debate on global warming), but does not get into detail.

*(Continued on p. 112.)*

ENCYCLOPÆDIA **Britannica** *Facts matter*

Search Articles

**global warming,** the phenomenon of increasing average air temperatures near the surface of Earth over the past one to two centuries. Since the mid-20th century, climate scientists have gathered detailed observations of various weather phenomena (such as temperature, precipitation, and storms) and of related influences on climate (such as ocean currents and the atmosphere's chemical composition). These data indicate that Earth's climate has changed over almost every conceivable timescale since the beginning of geologic time and that, since at least the beginning of the Industrial Revolution, the influence of human activities has been deeply woven into the very fabric of climate change.

Giving voice to a growing conviction of most of the scientific community, the Intergovernmental Panel on Climate Change (IPCC) reported that the 20th century saw an increase in global average surface temperature of approximately 0.6 °C (1.1 °F). The IPCC went on to state that most of the warming observed over the second half of the 20th century could be attributed to human activities, and it predicted that by the end of the 21st century the average surface temperature would increase by another 1.8 to 4.0 °C (3.2 to 7.2 °F), depending on a range of possible scenarios. Many climate scientists agree that significant economic and ecological damage would result if global average temperatures rose by more than 2 °C [3.6 °F] in such a short time. Such damage might include increased extinction of many plant and animal species, shifts in patterns of agriculture, and rising sea levels. The IPCC reported that the global average sea level rose by some 17 cm (6.7 inches) during the 20th century, that sea levels rose faster in the second half of that century than in the first half, and that—again depending on a wide range of possible scenarios. Many climate scientists agree that significant economic and ecological damage would result if global average temperatures rose by more than 2 °C [3.6 °F] in such a short time. Such damage might include increased extinction of many plant and animal species, shifts in patterns of agriculture, and rising sea levels. The IPCC reported that the global average sea level rose by some 17 cm (6.7 inches) during the 20th century, that sea levels rose faster in the second half of that century than in the first half, and that—again depending on a wide range of scenarios—the global average sea level could rise by another 18 to 59 cm (7 to 23 inches) by the end of the 21st century. Furthermore, he IPCC reported that average snow cover in the Northern Hemisphere declined by 4 percent, or 1.5 million square km (580,000 square miles), between 1920 niles), between 1920 and 2005.

The scenarios referred to above depend mainly on future concentrations of certain trace gases, called greenhouse gases, that have been injected into the lower atmosphere in increasing amounts through the burning of fossil fuels for industry, transportation, and residential uses. Modern global warming is the result of an increase in magnitude of the so-called greenhouse effect, a warming of Earth's surface and lower atmosphere caused by the presence of water vapour, carbon dioxide, methane, and other greenhouse gases. Of all these gases, carbon dioxide is the most important, both for its role in the greenhouse effect and for its role in the human economy. It has been estimated that, at the beginning of the industrial age in the mid-18th century, carbon dioxide concentrations in the atmosphere were roughly 280 parts per million (ppm). By the end of the 20th century, carbon dioxide concentrations had reached 369 ppm (possibly the highest concentrations in at least 650,000 years), and, if fossil fuels continue to be burned at current rates, they are projected

ENCYCLOPÆDIA
Britannica
*Facts matter*

Search Articles

to reach 560 ppm by the mid-21st century—essentially, a doubling of carbon dioxide concentrations in 300 years. It has been calculated that an increase of this magnitude alone (that is, not accounting for possible effects of other greenhouse gases) would be responsible for adding 2 to 5 °C (3.6 to 9 °F) to the global average surface temperatures that existed at the beginning of the industrial age.

A vigorous debate is in progress over the extent and seriousness of rising surface temperatures, the effects of past and future warming on human life, and the need for action to reduce future warming and deal with its consequences. This article provides an overview of the scientific background and public policy debate related to the subject of global warming. It considers the causes of rising near-surface air temperatures, the influencing factors, the process of climate research and forecasting, the possible ecological and social impacts of rising temperatures, and the public policy developments since the mid-20th century.

## *Climatic variation since the last glaciation*

 Global warming is related to the more general phenomenon of climate change, which refers to changes in the totality of attributes that define climate. In addition to changes in air temperature, climate change involves changes to precipitation patterns, winds, ocean currents, and other measures of Earth's climate. Normally, climate change can be viewed as the combination of various natural forces occurring over diverse timescales. Since the advent of human civilization, climate change has involved an "anthropogenic," or exclusively human caused, element, and this anthropogenic element has become more important in the industrial period of the past two centuries. The term *global warming* is used specifically to refer to any warming of near-surface air during the past two centuries that can be traced to anthropogenic causes.

To define the concepts of global warming and climate change properly, it is first necessary to recognize that the climate of Earth has varied across many timescales, ranging from an individual human life span to billions of years. This variable climate history is typically classified in terms of "regimes" or "epochs." For instance, the Pleistocene glacial epoch (about 2,600,000 to 11,700 years ago) was marked by substantial variations in the global extent of glaciers and ice sheets. These variations took place on timescales of tens to hundreds of millennia and ere driven by changes in the distribution of solar radiation across Earth's surface. The distribution of solar radiation is known as the insolation pattern, and it is strongly affected by the geometry of Earth's orbit around the Sun and by the orientation, or tilt, of Earth's axis relative to the direct rays of the Sun.

Worldwide, the most recent glacial period, or ice age, culminated about 21,000 years ago in what is often called the Last Glacial Maximum. During this time, continental ice sheets extended well into the middle latitude regions of Europe and North America, reaching as far south as present-day London and New York City. Global annual mean temperature appears to have been about 4–5 °C (7–9 °F) colder than in the mid-20th century. It is important to remember that these figures are a global average. In fact, during the height of this last ice age, Earth's climate was characterized by greater cooling at higher latitudes (that is, toward the poles) and relatively little cooling over large parts of the tropical oceans (near the Equator). This glacial interval terminated abruptly about 11,700 years ago and was followed by the subsequent relatively ice-free period known as the Holocene Epoch. The modern period of Earth's history is conventionally defined as residing within...

*Continues next page*

THE RHETORICAL
SITUATION

**Audience**
The audience for *Britannica* and this entry is readers who want an overview on a topic, in this case global warming. Readers are most likely from a general rather than an expert audience. They may use this entry as a jumping-off point for further research.

**Rhetorical appeals**
Mann and Selin establish their **ethos** as experts through their clear writing, authoritative tone, and bibliography of sources. Readers can also click on their names to see their qualifications to write on this topic.

The other contributors are "content editors" that *Britannica* uses for their subject knowledge and analytical abilities, to ensure the accuracy and currency of the article.

*(Continued on p.113.)*

Michael E. Mann, Henrik Selin, et al., for *Encyclopaedia Britannica, Global Warming*

ENCYCLOPÆDIA
**Britannica**
*Facts matter*

Search Articles

# Bibliography

## Documentaries

Of the several productions describing the scientific concepts behind the global warming phenomenon, *An Inconvenient Truth* (2006), produced by LAURIE DAVID, LAWRENCE BENDER, and SCOTT Z. BURNS and narrated by ALBERT GORE, JR., is the most lauded. A feature placing special emphasis on solutions that reduce carbon dioxide production is *Global Warming: What You Need to Know* (2006), produced by the Discovery Channel, the BBC, and NBC News Productions and narrated by TOM BROKAW. Other noted documentaries on global warming include two originally aired on PBS-TV: *What's Up with the Weather?* (2007), produced by JON PALFREMAN; and *Global Warming: The Signs and the Science* (2005), produced by DAVID KENNARD and narrated by ALANIS MORISSETTE.

*Michael E. Mann*

## Scientific Background

An excellent general overview of the factors governing Earth's climate over all timescales is presented in WILLIAM RUDDIMAN, *Earth's Climate: Past and Future* (2000). In addition, RICHARD C.J. SOMERVILLE, *The Forgiving Air: Understanding Environmental Change* (1996, reissued 1998), is a readable introduction to the science of climate and global environmental change. JOHN HOUGHTON, *Global Warming: The Complete Briefing* (1997), also offers an accessible treatment of the science of climate change as well as a discussion of the policy and ethical overtones of climate change as an issue confronting society. SPENCER WEART, *Discovery of Global Warming* (2003), provides a reasoned account of the history of climate change science.

A number of books present thoughtful discussions of global warming as an environmental and societal issue. Still prescient is an early account provided in BILL MCKIBBEN, *The End of Nature* (1989). Other good treatments include STEPHEN SCHNEIDER, *Laboratory Earth* (2001); ALBERT GORE, *An Inconvenient Truth* (2006); ELIZABETH KOLBERT, *Field Notes from a Catastrophe* (2006); EUGENE LINDEN, *The Winds of Change* (2006); TIM FLANNERY, *The Weather Makers* (2006); and MIKE HULME, *Why We Disagree About Climate Change: Understanding Controversy, Inaction and Opportunity* (2009). An excellent exposition for younger readers is found in ANDREW REVKIN, *The North Pole Was Here* (2007).

## Public Policy Background

STEPHEN H. SCHNEIDER, ARMIN ROSENCRANZ, and JOHN O. NILES (eds.), *Climate Change Policy: A Survey* (2002), is a primer on various aspects of the policy debate that explains alternatives for dealing with climate change. A broad analysis of the climate change debate is imparted in ANDREW E. DESSLER and EDWARD A. PARSON, *The Science and Politics of Global Climate Change: A Guide to the Debate* (2006). A summary of the quantitative aspects of greenhouse gas emissions designed to assist stakeholders and policy makers is provided in KEVIN A. BAUMERT, TIMOTHY HERZOG, and JONATHAN PERSHING, *Navigating the Numbers: Greenhouse Gas Data and International Climate Policy* (2005).

**ENCYCLOPÆDIA Britannica**
*Facts matter*

Search Articles

A somewhat more technical introduction to the science of climate change is provided in DAVID ARCHER, *Global Warming: Understanding the Forecast* (2006). More advanced treatments of the science of global warming and climate change are included in INTERGOVERNMENTAL PANEL ON CLIMATE CHANGE: WORKING GROUP I, *Climate Change 2007: The Physical Science Basis: Summary for Policymakers: Fourth Assessment Report* (2007); and INTERGOVERNMENTAL PANEL ON CLIMATE CHANGE: WORKING GROUP II, *Climate Change 2007: Climate Change Impacts, Adaptations, and Vulnerability: Fourth Assessment Report* (2007). Possible solutions to the challenges of global warming and climate change are detailed in INTERGOVERNMENTAL PANEL ON CLIMATE CHANGE: WORKING GROUP III, *Climate Change 2007: Mitigation of Climate Change: Fourth Assessment Report* (2007).

JOHN T. HOUGHTON, *Global Warming: The Complete Briefing*, 3rd ed. (2004), offers a perspective on climate change from one of the leading participants in the IPCC process. DANIEL SAREWITZ and ROGER PIELKE, JR., "Breaking the Global-Warming Gridlock," *The Atlantic Monthly*, 286(1):55–64 (2000), presents an alternative view on how to make progress on climate policy by focusing on reducing vulnerability to climate impacts.

Thoughtful discussions of the politics underlying the issue of climate change are provided in ROSS GELBSPAN, *Boiling Point* (2004); MARK LYNAS, *High Tide* (2004); and ROSS GELBSPAN, *The Heat Is On* (1998). The social justice implications involved in adapting the human population to changing climatic conditions are presented in W. NEIL ADGER et al. (eds.), *Fairness in Adaptation to Climate Change* (2006).

*Henrik Selin*

## THE RHETORICAL SITUATION

Mann and Selin appeal to readers' sense of **logos** (logic) by presenting the information in an accessible way; further, they provide specific data in relation to the topic, such as temperatures.

## Modes & media

**Mode = written and visual** The authors convey information in words, but also with charts and graphs. For example, they use a chart to explain temperature changes, and a video to illustrate greenhouse gases, showing how fossil fuels get released into the environment. These modes, along with animations, show readers the impact of pollutants on the environment.

**Medium = digital** There are pros and cons to providing information digitally. The pros are the many options for providing information. Digital encyclopedias also allow readers to connect through social media. For example, in the *Britannica* "Global Warming" entry, a share button allows readers to share the link on such sites as Twitter, Facebook, and LinkedIn, and to add the link to a social bookmarking site such as del.icio.us or Google. The cons are the ads. Because the entry is part of the free online resources *Britannica* provides, it is surrounded by ads. A printed encyclopedia would not include ads.

## THE GENRE'S CONVENTIONS

### Sources

Mann and Selin, who themselves are sources of information, do not provide footnotes, in-text citations, or a Works Cited list, but they do provide a bibliography and a list of links to external sites that connect readers to other sources that they recommend as authoritative.

ENCYCLOPÆDIA **Britannica** *Facts matter*

Search Articles

## Websites

### External Websites

- Common Questions About Climate Change - United Nations Environment Programme - World Meteorological Organization
- StopGlobalWarming.org
- A Paleo Perspective on Global Warming
  Discussion on paleoclimate research and global warming, and other issues regarding climate variability and change.
- U. S. Enviornmental Protection Agency - Global Warming
  Educational information on global warming and climate change, from the U.S. Environmental Protection Agency. Includes a primer on the greenhouse effect and recent trends in global climate; a glossary of climate change terms; material on the potential global warming impacts on health, water resources, and different ecosystems; and notes on local, national, and global actions to reduce climate change. Offers the contents of the quarterly newsletter "Inside the Greenhouse," a presentation on the impacts of climate change, and an inventory of U.S. emissions of carbon dioxide, methane, nitrous oxide, and other greenhouse gases.
- Environmental Education For Kids - Global Warming is Hot Stuff!
- Fact Monster - Global Warming
- How Stuff Works - Science - Global Warming
- NeoK12 - Educational Videos, Lessons and Games - Global Warming
- Science and Society - Global Warming
- National Geographic - Environment - What Is Global Warming?
- Think Quest - Global Warming
- National Aeronautics and Space Administration - Global Warming
- PBS Online - Savage Seas
- The Electronic Universe - Greenhouse Effect
- The Official Site of "An Inconvenient Truth"
- How Stuff Works - Science - How Does Global Warming Affect Hunting Season?
- How Stuff Works - Science - How Will Global Warming Affect Autumn?
- How Stuff Works - Science - Is Global Warming Destroying Mount Everest?
- How Stuff Works - Science - The Top 10 Worst Effects of Global Warming

## Questions: Analyzing *Britannica's* encyclopedia entry

**1. Purpose.** Although the topic of global warming is somewhat controversial, encyclopedists aim to inform—to take a neutral stance rather than try to persuade. What are some of the strategies the authors of the "Global Warming" entry use in order to avoid taking a position?

**2. Audience.** Who do you imagine is most likely to look up "global warming" in an online encyclopedia: a student, a businessperson, a teacher, or a scientist? What do you imagine his or her purpose might be?

**3. Rhetorical appeals.** Read an entry on a topic of your choice in *Wikipedia* and then read an entry on the same topic in another online encyclopedia. Compare the authors' techniques in the two entries. Do you notice them using similar methods to develop their ethos? What differences do you notice? Which entry sounds more authoritative, in your opinion? Why?

**4. Modes & media.** In what modes and media have you used encyclopedias? Do you have a preference for one mode or medium over another? Why?

**5. Elements of the genre.** As pointed out in the "Global Warming" annotations, encyclopedia entries serve as starting points for research. After reading the entry, what questions do you have about the topic? What are you curious about that you might want to research through other, more in-depth sources?

**6. Elements of the genre.** An encyclopedia entry about global warming is briefer than a book on the topic. As you read the *Britannica* entry excerpt, was there information you wished had been expanded upon? Why?

**7. Style.** Notice the neutral, third-person voice. How might your reading of this entry be different if the authors had written it in the first person?

**8. Design.** The entry is consistently formatted and designed so readers stay oriented. How important is it to you that information be easy to find in a reference work? Why? Can you think of examples of reference works that are not well designed?

**9. Sources.** In the *Britannica* entry, the authors rarely use attribution phrases such as "according to." How does this affect your reading of the entry? How might your experience as a reader be different if the entry were peppered with parenthetical notes and attribution phrases?

Michael E. Mann, Henrik Selin, et al., for *Encyclopaedia Britannica, Global Warming*

115

# Drafting an Encyclopedia Entry

---

## CHECKLIST: Drafting an Encyclopedia Entry
Thinking of drafting an encyclopedia entry? Ask yourself the following questions.

### WHAT'S MY RHETORICAL SITUATION?

☐ **Purpose.** What specific topic do I want to write about? Which subtopics do I want to write about? How will I define my topic and subtopics? Writing an entry about "fashion" implies that I will cover fashion over the course of history. Writing about "street fashion," however, significantly narrows the time period I would need to cover.

☐ **Audience.** Who are my readers? How many of them are experts on my topic? Nonexperts who have a mild interest in my topic? What questions will they expect my entry to answer? Are there technical terms I may need to define (or hyperlink to definitions)? What kinds of examples will my readers relate to?

☐ **Rhetorical appeals.** How will I establish my authority as a writer? What kinds of vocabulary, diction, and examples will I use to convey authority?

☐ **Modes & media.** Do I want readers to experience my entry in print or digital format? Do I want to include images or videos?

### WHAT GENRE CONVENTIONS MATTER?

☐ **Elements of the genre.** To keep my entry relatively brief, I will need to summarize other, longer works on the topic. Which works will I summarize? How will I make sure my writing is extremely precise? What terms might I need to carefully define?

☐ **Style.** How much do I want to develop my discussion of the topic? An entry geared toward a general audience (as in *Wikipedia*) will be less developed than one geared toward experts (as in *Medpedia*). Should I outline all the topics and subtopics I plan to cover? Then I can consider whether I'm over- or underdeveloping any of the subtopics, given who I imagine my audience to be.

☐ **Design.** How can I use titles and subtitles to make my entry easy to access for readers? If I create a digital entry, how will I use hyperlinks to direct readers to other entries?

☐ **Sources.** In addition to a list of sources, will I want to include a list of "additional resources" for readers who want to do their own research?

---

## PRACTICE  Want to experiment? Draft your own encyclopedia entry.

Are you an expert on a particular subject? Choose one that you're well versed in, and draft an encyclopedia entry on that topic based on what you already know and what you can learn by doing some research (that does not involve *Wikipedia* or any encyclopedia). Remember to include only facts and information that are largely uncontested by others who are well versed in the subject. You may want to include visual features to illustrate key concepts.

# CHARTS/INFOGRAPHICS

As writers, students, and professionals, we create charts—or any type of infographic, such as tables, graphs, and diagrams—to present information simply and visually. Anyone can create a chart, especially with software such as Microsoft Excel or shareware such as iCharts.

## Analyzing Charts/Infographics: What to Look For

THE RHETORICAL SITUATION

**Purpose**  Writers create charts to give a snapshot of complex information—and to draw attention to relationships among the items presented. If you are creating a chart, you might want to keep it simple. An effective way of achieving your purpose through an infographic is to create a chart with *x*- and *y*-axes.

When might you create a chart? Let's say you're thinking about majoring in engineering, but you're not sure which branch would be most lucrative. Because you are an excellent but rather obsessive student, you decide that the best way to represent this information is to create a bar chart (also known as a bar graph). In the PayScale example on page 118, the *x*-axis represents the range of salaries (in dollars); the *y*-axis represents the range of types of engineering. In this format, the data—which is clearly labeled—is easy to understand. Clearly, petroleum engineering majors have the highest earning potential, at least as of 2012, when PayScale created the graph. Note that in digital form, the graph links to PayScale's full methodology for creating it.

▲ CHART
The *x* and *y* axes.

Another reason to create a chart is to use it as a persuasive tool. A chart showing that incomes rise as education levels rise can be used to persuade lawmakers to invest more money in education, for example.

**Audience**  Graph creators know that their readers want information in a concise, easy-to-read format. They know readers might consult their chart for data that will help them make a decision, as in the salaries graph. To take another example, someone creating a chart that compares test scores of students admitted to graduate schools knows that readers are probably students choosing graduate schools to apply to.

CHART/INFOGRAPHIC ▶
**Harvard University,** Food Pyramid. *As printed in image and © 2008, Harvard University. NOTE: Harvard Health Publications does not endorse any products or medical procedures.*

BAR GRAPH ▶
**PayScale, Inc.,**
"Majors That Pay You Back." The left column (or *y* axis) lists specific majors; the bottom row (or *x* axis) shows salaries, making this chart clear and effective. Petroleum engineering, anyone? *PayScale.com.*

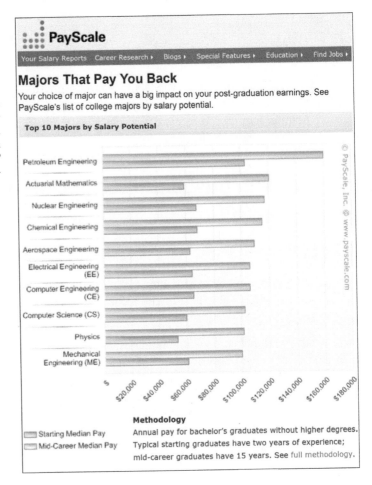

What types of information are best presented visually? Are there certain types of infographics (pie charts, graphs, etc.) that you prefer over others? Why?

**Rhetorical appeals**   Chart authors need to establish ethos by conducting research and presenting correct information in their infographics, in order to gain readers' confidence in the content. They can also appeal to audiences through logos, by using logical organization and smart, digestible design. In the example on page 119, job seeker Christopher Perkins appeals to readers' logic and pathos (in this case, through humor) by reimagining how to connect with his potential readers/employers with a visual resume.

**Modes & media**   Chart authors use visuals and text to share data. Often the visual content dominates and text is used mainly for labels. In terms of media, charts are communicated in print and digitally. Digital charts have the benefit of including hyperlinks to the chart's sources of information (as in the PayScale chart on engineering salaries above).

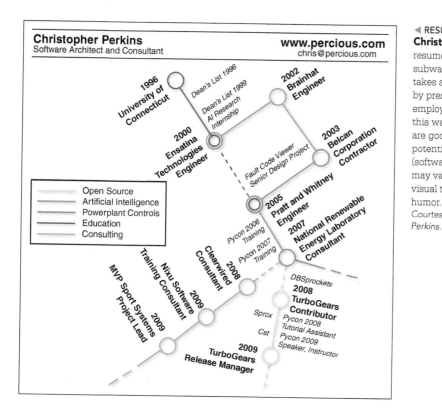

◄ RESUME
**Christopher Perkins,** resume designed as a subway map. Perkins takes a chance by presenting his employment history this way, but chances are good that his potential employers (software companies) may value his creative visual thinking and humor.
*Courtesy of Christopher Perkins.*

## THE GENRE'S CONVENTIONS

**Elements of the genre**   Chart makers compose works that are:

*Based on facts/data.* The information that writers present in charts is based on research that the writer draws on (such as existing statistics from a government Web site), or collects personally (through primary research such as interviews).

*Precise; clearly labeled and titled.* Chart makers provide specific values for each item they address and show readers exactly how items relate to each other. Chart makers choose titles that define the scope of the chart's content, convey purpose, or summarize their findings. For example, the chart on page 122 is titled "Why Does a Salad Cost More Than a Big Mac?" Within the chart, labels further clarify. For example, in a chart with *x*- and *y*-axes, both axes are labeled so readers/viewers know if numerical amounts are billions or thousands.

Have you ever seen a resume or other business document presented in a way that surprised you? What was it? Was it as informative as the more conventional version would have been?

*Illustrated with symbols that convey information.* Visual devices such as bars, lines, and sections or slices (of a pie chart) represent specific values and convey data clearly. Writers need to decide which type of chart works best for the information they're presenting. For example, line charts are best used when time is involved, because they can show trends over the course of a particular period.

*Supplemented with a key or footnotes when needed.* Chart makers sometimes provide a key (or legend) to let readers know what certain features of the visual mean. A key for a map defines each symbol; for example, tents might represent campgrounds. Footnotes connect readers to the sources of the chart's information.

**Style**   Chart makers make careful choices about style, including:

*What details to present.* Most chart makers don't include much detail; they usually provide a clear visual accompanied by brief text. The goal of chart writers is to make it easy for readers to absorb data quickly. Too much detail, especially for a general audience, might make it difficult for readers to see what's most important. However, if your audience is a group of specialists in a particular field who would like detail, then more in-depth data would be appropriate.

*What techniques, tone, and voice to use.* The best charts use simple, direct language, and the less the better. Chart makers use text judiciously, to provide a title, convey facts, label axes, and concisely explain symbols and colors in accompanying keys or legends. Their tone is neutral and objective.

**Design**   When chart makers lay out their work, they keep the following in mind:

*Simple is best.* The whole point is to make information accessible and digestible.

*Color is key.* Chart makers use color and shading to separate and highlight different pieces of information.

*The parts need to be arranged logically/spatially.* Chart makers lay out information and visuals in a way that shows readers what is most important to glean. In charts where there are multiple elements, or even multiple visuals that form one infographic, designers add white space between the elements to show separation, or place the elements near each other to show connections.

**Sources**   Charts are based on composers' knowledge or research. Readers assume that the chart maker is presenting reliable data based on specific sources. Many charts include a source or list of sources, which adds to their credibility and authority.

When it comes to charts, what is the happy medium between providing too many details and not enough?

For more coverage and examples of **infographics** and **maps,** see the Index of Genres on page G-1.

# Guided Reading: Chart/Infographic

## Physicians Committee for Responsible Medicine

### *Why Does a Salad Cost More Than a Big Mac?*

The Physicians Committee for Responsible Medicine (PCRM) is a nonprofit organization focused on promoting nutrition and good health. The editors at PCRM created the chart on page 122 to compare the cost of a salad with that of a Big Mac, and to determine why a salad is more expensive. PCRM's choice of a pyramid allows them to make an easy-to-digest comparison of data; it also brings to mind the food pyramid chart created by the U.S. Department of Agriculture, whose purpose is to direct people to eat healthier diets. (See the new and old pyramids online at *The Washington Post*.) *(Illustration on page 122: Courtesy of Physicians Committee for Responsible Medicine.)*

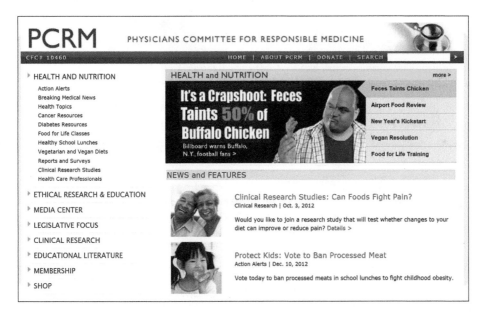

What is **PCRM**, the composer of the chart, doing?

THE RHETORICAL SITUATION

Purpose
Audience
Rhetorical appeals
Modes & media

*see page 123*

How do I know this is a **chart**?

THE GENRE'S CONVENTIONS

Elements of the genre
Style
Design
Sources

*see page 123*

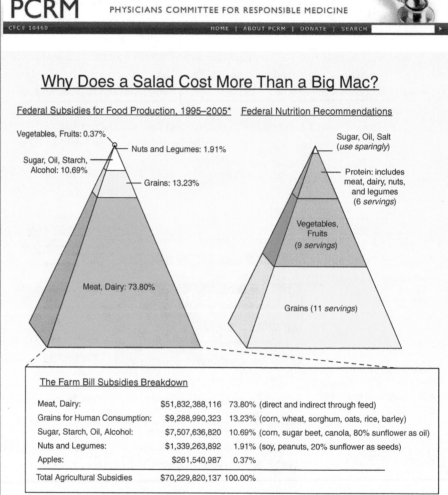

**PCRM** CFC# 10460 — PHYSICIANS COMMITTEE FOR RESPONSIBLE MEDICINE

HOME | ABOUT PCRM | DONATE | SEARCH

## Why Does a Salad Cost More Than a Big Mac?

### Federal Subsidies for Food Production, 1995–2005*

Vegetables, Fruits: 0.37%
Nuts and Legumes: 1.91%
Sugar, Oil, Starch, Alcohol: 10.69%
Grains: 13.23%
Meat, Dairy: 73.80%

### Federal Nutrition Recommendations

Sugar, Oil, Salt (*use sparingly*)
Protein: includes meat, dairy, nuts, and legumes (6 *servings*)
Vegetables, Fruits (9 *servings*)
Grains (11 *servings*)

#### The Farm Bill Subsidies Breakdown

| | | |
|---|---|---|
| Meat, Dairy: | $51,832,388,116 | 73.80% (direct and indirect through feed) |
| Grains for Human Consumption: | $9,288,990,323 | 13.23% (corn, wheat, sorghum, oats, rice, barley) |
| Sugar, Starch, Oil, Alcohol: | $7,507,636,820 | 10.69% (corn, sugar beet, canola, 80% sunflower as oil) |
| Nuts and Legumes: | $1,339,263,892 | 1.91% (soy, peanuts, 20% sunflower as seeds) |
| Apples: | $261,540,987 | 0.37% |
| Total Agricultural Subsidies | $70,229,820,137 | 100.00% |

*This calculation applies only to domestic food consumption. Therefore, exports and corn grown for ethanol are excluded. Also excluded is any federal support not specified in Title I of the Farm Bill. Therefore, disaster payments, conservation payments, and purchase for food assistance programs are not included.

SOURCES:
- Environmental Working Group, http://www.ewg.org/farm/region.php?fips=00000.
- Good, Darrell. "Corn: A Record Crop," Grain Price Outlook, No. 7, University of Illinois Extension, http://www.farmdoc.uiuc.edu/marketing/grainoutlook/html/101703/101703.html.
- Myers, Robert, Thomas Jefferson Agricultural Institute, http://www.jeffersoninstitute.org/pubs/sunflower_guide.pdf.
- USITC Publication 3350, September 2000, http://www.usitc.gov/er/nl2000/ER0922X1.HTM.
- USDA, industry statistics.
- Soy Stats online, United Soybean Board, http://www.soystats.com/2001/page_23.htm.
- World Resources Institute, http://earthtrends.wri.org/searchable_db/index.php?theme=8&variable_ID=1834&action=select_countries.

## THE RHETORICAL SITUATION

### Purpose

PCRM's purpose is to present complex information in a simple, digestible format. They also seek to persuade readers of a problem in terms of foods the U.S. government subsidizes (left pyramid) versus the foods Americans should be eating (right pyramid).

### Audience

Readers of this infographic want facts, and they want them efficiently presented. They may be general readers, healthcare professionals, lawmakers, voters, or anyone with a specific interest in food subsidies, nutrition, and government.

### Rhetorical appeals

The authors establish their **ethos** by identifying themselves as physicians, and therefore as health and nutrition experts. They further support that ethos with the precision of the information, their choice of sources, and the careful citing of sources.

The authors use logic (**logos**) by presenting the data in the pyramid charts, and also in the table below.

### Modes & media

**Mode = written and visual** The editors at PCRM use a combination of visuals and text to convey information and make an argument about federal subsidies and nutritional costs levied on consumers. At the top of the chart, they rely on the visual, juxtaposing two food pyramids (one of federal subsidies and one of nutrition recommendations). Below the food subsidies pyramid is a table that breaks down exact dollar amounts. Combining the table, graphic, and sources (at the bottom) provides rich information, boosting the persuasive power of the piece.

**Medium = digital** This information is geared toward a general online audience (anyone searching online for nutritional information, or even the cost of a Big Mac, might find this chart). If PCRM created the chart to be published in their own newsletter, the audience would be limited to physicians or other healthcare professionals. Though this infographic isn't interactive, many online charts like this are, allowing audiences to plug in certain information; can you imagine how the PCRM chart might be made interactive?

## THE GENRE'S CONVENTIONS

### Elements of the genre

**Based on data.** The PCRM authors draw on seven sources, including the USDA.

**Precise.** Percentages and numbers of items are precise (down to the decimal point); e.g., vegetables and fruits are listed as .37%, rather than rounded up to .4%.

**Clearly titled.** The words in the title convey the main point of the chart.

**Clearly labeled.** The labels clarify what each item is and its specific value (e.g., labels convey that grains make up 13.23% of subsidies).

**Uses symbols.** The two pyramids represent items and values related to federal subsidies versus those related to federal nutrition recommendations.

### Style

**Minimal detail** is used—but enough to make the information clear and authoritative. The two pyramids convey the essence of the information; the text provides concise information about subsidies.

PCRM's tone is **objective**. All information is presented as fact.

### Design

Color indicates the separation of categories (e.g., vegetables and fruits are green in the right-hand pyramid). Leader lines make clear how text and visuals relate. Information below the visuals is provided in list form and as a bulleted list for easy reading.

### Sources

PCRM's research draws on seven sources, which are listed at the bottom of the chart.

## Questions: Analyzing PCRM's chart/infographic

**1. Purpose.** How do the PCRM editors inform their readers about why a salad costs more than a Big Mac? To what extent are they presenting an argument?

**2. Audience.** Describe the audience that PCRM targets with this infographic. Is the target audience consumers? People interested in economics? Dieters? Vegetarians? Provide support for your answer.

**3. Rhetorical appeals.** One way the PCRM editors establish ethos is by listing the sources they used. How else is ethos established?

**4. Modes & media.** What are the advantages of making the chart available digitally? How might the PCRM editors revise the chart to take better advantage of a digital medium?

**5. Elements of the genre.** How does the title of the chart help shape the way you understand the information presented? Describe the tone of the title. To what extent does it reflect the conventions of the genre?

**6. Elements of the genre.** The chart has two visuals. What is the impact of the side-by-side presentation of these visuals?

**7. Style.** Describe the level of detail in this chart. Why do you think the PCRM editors chose to add another layer of detail with the table underneath the first graphic?

**8. Design.** How does the use of color relate to the information presented in the chart?

**9. Design.** Why is a pyramid an appropriate chart for presenting this information? What would be different if the PCRM editors had used a bar chart or a pie chart?

**10. Sources.** Why do you think the PCRM editors omitted any data from McDonald's in the chart?

# Drafting a Chart/Infographic

---

## CHECKLIST: Drafting a Chart/Infographic

Thinking of creating a chart or other infographic? Ask yourself the following questions.

### WHAT'S MY RHETORICAL SITUATION?

☐ **Purpose.** What financial experience that I've encountered might be interesting to represent in a chart? Why? Do I want to look at it from a personal angle or a more global perspective? What are all the considerations I need to take into account to represent the data that correspond to that experience?

☐ **Audience.** Who are my readers? Why should/will my chart matter to them? What do I want them to get out of it? And how will I reach them? Does my audience consist of general readers or specialists in the field? What level of detail will my chart need?

☐ **Rhetorical appeals.** How will I establish my authority and reliability as a writer? How will I convey my information so my readers believe my data? To what extent will I rely on logic to support my interpretations? How will I organize the information to convey the logic?

☐ **Modes & media.** Do I want readers to experience my chart primarily as a visual? How much text will accompany my chart? Do I want readers to access my chart digitally or in print? Why?

### WHAT GENRE CONVENTIONS MATTER?

☐ **Elements of the genre.** What types of data will I use to create my chart? Will I use colors or symbols in the chart? How will I represent those in my legend? Have I used sources based on research? Will I use footnotes to attribute those sources? Do I want my title to indicate my ultimate findings or present a question?

☐ **Style.** How will I keep my tone objective? What level of detail will I include in my chart?

☐ **Design.** How do I want to organize my chart spatially? Are there multiple visuals? Does each visual have accompanying text? Are colors appropriate for my chart? If so, what colors will help me convey my information? Is a bar chart or a line graph better for conveying my information?

☐ **Sources.** Is my chart based on my own knowledge or do I need to do research to gather data and statistics? How many sources do I need to draw on in order to present the information effectively?

---

## PRACTICE  Want to experiment? Draft your own chart or other infographic.

Think about how you spent time over the last week: doing homework, attending class, working, socializing, sleeping, eating, exercising, and so on. Then choose a visual way to represent this information, taking into account your data, what you want to convey and why, how you can best establish your ethos—and also your choices of text, images, color, and design.

The first newspapers were handwritten pages that reported on economic and social issues in Europe in the 1400s. The first successful English-language paper was *The Weekly Newes*, established in the 1620s; a little later, *The London Gazette* became the official newspaper of Great Britain (1666). In 1704, a bookseller and postmaster named John Campbell kicked off newspapers in America with *The Boston News-Letter*, an effort that was followed up more successfully in 1728 by Benjamin Franklin, who published *The Pennsylvania Gazette*, a paper considered to be *The New York Times* of the eighteenth century.

◀ PORTRAIT &
NEWSPAPER ▶

An issue of *The Pennsylvania Gazette*, personally managed by Benjamin Franklin. What would Franklin think about the Internet? Where would he get his news? *Both images: Library of Congress.*

Today, most cities have at least one local daily newspaper; Chicago, for example, has the *Chicago Sun-Times* and the *Chicago Tribune*. Daily newspapers are divided into sections on world, domestic, and local news; sports; business; science; health;

obituaries; and weather. Many have sections dedicated to editorials/opinions, food, travel, education, entertainment, and fashion, along with advice columns, comics, puzzles, and horoscopes. Smaller communities and organizations also publish newspapers on topics of interest to more specific audiences (such as the Boston area's *Wicked Local*, a consortium of local/community newspapers). Many publications are available online and include links to related stories and topics, as well as social media features that allow readers to post reactions to published stories.

Before the Internet, major newspapers were published once or twice a day. However, now that readers can check news headlines and follow stories online throughout the day, they expect constant updates. News reporting and publishing is now a 24/7 occupation; this makes us all better-informed citizens, but it also means that news agencies focused on breaking news are more vulnerable to misreporting and error. (For example, in 2011, in their zeal to break and update the story of the shooting of Arizona congresswoman Gabrielle Giffords, several news agencies reported that she was shot dead, though she survived the shooting. See the *Columbia Journalism Review*.)

While newspapers publish many kinds of writing—persuasive editorials, letters to the editor, advice columns, ads—at their core are factual news articles written by reporters. Reporters research their writing: They gather information for a story by conducting interviews, serving as eyewitnesses (reporting from the scene, for example), checking public records, and working with library and online sources. News journalists need to be able to back up the accuracy of their writing with facts from several reliable sources.

In news articles, writers present facts. In editorials, they present opinions. That said, the line between fact and opinion can blur, especially on broadcast news programs. Can you think of examples where a news report feels too much like an opinion piece? If so, how do you account for this?

## Analyzing News Articles: What to Look For

THE RHETORICAL SITUATION

**Purpose**   Journalists research and write news articles to inform readers of facts and events. Their purpose is to present true and fair accounts of issues and happenings, and to do so while adhering to ethical standards, such as those outlined by the Society of Professional Journalists.

Among the largest news providers are CNN, ABC, MSNBC, Fox News, the Associated Press, *The New York Times*, and *The Washington Post*. (For more news providers, see "Modes & media" below.) Depending on a news organization's size and scope, it might cover a range of world, national, and perhaps local news, and specific subject areas such as business, culture, science, and entertainment. Like any organization, each news provider has its own policies, agenda, and built-in biases. That said, ideally, the news articles that they publish or air are as fact based and objective as possible.

Keep in mind that news articles can appear in the context of other genres. In an online newspaper, for example, a news article might appear near an advertisement or an editorial or other opinion piece. It's a good practice to clarify for yourself what is informative fact-based reporting and what is editorial writing (see also Chapter 4).

**Audience** Journalists who write news articles know readers want to be informed about world events and issues, and to be kept up-to-date, especially online. They know that some readers will scan the first few paragraphs to get the main idea, so they need to include the most important material up front. Some readers who are especially interested—personally or professionally—in a given topic, however, will read for depth. They will read the entire article and also turn to related articles. Journalists keep that audience in mind as well.

**Rhetorical appeals** Journalists use ethos and logos to reach their audiences. A news publisher's reputation for "getting the story right" is crucial, as are the reputations of reporters associated with the publisher. If a reporter's credibility is seriously tarnished, his or her career in journalism will quickly end. In 2003, for example, promising *New York Times* reporter Jayson Blair was fired for plagiarizing parts of several news reports he had written. The *Times* called it "a low point in the 152-year history of the newspaper" and apologized profusely to its readers.

There is debate, both within the news industry itself and among readers and commentators, of what constitutes "news." The impact of reality television, which is cheaper to produce than dramas or news programs, is a factor, as is the mainstream appeal of celebrity and reality-star gossip. Whatever your opinion of the entertainment news published by *Gawker*, *TMZ*, and others, it's clear that the writers and editors at these organizations know how to appeal to their readers' pathos (emotions) with sensational headlines and stories about affairs, addictions, and arrests.

**Modes & media**   News articles can take many forms. Here, we're highlighting written news articles, because text can appear in print or digital formats. With the rise of digital news sites such as *The Huffington Post*, many print newspapers have moved online (see also "Purpose" on p. 127). Most traditional print newspapers have companion Web sites; for example, you can read many of the same stories in both the print and online versions of *The New York Times*, the *Wall Street Journal*, *The Washington Post*, and the *Los Angeles Times*, although some online content requires a subscription. The advantages of the online news article are that it can be updated instantly, can link to related articles and sources, and can be accompanied by video. Online publications also allow readers to post comments, making these sources much more interactive than print newspapers.

Traditional news outlets, such as those just mentioned, are not the only sources of news reports. News reports also commonly appear in news magazines, such as *Time, Newsweek/The Daily Beast, Slate, Salon*, and *Harper's*, and on blogs. Some news blogs, such as *This Just In*, are associated with a particular news outlet, in this case CNN. Others, such as the *Renewable Energy Law Blog*, report on news relevant to their readers; in the case of the *Renewable Energy Law Blog*, readers are clients and potential clients of the law firm that hosts the blog. In still other news blogs, writers report or comment on news, but they're not affiliated with a news outlet. Rather, these are individual blogs, such as *Not a Sheep, Jezebel*, and *Buzzfeed*, where bloggers present news snippets and then comment on them.

In addition to appearing in print and in digital formats, news stories can also take the form of audio and video reports. National Public Radio covers all the top stories that print and digital news outlets cover, but they of course do it in audio form. Many digital news outlets, such as MSNBC, also make videos of news coverage available online.

THE GENRE'S CONVENTIONS

## Elements of the genre

*Well researched and fact-checked*. As discussed above, the authority (or ethos) of the reporter, publisher, and content is crucial. Writers must be scrupulous in their research and fact-checking. A rule of thumb in journalism is to verify a report with at least three reliable sources. When an error is discovered in an article, journalists and publishers are usually quick to make a correction and apologize. For example, CNET News, a technology publication affiliated with CBS News, states their corrections policy on their Web site.

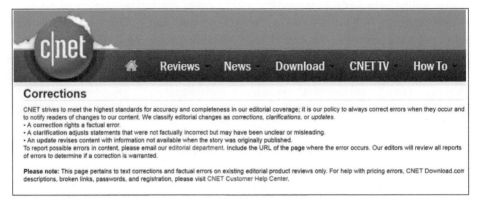

**Corrections**

CNET strives to meet the highest standards for accuracy and completeness in our editorial coverage; it is our policy to always correct errors when they occur and to notify readers of changes to our content. We classify editorial changes as *corrections, clarifications,* or *updates.*
• A correction rights a factual error.
• A clarification adjusts statements that were not factually incorrect but may have been unclear or misleading.
• An update revises content with information not available when the story was originally published.
To report possible errors in content, please email our editorial department. Include the URL of the page where the error occurs. Our editors will review all reports of errors to determine if a correction is warranted.

**Please note:** This page pertains to text corrections and factual errors on existing editorial product reviews only. For help with pricing errors, CNET Download.com descriptions, broken links, passwords, and registration, please visit CNET Customer Help Center.

*Usually aimed at a broad audience.* Most newspapers, news magazines, and news sites have a very broad readership with varying degrees of education, so the level of vocabulary in a news article must be appropriate for all. Most are written with a vocabulary considered to be ninth or tenth grade. *The New York Times,* however, is written at a twelfth-grade level of vocabulary and comprehension.

Think of the sources where you get your news. How would you characterize the writing? The vocabulary level? How do a journalist's style and word choice contribute to your reading experience?

*Opens with a concise summary in a lead (or lede) paragraph.* Most journalists begin their news articles with a paragraph that states the most important aspects of their story and grabs the reader's attention. In the rest of the article, reporters elaborate on what was presented in the opening paragraph. Because many readers skim rather than read a full article, the content of the lead paragraph is especially important.

*Presents information in order of importance.* Paragraphs that follow the lead and make up the body of the article provide details and supporting evidence from sources. Paragraphs closer to the beginning of the story provide details that are more important in understanding the essence of the story; those closer to the end, however, provide information that is less essential, given that some readers may not read the whole article to the end.

As explained in the "Style" section below, news journalists tend to structure their articles with an overview of the important information at the beginning, so readers can get information quickly.

*Includes quotations.* Journalists often quote sources directly to add flavor to their articles and to maintain the feel of "just the facts, ma'am." No one can accuse a reporter of misinterpreting what someone said if the reporter includes direct quotations.

*Written in short paragraphs.* Journalists often write in short paragraphs because they're easier to read than long ones. They're also easier on the eyes, especially considering the formats news articles are generally published in—either in narrow columns in print newspapers or online.

### Style

*Neutral tone/absence of personal opinion.* The goal of writing a news article is to report information. It's appropriate for news journalists to use a serious and fairly formal tone in their writing; of course, "formal" doesn't have to mean dry. It's also appropriate for journalists to refrain from editorializing, unless they are writing an editorial or hosting an opinion column, for example.

*Objective, third-person voice.* An objective stance conveys the cut-and-dry, fact-based nature of news articles. News journalists also use precise language in order to clearly communicate facts and details, and use the third person (*he/she/they*) rather than the first person (*I/we*).

Usually reporters write in the third person (*he/she/they*) because it is a neutral way to present facts. However, sometimes they use the first person (*I/we*). How might a journalist's use of *I* affect your reading of an article? What strategies might that writer use to persuade you that he or she is being objective?

*Just enough detail for the general reader.* Journalists use specific details to support their generalizations. In the annotated article by Nicholas Wade (p. 137), you'll notice that the writer is very specific about how cats lap water. However, Wade gives only the level of detail that a general reader can understand. For example, he explains that "the cat darts its tongue, curving the upper side downward so that the tip lightly touches the surface of the water. The tongue is then pulled upward at high speed, drawing a column of water behind it." A general reader can grasp this level of detail easily. A scientist or veterinarian may want more detail, but that level of detail would only be appropriate for a specialized audience of scientists or veterinarians.

### Design

*Attention-grabbing title/headline.* The title of a news article is called a headline. It is usually presented in much larger or bolder type than the story itself, and is brief and descriptive. Headlines are used to attract readers and are sometimes provocative; see, for example, the front page of the *New York Post*, a paper that is notorious for its over-the-top headlines. Compare that to the longer, more serious headline used by the BBC News on page 132.

▲ NEWSPAPER *New York Post,* front page. When it comes to unrestrained headlines, the *Post* rarely disppoints. *From the New York Post © 4/15/1983 NYP Holdings, Inc. All rights reserved.*

*Byline.* A byline is the presentation of the author's name, usually below the headline and above the text of the article. Sometimes the byline notes that the author is a correspondent or staff writer. Below, BBC News correspondent James Reynolds is credited for his report from Cairo.

NEWS ARTICLE ▶
**James Reynolds,**
byline at BBC News
(bbc.co.uk). Reynolds,
who has been with
the BBC since 1996,
is the group's Tehran
Correspondent. Note
also the headline for
Reynolds's report:
descriptive and
serious. Compare it to
the *Post* headline on
page 131.

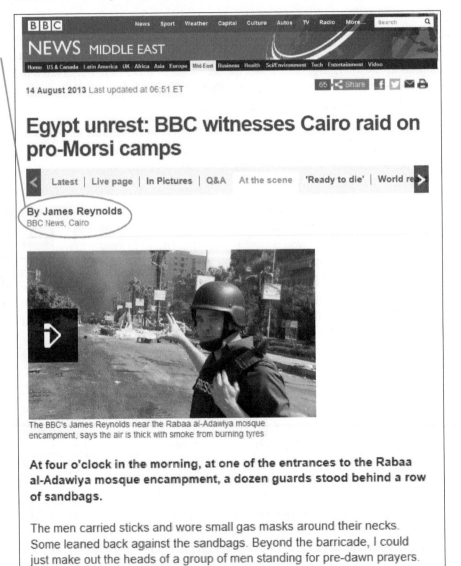

BBC
**NEWS** MIDDLE EAST

News  Sport  Weather  Capital  Culture  Autos  TV  Radio  More...  Search

Home  US & Canada  Latin America  UK  Africa  Asia  Europe  Mid-East  Business  Health  Sci/Environment  Tech  Entertainment  Video

14 August 2013 Last updated at 06:51 ET

65  Share  f  y  ✉  🖨

# Egypt unrest: BBC witnesses Cairo raid on pro-Morsi camps

◀  Latest | Live page | In Pictures | Q&A | At the scene | 'Ready to die' | World re▶

**By James Reynolds**
BBC News, Cairo

The BBC's James Reynolds near the Rabaa al-Adawiya mosque encampment, says the air is thick with smoke from burning tyres

**At four o'clock in the morning, at one of the entrances to the Rabaa al-Adawiya mosque encampment, a dozen guards stood behind a row of sandbags.**

The men carried sticks and wore small gas masks around their necks. Some leaned back against the sandbags. Beyond the barricade, I could just make out the heads of a group of men standing for pre-dawn prayers. No-one appeared to want to leave.

*Serif typeface.* A serif font has a very small flare at the stroke ends and corners of letters, while a sans serif font lacks these strokes. Print articles are often presented in serif fonts (such as in the print edition of *The New York Times*), while sans serif fonts, such as those used by BBC News (below) are a good choice for the readability of digital content. Compare a serif **A** to a sans serif **A**.

*Use of columns or chunking.* News sites such as the BBC's (see below) present articles in chunked sections that have their own headings. Digital content may be presented in multiple columns or on different sections of the grid with various ways to navigate the content. Print newspapers are limited to columns of no more than fifty-two characters wide.

*Images: photos, graphs, and multimedia components.* Many news articles, especially breaking news on a Web site, or a front-page story in a print paper, are con-

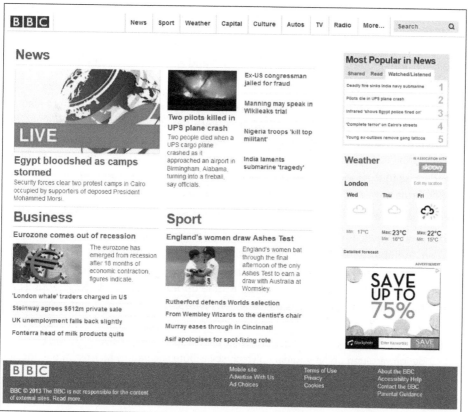

◀ NEWS SITE
**BBC News.** The layout chosen by the editors and designers at the BBC presents content in a clean, streamlined format. The consistent sans serif font for text and headings, the three-column grid, the chunking of text, and the use of images contribute to the readability and modern aesthetic.

textualized with photos, charts, graphs, and, in the case of the online source, video and other multimedia. This is true of the BBC News site (p. 133), where the main story (of August 14, 2013, about Egypt) features prominently and leads readers to plenty of related content and live video. A piece with a video or audio component usually includes an arrow icon or other visual element to indicate this; sometimes the video or audio itself is the news story.

News publishers use visual and multimedia to grab readers' attention, provide context, and enrich the content of print articles. For example, the article on page 134 reports on the civil-union ceremonies that took place after Colorado's civil-union law went into effect. The article features a large photo; a few paragraphs down are links to related stories. The featured photo and photo gallery give readers context for the event.

*Headers, footers, and tabs.* Designers of online news sites provide tabs and navigational menus and search boxes to keep readers oriented. The designers use repeated design features to reinforce the agency's identity. For example, a print newspaper's title appears on every page and in other elements, and titles, headers, and footers (which include the date and section, for example) help readers find what they need on the page.

*Use of color.* Online news sites include color images and video. Designers also use color typographically to direct attention toward particular content. Blue is used for hyperlinks (which turn a different color once you select them), red is sometimes used for breaking news headlines, and gray shading is sometimes used to orient readers as to their location within the content. Images and videos are shown in full color. Print newspapers, which are published on a thin paper called newsprint, are printed in black ink (such as *The New York Times*) or in color (such as *USA Today*).

**Sources** News reports are based on eyewitness accounts, authoritative published documents, interviews, and records. Most journalists indicate their sources within their news articles, using attribution phrases such as "according to" and linking directly to their sources. In his article on how cats drink, *New York Times* reporter Nicholas Wade writes:

> Cats, both big and little, are so much classier, according to new research by Pedro M. Reis and Roman Stocker of the Massachusetts Institute of Technology, joined by Sunghwan Jung of the Virginia Polytechnic Institute and Jeffrey M. Aristoff of Princeton. Writing in the Thursday issue of Science, the four engineers report. . . .

THE DENVER POST

# BREAKING NEWS

Weather: DENVER, CO | Now: 68°F | High: 75°F | Low: 56°F

| News | Sports | Business | Entertainment | Lifestyles | Opinion | Politics | Your Hub | Marketplace |

BOOKMARK | Print | Email

LOCAL NEWS

## Colorado couples celebrate midnight civil-unions ceremony

By Joey Bunch
*The Denver Post*

0
Tweet
 3.2k
 Like
0
+1
Submit

POSTED: 04/30/2013 10:16:47 PM MDT | UPDATED: 3 MONTHS AGO          343 COMMENTS

Getting personal with civil unions

Hundreds of Colorado gay and lesbian couples put an official government seal on their relationships in the early hours of Wednesday morning, after the state's civil-unions law took effect.

Shortly after midnight, whoops and cheers rang off the glassy interior of Denver's Wellington E. Webb Building and then again and again when each new set of 10 numbers flashed on a television monitor near the Clerk and Record's office, summoning the next in line to come apply for a license. With paperwork in hand, the couples returned to the atrium to exchange vows.

The couples gushed over their opportunity to hold the first piece of government acknowledgment of their relationships, granting them many of the same rights as married

Led by Denver Mayor Michael Hancock, Anna and Fran Simon are the first couple to take part in a civil union ceremony at the Webb Building in Denver, Colo., on May 1, 2013. (Craig F. Walker, The Denver Post)

couples.

The group represented a wide palette of ages and races, some in formal attire, some in jeans and T-shirts.

"Other people get to say fiancee and wife, and all we can say is girlfriend or partner," said Sarah Mutter, who made her commitment a government affair Tuesday night with her mate of four years, Isabel Aguirre.

Aguirre added, "This is a big step — for us to be taken as legally accepted."

Mayor Michael Hancock performed many of the first ceremonies,

**PHOTOS: COLORADO CIVIL UNIONS**

• View more photos from the Colorado civil union festivities in Denver from April 30-May 1, 2013.

**RELATED STORIES**

May 2:
• Colorado civil unions slower during the day after midnight parties
Apr 30:
• Colorado couples to make history as civil unions provide legal bonds
Apr 28:
• Colorado couples get ready to party Wednesday for civil unions
Apr 23:
• Civil union ceremonies scheduled to begin at midnight May 1 in Denver
Mar 24:
• Gay marriage ruling could bolster Colorado's new civil-unions law
• Supreme Court: Same-sex marriage case has echoes of Roe vs. Wade

Anthony Aragon and David Westman have their picture taken during the "The Civil Soiree" at the McNichols Building in Civic Center, Denver, Colo., April 30, 2013. (Craig F. Walker, The Denver Post)

Clark, said the evening was better than he could have hoped.

"What excitement people have after waiting decades for this night," he said. "It's overwhelming."

The excitement was palpable among the friends and family who gathered to witness.

"It's a proud night for my family," said Juan Moreno, who came to support his daughter, Hillary. "It's not right it took so long, because people shouldn't judge. Love is a hard enough thing to find."

The long line in front of the Wellington E. Webb building began forming at dusk, then swelled mightily when a celebratory dinner for 500 people let out across the street at about 10 p.m.

Though civil unions grant couples most of the same legal rights as marriage, Colorado voters banned same-sex marriages by approving a constitutional amendment in 2006.

Several speakers, including Hancock, said it's time for that to change. The U.S. Supreme Court could clear the way for that in its Defense of Marriage Act deliberations in June.

"We will not stop until our state residents ... have full marriage equality under the law," said Hancock, who received standing ovations at the beginning and end of his address to the crowd.

DeGette added, "It's way, way, way overdue."

DeGette is vice chair of the U.S. House of Representatives' LGBT Equality Caucus.

Among those in attendance at the pre-midnight ceremony was Robin Kniech, a Denver city councilwoman who is the first openly gay or lesbian member to be election to the City Council, and Debra Johnson, Denver's clerk and recorder.

Of Colorado's new civil-unions law that was then only hours away from taking effect, DeGette said, "We're going to fix one word in the statute, and that word is going to be wedding and marriage."

◄ ONLINE NEWS ARTICLE
A *Denver Post* article with color photos, videos, and links to related stories. The multimedia—and how it's laid out— enriches the reader's experience and provides supporting evidence and context.
*Story: Joey Bunch. Photos: Craig F. Walker. The Denver Post 5/2/2013.*

For more examples of **news articles** see the Index of Genres on page G-1.

Wade makes it clear that the information he draws on is a researched article from the journal *Science* and from the four researchers he names. Journalists, unlike the authors of peer-reviewed journal articles (p. 143), do not use academic documentation styles such as MLA or APA (pp. 395 and 415). Because news journalism is a popular genre and not a scholarly genre, it has a different set of conventions for documenting sources, such as the phrasing that Wade uses on page 134. In news journalism, the thinking is that the reader doesn't need the same level of detail about sources that scholarly audiences need. That said, online news providers and journalists can boost their ethos by linking to their sources.

# Nicholas Wade

## *For Cats, a Big Gulp with a Touch of the Tongue*

*The New York Times*, which has been publishing since 1851, is considered highly accurate and is regarded as one of the most authoritative newspapers available. Its Web site and print circulation make it one of the most widely read newspapers in the world. It has won over one hundred Pulitzer Prizes, the most prestigious reporting award given. Nicholas Wade is a science reporter for *The New York Times*. He has written several science books, including 2009's *The Faith Instinct*, about the scientific basis of religious faith. The following article appeared in the Science section of the *Times*; the online version includes links to sources, infographics, and video that support the text. *(Text and images on pp. 138–39, From* The New York Times, *November 11, 2010. Reprinted by permission.)*

▲ AUTHOR PHOTO
**Nicholas Wade,** *New York Times* reporter. *Naum Kazhdan/The New York Times/Redux Pictures.*

What is the composer, **Nicholas Wade**, doing?

THE RHETORICAL
SITUATION

Purpose
Audience
Rhetorical appeals
Modes & media

*see page 139*

How do I know this is a **newspaper article**?

THE GENRE'S
CONVENTIONS

Elements of the genre
Style
Design
Sources

*see page 140*

# The New York Times

## Science
### For Cats, a Big Gulp With a Touch of the Tongue

By NICHOLAS WADE
Published: November 11, 2010

It has taken four highly qualified engineers and a bunch of integral equations to figure it out, but we now know how cats drink. The answer is: very elegantly, and not at all the way you might suppose.

RECOMMEND
TWITTER
LINKEDIN
SIGN IN TO E-MAIL
PRINT
REPRINTS
SHARE

🔍 Enlarge This Image

Pedro Reis

Cutta Cutta, who inspired the study, belongs to a researcher at M.I.T.

Cats lap water so fast that the human eye cannot follow what is happening, which is why the trick had apparently escaped attention until now. With the use of high-speed photography, the neatness of the feline solution has been captured.

The act of drinking may seem like no big deal for anyone who can fully close his mouth to create suction, as people can. But the various species that cannot do so — and that includes most adult carnivores — must resort to some other mechanism.

Dog owners are familiar with the unseemly lapping noises that ensue when their thirsty pet meets a bowl of water.

The dog is thrusting its tongue into the water, forming a crude cup with it and hauling the liquid back into the muzzle.

**Multimedia**

📊 Graphic

A Study of Cat Lapping

**Connect With Us on Social Media**
@nytimesscience on Twitter.
· Science Reporters and Editors on Twitter

Like the science desk on Facebook.

Cats, both big and little, are so much classier, according to new research by Pedro M. Reis and Roman Stocker of the Massachusetts Institute of Technology, joined by Sunghwan Jung of the Virginia Polytechnic Institute and Jeffrey M. Aristoff of Princeton.

Writing in the Thursday issue of Science, the four engineers report that the cat's lapping method depends on its instinctive ability to calculate the point at which gravitational force would overcome inertia and cause the water to fall.

What happens is that the cat darts its tongue, curving the upper side downward so that the tip lightly touches the surface of the water.

The tongue is then pulled upward at high speed, drawing a column of water behind it.

*Continues next page*

# The New York Times

VIDEO »

More Video | Multimedia »

SCIENCE

**How Cats Lap**
The Biomechanics of Feline Water Uptake

Just at the moment that gravity finally overcomes the rush of the water and starts to pull the column down — snap! The cat's jaws have closed over the jet of water and swallowed it.

The cat laps four times a second — too fast for the human eye to see anything but a blur — and its tongue moves at a speed of one meter per second.

Being engineers, the cat-lapping team next tested its findings with a machine that mimicked a cat's tongue, using a glass disk at the end of a piston to serve as the tip. After calculating things like the Froude number and the aspect ratio, they were able to figure out how fast a cat should lap to get the greatest amount of water into its mouth. The cats, it turns out, were way ahead of them — they lap at just that speed.

To the scientific mind, the next obvious question is whether bigger cats should lap at different speeds.

The engineers worked out a formula: the lapping frequency should be the weight of the cat species, raised to the power of minus one-sixth and multiplied by 4.6. They then made friends with a curator at Zoo New England, the nonprofit group that operates the Franklin Park Zoo in Boston and the Stone Zoo in Stoneham, Mass., who let them videotape his big cats. Lions, leopards, jaguars and ocelots turned out to lap at the speeds predicted by the engineers.

The animal who inspired this exercise of the engineer's art is a black cat named Cutta Cutta, who belongs to Dr. Stocker and his family. Cutta Cutta's name comes from the word for "many stars" in Jawoyn, a language of the Australian aborigines.

Dr. Stocker's day job at M.I.T. is applying physics to biological problems, like how plankton move in the ocean. "Three and a half years ago, I was watching Cutta Cutta lap over breakfast," Dr. Stocker said. Naturally, he wondered what hydrodynamic problems the cat might be solving. He consulted Dr. Reis, an expert in fluid mechanics, and the study was under way.

At first, Dr. Stocker and his colleagues assumed that the raspy hairs on a cat's tongue, so useful for grooming, must also be involved in drawing water into its mouth. But the tip of the tongue, which is smooth, turned out to be all that was needed.

The project required no financing. The robot that mimicked the cat's tongue was built for an experiment on the International Space Station, and the engineers simply borrowed it from a neighboring lab.

## THE RHETORICAL SITUATION

### Purpose

As a science news reporter, Wade's purpose as author of this article is to explain recent findings about how cats drink.

### Audience

Wade's audience includes general news readers, online readers, *Times* fans, animal lovers, and science enthusiasts.

Also, as a science journalist, Wade may have his own following, so some readers may be his fans.

### Rhetorical appeals

Wade appeals to readers' sense of **ethos** through specific references to the work of four scientists who published an article in the journal *Science*.

He appeals to **pathos** by using humor, especially at the start of the article. He begins with a tongue-in-cheek statement: "It has taken four highly qualified engineers and a bunch of integral equations to figure it out."

He also appeals to readers' sense of logic (**logos**) by beginning with general statements about cats drinking water and then continuing with more specific details.

**Modes & media**

**Mode = written, visual, and video** Wade shares most information in words, but the photos of Cutta Cutta and the video illustrate his most

important points (note: scroll down to the video box on the *Times* page). Some news sites, such as *The Huffington Post*, present articles as videos that are introduced by a small amount of text.

**Medium = digital** Wade's article was published at *The New York Times* online and also in print. Among the advantages of the digital version of the article are the addition of video and the

links to other information, including the researched article that was Wade's source.

**Elements of the genre**

**Well researched and accurate.** Wade read a research report in *Science* and talked to the scientists who wrote it. He found out how the research was inspired, funded, and conducted.

**Opens with a lead paragraph** that sets up the article's subject: "[W]e now know how cats drink."

**Presents information in order of importance.** Wade begins with the researchers' findings: They discovered how cats drink, something previously unknown. "Cats lap water so fast that the human eye cannot follow what is happening, which is why the trick had apparently escaped attention until now."

Wade ends with information on how the research was funded, something fewer readers will be interested in.

**Includes quotations** to personalize the experience or information for the reader. The quote from Dr. Stocker shows what inspired his research: "Three and a half years ago, I was watching Cutta Cutta lap over breakfast."

**Short paragraphs** hold readers' attention.

**Style**

**Neutral/no opinions.** Wade doesn't indicate his personal opinion about how cats drink.

**Objective, third-person voice.** Wade reports what researchers

discovered, leaving himself out of the article. E.g., though he may be a dog owner himself, instead of writing "My dog," he writes "Dog owners are familiar" with the sounds dogs make when they drink.

**Just enough detail for the general reader.** Wade relates relevant details precisely, such as the formula used to calculate the drinking speed of cats: "The lapping frequency should be the weight of the cat species, raised to the power of minus one-sixth and multiplied by 4.6."

**Design**

**Appealing headline.** The title interests readers and conveys the gist of the article in a few words. Also,

the page presents the newspaper's title, the name of the section, and the date of publication.

**Byline.** Wade's name (rather than "staff writer") appears under the headline, which adds to his ethos.

**Friendly typeface.** *The New York Times* online uses a clean Georgia serif font designed specifically for easy screen reading.

**Columns and chunking.** The *Times* divides its Web page into columns—in this case the content and images are in one area; advertising (not shown here) is on the right.

**Images and multimedia.** A photo of Cutta Cutta gives readers a visual of the cat that inspired

the research, and a series of photos shows how cats drink. A video features the researchers explaining why they decided to study cats drinking.

**Sources**

**Sources are acknowledged.** Wade and the *Times* use hyperlinks to acknowledge sources. The names of the four engineers who wrote the report on cats are linked so readers can learn more about them. Linking to sources further conveys Wade's reliability and objectivity.

## Questions: Analyzing Wade's news article

**1. Purpose.** What is Wade's main purpose in writing this article? What are some of his secondary purposes? Identify passages in the article where these purposes are apparent.

**2. Purpose.** Notice how Wade uses a slightly humorous title for his science- and research-based article. Why does he do this?

**3. Audience.** How does Wade appeal to people who are not cat lovers?

**4. Rhetorical appeals.** The online version of Wade's article includes hyperlinks that connect readers with additional information, including a researched article in *Science* and the biographical profiles of the scientists who wrote it, which contributes to the ethos of Wade and his article. How else does Wade convey a sense of ethos?

**5. Rhetorical appeals.** Cats and kittens can be extremely cute and there are many online videos devoted to celebrating how adorable they can be. How does Wade approach the subject from a different angle? Are there any spots where Wade emphasizes their cuteness? If so, where—and to what end?

**6. Modes & media.** Do you read news primarily online or do you read print newspapers? Why?

**7. Elements of the genre.** How does the lead paragraph set the stage for the rest of the article?

**8. Style.** How does Wade convey scientific information in a way that a general audience can understand? If possible, watch the video embedded in the article. How does its content connect with Wade's article? What stylistic differences, if any, do you see between Wade's writing and the voice-over of the video?

**9. Design.** Notice that the images and video are neatly lined up on the left side of the article rather than interspersed within the article where they are mentioned. Why did the designers at *The New York Times* lay it out this way?

**10. Sources.** Make a list of all the sources Nicholas Wade consulted while writing this article. Are there any sources that surprise you? How can you categorize the sources? Are they primary? Secondary? Tertiary? (See Chapter 6.)

# Drafting a News Article

---

## CHECKLIST: Drafting a News Article
Thinking of drafting a news article? Ask yourself the following questions.

### WHAT'S MY RHETORICAL SITUATION?

- [ ] **Purpose.** What newsworthy event or issue do I want to report? Of all the people involved with the story, which person will be my focus? How can I bring the story and people to life for my readers?

- [ ] **Audience.** Who will read my article? How carefully will they read it? Why will they read it? What will they do with the information?

- [ ] **Rhetorical appeals.** How will I establish my authority as a writer? How will I logically connect ideas and details? How will I make sure that my use of pathos does not undercut my ethos?

- [ ] **Modes & media.** Will readers experience my article in print form or online? Do I want to include images or videos?

### WHAT GENRE CONVENTIONS MATTER?

- [ ] **Elements of the genre.** Which information is important enough to my readers that I should present it first? Which information is interesting but not as important?

- [ ] **Style.** How will I keep my tone objective and neutral? What level of detail will I include in my article?

- [ ] **Design.** How will I use headers and footers, titles, headlines, tabs, and other design features to keep my readers oriented? Will my article appear online? If so, what information will I hyperlink? How might I embed photos or videos into the layout?

- [ ] **Sources.** How much research will I need to do to compose this article? Are there people I'll need to talk to? Where will I need to go? Will I need to locate documents or records in a library or online?

---

**PRACTICE** Want to experiment? Draft your own news article.

Think of an event or issue on your campus that you'd like to report on. Who are the people associated with the event or issue? Arrange to interview at least two of those involved so you can include their voices and perspectives in your article. How will you quote them? What quotes will do the most to bring your article to life? Next, draft a short article for an online newspaper that conveys the big picture of the topic, as well as relevant details that will interest your readers. Be sure to create a catchy headline and to hyperlink to any sources you use (including the people you interview).

# PEER-REVIEWED JOURNAL ARTICLES

As a student, you've probably written a research paper or two. When you write research papers in the academic setting, your purpose is to investigate a specific topic, usually by examining what others have already said about it. You begin by drawing on a variety of sources, for example, articles from *EBSCOhost*. The articles from these journals are secondary sources. Once you've gathered your sources, you don't merely report what you've found: You also synthesize, compare, and analyze what has been said. You incorporate the voices of your sources in a systematic way, using quotations, citing sources in the body of your paper (or other composition), and listing them at the end. For some assignments, you might also respond to the sources you've researched by presenting and supporting your own argument. Like most writing, researched writing can also be persuasive. (For more on researched writing, see Chapter 5. For more on persuasive writing, see Chapter 4.)

What is the purpose of peer-reviewing? What makes a text authentically peer-reviewed?

Research papers do exist outside of the classroom, but they're not usually called "research papers"—and they are usually informed by primary research (that is, research conducted by the writer himself or herself). These papers may be called "articles," "professional researched reports," "scholarly journal articles," or "peer-reviewed journal articles." When we say a work has been "peer-reviewed," we mean that it has been read, critiqued, and approved by other experts/scholars.

Authors of peer-reviewed articles are scholars; they are recognized by other scholars as experts on the subject they're writing about. Many scholars are employed as professors at colleges and universities; others work in research laboratories. Research laboratories can be associated with universities, medical facilities (such as the Mayo Clinic), the government (such as the U.S. Naval Research Laboratory), for-profit organizations (such as Pfizer and other pharmaceutical companies), or nonprofit organizations (such as the Pew Research Center). Research laboratories and centers are sometimes referred to as "think tanks."

The organizations that publish peer-reviewed articles usually do so for a professional audience (rather than general readers). Two examples include *Nature*, a weekly science journal, and the Web site of the American Psychological Association, which compiles scholarly articles. Peer-reviewed articles are often presented at academic conferences, usually to audiences of peers and other experts on the subject.

Should a wiki—where content is read and edited by peers—be considered a peer-reviewed source in the same way that a scholarly journal is? Why or why not?

In these forums, scholars must cite their sources rigorously; a charge of plagiarism can easily end an academic career. The readers of peer-reviewed journal articles are usually other experts in a given field, but might sometimes include more general readers, such as students or other nonexpert readers interested in the topics covered.

# Analyzing Peer-Reviewed Journal Articles: What to Look For

## THE RHETORICAL SITUATION

**Purpose** Scholars write articles for peer-reviewed journals in order to share their research results with others in the same field. Sometimes scholarly writers present groundbreaking new research, such as a new drug or an alternative energy source. Other times, they present more subtle findings, such as a different way of looking at existing data.

Another purpose of scholarly writers is to persuade readers to see things the way they do. For example, when presenting data, a scholar may want to argue for his or her own particular interpretation of the data. Most scholarly articles are meant to both inform and persuade.

**Audience** Authors of scholarly articles usually write for a fairly narrow primary audience that includes researchers, professors, and other scholars who want to stay up-to-date in their fields. However, they also have secondary audiences in mind. For example, as a student, you might refer to a scholarly journal article as a source for a research paper. Peer-reviewed journals exist in every academic field, including the sciences, humanities, and social sciences. For example, Amy and Liz both read academic journals such as *College Composition and Communication*, which focuses on teaching and composition; they use *CCC's* journal articles to deepen their own understanding of writing and teaching research. Another example, this one in science, is ▼ *Nature*, the most widely read journal of its kind. For academics needing to keep abreast of major stories in the sciences, reading *Nature* is crucial, as it keeps them informed about new discoveries, developments, and research by other professionals.

> What scholarly journals are related to your major? To what extent do you relate to them as a reader?

ONLINE JOURNAL ▶
***Nature* Homepage.**
*Nature* is cited by more scientists than any other science journal. *Macmillan.*

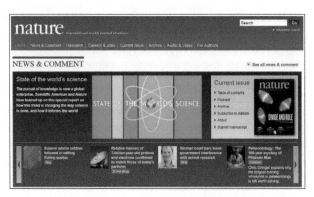

**Rhetorical appeals**   Scholars who write articles for peer-reviewed journals need to establish ethos by describing their research methods, explaining the data they collected and how they analyzed that information, and discussing their findings and conclusions in detail. They must also cite sources appropriately, taking into account the findings of others. And, because logic is important to scholarship and the writers' audience, writers must appeal to logos by building arguments that rest on tightly organized pieces of evidence and scrupulously researched data. Scholars must keep in mind that their readers will need to be convinced of the legitimacy of their research methods, the accuracy of their data collection, and the logic of their data analysis.

**Modes & media**   Scholarly articles are text based and may include visuals such as charts, graphs, and images to support and illustrate points. Journals are available in print and, increasingly, online; many articles that originate in print-based journals are available through subscription databases such as *EBSCOhost*, *JSTOR*, and *Project MUSE*. There are also a few scholarly journals that are only available digitally.

THE GENRE'S CONVENTIONS

## Elements of the genre

*Based on original research—or research of another expert or peer.* In a peer-reviewed journal article, scholars usually write about their own original research.

» First, they identify a question that needs to be answered (such as "How does living near a nuclear reactor affect birthrates?").

» Next, they design an experiment or research plan that will allow that question to be studied (for example, identifying nuclear reactors, collecting data on birthrates in the surrounding communities over time, interviewing obstetricians who practice in the surrounding communities, etc.).

» Then, they perform the research, analyze the data gathered in the research, and offer their interpretations in writing. Authors usually refer to related research by other scholars to contextualize their own work.

*Reviewed by others in the field for accuracy and reliability.* Scholarly articles are written by scholars, for scholars. During a process known as "peer review," other experts in the field review the article to check for clarity and style, but even more important, to make sure the research conducted is a legitimate means of measuring or studying the subject of the article. Peer reviewers might question, for instance, the validity of studying birthrates near nuclear reactors by merely interviewing people who live in the community. They would probably want more rigorous, objective data, such as hospital records documenting pregnancies, fertility rates, and births.

*Is thesis-driven.* Scholarly authors write to make a point about the research they've conducted—a point that usually has both informative and persuasive elements to it. For example, if an author's point is "drugs X, Y, and Z alleviate symptoms of condition A," she will go on to inform readers of how she drew that conclusion (how she conducted the research and analyzed the data) and will also—if the article is well researched and written—persuade readers that the drugs discussed in the article should be prescribed more often.

*Attributes sources/work of others.* Scholars who write articles for peer-reviewed journals summarize, paraphrase, and quote from their sources. When writers use other sources (outside of their own original research), they properly document the work/voices of others through in-text citations and Works Cited lists.

*Synthesizes sources.* Like a student writing a research paper, scholars must synthesize their sources in journal articles. That is, they pull together information across multiple sources to make their points.

*Uses formal and precise language.* Scholarly writers use formal language to convey the seriousness of their ideas and research. They also use precise language to communicate complex information accurately and in detail. In a scientific research study, the difference between .1 and .01 can be crucial.

### Style

*Descriptive title.* The title of a scholarly article needs to make clear what the article is about. In scientific fields, the more descriptive the better, such as "Hospital Mortality, Length of Stay, and Preventable Complications among Critically Ill Patients before and after Tele-ICU Reengineering of Critical Care Processes" (from *JAMA*). In the humanities, titles often have two parts: an imaginative or creative phrase, followed by a colon, and then a more descriptive phrase, such as "Black, White, and Blue: Racial Politics in B. B. King's Music from the 1960s" (an article by Ulrich Adelt, from *The Journal of Popular Culture*).

*Strong, authoritative voice and tone.* Authors of scholarly journal articles tend to use an authoritative voice and tone in their scholarly writing, which helps establish their ethos. For example, in "Status Struggles: Network Centrality and Gender Segregation in Same- and Cross-Gender Aggression," an article in *American*

Why do authors of scholarly articles tend to use long, descriptive titles? What are the benefits and drawbacks of such titles?

*Sociological Review*, authors Robert Faris and Diane Felmlee begin their article in a way that reinforces their expertise and authority:

> Aggression is commonplace in U.S. schools: bullying and other forms of proactive aggression adversely affect 30 percent, or 5.7 million, American youth each school year (Nansel et al. 2001). The National Education Association (1995) estimates that each weekday, 160,000 students skip school to avoid being bullied. This aggression has important consequences. Being victimized by bullies positively relates to a host of mental health problems, including depression (Baldry 2004), anxiety (Sharp, Thompson, and Arora 2000), and suicidal ideation (Carney 2000). —**Robert Faris and Diane Felmlee,** from "Status Struggles: Network Centrality and Gender Segregation in Same- and Cross-Gender Aggression," *American Sociological Review,* February 2011

*Use of detail.* Authors of scholarly articles use specific details to develop complex ideas. They also use details as evidence to back up their assertions. For example, in the article discussed above, Faris and Felmlee support general statements ("Aggression is commonplace in U.S. schools") with examples and evidence (bullying "affect[s] 30 percent, or 5.7 million, American youth each school year").

## Design

*Subheadings.* Many peer-reviewed journal articles are divided into sections by subheadings that make a long, complex article accessible. Subheadings also signal to the reader when the writer is about to turn his or her focus to another example or another aspect of the topic.

*Images.* Many scholarly articles include images, such as photos, charts, and illustrations, to convey complex information visually. Those that are published digitally can include hyperlinks to sources and other materials.

## Sources

*Types of sources used.* Scholarly writers must use sources that are authoritative and are appropriate to the topic and approach they've taken. For example, in the peer-reviewed article on page 148, the author draws heavily on movie reviews. This is appropriate because she discusses many films and their popular reception. Movie reviews would not be used for an article on molecular science, unless, for instance, the essay focuses on how molecular science is portrayed in films.

*Works Cited list.* Scholarly writers include a bibliography at the end of their articles. They list sources in the format dictated by the journal they're publishing in, or according to the format favored in their discipline's professional organization, such as the Modern Language Association (MLA style) and the American Psychological Association (APA style). For more on documentation, see Chapter 7.

For more examples of **academic writing,** including student work, see the Index of Genres on page G-1.

# Sika Dagbovie-Mullins

## *Mixed-Race Superstars*

Sika Dagbovie-Mullins is an assistant professor of English at Florida Atlantic University, where she teaches literature and researches the representation of mixed-race identity in literature and culture. Her article, originally titled "Star-Light, Star-Bright, Star Damn Near White: Mixed-Race Superstars," first appeared in 2007 in *The Journal of Popular Culture*, a scholarly, peer-reviewed journal. The journal, based at Michigan State University and published by the Popular Culture Association, presents the works of scholars in the field as well as in the related areas of literature, film studies, and African American studies. Dagbovie-Mullins's book *Crossing Black: Mixed-Race Identity in Modern American Fiction and Culture* was published in 2013.

*(Article: From The Journal of Popular Culture, Volume 40, Issue 2 (April 2007). Copyright © 2007 John Wiley and Sons. Reprinted by permission. Top banner: Courtesy of The Journal of Popular Culture.)*

ONLINE JOURNAL ▲
**The Journal of Popular Culture,** where Sika Dagbovie-Mullins published her article. *Courtesy of The Journal of Popular Culture.*

# THE JOURNAL OF POPULAR CULTURE

Submissions | Recent Articles | Editorial Board | FAQs | Subscribe | Advertise | Awards

### Star-Light, Star-Bright, Star Damn Near White: Mixed-Race Superstars

SIKA DAGBOVIE-MULLINS

In an episode of *The Chris Rock Show*, comedian Chris Rock searches the streets of Harlem to find out what people think of Tiger Woods.[1] When he asks three Asian storekeepers if they consider Woods Asian, one replies, "Not even this much," pressing two of his fingers together to show no space. This comic scene and the jokes that surround Woods's self-proclaimed identity reveal a cultural contradiction that I explore in this essay, namely the simultaneous acceptance and rejection of blackness within a biracial discourse in American popular culture. Though Woods's self-identification may not fit neatly into the black/white mixed-race identity explored in this project, he still falls into a black/white dichotomy prevalent in the United States. The Asian storekeepers agree with Rock's tongue-in-cheek suggestion that Tiger Woods is as black as James Brown, opposing sentiments like "The dude's more Asian than he is anything else" on an Asian American college Internet magazine ("Wang and Woods"). Woods cannot escape blackness (a stereotypical fried-chicken-and-collard-green-eating blackness according to Fuzzy Zoeller), and yet he also represents a multicultural poster boy, one whose blackness pales next to his much-celebrated multi-otherness.[2]

Through advertising, interviews, and publicity, biracial celebrities encode a distinct connection to blackness despite their projected (and sometimes preferred) self-identification. Drawing from Richard Dyer's *Stars*, I read biracial celebrities Halle Berry, Vin

*Continues next page*

What is the composer, **Sika Dagbovie-Mullins**, doing?

THE RHETORICAL SITUATION

Purpose
Audience
Rhetorical appeals
Modes & media

*see page 150*

How do I know this is a **peer-reviewed journal** article?

THE GENRE'S CONVENTIONS

Elements of the genre
Style
Design
Sources

*see page 150*

*(Continued on p. 152.)*

# THE JOURNAL OF POPULAR CULTURE

Diesel, and Mariah Carey by analyzing autobiographical representations, celebrity statuses, public reception, and the publicity surrounding each of the representations.[3] Dyer writes, "Stars are, like characters in stories, representations of people. Thus they relate to ideas about what people are (or are supposed to be) like" (*Stars* 22). Recognizing that we can never know how much agency stars have in their image, I acknowledge that biographies or interviews are not necessarily "truths." However, the interviews, career moves (e.g., movie roles or music), public reception, and publicity that I examine all play a part in creating a star's image. I argue that the reception of mixed-race celebrities in popular culture reflects a national inclination to define blackness. While laws have historically defined who is black, social laws also attempted to regulate blackness, ensuring that blacks "kept their place." Similarly, in contemporary popular culture, advertisers and media attempt to define blackness. For mixed-race celebrities, this means blackness is deemed acceptable only when it upholds stereotypical white preconceptions and desires.

During and after slavery, many whites thought that mulattos were intellectually superior to "pure" blacks, a notion that confirmed white supremacy. At the same time, some whites believed mulattos were psychologically unstable, suggesting that even one drop of black blood could lead to mental and other deficiencies. Though mixed-race men were often labeled rapists and murderers, mixed-race women were seen as lascivious seductresses. Some of these same stereotypes reappeared in nineteenth and twentieth century American literature. Sterling Brown was the first to name the literary stereotype the "tragic mulatto." In "Negro Character as Seen by White Authors" he describes the archetype as "a victim of divided inheritance and therefore miserable" (162). The persistence of this stereotype has continued in contemporary popular culture, revealing America's obsession with race mixing and mixed-race bodies. Like census statisticians, America does not know what to do with "mulattos." Historically and today, mixed-race individuals are used to explore, praise, or condemn the "racial unknown."

# THE JOURNAL OF POPULAR CULTURE

Though multiracial identity has become a modish identity that white Americans seek, desire, and fetishize, Americans still fear and loathe blackness, marginalizing and criminalizing black bodies. The fascination with mixed-race bodies is metaphorically synonymous to racial slumming in the late 1920s. Kevin Mumford explains, "the influx of white mainstream urbanites . . . temporarily participated in the interzones [black/white sex districts], usually for pleasure, and then returned to their homes and lives apart from the black/white vice districts" (133). Similarly, whites' obsession with black/white mixed-race bodies permits "consumption" of a more palatable form of blackness while allowing whites to return "home" or stay distanced from the supposedly less "attractive" aspects of black identity.

Some mixed-race celebrities are read as black, even when they distance themselves from blackness. Conversely, mixed-race celebrities who claim a black heritage often get labeled as multiracial, not black. In short, the contradictory desires of the American public and media, manifested in a simultaneous disavowal and celebration of mixed race, show both our discomfort and fascination with mixed-race people and their bodies in particular. In the entertainment industry, a star's biracial identity may fade, be tucked away, or even disappear according to audience perceptions and star construction. On the other hand, a mixed-race identity never satisfies. Berry may self-identify as black, yet the media often holds onto her multiracial background. Diesel's desire not to talk about his racial background unsurprisingly fuels more interest. Carey proudly asserts a biracial identity while alternately encoding blackness and "otherness" in the media. Although Berry is distinct from the two other celebrities in her constant embracing of and identification with blackness, the reception of all these celebrities groups them together. The hype surrounding Berry, Diesel, and Carey shows the inconsistencies of America's racial desires over whether to control blackness on the one hand or encourage racial harmony on the other, or perhaps to abandon race altogether.

*Continues next page*

---

**THE RHETORICAL SITUATION**

**Audience**

Readers are most likely to be educators, scholars, and/or researchers interested in race, identity, and celebrity. As readers of *The Journal of Popular Culture*, they are already interested in the topics that title suggests—such as film, television, and other areas of pop culture.

**Rhetorical appeals**

One way the author establishes her **ethos** is by providing a careful cultural analysis of the anecdote from *The Chris Rock Show*.

Dagbovie-Mullins appeals to readers' **logos** by reviewing historical aspects of her topic and using the quotations and source summaries she chooses to logically build toward her conclusion.

**Reviewed by peers.**
*The Journal of
Popular Culture,*
where the article
was published, is
a scholarly, peer-
reviewed journal
based at Michigan
State University.

**Is thesis-driven.**
Dagbovie-Mullins
begins by stating
the central issue she
will address. Her
thesis (spread over
several sentences)
provides her main
argument and its
consequences.

**Identifies and
synthesizes
sources.** The
author goes beyond
summarizing,
paraphrasing,
and quoting from
sources; she
synthesizes them to
make a point. E.g.,
when discussing
Halle Berry's role in
*Monster's Ball,* she
pulls together several
sources to make her
point.

(Continued on p. 154.)

# THE JOURNAL OF POPULAR CULTURE

## Claiming Halle Berry: Biracial or Black?

When Halle Berry won the Oscar for Best Actress in 2002, she became more widely recognized as an accomplished black actress. Berry's acceptance speech confirms her racial allegiance: "The moment is so much bigger than me. . . . It's [the Oscar] for every nameless, faceless woman of color that now has a chance because this door tonight has been opened." Despite Berry's claim, competing discourses on her ethnicity consume popular cultural discussions of her. In a 1994 interview with Lisa Jones, Berry makes clear, "I never once announced that I am interracial. I was never the one to bring it up. . . . Yet reporters constantly ask what childhood was like to an interracial person" ("Blacker" 60). Berry consistently identifies as African American, evoking an identity grounded in a black politics. Jones asks Berry if mixed-race children should choose a race. Berry replies, "You've got to identify with one group or the other. It is a political choice" (60). Berry learned this, she claims, from her white mother who advised her to "accept being black, embrace it" (Kennedy 28). Berry's biracial background follows her in her movie roles and public persona, evidenced perhaps in the approval she seems to give to stereotypes of mulatta women. The media's investment in reading Halle Berry within a biracial narrative assures a biracial script both within the movies and in pseudo-liberal discussions of race. She is more easily accepted in a "role," both cinematic and stereotypic, that is familiar to Americans—that of the exotic mixed-race woman.[4]

Donald Bogle's discussion of Dorothy Dandridge is particularly helpful in thinking about Halle Berry. Bogle describes Dandridge as having "the rich golden skin tone that had always fascinated movie audiences, black and white." He continues, "she was a destructive personality, schizophrenic, maddening, euphoric, and self-destructive," all characteristics that define what the tragic mulatta has become: a beautiful, licentious, yet confused and unhappy woman (166). Dandridge's roles in films like *Carmen Jones* (1954), *Island in the Sun* (1957), and *Tamango* (1957)

# THE JOURNAL OF POPULAR CULTURE

perpetuated the tragic mulatto stereotype around which her career became centered. Bogle asserts that Dandridge "epitomized the confused, unsatisfied movie star dominated by the publicity and lifestyle that informed her screen image" (174–75). Similarly, *Ego Trip's Big Book of Racism!,* a biting collection of satiric essays and lists, places Berry as number five in its "Top Ten Tragic Mulattos." The media unnecessarily emphasize her biraciality in any description of her misfortunes, including an abusive father and ex-boyfriend, two divorces, and a suicide attempt. The authors of *Ego Trip's* cite Berry's "emotionally wrenching turn as her troubled role model, Dorothy Dandridge" as partial evidence of her "tragic mulatto" status (Jenkins 81).

In an interview with Entertainment Television, Warren Beatty says, "She's a beautiful woman and she's the essence of that biracial thing in America that is so beautiful" ("Halle Berry"). Beatty, who acted with Berry in *Bulworth* (1998), romanticizes mixed-race identity as an American ideal, reducing Berry to the essence of a biracial "thing," no longer an individual but a notion or concept. Praising Berry as a national ideal inadvertently summons the history of black/white mixing in America, namely the sexual abuse of black women by white men during slavery. However, Beatty's comment also suggests a desire to interpret Berry within a "melting pot" framework, one that depoliticizes identity. This rhetoric abounds in multiracial literary interpretations, such as in Maria P. P. Root's assertion that "the accomplishment of complex identities by racially mixed persons gives us the hope that if individuals have been able to resolve conflicting values, claim identities, synthesize multiple heritages, and retain respect for individual heritages . . . perhaps it is possible for us eventually to do this as a nation" (347). Multiracial activists see a mixed-race Berry in the same way they view Tiger Woods, as an indication of racial harmony or what David L. Andrews and C. L. Cole describe as "racially coded celebrations which deny social problems and promote the idea that America has achieved

*Continues next page*

THE RHETORICAL
SITUATION

**Modes & media**

**Mode = written** The author's scholarly article is text based (it appears in print and as a PDF online) and includes no images or graphics. Some journals encourage authors to use images and graphics; this is especially true for business and economics journals that publish articles that analyze relationships among factors, and as you might expect, art journals make heavy use of images of the art being discussed. (See "Charts/ infographics" on p. 117.)

*(Continued on p. 155.)*

**THE GENRE'S CONVENTIONS**

**Documents sources.** The author provides in-text citations when drawing on outside sources.

**Uses formal language.** The author's choice of terms such as *self-proclaimed* and *discourse* adds to the serious feel of the writing.

**Uses precise language.** For example, Dagbovie-Mullins specifies that *Monster's Ball* "recycles nineteenth-century" images, clarifying that she sees the film in a particular historical context.

**Style**

**Descriptive title.** The author uses the title to grab attention and present the gist of her argument.

**Strong author's voice.** Dagbovie-Mullins refers to many sources but her voice stays in control; her voice doesn't get lost in the midst of quotations.

*(Continued on p. 156.)*

# THE JOURNAL OF POPULAR CULTURE

its multicultural ideal" (70).[5] Reading Berry in a biracial framework falls in line with historical and cinematic representations of mixed-race women and allows a white patriarchal system to prevail under the guise of politically correct rhetoric. In other words, other people define Berry and place her in a category that best satisfies white perceptions of race and mixed race.

The titles of articles on Berry reveal a tendency to read her as a modern day tragic mulatto. "Halle Berry, Bruised and Beautiful, Is on a Mission," "The Beautiful and Damned," "Am I Going to Be Happy or Not?" and even an unauthorized biography entitled *Halle Berry: A Stormy Life* all highlight Berry's troubled personal life, recalling mixed race literary characters whose beauty was rivaled only by their ugly misfortunes (Kennedy; Hirschberg; Haynes; Sanello). Though the media extol Berry's beauty, their accolades always urge references to her tragic life. Films including *The Flintstones* (1994), *Introducing Dorothy Dandridge* (1999), *X-Men* (2000), *Die Another Day* (2002), and *Monster's Ball* (2002) also subtly accentuate Berry's image as tragic or exotic. In the miniseries *Queen* (1993), Berry plays Alex Haley's grandmother, daughter of a white master and a black slave. The producers stayed "true" to Queen's racial background by choosing Berry for the part and remained loyal to the "tragic mulatress text: Not only does *Queen* drag out mulatto clichés from every B movie and paperback, it luxuriates in them with eerie aplomb" (Jones, *Bulletproof* 50). Yet even Berry's decidedly "monoracial" characters, like the role of Nina (a pro-black "fly girl") in *Bulworth*, repeat a tragic motif. Patricia Williams writes that Berry's role "never rises above the most ancient of clichés" by bordering "black and white," "hope and despair, good and bad, sane and insane; the positive and negative divided by two, multiplied by sex" (11). In the sci-fi comic-book-turned-movie *X-Men*, Berry's character again occupies an "in-between" space. Lynne D. Johnson asserts that Berry's role as Storm in *X-Men* did not surprise, given her mixed racial background: "Though not a tragic mulatto in the classic sense of the myth, being mixed in both the racial and

# THE JOURNAL OF POPULAR CULTURE

THE RHETORICAL
SITUATION

genetic mutation sense of the word, Storm is representative of this idea." In 2004, Berry played another mutant woman, *Catwoman*, first made famous by biracial actress Eartha Kitt in a 1960s television show. Like Berry's other films, *Catwoman* capitalizes on Berry's reputation as exotic, liminal, and hypersexual.[6]

Berry's casting as Leticia Musgrove in *Monster's Ball* prompted diverse reviews from moviegoers and critics. The reaction from the black community was mixed, mostly due to Berry's casting as a stereotypical black woman in a film that "unfolds like something that was written by Simon Legree, the slave owner in *Uncle Tom's Cabin*. Just hours after they meet, the black woman lustfully seduces the startled white man" (Wickham 15A).[7] While many reviews mention the clichés in *Monster's Ball*, most fail to mention the stereotypical image of black women.[8] Actress Angela Bassett declined the role, she claims, because "I wasn't going to be a prostitute on film. . . . I couldn't do that because it's such a stereotype about black women and sexuality" (Samuels 54). Bassett does not mention the stereotypes of mixed-race women implicit in Berry's portrayal of Leticia, a woman who wants Hank to "heal" her through sex. Here the movie recycles nineteenth-century images of black and mixed-race women as oversexual.[9] More specifically, the movie encourages the myth of mixed-race women "as lewd and lascivious as the men are idle, sensual, and dishonest" (Mencke 102). Though the film does not specifically label Leticia mixed race, her characterization urges such readings. Symbolically, the movie recalls the history of miscegenation yet, more specifically, the movie reinforces general perceptions of Halle Berry as biracial. One reviewer sarcastically claims that the film suggests blacks and whites will get along only when "black women are already half white, already measure up to the white beauty standard," like Halle Berry ("Monster Balls"). Berry's role in *Monster's Ball* speaks to Berry's own tragic mulatto image, and her image never strays far from the "biracial" characters she plays.

**Medium = print and digital** This piece originally appeared in both the print and digital versions of *The Journal of Popular Culture*. Subscribers to the print journal automatically get online access to the digital version of the journal, enabling readers to choose which medium they'd prefer to read an article in (there are no content differences between the versions). Some journals have developed apps for iPads and other mobile devices that allow readers to access the online version of an article on the go.

*Continues next page*

THE GENRE'S
CONVENTIONS

**Authoritative and declarative tone.** The author states her case with confidence. She sometimes uses first person to present her ideas as a researcher and scholar.

**Use of detail.** The author follows her generalizations with specific examples to back up her claims. E.g., she states that "The titles of articles on Berry reveal a tendency to read her as a modern day tragic mulatto" and then provides evidence: "'Halle Berry, Bruised and Beautiful, Is on a Mission,' 'The Beautiful and Damned,' 'Am I Going to Be Happy or Not?' and even an unauthorized biography entitled *Halle Berry: A Stormy Life* all highlight Berry's troubled personal life, recalling mixed race literary characters whose beauty was rivaled only by their ugly misfortunes."

(Continued on p. 158.)

# THE JOURNAL OF POPULAR CULTURE

As so many viewers and audiences have lamented, Hollywood representations of blackness have been limited and narrow. Movies have historically slighted actors who are "too black" and, simultaneously, shunned those who are "not black enough." Like Dorothy Dandridge and Lena Horne, Berry has been hindered by her lighter complexion, and sometimes deprived of movie auditions and offers for "black" roles. Berry's manager, Vincent Cirrincione, claims that when Berry auditioned for *Strictly Business* (1991), they told her to "get a tan" (Kennedy 28). Conversely, Cirrincione says other executives have told him "milk is milk until you add a little Hershey. It doesn't matter if you add a little Hershey or a lot" (Kennedy 28). More often than not, Berry does not signify real "blackness." Philip Kerr remarks that in *Monster's Ball*:

> I didn't see a black woman who looked, well, black. Am I the only one to have noticed? Halle Berry—who let's face it, is half-white—made a lachrymose, Oscar-winning thing about being a woman of colour, and yet the reality is that she looks no more like a person of colour than I do. Is it just me, or do most of the black women cast in Hollywood films, with their straight hair, thin lips and cappuccino-coloured skins, look just a little bit white? (44)

Kerr's offensive statement uses biology to classify Berry, relying on crude physical descriptions like "straight hair" and "thin lips" to declare Berry "not black." Though Kerr's criticism rightly addresses the prejudice against darker actresses, his critique also suggests a restrictive and monolithic view of blackness. Such physical stereotypes of African Americans neglect the wide array of physical characteristics and skin color within black communities. Berry cannot pass and does not "look" white as Kerr suggests; her physical markings represent those commonly associated with a person of color. That Berry self-identifies as black makes Kerr's statement particularly insulting in terms of his desire to read her as "half-white." The media criminalizes dark skin, associating darkness with poverty, ignorance, and physical ugliness. Cannot Leticia be poor, desperate, downtrodden, and still light skinned? Aside

# THE JOURNAL OF POPULAR CULTURE

from presenting narrow-minded views on race, Kerr's description shows that the public and critics invest in Berry's "whiteness."

Public discourses about Berry belabor her looks when referring to her celebrity allure. Charlie Kanganis, who directed Berry in *Race the Sun* (1996), compares Berry with "a double espresso machiatto, a dollop of shapely foam, a shower of cinnamon and cocoa." No other actress in "Cinema and the Female Star," a collection of reflections and tributes to actresses, is so objectified. Warren Beatty claims that people laugh when they first see Berry because "they don't know how else to react. They're not used to someone that beautiful" ("Halle Berry"). Literary descriptions of mixed-race women in early American fiction suggest a similar exceptional, almost unreal beauty. In Charles Chesnutt's novel, *The House Behind the Cedars* (1900), John, not yet recognizing Rena as his sister, describes her as "strikingly handsome, with a stately beauty seldom encountered" (7). These characterizations imply a uniqueness associated with mixed race that persists in popular culture. Lynn Hirschberg claims that Berry's beauty is "actually distracting; the perfection of her face would not seem to allow anything less than a perfect life" (26). Would people review Berry's beauty in the same way if she were "just black" (and not "biracial")? She represents the supposed mystique of mixed-race people, alluring because they symbolize a social taboo. Her image represents "black" and "not black," which unsettles and entices. A *Time* article begins, "Is it a curse to be beautiful?" continuing a familiar rhetoric about Berry's looks, one that intensified after *Monster's Ball* (Corliss 124-25). Descriptions of Berry's beauty intimate what has become a common boasting on numerous multiracial Web sites—that mixed-race people are "prettier." This notion gets directly and indirectly repeated in advertisements and magazines that use models who physically represent racial mixture. The point here is not to judge or critique Berry's beauty, but rather to examine why it attracts so much attention. Berry cannot be taken out of a historical context of mixed-race beauty images. Her image reflects back the fantasy that makes Americans both anxious and envious.

*Continues next page*

# THE JOURNAL OF POPULAR CULTURE

## Multiracial to the Rescue: Vin Diesel

When Tiger Woods gained notoriety, he was proclaimed the new multiracial face of America. Andrews and Cole maintain that Woods represents the "latest in America's imagined realization of its ideals (agency, equality, responsibility, and freedom) and its imagined transformed sense of national self (America has become the world that came to it)" (73). Yet Vin Diesel's recent explosion in Hollywood has introduced an even "better" Tiger Woods, because unlike Woods, Diesel refuses to name himself racially. Diesel, a self-described "mystery man," represents an amalgamation of all races, literally in his racial ambiguity and symbolically in his equally racially vague movie roles. In short, he is "everyman." His image enacts America's desired "other": multiracial, de-politicized, and lacking any serious racial allegiance.

When asked about his background, Diesel firmly describes himself as "multicultural." Diesel's name change from Mark Vincent to Vin Diesel seems to corroborate his racial ambiguity or at least encourage a multiracial reading of this ethnicity as "Vin" is a stereotypical Italian American name. ("Diesel" refers to the slang term, "cock diesel," describing a man's muscular physique.) Diesel explains that this nickname emerged when he worked as a bouncer: "We all had nicknames. It was wonderful to detach a little bit" (Tesoriero 61). As an actor, Diesel appears to detach from any racial group. Rumors abound about his Italian mother and African American father, but he maintains, "I want to keep my mystery" (Kirkland). Diesel denies "hiding anything": "It's not that I don't want people to know anything. It's just that I would rather spend more time talking about more productive things that relate to the film [XXX]" (Kirkland). Diesel's silence seems a strategic response not just to advertisers but also to the broader cultural pattern that advertisers respond to, namely multiculturalism. One advertising executive asserts, "Both in the mainstream and at the high end of the marketplace, what is perceived as good, desirable, successful is often a face whose heritage is hard to pin

# THE JOURNAL OF POPULAR CULTURE

down" (La Ferla). Diesel confirms what Danzy Senna jokingly calls "mulatto fever," telling one reporter that his "ambiguous, chameleon-like ethnicity" is "cool" (Thrupkaew). His production company, One Race, enforces his raceless image, reminiscent of Jean Toomer's early twentieth century proclamation, "I am at once no one of the races, and I am all of them." Diesel's explanation of his racial background captures how his image reflects America's desire for ethnic homogeneity. He presents no controversy and gives no reminders of black/white miscegenation.

Diesel's relationship with the black community seems dubious considering his reticence to claim any identity. Samuel Jackson, who stars with Diesel in *XXX*, tells *People Weekly*, "There's an air of mystery and danger about Vin, but he also has a little bit of the just-like-us quality" (Miller 87). Perhaps "just-like-us" speaks to the African American colloquial belief, "we know our own." Jackson's comments imply Diesel's blackness ("just-like-us") but also suggest his multiracial background ("air of mystery"). Despite claiming a nebulous "multicultural" description, Diesel has been somewhat accepted by the black community, at least superficially in terms of his appearances as a presenter at the 2002 NAACP Image Awards and his inclusion in *Ebony*'s 2003 top Black moneymakers list. This acceptance is, however, limited. A forum on bet.com (Black Entertainment Television) which posed the following question, "If Vin Diesel has any Black heritage, should he claim it publicly?" and articles such as "Outing Diesel" repeat a familiar resentment with celebrities who do not outwardly claim the black community (Hill). Still, that Diesel's refusal to acknowledge (or disclaim) blackness (or any race) has incited less anger and uproar than Tiger Woods's self-termed "Cablinasian" perhaps speaks to America's desire to forget about racial divisions. Similarly, publicity surrounding Vin Diesel exposes America's desires to be like Diesel, "of no particular place, and at the same time, able to be anywhere and be anything" (Iverem).

*Continues next page*

Sika Dagbovie-Mullins, *Mixed-Race Superstars*     159

# THE JOURNAL OF POPULAR CULTURE

Diesel's recent movies, with their over-the-top action and "heroes" of superhuman strength, seem geared toward teenagers. Diesel says he claims a "multicultural" identity because of his young audience: "I support the idea of being multicultural primarily for all the invisible kids, the ones who don't fit into one ethnic category and then find themselves lost in some limbo" (Iverem). Homi Bhabha contends that "the multicultural has itself become a 'floating signi-fier' whose enigma lies less in itself than in the discursive uses of it to mark social processes where differentiation and condensa-tion seem to happen almost synchronically" (31). Diesel repre-sents Bhabha's explication of the multicultural. The celebration over his fame both depends upon his difference as "Hollywood's new superhero: a self-made man unconfined by racial categories" (Thrupkaew) and his ability to relate to Americans as "multiethnic Everyman, a movie star virtually every demographic can claim as its own" (Svetkey 5). Diesel is a floating signifier, and, as *Boiler Room* director Ben Younger claims, "People seem to make him into whatever they want him to be" (Svetkey 5). Unlike Berry who cannot "pass," Diesel's racially uncertain physical characteristics allow him to pass as various ethnicities in his movies. For example, he plays an Italian in *Saving Private Ryan* (1998) and in *The Fast and the Furious* (2001), and a racially ambiguous person in *Boiler Room* (2000), *Pitch Black* (2000), and *The Chronicles of Riddick* (2004). While critics have charged Diesel with passing, others applaud his savvy marketing skills. Diesel admits, "Being multicul-tural has gone from the Achilles' heel of my career to my strength." He describes the world as a "big melting pot," deducing that "peo-ple are ready for a hero who is more ambiguous" (Thrupkaew).

*XXX*'s advertising refers to its main character, Xander Cage, as "a new breed of secret agent," a seemingly intentional though oblique reference to Diesel's mixed-race background and his emergence in a genre once dominated by now outdated white action stars like Arnold Schwarzenegger, Sylvester Stallone, and Bruce Willis (A. White). Similar descriptions follow Diesel, naming him a new

# THE JOURNAL OF POPULAR CULTURE

"multicultural hero" (Mora) and the "first truly All-American action hero" (A. White). Director Rob Cohen (*XXX* and *The Fast and the Furious*) maintains, "It has taken America a long time to acknowledge the new face of America . . . and to some degree, Vinny is that new face" (Kirkland). Such descriptions recall *Time*'s 1993 special issue cover, "The New Face of America," featuring a future mixed race, computer-made American woman. Suzanne Bost argues that *Time*'s female creation "charms . . . and yet she is taboo, bloodless, impure" (1). Lauren Berlant suggests that "new faces" like the *Time* cover respond to "problems of immigration, multiculturalism, sexuality, gender, and trans(national) identity that haunt the U.S." (398). What does it mean that this new representative (noncomputerized) face is a man, a "He-man" no less? Diesel's image, in part created through his movie roles, represents America's assimilation and capitalist impulses. In other words, his image encourages the idea that race is a commodity that people can trade, buy, or sell, virtually "e-racing" national histories of racialization. Henry Giroux writes, "National identity in the service of a common culture recognizes cultural differences only to flatten them out in the conservative discourse of assimilation and the liberal appeal to tolerance" (182). The suggestion that Diesel stands for "everyman" attempts to create a national identity that eliminates difference. Santiago Pozo, CEO of Arenas Entertainment, tells *Time*, "In the past, John Wayne and Jimmy Stewart were the face of America. . . . Today it's The Rock or Vin Diesel" (Tesoriero 61). Such a comparison suggests that biracial celebrities like The Rock or Diesel evoke a "multiracial sameness," a sugar pill oxymoron that ends up surreptitiously recentering white normative American identity.

## Mariah Carey as Biracial Fantasy

If Halle Berry is America's prized mulatta, then Mariah Carey is her lascivious tragic sister. Carey's image depends on her exploitation of the mulatta stereotype.[10] On the one hand, she represents

*Continues next page*

# THE JOURNAL OF POPULAR CULTURE

the alienated racial outsider in songs such as "Outside" (from the *Butterfly* album) where she bemoans the difficulties of not belonging. On the other hand, she exploits the notion of the racially ambiguous seductress, wearing next to nothing in music videos and publicity photos. Since Carey's self-titled debut album in 1990, she has publicly performed various "roles" including white ingenue, biracial outsider, black hiphopper, and erotic/exotic "other." Kate Lanier, a script-writer for Carey's film, *Glitter* (2002), asserts that "a lot of mixed-race girls and young women . . . hold Mariah up as a hero." Lanier claims this makes Carey "proud" because "for a long time she was encouraged to play up her white side. Since she has been allowed creative freedom, she has related more to black culture" (Beller 13). Carey's image both deflects and confirms blackness, creating an "in-between" status she teases in terms of her racialized sexuality. She wears biracial stereotypes like a black-face "costume," allowing audiences to explore racial and sexual fantasies while maintaining racial stereotypes.

Music reviews and articles have paid close attention to Carey's overt sexuality and racial shifts in a popular culture context. Vincent Stephens observes: "Along with genre changes, Carey has taken on a more sexualized visual persona and has become more outspoken about her multiracial heritage and struggles for artistic freedom" (234). Caroline Streeter sees Carey "transform[ing] from white to black before our very eyes" (311). Indeed, Carey's album covers trace her shifting racial movements from what Lisa Jones calls "a rainbow body of African descent, skin toasted almond and hair light brown" to her current whitewashed blond pin-up look (*Bulletproof* 200). While other ethnic stars such as Jennifer Lopez or Beyoncé sport blond hair, Carey's hair transformation seems particularly racially motivated considering the initial marketing of Carey that concealed her blackness. In 1990, music critics labeled Carey a "white Whitney Houston" until outside pressures prompted her record company to make a statement. Carey cleared up misconceptions at a press confer-

# THE JOURNAL OF POPULAR CULTURE

ence where she declared, "My father is black and Venezuelan. My mother is Irish and an opera singer. I am me" (Jones *Bulletproof* 197). Following Carey's public disclosure, black publications ran articles such as "Mariah Carey Tells Why She Looks White but Sings Black" in *Jet*, and "Mariah Carey: Not Another White Girl Trying to Sing Black" in *Ebony* (Norment), seemingly attempting to assure black audiences that Carey was not trying to pass or disregard her black ancestry. However, Carey's later physical transformation suggests an effort to depart visually from "black" and to reflect white standards of beauty.

Despite publicly claiming a multiracial heritage, Carey admits that her physical hints of blackness made her self-conscious. Recalling her *Butterfly* (1997) album cover, Carey shares that she felt pressured to cover up her face "because I had been told I looked horrible and too ethnic with my face showing" (Grigoriadis 194). As Carey's hair turns straighter and blonder, she increasingly signifies "whiteness" while contradictorily maintaining a position as ethnic "other" vis-a-vis her public assertions of biracialism. Richard Dyer suggests that "blondeness is racially unambiguous" and "the ultimate sign of whiteness" (*Heavenly* 44, 43). Carey represents a racial anomaly because her image simultaneously projects different racial tropes. These competing discourses establish Carey in a biracial narrative that depends upon her liminality.

Musically, Carey has moved from pop to hip-hop, in some ways a symbolic shift from white to black. After Carey divorced then Sony Music president Tommy Mottola, her music and image changed drastically. Carey claims that her *Butterfly* album symbolizes her feelings of personal and professional freedom impelled by her divorce. As she explained it in 1997, "I feel more free to put more of myself into my music" (Thigpen 113). With *Butterfly*, Carey has worked with more hip-hop artists and producers to tap into her "broad demographic." As she observes, "I have an audience that's urban and one that's Middle America." She continues, "So I have to really be a little bit conscious of the fact that

*Continues next page*

# THE JOURNAL OF POPULAR CULTURE

it's broad, and also it's diverse in terms of the racial thing. I am anyway, being a mixed person racially" (Carey, Interview by Ehrlich 338). On *Rainbow* (1999), Carey collaborated with hip-hop artists and rappers including Jay-Z, Usher, Da Brat, Missy Elliott, and Snoop Dogg. Carey's earlier albums *Mariah Carey* (1990), *Emotions* (1991), and *Daydream* (1995) demonstrated her penchant for love ballads and cross-over pop songs, save for Carey's "Dreamlover" remix with Ol' Dirty Bastard on *Daydream*. Earlier albums also feature Carey in her pre-blonde days, suggesting that Carey's physical transformation heightened after she professionally embraced black culture. In a 2002 MTV interview Carey revealed, "Most of my friends and most of the music I listen to and most of my influences are R&B and hip-hop" ("Mariah Carey: Shining"). Still, Carey's most hip-hop albums visually emphasize her whiteness, such as *Charmbracelet* which shows her with platinum streaks.

Carey constructs a stereotypical mulatta trope in public discussions of her biraciality. Inside the *Rainbow* CD liner Carey's message to fans expresses her desire for people of all races and hues to live with one another happily and without conflict. Her words both reveal her vision of racial unity and explain why multiracial organizations herald her as an ideal biracial "spokesperson," In "My Saving Grace," on *Charmbracelet*, Carey positions herself as tragic, discussing how during her childhood she felt confused and suffered from low self esteem due to her mixedness. In general, she laments over the media's and public's obsession with her racial identity yet openly discusses her feelings of racial alienation and isolation. She shares always feeling "so separate from everybody, even if I never talked about it" (Udovitch 34). She attributes this alienation to various reasons: "Because my father's black and my mother's white. Because I'm very ambiguous-looking." Carey has claimed multiple descriptors including "person of color" and the glib, "I view myself as a human being" (Farley 75). Yet despite Carey's supposed desires to put the issue of her racial

# THE JOURNAL OF POPULAR CULTURE

background to rest, she often brings it up in interviews and has appeared on national shows like *Oprah* to discuss such issues. In an *Oprah* show entitled "Mariah Carey Talks to Biracial Teens," Carey announces herself as somewhat of a multiracial nationalist, claiming, "I bond with mixed people" (7). Yet, Carey frequently exploits biracial stereotypes, betraying her role model status.

Carey's hypersexuality intensifies as she encodes "whiteness" via her album covers and "blackness" via her music, symbolically evoking the "warring" racial divisions and libidinous nature of the mulatta stereotype. Magazine photos play up her sexuality so that her overall image combines multiple representations: mulatta sex kitten, black performer, and white pin-up. However, Carey and her music are not considered "black" in the same way, for example, that Mary J. Blige represents "blackness." And physically, Carey is too ethnic to be a white sex symbol. The result places Carey in an in-between, mixed-race seductress narrative. For example, the *Rainbow* CD liner opens up to reveal a photo which exploits Carey as a heterosexual male fantasy: she suggestively lies on a bed in white cotton underclothes, wearing stiletto heels and licking a heart-shaped lollipop. A nearby phone lying off the hook may suggest Carey's possible roles as phone sex operator or prostitute. Magazine photos of Carey (as in *Vibe* March 2003) (Ogunnaike) are not just revealing, but border on soft porn. In one photo she wears a trench coat, partly opened to reveal her naked body. Another frames Carey lying on a couch, one hand on her breast, the other suggestively positioned below her stomach. Still another shows Carey in an unzipped miniskirt and unzipped midriff top, suggestively looking downwards at her skirt. While many pop stars like Christina Aguilera and Britney Spears also wear skimpy and sexy clothing, Carey's provocative style of dress is coupled with a publicized troubled multiracial identity, making her sexuality fetishized and tragic. Tellingly, Carey cites Marilyn Monroe, a star whose name virtually equaled sex in the 1950s and who began her career as a pin-up, as the

Continues next page

# THE JOURNAL OF POPULAR CULTURE

person she most admires.[11] Not surprisingly, Barbara Walters symbolically likens the two, calling Carey "a soldier's pin-up girl come to life" while describing her Kosovo trip to visit U.S. troops (Carey, "Surviving").

Carey's semi-autobiographical box office failure, *Glitter*, confirms her racialized sexuality despite its attempts to critique biracial clichés. In one scene the music video director explains his idea for the main character's video: "She is not black, she is not white, she is exotic, OK?" This same theme follows representations of Carey's public and private life. In July 2001, Carey appeared on MTV's *Total Request Live* (*TRL*) pushing an ice-cream cart in a "Loverboy" (the name of *Glitter*'s first single) T-shirt and heels. She proceeded to perform a pseudo striptease, taking off her T-shirt to reveal a hidden skimpy outfit. Entertainment reporters and tabloids ridiculed Carey for her bizarre behavior and incoherent ramblings to *TRL* host, Carson Daly. Accordingly, *Ego Trip's Big Book of Racism!* comically named Carey their number one "Tragic Mulatto" for, among other things, "a propensity for 'whorelike attire,' a nervous breakdown, a mocked and derided cinematic debut, and a failed soundtrack" (Jenkins et al. 81). Such descriptions urge the question, what role does Carey have in sexualizing her image? Carey reports feeling "constantly amazed" regarding her portrayal as "very loose morally and sexually," an ironic statement considering that Carey invites such readings in nearly all recent publicity photos and public outings ("Mariah Carey Discusses" 58). Though we can never know how much agency stars exert over their image, Carey seems to perpetuate wittingly an oversexual public persona. She represents a historically comfortable vision of mixed race women. Carey poses little threat to racial hierarchy because she fits a mold that showcases just enough "blackness" to intrigue but not enough to appear definitive or political.

# THE JOURNAL OF POPULAR CULTURE

## New Faces, Old Masks

The media commodifies biracialism by using "new" celebrity faces: Diesel's movie posters that target a younger, more multicultural and multiracial generation and Carey's seemingly produced and packaged embodiment of the mulatta seductress in videos, albums, and magazines. Despite Berry publicly announcing a black identity, her image still "sells" biracialism through media representations of her life and less obviously via her stereotyped movie roles. In this sense, all three stars symbolically represent the "multiracial neutral" in that their images "sell" the idea of racial pluralism and freedom, and yet their images remain "Other," available for audiences and consumers of all racial backgrounds to "claim" or "own." The popularity of these stars does not reflect a more racially tolerant or progressive America. Like the cliché "some of my best friends are black," which attempts to prove a supposed lack of racism, the multiracial craze only superficially embraces the dark "Other." Liberals and conservatives alike have repeatedly placed idealistic expectations on mixed-race individuals in discussions of racism and multiculturalism. Though expectations differ, this pattern gets repeated in a popular culture context with mixed-race stars. Thus, Tiger Woods is not just a superb athlete of color, but an emblem of racial harmony, the Great Multiracial Hope. When stars' images do not fit our vision, we force them into familiar stereotypes that satisfy other expectations. Halle Berry's image may not represent racial unity, but at least it does not depart from what we have learned to expect from mixed-race women. In a popular culture context, biraciality "works" for people who do not really want to confront racial issues when it exploits difference under the guise of celebrating diversity. The "new" faces of America have no racial responsibilities, loyalties, or obligations. People admire them for their beauty, celebrate them as America's future, and envy their "cool" multiracial status. However, old masks lurk alongside interpretations of what new faces represent, namely racial stereotypes. Until power relations equalize, any celebration of mixed race needs to recognize those who are not celebrating or benefiting from

*Continues next page*

# THE JOURNAL OF POPULAR CULTURE

America's longtime fascination. Questioning what it means to be black or part-black allows one to be critical of traditional assumptions about racial identification and realize the urgency of racial responsibility in a society built upon racial inequality.

## NOTES

1. See *Best of the Chris Rock Show*.

2. In 1997, golfer Fuzzy Zoeller made a racist joke during the 62nd Masters golf tournament in Augusta, Georgia. He reportedly joked that he hoped fried chicken and collard greens would not be served at the next year's tournament should Tiger win and choose the menu.

3. My essay focused on these particular celebrities because they have represented multiple racial tropes in popular culture and in their work. Their immense popularity, I argue, is also connected to their "otherness." These stars differ from other biracial stars, such as Alicia Keys, whose blackness often foregrounds their public image. This essay was written after Mariah Carey's 2002 album and after Vin Diesel's and Halle Berry's 2004 films.

4. In his classic book, *Toms, Coons, Mulattoes, Mammies, and Bucks*, Donald Bogle examines the persistence of these five common stereotypes of African Americans on film. Bogle cites *The Debt* (1912) as one of the earliest film representations of the tragic mulatto. Like the literary stereotype, the mulatta on film was often near white, exceedingly beautiful, exotic, and doomed as a result of her mixed race.

5. Such perceptions abound in Web sites and often show up in online discussions, particularly following Berry's Oscar speech, which angered many people who self identify as multiracial. For example, responding to a post in a "Moms of Biracial Children" forum on Commitment.com, one woman writes, "I didn't watch the awards but it's pretty sad that she had to put a label on the [Black] community she was thanking. . . . It's comments like that continues the separatism of races." Another respondent writes, "My daughter a beautiful little girl loves Halle Berry and couldn't understand why she only said she was black. I think it was a very confusing statement." See "Did Halle Berry Forget Her Mom Is White?" for other postings.

6. Continuing her portrayal of "liminal" characters, Berry says she is preparing for a movie entitled *The Guide*, playing "a spiritual woman—half Native American, half African-American—who guides people through times of crisis" (Ritz 128). Most recently, she portrayed Zora Neale Hurston's mixed-race character, Janie, in Oprah Winfrey's television rendition of *Their Eyes Were Watching God*.

7. See, for example, the online discussion, "Bassett: 'Monster' Role Was Demeaning."

8. For a sample of reviews on *Monster's Ball*, see Roger Ebert, Leslie Felperin, Lisa Schwarzbaum, and Stephanie Zacharek.

# THE JOURNAL OF POPULAR CULTURE

9. In *Ar'n't I a Woman?: Female Slaves in the Plantation South*, Deborah Gray White argues that the jezebel stereotype that emerged during slavery was used to justify the sexual exploitation of black women. The stereotype suggested that black women were promiscuous and invited rape and sexual abuse.

10. Ironically, an April 2005 *Essence* article on Mariah Carey begins, "This 'mulatto' is hardly tragic" (121). See Joan Morgan.

11. See "All Mariah" on Carey's homepage (www.mariahcarey.com).

## Works Cited

"All Mariah." *Mariah Carey*, www.mariahcarey.com. Accessed 19 Mar. 2004.

Andrews, David L., and C. L. Cole. "America's New Son: Tiger Woods and America's Multiculturalism." *Sport Stars: The Cultural Politics of Sporting Celebrity*, edited by David L. Andrews and Steven J. Jackson, Routledge, 2001, pp. 70-86.

"Bassett: 'Monster' Role Was Demeaning." *The Black Web Portal*, www.blackwebportal.com/forums/. Accessed 28 Mar. 2004.

Beller, Thomas. "The New M.C." *Elle*, July 2001, p. 13.

Berlant, Lauren. "The Face of America and the State of Emergency." *Disciplinarity and Dissent in Cultural Studies*, edited by Carey Nelson and Dilip Parameshwar Gaonkar, Routledge, 1996, pp. 397-439.

Berry, Halle. "Halle Berry Dishes the Dirt." Interview by David A. Keeps, *Marie Claire*, Feb. 2002, pp. 52-59.

*Best of the Chris Rock Show*. HBO, 1999. DVD.

Bhabha, Homi K. "Culture's in Between." *Multicultural States: Rethinking Difference and Identity*, edited by David Bennett, Routledge, 1998, pp. 29-36.

Bogle, Donald. *Toms, Coons, Mulattoes, Mammies, and Bucks*. Continuum, 2003, pp. 166, 174-75.

Bost, Suzanne. *Mulattas and Mestizas: Representing Mixed Identities in the Americas, 1850-2000*. U of Georgia P, 2005, p. 1.

Brown, Sterling B. "Negro Character as Seen by White Authors." *Journal of Negro Education*, 2 Apr. 1933, p. 162.

*Continues next page*

# THE JOURNAL OF POPULAR CULTURE

Carey, Mariah. "Outside." *Butterfly*, Columbia, 1997.

---. *Rainbow*. Columbia, 1999. CD.

---. Interview by Dimitri Ehrlich, *Interview*, Oct. 1999, pp. 338-39.

---. "My Saving Grace." *Charmbracelet*, Island Def Jam,
2002. CD.

---. "Surviving the Glare: Celebrities Who Prevailed After Scandal."
Interview with Barbara Walters, *20/20*, ABC, 9 May 2002.

Chambers, Veronica. "Mariah on Fire." *Newsweek*, 15 Nov.
1999, pp. 80-81.

Chesnutt, Charles W. *The House Behind the Cedars*. 1900.
Modern Library, 2003, p. 7.

Corliss, Richard. "Halle Berry: Monster's Ball." *Time*, 21 Jan.
2002, pp. 124-25.

"Did Halle Berry Forget Her Mom Is White?" *Moms of Biracial
Children*, 11 Sept. 2000, www.commitment.com/boards/
boardMB/MBbrmsgs/142.html. Discussion list post.

Dyer, Richard. *Stars*. British Film Institute, 1979, p. 22.

---. *Heavenly Bodies: Film Stars and Society*. St. Martin's Press,
1986, pp. 43-44.

Ebert, Roger. "*Monster's Ball* Review." Review of *Monster's Ball*,
directed by Marc Forster, *Chicago Sun-Times*, 1 Feb. 2002,
www.suntimes.com/ebert/ebert_reviews/2002/02/020101/html.

Farley, Christopher John. "Pop's Princess Grows Up." *Time*, 25
Sept. 1995, p. 75.

Felperin, Leslie. "*Monster's Ball* Review." Review of *Monster's
Ball*, directed by Marc Forster, *Sight and Sound*, June 2002,
sec. 12, p. 46.

Giroux, Henry A. "The Politics of National Identity and the
Pedagogy of Multiculturalism in the USA." *Multicultural
States: Rethinking Difference and Identity*, edited by David
Bennett, Routledge, 1998, p. 182.

*Glitter*. Directed by Vondie Curtis-Hall, Twentieth Century Fox,
2001.

Grigoriadis, Veronica. "The Money Honey." *Allure*, Sept. 2001,
p. 194.

# THE JOURNAL OF POPULAR CULTURE

"Halle Berry." *Road to the Red Carpet*. Entertainment Television, 3 May 2003.

Haynes, Esther. "Am I Going to Be Happy or Not?" *Jane*, Dec. 2003, pp. 126-28.

Hill, James. "'Outing' Diesel." *Black Entertainment Television*, 2 Aug. 2002, www.bet.com.articles/o,,c3gb3453-4121,00.html.

Hirschberg, Lynn. "The Beautiful and Damned." *The New York Times Magazine*, 23 Dec. 2001, p. 26.

Iverem, Esther. "A Monster Love." Review of *Monster's Ball*, directed by Marc Forster, 21 Feb. 2002, *Seeing Black*, www.seeingblack.com/x022102/monstersball.shtml.

Jenkins, Sacha, et al. *Ego Trip's Big Book of Racism!* Regan Books, 2002, p. 81.

Johnson, Lynne D. "Bearing the Black Female Body as Witness in Sci-Fi." *Pop Matters*, 1 Dec. 2003, www.popmatters.com/columnsjohnson/031218.shtml.

Jones, Lisa. "The Blacker the Berry." *Essence*, June 1994, p. 60.

---. *Bulletproof Diva: Tales of Race, Sex, and Hair*. Doubleday, 1994, pp. 50, 197, 200.

Kanganis, Charlie. "Halle Berry." Cinema and the Female Star: A Symposium, Part 1, *Senses of Cinema*, 23 Dec. 2002, www.sensesofcinema.com/contents/02/23/symposium1.html#berry.

Kennedy, Dana. "Halle Berry, Bruised and Beautiful, Is on a Mission." *The New York Times*, 10 Mar. 2002, pp. 2A+.

Kerr, Philip. "A Shocking Cheek." *New Statesman*, 17 June 2002, p. 44.

Kirkland, Bruce. "Word's Out: Vin's In." *Toronto Sun*, 4 Aug. 2004, www.canoe.ca/JamMoviesArtistsD/diesel_vin.html.

La Ferla, Ruth. "Generation E.A.: Ethnically Ambiguous." *The New York Times*, 28 Dec. 2003, sec. 9, pp. 1+.

"Mariah Carey Discusses Her Sex Life, Race, Career." *Jet*, 31 May 2000, pp. 56-60.

"Mariah Carey: Shining Through the Rain." Interview by John Norris, MTV, 3 Dec. 2002.

*Continues next page*

## THE JOURNAL OF POPULAR CULTURE

"Mariah Carey Talks to Biracial Teens." *Oprah*, ABC, 27 Dec. 1999. Transcript.

"Mariah Carey Tells Why She Looks White but Sings Black." *Jet*, 4 Mar. 1991, pp. 56-57.

Mencke, John G. *Mulattoes and Race Mixture: American Attitudes and Images, 1865-1918*. Umi Research Press, 1979, p. 102.

Miller, Samantha. "XXX Appeal." *People*, 19 Aug. 2002, vol. 58, no. 9, pp. 87-88.

"Monster Balls." Review of *Monster's Ball*, directed by Marc Forster, *Metaphilm*, 29 Feb. 2004, www.metaphilm.com/index.php/detail/monsters_ball/.

Mora, Renee Scolaro. Review of *XXX*, directed by Rob Cohen, *Pop Matters*, 9 Aug. 2002, www.popmatters.com/film/reviews/x/xxx.shtml.

Morgan, Joan. "Free at Last." *Essence*, Apr. 2005, p. 121.

Mumford, Kevin J. *Interzones: Black/White Sex Districts in Chicago and New York in the Early Twentieth Century*. Columbia UP, 1997, p. 133.

Norment, Lynn. "Mariah Carey: Not Another White Girl Trying to Sing Black." *Ebony*, Mar. 1991, pp. 54-58.

Ogunnaike, Lola. "Through the Fire." *Vibe*, Mar. 2003, pp. 113-20.

Pappademas, Alex. "Over the 'Rainbow': A Tale of Two Mariahs." *Boston Phoenix*, 22 Nov. 1999, weeklywire.com/ww/11-22-99/boston_music_2.html.

Prince. "Controversy." *Controversy*, Warner Bros., 1981. CD.

Ritz, David. "Heart to Heart." *Essence*, Dec. 2002, pp. 128+.

Root, Maria P. P. "From Shortcuts to Solutions." *Racially Mixed People in America*, edited by Maria P. P. Root, Sage, 1992, pp. 342-47.

Samuels, Allison. "Angela's Fire." *Newsweek*, 1 July 2002, p. 54.

Sanello, Frank. *Halle Berry: A Stormy Life*. Virgin Books, 2003.

Schwarzbaum, Lisa. Review of *Monster's Ball*, directed by Marc Foster, *Entertainment Weekly*, Issue 639, Feb. 2002, p. 47, *EBSCOhost*, doi: 6056917.

# THE JOURNAL OF POPULAR CULTURE

Stephens, Vincent. Review of *Rainbow*, by Mariah Carey, *Popular Music & Society*, Summer 2003, sec. 26, pp. 234-35.

Streeter, Caroline A. "The Hazards of Visibility: 'Biracial Women,' Media Images, and Narratives of Identity." *New Faces in a Changing America: Multiracial Identity in the 21st Century*, edited by Loretta I. Winters and Herman L. DeBose, Thousand Sage, 2003, pp. 301-22.

Svetkey, Benjamin. "Vin at All Costs." *Entertainment Weekly*, 2 Aug. 2002, p. 5.

Tesoriero, Heather Won. "The Next Action Hero." *Time*, 5 Aug. 2002, pp. 61-62.

Thigpen, David E. Review of *Butterfly*, by Mariah Carey, *Time*, 15 Sept. 1997, p. 113.

Thrupkaew, Noy. "The Multicultural Mysteries of Vin Diesel." *Alternet*, 16 Aug. 2002, www.alternet.org/story.html?StoryID=13863.

Udovitch, Mim. "An Unmarried Woman." *Rolling Stone*, 5 Feb. 1998, pp. 30-32.

"Wang and Woods." *Asian American E-Zine*, Stony Brook University, 11 Dec. 2002, www.aa2sbu.org/aaezine/articles/sports/12-WangAndWoods.shtml.

White, Armond. Review of *XXX*, directed by Rob Cohen, *New York Press*, www.nypress.com/15/33/film/film2.cfm. Accessed 4 Mar. 2004.

White, Deborah Gray. *Ar'n't I a Woman?: Female Slaves in the Plantation South*. Norton, 1984.

Wickham, DeWayne. "Bassett Criticism Has Its Merit." *USA Today*, p. 15A.

Williams, Patricia. "Bulworth Agonistes." *The Nation*, 7 June 1998, p. 11.

Zacharek, Stephanie. Review of *Monster's Ball*, directed by Marc Forster, *Salon*, 4 Jan. 2002, archive.salon.com/ent/movies/review/2002/01/04/monsters_ball/.

# Questions: Analyzing Dagbovie-Mullins's peer-reviewed journal article

**1. Purpose.** Dagbovie-Mullins discusses Halle Berry, Vin Diesel, and Mariah Carey, but how does she make it clear from the beginning that she's not writing about these actors as entertainers? What seems to be her main purpose? Does she seem to have secondary purposes?

**2. Audience.** What are some features of this paper that make it clear that she's writing for other scholars, rather than, say, general readers of *People* magazine, who might also be interested in reading about Halle Berry, Vin Diesel, and Mariah Carey? How would the author need to revise for a *People* magazine audience?

**3. Rhetorical appeals.** How does Dagbovie-Mullins establish her authority on the topic she writes about?

**4. Rhetorical appeals.** How does the author appeal to your sense of logic in presenting examples and details to support her points? What are some specific details she uses that appeal to your sense of logos?

**5. Modes & media.** This particular article does not include any images, although there are thousands of images of Halle Berry, Vin Diesel, and Mariah Carey available. Why do you think the author opted not to integrate images into her article?

**6. Elements of the genre.** What is Dagbovie-Mullins's thesis? How easy was it for you to locate her thesis? What cues does she use in her introduction to indicate that the thesis is coming?

**7. Elements of the genre.** Do you have to be familiar with the author's sources to understand her point? Explain.

**8. Style.** Celebrities are typically considered more appropriate subjects for gossip magazines than scholarly journals. How does the author present celebrities as appropriate subjects for a researched article?

**9. Design.** Dagbovie-Mullins uses subheadings to break the article up into chunks. Did you find these helpful? Did you want fewer or more of them? Why or why not? Also note that some subheadings are questions, while others could be considered thought-provoking statements ("Multiracial to the Rescue: Vin Diesel"). How did these subheadings work on you as a reader? Did they make you want to keep reading? Explain.

**10. Sources.** Note the extensive Works Cited list. Glance through the list of sources and note how many seem to be scholarly sources and how many seem to be other types of sources. How does the use of nonscholarly sources seem appropriate or inappropriate for this article?

# Drafting a Peer-Reviewed Journal Article

---

## CHECKLIST: Drafting a Peer-Reviewed Journal Article Thinking of drafting a peer-reviewed journal article? Ask yourself the following questions.

### WHAT'S MY RHETORICAL SITUATION?

☐ **Purpose.** What topic have I researched that I could inform other experts about? Have I discovered something about the topic that others like me might find interesting or conducive to their own research? Do I want to persuade readers of something? To effectively persuade readers, what will I need to inform them about?

☐ **Audience.** My readers will be experts on my general topic, but they won't know as much as I do about the aspect I'm writing about. How much background information will they need? What kind of terminology will they expect? How will my readers use the information I present?

☐ **Rhetorical appeals.** How will I establish my authority as a writer? How will I build a case for my conclusions using logic? Will I need to cite sources to establish myself as an expert? What kinds of sources will help me build my case?

☐ **Modes & media.** Can some of the information I present be shown with a chart or graphic? Do I want readers to access my article in print or digitally? Or do I want to make both options available?

### WHAT GENRE CONVENTIONS MATTER?

☐ **Elements of the genre.** How can I make sure my thesis is clear and declarative? How will I refer to my sources? How can I synthesize my sources to show readers how they are in conversation with each other?

☐ **Style.** How can I project an authoritative voice? How much detail will I need to provide so that readers will understand the complexity and validity of my research?

☐ **Design.** How will I use subheadings to present my information in chunks? Will I use images to illustrate points?

☐ **Sources.** Will my readers expect sources to be cited in MLA style, APA style, or another format? Will my readers respect the types of sources I've referred to?

---

## PRACTICE Want to experiment? Draft your own peer-reviewed journal article.

Think about a topic you are researching for this class or another class. What are some of the issues surrounding your topic? Draft an opening paragraph that establishes you as an authority and also makes it clear that you are writing for fellow students rather than a general audience.

# 4 PERSUASIVE GENRES

## CONTENTS

e.For e-Pages content, visit **bedfordstmartins.com /bookofgenres.**

TRY TO SEE THINGS FROM MY POINT OF VIEW.

POLITICAL CARTOON ▶
**Rex F. May.** *Reprinted by permission of Rex May.*

Open your Web browser, page through any magazine, or take a walk to the coffee shop, and you will be barraged by texts and media created to persuade you—to think something, do something, like something, or buy something. Depending on the source you look at, city-dwelling Americans see between three thousand and five thousand ads per day.*

For an Index of Sources & Contexts for material referenced in this chapter, see the e-Pages at **bedfordstmartins.com /bookofgenres.**

Online, advertisers individualize their messages to you. For example, when you log on to Amazon.com you are greeted with a list of recommendations based on your previous purchases. On Facebook, the ads on your page are generated according to your likes and dislikes, and other information you provide in your profile and posts.

While advertising is probably the most pervasive of persuasive genres, there are lots of other kinds of texts that we create at home, work, and school in order to convince others to see things our way. In fact, you could argue that almost every communication—a text message to a friend about what movie to see, an online posting of a cute kitten or puppy, a Match.com profile, an editorial on Fox News about the economy, a joke made on *The Simpsons* about the editorial on Fox News, or even a chapter in a textbook—has persuasive elements built into it.

## The Rhetorical Situation

### Purpose: Why write to persuade?

When we write to persuade, we do so because we want to convince our readers of something—usually to agree with us about a topic, issue, or idea, or to take a specific action. As a student, when you write a paper in which you take a stance on an issue or you give a speech in which you ask your audience to do something, you are writing to persuade. As a professional, when you apply for a job, you craft a resume and cover

▲ AD
**Match.** Have ads like this popped up in your browser window? According to Match, "1 in 3" relationships start online." *Courtesy of Match.*

*According to a study done by the journal *Pediatrics*, "The average young person views more than 3,000 ads per day on television (TV), on the Internet, on billboards, and in magazines" (see "Children, Adolescents, and Advertising," December 1, 2006). According to an article by Walter Kirn, published in *The New York Times Magazine*, "[R]esearchers estimate that the average city dweller is exposed to 5,000 ads per day, up from 2,000 per day three decades ago" (see "Here, There, and Everywhere," February 11, 2007).

**STAY ALIVE!**
**DON'T TEXT & DRIVE**

letter and make a convincing case for yourself during your interview in order to persuade the person hiring that you are the best candidate. A persuasive text can be as simple as a six-word slogan.

## Audience: How do we persuade others?

As citizens of a democracy, we may read persuasive texts, such as editorials, to help us figure out our own positions on specific issues. For instance, during election season, you might pay close attention to the opinion pages of local and national newspapers. The editorial boards of these newspapers publish editorials in which they try to convince you who to vote for, how to think of specific issues, and why.

Like the editorial board of *The New York Times*, any time you want to persuade your audience, you need to lay out your ideas, anticipate possible objections, and support your argument with relevant information. As with reporting information (see Chapter 3), accuracy is important when it comes to persuading others. Backing up your ideas and claims with correct information, gathered from reliable sources, will make your argument stronger.

The *Times* editorial board was well aware of their audience—which tends to be liberal, Democratic, and educated—when they wrote the piece on page 179 during the 2008 presidential election. The editors wrote: "We believe [Barack Obama] has the will and ability to forge the broad political consensus that is essential to finding solutions to this nation's problems." They supported their argument by contrasting Obama with his opponent, John McCain, and by providing carefully chosen details of Obama's platform and the choices he made as a senator.

## Rhetorical Appeals: How do we use ethos, logos, and pathos to persuade?

Whether you want to convince others to agree with you on an important issue, to date you, to vote for your candidate, or to

What texts in your immediate surroundings (billboards, ads, etc.) are meant to persuade you of something? What persuasive techniques are evident? Which texts are most convincing? Why?

## EDITORIAL

### Barack Obama for President

Published: October 23, 2008

Hyperbole is the currency of presidential campaigns, but this year the nation's future truly hangs in the balance.

**Multimedia**

Interactive Feature
New York Times Endorsements Through the Ages

**Related**

Times Topics: Barack Obama

The United States is battered and drifting after eight years of President Bush's failed leadership. He is saddling his successor with two wars, a scarred global image and a government systematically stripped of its ability to protect and help its citizens — whether they are fleeing a hurricane's floodwaters, searching for affordable health care or struggling to hold on to their homes, jobs, savings and pensions in the midst of a financial crisis that was foretold and preventable.

As tough as the times are, the selection of a new president is easy. After nearly two years of a grueling and ugly campaign, Senator Barack Obama of Illinois has proved that he is the right choice to be the 44th president of the United States.

Mr. Obama has met challenge after challenge, growing as a leader and putting real flesh on his early promises of hope and change. He has shown a cool head and sound judgment. We believe he has the will and the ability to forge the broad political consensus that is essential to finding solutions to this nation's problems.

In the same time, Senator John McCain of Arizona has retreated farther and farther to the fringe of American politics, running a campaign on partisan division, class warfare and even hints of racism. His policies and worldview are mired in the past. His choice of a running mate so evidently unfit for the office was a final act of opportunism and bad judgment that eclipsed the accomplishments of 26 years in Congress.

Given the particularly ugly nature of Mr. McCain's campaign, the urge to choose on the basis of raw emotion is strong. But there is a greater value in looking closely at the facts of life in America today and at the prescriptions the candidates offer. The differences are profound.

Mr. McCain offers more of the Republican every-man-for-himself ideology, now lying in shards on Wall Street and in Americans' bank accounts. Mr. Obama has another vision of government's role and responsibilities.

In his convention speech in Denver, Mr. Obama said, "Government cannot solve all our problems, but what it should do is that which we cannot do for ourselves: protect us from harm and provide every child a decent education; keep our water clean and our toys safe; invest in new schools and new roads and new science and technology."

Since the financial crisis, he has correctly identified the abject failure of government regulation that has brought the markets to the brink of collapse.

#### The Economy

The American financial system is the victim of decades of Republican deregulatory and anti-tax policies. Those ideas have been proved wrong at an unfathomable price, but Mr. McCain — a self-proclaimed "foot soldier in the Reagan revolution" — is still a believer.

Mr. Obama sees that far-reaching reforms will be needed to protect Americans and American business.

Mr. McCain talks about reform a lot, but his vision is pinched. His answer to any economic question is to eliminate pork-barrel spending — about $18 billion in a $3 trillion budget — cut taxes and wait for unfettered markets to solve the problem.

Mr. Obama is clear that the nation's tax structure must be changed to make it fairer. That means the well-off Americans who have benefited disproportionately from Mr. Bush's tax cuts will have to pay some more. Working Americans, who have seen their standard of living fall and their children's options narrow, will benefit. Mr. Obama wants to raise the minimum wage and tie it to inflation, restore a climate in which workers are able to organize unions if they wish and expand educational opportunities.

Mr. McCain, who once opposed President Bush's tax cuts for the wealthy as fiscally irresponsible, now wants to make them permanent. And while he talks about keeping taxes low for everyone, his proposed cuts would overwhelmingly benefit the top 1 percent of Americans while digging the country into a deeper fiscal hole.

#### National Security

The American military — its people and equipment — is dangerously overstretched. Mr. Bush has neglected the necessary war in Afghanistan, which now threatens to spiral into defeat. The unnecessary and staggeringly costly war in Iraq must be ended as quickly and responsibly as possible.

While Iraq's leaders insist on a swift drawdown of American troops and a deadline for the end of the occupation, Mr. McCain is still talking about some ill-defined "victory." As a result, he has offered no real plan for extracting American troops and limiting any further damage to Iraq and its neighbors.

Mr. Obama was an early and thoughtful opponent of the war in Iraq, and he has presented a military and diplomatic plan for withdrawing American forces. Mr. Obama also has correctly warned that until the Pentagon starts pulling troops out of Iraq, there will not be enough troops to defeat the Taliban and Al Qaeda in Afghanistan.

Mr. McCain, like Mr. Bush, has only belatedly focused on Afghanistan's dangerous unraveling and the threat that neighboring Pakistan may quickly follow.

Mr. Obama would have a learning curve on foreign affairs, but he has already showed sounder judgment than his opponent on these critical issues. His choice of Senator Joseph Biden — who has deep foreign-policy expertise — as his running mate is another sign of that sound judgment. Mr. McCain's long interest in foreign policy and the many dangers this country now faces make his choice of Gov. Sarah Palin of Alaska more irresponsible.

Both presidential candidates talk about strengthening alliances in Europe and Asia, including NATO, and strongly support Israel. Both candidates talk about repairing America's image in the world. But is seems clear to us that Mr. Obama is far more likely to do that — and not just because the first black president would present a new American face to the world.

Mr. Obama wants to reform the United Nations, while Mr. McCain wants to create a new entity, the League of Democracies — a move that would incite even fiercer anti-American furies around the world.

Unfortunately, Mr. McCain, like Mr. Bush, sees the world as divided into friends (like Georgia) and adversaries (like Russia). He proposed kicking Russia out of the Group of 8 industrialized nations even before the invasion of Georgia. We have no sympathy for Moscow's bullying, but we also have no desire to replay the cold war. The United States must find a way to constrain the Russians' worst impulses, while preserving the ability to work with them on arms control and other vital initiatives.

Both candidates talk tough on terrorism, and neither has ruled out military action to end Iran's nuclear weapons program. But Mr. Obama has called for a serious effort to try to wean Tehran from its nuclear ambitions with more credible diplomatic overtures and tougher sanctions. Mr. McCain's willingness to joke about bombing Iran was frightening.

#### The Constitution and the Rule of Law

Under Mr. Bush and Vice President Dick Cheney, the Constitution, the Bill of Rights, the justice system and the separation of powers have come under relentless attack. Mr. Bush chose to exploit the tragedy of Sept. 11, 2001, the moment in which he looked like the president of a unified nation, to try to place himself above the law.

Mr. Bush has arrogated the power to imprison men without charges and browbeat Congress into granting an unfettered authority to spy on Americans. He has created untold number of "black" programs, including secret prisons and outsourced torture.

The president has issued hundreds, if not thousands, of secret orders. We fear it will take years of forensic research to discover how many basic rights have been violated.

Both candidates have renounced torture and are committed to closing the prison camp in Guantánamo Bay, Cuba.

But Mr. Obama has gone beyond that, promising to identify and correct Mr. Bush's attacks on the democratic system. Mr. McCain has been silent on the subject.

Mr. McCain improved protections for detainees. But then he helped the White House push through the appalling Military Commissions Act of 2006, which denied detainees the right to a hearing in a real court and put Washington in conflict with the Geneva Conventions, greatly increasing the risk to American troops.

The next president will have the chance to appoint one or more justices to a Supreme Court that is on the brink of being dominated by a radical right wing. Mr. Obama may appoint less liberal judges than some of his followers might like, but Mr. McCain is certain to pick rigid ideologues. He has said he would never appoint a judge who believes in women's reproductive rights.

#### The Candidates

It will be an enormous challenge just to get the nation back to where it was before Mr. Bush, to begin to mend its image in the world and to restore its self-confidence and its self-respect. Doing all of that, and leading America forward, will require strength of will, character and intellect, sober judgment and a cool, steady hand.

Mr. Obama has those qualities in abundance. Watching him being tested in the campaign has long since erased the reservations that led us to endorse Senator Hillary Rodham Clinton in the Democratic primaries. He has drawn in legions of new voters with powerful messages of hope and possibility and calls for shared sacrifice and social responsibility.

Mr. McCain, whom we chose as the best Republican nominee in the primaries, has spent the last coins of his reputation for principle and sound judgment to placate the limitless demands and narrow vision of the far-right wing. His righteous fury at being driven out of the 2000 primaries on a racist tide aimed at his adopted daughter has been replaced by a zealous embrace of those same win-at-all-costs tactics and tacticians.

He surrendered his standing as an independent thinker in his rush to embrace Mr. Bush's misbegotten tax policies and to abandon his leadership position on climate change and immigration reform.

Mr. McCain could have seized the high ground on energy and the environment. Earlier in his career, he offered the first plausible bill to control America's emissions of greenhouse gases. Now his positions are a caricature of that record: think Ms. Palin leading chants of "drill, baby, drill."

Mr. Obama has endorsed some offshore drilling, but as part of a comprehensive strategy including big investments in new, clean technologies.

Mr. Obama has withstood some of the toughest campaign attacks ever mounted against a candidate. He's been called un-American and accused of hiding a secret Islamic faith. The Republicans have linked him to domestic terrorists and questioned his wife's love of her country. Ms. Palin has also questioned millions of Americans' patriotism, calling Republican-leaning states "pro-America."

This politics of fear, division and character assassination helped Mr. Bush drive Mr. McCain from the 2000 Republican primaries and defeat Senator John Kerry in 2004. It has been the dominant theme of his failed presidency.

The nation's problems are simply too grave to be reduced to slashing "robo-calls" and negative ads. This country needs sensible leadership, compassionate leadership, honest leadership and strong leadership. Barack Obama has shown that he has all of those qualities.

buy your product, you will be most persuasive if you relate to your audience through the rhetorical appeals—ethos, logos, and pathos.

*Ethos*, the authority and trustworthiness that you establish as a writer, composer, or speaker, is crucial when you want to persuade others. For example, if your boss asks you to review several possible locations for an important fund-raising event and recommend one, you will want to establish yourself as dedicated to getting a high-quality venue for a reasonable price. To do this, you'll need to demonstrate that you've taken the assignment seriously, studied the options objectively, and weighed your company's needs and priorities carefully.

Here's another example. Way back in 1981, horror writer Stephen King wrote an essay about why horror films are popular. Because he was already established as a best-selling horror author with titles like *Carrie* (1974) and *The Shining* (1977), both of which had already been made into successful horror movies, he had instant credibility, with which he developed an ethos as an expert on his subject. He went further than that, however, citing many examples throughout the essay to establish that he knows more than just his own experience. Here is an excerpt from the essay:

> We also go to re-establish our feelings of essential normality; the horror movie is innately conservative, even reactionary. Freda Jackson as the horrible melting woman in *Die, Monster, Die!* confirms for us that no matter how far we may be removed from the beauty of a Robert Redford or a Diana Ross, we are still light-years from true ugliness.
> —**Stephen King,** from "Why We Crave Horror Movies"

King furthers his ethos by taking his subject seriously and speaking specifically about it.

*Logos*, the logical chain of reasoning that you provide for readers, is extremely important when you are making any kind of argument. Imagine you are taking a car for a test drive to decide whether you will buy it. You might mention to the salesperson that you are interested in a car that won't be too bad for the environment. The salesperson might then present you with some facts about the mileage the car gets, the measures the manufacturer has taken at the factory to protect the

Are there particular types of persuasive texts you automatically trust? Distrust? Why?

environment, and the paper-free policy the dealership has initiated by conducting as much business as possible electronically. By talking to you about these factors, the salesperson is creating a chain of reasoning that—she hopes—will lead you to conclude that the car you are driving is an environmentally responsible choice.

Let's look at an example of a verbal argument made by media scholar Johanna Blakley. She gave a presentation about social media that was videotaped and published online by TED, a nonprofit open-source site devoted to "ideas worth spreading." In her TED talk, Blakley makes a case for how people connect. She says:

> [People] don't aggregate around age, gender, income. They aggregate around the things they love, the things that they like. And if you think about it, shared interests and values are a far more powerful aggregator of human beings than demographic categories. I'd much rather know whether you like *Buffy the Vampire Slayer* rather than how old you are. That would tell me something more substantial about you.
> —**Johanna Blakley,** from "Social Media and the End of Gender"

Notice how—after making her claim that people aggregate around their interests—she gives a specific example about interest in *Buffy the Vampire Slayer* being a better indicator than age of how much people have in common with each other.

*Pathos* is the appeal that you use when you want to evoke your readers' emotions. This comes in handy when you are trying to persuade someone to do something. An appeal to pathos connects you with your audience, and vice versa. For example, when a salesperson asks you about yourself and then tells you a bit about himself and you find some commonalities, that salesperson is appealing to your pathos. When he later tells you that he loves the stereo you are looking at, you're more likely to buy it because you've already identified with him.

Advertisers often appeal to pathos. For example, a commercial for Tide Free & Gentle detergent begins with a little girl trying on pairs of tights as a motherly woman's voice says:

> "Picking the right tights isn't always easy. Picking a free detergent is."

As the commercial continues, the girl frolics around her room, posing in front of her mirror in different pairs of tights, as the motherly voice continues talking about how Tide Free & Gentle detergent will ensure that whichever tights the girl picks, they will be clean and free of anything that can irritate her skin.

By focusing on the cuteness and innocence of the little girl, the ad equates a mother's desire to keep her daughter safe with choosing Tide Free & Gentle detergent. The advertisers associate protectiveness and love with the detergent itself.

## Modes & Media: How can they help you persuade?

Following is a breakdown of the modes and media of some of the compositions presented in this chapter:

| PERSUASIVE GENRES | Mode | Medium |
| --- | --- | --- |
| **AD**<br>Match.com (p. 177) | **VISUAL AND WRITTEN** | **DIGITAL** |
| **BUMPER STICKER**<br>Imagina Productions, "Don't Text & Drive" (p. 178) | **WRITTEN** | **PRINT** |
| **ONLINE EDITORIAL**<br>*The New York Times* Editorial Board, "Barack Obama for President" (p. 179) | **VISUAL AND WRITTEN** | **DIGITAL** |

| ONLINE & TV AD | VISUAL AND AUDIO | DIGITAL |
|---|---|---|
| Tide Free & Gentle detergent commercial (p. 182) | | (ONLINE AND ON TELEVISION) |

## The Genre's Conventions

### Elements of the Genre: What does all persuasive writing have in common?

Persuasive writers aim to change the reader's or viewer's mind in some way. Different authors and artists may use different strategies for achieving this, but most effective persuasive communication has two elements in common:

1. *Makes an explicit argument/position statement.* When writers state exactly what they'd like readers or viewers to do or think, then there is no guesswork involved. Many persuasive writers present an explicit position statement, such as "Voters should support Proposition 2 because it will reduce taxes in the long run." Others may strongly imply, but not explicitly state, the case they're making. The text of an ad won't always say, "Buy this product," but you get that idea from the use of persuasive images and text; ad writers make clear what they're trying to persuade you of, often without using direct language.

2. *Taps into audiences' values and emotions.* Most persuasive writers appeal to their readers' or viewers' sensibilities in some way. While this is true of most writers, it's particularly true of writers who want to persuade; it's essential to tap into ethos, pathos, and/or logos. Ethos is especially important because most readers will not be convinced by an unreliable author.

### Style: How does it help you persuade?

When you want to persuade others, present your ideas in a way that will hold your readers' (or listeners' or viewers') attention. You will need their attention before you can make your specific arguments. You can do this with certain stylistic techniques—as well as through the voice and tone you use.

Let's look at an example. On January 8, 2011, Congresswoman Gabrielle Giffords and eighteen others were shot in a supermarket parking lot in Tucson, Arizona. Six people died. A few days later, President Obama gave a speech in Tucson that paid tribute to the injured and killed; the speech was also designed to persuade Americans not to blame each other or a particular political party for the tragedy (though the gunman was later described as mentally ill by the judge at his sentencing, early reports had circulated that his politics had inspired his actions). He began with a greeting to those present, noted the occasion for the speech, and said something about each person killed in the shooting. Then Obama moved on:

> [A]t a time when our discourse has become so sharply polarized—at a time when we are far too eager to lay the blame for all that ails the world at the feet of those who happen to think differently than we do—it's important for us to pause for a moment and make sure that we're talking with each other in a way that heals, not in a way that wounds. . . .
>
> Yes, we have to examine all the facts behind this tragedy. We cannot and will not be passive in the face of such violence. We should be willing to challenge old assumptions in order to lessen the prospects of such violence in the future. But what we cannot do is use this tragedy as one more occasion to turn on each other. That we cannot do. That we cannot do.
>
> As we discuss these issues, let each of us do so with a good dose of humility. Rather than pointing fingers or assigning blame, let's use this occasion to expand our moral imaginations, to listen to each other more carefully, to sharpen our instincts for empathy and remind ourselves of all the ways that our hopes and dreams are bound together.
>
> —**Barack Obama,** from his speech "Together We Thrive: Tucson and America," University of Arizona, January 12, 2011

Notice the structure of the excerpt above. Obama moves from providing context to actively presenting an argument to his listeners. One of his techniques is to use repetition to reinforce what he says. For example, he uses the phrase "at a time when" twice in the first sentence to keep listeners engaged; he uses the line "we cannot do" three times in order to emphasize his case that we cannot "turn on each other" during a divisive moment. Notice, too, the mix of long and very short sentences that create variety for listeners.

In this speech, Obama's tone is friendly but also serious and presidential.

## Design: What is the best format for persuading?

Consider the Nike logo. Ever wonder who designed it? As it happens, in 1971 a graphic arts student at Portland State University named Carolyn Davidson created the Nike swoosh symbol, which became one of the most successful logos of all time. Years later, the ad firm Wieden + Kennedy penned the slogan "Just Do It." The campaign is noted by *Advertising Age* as one of the Top 100 Advertising Campaigns of the twentieth century. Why? Because the swoosh design and the slogan are clear, simple, and memorable. These are the qualities that make the campaign persuasive.

The design of a piece can contribute to its persuasiveness or work against it. Consider someone trying to convince you that he is a calm and patient person. Imagine that he is wearing a bright red T-shirt with the slogan "Don't think! Just *act*!" Chances are that the design of this person's wardrobe would work against persuading you that he is calm and patient.

## Sources: What research should you draw on to persuade others?

To be persuasive, use sources to develop your credibility, to draw on for facts, and to support your claims and objectives. For example, if Liz wants to persuade her dean to send her to a conference, she'll need to do some research about the conference and then make a case for how the conference and the dean's goals are related.

In the composition on page 186, artist Dominic Episcopo aims to persuade viewers that, figuratively, America is "made of meat." In creating this piece, which is part of his "Meat America" series, he may have had in mind any or all of the following factors: high U.S. obesity rates, high levels of cholesterol and heart disease, or the country's dependence on a system of raising cattle that is hard on the environment and animals.

To support the argument he makes in his sculpture, Episcopo could draw on sources of information on meat consumption in the United States and its effects. For example, he could draw on the data in the chart on page 187 that shows the rise of Americans' beef consumption—from 63 pounds per person per year in 1950 to 85.56 pounds per person in 2010 (with the greatest consumption in 1975). Published by the Humane Society, this chart uses government census and USDA data, which makes it a particularly solid source.

◀ PHOTO
▶ SCULPTURE &
▼ WEB SITE
**Dominic Episcopo,**
"United Steaks of America" (right), a work included at meatamerica.com (bottom). *Three images: Dominic Episcopo.*

MEAT AMERICA | by Dominic Episcopo

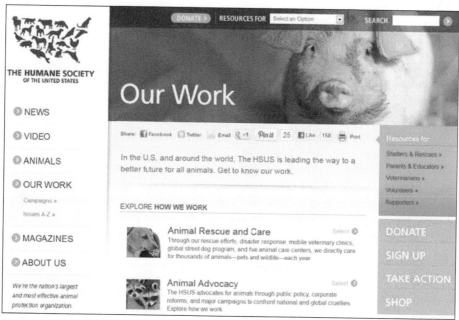

When you write to persuade, how do you use sources to support your argument? What types of sources are most persuasive? Why?

▲ WEB SITE & ▼ CHART

**The Humane Society of the United States,** "U.S. Per Capita Meat Consumption" and humanesociety.org. *The Humane Society of the United States homepage.*

# ADVERTISEMENTS

How do you know when you are (or aren't) the target audience for an ad? Have you ever been offended or alienated by an ad? If so, why?

An advertisement is any text created to persuade consumers to purchase a product or service. Print advertising is as old as the first newspapers, which appeared in England in the 1600s. Today, ads are everywhere and are presented in a variety of print and digital media. Advertisers spend large amounts of money to research potential customers and then tailor and distribute sales messages that will appeal to those consumers and translate into sales. The money they spend on Web advertising, in particular, is on the rise, especially display ads (banners and video ads). The Interactive Advertising Bureau (IAB), in its 2012 report, indicates record online ad revenues, with a 15 percent and more than $1 billion increase over 2011. The *Los Angeles Times* and eMarketer.com report that while advertisers still spend on print ads, they're spending more of their budgets on digital ads; by 2016 online ad spending is likely to nearly double ($62 billion), leaving print far behind ($32 billion).

CHART ▶
**eMarketer.com/Los Angeles Times,** "U.S. Print vs. Online Ad Spending, 2011–2016." *eMarketer, Inc.*

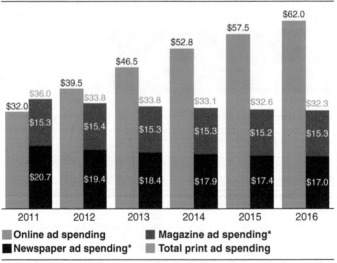

US Print vs. Online Ad Spending, 2011–2016
*billions*

| Year | 2011 | 2012 | 2013 | 2014 | 2015 | 2016 |
|------|------|------|------|------|------|------|
| Online ad spending | $32.0 | $39.5 | $46.5 | $52.8 | $57.5 | $62.0 |
| Total print ad spending | $36.0 | $33.8 | $33.8 | $33.1 | $32.6 | $32.3 |
| Magazine ad spending* | $15.3 | $15.4 | $15.3 | $15.3 | $15.2 | $15.3 |
| Newspaper ad spending* | $20.7 | $19.4 | $18.4 | $17.9 | $17.4 | $17.0 |

■ Online ad spending  ■ Magazine ad spending*
■ Newspaper ad spending*  ■ Total print ad spending

Note: eMarketer benchmarks its US online ad spending projections against the IAB/PWC data, for which the last full year measured was 2010; eMarketer benchmarks its US newspaper ad spending projections against the NAA data, for which the last full year measured was 2010; *print only
Source: eMarketer, Jan 2012
136019                                                         www.eMarketer.com

# Analyzing Advertisements: What to Look For

**Purpose**   To sell their products and services, companies need to publicize information about what they're offering. They also need to win business from competitors. For example, the well-known Progressive auto insurance commercials advertise the company's "comparison shopping" feature, as shown below, to inform shoppers of their rates versus those of other carriers and support their claim that with Progressive, "You could save over $475 on car insurance."

◀ ONLINE AD
**Progressive,**
"Compare Rates."
*Courtesy of Progressive.*

**Audience**   When major advertising firms such as the Ad Agency, Arnold Worldwide, and Wieden + Kennedy create ads, they have a very clear picture of their target market, and they aim their branding, visuals, messages, and other persuasive tools squarely at that market. For example, the Old Spice commercials of 2010, featuring the actor Isaiah Mustafa, clearly target a young, tech-savvy, heterosexual female demographic. The creators of these quirky ads (Wieden + Kennedy) dusted off an old brand of men's cologne and made it more appealing to a new audience by using humor, personality, and a supersuave ladies' man. Originally released on YouTube and then as a Super Bowl commercial, the "Old Spice Guy" ad went viral within a few days, getting more than thirty-four million views in less than a week.

In the ad, Mustafa says: "Hello, ladies, look at your man, now back to me, now back at your man, now back to me. Sadly, he isn't me, but if he stopped using ladies' scented body wash and switched to Old Spice, he could smell like he's me. Look down, back up, where are you? You're on a boat with the man your man could smell like. What's in your hand, back at me. I have it, it's an oyster with two tickets to that thing you love. Look again, the tickets are now diamonds. Anything is possible when your man smells like Old Spice and not a lady. I'm on a horse." Then comes the voiceover: *"Smell like a man, man. Old Spice."*

**Rhetorical appeals**    Advertisers use appeals to ethos (authority), logos (logic), and pathos (emotion). Many ads that feature expert testimonials or celebrity endorsements, for example, make use of ethos; if you trust the expert giving the testimonial, you are more likely to trust the product. A product that has been long established, such as Old Spice, which has been around for more than seventy years, has its own built-in ethos. The advertisers of Old Spice further establish its ethos by emphasizing the macho quality of the product and choosing a super-fit actor with a deep voice to star in the commercial. The advertisers also appeal to viewers' sense of pathos—tapping into their desire to buy the product, even though it is a nonessential item.

**Modes & media**    As more reading and viewing happen online, more advertising will happen there too. A digital ad, such as the Old Spice commercial mentioned above, has the potential to spread through social media and YouTube, giving advertisers more "bang for the buck." In terms of the medium, some online ads are static (e.g., display ads that don't move) while others are videos or animations that incorporate sound. There are even reports of a new medium called "smell-vertising": a product's scent is broadcast in an area with potential consumers of the product.

Think of an ad that features a visual image that doesn't directly relate to the product being promoted. What is the product? The visual? Why might the ad creators have made this choice?

### Elements of the genre

*Headlines*. Advertisers use headlines to immediately attract the reader's attention. The headline often conveys the product's benefits through concise language. Additionally, advertisers pay special attention to the placement of the headline, ensuring that it is not obscured or overwhelmed by a visual element. In the case of some electronic ads, a headline may be read aloud by a narrator.

*Visuals*. Graphics work together with the headline to attract the reader. They also illustrate the point or provide visual evidence that supports the product's claim. In television commercials, advertisers edit the visuals to hold viewers' attention, maintaining a quick pace and not lingering for too long on one image.

*Ad copy*. Advertisers use the words of an advertisement, or ad copy, for specific purposes. They use a headline to get a consumer's attention and then draw the reader in further with an intriguing subheading. Copy that is not a headline or heading is called body text, and it tells about the benefits of the product or service and either implicitly or explicitly tells the consumer to make a purchase. Digital and TV ads also feature ad copy—it can be spoken and/or animated on the screen.

*Advertising slogans*. Advertisers often associate sayings or phrases with a product. For example, Nike's slogan is "Just Do It."

*Signature*. Usually found toward the bottom of a print ad, the signature includes the advertiser name and contact information. In digital and TV ads, contact information is not normally provided, but the brand and product name is made clear.

### Style

*Technique*. The writing tends to be brief and directive. For example, in the original Smokey the Bear advertisements, Smokey addresses the reader: "Only YOU can prevent forest fires!" Words are usually secondary to visuals. Visuals are carefully selected as persuasive tools (see "Design" below). Because digital and TV ads are very short (usually thirty seconds or less), words are limited.

*Details*. Advertisers usually keep details (and words, in general) to a minimum.

*Voice and tone*. In a commercial, voice and tone can give the viewer an impression of the product's benefits. For example, if a company is promoting its product's ability to relieve stress, then the tone of the ad is usually soothing. If a financial company is advertising its services, then the tone is usually reassuring. Written ad copy conveys its tone through word choice and phrasing, while digital and TV ads convey tone through vocal intonation, pacing, and the qualities of the voice itself (male or female, deep or high, etc.).

### Design

*Visual of the product.* Advertisers need to provide an image of what they're selling so consumers can identify and purchase it. If the product is less tangible (or not an object), such as an auto insurance policy, then some kind of visual emphasizes the message. For example, in some Geico ads, a caveman is the main visual, emphasizing how easy it is to purchase auto insurance.

*Additional pathos-building images.* Advertisers use visuals to convey ideas and tap into viewers' emotions. For example, in a commercial for Abilify (a drug used mainly to treat depression), the advertiser presents "before" and "after" images. The commercial begins with a series of people looking stressed, sad, and unable to do anything. The drug is introduced, followed by a series of visuals showing the same people engaged with life and smiling.

*Color.* Advertisers can further appeal to pathos by using images and colors associated with particular emotions.

For more examples of **advertisements,** see the Index of Genres on page G-1.

*Product logos.* Advertisers carefully design product logos to convey particular ideas and values about a product. For example, the Nike swoosh indicates speed and movement. All Nike products and advertisements feature the swoosh, which is instantly identifiable and long established.

*Layout.* In a print-based ad (or a static Web ad), the layout orients the reader and establishes the most important pieces of information. The main visual and headline are the most prominent in the advertisement; contact info and fine print are usually somewhere toward the bottom of the piece. Advertisers use similar principles in digital and TV commercials to make the featured product and message clear and conspicuous.

**Sources**    Advertising agencies conduct market research before creating ad campaigns so they can most efficiently identify and target their main audience and tailor their overall message accordingly. Once they've identified some possible directions for the content and design, they may ask a test audience to determine which ad will be most successful. Sources noted within an ad can include a company Web site where consumers can find more information about the product.

# Danone/Evian and Havas Worldwide

## *Detox with Evian*

The Evian brand of spring water is promoted as a natural product "from the heart of the French Alps." The Danone company introduced Evian to the United States in the 1970s, mostly in luxury hotels and expensive restaurants. Since then, they have associated the brand with luxury and have often used celebrities and people from the fashion industry to build its appeal.

Among the many ads for Evian is the notable "Detox" campaign of 2006. This campaign stressed the health benefits of drinking Evian, arguing that the water helps people maintain youthfulness and purity. Youthfulness is a theme that recurs in Evian's campaigns, including their current "Live Young" campaign that invites customers to post photos and participate in a video campaign.

To create the "Detox" campaign, Danone/Evian worked with the ad firm Havas Worldwide (formerly known as Euro RSCG). The firm also created Evian's popular "Live Young" campaign. Havas Worldwide creates ads and marketing plans for many major companies and is one of the largest advertising and marketing agencies in the world.

Danone/Evian also hired a firm called Codegent to create the digital marketing pieces for the "Detox" campaign. Copy on Codegent's site reads: "We've worked on Evian campaigns for a couple of years, now: the Detox with Evian campaign that was in conjunction with the on-pack promotion and the Evian Live Young campaign which also featured TV advertising. Bringing brands to life online, it's a great job."

Annotations in the margins of the Evian ad on page 194 point out the choices that Evian made in terms of their purpose, sense of audience, and use of rhetorical appeals. You'll also see notes on how this work reflects the conventions of the advertising genre—in terms of its persuasive appeal and specific techniques. *(Source for image on p. 194: various publications.)*

▲ WEB SITE
Danone, owner of Evian spring water.

What are the composers of the ad, **Havas Worldwide**, doing?

THE RHETORICAL SITUATION

Purpose
Audience
Rhetorical appeals
Modes & media

*see page 195*

How do I know this is an **advertisement**?

THE GENRE'S CONVENTIONS

Elements of the genre
Style
Design
Sources

*see page 195*

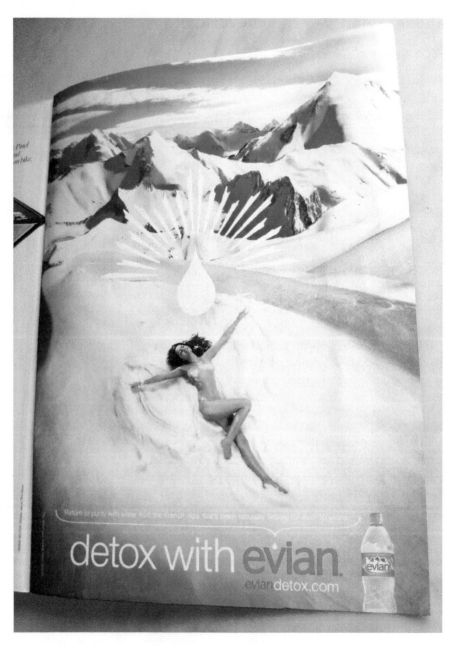

The ad copy reads: "Return to purity with water from the French Alps that's been naturally filtered for over 15 years."

## Purpose

Havas Worldwide, the creators of this ad (hired by Danone/Evian), hope to persuade consumers to buy Evian water.

## Audience

The ad creators are aiming at people looking for health benefits and/or people who want to "detoxify." (Note that this ad appeared right after New Year's Eve 2006, and the idea of detoxifying had been very popular that year.) The audience reads magazines (where the print ad appeared) and spends time online (notice the Evian URL in the ad copy).

## Rhetorical appeals

The ad appeals mainly to readers' **pathos** (emotion)—by displaying a beautiful landscape and model, and by equating both with Evian. The model's nudity implies snow-angel-grade purity. It also—in combination with the giant falling drop—suggests sex. The idea of "detoxing" also plays on readers' worries about health and an "impure" lifestyle.

The ad also conveys Evian's **ethos** through the presentation of the bottle and the emphasis on branding.

## Modes & media

**Mode = written and visual** The advertisers use visuals and a small amount of text to persuade viewers to purchase Evian water. Evian's "Detox" campaign stresses the purity and health benefits of the water, so both the visuals and text convey this point. The text emphasizes this through the headline ("Detox with Evian") and also the body copy ("Return to purity"). The visuals make the claim with pictures of snow-covered alps and a beautiful woman.

**Medium = print and digital** While this ad appeared in print magazines, it can also be found digitally. Evian's campaigns are designed not only for print, but also for TV and the Internet.

## Elements of the genre

Presents an argument (visual and textual) for purchasing a product.

The headline, "Detox with Evian," is brief, direct, and directive. The ad copy, "Return to purity with water from the French Alps that's been naturally filtered for over 15 years," suggests the benefits of the water and the process used to filter it; the writers also used directive language (i.e., "Return").

## Style

Brief text, with an emphasis on visuals. A central image—a naked woman making a snow angel in the Alps—is used to sell the Evian water.

## Design

Color is used to create drama and focus attention. The writers and designers chose cool tones—blue and white—for the snow and water to suggest purity, and chose bright colors—red and pink—for the product name and product shot to highlight the brand.

**The layout focuses** on the woman's body; the composition suggests purity but also sexuality to entice consumers.

The spatial arrangement emphasizes the Alps, where the water originates. The placement of the woman below the mountain suggests that drinking water that comes from the mountain can make you young and beautiful.

The use of a sans serif typeface and lowercase letters suggests freshness and a contemporary quality. The clean lines of the font reinforce the pure/natural message.

## Sources

Havas Worldwide most likely researched a variety of images before choosing the final one. The source of the water itself (the Alps) also plays into the choice of setting/backdrop for the ad.

## Questions: Analyzing Danone/Evian and Havas Worldwide's advertisement

**1. Purpose.** What information did the creators of the ad provide (textually and visually) about Evian water? How interesting is the information? How persuasive is it? Explain.

**2. Audience.** How do the various images in the ad speak to its audience? Who is the primary target audience for this ad? Is there only one audience or are several audiences being addressed by the ad? Why do you think so?

**3. Rhetorical appeals.** How many different ways is the concept of "purity" conveyed in the ad? How is this used to persuade the audience?

**4. Rhetorical appeals.** Why do the ad's creators focus on Evian water's "detoxifying" properties? And what does this suggest about Evian's target audience?

**5. Rhetorical appeals.** Look up the word *detox* in a dictionary. Which of the definitions listed seems most appropriate in the case of the ad? Why?

**6. Modes & media.** The ad copy mentions the French Alps but does not mention the woman, although both are central visuals in the ad. Why do you think the creators chose not to include the woman in the ad copy?

**7. Elements of the genre.** The ad headline is very brief and directive. Does it have the same catchiness as the Nike slogan "Just Do It"? Why or why not?

**8. Elements of the genre.** What is the relationship between the visual images and the text? If the bottom portion of the ad with the text were eliminated, what would your reaction to the image be? How does your reaction change when you see the text?

**9. Style.** How would you characterize the tone of the ad copy? Does the tone fit the advertisement's purpose? Why or why not?

**10. Design.** Describe the visuals in the ad. What do the visuals suggest about what the advertisers want consumers to think/believe/feel about Evian?

**11. Design.** Water drops are used twice in the ad. What purpose do they serve?

**12. Sources.** Is it effective to use an image of the mountains where Evian water comes from as a backdrop in the ad? Why or why not?

# Drafting an Advertisement

---

## CHECKLIST: Drafting an Advertisement Thinking of creating an ad? Ask yourself the following questions.

### WHAT'S MY RHETORICAL SITUATION?

☐ **Purpose.** What product do I use that I want to convince others to use? What are the reasons to use that product? Why would someone besides me want to use the product?

☐ **Audience.** Who are the people in my target audience? Who will use the product? When will they use the product? Where will they use the product? How will they use the product?

☐ **Rhetorical appeals.** How will I establish my credibility in my advertisement? How will I illustrate the product's reliability and ethos? How will I use emotions to persuade my reader to use the product? To what extent will I use logic to support my claim about the product?

☐ **Modes & media.** Will my ad be print-based or digital or made for TV? How will I use visual images to persuade? Will I use one primary image or others that are secondary? How will my text work with my images? Will text explain visuals? Complement them? Will I use animation?

### WHAT GENRE CONVENTIONS MATTER?

☐ **Elements of the genre.** Will my visuals be literal or symbolic? What type of catchy slogan can I create to make my product memorable? Will I use the slogan as my headline or within the ad copy?

☐ **Style.** What tone will work best for selling my product? How will my intended audience respond to my tone?

☐ **Design.** What typeface should I use? What size type will work best with my visuals? How can I use layout in order to feature the most important elements and leave the least important for final viewing? How can I use color and other design elements to guide my viewers' experience?

☐ **Sources.** What kind of market research will I conduct? Will I test out my headline/slogan on a potential audience? Will I show them a series of visuals to see which is most persuasive?

---

## PRACTICE Want to experiment? Draft your own advertisement.

Think of a product you consume or use, such as an energy drink, candy bar, computer, or article of clothing. Create a draft of a print advertisement that highlights a specific property/aspect of that product, such as the detoxifying properties of Evian. Use symbolic visuals to sell your product. Alternatively, create a digital or TV ad in which you use images, sound, and text.

# EDITORIALS & OPINION PIECES

Editorials are related to **news articles**. Both types of writing are presented by news organizations (such as *The New York Times*, CNN, and your campus paper); however, editorials present opinions (which are subjective) and articles present facts (which are objective). For more on **news articles,** see the Index of Genres on page G-1.

Editorials and opinion pieces are texts that convey a writer's opinion on a particular topic, sometimes a controversial topic. This type of writing can be called by different names, such as *opinions, perspectives, commentaries,* and *viewpoints,* and can take the form of a letter to the editor or an online comment in response to an issue or other piece of writing.

Editorials appear in newspapers and magazines, on TV and radio, and in blogs and other online publications. Editorials also include editorial cartoons. An editorial represents the opinion of a news agency's editorial board, and therefore represents the opinion of the publisher. An opinion piece, on the other hand, could take the form of opinion columns by regular featured writers, and letters from readers in which they share their views. Many newspapers, such as the *Denver Post*, feature editorials and opinion pieces side by side; the *Denver Post* calls the page simply the Opinion Page. If your school publishes a newspaper, it probably also includes a section dedicated to editorials or opinions.

EDITORIAL PAGE ▶
The *Denver Post*
Opinion page. *Printed
with permission from
The Denver Post.*

## Analyzing Editorials & Opinion Pieces: What to Look For

THE RHETORICAL SITUATION

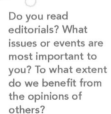

Do you read editorials? What issues or events are most important to you? To what extent do we benefit from the opinions of others?

### Purpose

*Individual writers.* An average citizen or student who writes an editorial or letter to the editor does so to convey his or her view on a specific issue, with the intent of persuading other readers. For example, in one issue of the *Oregon Daily Emerald,* a University of Oregon student wrote a column titled "Students Should Have Wider

**denverpost.com** Opinion

## Editorial: Trim feds' role in policing pot

As more and more states legalize medical marijuana, it's time for Congress to end the conflict between federal and state law.

By The Denver Post                    POSTED: 06/25/2011 01:00:00 AM MDT

The nation's marijuana laws are an overlapping mess. Possession is illegal under federal law while an impressive list of states, including Colorado, brazenly defy Washington's edict by allowing marijuana for medical use. Congress should have resolved this conflict years agobut now at last it has its chance.

A bill, whose sponsors include Rep. Jared Polis, D-Boulder, would not legalize marijuana, but rather remove it from the federal government's list of controlled substances. That would enable states that have legalized medical marijuana — which include such major population centers as California, New Jersey and Michigan — to craft and enforce their own laws without conflict with the feds.

Those states may be operating outside of federal law, but it's with their citizens' consent. State and local officials, as well as dispensaries and their clients, deserve a reprieve from this twilight zone in which federal authorities could change their mind at any moment and charge them with crimes.

Earlier this year, the clash between state and federal law came into sharp focus when federal prosecutors essentially fired warning shots at proposals in several states despite previous assurances they would not target those who followed state laws.

John Walsh, U.S. attorney for Colorado, took issue with a proposed law that would have created a license for large-scale marijuana-infused manufacturing facilities. Similarly, other U.S. attorneys threatened enforcement of federal law against big operations.

The result was trepidation among medical marijuana business owners who had operated in line with what they thought was a relaxation of federal enforcement.

We haven't and won't defend the ambition of medical marijuana businesses that seem determined to interpret the 2009 Justice Department pronouncement in the most expansive light.

We also have said on several occasions that we do not think voters were approving back-door legalization when they supported a 2000 state constitutional amendment allowing medical marijuana. Indeed, straight-up legalization failed overwhelmingly in Colorado in 2006 and would probably fail again if voters are given another shot at the issue in 2012.

If voters were to approve legalization, of course, the conflict with federal law would only sharpen.

That's why we think this congressional measure makes sense.

To be sure, the bill still would allow for some federal enforcement — in cases, for instance, of trafficking between states. But mostly it would take the feds out of the enforcement equation.

Such a change would all but eliminate the confusion between state and federal law and allow for clear enforcement of established rules.

---

Gun Liberties," in response to an article discussing how the university campus prepares for a campus shooting. The student's purpose is clear—as is his opinion.

The same is true for an individual columnist—a staff or syndicated writer for a specific newspaper, magazine, or other news organization; that is, the columnist conveys his or her own opinion in the editorial and not the opinion of a publisher, though there is some gray area here because the writers are usually employed by the publisher.

*Editorial board writers.* Texts that are written by the editorial board of a newspaper or magazine convey the opinion of the publisher. These editorials are intended to educate and persuade readers to agree with a specific idea and/or to take a specific action. For example, in the *Denver Post* editorial "Trim Feds' Role in Policing Pot," the *Post* argues in support of a congressional measure that would eliminate marijuana from the federal government's list of controlled substances. The editorial boards of most newspapers reflect a conservative or liberal point of view through their editorials; for example, the editorial board of *The New York Times* has a reputation for being fairly liberal, while the editorial board of the *News-Gazette* of Champaign-Urbana, Illinois, has a reputation for being conservative.

**Audience**    Anyone with access to newspapers, magazines, television, radio, or the Internet can access editorials and opinion pieces. As a reader, you might scan the

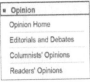

E-mail | Print | RSS

# When teachers cut class

Remember those days when your teacher unexpectedly called in sick? Some hapless substitute walked in, briefly struggled to teach a lesson and then surrendered class time to "study hall."

Despite anecdotal and academic evidence that students don't learn as much from substitutes, many school districts appear to have a problem with truant teachers, especially on sunny Fridays. An *Orlando Sentinel* reporter recently found that one district had 35% more teachers sick on Fridays than Wednesdays. A Minneapolis reporter found similar absentee problems there.

Besides hurting kids' education, these suspicious absences deplete school funds that could be spent on other education priorities. Substitutes generally cost districts $60 to $100 a day.

Academic and financial costs incurred when teachers skip class argue for tougher attendance measures. But a recent *Education Week* survey of superintendents found little taste for confronting teachers' unions. One Florida superintendent threw up her hands in helplessness. She had no choice but to accept the word of teachers that they were sick, she said, and challenging teachers on skipping school wasn't something she was going to make into an "issue."

That's not good enough, especially considering recent evidence from researchers at Duke and Harvard universities confirming what common sense already suggests: Teacher absences affect student performance. The Harvard study found that 10 days of teacher absence is equivalent to a student drawing a rookie teacher rather than a second-year teacher. The Duke University study of North Carolina schools found similar results.

A few superintendents have launched programs to reward teachers who take fewer sick days than the contract allows. Other programs pay bonuses to schools that reduce their overall absence rates.

None of this should be necessary. Most teachers work hard in demanding jobs for modest pay, but they get home for dinner, have plenty of school holidays and breaks, and get summers off. It's grossly unprofessional for those who aren't really ill to take long weekends during the school year.

Perhaps supervisors need to start treating truant teachers like children and demanding notes from their parents and doctors.

opinion pages of newspapers regularly, or mainly during an election or controversy, in order to read the opinions, analysis, and interpretations of others on these issues.

Writers of editorials keep their readers—primary and secondary audiences—in mind as they compose. For example, the editorial board of *USA Today* published an editorial titled "When Teachers Cut Class" (May 1, 2008), aimed primarily at a conservative audience of parents, taxpayers, and citizens opposed to teachers' unions; it is also aimed at the teachers they critiqued in the editorial. Among the responses

| ■ Opinion |
| Opinion Home |
| Editorials and Debates |
| Columnists' Opinions |
| Readers' Opinions |

E-mail | Print |  RSS

## Time to show respect to America's educators

I take exception to USA TODAY's characterization of teachers in its editorial about high sick-leave rates in school districts on Fridays ("When teachers cut class," May 1).

After the terrorist attacks on Sept. 11, 2001, I pondered what I would do if my job situation changed. I went back to school and earned a master's degree in education.

Having spent nearly 30 years in business, where responsibilities are well-defined and employees are compensated for their work, I sometimes look at the options in teaching and wonder why such an important job is so poorly compensated yet receives more criticism than respect from the American public.

No one seems to consider that many teachers are the breadwinners in their families. Summers are often spent taking courses to keep up with licensure renewal or mandates.

Teachers don't exit school on the day students are released for the summer or return on the same day in the fall when students arrive. There are reports to complete, rooms to organize and lesson plans to write. Teachers spend hours writing lesson plans and aligning them to standards. I have done this, and it requires much effort.

Every teacher I know works hard to achieve success for his or her students. In business, we are expected to suffer failures in the pursuit of success. Teachers are held to a standard of 100%, and I cannot think of another profession, even medicine, that mandates 100% success, pays little and then harps when a person takes a day off — personal, sick or otherwise.

Myra Warne

Zanesville, Ohio

Do you listen to editorials read on the radio? What is your experience as a listener? As a writer, how would you decide on the best mode and medium for your editorial message?

to the editorial was a letter to the editor from Myra Warne, an Ohio teacher who took exception to *USA Today*'s opinion.

**Rhetorical appeals**   Editorial and opinion piece writers rely most on ethos and logos to persuade readers of the validity of their positions. As shown on page 200, the editorial board at *USA Today*, for example, uses evidence to appeal to readers' sense of logic. If the reader accepts the results of the university studies about the ill effects of teacher absences on student learning, then the reader should make the logical leap that teacher absences need to be dealt with seriously. Myra Warne responds to the editorial using a variety of appeals, including pathos. She establishes her ethos by discussing all her years in business, establishing her expertise in the work world. Additionally, she appeals to readers' emotions by illustrating the amount of work teachers do during the summer when they are not working, hoping that her readers sympathize with the dedication of teachers.

**Modes & media**   Newspaper editorials and opinion pieces are usually presented as written texts; sometimes they're accompanied by a small photo of the writer to establish the writer's credibility. Some editorials include charts or other infographics. Some editorials are presented as audio texts, such as the commentaries offered by National Public Radio. Editorials and opinion pieces can be found both in print, such as in newspapers and magazines, and digitally, such as on the sites for *The New York Times* and NPR.

## THE GENRE'S CONVENTIONS

**Elements of the genre**   Editorial and opinion piece writers do the following:

*Clearly present their work as opinion writing.* The distinction between an editorial or opinion piece and a news article is important: Editorials or opinion pieces are opinions based on research and analysis, whereas news articles are objective reporting based on research. That is, editorials reflect a personal view while news articles are supposed to be totally free of opinion. Editorials or opinion pieces are usually clearly labeled as *editorials* (or with another name such as *opinion, viewpoint, perspective,* or *commentary*).

*Write concisely.* An editorial or opinion piece is typically about five or so paragraphs long, which means the author needs to make his or her point quickly.

*Begin with an introduction that gets readers' attention.* For example, the authors of the *USA Today* piece on teachers' cutting class opens with a rhetorical question asking readers, "Remember those days when your teacher unexpectedly called in sick?" followed by a remark about the useless substitute. Immediately, readers are reminded of their own experiences and identify with the writers.

*Identify and address counterarguments.* Editorial and opinion piece writers make their strongest cases when they anticipate objections and opposition to their views. In the *Denver Post* editorial arguing for state control of marijuana (p. 199), the writers anticipate that readers might bring up the fact that state marijuana laws operate in conflict with federal laws. In response to this, the writers argue, "Those states may be operating outside of federal law, but it's with their citizens' consent."

*Offer potential solutions.* Often after explaining a problem, writers will examine potential solutions and suggest one over another. In the *USA Today* editorial, the writers mention some solutions but then conclude that the best one would be for teachers to simply stop taking sick days unless they are sick.

*Close with a simple but memorable statement.* For example, the final paragraph of the *USA Today* editorial is particularly memorable because of the writers' tone—and the sarcastic suggestion that, like absent children, absent teachers should provide a sick note from their parents.

*Invite readers to respond.* Many online editorials, such as the *USA Today* editorial, become discussion starters in which hundreds or even thousands of readers post replies to the original editorial and to other posts.

**Style**   Editorial and opinion piece writers do the following:

*Include concise detail.* Editorial and opinion piece writers use specific facts throughout their texts to support their position. Because they are making a case, they need to use enough evidence to convince readers, but they still need to keep the entire piece fairly brief.

*Use a variety of techniques.* To engage and persuade readers, editorial and opinion piece writers:

» Include quotations from experts to support their claims.

» Avoid errors in reasoning; such errors are known as logical fallacies. Here are some of the most common types:

   » *Red herring*: Distracting the reader from the real issue being argued; for example, "Global warming needs to be addressed, but people are struggling with gas prices."

   » *Ad hominem*: Attacking the person making an argument instead of addressing the argument; for example, "She says women should have equal rights, but look at how ugly she is."

   » *Hasty generalization*: Extrapolating unrealistically from one example; for example, "He lied; therefore all men are liars."

   » *Slippery slope*: Assuming that if one step is taken, then all sorts of catastrophic results will inevitably follow; for example, "If we increase taxes by 1 percent today, tomorrow our children will be paying more in taxes than they take home."

> » *Circular reasoning*: Defining a word by using the word, where the start is the same as the ending; for example, "The reason we should outlaw guns is that guns should be made illegal."

> » *Post hoc*: Confusing chronology with causality; for example, "The cat peed on the bedspread because I just washed it."

» Use analogies and refer to cultural and historical events so that readers will identify with the issue.

» Avoid jargon and instead use language that will appeal to readers who may not be familiar with the issue.

» Use rhetorical questions to spark readers' attention.

*Convey a clear, personable voice and tone.* Writers use clear, persuasive language as they present their opinions and support them with facts. Editorial writers often write in the first person (*I*) and in a friendly and inviting tone to reach a wide readership.

**Design**    Editorial and opinion piece writers—and the designers they work with—do the following:

*Write clear, interesting headlines.* Whether they're published in print or online, editorials, like news articles, are presented with a headline designed to get readers' attention and to make it clear what the editorialist is writing about. Editorials and opinion pieces are also clearly labeled as such, or with other terms, such as *opinions* or *commentaries*, that denote subjective writing.

*Repeat design features on the page.* Whether you're reading an editorial or opinion piece in print or online, you'll see certain design elements on every page; these elements include the name of the newspaper, perhaps presented as a logo or otherwise branded, at the top and bottom of the page. This helps the writers and designers establish the news organization's identity. You might also find a heading indicating what part of the paper or site you've navigated to ("Editorial," "Opinion," etc.). The date also appears in these spots for easy reference.

How do editorial writers use sources to support their arguments? What sources are most persuasive? Can anecdotal evidence be as convincing as statistical data?

Note: Design features of editorials and opinion pieces are generally similar to those of newspaper articles. See Chapter 3, page 131, for more on news article design.

**Sources**   Editorial and opinion piece writers do the following:

*Refer to specific examples.* The editorial board of *USA Today* offers several specific pieces of evidence to make their point (p. 200), such as the actual cost of substitutes, the results of the *Education Week* survey, and the results of the Harvard and Duke studies. The writers make the case by offering a variety of support from credible sources.

*Use attribution phrases.* Editorialists present evidence to support their points, often using attribution phrases to let readers know where the data came from. For instance, in the *USA Today* editorial, "An *Orlando Sentinel* reporter recently found" cues readers that the source of the information on the most common sick days is an *Orlando Sentinel* article.

## Guided Reading: Opinion Piece

## Katha Pollitt

### *Adam and Steve—Together at Last*

Katha Pollitt is a regular columnist for *The Nation* magazine, where she writes an opinion column called "Subject to Debate," which has won the National Magazine Award for Columns and Commentary. *The Nation*, like Pollitt's column, tackles political and social issues, usually from a left-wing political perspective. Pollitt's work has appeared in other magazines including *Harper's* and *The New Yorker*. Her persuasive essay "Adam and Steve—Together at Last" first appeared in the December 15, 2003, issue of *The Nation*. The essay disputes the legitimacy of arguments against same-sex marriage. Although same-sex marriage is legal in many countries, such as Canada and South Africa, it has been a controversial issue in the United States, with supporters claiming that allowing same-sex unions extends basic rights to homosexuals, and opponents maintaining that legalizing same-sex unions would jeopardize all marriages. *(Pages 206–08: Text © Katha Pollitt. Art Courtesy of* The Nation.*)*

▲ AUTHOR PHOTO
**Katha Pollitt.**
*Christina Pabst.*

**What is the composer, Katha Pollitt, doing?**

THE RHETORICAL
SITUATION

Purpose
Audience
Rhetorical appeals
Modes & media

*see page 207*

**How do I know this is an opinion piece?**

THE GENRE'S
CONVENTIONS

Elements of the genre
Style
Design
Sources

*see page 207*

# Nation.

HOME | BLOGS | COLUMNISTS | CURRENT ISSUE | MAGAZINE ARCHIVE | MULTIMEDIA          COMMUNITY | NATION BUILDERS | STUDENTS

POLITICS | WORLD | BOOKS & ARTS | ECONOMY | ENVIRONMENT | ACTIVISM | SOCIETY | LIVED HISTORY | NEW YORK: THE GILDED CITY

## Adam and Steve--Together at Last

Will someone please explain to me how permitting gays and lesbians to
marry threatens the institution of marriage?

*Katha Pollitt*

Will someone please explain to me how permitting gays and lesbians to
marry threatens the institution of marriage? Now that the Massachusetts
Supreme Court has declared gay marriage a constitutional right, opponents really have to get their arguments in line. The most popular theory,
advanced by David Blankenhorn, Jean Bethke Elshtain, and other social
conservatives is that under the tulle and orange blossom, *marriage* is
all about procreation. There's some truth to this as a practical matter—
couples often live together and tie the knot only when baby's on the way.
But whether or not marriage is the best framework for child-rearing,
having children isn't a marital requirement. As many have pointed out, the
law permits marriage to the infertile, the elderly, the impotent, and those
with no wish to procreate; it allows married couples to use birth control,
to get sterilized, to be celibate. There's something creepily authoritar-
ian and insulting about reducing marriage to procreation, as if intimacy
mattered less than biological fitness. It's not a view that anyone outside a
right-wing think tank, a Catholic marriage tribunal, or an ultra-Orthodox
rabbi's court is likely to find persuasive.

So scratch procreation. How about: Marriage is the way women domesticate
men. This theory, a favorite of right-wing writer George Gilder, has some
statistical support—married men are much less likely than singles to kill
people, crash the car, take drugs, commit suicide—although it overlooks such
husbandly failings as domestic violence, child abuse, infidelity, and abandonment. If a man rapes his wife instead of his date, it probably won't show up
on a police blotter, but has civilization moved forward? Of course, this view

THE
Nation.

HOME | BLOGS | COLUMNISTS | CURRENT ISSUE | MAGAZINE ARCHIVE | MULTIMEDIA          COMMUNITY | NATION BUILDERS | STUDENTS

POLITICS   WORLD   BOOKS & ARTS   ECONOMY   ENVIRONMENT   ACTIVISM   SOCIETY   LIVED HISTORY   NEW YORK: THE GILDED CITY

of marriage as a barbarian-adoption program doesn't explain why women should undertake it—as is obvious from the state of the world, they haven't been too successful at it, anyway. (Maybe men should civilize men—bring on the Fab Five!) Nor does it explain why marriage should be restricted to heterosexual couples. The gay men and lesbians who want to marry don't impinge on the male-improvement project one way or the other. Surely not even Gilder believes that a heterosexual pothead with plans for murder and suicide would be reformed by marrying a lesbian?

What about the argument from history? According to this, marriage has been around forever and has stood the test of time. Actually, though, marriage as we understand it—voluntary, monogamous, legally egalitarian, based on love, involving adults only—is a pretty recent phenomenon. For much of human history, polygyny was the rule—read your Old Testament—and in much of Africa and the Muslim world, it still is. Arranged marriages, forced marriages, child marriages, marriages predicated on the subjugation of women—gay marriage is like a fairy tale romance compared with most chapters of the history of wedlock.

The trouble with these and other arguments against gay marriage is that they overlook how loose, flexible, individualized, and easily dissolved the bonds of marriage already are. Virtually any man and woman can marry, no matter how ill assorted or little acquainted. An eighty-year-old can marry an eighteen-year-old; a john can marry a prostitute; two terminally ill patients can marry each other from their hospital beds. You can get married by proxy, like medieval royalty, and not see each other in the flesh for years. Whatever may have been the case in the past, what undergirds marriage in most people's minds today is not some sociobiological theory about reproduction or male socialization. Nor is it the enormous bundle of privileges society awards to married people. It's love, commitment, stability. Speaking just for myself, I don't like marriage. I prefer the old-fashioned ideal of monogamous free love, not that it worked out particularly well in my case. As a social mechanism, moreover, marriage seems to me a deeply

*Continues next page*

*Katha Pollitt, Adam and Steve—Together at Last*

THE RHETORICAL
SITUATION

**Purpose**

Pollitt wants to convince readers that gay marriage should be accepted as a "constitutional right."

**Audience**

Pollitt's readers are interested in the gay marriage debate. They may be socially liberal or conservative; if they are regular readers of *The Nation*, they're probably socially liberal.

THE GENRE'S
CONVENTIONS

**Elements of the genre**

Pollitt makes it clear that this is an opinion piece, beginning with the tone of her title, a play on Adam and Eve, and her first sentence: "Will someone please explain to me. . . ." She goes on to **relate her opinions** on gay marriage.

Pollitt **grabs attention** by starting with a question and a reference to a court decision.

*(Continued on p. 208.)*

**THE RHETORICAL
SITUATION**

**Rhetorical appeals**
By pointing out that
"having children
isn't a marital
requirement," Pollitt
appeals to **logos;** she
shows that it isn't
logical to disallow
same-sex marriages
on the basis that
same-sex couples
can't have children
together.
*(Continued on p. 209.)*

**THE GENRE'S
CONVENTIONS**

She strengthens
her position when
she identifies
and critiques
counterarguments.

**She closes with a
strong statement:**
"Gay marriage—it's
not about sex, it's
about separation of
church and state."
This simple line is
likely to stick with
readers long after
they've forgotten
Pollitt's specifics.

# Nation.

HOME | BLOGS | COLUMNISTS | CURRENT ISSUE | MAGAZINE ARCHIVE | MULTIMEDIA       COMMUNITY | NATION BUILDERS | STUDENTS

POLITICS    WORLD    BOOKS & ARTS    ECONOMY    ENVIRONMENT    ACTIVISM    SOCIETY    LIVED HISTORY    NEW YORK: THE GILDED CITY

unfair way of distributing social goods like health insurance and retirement checks, things everyone needs. Why should one's marital status determine how much you pay the doctor, or whether you eat cat food in old age, or whether a child gets a government check if a parent dies? It's outrageous that, for example, a working wife who pays Social Security all her life gets no more back from the system than if she had married a male worker earning the same amount and stayed home. Still, as long as marriage is here, how can it be right to deny it to those who want it? In fact, you would think that, given how many heterosexuals are happy to live in sin, social conservatives would welcome maritally minded gays with open arms. Gays already have the baby—they can adopt in many states, and lesbians can give birth in all of them—so why deprive them of the marital bathwater?

At bottom, the objections to gay marriage are based on religious prejudice: The marriage of man and woman is "sacred" and opening it to same-sexers violates its sacral nature. That is why so many people can live with civil unions but draw the line at marriage—spiritual union. In fact, polls show a striking correlation of religiosity, especially evangelical Protestantism, with opposition to gay marriage and with belief in homosexuality as a choice, the famous "gay lifestyle." For these people gay marriage is wrong because it lets gays and lesbians avoid turning themselves into the straights God wants them to be. As a matter of law, however, marriage is not about Adam and Eve versus Adam and Steve. It's not about what God blesses, it's about what the government permits. People may think *marriage* is a word wholly owned by religion, but actually it's wholly owned by the state. No matter how big your church wedding, you still have to get a marriage license from City Hall. And just as divorced people can marry even if the Catholic Church considers it bigamy, and Muslim and Mormon men can only marry one woman even if their holy books tell them they can wed all the girls in Apartment 3G, two men or two women should be able to marry, even if religions oppose it and it makes some heterosexuals, raised in those religions, uncomfortable.

Gay marriage—it's not about sex, it's about separation of church and state.

## THE RHETORICAL SITUATION

Pollitt establishes her **ethos** by writing with authority and showing her familiarity with historical facts and theories (such as those put forth by Blankenhorn and Elshtain).

### Modes & media

**Mode = written** The digital version also includes a visual, a small headshot of Pollitt. Most editorials and opinion pieces are written or audio. Words are vital to an editorialist making his or her point because the specificity and clarity of the editorialist's position is so important.

**Medium = print and digital** The content is the same in both versions, but the design and context are different. In the print version, the essay gets one complete page of the magazine. In the digital version, the column shares space with a menu bar at the top and several items that occupy the left-hand side of the screen, including a small headshot of Pollitt and links to related articles on *The Nation*'s Web site. These differences result from the varying needs and desires of print and digital editorial audiences.

## THE GENRE'S CONVENTIONS

### Style

Pollitt **uses specific facts** to back up her views; e.g., she provides details of aspects of George Gilder's theories and refers to other source texts, including the Bible.

She **uses rhetorical questions** effectively; for example, to hold the reader's interest, she asks, "Why should one's marital status determine how much you pay the doctor?"

**Her tone is personal and informal.** For example, she writes, "Speaking just for myself, I don't like marriage."

### Design

The "Subject to Debate" **headline and its visual design draw readers in.** For easy reference, *The Nation*'s title appears at the top of the page. In the online version of this article, there are "About the Author," "Also by the Author," and "Related Topics" headings to orient readers within the site and expand their reading.

### Sources

Pollitt **refers to several specific sources** (the voices of opposition), such as David Blankenhorn, the founder and president of the socially conservative Institute for American Values, and ethics professor Jean Bethke Elshtain, as well as the Old Testament. While sources are linked in some online editorials and opinion pieces, that's not the case here.

## Questions: Analyzing Pollitt's opinion piece

**1. Purpose.** Does Pollitt convince you that gay marriage is "not about sex, it's about separation of church and state"? Why or why not?

**2. Audience.** How do you think a person opposed to gay marriage might respond to Pollitt's essay?

**3. Rhetorical appeals.** List the counterarguments Pollitt addresses. Do you think she's left out any? If so, why do you think she chose to focus on the ones she did?

**4. Rhetorical appeals.** How does Pollitt build her case? How does she appeal to her audience using logos?

**5. Rhetorical appeals.** To what extent does Pollitt come across as authoritative and knowledgeable? What does she do to convince you she is (1) authoritative and knowledgeable or (2) lacking in authority and knowledge? Explain.

**6. Modes & media.** Imagine that Pollitt had included a large black-and-white photo of two men kissing at the top of the essay. How would the addition of this image add to or detract from the effectiveness of the editorial?

**7. Elements of the genre.** Although Pollitt's essay doesn't feature a clearly stated position or thesis statement at the beginning, how does she make her position clear from the beginning? Where does Pollitt state her position most clearly?

**8. Elements of the genre.** How do the organization and paragraph structure help you pick out the specific counterarguments Pollitt addresses in her column?

**9. Style.** How would you characterize the tone of Pollitt's essay? How does it affect you as a reader? Do you think anyone would consider her language inflammatory? How does this work for or against her position?

**10. Style.** What does the title allude to? Why is that allusion appropriate for this essay?

**11. Design.** The final sentence is set off in its own paragraph. How does this add to the impact of Pollitt's conclusion?

**12. Sources.** Pollitt does not cite sources in every paragraph. How does she convince you that she is familiar with source material about, say, the history of marriage, without directly citing sources?

# Drafting an Editorial or Opinion Piece

---

## CHECKLIST: Drafting an Editorial or Opinion Piece Thinking of writing an editorial? Ask yourself the following questions.

### WHAT'S MY RHETORICAL SITUATION?

☐ **Purpose.** What is my purpose? And what do I want to persuade others to think or do? Do I want readers to see things from a different perspective? To take action? Do I want them to completely change their minds on an issue? How feasible is it to try to change a person's mind?

☐ **Audience.** Who am I trying to persuade? What are my audience's concerns about the issue I'm writing about? What do they fear? What is their stake in the issue (what do they personally have to risk losing if they do what I want)?

☐ **Rhetorical appeals.** How will I establish myself as reasonable and authoritative on this issue? How can I use organization to appeal to my audience's sense of logos? Will my audience respond to emotional appeals or will I seem manipulative if I appeal to pathos?

☐ **Modes & media.** Will I use written words or audio or video to convey my point? Based on the audience I have in mind—are they more likely to read or listen to an editorial in print, on the radio, or on the Internet?

### WHAT GENRE CONVENTIONS MATTER?

☐ **Elements of the genre.** How can I make it clear that I'm writing an opinion piece? How can I get my audience's attention immediately and show them how important and relevant this issue is to their lives? Which potential objections and counterarguments should I address? How can I make the closing of my editorial memorable?

☐ **Style.** Would it help to support my case by bringing in quotations from experts? Are there analogies that I could use that would appeal to my readers? What types of rhetorical questions would be most compelling for my editorial? How will I keep my language persuasive yet friendly?

☐ **Design.** Do I want to design a heading or logo for my column to identify myself as the author? How can I use a heading, logo, or other design element to develop my ethos?

☐ **Sources.** What kinds of sources will be most useful and most interesting and persuasive to my audience? How might I bring in sources to address potential objections and opposing arguments?

---

## PRACTICE Want to experiment? Draft your own editorial or opinion piece.

Think about an issue you care deeply about. Think about what your position is on the issue. Then brainstorm a list of reasons/evidence that supports your position. What are some of the counterarguments? Do research so that you can provide some support, as Pollitt does with different theorists and their positions. Then combine your research and ideas into an editorial or opinion piece that convinces your audience that your position is a valid one.

# RESEARCHED ARGUMENTS

A researched argument is any work in which a writer presents an argument and backs it up with solid sources. Most academic research papers are researched arguments (see also the peer-reviewed journal article discussed in Chapter 3, p. 148). Writers of researched arguments do the following:

» Investigate a topic and work with sources

» Make a specific and persuasive case about that topic

» Incorporate in their writing voices of their sources through summary, para-phrase, and quotation

» Cite those sources in the body of the composition

» List the sources at the end

When you read an argument text, are you more swayed by personal opinion and anecdote or research as support? Does it depend on the subject matter? Your expertise on the subject? The genre itself? Explain.

The main purpose of writing a researched argument is to persuade your readers of the merits of your argument. Drawing on and citing your sources builds a case for your argument.

Researched arguments appear in the same places that research papers do: in the classroom, in peer-reviewed journals, in magazines, and on the Internet in the form of blog entries and other argumentative pieces. Depending on the level of research they've conducted and where they publish their work, authors of this genre may be scholars, recognized by other scholars as experts on the subject they are writing about, or they may be reporters, bloggers, or other types of experts on their subject. For example, an experienced snowboarder who researches different snowboarding designs and blogs in favor of one would be considered an expert on the subject she's writing about.

For more examples of **researched compositions**, see the Index of Genres on page G-1.

At work, researched arguments often take the form of reports or memos. When an employee wants to persuade an organization to change a policy or procedure, he may write a memo or report in which he refers to specific research or to policies at similar organizations.

# Analyzing Researched Arguments: What to Look For

THE RHETORICAL SITUATION

**Purpose**   We write researched arguments because we want to persuade others to share our point of view on a topic. We may be looking for readers to simply agree, or maybe to take a specific action. When you write a researched argument, you begin by conducting research in hopes that the quality and quantity of the data you present will convince readers. For example, Liz had the following experience: her department at Metro State recently considered whether or not to change the amount of credit students will receive for certain AP scores. Liz and a colleague argued their position on how much credit Metro State should give students in a memo to the department that cited the AP credit policies of several other similar universities and colleges. Their purpose was to get their colleagues to agree with them and to take action.

Do any of the blogs you read feature researched arguments? How persuasive do you find them? Have you ever changed your view on a topic because of a researched argument you read on a blog?

Henry Fong, host of the blog *FitBomb*, writes to persuade readers to adopt or at least consider the exercise and eating plans he favors. In the post on page 214, he argues for the Paleo Diet, citing research to back up his views on the benefits of "eating like a caveman." As you can see, he uses hyperlinks to cite his sources, furthering his ethos and logos. This is an example of a researched argument presented as a blog post.

**Audience**   Authors of researched arguments usually write for others who are interested in the topic being discussed. Readers may or may not agree with the argument the writer proposes, but they're generally curious enough to read about the perspectives of others. If you're an expert writing a researched argument for a peer-reviewed journal, then your audience is other experts. If you're writing a memo or report at work, then your audience is your colleagues. If you're writing a blog, such as Henry Fong does at *FitBomb*, you're writing for others who most likely share your enthusiasm for fitness—but who may or may not agree with everything you propose.

☞ **Attention, researchers & writers!**

Poorly integrated and cited research casts doubt on you as an author and seriously compromises your ethos—while a smart use of sources does a lot to build it. See Chapter 7 for more on integrating and citing sources.

In the case of the *FitBomb* post on the Paleo Diet, it's clear the author is aware of his readers' potential skepticism. The Q&A format he adopts for the argument takes into account potential objections, and he addresses the reader directly: "What? Not good enough? I hear you. Frankly, I resisted going Paleo for quite a while."

BLOG POST ▶
**Henry Fong,** "What
Is the Paleo Diet?," a
researched argument
at *FitBomb*. All images
on pages 214–22. Henry
Fong/Fitbomb.com.

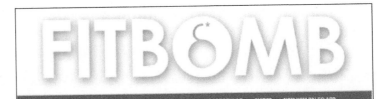

START HERE    ABOUT    CROSSFIT    WHAT IS THE PALEO DIET?    MOST POPULAR    SHIRTS    NOM NOM PALEO APP

## What Is The Paleo Diet?

### INTRODUCTION

Even after eating this way for years, we still manage to catch
some of our dining companions off-guard. Their eyebrows
shoot up when we order our food sans bread, pasta, rice,
polenta or beans. The questions are always the same:

"Are you on Atkins or something?"

"Trying to lose weight?"

"You don't even eat *whole* grains?"

"What the hell is the matter with you?"

Well, here exactly is the matter with me: I EAT PALEO. As in
the Paleolithic (or "Paleo") Diet. You may have heard of it as
the Caveman Diet.

If you're feeling bookish, Loren Cordain's "The Paleo Diet" and Mark
Sisson's "The Primal Blueprint" introduced the concept of ancestral
eating approaches to tons of people. (Sisson, in particular, is an
excellent resource for tips and information on implementing this type of
nutritional template. Check out his massively popular site, Mark's Daily
Apple, for more.)

If you'd rather gaze into a computer screen, start with Cordain's Paleo
Diet FAQ, Sisson's how-to on living "Primally," and J. Stanton's "Eat
Like a Predator, Not Like Prey." This page on Melissa McEwen's site
also contains lots of useful resources for newbies. Hivelogic's Paleo
link primer is a great starting point, too. (And I'm not just saying that
'cause my wife's blog is listed as a Paleo cooking resource.)

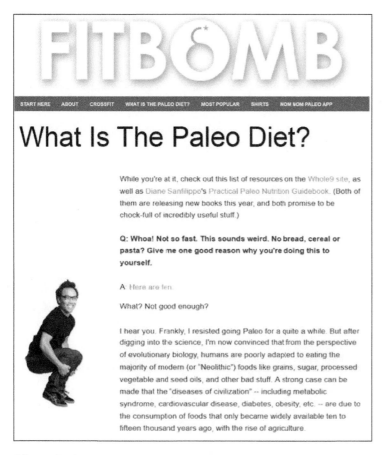

**FITBOMB**

START HERE   ABOUT   CROSSFIT   WHAT IS THE PALEO DIET?   MOST POPULAR   SHIRTS   NOM NOM PALEO APP

# What Is The Paleo Diet?

While you're at it, check out this list of resources on the Whole9 site, as well as Diane Sanfilippo's Practical Paleo Nutrition Guidebook. (Both of them are releasing new books this year, and both promise to be chock-full of incredibly useful stuff.)

**Q: Whoa! Not so fast. This sounds weird. No bread, cereal or pasta? Give me one good reason why you're doing this to yourself.**

A: Here are ten.

What? Not good enough?

I hear you. Frankly, I resisted going Paleo for a quite a while. But after digging into the science, I'm now convinced that from the perspective of evolutionary biology, humans are poorly adapted to eating the majority of modern (or "Neolithic") foods like grains, sugar, processed vegetable and seed oils, and other bad stuff. A strong case can be made that the "diseases of civilization" -- including metabolic syndrome, cardiovascular disease, diabetes, obesity, etc. -- are due to the consumption of foods that only became widely available ten to fifteen thousand years ago, with the rise of agriculture.

**Rhetorical appeals**   When writing a researched argument, authors can establish ethos by:

» Describing their research methods

» Explaining the data they collected and how they analyzed it

» Discussing their findings and conclusions in detail

» Citing their sources appropriately

» Writing as directly and persuasively as possible

Writers can establish logos by:

» Stating their position clearly

» Stating each aspect of their argument clearly—and in an order that makes sense

» Anticipating and addressing objections

» Supporting their claims with evidence—including the views of others (drawn from their sources)

The author of the *FitBomb* post outlines his information and argument clearly. He explains what the diet is, and also makes a case for adopting the diet.

As this book goes to press, Henry Fong of *Fitbomb* presents his information on the Paleo Diet in the following parts, which are in turn broken out into a Q&A format:

Introduction

1. What to Eat and Why

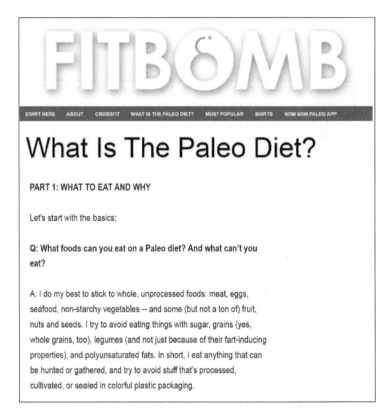

**What Is The Paleo Diet?**

**PART 1: WHAT TO EAT AND WHY**

Let's start with the basics:

**Q: What foods can you eat on a Paleo diet? And what can't you eat?**

A: I do my best to stick to whole, unprocessed foods: meat, eggs, seafood, non-starchy vegetables -- and some (but not a ton of) fruit, nuts and seeds. I try to avoid eating things with sugar, grains (yes, whole grains, too), legumes (and not just because of their fart-inducing properties), and polyunsaturated fats. In short, I eat anything that can be hunted or gathered, and try to avoid stuff that's processed, cultivated, or sealed in colorful plastic packaging.

Do you prefer an author to sound like a know-it-all or would you rather an author admit that he or she doesn't know everything about the topic?

2. What's Wrong with What We Eat?

3. You Aren't What You Eat (So Eat Some Fat)

4. Why I Eat Paleo

5. Mythbusting

6. Foods to Avoid and Why

7. Transitioning to Paleo

What voice and tone are appropriate for a researched argument? How might this vary, depending on context and medium?

Whether or not you agree with his take on "eating like a caveman," the author of the *FitBomb* post appeals to readers by doing much of what is described in the above section on ethos and logos. Further, he appeals to pathos through his use of humor, as in the excerpt that follows.

**Modes & media**   Researched arguments published as articles in peer-reviewed journals, as memos, and as reports are text based and may include visuals such as charts, graphs, and images to support and illustrate points. These types of pieces can be available in print or online. For example, the memo about AP scores that Liz wrote was circulated by e-mail. Blog entries, of course, are digital.

## Elements of the genre

*Author states a thesis or makes a clear claim.* To make a position clear, a writer can (1) indicate the topic at hand and his or her position on it right in the title, (2) provide a clear thesis, doing so right at the beginning, or (3) combine both. In the *FitBomb* post on the Paleo Diet, the author uses clear subheadings for the various sections. In the section titled "What Really Causes Obesity?" he answers the question in a clear thesis in paragraph 1:

> The short answer: Excess carbohydrates. Especially sugar.

This clearly shows that the writer will argue against the commonly held belief that consuming too much fat leads to obesity; instead, he will argue that sugar causes us to be overweight.

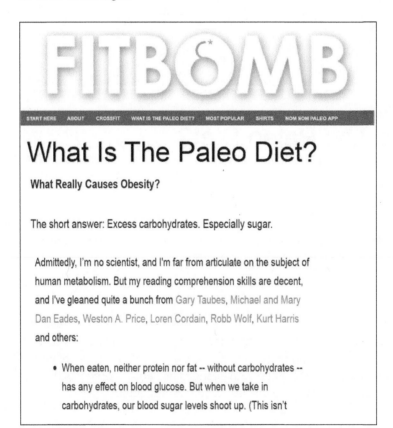

*Authors present an argument.* For example, the *FitBomb* blogger writes to explain the Paleo Diet—but mainly to persuade readers to adopt it. He supports his main argument with seven sections—moving from what the diet is, to what research shows about the diet, to why he likes it—and ends with advice on how readers can transition to it themselves. In each part of his argument, the writer supports himself with evidence.

*Authors base their arguments on solid research.* All researched writing relies on research of some kind. Most writers support their ideas by drawing on the research of others—of experts and leaders in the field. As a student, unless you do primary research (such as conducting interviews), you most likely draw on the research of others in your researched writing.

Some authors—mainly academics writing for peer-reviewed journals—draw on their own research, particularly if they've conducted a study or survey of some kind that brings in data. Arguments for peer-reviewed journals are usually written in a formal style using precise language. They are also reviewed by others in the field for accuracy and reliability. (For more on peer-reviewed journal articles, see Chapter 3.)

When Liz and Amy present papers at conferences, they draw on and cite specific research done by academic experts and colleagues to support their arguments. The *FitBomb* blogger cites more than two hundred sources, including research by established experts, such as the Weston A. Price Foundation, which focuses on nutrition education.

*Authors address counterarguments.* To build logos, writers need to acknowledge contrasting or opposing arguments and either (1) refute them by exposing their holes or presenting evidence that outweighs them or (2) concede that they are legitimate and then explain why, despite this legitimacy, the audience should take the author's position. In Liz's AP score memo, she conceded to the opposing argument that some students with AP scores of 3 in English might no longer apply to Metro State if they wouldn't receive credit for a composition class. However, she explained that in the long run, these students would actually be more successful if they were required to take a composition class at Metro State.

*Authors synthesize and attribute the work of others.* As noted above, citing sources—and specific examples—builds ethos. It's also a good idea to pull information from multiple sources and to synthesize it by showing readers how these sources align and differ. When a writer relies on only one source, it makes the argument look weak to readers, and therefore much less persuasive. (For more on synthesizing sources, see Chapter 7.)

## Style

*Authors title their work to make their position clear.* Authors of researched arguments title their work to make clear the topic they're writing about and what their position is. For example, for her memo subject line, which serves as the memo's title, Liz wrote: "Why we should raise AP scores for composition credit."

*Authors write with authority.* Writers use a strong voice and tone to convey expertise on a topic, support their ethos, and persuade their readers.

*Authors get readers' attention with simple but memorable introductions and closing statements.* For example, the *FitBomb* blogger starts with an anecdote.

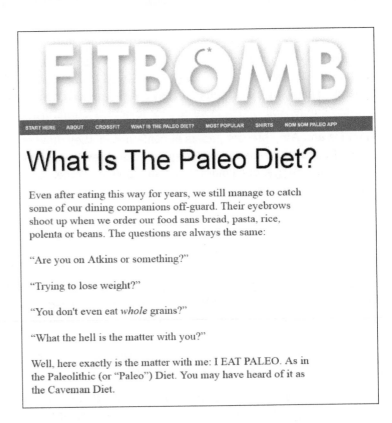

**START HERE**   **ABOUT**   **CROSSFIT**   **WHAT IS THE PALEO DIET?**   **MOST POPULAR**   **SHIRTS**   **NOM NOM PALEO APP**

## What Is The Paleo Diet?

Even after eating this way for years, we still manage to catch some of our dining companions off-guard. Their eyebrows shoot up when we order our food sans bread, pasta, rice, polenta or beans. The questions are always the same:

"Are you on Atkins or something?"

"Trying to lose weight?"

"You don't even eat *whole* grains?"

"What the hell is the matter with you?"

Well, here exactly is the matter with me: I EAT PALEO. As in the Paleolithic (or "Paleo") Diet. You may have heard of it as the Caveman Diet.

Toward the end of his argument, the blogger concedes that the Paleo Diet isn't for everyone, but he does so with humor—subtly critiquing the "low-fat approach" and presenting a mental image of grass-fed beef, a central part of the Paleo Diet.

I have a number of friends who are committed to strict calorie-counting as a weight loss strategy, and I know plenty of others who've adopted the "everything in moderation" approach to eating. Some still look to egg-white omelets and low-fat (but high-sugar) cookies for weight loss purposes. If they're happy with those approaches, then that's their choice. I'm not going to force-feed them grass-fed beef. (I'm saving that stuff for me!)

*Authors use detail.* The more specific writers are—in terms of both the main point and the research they're drawing on—the better and more persuasive the argument.

## Design

*Authors use subheadings.* Many writers divide their arguments into sections with subheadings that make a long, complex piece easier to navigate. (See p. 216.) Subheadings also signal readers that an author is shifting his or her focus.

*Authors support their arguments with images.* Photos, charts, and illustrations convey complex information visually—and can serve as sources. For example, the *FitBomb* blogger uses images to back up his argument about the Paleo Diet, such as the infographic on page 222, taken from a like-minded site, PaleolithicDiet.com.

## Sources

*Authors curate sources carefully.* Authors of researched arguments use sources that their readers will respect. When Liz wrote the AP credit memo, she knew her audience—colleagues in the English department—would be swayed by what other English departments do. In the case of the *FitBomb* post, the author draws on sources by writers he identifies as experts on the Paleo Diet.

*Authors cite sources—according to genre conventions.* An author of a peer-reviewed journal article would include a bibliographic list at the end of the article and use parenthetical citations throughout. A blogger simply embeds links to his or her sources, as the *FitBomb* blogger does.

For more examples of **researched writing** and **academic writing,** including student work, see the Index of Genres on page G-1.

## Chase Dickinson (Student)

### *Are Kids on a One-Way Path to Violence?*

Chase Dickinson, a student from Herriman, Utah, wrote the following researched argument when he was a freshman at Weber State University, where he studied geoscience. As he mentions in the following essay, Dickinson worked for a video game vendor called Play N Trade, which factors into the argument he makes about video games in "Are Kids on a One-Way Path to Violence?" The essay, which he wrote for his English composition course, was also published in Weber State's journal of student work, called *Weber Writes*, edited in 2010 by Scott Rogers and Sylvia Newman.

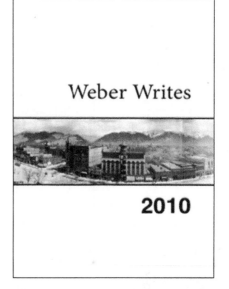

▼ STUDENT PHOTO, JOURNAL COVER, ▶ & UNIVERSITY WEB SITE ▼
**Chase Dickinson;** *Weber Writes*, the student journal that published Dickinson's researched essay; and Weber State University's site. *Author photo: Chase Dickinson. Journal cover: Weber State University. Web screen: Weber State University.*

What is the
composer,
**Chase
Dickinson**,
doing?

THE RHETORICAL
SITUATION

Purpose
Audience
Rhetorical appeals
Modes & media

*see page 225*

How do I
know this is
**a researched
argument**?

THE GENRE'S
CONVENTIONS

Elements of the genre
Style
Design
Sources

*see page 226*

# Chase Dickinson
## *Are Kids on a One-Way Path to Violence?*

In the popular video game *Grand Theft Auto* (GTA), players are thrust into a world without laws, free to do just about anything they want. Stealing cars, killing civilians, and causing general mayhem are common occurrences in the fictitious world of Liberty City (Rockstar Leeds). In fact, GTA is about as lawless as games get. But can a game such as *Grand Theft Auto* actually fuel real-world violence? There are many who believe so, and violent video games have therefore become a hotly debated topic in today's headlines.

If you were to listen to politicians and critics, the relationship between video games and crime is blatantly clear: children who play video games will either become more aggressive or actually commit real-world acts of violence. According to the lawyers of Lee Malvo, the young "DC Sniper," Malvo learned to shoot by playing "very realistic and gory" video games. These games were also said to have "desensitized (him) . . . to train him to shoot human forms over and over" (qtd. in Provan). Another popular argument against violent video games comes in the form of the infamous Columbine shootings in which Dylan Klebold and Eric Harris killed thirteen students and injured twenty-three more before killing themselves. During the investigation that followed, it was discovered that both teenagers enjoyed playing the bloody first-person shooter *Doom*, and that they went on the rampage shortly after their parents took the game away from them. It has also been speculated that the pair created a level in *Doom* with the same layout as their school in order to plan out their attack (Mikkelson). Yet another argument finds Jack Thompson, a leader in the fight against violent video games, blaming the Virginia Tech shooting on the first-person shooter *Counter-Strike*, saying that once again the shooter trained for his crime by playing the popular first-person shooter (qtd. in Benedetti).

Dickinson, *One-Way Path to Violence?* *Continued*  ~Thesis~

¶ With video games rapidly gaining popularity, we have to ask ourselves if these crimes are actually caused by the increasing violence in games. While there are many who tend to think so, I believe that it is not the fault of the games themselves, but the lack of parental supervision and interaction with today's youth. Also, preexisting mental disorders have been found to play a huge role in how different people will react to video games. "

Take, for example, the DC sniper shootings. *Halo*, the game that Malvo supposedly used to prepare for his crimes, employs the use of unrealistic guns to shoot giant alien bugs (Bungie). Such actions are hardly effective ways to learn how to shoot a sniper rifle at human beings. Malvo even admitted that he trained by shooting a real gun at makeshift targets with paper plates for heads (Provan). Similarly, the claims that the Columbine shooters created a level with their school's layout were never found to be true. In fact, all of the levels they made were later found on their Web site, and all of them were based on fictitious locations on alien planets (Mikkelson). Lastly, no one was ever reported to have seen Seung-Hui Cho, the Virginia Tech shooter, playing any video games. His roommate told *The New York Times* that he would sometimes enter Cho's room and find Cho sitting at his desk, staring into nothingness (Biggs). He wasn't staring at a computer and playing *Counter-Strike*, but was rather staring at nothing at all.

In addition, Seung-Hui Cho had been diagnosed with selective mutism, a severe anxiety disorder, as well as major depressive disorder (Adams). The DC shooter had a long history of anti-social and criminal behavior, including the torturing of small animals (Kutner 8). Similarly, FBI investigations were able to conclude that Klebold was significantly depressed and suicidal, and Harris was a sociopath (Kutner 8).

Ultimately, it falls upon the parents to filter what gets to their kids, and, when a known mental problem exists, parents should be that much more strict on what their kids play. As an avid

**Purpose**

Dickinson wants to persuade readers that video games do not cause violent behavior in mentally healthy children.

**Audience**

His readers are his instructor, his classmates, and the students at Weber State University who read the journal *Weber Writes*.

**Rhetorical appeals**

Dickinson develops his **ethos** by stating that he is a gamer himself and that he's even worked in the industry.

By noting that the DC Sniper trained at a shooting range, Dickinson appeals to readers' sense of **logos** to question the connection between the DC Sniper and his video game experience.

*Continues next page*

Chase Dickinson (Student), *Are Kids on a One-Way Path to Violence?*

Dickinson, *One-Way Path to Violence?* *Continued*

THE GENRE'S
CONVENTIONS

**Elements of the
genre**

**States a thesis or
makes a clear claim.**
Dickinson's is "I
believe that [violent
behavior in people
who play video
games] is not the
fault of the games
themselves, but
the lack of parental
supervision and
interaction with
today's youth."

**Presents an
argument based
on research.**
He presents
his argument
in paragraph 3
and develops it
in subsequent
paragraphs—
reasoning that
the DC Sniper,
Columbine shooters,
and Virginia Tech
shooter had histories
of mental illness,
and that is what
the crimes should
be attributed to.
He argues that
parents should
monitor children's
use of games and
take mental health
into account when
deciding what their
children can handle.

*(Continued on p. 228.)*

gamer myself, and as someone who has worked in the industry,
I understand the sense of accomplishment received from a well
placed shot in *Modern Warfare* just as much as I understand
that video games are not real. I was personally raised buying
and playing games under the supervision of my parents, and
am a strong supporter of such supervision. Even so, according to the anti-videogame activist Jack Thompson and others
with his mindset, I should be a ball of boiling hatred ready to
explode at the slightest provocation (Musgrove).

Contrary to the claims of many naysayers, it is becoming easier
to filter what a child does and does not play. A rating system
implemented by the Entertainment Software Rating Board
(ESRB) provides a fantastic way for parents to monitor what
their kids are playing. This rating system issues an age range for
each game, disclosing the full contents of the game. The most
common ratings include E (Everyone, suitable for everyone age
six and older), T (Teen, suitable for ages thirteen and older), and
M (Mature, suitable for ages seventeen and older). The AO rating (Adult Only) is the only one higher than the M rating, and
is actually considered to be a death sentence for games because
brick-and-mortar stores will not sell them. AO- and M-rated
games are the ones that come under the most fire from the
media because they contain the most violent and bloody content.
However, many people don't realize that in order to purchase an
M-rated game from any major retailer, the customer must be at
least seventeen years of age. Because of this age restriction, it is
harder for young children to get their hands on violent content
without parental approval (Entertainment Software Assoc.).

There is no denying that video games have matured since their
introduction in the '70s. Back then, games meant playing *Pong*
or *Space Invaders* with friends and family. Today, games are
becoming more and more complex, with violence playing a
large role in almost all modern titles. Still, with parents staying involved in their kids' lives, it is possible to filter violent
content and keep it to a minimum, which can prevent any type

Dickinson, *One-Way Path to Violence?* Continued

THE RHETORICAL
SITUATION

**Modes & media**

**Mode = written**
Dickinson's
assignment
specified that he
write an essay;
however, sometimes
assignments allow
students the latitude
to choose another
mode, such as video
or audio essay.
Dickinson could have
included visuals with
his essay, perhaps
screen shots of
the video games
mentioned in the
essay or mug shots
of the DC Sniper.

**Medium = print**
Again, Dickinson
was required by
his assignment to
produce an essay
in print form,
but researched
arguments often
appear digitally, on
blogs, for example.

of aggressive behavior from developing. And with resources such as ESRB, it is becoming easier and easier to keep children from playing games that are not age appropriate. Rather than focusing on trying to ban video games for their so-called influence on violent crime, an emphasis on parental supervision should be implemented in the fight against modern-day crime.

## Works Cited

Adams, Duncan. "The Alienation and Anger of Seung-Hui Cho." *The Roanoke Times*, 31 Aug. 2007, www.roanoke .com/vtinvestigation/wb/130177.

Benedetti, Winda. "Were Video Games to Blame for Massacre?" *MSNBC.com*, 20 Apr. 2007, www.roanoke .com/vtinvestigation/wb/130177.

Biggs, John. "Why Video Games Don't Cause Violence." *CrunchGear.com*, 18 Apr. 2007, techcrunch.com/2007/ 04/18/why-video-games-dont-cause-violence/.

Bungie, developer. *Halo: Combat Evolved*. Microsoft Studios, 15 Nov. 2001, www.halowaypoint.com/en-us.

Entertainment Software Association. *Entertainment Software Rating Board*, www.esrb.org. Accessed 27 Jan. 2001.

Kutner, Lawrence, and Cheryl Olson. *Grand Theft Childhood: The Surprising Truth About Violent Video Games and What Parents Can Do*. Simon & Schuster, 2008, p. 8.

Mikkelson, Barbara. "Columbine Doom Levels." *Snopes.com*, 1 Jan. 2005, www.snopes.com/horrors/madmen/doom.asp.

Musgrove, Mike. "Va. Tech: Dr. Phil and Jack Thompson Blame Video Games." *The Washington Post*, 17 Apr. 2007, voices.washingtonpost.com/posttech/2007/04/va_tech_dr _phil_jack_thompson.html.

Provan, Alexander. "The Education of Lee Boyd Malvo." *Bidoun*, 13 Jan. 2009, www.bidoun.org/magazine/16-kids/ the-education-of-lee-boyd-malvo-by-alexander-provan/.

Rockstar Leeds and Rockstar North, developers. *Grand Theft Auto: Liberty City Stories*. Rockstar Games, Capcom, 24 Oct. 2005, www.rockstargames.com/libertycitystories.

**Dickinson, *One-Way Path to Violence?* Continued**

THE GENRE'S CONVENTIONS

**Acknowledges counterarguments.** For example, in paragraph 2, the author mentions that lawyers claimed there were connections between their clients' violence and use of video games.

**Refutes or concedes counterarguments.** For example, in paragraphs 4 and 5, the author discredits the links others have made between specific criminals and video game habits.

**Cites specific examples, synthesizing them into his main argument.** Rather than being general, the author specifies shooters (DC Sniper, Columbine, and Virginia Tech) and particular games (*Grand Theft Auto*, *Doom*, *Halo*, and *Counter-Strike*).

### Style

**Descriptive title.** Dickinson's title makes it clear that his essay deals with kids and violence.

**Gets readers' attention in the introduction.** Dickinson accomplishes this by stating that players are "free to do just about anything they want" in the game *Grand Theft Auto*.

**Closes with a simple, memorable statement.** His final sentence reads: "Rather than focusing on trying to ban video games for their so-called influence on violent crime, an emphasis on parental supervision should be implemented in the fight against modern-day crime."

**Strong authoritative voice and tone.** The author chooses to avoid phrases such as "I think" and "in my opinion" but is still present in the essay.

**Uses detail.** For example, he names the names of violent criminals and identifies the games they're associated with.

### Design

For this brief essay, the author decided that subheadings and explanatory notes would be inappropriate. When he submitted it for class, it was double-spaced. For use in *Weber Writes*, it was single-spaced to conform to that journal's design.

### Sources

Using the MLA style of documentation, the author cites sources in the body of the text and at the end in a Works Cited list. His sources are varied and include video games, works by scholars and journalists, and the fact-checking site Snopes.com. (For help with documenting sources, see Ch. 7. For guidance on the MLA style, see pp. 393–414.)

## Questions: Analyzing Dickinson's researched argument

**1. Purpose.** Has Dickinson persuaded you that video games cannot be conclusively linked to violent behavior in players? Why or why not?

**2. Audience.** Besides Dickinson's professor and classmates, who else do you think might be an appropriate audience for this essay? Would Dickinson need to revise his essay to make it accessible for other audiences?

**3. Rhetorical appeals.** What are two techniques Dickinson uses to develop his ethos?

**4. Rhetorical appeals.** Dickinson's appeals to ethos and logos are discussed in the annotations. Can you find any appeals to pathos in the essay?

**5. Modes & media.** How would the inclusion of screen shots of the video games mentioned add to or detract from the essay?

**6. Elements of the genre.** How effective do you think Dickinson's refutation of the counterarguments is? Can you think of other refutations he could have used?

**7. Style.** Dickinson begins his essay by stating that players are "free to do just about anything they want" in *Grand Theft Auto*. What are some other ways Dickinson could have gotten readers' attention at the very beginning? For example, how could a reference to one of the criminals mentioned in the essay be used in the introduction?

**8. Style.** Dickinson writes in a strong, declarative voice rather than in a tentative "I'm just a student" voice. Find two or three sentences that are particularly strong and analyze the techniques Dickinson uses to come across as authoritative in these sentences.

**9. Design.** Because this is a short essay, Dickinson opted against using subheadings. If the essay were developed into a longer one, say fifteen pages, what are some subheadings he might use?

**10. Sources.** Look over Dickinson's Works Cited list. Are there some sources that appear to be more reliable than others?

# Drafting a Researched Argument

---

**CHECKLIST: Drafting a Researched Argument** Thinking of writing a researched argument? Ask yourself the following questions.

☐ **Purpose.** What topic am I researching that might lend itself to an argument? What are some potential persuasive claims I could make about that topic? Have I discovered something about the topic that would contribute to other scholarly research?

☐ **Audience.** Assuming my readers are my classmates and professor—I need to think about how much they already know about my topic. How much background information will they need? What kind of terminology will they expect? How will they use the information I present?

☐ **Rhetorical appeals.** How will I establish my authority as a writer? How will I build a case for my conclusions using logic? What kinds of sources establish me as an expert and work to build my case?

☐ **Modes & media.** Can some of the information I present be shown visually with a chart or graphic? Do I want readers to access my article in print or digitally? Or do I want to make both options available?

☐ **Elements of the genre.** How will I make my thesis clear and declarative? How will I refer to my sources? How can I synthesize my sources to show readers that my sources are in conversation with each other?

☐ **Style.** How can I project an authoritative voice? How much detail will I need to provide so that readers understand the complexity and validity of my research?

☐ **Design.** How will I use design elements to my advantage? Will I use subheadings to organize and chunk information? Will I use images to illustrate points?

☐ **Sources.** Will my readers expect me to cite my sources in MLA, APA, or another format? Will my readers respect the types of sources I've referred to?

---

**PRACTICE** Want to experiment? Draft your own researched argument.

Think of a controversial topic you are curious about, perhaps even a bit uninformed about. Maybe campaign finance reform, the safety of bottled water, or the future of AIDS research. Ask your instructor or a librarian to help you find three reliable sources on the subject. Read the sources and then draft an argumentative thesis statement in which you take a position on the topic. Sketch out at least two counterarguments and your refutations of them.

# AUTHOR'S/ARTIST'S STATEMENTS

Composers of all sorts often write a statement for their audience that explains their inspirations, intentions, and choices in their creative and critical processes. The liner notes that come with a CD, the program you receive at the theater or symphony, the Director's Commentary on a DVD, the Artist's Statement pinned to the wall at an art gallery—these are all forms of Authors' or Artists' Statements.

What are some examples of Authors' or Artists' Statements that you've seen lately? How does understanding a composer's perspective and intent contribute to how you relate to their work?

The magazine *Cook's Illustrated* is in the business of providing recipes, often with accompanying critical discussions. The point of the discussion—or what you could call a Cook's Statement—is to explain and discuss what went into the creation of the recipe, what went well, and what could have gone better, for example, and to discuss process. In the following discussion of the recipe for Thai Grilled-Beef Salad, recipe writer Andrew Janjigian explains what his goals were and the thought processes behind the decisions he made as he tinkered with the recipe. Janjigian is an associate editor for *Cook's Illustrated* and also works for America's Test Kitchen.

An Author's or Artist's—or Cook's—Statement assists the reader in understanding the process that led to the product. If you've watched a DVD recently, you may have found a Director's Commentary included along with the feature film or documentary. In Director's Commentaries (or Statements), the director—or an actor, choreographer, or other person associated with the film—talks about the considerations that went into making the film, such as casting, lighting, music, and blocking. The Director's Commentary, like an Author's Statement, makes visible, to some extent, the behind-the-scenes work that is invisible in the final product.

When our students create assignments—whatever genre or media they create in—we ask them to write an accompanying Author's or Artist's Statement that can give us insight into what they set out to do, how they did it, and what they might do to further improve the piece.

▲ AUTHOR PHOTO
**Andrew Janjigian.** *America's Test Kitchen.*

## Thai Grilled-Beef Salad

Our goal was to look no further than the supermarket to replicate this salad's complex range of flavors and textures. Along the way, we learned a neat trick for grilling meat.

BY ANDREW JANJIGIAN

A scoop of rice turns this steak salad into a meal.

### High-Steaks Decisions

### Five Tastes of Thai Grilled-Beef Salad—and One More

One of the keys to this salad is balancing the signature flavor elements of Thai cuisine. In addition to achieving this we added one more complementary flavor: the earthiness of toasted cayenne and sweet paprika.

| HOT | SOUR | SALTY | SWEET | BITTER | EARTHY |
|---|---|---|---|---|---|

### Falling Water

### Well Dressed

**THAI GRILLED-BEEF SALAD**
SERVES 4 TO 6

1 teaspoon sweet paprika
1 teaspoon cayenne pepper
1 tablespoon white rice
3 tablespoons lime juice (2 limes)
2 tablespoons fish sauce
2 tablespoons water
½ teaspoon sugar
1 (1½-pound) flank steak, trimmed
Salt and white pepper, coarsely ground
4 shallots, sliced thin
1½ cups fresh mint leaves, torn
1½ cups fresh cilantro leaves
1 Thai chile, stemmed and sliced thin into rounds
1 seedless English cucumber, sliced ½ inch thick on bias

### Unbeatable Thai Trick: Knowing When to Flip

TIME TO FLIP

Look The Moisture Beads
Video available FREE for 4 months at www.CooksIllustrated.com/aug11

---

# Analyzing Author's/Artist's Statements: What to Look For

## THE RHETORICAL SITUATION

**Purpose**   The purpose of an Author's Statement is for an author (or artist or other composer) to discuss the decisions and choices he or she made in composing a specific text or other work. Let's say you've created an ad or a documentary film for your course. By writing an accompanying Author's or Artist's Statement, you can persuade your readers to see your finished piece in a particular way. A successful Author's Statement reflects your understanding of your chosen genre (and the elements, style, design, and use of sources that characterize it)—and of your specific rhetorical situation (your reasons for composing, your audience, how you use rhetorical appeals, and your choice of mode and medium).

Following is an example of a Director's Statement. It relates to the film *The Social Network*, directed by David Fincher. In the Director's Commentary for the film (included on the DVD), Fincher aims to persuade viewers that his choice in how to cast the main character was motivated by his desire to be realistic:

> I was looking for somebody who could just come out of the gates and be relentlessly who he is, and um, this QuickTime of an audition ended up on my computer and I turned it on and I watched Jesse Eisenberg. I think he did two takes of this scene, and I just thought, "Wow, like, that's pretty undeniable," and I remember dragging Aaron [Sorkin, the screenwriter on the film] into my office and saying, "Just watch this," and he looked at it and he said, "Well, our job's done."
>
> —**David Fincher**, from Director's Commentary for *The Social Network*

If you're writing an Author's Statement in an academic setting, your main purpose is to inform and persuade readers—your peers, your instructor, your audience—of the critical and creative thought you put into your composition.

**Audience**  The audience for an Author's Statement is usually a particularly engaged and interested reader or viewer. Not everyone who saw the film *The Social Network* listened to David Fincher's Director's Commentary. Only the most interested viewers did; the ones who wanted to better understand the behind-the-scenes process. In an academic setting, your audience is made up of invested and critical readers and viewers, such as your professor and peers, who want to confirm that you've made deliberate choices throughout your composing process.

**Rhetorical appeals**  In an Author's Statement, writers persuade readers by appealing mainly to logos and ethos. The author's credibility (ethos) is particularly important because, as with most persuasive pieces, the writer needs to come across as honest and thoughtful. Authors can establish ethos through the reasoning (logos) they present in their Authors' Statements. When writers logically present evidence to readers about the choices they made in organizing and presenting their work, readers are more likely to accept the claims the author makes.

To persuade, composers may sometimes appeal to their audience's emotions. For example, if a composer wrote a piece of music as a memorial and wanted it performed a certain way, that message would appear in the program.

**Modes & media**  Authors choose modes and media for their Statements that are appropriate for those of the work they're discussing. An artist showing work online would probably create a digital Artist's Statement, whereas an artist showing work in a brick-and-mortar gallery would probably print out a text-based statement to hang next to his or her masterpieces.

Analyzing Author's/Artist's Statements: What to Look For

THE GENRE'S CONVENTIONS

**Elements of the genre**   In their Authors' and Artists' Statements, writers do the following:

*Discuss a specific composition—and make an argument.* In an Author's or Artist's Statement, writers discuss a particular composition—such as an essay, painting, photo, documentary, ad, or other work. They refer directly to that work and provide specific details as they explain the "what, why, and how" of their creation. For example, in the Cook's Statement example from *Cook's Illustrated*, Andrew Janjigian explains that he set out to create a dressing that would successfully blend "the four Thai flavor elements: hot, sour, salty, and sweet." He then explains how he did that.

Writers also make a case for their compositions in order to persuade readers to see their work in a particular way. For example, David Fincher (p. 233) wants us to believe his casting was motivated by a desire for realism. Andrew Janjigian wants us to see that his beef salad recipe succeeds in blending desired flavors.

*Address readers directly.* Writers use the *I* construction, which allows them to speak plainly to readers about their choices. They also refer to the works they're discussing in the Statement as "my essay" (or "my painting," "my photograph," etc.), indicating their ownership of the composition and the choices they made.

*Explain their choice of genre—and how they worked with its conventions.* The Author's or Artist's Statement is a place for a composer to explain why he or she chose to work in a particular genre. For example, let's say that for your composition course, you chose to write an opinion piece on gun control. In a separate statement, submitted with your opinion piece, you might explain to your instructor and classmates why you chose this genre. Pointing out your specific choices builds your ethos and persuasiveness. You might note, for example, that the opinion piece was the best choice of genre, because it allowed you to:

» Clearly present your opinion on the topic of gun control (and write in the first person)

» Be brief (just a few paragraphs) and lively

» Deal with potential objections and offer potential solutions

» Invite readers to respond

What are some arguments a musician might make about a song or album? What are some claims a fashion designer might make about a new line of clothing?

Alternatively, maybe you created a photo essay, for your class or a wider audience. An accompanying statement—in which you explain why you found the photo essay to be the best way to communicate your ideas about gun control—would go a long way toward helping your viewers get the most out of your work.

*Discuss their specific rhetorical situation—and related choices.* The Author's or Artist's Statement gives you, as a composer, an opportunity to explain to audiences:

» Your purpose: why you composed the work—on that specific topic, in that specific way

» Your audience and use of rhetorical appeals: what you understand about your readers and how you connected with them through choices regarding ethos, pathos, and logos

» Your mode and medium: why you chose them and how they benefit your work overall

For example, if you created a collage—perhaps on the topic of body art and identity—in your Artist's Statement, you could explain to viewers:

» Your purpose or main point in creating a collage on the relationship between body art and identity—and what the relationship is

» Why you chose specific central images, how they contribute to your message, and how you hope your viewers will read them and relate to the collage overall

» How you wanted to connect with your viewers through pathos, logos, and ethos (for example, your arrangement of images might appeal to their logic or emotions)

» Why you decided to create the collage, say, in a digital format

*Reflect on their compositions—and discuss successes and limitations.* Writers use Authors' Statements as an opportunity to look back at a composition and to evaluate the extent of their achievement; they might also note what they would have done differently or better. For example, say you created an advertisement showing how marines achieve strength without steroids. You might note in an accompanying Author's Statement that you felt you'd succeeded in providing a captivating visual, an original slogan, and an emotional appeal. On the other hand, don't hesitate to mention in your Statement places where you could improve your work editorially or technically. The point here is to do your best and reflect on what you did well and talk about what you'd like to improve. This all adds to your ethos as a composer and to the persuasiveness of your work.

*Provide context.* In the Author's or Artist's Statement, it's useful for writers to give some background on their composition (their editorial or collage, etc.), such as how they became interested in the topic, what their inspirations were, or, if they've created a series of related works, how the piece fits in with other pieces. Andrew Janjigian explains in his Cook's Statement that he decided to create his own beef salad recipe because he hadn't found one that came close to achieving the quality of beef salads he'd eaten in Thai restaurants.

**Style**   Statement authors do the following:

*Use detail.* The persuasive and critical nature of the Statement depends on the use of specific detail. Janjigian, for example, names particular ingredients that he tried and describes the exact result he got, such as in his discussion of what happened when he used cayenne pepper instead of powdered Thai bird chiles: "Just ½ teaspoon of cayenne, in fact, overpowered the meat's smoky char."

*Write in a tone that builds ethos.* In their Statements, authors use critical, analytical language to make their points. They choose words related to their subject of inquiry to establish themselves as experts. When you write such a Statement, even though you're writing in the first person (*I*), use a serious, straightforward tone to emphasize that you have made deliberate, thoughtful choices.

**Design**   Authors' Statements can often look very much like an academic essay, with indented paragraphs and little or no decoration except for subheadings that offer structure and organization. However, a writer might choose to design an Author's Statement to reflect the genre of the composition. For example, an Author's Statement might take the form of a letter written to a professor, a Director's Commentary, or a one-page Artist's Statement.

**Sources**   The most persuasive authors discuss the sources that informed their composing process. For example, in his Statement, student Michael Kipp mentions specific sources by title or author's name, including page numbers. Depending on the audience, sources may be cited according to MLA or APA or other academic formats, as in Michael Kipp's Statement on page 238. An artist who is inspired by another artist usually names his or her inspiration and cites specific works by that artist.

Besides the essay format, what other forms might you use for an Author's or Artist's Statement? When might writing a song for this purpose be appropriate? Are there forms that would never work as a Statement? What forms? Why?

## Michael Kipp (Student)

### Artist's Statement: Why and How I Created My Collage: "Thank You"

Michael Kipp, a student at Red Rocks Community College, became interested in the concept of gratitude and happiness when he took a psychology course and studied positive psychology. As part of a second-semester research-based composition class, Kipp decided to focus his semester-long multigenre project on the idea of gratitude, looking at research in the field and reflecting on his own experience with feeling gratitude. One of the pieces Kipp created for the project was a collage illustrating gratitude. Accompanying the collage is his Artist's Statement, analyzing the choices he made in creating the collage, such as design and organization, and illustrating how his collage achieves his purpose and uses rhetorical appeals to persuade his audience. *("Artist's Statement: Why and How I Created My Collage: 'Thank You.'" Reprinted Courtesy of Michael Kipp.)*

▲ STUDENT
AUTHOR PHOTO &
◀ COLLAGE
**Michael Kipp** and his composition, *Thank You*, the subject of his Artist's Statement on page 238. *Michael Kipp.*

What is the composer, **Michael Kipp**, doing?

THE RHETORICAL SITUATION

Purpose
Audience
Rhetorical appeals
Modes & media

*see page 239*

How do I know this is an **Artist's Statement**?

THE GENRE'S CONVENTIONS

Elements of the genre
Style
Design
Sources

*see page 239*

# Michael Kipp
## *Artist's Statement: Why and How I Created My Collage: "Thank You"*

"Psychologists have repeatedly shown that perceptions are more important than objective reality" ("Positive Thinking"). That statement embodies the message behind my collage. It ties in with messages from other research I've done on the science of happiness, including my reading of the article "Psychological Research: Gratitude," by Jerry Lopper. In that piece, Lopper quotes psychologist and researcher Dr. Alex Wood as saying: "Gratitude is a life orientation towards noticing and appreciating the positive in the world." What Wood suggests is that feeling grateful requires mental work (Emmons, *Thanks!* 6). Gratitude is a part of our perception, a "life orientation," and without effort that perception will not arise or be maintained. Thus, to have an attitude of gratefulness, we must change our outlook on life. My purpose in creating this collage is to promote the idea that we make choices about how we perceive experience, and that practicing gratitude can make us happier.

My intended audience for my collage is made up of people who like art, psychology, and philosophy, who appreciate the abstract expression of concepts, and who may be persuaded to think about how a grateful attitude could be more important than one's objective reality—and how they may practice that in their own life to be happier.

In my collage I used *pathos* to convey these ideas—I wanted to sway my viewers emotionally, to cause them to feel curious and inspired when looking at the collage. I did this through my choices of composition, colors, and subjects, which are discussed in depth below. I used striking contrast and positioned the objects in ways the viewer might not expect, thereby drawing attention to them. I also used *logos* by putting the piece together in a logical manner, and by grounding my concept in positive psychology research. Furthermore, by connecting

Kipp, *Artist's Statement*, Continued

my audience with research on the power of the perception (in para. 1), I ask viewers to think about how the collage illustrates that concept. My goal is that my audience will ponder what each part of the collage represents and come to logical conclusions about the collage's representation of gratitude.

During my research, the following passage stood out for me: "A grateful outlook does not require a life full of material comforts but rather an interior attitude of thankfulness regardless of life circumstances" (Emmons and Shelton, 465). I wanted to convey this idea visually in my collage by emphasizing contrasting experiences; a negative or challenging objective reality is represented by the black background that encompasses and surrounds the sitting figure, which is asymmetrically placed within the piece. The figure herself is creating a positive perception of her reality, which is represented by the landscape and the rainbow that arches upward and out—drawing the eye forward and to a higher point. The figure is practicing gratitude, a habit which is documented in a recent study as raising a person's outlook and affect (Martinez-Marti et al. 893).

The landscape in my collage refers to the fact that grateful people experience a positive memory bias—they are more likely to recall positive memories, similar to the negative memory bias experienced in depression (Watkins 63). The idea of creation is also suggested by the plant and the roots that surround the woman's head. Her efforts to be thankful and practice gratitude nourish the plant and support its upward growth, changing her reality, subjective and objective, for the better. The figure's pose is reminiscent of *The Thinker*, a nineteenth-century sculpture by Rodin, which suggests that changing one's attitude takes intentional, active thought. "People adapt quickly to positive changes in their lives and thus derive diminishing happiness returns" ("Positive Thinking"), so it may be that practicing gratitude helps counteract that adaptation.

*Continues next page*

## THE RHETORICAL SITUATION

### Purpose

Kipp's purpose is to persuade readers that "practicing gratitude can make us happier" and that his collage furthers that goal. He wants readers to know that he made thoughtful decisions when composing the collage.

## THE GENRE'S CONVENTIONS

### Elements of the genre

Kipp **discusses a specific composition** (his collage)—and makes an argument about it. He supports claims with evidence; for example, Kipp discusses how he used color and composition in the context of Emmons and Shelton's concept of an "interior attitude of thankfulness."

Kipp **addresses readers directly** (e.g., "I considered adding words") and uses *my* throughout (e.g., "my collage" and "my research").

*(Continued on p. 240.)*

Michael Kipp (Student), *Artist's Statement*     **239**

Kipp, *Artist's Statement*, Continued

THE RHETORICAL
SITUATION

**Audience**

His readers are his
instructor and fellow
students. They want
to know why he
created a collage
and what research
informed it.

THE GENRE'S
CONVENTIONS

Kipp **explains why
he created a collage**
and how he worked
with established
conventions. For
example, he writes
that choosing this
genre meant he
could use a variety
of images—and
also use a black
background as part
of the composition.

He **talks about
his rhetorical
situation**—and
specific related
choices. For
example, he appeals
to his audience
through pathos,
hoping they "feel
curious and inspired"
when viewing the
collage.

The embracing arms in the collage represent several things: first, they represent the tendency for people who practice gratitude to be more prosocial, more likely to help others or return a favor, than less grateful people (Tsang 139). They also represent the positive social benefits we receive when we regularly practice gratitude (Watkins et al. 65). Finally, they represent that gratitude is an acknowledgment that one is dependent on others (Emmons and Shelton 463). The angle of the arms above the rainbow creates a triangle that leads the eye to the point where they get close together and hit the frame. The picture frames suggest that gratefulness is a frame of mind. What is outside that frame is objective reality. The parallel lines created by the frames again pull the eye upward; their top ends create a diagonal line with the part of the plant where the last leaf connects to the stem, as well as the top of the mountain, which pulls the eye back to the left center of the piece, and finally back to the central figure. The shelf the books rest on and the bench the woman sits on repeat the parallel lines created in the frames, but are perpendicular to them. The red "Thank You" at the bottom of the piece pulls in the warm colors in the arms at the opposite side and serves as a sort of name tag—indicating that the collage is based on thankfulness, as is the woman's perception of her life.

All of these pieces contribute to the composition of my collage—even the use of a canvas was intentional, enhancing the idea of active creation. I chose to create a collage because even though I am unfamiliar with the genre, I am familiar with painting and drawing, so I have some, although limited, background in composition and got to try something new. I also wanted to create in a medium other than text or a computer-based visual. Collages often have more cut out pieces pasted together, but the more I added, the less I felt like the collage conveyed the intended message. Covering too much of the black background defeated the purpose of that background—the negative space is as important as the positive space. I considered adding words, but found that the collage was more powerful without text—this is also why I moved "Thank You" off the canvas; it complements the idea behind the picture, but is not included within the composition itself. In a future iteration of the collage, I would probably add the quote that I began this statement with: "Psychologists have repeatedly shown that perceptions are more important than objective reality" ("Positive Thinking"). I think it would give the viewer more to think about, particularly because it is the quote that inspired the entire piece. It also extends the ideas I've presented, asking viewers not only to feel and practice gratitude, but to affect their own experiences of reality by doing so.

## Works Cited

Emmons, Robert A. *Thanks! How the New Science of Gratitude Can Make You Happier*. Houghton Mifflin Harcourt, 2007. *Google Books*, books.google.com/books?id=tGCcH2l4jUUC.

Emmons, Robert A., and Charles M. Shelton. "Gratitude and the Science of Positive Psychology." *Handbook of Positive Psychology*, edited by C. R. Snyder and Shane J. Lopez, Oxford UP, 2002, pp. 459-71.

Lopper, Jerry. "Psychological Research: Gratitude." *Suite101*, 19 May 2008, www.suite101.com/content/psychological-research-gratitude-a54399.

Martinez-Marti, et al. "The Effects of Counting Blessings on Subjective Well-Being: A Gratitude Intervention in a Spanish Sample." *Spanish Journal of Psychology*, vol. 13, no. 2, 2010, pp. 886-96, www.ucm.es/info/psi/docs/journal/v13_n2_2010/art886.pdf.

Continues next page

### THE RHETORICAL SITUATION

**Rhetorical appeals**
Kipp establishes his credibility, or **ethos,** in paragraph 1 by showing he's done research on positive psychology, including quotes from experts.
*(Continued on p. 242.)*

### THE GENRE'S CONVENTIONS

Kipp **reflects on his successes and limitations.** For example, he mentions that though he has a "limited" background in design and visual composition, he was pleased by achieving a "striking contrast" for viewers through his positioning of images.

Kipp **provides context** by discussing his interest in the concept of gratitude and his goal to show readers "that practicing gratitude can make us happier."

Kipp, *Artist's Statement*, Continued

Pursuit of Happiness. "Positive Thinking: Optimism and
Gratitude." *The Pursuit of Happiness*, www.pursuit-of
-happiness.org/science-of-happiness/positive-thinking/.
Accessed 26 Nov. 2012.

Rodin, Auguste. *The Thinker*. 1880-81, Cleveland Museum of
Art, Cleveland. Bronze sculpture.

Tsang, Jo-Ann. "Gratitude and Prosocial Behaviour: An
Experimental Test of Gratitude." *Cognition and Emotion*,
vol. 20, no. 1, 2006, pp. 138-148, www.academia.edu/
365898/Gratitude_and_prosocial_behavior_An_experimental
_test_of_gratitude.

Watkins, Philip C., et al. "Counting Your Blessings:
Positive Memories among Grateful People." *Current
Psychology*, vol. 23, no. 1, 2004, pp. 52-67. *JSTOR*, doi:
10.1007/512144-004-1008-2.

## THE RHETORICAL SITUATION

Kipp appeals to **logos** by explaining his choices logically and using evidence from his collage to support his claims. For example, when he discusses his use of **pathos**, he shows how he used contrast and layout to make readers curious.

### Modes & media

**Mode = written**
Kipp uses only words to make his case for his collage. He uses both his own analysis and outside research to deliver his reflections and analysis.

**Medium = print**
Because Kipp composed his statement as a researched academic essay, he chose to print it out and submit it to his instructor that way. Of course, he could also have submitted the statement digitally. In digital format, readers could easily click on the sources in his Works Cited page, for example.

## THE GENRE'S CONVENTIONS

### Style

Kipp **uses specific detail.** For example, he talks about the image of embracing arms, and what they represent in terms of gratitude, how their angle orients the reader toward a certain point, and how the arms relate to the frame.

His **word choice reflects his critical thought** (e.g., *intentional, sway, ponder, grounding, bias*).

### Design

Kipp structures and designs his statement as a traditional researched essay with an introduction, body paragraphs, conclusion, parenthetical citations, and Works Cited list.

### Sources

Kipp's sources for the Artist's Statement are the collage itself and the research he conducted on gratitude. He refers to source material, such as a study by Martinez-Marti, Avia, and Hernandez-Lloreda, and relates that back to his collage.

He cites his sources per MLA style using parenthetical in-text citations and a Works Cited list—and connects them to the decisions he made in composing his collage.

## Questions: Analyzing Kipp's Artist's Statement

**1. Purpose.** How does Kipp convince you that his collage illustrates that "practicing gratitude can make us happier"?

**2. Audience.** Although the primary audience for the piece is Kipp's instructor, are there other audiences that might be interested in reading the piece? If so, who? Why?

**3. Rhetorical appeals.** One of the ways Kipp establishes his ethos is by including research. How else does he establish his ethos?

**4. Rhetorical appeals.** Why would it be inappropriate for Kipp to use pathos in an Artist's Statement? Are there any circumstances where pathos might be appropriate for an Artist's Statement? What circumstances? Why?

**5. Modes & media.** How would including visuals enhance Kipp's Artist's Statement? Where might he incorporate visuals?

**6. Elements of the genre.** What types of evidence does Kipp use to support his claims? How effective is the evidence? Are there places where he might have included different evidence? If so, where and what?

**7. Elements of the genre.** Throughout the statement, Kipp shows how research influences his choices and motivations. Do you learn anything about Kipp's own personal motivation for exploring this subject? If so, how? If not, what would this add to the Artist's Statement?

**8. Style.** How does Kipp use language to establish his credibility?

**9. Design.** Kipp chose to submit his Artist's Statement in a traditional academic essay form. Would the piece be strengthened if he had used subheads and divided the Artist's Statement into sections? If so, what would be the different sections?

**10. Sources.** What are the different purposes the research serves in Kipp's Artist's Statement?

# Drafting an Author's/Artist's Statement

---

## CHECKLIST: Drafting a Statement
Thinking of drafting an Author's/Artist's Statement? Ask yourself the following questions.

### WHAT'S MY RHETORICAL SITUATION?

☐ **Purpose.** What is the central claim I want to make about my piece? What particular elements do I need to justify? What choices did I make as I created the piece? What motivated me to create the piece?

☐ **Audience.** Am I writing this Statement for my instructor? For fellow students? Will my Statement be read by people outside the academic setting? If so, how will this affect what I write?

☐ **Rhetorical appeals.** What makes me a credible writer on this subject? How will I show readers my credibility? How will I organize my information to support my claims?

☐ **Modes & media.** Will I present my Statement only in written form? Is it appropriate to incorporate visuals? If so, what types of visuals? How would the inclusion of audio enhance my Statement? Would it be appropriate to just use audio? Do I want to present my work in print or digital form?

### WHAT GENRE CONVENTIONS MATTER?

☐ **Elements of the genre.** What persuasive point do I want to make about my piece? How can I support that point with specific examples and details from my composition and process? Are there aspects of the context that readers should know to fully understand and appreciate my work?

☐ **Style.** How can I use my tone to convey the seriousness with which I view my work? What details can I use to support the generalizations I make?

☐ **Design.** How will I organize my Statement? What visuals should I include? Should I use subheadings, or is my Statement short enough that subheadings aren't necessary?

☐ **Sources.** Is the piece I composed informed by source material? What inspired me? Where did I get the facts and information that I used? Will my audience expect formal citations?

---

**PRACTICE** Want to experiment? Draft your own Author's/Artist's Statement.

Look at a piece you wrote earlier in the semester or for another class. Reflect on the choices you made as you thought through and created the piece. Where did you put most of your energy and why? Where did you get your ideas? What did you tinker with? Then draft a brief statement in which you discuss your process and thoughts.

# COLLAGES/VISUAL ARGUMENTS

Collage is an art form that involves gluing pieces of paper, ribbon, newspaper, photos, gems, buttons, and other small items to a paper, poster board, wood, or canvas background. Artists use a combination of everyday or "found" materials, assembling them to create a piece of art. Collage techniques have been used since tenth-century Japanese calligraphers glued colored pieces of paper to their poems; today, scrapbookers and other DIY artists use collage techniques.

Have you ever made a collage? If so, why? And for what audience? What was the overall message of your collage?

Iconic artists, including Pablo Picasso (1881–1973), have used collage to express ideas—and to make arguments. One of Picasso's well-known collages is *Guitar, Sheet Music, and Glass*, completed in 1912, in which the artist glued pieces of sheet music and newspaper to a background.

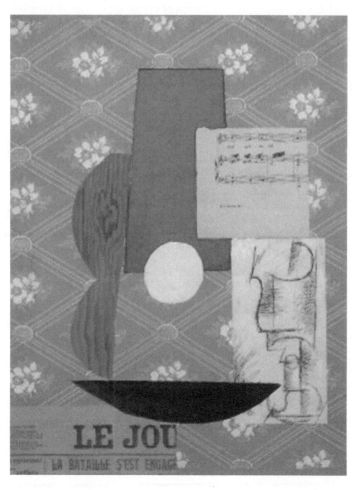

◀ COLLAGE
**Pablo Picasso**, *Guitar, Sheet Music, and Glass* (1912). © McNay Art Museum/ Art Resource, NY.

Let's look at Picasso's collage as a visual argument. What is Picasso arguing? And what choices make his argument(s) clear? Let's look at two of the choices he made.

1. Picasso chose to represent the objects in the collage in an abstract, rather than a realistic, way. Possible argument: Picasso is making a case for a break from traditional forms of art such as lifelike or still-life painting.

2. Picasso chose to use everyday materials drawn from everyday life (wallpaper, a cast-off piece of sheet music, etc.). Possible argument: Picasso is making the case for the value of the everyday in fine art. (This was a revolutionary idea back in 1912.)

What are some other examples of visual arguments? This book is filled with them— ads, comics, bumper stickers, photos, and other images. While the focus of this section is on the collage as a visual argument, much of the advice here also pertains to any type of visual argument.

POLITICAL CARTOON ▶
**Rex F. May (a.k.a. Baloo),** "My Point of View." *Reprinted by permission of Rex May.*

# Analyzing Collages/Visual Arguments:
# What to Look For

**Purpose**  We (artists, nonartists, students) create visual artwork, including collages, in order to convey ideas or aesthetic concepts—and often to make a visual argument or commentary on a controversial issue, a moment in time, or a cultural theme. Some collage artists, for example, choose a particular shape for their composition to emphasize their point.

**Audience**  Visual artists often appeal to a particular audience through their choice of subject. For example, the artist Kara Walker, who works with issues of race and gender, knows that her art appeals to people who are interested in slavery, racism, and feminism. In her piece on page 248, Walker superimposes a figure over an illustration from *Harper's Pictorial History of the Civil War: Volume 2* that is rendered in a woven tapestry.

▼ ARTIST PHOTO
**Kara Walker** with her work at her 2006 installation at the Metropolitan Museum of Art. *Librado Romero/ The New York Times/ Redux Pictures.*

▲ COLLAGE

**Kara Walker,** *A Warm Summer Evening in 1863*. To create this work, Walker superimposed a figure against a woven tapestry rendering of an illustration from *Harper's Pictorial History of the Civil War*. The illustration, from the second volume of Harper's history (of September 1862 through December 1867), includes the following caption: "THE RIOTERS BURNING THE COLORED ORPHAN ASYLUM. CORNER OF FIFTH AVENUE AND FORTY-SIXTH STREET, NEW YORK CITY." (See archive.org/details/harperspictorial02guer.) *Artwork © Kara Walker/Image courtesy of Sikkema Jenkins & Co., New York.*

**Rhetorical appeals**   Visual composers use image, line, color, and other visual elements to express concepts and arguments. Depending on an artist's main point—and how he or she chooses to reach viewers—the artist will emphasize ethos, pathos, or logos. For example, the composer of the *Business Collage* on page 251 appeals to viewers' sense of logos by creating a chain of reasoning for the reader. The "$" and "Only" on the glasses in the collage tell the reader that the consumer organizes the world according to money and perceived bargains. Additionally, the composer appeals to viewers' sense of pathos by presenting a relationship between the pressure of consumerism (as symbolized by the coupons) and addictive behavior (as symbolized by the cigarette and the beckoning finger). The piece is persuasive because of the textual messages, the visual representation of a consumer, and the juxtaposition of all the elements.

The *Coffee Break* collage below was created in response to a contest called the NASA Remix Challenge. The composer combined real NASA photos and a picture of a café on Route 66. The artist establishes ethos by using real photos to remix ideas about the moon landing, and also appeals to viewers' pathos through humor. The original caption reads: "After 109 hours, 39 minutes in the lunar module, Neil Armstrong and Buzz Aldrin enjoy a double cafe mocha." The collagist persuades the viewer that Starbucks has no boundaries—they will even take their product to the moon.

**Modes & media**   Visual composers use a variety of visual elements to create their work. Collagists, specifically, cut images out of magazines, incorporate found objects and fabrics, and work with photos to create their assemblages. When text is a part of a collage, it is usually "found text" taken from something else rather than written specifically for the collage. Collages are delivered in a variety of media—in galleries, print magazines, and digital collections.

Visual composers arrange images in certain ways to create connections. Have you ever seen two images side by side and been struck by the combination? How does seeing an image on its own—or paired with another—alter how you experience it?

◀ COLLAGE
**Jerry Taylor,** *Coffee Break. "Coffee Break"* NASA remix, Jerry Taylor (jrtcel).

**Elements of the genre**   Visual composers do the following:

*Convey a theme.* If you think of a visual work as an argument, then the visual artist, like an editorial writer or film reviewer, for example, creates works that convey a central idea or commentary. In collages, artists juxtapose different images or use shape and form to convey a theme. For example, among the images the *Business Collage* artist chooses are a dollar sign and a price tag, which contribute to the overall commentary on greed, consumption, and "business."

*Connect with culture and history.* Visual artists—especially those making an argument—often create or incorporate images that allude to a cultural or historical phenomenon. For example, in one of her collages, Kara Walker features an image of Ulysses S. Grant, the eighteenth U.S. president and commander of the Union army in the Civil War, and pastes onto it an image of an African American woman. Walker's collage makes clear the differences between her perspective and that of the nineteenth-century creators of the Grant image, and puts her work in the context of the Civil War.

*Use layers and juxtapose images and materials.* By definition, collages are composed of a variety of objects. Collagists use a variety of objects to bring texture and dimensionality to their work. All visual artists, especially those presenting an argument, consider how presentation and positioning of different items affect how viewers see the work.

*Use color to direct the attention of the viewer.* In Kara Walker's collage, the superimposed silhouette stands out against the pale background image. Collage artists use the same principles as composers of advertisements, who might contrast the color of the text with the background of the page or screen so that the text is more prominent for the viewer.

*Assemble parts.* When artists assemble a collage, they use a variety of materials, such as scissors, glue, newspapers, magazines, books, and paint. Because you can make a collage out of anything, you can use materials you find in the kitchen or at a bus stop. For example, the Romanian-born Swiss artist Daniel Spoerri uses familiar objects in his pieces, such as kitchen plates and leftover food. Although collagists have the broadest range of materials, all visual artists use a variety of materials to assemble their pieces.

**Style**   Visual composers do the following:

*Present varying degrees of detail*. The amount of detail in a visual argument varies. In Picasso's collage (p. 245), he uses just a few elements to create his piece. In the *Coffee Break* collage (p. 249), the artist uses detail to emphasize the Starbucks brand.

*Convey a tone*. Artists convey their attitudes toward the subjects of their work. Some artists use parody to persuade viewers, for example, the creator of the *Coffee Break* collage.

**Design**   Visual composers do the following:

*Vary the size and shape of their compositions*. Collage artists, like other visual artists, are not limited by a particular size or form for their creations. Some pieces might be the size of a sheet of paper, while others might occupy an entire wall. In collage, in particular, by using shape in a deliberate way the artist conveys a point.

*Embrace (or reject or remix) traditional artistic conventions*. Collagists generally follow the conventions of visual art, in terms of balance, contrast, and perspective. These conventions allow the artist to make sure that nothing in the piece gets more attention than he or she wants it to. Artists generally divide their canvases into sections. For example, the collagist who created *Coffee Break* divides his work into thirds, with each astronaut on the outer third of the piece. This keeps the artist from putting an image right smack in the middle, where it would dominate the piece. As with other art forms, when artists violate the rules of perspective and other conventions, they do it with a purpose, to call attention to the violation.

*Present patterns/repeat certain elements*. All visual artists must give their work a sense of order or coherence. This is true of collagists, whose works are made of seemingly random pieces, but which can be given order through the repetition of elements such as color or shape. The *Business Collage*, for instance, is held together visually by the predominant use of black and white, and by the curved

▲ COLLAGE **Stock Artist, Business Collage.** *CSA Images/ Printstock Collection/Getty Images.*

shapes of the ears, chin, and glasses. Other artists use similar strategies, repeating shapes and colors to give a piece an overall sense of unity.

*Use lines (or not).* Collagists use the lines created by the edges of the images they've assembled to direct the audience's attention to particular elements, just as an arrow would. Notice, for example, how the flagpole in *Coffee Break* directs your attention to both the café flag and the astronaut's arm. Visual artists working in other media use lines similarly. Click through a museum Web site and find a painting and notice how the lines in the painting direct your attention.

**Sources**   To create collages, artists do the following:

*Incorporate found objects.* The cutouts and items that a collagist uses are considered "found objects" because they are not created for artistic purposes; rather, they are items that have been repurposed by an artist. Source material is often paper based, such as photos and cutouts from magazines and newspapers, but can be any item an artist chooses. Collage artists have used small objects like buttons and ribbons, parts of items like tree branches, and larger items, too. Visual artists working in other media get ideas and inspiration from many sources; for example, an artist might paint a portrait based on a photograph of a person or place.

*Incorporate cultural materials.* Artists may include cultural and historical materials such as documents and images.

Look around you and find three visual pieces in any medium—posters, ads, billboards, and so on. Which pieces are divided into thirds? What is the effect?

# Richard Hamilton

## *Just What Is It That Makes Today's Homes So Different, So Appealing?*

On page 254 is a collage created in 1956 by artist Richard Hamilton (1922–2011), entitled *Just What Is It That Makes Today's Homes So Different, So Appealing?* The dimensions of the original are 10¼ × 9¾ inches. When the collage was first displayed as part of an exhibit titled *This Is Tomorrow*, the image of the tape player in the collage had a sound source behind it, making the piece not just a collage but a multimodal composition. The *This Is Tomorrow* exhibit kick-started the pop art movement, and *Just What Is It That Makes Today's Homes So Different, So Appealing?* became one of the most recognized pieces of pop art ever produced. Pop art raised everyday materials and techniques to art status, featuring more ingenuity and cleverness than high art sensibility. The background of this collage is a flooring ad torn from a 1950s *Ladies' Home Journal*. *(Image on page 254: © R. Hamilton. All Rights Reserved, DACS and ARS 2015. Also: Kunsthall Tübingen, Collection Zundel.)*

What do you think of pop art? Is everyday or "lowbrow" life worth looking at? How do the sensibilities of Hamilton, "the father of pop art," compare with your own? Learn more in his obituaries in digital editions of the *Guardian* and *The New York Times.*

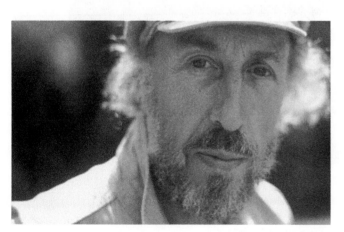

◀ ARTIST PHOTO
**Richard Hamilton.**
*Chris Morphet/Getty Images.*

Hamilton, *Today's Homes, Continued*

What is the composer, **Richard Hamilton**, doing?

THE RHETORICAL SITUATION

Purpose
Audience
Rhetorical appeals
Modes & media

*see page 255*

How do I know this is a **collage/visual argument**?

THE GENRE'S CONVENTIONS

Elements of the genre
Style
Design
Sources

*see page 255*

**Hamilton, *Today's Homes*, Continued**

## THE RHETORICAL SITUATION

### Purpose

Hamilton makes an argument about 1950s domesticity, sexuality, and consumerism. He wants to persuade us that having all the new consumer culture wouldn't lead to a perfect life—it would merely lead to a perfect-*looking* life. He also comments on 1950s body ideals.

### Audience

His viewers appreciate visual art, pop culture, and humor. When the piece was originally displayed in 1956, many audience members were probably curiosity seekers attracted by the hoopla around the exhibit.

### Rhetorical appeals

The artist appeals to **pathos** by presenting erotic images—a bodybuilder and a nude woman on a couch—in a domestic situation. He establishes his **ethos** by including items that might be found in a home in the late 1950s.

### Modes & media

**Mode = visual and audio** The visual aspect is most obvious. When the piece was exhibited in 1956 in *This Is Tomorrow*, it also had an audio element because of the sound source behind the radio.

**Medium = paper** In the original exhibition, the piece was viewed face-to-face. Reproductions can be conveyed in print, as in this book, or digitally, as in images of the piece on the Internet. Artwork typically makes a more profound impression when viewed face-to-face, in part because a small reproduction in a book simply can't make the same impact as a large piece can in person. Textures that are evident in a face-to-face viewing are usually lost in print or digital renderings.

## THE GENRE'S CONVENTIONS

### Elements of the genre

**Presents a theme.** Hamilton's collage connects 1950s home life with romance (e.g., the framed comic book page), convenience (e.g., the canned ham), and tradition (e.g., the formal portrait on the wall).

**Connects with history and culture.** The images from 1950s pop culture invite viewers to make associations. For example, the canned ham connects with World War II, when fresh meat was scarce and convenience foods like Spam hit the market.

**Layers images.** The artist cut images from ads and magazines, then arranged them into a layered composition.

**Works with color.** Hamilton chooses mainly black and white, but uses color very deliberately. For example, the Tootsie Pop and the framed comic stand out.

**Assembles the pieces.** Hamilton used a transparent material to attach the pieces, so that it would not interfere with the visual impact.

### Style

**Brings in specific detail.** For example, the artist makes sure the brands of the canned ham and lollipop are visible.

**Conveys a tone and attitude.** Most living rooms don't feature a naked bodybuilder holding a giant lollipop, yet Hamilton uses images such as these to create an ironic and satirical tone.

### Design

**Consciously uses size and shape.** Hamilton works with scale to create emphasis—note the different sizes of the women in the image.

**Works with traditional art conventions.** While this collage looks very modern, Hamilton conforms to established principles of balance, contrast, and perspective.

**Repeats elements.** For example, the rectangular shapes (the couches) highlight the idea that people are constrained by consumerism rather than liberated by it.

**Uses lines.** Hamilton creates strong horizontal and vertical lines with the edges of the cutouts, such as the couch, window, portrait, and framed comic.

### Sources

The collage is made up of clippings from magazines (e.g., *Ladies' Home Journal*) and advertisements of the time.

## Questions: Analyzing Hamilton's collage

**1. Purpose.** Hamilton is considered a creator of pop art. In an interview, he said that he considered pop art to be "popular (designed for a mass audience); transient (short-term solution); expendable (easily forgotten); low cost; mass produced; young (aimed at youth); witty; sexy; gimmicky; glamorous; and last but not least, Big Business." In what ways does Hamilton's collage seem consistent with his thoughts on pop culture? Explain.

**2. Purpose.** Hamilton's collage is titled *Just What Is It That Makes Today's Homes So Different, So Appealing?* How does the title direct your thinking about the artist's point in making the collage? How effective is the title? Why?

**3. Audience.** The collage uses images current for audiences in 1956. View some of the modern adaptations created by students at Joliet Junior College at www.redmagazine.com/web2012/feature_what_the.html. How do you think the audiences for Hamilton's collage and the students' collages are similar and/or different?

**4. Rhetorical appeals.** How does Hamilton appeal to your emotions? What emotions is he appealing to and how?

**5. Rhetorical appeals.** What other rhetorical methods does Hamilton use to try to persuade us, his viewers, of his take on 1950s domestic culture?

**6. Modes & media.** You are viewing this piece at a smaller size than the original. Check out a bigger version of this collage from the Tate museum site, in London. What details do you notice in it that you didn't notice when you looked at the small printed reproduction in the book?

**7. Elements of the genre.** What ideas or themes do you notice in the collage?

**8. Style.** What difference would it make if the canned ham and lollipop weren't associated with particular brands?

**9. Style.** Do certain parts of the collage seem to attract more of your attention? For example, do your eyes more readily go to the romance comic book page on the wall or to the Tootsie Pop acting as a loincloth? Why?

**10. Design.** How many different materials can you identify in the collage? How does the use of different materials affect you as a viewer?

**11. Design.** How do the lines and use of color in the collage direct your attention toward particular elements?

**12. Sources.** The collage is made up of "found objects" rather than created from scratch. How does the fact that the collage is constructed of rather mundane scraps from magazines and advertisements, rather than painted or drawn, lend meaning to it? Keep in mind that the purposes and audiences for the scraps are probably different from the purposes and audiences of the collage. For example, the Tootsie Pop cutout in the collage was probably originally intended for an advertisement, not an artistic collage.

# Drafting/Sketching a Collage/Visual Argument

## CHECKLIST: Planning a Collage

Thinking of sketching out a collage or other visual argument? Ask yourself the following questions.

### WHAT'S MY RHETORICAL SITUATION?

☐ **Purpose.** What idea do I want to represent in a collage or other visual argument? Do I want to persuade others about a political issue? Do I want my viewers to take some type of action? What themes might I use to advance my ideas or arguments?

☐ **Audience.** Will my collage or other visual argument be viewed in a public space? Private space? What type of viewer is interested in my subject? Who do I want to influence?

☐ **Rhetorical appeals.** How will I establish my credibility? How will I persuade my viewer? Do I want to appeal to viewers' emotions through humor? Do I want to shock viewers? How will I organize my material to appeal to viewers' sense of logos?

☐ **Modes & media.** To create a visual argument, will I use only visuals, such as photographs? Will I incorporate text? Will the text be something I create or something I take from existing material? Do I want viewers to see the piece face-to-face, such as hanging on a wall? Or do I want to digitize the piece so that anyone can view it?

### WHAT GENRE CONVENTIONS MATTER?

☐ **Elements of the genre.** What theme do I want to convey? How can I use shape, color, image, and other elements to convey this theme? What connotations and cultural associations do I want my audience to catch?

☐ **Style.** How can I layer and juxtapose materials to add dimensionality? What colors will convey my point? What materials will I use to put everything together? How much detail will I need to persuade my audience? Do I want to convey a satirical tone? A serious tone? Some other tone?

☐ **Design.** What size and shape will my visual argument be? Is there a particular shape I can use to convey my point? How will I use balance, contrast, perspective, and line to focus my audience's attention on particular elements? What elements can I repeat to give the piece a sense of order?

☐ **Sources.** What sources will I use? Should I consider cutting photos or pictures out of magazines, or printing images from the Internet (or embedding them if I'm creating a digital file)? What about objects, such as buttons, jewelry, or scraps? How about found objects such as a grocery list, a cocktail napkin, or a restaurant's bar coaster? Are there particular cultural or historical associations that I'd like my audience to make? If so, I need to consider working with (or from) these types of materials.

# PRACTICE Want to experiment? Sketch your own collage.

Think of a point you'd like to argue about modern life, such as "social networking is making us lose our ability to communicate in person," and create a collage to make your argument. Begin by going through some magazines and cutting out images that you think will assist in making your point. Play with different ways of arranging the images together, overlapping them in different ways. Then think about other items you might want to add, such as buttons and pins, scraps of fabrics or other materials, printouts of images from the Internet, photos, or jewelry (for example, to make the argument mentioned about social networking, you might want to find and print out from the Internet an image of an old-fashioned calling card).

Alternatively, create a digital collage. Instead of cutting out images from magazines, find images online and incorporate them or take your own digital photos. Instead of buttons, pins, and fabric scraps, you can use a photo-editing application to create different effects, such as blurred photo edges or the addition of a particular pattern, similar to a pattern added with a rubber stamp in a traditional collage.

ACCESS FAR MORE BOOKS, ARTICLES, DOCUMENTS, REPORTS, MULTIMEDIA, AND VISUAL RESOURCES THAN SCHOLARS OF THE PAST.

EVEN WHEN YOU'RE WORKING WITH A LOT OF SOURCES, YOU'RE LOOKING FOR THE BEST SOURCES POSSIBLE.

SEEK OUT BOTH QUANTITY AND QUALITY.

WITH SO MUCH INFORMATION OUT THERE, YOU NEED TO DO **DETECTIVE WORK** TO FIGURE OUT WHICH SOURCES TO USE.

DON'T MAKE THE MISTAKE OF RUSHING THROUGH THE PROCESS OF FINDING SOURCES.

I-43

BUT IF YOU WRITE A TELL-ALL BOOK YEARS LATER, THAT WON'T BE A PRIMARY SOURCE ANYMORE.

RIGHT?

ACTUALLY, IF I WITNESSED OR PARTICIPATED IN AN EVENT, HISTORIANS WOULD CONSIDER MY ACCOUNT A **PRIMARY SOURCE**...

...NO MATTER WHEN THE ACCOUNT WAS WRITTEN.

EXPERIMENTAL RESULTS AND FIELD RESEARCH ARE ALSO PRIMARY SOURCES THAT OTHER RESEARCHERS CAN BUILD ON.

GOVERNMENT DOCUMENTS CAN BE IMPORTANT PRIMARY SOURCES FOR RESEARCH PROJECTS AS WELL.

A PRIMARY SOURCE DOESN'T NEED TO BE A WRITTEN TEXT, EITHER.

PAINTINGS, SOUND RECORDINGS, FILMS, BUILDINGS -- ALL OF THESE AND MORE CAN BE PRIMARY SOURCES YOU MIGHT EXPLORE IN A CLASS OR IN OTHER WRITING CONTEXTS.

BLUEPRINTS

A **SECONDARY SOURCE** IS A SOURCE THAT DESCRIBES, ANALYZES, OR INTERPRETS A PRIMARY SOURCE.

BOOKS AND ARTICLES ABOUT LITERATURE, SCIENCE, OR ART MIGHT BE CONSIDERED SECONDARY SOURCES.

2

SO IF I WROTE AN ESSAY ABOUT ARTHUR MILLER'S *THE CRUCIBLE*, WHICH WAS ABOUT THE SALEM WITCH TRIALS IN MASSACHUSETTS IN 1692...

...AND USED A SCHOLARLY ARTICLE FROM A JOURNAL OF THEATER STUDIES...

...MILLER'S PLAY WOULD BE A **PRIMARY SOURCE**, AND THE JOURNAL ARTICLE WOULD BE A **SECONDARY SOURCE**.

RIGHT! THE ARTICLE PROVIDES AN INTERPRETATION OF MILLER'S PLAY.

WHAT'S TRICKY IS THAT A SECONDARY SOURCE IN ONE SITUATION MIGHT BE A PRIMARY SOURCE IN ANOTHER.

FOR EXAMPLE, THE SAME ARTICLE YOU'RE USING AS A SECONDARY SOURCE FOR YOUR PROJECT ON *THE CRUCIBLE* COULD BE A **PRIMARY SOURCE** FOR A RESEARCH PROJECT ON THE AUTHOR OF THE ARTICLE.

A SUBJECT LIKE THE SALEM WITCH TRIALS CAN INTEREST RESEARCHERS IN MANY FIELDS.

INDEED, SCHOLARS LOOK FOR DIFFERENT KINDS OF EVIDENCE IN APPROACHING THE SAME SUBJECT...

...AND THEY MAY EVEN DRAW DIFFERENT CONCLUSIONS FROM THE SAME EVIDENCE.

Bettmann/Getty Images

HISTORIANS WHO STUDY RACE LOOK AT HOW PERCEIVED RACIAL DIFFERENCES AND STEREOTYPES ABOUT SLAVES MIGHT HAVE PLAYED INTO THE PURITANS' HYSTERIA ABOUT WITCHES.

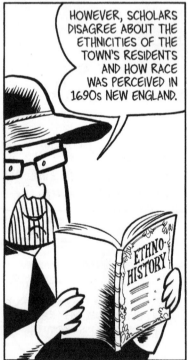

HOWEVER, SCHOLARS DISAGREE ABOUT THE ETHNICITIES OF THE TOWN'S RESIDENTS AND HOW RACE WAS PERCEIVED IN 1690s NEW ENGLAND.

ETHNO-HISTORY

ECONOMISTS MIGHT LOOK AT SUPPLY AND DEMAND TO UNDERSTAND THE EVENTS THAT TOOK PLACE IN SALEM VILLAGE, PARTICULARLY WHEN CROPS FAILED OR VILLAGERS SQUABBLED OVER PROPERTY RIGHTS.

SOMETIMES EVEN THE "FACTS" OF HISTORICAL CASES MAY BE OPEN TO DEBATE.

RAINFALL STATISTICS AND THE LOCATIONS OF PROPERTY LINES WEREN'T RECORDED AS CAREFULLY IN 1692 AS THEY ARE TODAY.

JOURNAL of ECONOMIC PERSPECTIVE

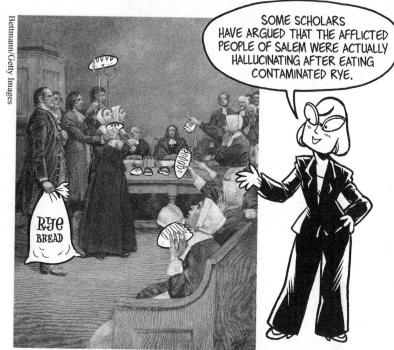

RYE BREAD

SOME SCHOLARS HAVE ARGUED THAT THE AFFLICTED PEOPLE OF SALEM WERE ACTUALLY HALLUCINATING AFTER EATING CONTAMINATED RYE.

YOU SHOULD CONSULT MULTIPLE SOURCES TO GET A SENSE OF THE SCHOLARLY DEBATES SURROUNDING YOUR RESEARCH TOPIC. NOT EVERYONE AGREES THAT WHAT THE PURITANS ATE WAS TO BLAME FOR THE SALEM WITCH HYSTERIA.

JOURNAL of RYE
R.Q.
RYE QUARTERLY
STUDY: Rye Best for Grilled Cheese

CAST A WIDE NET FOR YOUR RESEARCH AND READ THROUGH ALL THE LIBRARY RECORDS OR SEARCH SCREENS. DON'T STOP AT THE FIRST PAGE OF RESULTS.

OF COURSE, IF YOU TURN UP THOUSANDS OF GOOGLE HITS, YOU NEED TO NARROW YOUR SEARCH, BEFORE YOU READ THROUGH THE RESULTS.

HMMM...

BIBLIOGRAPHY
Aaronson, Albert
Alabaster, Arthur
Amand, Alexandra
Anderson, Alice
April, Anders
Arlington, Alan
Atwood, Ambrose
that's it!

Issue 2 • Research: More Than Detective Work

## DECIDING WHICH SOURCES TO TRUST

A WRITER REGARDED AS AN EXPERT MAY OFTEN BE CITED BY OTHERS.

To: Luis
From: Cindy

Hey, check o[ ]
this blog abou[ ]
Arthur Mille[ ]
H's RAD!
http://www.arthur[ ]
Later!
Cindy

[REPLY] [DELETE]

**Reference + Information**

A LIBRARY'S CATALOG AND DATABASES CAN SHOW THE ACADEMIC WORK THAT A PARTICULAR AUTHOR HAS PUBLISHED.

YOU CAN USE AN INTERNET SEARCH ENGINE TO FIND OUT ABOUT WRITERS WHO AREN'T ACADEMICS.

MANY AUTHORS HAVE PERSONAL WEB PAGES WITH INFORMATION ABOUT THEIR WORK.

CHECK A SOURCE'S DATE OF PUBLICATION.

A RECENT BOOK OR ARTICLE IS LIKELY TO CONTAIN REFERENCES TO THE MOST CURRENT RESEARCH.

DISCIPLINES SUCH AS THE SCIENCES MAY REQUIRE UP-TO-DATE SOURCES, SINCE KNOWLEDGE IN THOSE DISCIPLINES CHANGES RAPIDLY.

the BENEFITS of LEECHES 1756

IN OTHER DISCIPLINES, SUCH AS HISTORY, OLDER ACCOUNTS MIGHT SOMETIMES BE APPROPRIATE.

A WORD OF CAUTION: THINK CAREFULLY ABOUT POPULAR PERIODICALS.

IF YOUR BEST SOURCE IS A NEWSPAPER ARTICLE, YOU SHOULD PROBABLY KEEP LOOKING.

POPULAR NEWS

She Sings!

JOURNALISTS OFTEN HAVE GOOD GENERAL KNOWLEDGE...

...AND GOOD WRITING SKILLS...

BUT MOST REPORTERS AREN'T SPECIALISTS WITH IN-DEPTH KNOWLEDGE OF THE TOPIC.

INSTEAD, SEE IF THE NEWSPAPER ARTICLE MENTIONS A PROFESSOR, A GOVERNMENT OFFICIAL, OR ANOTHER EXPERT ON THE TOPIC, AND THEN SEARCH FOR INFORMATION FROM THESE SPECIFIC SOURCES.

ADS

## SUMMARY     PARAPHRASE     QUOTATION

SETTING UP CONTEXTS AND PROVIDING BACKGROUND INFORMATION

GIVING A SENSE OF THE AUTHOR'S ARGUMENT

DRAWING ATTENTION TO SOMETHING PARTICULARLY EVOCATIVE OR INSIGHTFUL IN THE AUTHOR'S OWN WORDS

LET'S TALK ABOUT SUMMARIZING, PARAPHRASING, AND QUOTING -- HOW TO DO THEM, WHEN, AND WHY.

## SUMMARIZING

PRESENTS A CONCISE, GENERAL SENSE OF WHAT YOUR SOURCE IS ABOUT.

OFTEN, SUMMARIZING GIVES A BROAD OVERVIEW OF MATERIAL THAT IS NOT IN DISPUTE.

HERE'S A SUMMARY THAT USES CONTENT FROM A WIKIPEDIA ARTICLE:

"The history of detective fiction dates back to 1841, when Edgar Allan Poe introduced Monsieur C. Auguste Dupin in the short story 'The Murders in the Rue Morgue.' Today it includes the police procedural, the legal thriller, the courtroom drama, the locked room mystery, hard-boiled fiction, the noir novel, and the 'cozy,' in which sex and violence are downplayed. In the 'cozy,' the protagonist is often a female amateur, and humor and social satire might be important parts of the narrative."

WIKIPEDIA

**PARAPHRASING** SHOULD GIVE THE READER A MORE COMPLETE SENSE OF THE AUTHOR'S ARGUMENT AND MORE OF THE FLAVOR OF THE ORIGINAL THAN A SUMMARY.

AND EVEN THOUGH A PARAPHRASE IS "IN YOUR OWN WORDS," THE IDEAS CAME FROM SOMEWHERE ELSE -- SO YOU'LL HAVE TO CITE YOUR SOURCE.

HERE'S A PARAPHRASE OF PART OF A CHAPTER IN THE BOOK *CITY OF QUARTZ,* A HISTORY OF LOS ANGELES.

AUTHOR MIKE DAVIS CLAIMS THAT NOIR STORIES ABOUT CRIME AND THE ILL EFFECTS OF CAPITALISM REFLECT MANY DIFFERENT INFLU-ENCES FROM THE TIME OF THE GREAT DEPRESSION, WORLD WAR II, AND THE PERIOD THAT FOLLOWED.

DAVIS ARGUES THAT IMMIGRANT WRITERS, COMPOSERS, FILMMAKERS, AND ARTISTS FLEEING HITLER'S GERMANY PLAYED A ROLE IN DEVELOPING CERTAIN ASPECTS OF THE NOIR DETECTIVE GENRE, BUT HE INSISTS THAT FEW OF THEM ACTUALLY PARTICIPATED IN THE GRITTY URBAN LIFESTYLES OF LOS ANGELES IN THE 1940s.

UNLIKE MANY CRITICS, DAVIS ASSERTS THAT LOCAL LOS ANGELES AUTHORS PLAYED A MAJOR ROLE IN DEVELOP-ING WHAT CAME TO BE KNOWN AS "L.A. NOIR."

HE SAYS THAT THESE LOCAL WRITERS KNEW MUCH MORE ABOUT THE SCANDALS OF THE CITY -- POLICE CORRUPTION, REAL ESTATE AND OIL SPECULATION, AND ANTI-LABOR AND ANTI-IMMIGRANT POLITICS -- THAN OUTSIDERS COMING FROM EUROPE DID.

WOW!

THAT PARAPHRASE REALLY GAVE ME A SENSE OF DAVIS'S ARGUMENT AND OF WHY HIS SCHOLARSHIP IS DISTINCTIVE.

SO, WHEN YOU FIND A SOURCE THAT IS REALLY SIGNIFICANT FOR YOUR RESEARCH, EVEN IF YOU DISAGREE WITH IT, YOU MIGHT WANT TO SPEND SOME TIME CAREFULLY PARAPHRASING IT IN YOUR OWN WORDS.

PARAPHRASE    SUMMARY

REMEMBER #2 **PARAPHRASE** to give a sense of the author's ARGUMENT.

NOW, **QUOTING** COMES IN HANDY WHEN YOUR SOURCES SAY SOMETHING PARTICULARLY **EVOCATIVE**...

...OR **INSIGHTFUL**...

...OR WHEN YOU WANT TO CALL ATTENTION TO A WRITER'S **LANGUAGE**.

GENIUS!

YOU CAN QUOTE A SHORT PASSAGE OR EVEN JUST A SIGNIFICANT KEYWORD.

IF YOU CHOOSE TO PRESENT A LONG QUOTATION, MAKE SURE THAT YOU HAVE ENOUGH TO SAY ABOUT THE PASSAGE TO SHOW WHY IT'S WORTH REPRODUCING IN ITS ENTIRETY.

FOR INSTANCE...

LAUGHING in the JUNGLE LOUIS ADAMIC

LAUGHING IN THE JUNGLE, A BOOK ABOUT LOS ANGELES BY IMMIGRANT WRITER LOUIS ADAMIC, HAS A DISTINCTIVE WRITING STYLE AND MANY JUICY PASSAGES TO CHOOSE FROM.

I-57

*In this case, Tom Gammill, creator of The Doozies.

YOU SHOULD **TALK** TO US IF YOU'RE HAVING TROUBLE HANDLING A PROJECT.

PRESENTING OTHERS' WORK AS YOUR OWN IS A TERRIBLE IDEA FOR A LOT OF REASONS.

FOR ONE THING, IT'S **PLAGIARISM.**

BUT JUST A COUPLE OF PAGES BACK YOU GUYS WERE TALKING ABOUT QUOTING FROM SOURCES.

BUT YOU NEED TO TELL READERS WHERE YOU FOUND YOUR SOURCES, NOT PRETEND YOU CREATED THE WORK YOURSELF.

AND YOU ALSO NEED TO EVALUATE AND INTERPRET MATERIAL THAT YOU FIND AND INTEGRATE IT INTO YOUR OWN TEXT.

YOU DON'T JUST INSERT SOURCES WITHOUT ANY ANALYSIS OR REFLECTION!

IF YOU ARE GOING TO QUOTE SOMEONE ELSE'S WORK, HAVE A GOOD REASON FOR REPRODUCING IT EXACTLY.

=SIGH=

THAT MAKES SENSE.

I GUESS WE KNEW ALL THAT, BUT DESPERATION MAKES PEOPLE DO CRAZY THINGS SOMETIMES.

IT'S NOT ALWAYS EASY TO CITE YOUR SOURCES.

OUR STUDENTS HAVE TROUBLE WITH IT ALL THE TIME.

HOW DO I CITE A VIDEO I WATCHED **ONLINE?**

WHAT ABOUT A **COMIC?**

Issue 2 • Research: More Than Detective Work

**Search**

fracking

SEARCH CLICK

WHAT ABOUT THIS?

"DOES FRACKING ROCK OR DOES FRACKING SHAKE US UP?"

IT'S THE FIRST RESULT.

FRACK ATTACK!

play the GAME!

COOL WEB SITE. IT MAKES A **STRONG ARGUMENT** USING ANIMATION.

YEAH, THEY EVEN HAVE A VIDEO GAME THAT SHOWS HOW GEOLOGICAL FORCES INTERACT.

BUT THE WEB SITE DOESN'T CITE THE SOURCES FOR ALL THE STATISTICS THEY LIST.

I CAN'T FIGURE OUT WHO **SPONSORS** THE SITE.

OH, HERE IT IS! "COURTESY OF **FRACK ATTACK**, THE MOVIE."

THIS RESEARCH DOESN'T SEEM ALL THAT **OBJECTIVE**. PARTICULARLY IF IT'S PROMOTING A FILM.

THIS VIDEO GAME IS **INTRIGUING**, THOUGH.

Stress Determination by Hydraulic Fracturing in Subsurface Waste Injection

R. G. Wolff, J. D. Bredehoeft, W. S. Keys, Eugene Shuter

Journal (American Water Works Association), Vol. 67, No. 9, Ground-Water Recharge (September 1975), pp. 519-523

legislation/regulation: Hydraulic Fracturing: Is Regulation Needed?

Frederick W. Pontius

Journal (American Water Works Association), Vol. 101, No. 9 (September 2009), p. 24, 26, 28, 30, 32

TWO OF THESE ARTICLES ARE FROM A JOURNAL FROM THE AMERICAN WATER WORKS ASSOCIATION.

IT MIGHT TAKE SOME INVESTIGATING TO LEARN HOW OBJECTIVE THOSE ARTICLES ARE.

YEAH, IT'S TIME TO DIG DEEPER!

click! click! ding!

ha ha

I'M ALMOST AT THE DEPOSIT!

+ 500

ANYWAY... ...YOU CAN SEARCH JUST FOR THE PEER-REVIEWED ARTICLES FROM THAT JOURNAL, WHICH CAN BE SEPARATED FROM FEATURE ARTICLES ON WATER MANAGEMENT OR INDUSTRY NEWS.

YOU CAN ALSO DO SOME RESEARCH ON THE ORGANIZATION. HERE'S WHAT THEIR WEB SITE SAYS:

Established in 1881, the American Water Works Association is the largest nonprofit, scientific and educational association dedicated to managing and treating water, the world's most important resource.

BUT A NONPROFIT ORGANIZATION ISN'T NECESSARILY OBJECTIVE.

HOW ABOUT THIS...

next 50 years with current technologies. *Science* 305:968–972.
2. Tour JM, Kittrell C, Colvin VL (2010) Green carbon as a bridge to renewable energy. *Nature Mater* 9:871–874.
3. Kerr RA (2010) Natural gas from shale bursts onto the scene. *Science* 328:1624–1626.
4. Raupach MR, et al. (2007) Global and regional drivers of accelerating $CO_2$ emissions. *Proc Natl Acad Sci USA* 104:10288–10293.
5. US Energy Information Administration (2010) *Annual Energy Outlook 2010 with Projections to 2035* (US Energy Information Administration, Washington, DC), DOE/EIA-0383; http://www.eia.doe.gov/oiaf/aeo/pdf/0383(2010).pdf.
6. US Environmental Protection Agency (2011) Hydraulic Fracturing. (US Environmental Protection Agency, Washington, DC), http://water.epa.gov/type/groundwater/uic/class2/hydraulicfracturing/.
7. Kargbo DM, Wilhelm RG, Campbell DJ (2010) Natural gas plays in the Marcellus shale: Challenges and potential opportunities. *Environ Sci Technol* 44:5679–5684.
8. Revesz KM, Breen KJ, Baldassare AJ, Burrus RC (2010) Carbon and hydrogen isotopic evidence for the origin of combustible gases in water supply wells in north-central Pennsylvania. *Appl Geochem* 25:1845–1859.
9. Zoback M, Kitasei S, Copithorne B Addressing the environmental risks from shale gas development. *Worldwatch Institute Briefing Paper 1* (Worldwatch Inst, Washington, DC), http://blogs.worldwatch.org/revolt/wp-content/uploads/2010/07/Environmental-Risks-Paper-July-2010-FOR-PRINT.pdf.
10. Pennsylvania Department of Environmental Protection, Bureau of Oil and Gas Management (2010) 2009 Year End Workload Report. (Pennsylvania Dept of Environmental Protection, Bureau of Oil and Gas Management, Harrisburg, PA), http://www.dep.state.pa.us/dep/deputate/minres/oilgas/2009%20Year%20End%20Report-WEBSITE.pdf.
11. Colborn T, Kwiatkowski C, Schultz K, Bachran M (2010) Natural gas operations from a public health perspective. *Hum Ecol Risk Assess*, in press.
12. Pennsylvania Department of Environmental Protection (2011) Private Water Wells in Pennsylvania. (Pennsylvania Dept of Environmental Protection, Harrisburg, PA), http://www.dep.state.pa.us/dep/deputate/watermgt/wc/Subjects/SrceProt/well/.
13. Eltschlager KK, Hawkins JW, Ehler WC, Baldassare F (2001) *Technical Measures for the Investigation and Mitigation of Fugitive Methane Hazards in Areas of Coal Mining* (US Dept of the Interior, Office of Surface Mining Reclamation and Enforcement, Pittsburgh).
14. Schoell M (1980) The hydrogen and carbon isotopic composition of methane from natural gases of various origins. *Geochim Cosmochim Acta* 44:649–661.
15. Bernard BB (1978) Light hydrocarbons in marine sediments. PhD Dissertation (Texas A&M Univ, College Station, TX).
16. Jenden PD, Drazan DJ, Kaplan IR (1993) Mixing of thermogenic natural gases in northern Appalachian Basin. *Am Assoc Pet Geol Bull* 77:980–998.
17. Laughrey CD, Baldassare FJ (1998) Geochemistry and origin of some natural gases in the Plateau Province Central Appalachian Basin, Pennsylvania and Ohio. *Am Assoc Pet Geol Bull* 82:317–335.
18. Osborn SG, McIntosh JC (2010) Chemical and isotopic tracers of the contribution of microbial gas in Devonian organic-rich shales and reservoir sandstones, northern Appalachian Basin. *Appl Geochem* 25:456–471.
19. Repetski JE, Ryder RT, Harper JA, Trippi MH (2006) Thermal maturity patterns in the Ordovician and Devonian of Pennsylvania using conodont color alteration index (CAI) and vitrinite reflectance (%Ro). *Northeastern Geology Environmental Sciences*

and biogenic methane: Upper Devonian... *Cosmochim Acta* 62:1699–1720.
21. Engelder T, Lash GG, Uzcategui RS (2009) Middle and Upper Devonian gas shale... *Bull* 93:857–889.
22. Pennsylvania Department of Environmental Protection, Harrisburg... pa.us/dep/deputate/minres/oilgas/new...
23. New York State Department of Health... (2009) (New York State Dept of Health) mental Generic Environmental Statement the Marcellus Shale and other Lo... Well Permit Issuance for Horizontal... riverkeeper.org/wp-content/uploads/20... 3-NYSDOH-Environmental-Radiation-M...
24. Taylor LE (1984) Groundwater Resources sylvania: Water Resources Report 58. (... Office of Parks and Forestry—Bureau of... PA) 139.
25. Williams JH, Taylor L, Low D (1998) H... Glaciated Valleys of Bradford, Tioga,... sources Report 68. (Commonwealth of... Resources, Harrisburg, PA) p 89.
26. Kendall C, Coplan TB (2001) Distribut... across the United States. *Hydrol Proc...*
27. Van Stempvoort D, Maathuis H, Jaw... fugitive methane in groundwater link... 43:187–199.
28. Taylor SW, Sherwood Lollar B, Wass... surface aquifers: Implications for leak... 34:4727–4732.
29. Cramer B, Schlomer S, Poelchau HS (2... the release of natural gas from groun... tions, London), 447–455.
30. Geyer AR, Wilshusen JP (1982) Engine... environmental geology supplement... Geological Survey. (Dept of Environm... ment, Harrisburg, PA).

31. Etiope G, Martinelli G (2002) Migration of carrier a... overview. *Phys Earth Planet Inter* 129:185–204.
32. Aravena R, Wassenaar LI (1993) Dissolved organic ca... confined aquifer, southern Ontario, Canada: Carbon... subsurface sources. *Appl Geochem* 8:483–493.
33. Coleman DD, Liu C, Riley KM (1988) Microbial me... sediments and glacial deposits of the Illinois, USA.
34. Alexander SS, Cakir R, Doden AG, Gold DP, Root SI (2...

COMING UP IN THE NEXT EXCITING EPISODE OF **REFRAME**

"Am I **MISSING** something?"

# "RESEARCH"

### 1 CONNECTIONS

TO GET STARTED AS A RESEARCHER, LOOK FOR AN ENTRY POINT THAT APPEALS TO YOU. YOU CAN LOOK AT A VARIETY OF BACKGROUND SOURCES OR BEGIN WITH A PERSONAL CONNECTION THAT DRAWS YOU TO YOUR TOPIC.

MARISSA OSATO WANTED TO RESEARCH JAPANESE INTERNMENT CAMPS DURING WORLD WAR II BECAUSE OF A PERSONAL CONNECTION: HER GRANDMOTHER HAD LIVED IN ONE OF THE CAMPS.

Gesensway, Deborah, and Mindy Roseman. *Beyond Words: Images from America's Concentration Camps.* Cornell UP, 1987.

Kuramitsu, Kristine C. "Internment and Identity in Japanese American Art." *American Quarterly*, vol. 47, no. 4, Dec. 1995, pp. 619-58. JSTOR, doi:10.2307/2713369.

Matsuda, Ted. "Contemporary Accounts and Documents (Photocopies), 1942-1976 and Undated." Mitsuye Yamada Papers, MS-R71, Box 1, Folder 6, Special Collections and Archives, The U California Irvine Libraries, Irvine.

Osato, Mollie. Bird pins. Circa 1943-45. Photograph by Marissa Osato.

Osato, Mollie. Personal interview. 14 May 2006.

*Something Strong Within.* Directed by Robert A. Nakamura, Japanese American National Museum, 1994.

IDEAS AND SOURCES CAN LEAD TO UNEXPECTED PLACES. YOUR RESEARCH MIGHT EVEN END UP HELPING OTHER RESEARCHERS SOMEDAY!

SEE WHERE **YOUR** RESEARCH TAKES YOU.

# DRAWING CONCLUSIONS

The following assignments ask you to practice finding,
evaluating, and responding to research sources.

**1** Look at Liz's detective map on p. I-37.
Try to follow the arrows and construct
a version of her investigation, writing
out a step-by-step narrative that
describes the process.

Think about the organization of your
details, and craft a story that makes
some kind of sense even when the
illustrations are outlandish.

**2** Choose a current event that you already know a
little bit about, and spend some time gathering what
you believe are unreliable resources on that topic --
perhaps a biased news site or a personal blog.

Once you've gathered some examples, try to think
of instances in which these resources might be
useful, depending on what aspect of the event is
being discussed.

On the other end of the spectrum, are there ever
instances when "reputable" sources of information might
**NOT** be suitable for a particular piece of writing?

**3**

Choose a historical event and search for as many different kinds of sources on the topic as you can -- primary and secondary, fiction and nonfiction, multimedia, digital, etc.

As you gather your list, brainstorm ways you can evaluate the usefulness or relevance of each source. What are your methods for finding different sources? What kinds of sources are easier or more difficult to find?

**4**

A good way to begin creating a research-based argument is to find a position that you will refute or critique. Think about your position on some significant aspect of the event you began researching in question 3.

Find a source that takes a thoughtful position that differs from your own. Summarize that source's argument fairly, and then sketch out a chart or an outline of your response.

PART 2
# COMPOSING IN GENRES
## FROM START TO FINISH

# 5

# EXPLORING TOPICS & CREATING A RESEARCH PROPOSAL

## CONTENTS

▲ STUDENT AUTHOR
**Jasmine Huerta.**
*iStockphoto.*
RESEARCH PROPOSAL ▶
**Jasmine Huerta,**
Diabetes Project.

---

ENG 101, Professor Braziller

**Research Proposal Assignment: What Is Your Focus?**

Jasmine Huerta
Professor Amy Braziller
English 101
October 6, 20—

Research Proposal

1. Your research question

    How can diet—specifically, monitoring the intake of sugar, calories, and sodium—help someone with diabetes manage the disease and avoid taking insulin?

2. A working title for your project

    The working title for my project is "Living with Diabetes: Diet Is the Answer." I chose this topic because although some people are predisposed to diabetes because of genetics, they do have some control over the situation. For example, through their choices related to food and diet they can manage or perhaps even prevent the disease.

# CHOOSING A TOPIC THROUGH BASIC RESEARCH

The Internet offers an unlimited source of topics, and beginning your reading can be exciting but overwhelming: You can easily locate millions of resources on any topic simply by doing a quick online search. That's why it's important to go about the process in an orderly fashion. This chapter will show you the steps you need to take.

Whenever you write—as a student in a composition classroom or a professional in a workplace—you focus on a specific topic. Sometimes you may be provided with a general theme or a specific topic or issue. For example, your instructor might ask you to respond to an essay you've read for class, or your manager at work might ask you to share your plans to improve business or increase sales in the next quarter. Other times, most often in the course of college work, you get to start from scratch and choose a topic purely out of your own interest and curiosity.

So how do you choose a topic? Where should you start? One place might be this book. The Index of Themes (p. T-1) organizes every reading in this text by topic, and the Index of Genres (p. G-1) will help you see the relationship between topic choice and genre choice.

*What issues do you care most about? What have you blogged or posted about lately? What topics from the news or your studies keep you up at night? What would you like to learn more about?*

## 1. Brainstorm Topic Ideas: Read, Talk, Sketch, Enjoy.

The best way to get started on identifying a topic that is meaningful to you is to get your ideas flowing. Here are some ways to do that.

Begin by reading for ideas, and discuss those ideas with others.

**Do some preliminary reading online, but be disciplined about it**   Googling your topic is a way to explore your initial ideas, but at this stage, limit yourself to a few major sources in order to get a flavor for the topic. Some general sources might be *Salon, Slate, The New York Times,* or CNN. If you want to skim scholarly sources, try Google Scholar (scholar.google.com). If you go to *Wikipedia,* be sure to look at the source links for the entries you read. That's where you'll find the best leads. And don't be all day about it: Remember, you're generating ideas, not surfing mindlessly. For example, let's say you are interested in the topic of road rage: the problem of aggressive driving. While the *Wikipedia* "Road Rage" entry (see p. 262) may not be exceptionally informative (or particularly trustworthy), the "Sources," "Further reading," and "External links" sections can connect you to better sources, such as the National Highway Traffic Safety Administration's campaign to stop aggressive driving (see p. 263), and AAA's (the Automobile Association of America's) study on controlling road rage.

*For an Index of Sources & Contexts for material referenced in this chapter, see the e-Pages at* **bedfordstmartins .com/bookofgenres.**

WIKIPEDIA ENTRY ▶
**Wikipedia,**
"Road Rage." While
a wiki entry may not
be totally reliable,
it can be a starting
point. *Photo by Mario
Roberto Duran Ortiz
Mariordo. The Wikipedia
trademark is licensed
under CC BY-SA 3.0.
(Author User: Paul
Stansifer, User: Nohat,
Philip Metschan.)*

WIKIPEDIA ENTRY ▶
**Wikipedia,**
"Sources" section of
"Road Rage" entry.
Here you will find a
list of books, articles,
and the U.S. National
Highway Traffic Safety
Administration, an
authority on road
rage. (See p. 265.)
*CC BY-SA 3.0.*

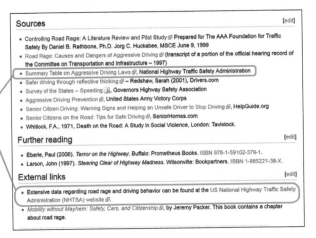

**Talk to people**   Discuss your topic ideas and questions with classmates, friends, family, and coworkers to find out what others have to say about the topic you're considering. Often, explaining why you're interested in a topic can help you focus. When others ask you to clarify your ideas, you will often discover what you really want to say.

Continue to generate ideas through brainstorming and sketching techniques.

**Make a list**   What do you care most about? Begin by making a list of things you are passionate about, your pet peeves, things you are curious about, things you don't understand, or things you'd like to change about the world. From your initial

◄ WEB SITE
**National Highway Traffic Safety Administration,** "Stop Aggressive Driving." The "Sources" and "External Links" sections of *Wikipedia*'s "Road Rage" entry point readers to this authoritative government source (nhtsa.gov/ Aggressive). *Courtesy of the National Highway Traffic Administration.*

list, force yourself to double or triple the size of the list. Often the best topic ideas are the less obvious ones—ideas that will come to you when you push yourself to keep listing.

**Freewrite**  If you've identified a general topic area, or some of the ideas you've generated in your lists interest you, try freewriting. The goal here is to get your ideas written down, without judging what you're writing, or editing yourself, or trying to write beautifully. Experiment by making yourself write nonstop for ten to thirty minutes. As you keep your fingers moving, don't worry about making sense, or about readers being confused or impressed. No one is going to read this document but you. When you take away the pressure of producing smooth prose, you may be surprised to see the ideas you generate.

**Mind map**  Like list making and freewriting, mind mapping gives you a creative format for sketching out your early ideas about a topic. To begin, write the topic or idea you are exploring in the middle of a blank piece of paper (alternatively, you can use mind-mapping software such as MatchWare OpenMind or a free Web-based mind-mapping application such as Bubbl.us). As you think of details and related ideas, write them around the central topic, connecting them with lines that indicate their relationships.

Ideas come out of conversations. What comes up in your talks with friends? What was the topic of your last discussion or disagreement? What are some of your unresolved questions about the topic?

# Guided Process: How to Choose a Topic

## Sharon Freeman (Student)

### *From Coffee to Germs*

▲ STUDENT AUTHOR
**Sharon Freeman.**
Here we look at
this student's early
brainstorming on a
possible research
topic (germs).
*Shutterstock.*

Below are three lists made by student Sharon Freeman. In the first list, she simply wrote down everything on her mind. For the second list, she wrote a question or two about each topic. By the third, she focused on germs and specific questions related to that topic.

**TOPIC BRAINSTORM 1**

Coffee

Chocolate

Democracy

Taxes

Germs

**TOPIC BRAINSTORM 2**

**Coffee**—is it worth it to pay more for organic or sustainably grown coffee?

**Chocolate**—is dark chocolate really good for you?

**Democracy**—how much say do citizens have compared with corporations these days? How much difference do huge campaign contributions make in how politicians vote and make laws?

**Taxes**—how much do I really pay in taxes (income taxes, sales taxes, property taxes, etc.), and how does it all get spent?

**Germs**—is antibacterial soap really necessary?

**TOPIC BRAINSTORM 3**

Germs

Do I need to use antibacterial soap, or does it make things worse?

Do you need both antibacterial soap and hand sanitizer, or just one?

How much money do people spend these days on antibacterial products and is it all just a hoax?

Aren't some germs actually good for you?

Has anyone actually gotten sick from someone at the gym not wiping down a machine? Seriously, what can you catch from someone else's sweat?

Why do some people get colds and other people don't?

How contagious are you when you have a cold? Should you really skip class and work?

How can you build your immunity against colds?

After brainstorming, Sharon did some freewriting about germs:

**TOPIC FREEWRITE: "GERMS"**

It seems like everyone I know is obsessed with germs. My roommate has little bottles of hand sanitizer stashed everywhere and she's constantly using the stuff and offering it to me. I feel weird when I say no, but honestly, I'm suspicious of the stuff. I wash my hands before cooking or eating and of course, after using the bathroom, and I almost never get sick, so it seems to me that I'm doing everything I need to do. What would spending money on hand sanitizer and obsessing over germs do for me? I think it's a moneymaking scheme. The companies that make soap now want to sell us soap AND hand sanitizer. And now we have to pay extra to get antibacterial soap, too. My parents don't use that and they're perfectly healthy. My dad hasn't had a cold in twenty years.

Sharon also sketched out a mind map in order to explore different views and aspects of her topic. In the map below, she broke out "Germs" into two aspects or subtopics:

**TOPIC MIND MAP: "GERMS"**

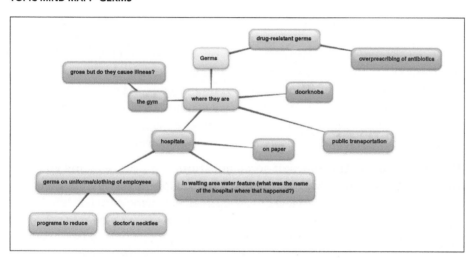

At this point, Sharon is ready to test some of her questions with some preliminary research, with a focus on:

1. Where germs are

2. How germs become drug resistant

From there, she focuses on the first subtopic—where germs are—and further breaks it down into aspects she could explore (in darker green):

» The gym

» Public transportation

» Hospitals

» Doorknobs

When you research a topic, how do you know what is fact and what is opinion (an argument supported with facts)? If you wanted just plain facts about how germs are spread—and not, say, an argument for or against hand sanitizers—what sources would you turn to? Medical reports? Editorials?

Sharon Freeman, *From Coffee to Germs*

265

Next, Sharon focuses on hospitals—and programs that hospitals could adopt for reducing the spread of germs among staff and patients. For example, "asking doctors not to wear germ-transporting neckties" could branch off the "programs to reduce" bubble.

There are still plenty of unexplored topic areas represented in this map. For example, Sharon could go back to her "Germs" bubble and add other aspects, such as the views of scientists, parents, and schools. Or she could focus on the relationship between drug-resistant germs and the use of hand sanitizer.

## 2. Explore Topic Ideas through Preliminary Research: Ask Yourself, Who's Saying What?

Once you've identified a topic area (road rage, germs, or something else), you're ready to dig a little deeper to better understand it. Keep a few possibilities in mind and conduct preliminary research on several related topics (or subtopics) so you can make an informed decision about which one to commit to; the viability of each topic will depend on what you find out at this point. As with the preliminary reading you did during brainstorming, you'll continue to draw on sources written for nonexperts. Later in your process, you'll move on to more specialized sources. As you conduct preliminary research, focus on the following:

**Words and facts: Ask yourself some questions. Are there terms you need to define? And what are the facts?**   For example, if you are exploring road rage, you might ask yourself: How do law enforcement agencies define "road rage"? When is this term used, and why? Are there degrees of road rage that police recognize? And how does the court system define and prosecute road rage? For ex- ▶ ample, the Automobile Association of America (AAA), in a report it commissioned (see p. 267), makes a distinction between "road rage" and "aggressive driving."

As you gather facts, ask yourself: How many incidents of road rage have been recorded nationally? How many in your state, city, or neighborhood? What were the circumstances? What were the repercussions?

**Opinions: Find out what others have to say on the subject, and notice what evidence they use to support their opinions**   In addition to facts, what opinions surround your topic? Who writes about the topic, and why are they concerned? On what sources do they base their statements or arguments? What sources do they draw on? And what sources might you want to use, too? In relation to the road rage topic, you might find out that some psychologists consider road rage a mental health issue, or that law enforcement in different places defines road rage as a crime, depending on whether someone is injured or killed. Source material for road rage might include legal statutes and news reports of incidents.

### RESEARCH  ABOUT  MEDIA CENTER  STORE

Home › About › About the AAA Foundation for Traffic Safety

## ABOUT THE AAA FOUNDATION FOR TRAFFIC SAFETY

The AAA Foundation for Traffic Safety was founded in 1947 by AAA to conduct research to address growing highway safety issues. The organization's mission is to identify traffic safety problems, foster research that seeks solutions and disseminate information and educational materials.

The Foundation has funded over 250 projects designed to discover the causes of traffic crashes, prevent them, and minimize injuries when they do occur. Knowledge is the first step to becoming a better driver. The Foundation's studies have shown that understanding the risks of driving and one's own limitations can prevent crashes. The Foundation's materials seek to give drivers new skills, sharpen old ones, and change attitudes as the first step to changing behaviors. Additionally, AAAFTS research is used to create focused, high-impact educational materials for drivers, pedestrians, bicyclists and road users of all ages.

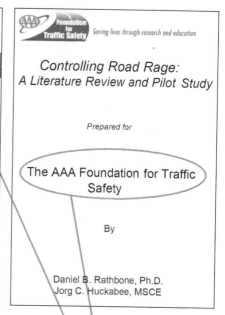

*Controlling Road Rage:*
*A Literature Review and Pilot Study*

*Prepared for*

The AAA Foundation for Traffic Safety

By

Daniel B. Rathbone, Ph.D.
Jorg C. Huckabee, MSCE

*Controlling Road Rage: A Literature Review and Pilot Study*

**Executive Summary**

This report discusses results of a literature review and pilot study on how to prevent aggressive driving and road rage. The study *"Controlling Road Rage: A Literature Review and Pilot Study"* defines road rage as "an incident in which an angry or impatient motorist or passenger intentionally injures or kills another motorist, passenger, or pedestrian, or attempts or threatens to injure or kill another motorist, passenger, or pedestrian." It must be emphasized that "road rage" and "aggressive driving" are not synonymous. Road rage is uncontrolled anger that results in violence or threatened violence on the road; it is criminal behavior. Aggressive driving does not rise to the level of criminal behavior. Aggressive driving includes tailgating, abrupt lane changes, and speeding, alone or in combination. These potentially dangerous behaviors are traffic offenses, but are not criminal behavior.

The facts that the AAA authors present are drawn from research about road rage. They begin by defining terms and differentiating "road rage" from "aggressive driving."

▲ REPORT **Daniel B. Rathbone and Jorg C. Huckabee,** *Controlling Road Rage: A Literature Review and Pilot Study.* This report was prepared for the AAA Foundation for Traffic Safety. *Courtesy of the AAA Foundation.*

As you gather opinions on your topic, ask yourself: What are the advantages of—and motivations behind—each argument? For example, an organization that wants to stop road rage might define it as a mental health issue; this might make it easier for them to get funding for a safe driving program.

**Your perspective: Form your own arguments in response to others**  As you research, you will begin to form your own ideas and opinions about your topic. For example, learning how others define road rage might lead you to form your own definition. Or learning how psychologists understand and treat road rage could lead you to put forth an argument on how it should be handled by law enforcement. In other words, you will naturally begin responding to the ideas of others and kicking around possible arguments.

**Conflicting views: Notice who disagrees about your topic**  When you begin reading sources related to your topic, you might begin to notice that there are viewpoints that stand opposed to each other. Furthermore, as you dig into these disagreements, you might realize that the differing viewpoints are well researched and should not be immediately dismissed. In the case of road rage, you might find one article by a psychologist arguing that road rage is a result of a mental disorder and another article written by a sociologist claiming that road rage is not a mental condition, but rather a cultural condition based on societal behavior. Discovering well-researched, well-reasoned opposing stances related to your topic forces you to accept that there is not necessarily one "correct" viewpoint; reasonable people can disagree.

**The irrational: Avoid arguments that are just too "out there"**  In the course of your research, you may stumble upon the ideas of people who are unreasonable, ill informed, or both. For example, say you are researching *Apollo 11*, the first manned landing on the moon, in 1969, and the cultural impact of this event. You may encounter arguments by those who believe the landing was a hoax, despite factual evidence to the contrary. Moon landing deniers are considered by most people to be out of touch with reality; in this case, pursuing this strand of research is not worthwhile. Keep a critical eye as you read sources.

**Comfort zone: Use sources that are right for you**  While there is plenty of source material on the topics of road rage and *Apollo 11*, other topics, especially those that are very narrow or specialized, can be problematic. In certain cases, the information you need might be held in archives or scientific labs that you don't have access to; another problem is that the information you find might be so complex that you can't understand it. For example, a scholarly journal article on advanced economic theory is probably not an appropriate source for your purposes (unless you happen to be an expert in this area).

**Detective work: Keep an eye out for subtopics**  In your preliminary research you'll uncover subtopics you hadn't thought of before. For example, you may not have known that the phenomenon of road rage is discussed and researched by doctors and psychologists; a subtopic of road rage might be personality predictors for road rage.

**The search: Pay attention to key terms**  As you conduct preliminary research, you'll notice that certain terms pop up. For example, if you research road rage, you'll see that *defensive driving*, *aggressive driving*, *reckless driving*, and *intermittent explosive disorder* are terms that appear frequently in source materials. Follow up on these key terms by using them in your searches of the Internet and library databases.

**What works: Test the viability of your topic by asking yourself a few questions** Following is an assignment we give our students during their preliminary research phase. It includes the responses of a student, Jasmine Huerta, whose research topic is diabetes. (Note: We will see more of her work on this project later in the chapter.)

Through answering the assigned questions, Jasmine realizes that she has several interesting potential research questions to pursue. The list of key terms helped her continue and refine her research. She realized that the glycemic index is not 100 percent accepted, which surprised and intrigued her. By using the Internet to find key terms, exploring some of these potential subtopics, previewing and reading sources, and then reflecting on her process and discoveries, Jasmine narrows her topic from diabetes to the role of nutrition in the diabetic patient.

---

**ENG 101, Professor Braziller**

**Topic Assignment: What Is Your Topic? How Viable Is It?**

Jasmine Huerta
Professor Amy Braziller
English 101
September 26, 20—
Topic Idea: Diabetes

You've begun your preliminary research. Now, respond to the following questions to see how workable your topic may be.

1. What is the general topic area you are considering?

   I am interested in researching and writing about diabetes.

2. Why? Are you truly fascinated/curious/passionate about the topic? How did you become interested in this topic? (If your answer is no, explain why and then move on to the next topic without answering any more questions.)

   Diabetes runs in my family, so it's something I want to understand more about in case I am faced with it at some point. My six-year-old cousin has type 1 diabetes. My mother had gestational diabetes when she was pregnant with me. Most recently, my grandfather, who is a bit overweight (as is my cousin), was diagnosed with diabetes. I'm wondering if I am just destined to develop it at some point because of my family history. I also wonder if perhaps there are things I can do to prevent the disease, since I presently don't have diabetes. I worry about both my cousin and grandfather, so I'd like to see if there are some things they could do to keep their diabetes under control, rather than just relying on traditional medicine.

3. What surprising facts have you gathered so far about your topic? What further questions do you have that you need answered with data? And what sources are you thinking of using?

*Continues next page*

▲ STUDENT AUTHOR
**Jasmine Huerta.**
In this chapter, we follow this student as she chooses and investigates a topic (diabetes). Jasmine appears next on page 277.
*iStockphoto.*

◀ TOPIC ASSIGNMENT
**Jasmine Huerta.**
Shown here are Jasmine's very early ideas about her diabetes project and some information on what she's discovered during preliminary research.

Huerta, *Topic Assignment,* *Continued*

Surprising facts/data:

- According to *Wikipedia*'s entry "Diabetes" (accessed on 9/20/13): "Diabetic patients with neuropathic symptoms such as numbness or tingling in feet or hands are twice as likely to be unemployed as those without the symptoms."

- A link found on the American Diabetes Association to an article on SmartBrief .com stated that those who are exposed to secondhand smoke have a greater risk of contracting diabetes.

- According to an article about lifestyle and home remedies, found on the Mayo Clinic's page, diabetes can contribute to gum infections.

Potential sources:

- *Wikipedia*

- American Diabetes Association

- Mayo Clinic

4. Do reasonable people disagree about the topic? If so, what aspects of the topic do they disagree about? Who disagrees with whom? Name names. Articulate at least three positions you have found. (If your answer is no, explain why and then move on to the next topic without answering any more questions.)

There seems to be a bit of a debate about what makes the best approach for a diabetic diet. While surfing around on the Internet, one of the big debates I found discussed the glycemic index and how it relates to managing diabetes. It seems that people used to think you just had to avoid high-sugar foods, but after reading a few articles, I realized that many researchers want to look more closely at using the glycemic index (taking into account carbohydrates) in working with diabetic diets.

In an article titled "Low–Glycemic Index Diets in the Management of Diabetes," Miller et al. argue that this is a positive approach. I found an editorial written by Marion Franz in the publication *Diabetes Care* that argues with this approach: "The Glycemic Index: Not the most effective nutrition therapy intervention." In the Mayo Clinic's advice column, "Ask a Diabetes Specialist," someone wrote to Dr. Maria Collazo-Clavel, asking, "Is the glycemic-index diet useful for people with diabetes?" She responds that it's very complicated to use this as a measure, cautioning that it might not be the best approach for everybody.

5. Is the topic researchable in the time you have? Will you be able to conduct primary research? (If your answer is no, explain why and then move on to the next topic without answering any more questions.)

I don't see any issues with researching the topic this semester. In a short amount of time I was able to find many sources and potential ideas. Primary research also should be easy. As I mentioned in my answer above, I have a number of family members who deal with diabetes. I can easily interview them. I also would like to contact a doctor who treats people with diabetes and arrange an interview, perhaps by phone or e-mail. Another possibility for primary research is to find some blogs written by diabetics, so I could draw on some of their firsthand experiences.

Huerta, *Topic Assignment,* *Continued*

6. What are some subtopics that have emerged in your research?

- Nutrition to manage diabetes

- Medication to manage diabetes

- Alternative treatments for diabetes

- Prevention of diabetes

- Social issues connected to diabetes

7. What questions might you pursue in further research, based on what you've discovered during preliminary research?

- What types of diets are best for people with diabetes?

- How can diet prevent someone from getting diabetes if he or she has a family history of diabetes?

- How can following certain nutritional guidelines make diabetes go away?

- How can alternative treatments or natural medications be used instead of insulin?

- What countries have the highest rate of diabetes? What contributes to the high rate?

8. What are some key terms that keep coming up in relation to this topic?

- glycemic index

- metabolism

- blood sugar

- hypertension

- obesity

- glucose monitoring

- insulin

## 3. Commit to a Single Viable Topic: What Are You Most Curious About?

Once you've identified a general topic area, it's time to commit to one specific topic within it. The "What Is Your Topic? How Viable Is It?" assignment (p. 269) can assist you with this choice, as can the following questions:

**Is your topic compatible with your assignment? And can you make a strong argument about it?**   If your instructor has given you an assignment, read it carefully and consider the degree to which your topic will work. If you've

Attention, researchers! Looking for something to argue about?

Almost any topic offers argumentative angles: The key is to find the angles.

For example, while "reading" may not seem like the most provocative topic, a quick Google search reveals that it's the subject of much debate. Some questions around this debate include: Do college students read more or less than in the past? Is online reading cognitively different from reading books? What is the relationship between how much we read and our development of critical thinking skills?

The point is to keep an open mind to topics that seem vanilla. You may find some spice under the surface.

been asked to make an argument, you might find yourself gravitating toward controversial issues—such as gun control, abortion, and censorship. However, we urge you to consider other, less obvious topics. For example, if you are interested in the subject of gun control, rather than choosing the topic of concealed weapons and constitutional rights, you might take the topic of gun control and examine the power that gun control groups, such as the NRA, hold in the political arena.

**Do you like your topic enough to stick with it?**  If you are not truly curious about your topic, you probably won't remain interested in your research beyond the first week or so. Choose something you really want to learn about, that has some connection to you and your life.

**What is your deadline, and how will it affect your plans for research?** If your completed project is due in two weeks, choose a topic for which there is plenty of information that you can access easily. If you have more time, say an entire fifteen-week semester, you have the luxury of using a range of sources, and conducting interviews or surveys, for example, so you can select your topic accordingly. On the other hand, if your topic is so obscure that your only sources need to be ordered through interlibrary loan (which can take several weeks), it is not a good topic for either a two-week or fifteen-week deadline.

**Will you find appropriate sources for your topic?**  Some topics are so current that there is little or no published research available. For example, a friend who works in the field of bioengineering might tell you that scientists are developing crops with deeper roots to reduce the amount of carbon dioxide in the atmosphere, but because the research has just begun, there are no published articles about it. In this case, you might want to shift your topic toward an aspect of bioengineering that is more researchable in the present.

## 4. Form a Working Research Question—and Refine as You Go.

**What's your general topic? What questions will move you from a basic, broad idea to more specific ideas?**  Creating research questions focuses your attention from a general topic to a specific aspect of the topic, as follows:

| | |
|---|---|
| GENERAL TOPIC | Race |
| WORKING RESEARCH QUESTIONS | Is the criminal justice system in the United States racist? |
| | Is racial profiling a form of racism? |
| | What is it like to be an immigrant in America? |

While you'll ask (and answer) lots of questions in your research, your "research question" is the big question, the one that you are ultimately interested in answering. Once you've done some preliminary searching—and have a sense of what people are saying about your topic and what some of the subtopics are—you can formulate a working research question. As you continue your research, you will refine your question. For instance, you might decide to begin as follows:

WORKING RESEARCH QUESTION | Is racial profiling a form of racism?

But as you discover more about your topic, you might revise your question to reflect what you're learning, as follows:

REVISED RESEARCH QUESTION | Does racial profiling help or hinder law enforcement policies?

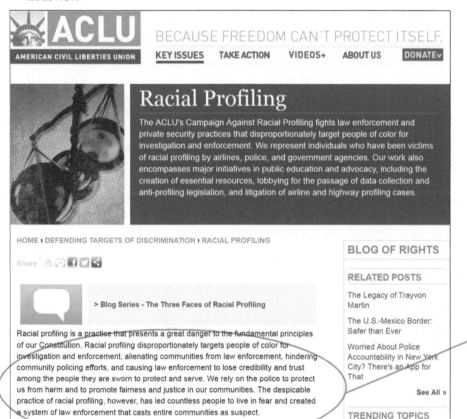

◀ WEB SITE
**The American Civil Liberties Union.** The ACLU is an excellent resource for racial profiling data and perspectives. *American Civil Liberties Union.*

The ACLU argues that the practice of racial profiling hinders law enforcement and alienates communities.

**What questions—focused on finding facts and defining terms—can move you toward a final research question?** As you begin your research, many of your questions will be focused on gathering facts and defining terms. If, as in the example above, you're researching the general topic of race, you will ask questions at the outset such as the following:

| | |
|---|---|
| QUESTIONS TO HELP YOU UNCOVER FACTS & TERMS | What is the definition of *race*? |
| | What is the difference between *race* and *ethnicity*? |
| | Has the definition of *race* changed over time? |
| | What statistical data is there concerning race in the United States? |

Your research question, however, should focus on more complex *analysis*. Following are some examples of revised, more final research questions:

| | |
|---|---|
| RESEARCH QUESTIONS | How is race portrayed in the news media? |
| | What are the real-life effects of the news media's portrayal of race? |
| | What can news media outlets do to ensure that race is portrayed responsibly? |
| | What would happen if the portrayal of race in the news media were regulated by a governing body? |

Notice how these questions require extensive research and even speculation, especially the last question. These would make solid research questions, while the first set of questions would not, although they would be useful questions to ask in the course of researching one of the questions in the second list.

Let's look at another example. Imagine you are researching graphic novel heroes. As you begin to familiarize yourself with your topic, you might ask:

| | |
|---|---|
| QUESTIONS TO HELP YOU UNCOVER FACTS & TERMS | When did graphic novels become popular? |
| | What are some popular themes in graphic novels? |
| | What are the most commercially successful graphic novels? |
| | Who is the audience for the most commercially successful graphic novels? |

With the answers to these questions, you can then focus on answering more critical, complex research questions, like these:

RESEARCH QUESTIONS   How do graphic novels subvert female stereotypes?

How does the portrayal of females in graphic novels differ from the portrayal of females in comic books?

How do graphic novels extend and build upon the archetypes of comic books?

How does the subversion of female stereotypes in graphic novels affect female readers?

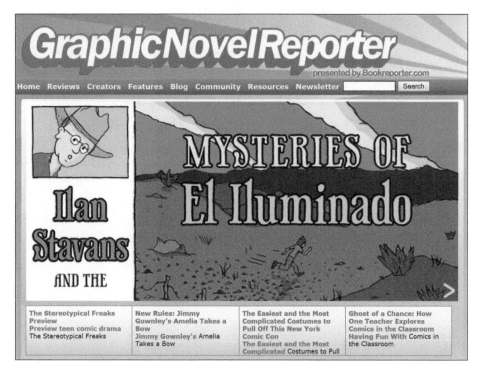

◀ WEB SITE
***Graphic Novel Reporter*** is a good source for facts and opinions on graphic works, and for investigating the themes, assumptions, and stereotypes built into graphic novels. *Copyright 2008–2015, GraphicNovelReporter.com. All rights reserved.*

As with the research questions about race, the final questions about graphic novels are much more focused on analysis than on simple fact-finding.

What is the general topic of your research? What are your questions about it so far? Which questions have to do with finding facts? Which ones are more about analysis? What, in your early research, has surprised you most?

The chart below shows some working research questions as they move from general concepts drawing on facts to more complex ideas involving speculation. As you read from left to right, you can see beginning/working research questions evolving into more final research questions. Notice also that as the questions get more speculative, they also become more debatable and argumentative.

**QUESTIONS TO HELP YOU UNCOVER FACTS & TERMS**

**RESEARCH QUESTIONS**

Broad/general ⟶ Specific, analytical, complex

| TOPIC: **Race** | What is the definition of *race*?<br><br>What is the difference between *race* and *ethnicity*? | ▶ Has the definition of *race* changed over time? | ▶ How is race portrayed in the news media?<br><br>What are the effects of the news media's portrayal of race? | ▶ What can news media outlets do to ensure that race is portrayed responsibly? | ▶ What would happen if the portrayal of race in the news media were regulated by a governing body? |

Broad/general ⟶ Specific, analytical, complex

| TOPIC: **Graphic novels** | When did graphic novels become popular?<br><br>What are the most commercially successful graphic novels?<br><br>Who is the audience for the most commercially successful graphic novels? | ▶ What are some popular themes in graphic novels? | ▶ How do graphic novels subvert female stereotypes?<br><br>How does the portrayal of females in graphic novels differ from the portrayal of females in comic books? | ▶ How do graphic novels extend and build upon the archetypes of comic books? | ▶ How does the subversion of female stereotypes in graphic novels affect female readers? |

▲ CHARTS

**Refining a research question.** This chart shows the movement from broad topic questions to more specific research questions. Notice the movement from "What is race?" to "What if the government had a say in the portrayal of race in the media?"

CHECKLIST Refining Your Research Question

What are the qualities of a really good research question?

☐ **It is open-ended,** meaning it cannot be answered with a simple yes, no, or maybe, or a single number.

☐ **It uses specific, rather than general, terms.**

☐ **It can be answered in the time you have—and with the resources you have access to.** You might have a fascinating and specific research question, but if you can't feasibly research it in the time you have, it just won't work.

☐ **It is one you really want to find answers to.** The best research grows out of curiosity. No matter how good your research question is, if it isn't backed up by your genuine interest, it won't lead you to rich, interesting research.

# MOVING FROM A RESEARCH QUESTION TO A PROPOSAL

Now that you've got an understanding of how to explore a topic and form working research questions, let's look at some next steps. In the following Guided Process, we circle back to Jasmine Huerta (remember her from the assignment on p. 269?) to see how she proceeds in her research on diabetes.

## Guided Process: How to Research a Topic

### Jasmine Huerta (Student)

*Diabetes Project*

While you may not follow every step that Jasmine takes as you work on your own research topic, tracing her process (through p. 296) may give you ideas for how to proceed.

## Exploring a Topic: Diabetes

When Jasmine got started on her project, she knew she wanted to write about diabetes, but she wasn't sure how to focus. So she began with a few broad questions:

QUESTIONS TO HELP YOU UNCOVER FACTS & TERMS

What causes diabetes? Who is affected by it, and why?

What are the statistics of diabetes in the United States and around the world?

What is the latest medical research on diabetes?

What alternative treatments are there (as opposed to insulin)?

How can people avoid getting diabetes?

What is the relationship between nutrition and diabetes?

What is the relationship between metabolism and diabetes?

What is the role of glucose and the glycemic index?

▲ STUDENT AUTHOR
**Jasmine Huerta** moves from her working research question to a final proposal in this Guided Process section. *iStockphoto.*

From these fact-finding questions, which she investigated through research (we'll outline this process in a moment), Jasmine began to narrow the scope of her topic from the list of questions above to:

WORKING RESEARCH QUESTION

What is the relationship between nutrition and diabetes?

After still more research and analysis, she pursued this question:

REVISED RESEARCH QUESTION    How can diet—specifically, monitoring the intake of sugar, calories, and sodium—help someone with diabetes manage the disease and avoid taking insulin?

Ultimately, Jasmine moved from a research question to the argument she made in her final paper, which also became her title:

FINAL RESEARCHED ARGUMENT    Getting off insulin: A case for a nutritional approach for managing diabetes

▼ *WIKIPEDIA* ENTRY
**"Diabetes mellitus."**
Jasmine reads through this entry with special attention to the "References" and "External links" sections for further resources— as well as the "Management" and "Lifestyle" portions for information on diet, which are shown on page 279. *The Wikipedia trademark is licensed under CC BY-SA 3.0. (Author User: Paul Stansifer, User: Nohat, Philip Metschan.)*

# Finding Facts about Diabetes

What was Jasmine's process? First, through her early reading, and as a person with a family history of the disease, Jasmine realizes that what interests her most are the dietary concerns of diabetics. With this in mind, she begins to explore a few more sources.

*Wikipedia* is her starting point. Even though her instructor has cautioned the class against using *Wikipedia* as a source (see our advice about *Wikipedia* on p. 406), Jasmine sees it as a good starting point for general information, and perhaps some leads related to dietary concerns. She begins with the "Diabetes mellitus" page (when she typed in "Diabetes," she was redirected there). ▼

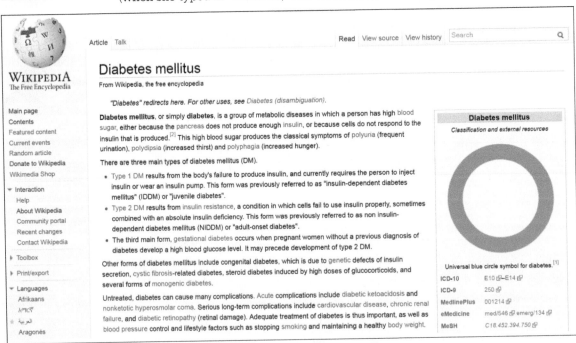

After reading through the overview, Jasmine realizes that she needs information about the differences between type 1 diabetes and type 2 diabetes (which the entry explains is the more common form, and the one that can be treated through diet). She discovers she'll also need to explore diabetes in terms of blood glucose levels, metabolism, body weight, and insulin.

Of particular interest are the "References" and "External links" sections of the "Diabetes mellitus" page, which offer Jasmine a head start on exploring other sources.

---

## References

1. ^ "Diabetes Blue Circle Symbol" ⊕. International Diabetes Federation. 17 March 2006.
2. ^ *a b c d* Shoback, edited by David G. Gardner, Dolores (2011). *Greenspan's basic & clinical endocrinology* (9th ed.). New York: McGraw-Hill Medical. pp. Chapter 17. ISBN 0-07-162243-8.
3. ^ *a b* Williams textbook of endocrinology (12th ed.). Philadelphia: Elsevier/Saunders. pp. 1371–1435. ISBN 978-1-4377-0324-5.
4. ^ Lambert, P.; Bingley, P. J. (2002). "What is Type 1 Diabetes?". *Medicine* **30**: 1–5. doi:10.1383/medc.30.1.1.28264 ⊕. Diabetes Symptoms ⊕ edit
5. ^ Rother KI (April 2007). "Diabetes treatment—bridging the divide". *The New England Journal of Medicine* **356** (15): 1499–501. doi:10.1056/NEJMp078030 ⊕. PMID 17429082 ⊕.
6. ^ *a b* "Diabetes Mellitus (DM): Diabetes Mellitus and Disorders of Carbohydrate Metabolism: Merck Manual Professional" ⊕. Merck Publishing. April 2010. Retrieved 2010-07-30.
7. ^ Dorner M, Pinget M, Brogard JM (May 1977). "Essential labile diabetes" (in German). *MMW Munch Med Wochenschr* **119** (19): 671–4. PMID 406527 ⊕.
8. ^ Lawrence JM, Contreras R, Chen W, Sacks DA (May 2008). "Trends in the prevalence of preexisting diabetes and gestational diabetes mellitus among a racially/ethnically diverse population of pregnant women, 1999–2005". *Diabetes Care* **31** (5): 899–904. doi:10.2337/dc07-2345 ⊕. PMID 18223030 ⊕.

## External links

- Diabetes ⊕ at the Open Directory Project
- American Diabetes Association ⊕
- IDF Diabetes Atlas ⊕
- National Diabetes Education Program ⊕

◀ WIKIPEDIA
ENTRY DETAIL
**"Diabetes mellitus."**
The "References" and "External links" sections provide Jasmine with authoritative resources, including the American Diabetes Association, which she will investigate (see p. 281). *The Wikipedia trademark is licensed under CC BY-SA 3.0. (Author User: Paul Stansifer, User: Nohat, Philip Metschan.)*

---

In addition, the "Lifestyle" section of the page links her to another entry titled "Diabetic diet."

## Management

*Main article: Diabetes management*

Diabetes mellitus is a chronic disease which cannot be cured except in very specific situations. Management concentrates on keeping blood sugar levels as close to normal ("euglycemia") as possible, without causing hypoglycemia. This can usually be accomplished with diet, exercise, and use of appropriate medications (insulin in the case of type 1 diabetes, oral medications, as well as possibly insulin, in type 2 diabetes).

Patient education, understanding, and participation is vital, since the complications of diabetes are far less common and less severe in people who have well-managed blood sugar levels.[24][25] The goal of treatment is an HbA1C level of 6.5%, but should not be lower than that, and may be set higher.[26] Attention is also paid to other health problems that may accelerate the deleterious effects of diabetes. These include smoking, elevated cholesterol levels, obesity, high blood pressure, and lack of regular exercise.[26] Specialised footwear is widely used to reduce the risk of ulceration, re-ulceration, in at-risk diabetic feet. Evidence for the efficacy of this remains equivocal, however.[27]

## Lifestyle

*See also: Diabetic diet*

There are roles for patient education, dietetic support, sensible exercise, with the goal of keeping both short-term and long-term blood glucose levels within acceptable bounds. In addition, given the associated higher risks of cardiovascular disease, lifestyle modifications are recommended to control blood pressure.[28]

## Medications

**Oral medications**

*Main article: Anti-diabetic medication*

Metformin is generally recommended as a first line treatment for type 2 diabetes, as there is good evidence that it decreases mortality.[29] Routine use of aspirin, however, has not been found to improve outcomes in uncomplicated diabetes.[30]

**Insulin**

*Main article: Insulin therapy*

◀ WIKIPEDIA
ENTRY DETAIL
**"Diabetes mellitus."**
The "Management," "Lifestyle," and "Medications" sections refer Jasmine to related entries. She notices that the "Lifestyle" section links to an entry for "Diabetic diet," which she decides to check out (see p. 280). *The Wikipedia trademark is licensed under CC BY-SA 3.0. (Author User: Paul Stansifer, User: Nohat, Philip Metschan.)*

Create account   Log in

Article   Talk

Read   Edit   View history

Search

# Diabetic diet

From Wikipedia, the free encyclopedia

There is much controversy regarding what diet to recommend to sufferers of diabetes mellitus. The **'diet'** most often recommended is high in dietary fiber, especially soluble fiber, but low in fat (especially saturated fat). Recommendations of the fraction of total calories to be obtained from carbohydrate intake range from 1/6 to 75% – a 2006 review found recommendations varying from 40 to 65%.[1] Diabetics may be encouraged to reduce their intake of carbohydrates that have a high glycemic index (GI), although this is also controversial.[2] (In cases of hypoglycemia, they are advised to have food or drink that can raise blood glucose quickly, such as lucozade, followed by a long-acting carbohydrate (such as rye bread) to prevent risk of further hypoglycemia.) However, others question the usefulness of the glycemic index and recommend high-GI foods like potatoes and rice.

Display showing low fat and/or high fiber foods

**Contents** [hide]

1 History
2 Exchange scheme
3 Later developments
4 Carbohydrates
5 Low-carbohydrate alternatives
6 Vegan/vegetarian
7 Timing of meals
8 Special diabetes products
9 Alcohol and drugs
10 Specific diets
11 See also
12 Further reading
13 References
14 External links

Display showing refined, high fat/carbohydrate foods

## History     [edit]

There has been long history of dietary treatment of diabetes mellitus – dietary treatment of diabetes mellitus was used in Egypt as long ago as 3,500 B.C., and was used in India by Sushruta and Charaka more than 2000 years ago. In the eighteenth century, these authors note, John Rollo argued that calorie restriction in the diabetic diet could reduce glycosuria in diabetes. However, more modern history of the diabetic diet may begin with Frederick Madison Allen, who, in the days before insulin was discovered, recommended that people with diabetes ate only a low-calorie diet to prevent ketoacidosis from killing them. This was an approach which did not actually cure diabetes, it merely extended life by a limited period. The first use of insulin by Frederick Banting in 1922 changed things, and at last allowed patients more flexibility in their eating.

Jasmine looks closely at the "External links" section of the *Wikipedia* page (p. 279) and decides to investigate the American Diabetes Association. She finds out that the ADA is a nonprofit group whose purpose is to control diabetes, especially through improving healthcare access and funding research and prevention.

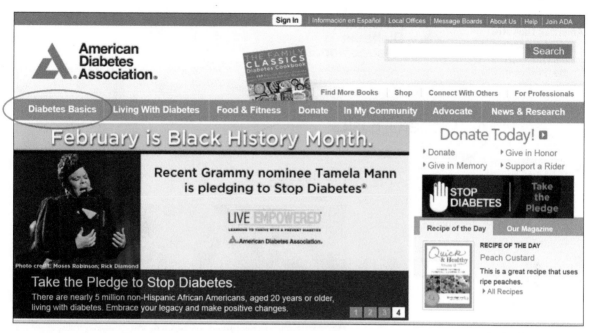

The ADA site is organized into topics, including "Diabetes Basics," which in turn is broken down into related subtopics. In this section, Jasmine uncovers some interesting data, including:

» Prediabetes is a condition that develops prior to type 2 diabetes.

» Seven million people in the United States have undiagnosed diabetes.

» It is a myth that people get diabetes just because they eat too much sugar.

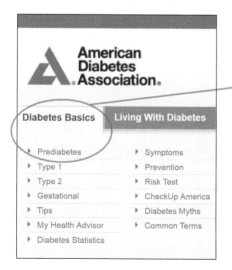

◀ WEB SITE DETAIL
**American Diabetes Association.** Jasmine is especially interested in the "Diabetes Basics" category and wonders what the ADA has to say about prediabetes, type 1, and type 2. *Copyright 2015 American Diabetes Association. From diabetes.org. Reprinted with permission from The American Diabetes Association.*

▲ WEB SITE
**American Diabetes Association.** Jasmine investigates the ADA site, where she focuses on the following content categories: "Diabetes Basics," "Prediabetes," "Living with Diabetes," "Recently Diagnosed," "Food & Fitness," and "MyFoodAdvisor," as shown below and through page 186. *Copyright 2015 American Diabetes Association. From diabetes.org. Reprinted with permission from The American Diabetes Association.*

Jasmine is also interested in "Living With Diabetes," which is broken down into
smaller topic areas.

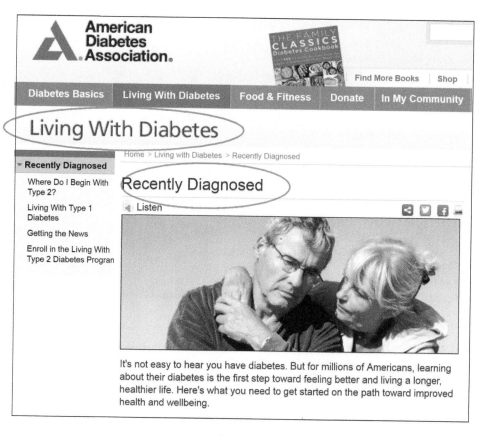

She's especially drawn to the "Food & Fitness" section, because of her interest in nutrition.

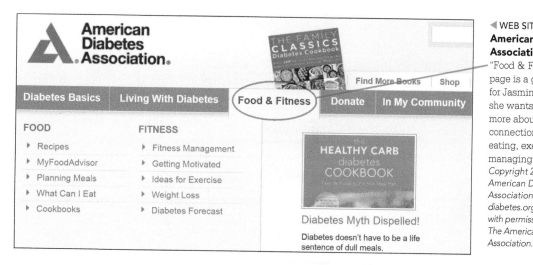

In the "Food & Fitness" section, Jasmine is surprised by the emphasis on recipes and meal planning as ways to control the disease. She finds the following information especially interesting:

» Beans, berries, and tomatoes are diabetes "superfoods."

» We shouldn't just look at the sugar content on food labels. It's more useful to examine the total carbohydrate number.

» Recipes for diabetics are not dull. The site includes recipes for Texas Tuna Burger, Asian Roast Pork Sliders, and Whole-Wheat Pancakes.

WEB SITE DETAIL ▶
**American Diabetes Association.** On the "MyFoodAdvisor" page, Jasmine is thrilled to find specific recipes and nutritional advice. *Copyright 2015 American Diabetes Association. From diabetes.org. Reprinted with permission from The American Diabetes Association.*

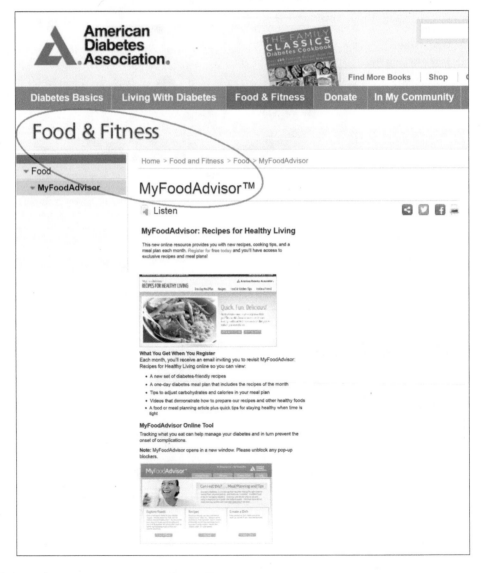

As Jasmine continues to read through the ADA site, she gets more absorbed in the idea that eating specific kinds of foods can assist in managing diabetes. She decides her next step is to find more information on nutrition, maybe even some more recipes designed for diabetics. A hospital or research facility might be another good source, she thinks, and she decides to check out the Mayo Clinic site.

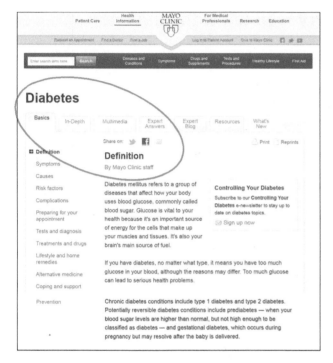

◀ WEB SITE
**Mayo Clinic.** On their "Diabetes" page, the Mayo Clinic provides a definition of the disease. Jasmine is interested to see how this information compares to that of the ADA. *Mayo Foundation for Medical Education and Research.*

There she finds information on diabetes, along with meal plans and recipes. She gets even more interested in the relationship between diet and diabetes management.

◀ WEB SITE DETAIL
**Mayo Clinic.** On the "Diabetes meal plan recipes" page, Jasmine is pleasantly surprised by the range of foods that the Mayo Clinic recommends. *Mayo Foundation for Medical Education and Research.*

The following recipe, among many others, catches her eye.

WEB SITE DETAIL ▶
**Mayo Clinic.**
Jasmine finds that the
recipes are created
by Mayo Clinic
staff and include
specific pointers
from a dietitian. *Mayo
Foundation for Medical
Education and Research.*

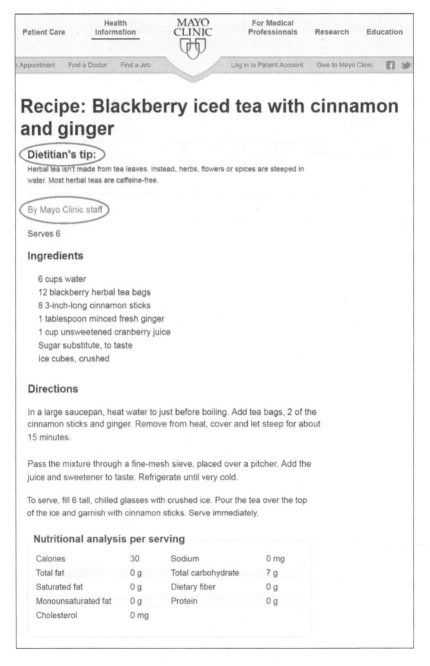

The recipe itself, and the surrounding information, presents Jasmine with a few things to think about. First, the "Dietitian's tip" mentions that most herbal teas are caffeine-free, which makes her wonder about the connection between caffeine and the health of a diabetic. She also notices the use of cinnamon and ginger and wonders how these natural ingredients might benefit a diabetic. In the nutritional analysis of the recipe, Jasmine sees that the drink is low in calories and does not contain any sodium. She wonders if these are important concerns; before she started browsing recipes at the ADA and the Mayo Clinic, Jasmine knew that diabetics should avoid sugar, but she hadn't been taking sodium and calorie content into consideration.

At this point, Jasmine's working research question has evolved from:

WORKING RESEARCH QUESTION        What is the relationship between nutrition and
                                 diabetes?

to:

REVISED, MORE SPECIFIC,          How can diet—specifically, monitoring the intake of
WORKING RESEARCH QUESTION        sugar, calories, and sodium—help someone
                                 with diabetes manage the disease?

Now that Jasmine has done some exploratory, informational reading, she's ready to see what others have to say about managing diabetes through diet. She moves on to look for sources that will offer viewpoints and arguments about diabetes and nutrition.

## Gathering Opinions about Diabetes

Jasmine looks for other sources—including a journal article, a Web site, and a You-Tube video—to provide current viewpoints on nutrition as prevention/treatment for diabetes.

## 1. American Diabetes Association.

At the ADA site, Jasmine finds an article (in their journal, *Diabetes Care*) that provides the organization's position on diabetes and nutrition. The ADA argues:

> There is not sufficient, consistent information to conclude that low–glycemic load diets reduce the risk for diabetes.
>
> —**ADA,** from "Nutrition Recommendations and Interventions for Diabetes"

JOURNAL ARTICLE/ ▶
POSITION STATEMENT
**American Diabetes
Association.** Jasmine
goes back to the
ADA to see if that
organization offers
any opinions or
recommendations
about diabetes
and nutrition. She
finds this position
statement. (Shown
here: the introductory
paragraph and
recommendations.)
*Copyright 2015
American Diabetes
Association. From
diabetes.org. Reprinted
with permission from
The American Diabetes
Association.*

## Diabetes Care

Home | Current Issue | Archive | Contact Us | Subscribe | Help | Alerts |

## Nutrition Recommendations and Interventions for Diabetes
### A position statement of the American Diabetes Association

### American Diabetes Association

Medical nutrition therapy (MNT) is important in preventing diabetes, managing existing diabetes, and preventing, or at least slowing, the rate of development of diabetes complications. It is, therefore, important at all levels of diabetes prevention (see Table 1). MNT is also an integral component of diabetes self-management education (or training). This position statement provides evidence-based recommendations and interventions for diabetes MNT. The previous position statement with accompanying technical review was published in 2002 (1) and modified slightly in 2004 (2). This statement updates previous position statements, focuses on key references published since the year 2000, and uses grading according to the level of evidence available based on the American Diabetes Association evidence-grading system. Since overweight and obesity are closely linked to diabetes, particular attention is paid to this area of MNT.

**Recommendations**

- Among individuals at high risk for developing type 2 diabetes, structured programs that emphasize lifestyle changes that include moderate weight loss (7% body weight) and regular physical activity (150 min/week), with dietary strategies including reduced calories and reduced intake of dietary fat, can reduce the risk for developing diabetes and are therefore recommended. (A)

- Individuals at high risk for type 2 diabetes should be encouraged to achieve the U.S. Department of Agriculture (USDA) recommendation for dietary fiber (14 g fiber/1,000 kcal) and foods containing whole grains (one-half of grain intake). (B)

- There is not sufficient, consistent information to conclude that low–glycemic load diets reduce the risk for diabetes. Nevertheless, low–glycemic index foods that are rich in fiber and other important nutrients are to be encouraged. (E)

- Observational studies report that moderate alcohol intake may reduce the risk for diabetes, but the data do not support recommending alcohol consumption to individuals at risk of diabetes. (B)

## 2. The Joslin Diabetes Center.

At this site, Jasmine read the views of Amy Campbell, a Joslin nutritionist and the coauthor of a book titled *16 Myths of a Diabetic Diet*. Campbell states that there is no such thing as a "diabetic diet." Jasmine finds the following quote from Campbell on a Joslin page titled "The Truth about the So-Called 'Diabetes Diet'":

> A person with diabetes can eat anything a person without diabetes eats.
>
> —**Amy Campbell,** from "The Truth about the So-Called 'Diabetes Diet'"

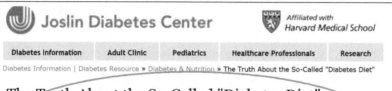

**Joslin Diabetes Center**
Affiliated with *Harvard Medical School*

| Diabetes Information | Adult Clinic | Pediatrics | Healthcare Professionals | Research |

Diabetes Information | Diabetes Resource » Diabetes & Nutrition » The Truth About the So-Called "Diabetes Diet"

### The Truth About the So-Called "Diabetes Diet"

Despite all the publicity surrounding new research and new nutrition guidelines, some people with diabetes still believe that there is something called a "diabetic diet." For some, this so-called diet consists of avoiding sugar, while others believe it to be a strict way of eating that controls glucose. Unfortunately, neither are quite right.

The "diabetes diet" is not something that people with type 1 or type 2 diabetes should be following. "That just simply isn't how meal planning works today for patients with diabetes," says Amy Campbell, MS, RD, LDN, CDE, a nutritionist at Joslin and co-author of *16 Myths of a Diabetic Diet*.

"The important message is that with proper education and within the context of healthy eating, a person with diabetes can eat anything a person without diabetes eats," Campbell states.

**What's the truth about diabetes and diet?**

We know now that it is okay for people with diabetes to substitute sugar-containing food for other carbohydrates as part of a balanced meal plan. Prevailing beliefs up to the mid-1990s were that people with diabetes should avoid foods that contain so-called "simple" sugars and replace them with "complex" carbohydrates, such as those found in potatoes and cereals. A review of the research at that time revealed that there was relatively little scientific evidence to support the theory that simple sugars are more rapidly digested and absorbed than starches, and therefore more apt to produce high blood glucose levels.

◀ RESEARCHED ARGUMENT
**Joslin Diabetes Center and Amy Campbell.**
At the Joslin Diabetes Center page, Jasmine is surprised to see an argument against "the so-called 'diabetes diet.'" It seems to contrast with what she's read elsewhere at the American Diabetes Association Web site. *Copyright © 2012 by Joslin Diabetes Center (www.Joslin.org). All rights reserved. Reprinted with permission.*

## 3. Nature's Factory Products.

On YouTube, Jasmine finds a video produced by a business called Nature's Factory Products, which makes aloe vera–based products and markets them for various ailments. Jasmine was surprised by the company's claim that aloe helps treat diabetes. In their video, "How Aloe Vera can help Diabetics," the manufacturer claims that:

> Aloe vera can help regulate blood sugar levels and control inflammation caused by diabetes.
>
> —**Nature's Factory Products**

While she is skeptical about Nature's Factory Products' claims, Jasmine doesn't dismiss their argument altogether. She decides to keep this source in mind and to fact-check the claims made in the video by researching medical studies.

Now that she's gathered some facts and arguments about diabetes, Jasmine decides to meet with her instructor to talk about a final research question and plan her research proposal.

VIDEO AD ▶
**Nature's Factory Products, From "How Aloe Vera Can Help Diabetics."**
Jasmine discovered a video on YouTube by a company that makes nutritional supplements. In the video advertisement, Nature's Factory Products addresses the question: "What is Aloe Vera?" and argues that among its many benefits, the plant helps reduce blood sugar. Jasmine is intrigued by this and by the claims that aloe vera may improve the circulation, immune systems, and overall internal health of diabetics. She decides to keep this source in the mix—and to verify some of the claims made by Nature's Factory Products. She'll do this by reading medical studies on the relationship between aloe vera—and potential health benefits to diabetic patients.

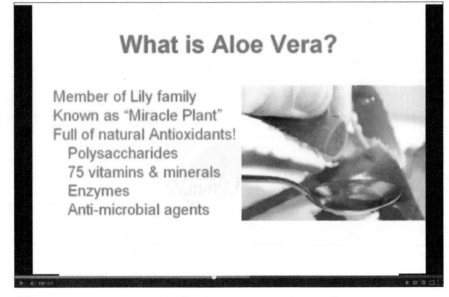

**What is Aloe Vera?**

Member of Lily family
Known as "Miracle Plant"
Full of natural Antioxidants!
Polysaccharides
75 vitamins & minerals
Enzymes
Anti-microbial agents

CHECKLIST Choosing a Topic

**As you start your research, consider following these steps:**

☐ **Brainstorm topic ideas.**

   ☐ Read what others have said.

   ☐ Google your topic (but stay focused).

   ☐ Discuss what you find with others.

☐ **Start writing informally.**

   ☐ Make a list of topics that interest you, then double it, then double it again.

   ☐ Freewrite about your topic.

   ☐ Sketch out a mind map.

☐ **Do preliminary research.**

   ☐ Ask questions of fact and definition so that you will understand the more complex research you do later.

   ☐ What arguments have others made about your topic? How do they support their views?

   ☐ Note key terms to aid in later research.

☐ **Commit to a topic. Consider these factors:**

   ☐ Is the topic compatible with the assignment?

   ☐ Have you found an argumentative angle?

   ☐ Will you stay interested in this topic?

   ☐ Are there enough appropriate sources available for you to research in the time you have?

   ☐ Overall, how viable is the topic? (See Jasmine Huerta's assignment, "What Is Your Topic? How Viable Is It?" on p. 269.)

☐ **Form a research question. Consider these factors:**

   ☐ Does your question focus more on stating facts and defining terms? Or are you making an argument? Providing an analysis?

   ☐ Is your question open-ended?

   ☐ Is your question specific enough? If not, how will you move from a general question to a more specific one?

   ☐ Are you truly interested in finding answers to this question?

   ☐ What are some challenges you may come up against as you research this question, and how can you deal with these challenges?

# Creating a Research Proposal

A research proposal sets forth a writer's rationale for choosing a particular research question. For Jasmine, the proposal gives her an opportunity to fine-tune her research question and her focus. Your instructor may ask you to turn in a proposal or a working bibliography that outlines your sources (pp. 297–300). Or your instructor might simply ask you to think about your research before looking more carefully at sources.

Even if your instructor does not assign a formal research proposal, it can be a great tool for use in planning your project. Following is a research proposal assignment that we give our students.

ASSIGNMENT ▶
**Research Proposal.**
Creating a research proposal is a great way to help you focus and plan. See below for Jasmine's completed assignment.

**ENG 101, Professor Braziller**

**Research Proposal Assignment: What Is Your Focus?**

This proposal will help you solidify your ideas for your semester's research. Your proposal should be approximately two double-spaced pages in MLA manuscript format. Your proposal should include the following:

1. Your research question

2. A working title for your project

3. A summary of your project. Identify your topic and describe what you will be looking at in terms of the topic. Include some key terms and additional questions that will guide your research.

4. A description of your purpose for working on this project. Why did you choose this topic? What do you hope to learn from this project?

5. A discussion of the key challenges you will face or you imagine you will face. What concerns do you have regarding the research/project?

Following is Jasmine's research proposal, in response to the above assignment.

▲ STUDENT AUTHOR
**Jasmine Huerta.**
*iStockphoto.*

ASSIGNMENT ▶
**Research Proposal.**
Jasmine has explored her topic and gathered facts and opinions from some solid sources, and she is now ready to share her ideas for what she plans to do next.

**ENG 101, Professor Braziller**

**Research Proposal Assignment: What Is Your Focus?**

Jasmine Huerta
Professor Amy Braziller
English 101
October 6, 20—

Research Proposal

1. Your research question

   How can diet—specifically, monitoring the intake of sugar, calories, and sodium—help someone with diabetes manage the disease and avoid taking insulin?

2. A working title for your project

   The working title for my project is "Living with Diabetes: Diet Is the Answer." I chose this topic because although some people are predisposed to diabetes because of genetics, they do have some control over the situation. For example, through their choices related to food and diet they can manage or perhaps even prevent the disease.

3. A summary of your project. Identify your topic and describe what you will be looking at in terms of the topic. Include some key terms and additional questions that will guide your research.

   I plan to research and write about different ways you can control diabetes through nutritional choices. While there are medications used to control the disease, such as insulin, I'm more curious about natural approaches, such as diet. I want my readers to understand that diabetes doesn't have to be a death sentence and that even if you are predisposed to it, there are some simple things you can do to keep it from taking over your life or causing other health issues.

I also think, based on my research, that diet and nutrition might be just as powerful as insulin for some people. I wonder if doctors are too quick to prescribe insulin.

Much of the debate around diabetes has to do with the connection between diabetes and obesity. I wonder to what extent diabetes can be prevented by a healthy diet, one that helps people avoid obesity. Also, are there specific foods that children need to avoid? Are these different from what older people should avoid?

Besides researching different diabetes-related diets, I want to find out how people learn about these diets. Are there specific programs, initiatives, or educational tools used to get this information out to the public? How might schools and doctors share this information?

Following are some **key terms** I've discovered during my preliminary research: *glycemic index, metabolism, blood sugar, hypertension, obesity, glucose monitoring,* and *insulin.*

Following are some of the **questions that will guide my research:**

- What diets are best for diabetics?
- What foods do diabetics need to avoid?
- Can diet cure diabetes? If so, how?
- Can diet prevent someone from getting diabetes, even if he or she has a family history of the disease? If so, how?
- Can diet prevent someone's diabetes from getting worse? If so, how?
- Can dietary changes prevent or reduce a diabetic's dependence on insulin?

4. A description of your purpose for working on this project. Why did you choose this topic? What do you hope to learn from this project?

Diabetes runs in my family, so it's something that is very close to me. My cousin, who is only six years old, has type 1 diabetes. Just last month, my grandfather, who is somewhat overweight, but definitely not obese, was diagnosed with diabetes. When my mother was pregnant with me, she had gestational diabetes.

I believe I may be predisposed toward the disease, and I want to find out what I can do to avoid it. I also want to help my family by sharing what I learn—especially in terms of natural alternatives rather than traditional medicine.

5. A discussion of the key challenges you will face or you imagine you will face. What concerns do you have regarding the research/project?

My biggest challenge so far has been making sense of some terms I've encountered in my research. Some articles go into a lot of detail about the relationship of the glycemic index to insulin levels. Authors of these pieces also use technical terms such as *pancreatic islet cells, resistant starches,* and *macronutrients.*

Another challenge I might face is that my topic may be too narrow. Based on my research so far, it seems that many sources say yes, diet does contribute to diabetes prevention and management. But how might I expand on that? Will I end up just listing foods to eat and not to eat?

I think that trying to figure out if nutritional changes can actually replace insulin as treatment gives my project a good argumentative angle, but I am a little worried that I may end up arguing more strongly against insulin than I really want to.

I am also afraid of getting sidetracked and focusing too much on the obesity problem, especially in regard to children, and losing my focus on diabetes. While obesity is related, I really want to focus on preventing and managing the disease— and not so much on the causes of diabetes. While it's important to understand some of the causes, especially as they relate to nutrition, I'm more interested in prevention and treatment.

Now that Jasmine has written her proposal and submitted it to her instructor, she is ready to begin the next stage of her research.

## CHECKLIST Creating a Research Proposal

What does a good research proposal do?

☐ **It assists you in organizing your project,** and includes five major components:
  - Research question (the main thrust of your research)
  - Working title
  - Summary of the project (a sketch of the research you've done, the questions you've raised, and the possible direction you will take, including the potential argument you may make)
  - Overall purpose (why you want to pursue this topic and project)
  - Potential challenges

☐ **It shows that you have a clear focus for your research.** Your research question and working title are specific, showing your reader the angle you are researching. Throughout the proposal, you include details rather than vague generalities. For example, Jasmine doesn't just write, "I want to learn how people find out about these diets." She adds these details: "Are there specific programs, initiatives, or educational tools. . . ."

☐ **It illustrates that you have done some preliminary research.** Your summary includes key terms that you discovered while doing research. While Jasmine might have previously thought of the key terms *obesity* and *insulin*, she probably had not considered such terms as *glycemic index* and *glucose monitoring*.

☐ **It gives reasons why you have selected your area of research.** By communicating why you chose your topic, your reader understands your choice, and you see why this research matters to you. By articulating these reasons, you stay more engaged.

☐ **It shows that you have considered potential challenges.** Anticipating challenges prepares you for the bumps you might hit during research. Additionally, a good research proposal tells your reader about those challenges so that you might be given assistance. For example, when Jasmine writes that she has encountered technical terms such as *pancreatic islet cells*, her reader might point her to resources where she can get help deciphering these terms.

# ORGANIZING YOUR SOURCES

Once you have a research question and a rough plan (as Jasmine does), you'll begin to gather and read more sources. In the next chapter, we're going to take you deeper into the research process. But before that, here's some advice on staying organized.

Be sure to keep track of every source you look at so that you can:

» Easily retrieve sources to verify facts

» Check that you aren't plagiarizing

» Make connections among sources

» Document your sources in your final paper

## Use Simple Strategies: E-mail, Bookmark, Copy/Paste, Screen Capture

Following are some strategies for keeping track of your sources:

**E-mail sources you find online to yourself.**   Store the e-mails in a folder on your computer.

**Bookmark sources on your computer.**   Create folders for your bookmarks.

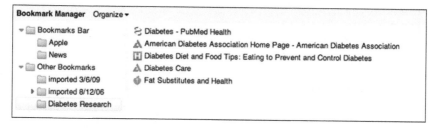

◀ BOOKMARK TOOLS
Featured on most PCs.

**Use social bookmarking tools.**   Sites such as Diigo have bookmarking/information storage functions.

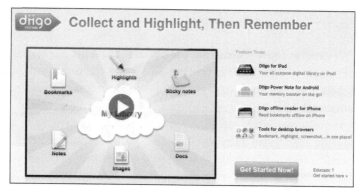

◀ BOOKMARK TOOL
**Diigo.**
*Courtesy of Diigo.*

**Copy and paste content from Web sites into a Word document.** Below is a Word document into which we've pasted a section of the text of a commencement speech by the late novelist, David Foster Wallace, published by Kenyon College.

WORD DOCUMENT ▶
David Foster Wallace's 2005 commencement speech at Kenyon College, "This is Water," copied/pasted from *Kenyon College Alumni Bulletin.* Kenyon College. Hill Nadell Literary Agency.

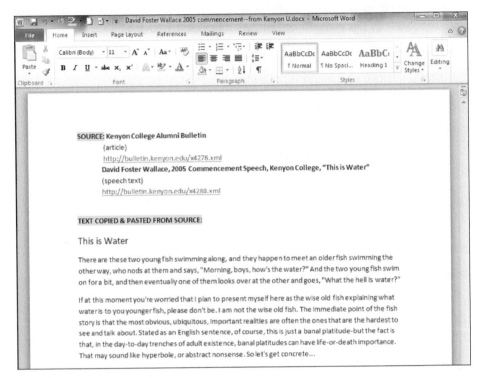

**Attention, researchers! A note on cutting and pasting.**

If you copy and paste from a source, do so very carefully. Make sure you have a way of reminding yourself which words belong to others—and which ones belong to you. Review page 392 in Chapter 7 to see how cutting and pasting *can lead to inadvertent plagiarism.* If you decide you want to capture something exactly from a Web site, then copy and paste as above, highlighting the source information.

**Create screen captures of online content.** For this option, you would capture screens of your sources and paste them into a Word document (or save the screens as image files). We highly recommend this method of recording source material. Why? Because it prevents any potential confusion about what content came from where—and prevents you from inadvertently mixing up your own words with those from your source. A screen capture of the David Foster Wallace commencement speech as it appears online is on page 297.

# Create a List of Sources: Keep a Working Bibliography

We also highly recommend that you create a working bibliography—or, even better, an annotated working bibliography, which includes more detail. A working bibliography is simply a list of the sources you've gathered and plan to refer to. Keeping a list will provide you with the information required by all documentation styles, including MLA and APA (see p. 395 for Modern Language Association style and p. 415 for American Psychological Association style).

Your working bibliography, which you add to and revise as you research, will be the basis for your final Works Cited list and in-text citations. It will also help you evaluate your sources as a group, so you can make sure they represent a good range and so you can make any useful connections among your sources. (For information on evaluating and integrating sources, see Chapters 6 and 7.)

## Better Yet, Keep an Annotated Working Bibliography

An annotated bibliography is a working bibliography (a list of your sources) that includes your own brief notes about each source. In your annotations, you summarize each source, capturing its essence in a few sentences. If the source is argumentative, you also note the main points of the writer's argument. In addition, note the potential reliability of the source: Is it from a reliable site, news organization, or publication? Was it created by a source you can trust? How well do the source and its author fit with your research? What might the source add? What might be its drawbacks? (For details on evaluating sources, see Chapter 6.)

# Guided Process: How to Create a Bibliography

## Jasmine Huerta (Student)

*Diabetes Project: Bibliography*

▲ STUDENT AUTHOR
**Jasmine Huerta.**
*iStockphoto.*

## Jasmine's Working Bibliography

Below is Jasmine's working bibliography for her project on nutrition and diabetes. In this case, Jasmine uses the MLA style of documentation. Her bibliography, ultimately, will become her MLA-style Works Cited list.

Jasmine writes of her working bibliography:

> I pulled together a good range of dependable sources—including, for example, a peer-reviewed journal called *Diabetes Care*, the American Diabetes Association, and the Harvard School of Public Health. My sources are connected: Three focus on diabetes and the glycemic index and two focus specifically on low-glycemic foods. I made sure to include the detailed source information my instructor expects, and in MLA format.

Huerta 1

Working Bibliography/Works Cited
(for diabetes project-in-progress)

Brand-Miller, Jennie, et al. "Low–Glycemic Index Diets in the Management of Diabetes." *Diabetes Care*, vol. 26, no. 8, 2003, pp. 2261-67, care.diabetesjournals.org/content/26/8/2261.long.

"Diabetes Mellitus." *Wikipedia*, en.wikipedia.org/wiki/Diabetes_mellitus. Accessed 15 Sept. 2013.

"Glycemic Index and Diabetes." *American Diabetes Association*, www.diabetes.org/food-and-fitness/food/planning-meals/glycemic-index-and-diabetes.html. Accessed 15 Sept. 2013.

"Glycemic Index and Diabetes: Low-Glycemic-Index Foods." *WebMD Diabetes Health Center*, WebMD, diabetes.webmd.com/glycemic-index-good-versus-bad-carbs. Accessed 15 Sept. 2013.

"Simple Steps to Preventing Diabetes." *The Nutrition Source*, Harvard School of Public Health, www.hsph.harvard.edu/nutritionsource/diabetes-prevention/preventing-diabetes-full-story/index.html. Accessed 15 Sept. 2013.

# Jasmine's Annotated Bibliography

Here is how Jasmine describes her process:

I began each entry with a basic summary. In my summaries, I note specific examples, such as unfamiliar terms or important evidence. I've also indicated my evaluation of how dependable each source is. When I quoted exact language from a source, I used quotation marks. I also made connections among my sources.

---

Huerta 1

### Annotated Working Bibliography/Works Cited

Brand-Miller, Jennie, et al. "Low–Glycemic Index Diets in the Management of Diabetes." *Diabetes Care*, vol. 26, no. 8, 2003, pp. 2261-67, care .diabetesjournals.org/content/26/8/2261.long.

The authors explore the controversy about whether a low-glycemic diet actually helps someone manage his or her diabetes. The article presents the research methods used, along with the results. Ultimately, the results of their study show that a low-glycemic diet did help patients manage their diabetes—in contrast to patients whose diets consisted of high-glycemic foods. The article is filled with unfamiliar terms such as "acarbose therapy." At the end is a list of footnotes and references that will be useful as I continue my research. This is a very reliable source because *Diabetes Care* is a peer-reviewed journal; also, the use of documentation reinforces the authors' ethos.

"Diabetes Mellitus." *Wikipedia*, en.wikipedia.org/wiki/Diabetes_mellitus. Accessed 15 Sept. 2013.

This article gives a very comprehensive overview of diabetes. It begins by briefly explaining the different types of diabetes, such as types 1 and 2. It also includes a discussion of symptoms, causes, and ways to control the disease. Throughout the article, there are numerous hyperlinks to other Wikipedia pages that explain concepts further. Since I'm focusing on nutrition, I found the hyperlink to the "Diabetic Diet" page most useful, since this page included information on various diets and potential research sources. *Wikipedia* gears its information to someone beginning research, looking for possible angles to explore related to the topic. Additionally, it establishes its reliability by providing many source references at the end of the article. Many of the references were from medical journals.

"Glycemic Index and Diabetes." *American Diabetes Association*, www.diabetes .org/food-and-fitness/food/planning-meals/glycemic-index-and-diabetes .html. Accessed 15 Sept. 2013.

The ADA's page on the glycemic index and its relationship to diabetes is an informative summary on the topic. It has three subheads, so readers can immediately find information: "What is the glycemic index?" "What

*Continues next page*

---

### Attention, bibliographers!

The latest MLA guidelines require writers to include source URLs without http:// as is shown in Jasmine's bibliographies. Including URLs (or embedding hyperlinks in your paper) leaves no room for confusion about where you obtained information, and makes it easier and faster for your readers to check your sources. For sources accessed through a database such as *JSTOR*, provide a DOI, if available, rather than a URL. (See also Chapter 7.)

For online sources that do not include a date, include in your Works Cited list an "Accessed" date, as Jasmine does.

**Huerta,** *Annotated Bibliography,* *Continued*

affects the GI of a food?" And, "Is the GI a better tool than carbohydrate counting?" The article discusses how the glycemic index is affected by many things and is not simply determined by a food's type. For example, factors such as length of ripening and cooking time affect a food's glycemic index. The article is written for a general reader, so I found that I could understand all its terms and get a beginning grasp of the glycemic index. This article, too, is very reliable since the American Diabetes Association is a respected and noted organization related to the field.

"Glycemic Index and Diabetes: Low-Glycemic-Index Foods." *WebMD Diabetes Health Center*, diabetes.webmd.com/glycemic-index-good-versus-bad-carbs. Accessed 15 Sept. 2013.

WebMD's article provides a good overview of the glycemic index. The article briefly discusses how a diet of high-glycemic-index foods (pasta, rice) can contribute to weight gain and health issues. The article encourages readers to choose low-glycemic-index foods (vegetables, fruits) for a healthier diet. While the article tends to be fairly general, it does bring up some useful points; for example, it explains that several factors might alter the glycemic index, such as the combination of foods eaten. I trust the information presented here since WebMD is a trusted Web source for medical information, especially in terms of providing basic ideas to readers.

"Simple Steps to Preventing Diabetes." *The Nutrition Source*, Harvard School of Public Health, www.hsph.harvard.edu/nutritionsource/diabetes-prevention/ preventing-diabetes-full-story/index.html. Accessed 15 Aug. 2013.

This article focuses on ways to prevent type 2 diabetes. It gives statistics on the number of people affected by the disease and lists illnesses that the disease may cause, such as blindness. Prevention strategies are offered, such as diet and exercise. The writers sum up these strategies by saying, "Stay lean and stay active." This article, like the Brand-Miller piece, also includes a list of references, so I will add that to my potential project sources. Since this piece was published by a Harvard University site, I trust the information presented.

# Drafting a Research Question, Proposal, & Bibliography

---

**CHECKLIST: Beginning Your Research** As you begin drawing on sources, forming your research questions, drafting your research proposal, and creating a bibliography, ask yourself the following questions.

### WHAT'S MY RHETORICAL SITUATION?

☐ **Purpose.** What am I learning as I research? And how can I develop what I'm learning into a solid research question? Once I identify a research question, I'll need to refine it. Does it simply focus on facts (if so, it's not refined enough)? Or is it geared toward analysis and argument (if so, I'm heading in the right direction)? Once I come up with a research plan, I need to clearly articulate my approach, purpose, and potential challenges in my research proposal.

☐ **Audience.** What expectations will my readers (my instructor, classmates, and any audience beyond) have regarding the quality of my sources? (See Chapter 6 for more on evaluating source quality.) As I gather sources into an annotated bibliography, how can I make certain that my notes on each source show readers its potential usefulness?

☐ **Rhetorical appeals.** As I begin research, how will I know whether to trust an author and source? What about a given author and source gives me confidence, or doubts? What techniques and appeals do authors use that I can adopt for my own purposes? To what degree do they use logos (logic) and pathos (emotion) to reach readers? As I draft my research question, proposal, and bibliography, I need to make a solid case for my readers. Do I convey the reliability of my sources in my proposal and bibliography?

☐ **Modes & media.** How do modes and media come into play as I'm reading and choosing sources? My sources should represent a range of modes and media.

### HOW DOES GENRE MATTER?

☐ **Elements of genres.** As I look at potential sources, I need to ask: Does the author of this source draw on other sources? Does the author document the work of others? For example, I'd expect a journalist to attribute quotations to specific people in a news article, but bloggers may not be meticulous about naming people quoted. How many different genres should I include among my sources—and in my bibliography?

☐ **Style.** When I look at a potential source, how much attention should I pay to the author's style? Are informal first-person pieces the right fit for my topic? Do I need to gather sources written in a variety of styles? To what extent do tone and level of detail contribute to a source's reliability? I should note each author's style and tone in my annotated bibliography.

☐ **Design.** When I look at a potential source, how important are design considerations? Some sources are very visual and graphically designed, but I should find a good mix.

☐ **Sources.** What makes a source particularly trustworthy? For example, if an author draws on documented sources, I may want to pay more attention to that text. If a source is drawn on by more than one author, I should check out that source and consider adding it to my working bibliography and commenting on it in my research proposal. I also need to record my source information carefully, keeping in mind the documentation style I will use (MLA, APA, or other).

**PRACTICE** Want to experiment? Draft a research proposal. Create a working bibliography and annotate it.

Find a topic that interests you and work through the points in the above checklist until you develop a research question you are interested in. Then do the following:

1. Draft a research proposal for your professor that includes:
   - A working title for your project (you can always change the title later, when you have a better idea of what your finished project will actually cover).
   - A summary of the project, including which aspects of the topic you will research.
   - A list of the keywords you've identified in the research you've done so far.
   - A discussion of your purpose in working on the project. This is where you'll discuss why you are interested in answering the research question.
   - A discussion of the challenges you anticipate facing in your project and strategies you can use to deal with them.

2. Keep a working bibliography of all the sources you use, even ones you think you won't refer to in your final written report. You never know.

3. Annotate three sources you find particularly interesting or thought provoking. In your annotation, discuss:
   - What the summary is about
   - The argument the source makes
   - How reliable you judge this source to be and why
   - How this source might be used in your project

# EVALUATING & CHOOSING SOURCES

## CONTENTS

◀ SOURCE

**Wikipedia.**

What is a source? In this chapter we look at a range of them—including popular general sources, such as *Wikipedia*, and specialized academic sources, such as a journal published by the American Psychological Association. *The Wikipedia trademark is licensed under CC BY-SA 3.0. (Author User: Paul Stansifer, User: Nohat, Philip Metschan.)*

In Chapter 5, we discussed how to begin your research to explore topics—and ultimately to come up with a research question and proposal. We assume in this chapter that you've done your preliminary research, you have a topic, and you are ready to focus in on an important aspect of that topic. In the following pages, we will discuss research in greater depth, covering how to identify a source that is appropriate, reliable, and useful to you.

# GETTING STARTED WITH SOURCES

## What Are Sources?

For an Index of Sources & Contexts for material referenced in this chapter, see the e-Pages at **bedfordstmartins.com /bookofgenres.**

The word *source* comes from the Anglo-French word *surse*, which means "to rise or to begin." Think of a source as a starting point. To cook something you've never made before, you might first refer to a cookbook, an online recipe database, or the Food Channel for inspiration. To plan a trip, you might begin with sources including maps, photos, and brochures. To begin a research paper, you might refer to Google and online databases such as *EBSCOhost* and *ProQuest*, and consult research librarians and professors to shape and define your ideas and narrow your topic.

LIBRARY HOMEPAGE ▶
**Auraria Library Homepage.** This library serves the Metropolitan State University of Denver and other institutions in the Denver area. Like most libraries, this one offers access to a range of databases, organized by title and subject area. *Auraria Library.*

What research have you done for other courses? Where did you seek advice? What sources worked especially well? What do you wish you'd done differently or better?

In the context of this book, we see everything you read (or view, or listen to, or experience in any way), every text you encounter, every conversation you have, as a potential source for your writing. When you compose—whether in college or on the job—you draw on sources for information and opinions. These sources do more than get you started; they are also the texts that you'll converse with throughout your composing process, from your earliest topic ideas to your final project. (For more on early topic ideas, see Chapter 5. For information on later stages of research and writing, see Chapter 7.)

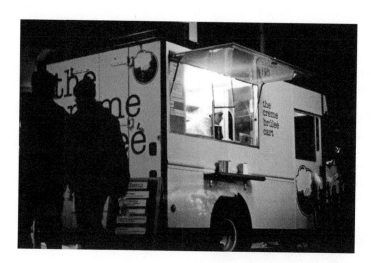

◀ ARTIFACT
**The Crème Brûlée truck,** also known as the Crème Brûlée Cart, is based in San Francisco. Researching food? A food truck or other eatery can be a valuable source of firsthand information. *The Crème Brûlée Cart.*

Can a food truck be a source? Sure. Especially if you're researching the trend of food trucks, or the growing number of people who identify themselves as "foodies." Maybe you're interested in comparing the old-time ice cream truck to the phenomenon of the food truck. Depending on your argument, you might use the truck as a starting point for your research, talking with its chef or operator to learn more about the business: its operation, clientele, and profitability. Or maybe about the food itself: the source of its ingredients and its nutritional value. (See Cremebruleecart .com: Better Living through Dessert.)

## Where Do I Find Sources?

Sources are everywhere. Imagine that a friend tells you about an upcoming debate about the presence of the ROTC on campus; because she has provided you with information, your friend is a source. Let's say you become interested in the ROTC debate and decide to search your online campus newspaper for articles and editorials on the topic. Your campus paper and the materials it contains are sources.

STUDENT NEWSPAPER : ▶
EDITORIAL PAGE
***Accent: The Student
Voice of Austin
Community College.***
Here a student offers a
commentary on women's
healthcare in the state of
Texas, which has some
of the most restrictive
reproductive health
policies in the country.
Your own campus
publication may provide
an excellent source for
ideas, facts, and opinions
on your topic. *Courtesy of
The Accent (theaccent.org).*

From there, you could learn more by talking to a member of the ROTC or a military recruiter, or a local activist organization opposed to military recruiting. The people you talk with and the discussions you have with them are sources.

## What Can Sources Do for Me?

For one thing, they help you make decisions. You use sources all the time—not only to inform your school and work projects, but to aid you in making informed choices. For example, you want to choose a movie to see this weekend. You'd probably consult a variety of sources: Maybe you'd read film reviews, watch current movie trailers, or talk with a film-buff friend. Or imagine you're shopping for a car. You would probably do some research; you would probably visit some manufacturers' sites, talk to your mechanic and other car owners, or visit dealerships for test drives. You might check out the advice at Cars.com.

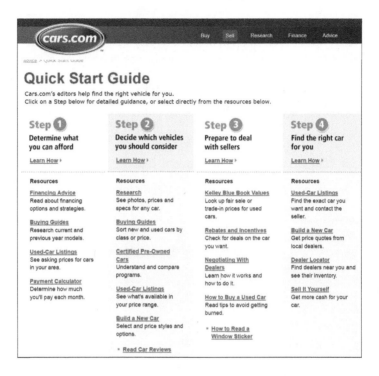

◀ WEB PAGE
**Cars.com, "Quick Start Guide."** We all draw on sources to conduct research in daily life, perhaps using consumer sites such as this one. Solid information helps us make better decisions. *Courtesy of Cars.com.*

Now that you have a sense of what sources are, the rest of this chapter will show you how to:

» Locate and preview sources

» Identify sources in terms of general versus specialized academic; and of primary versus secondary

» Read sources critically, with attention to author, purpose, audience, and other rhetorical concerns

» Evaluate what sources will be best for your own research and writing

## What's a General Source?
## What's a Specialized Academic Source?

When you look at a source, think about who created that text, and for what purpose and for what audience. That will guide you as to when and how to use that source.

### General Sources

General sources are aimed at a general audience; that is, they're written by knowledgeable authors and are meant to be understood by nonexperts. For example, a

Did you ever start reading a source and realize that you were in over your head? What were the indicators? Have you ever had the opposite experience—you started reading a source and realized it was much too simple? What were the indicators?

journalist who regularly covers local politics for your newspaper might write a piece to inform readers about a scandal at city hall. To get the gist of the story, you don't have to know anything about local politics or politicians. General sources help you:

» Begin to understand the overall topic

» Begin to see what the subtopics are

» Discover keywords

» Find the different conversations that are related to the topic

» Begin to explore your research questions

ARTICLE: ▶
GENERAL SOURCE
*Psychology Today.*
Amy Alkon's article,
"The Truth about
Beauty," is aimed at
a general audience.
*Courtesy of* Psychology Today. *Photo by Art
Steiber/August Images.*

An example of a general source is "The Truth about Beauty," an article written by Amy Alkon, a journalist and writer for the magazine *Psychology Today.* Alkon's purpose is to persuade her audience, primarily middle-aged women, about how men define beauty. Her ultimate goal in the article is to empower women so that they can understand their choices and the effects of their choices when it comes to beauty and landing a man. This is an example of a general source.

## Specialized Academic Sources

These sources are aimed at (you guessed it!) specialized academic readers. They are usually written by scholars and other experts—professors, scientists, doctors, and researchers—who have studied the subject extensively. An example of a specialized academic source is an article from *JAMA* (*The Journal of the American Medical Association*) on a new clinical trial and its success. Readers of such an article would include doctors interested in new treatments that they can incorporate in their own practice. Although academic articles are aimed at people with expertise on a given subject, that doesn't mean you should avoid these sources. They may include information that you can use—and may become easier to understand as you deepen your research and gain an understanding of your topic (and associated terms and vocabulary). You might turn to these sources once you've built a foundation of understanding with your general sources. Specialized academic sources help you:

» Delve into a topic in depth

» See how experts view the subject

» Access the latest research in the field

» Access critiques of research in the field

» Find other academic sources through Works Cited lists and bibliographies

▲ WEB SITE & ARTICLE ▶: SPECIALIZED ACADEMIC SOURCE
**American Psychological Association.** This article from the *Journal of Personality and Social Psychology* is aimed at an audience of experts. *The APA Web site screenshots are reproduced with permission. Copyright © 2013 by the American Psychological Association, all rights reserved. No further reproduction or distribution is permitted without written permission from the American Psychological Association.*

An example of a specialized academic article is a piece on self-esteem development by Ruth Yasemin Erol and Ulrich Orth (see p. 309), which appeared in the American Psychological Association's publication, the *Journal of Personality and Social Psychology*. In the article, the authors examine the ways that early self-esteem affects health and happiness in later life. The primary audience for this piece consists of psychology and sociology scholars interested in social behavior.

 **Attention, researchers! A word about specialized sources.**

In addition to specialized academic sources, depending on your topic, you might also deal with specialized technical sources, such as technical manuals or drawings. For example, if you are researching ecotourism, you might use as a source a schematic drawing of a water treatment plant, one that an engineer might refer to on the job.

## What Are Primary & Secondary Sources? Tertiary Sources?

**What kinds of sources do you use every day that would be considered primary sources? What about secondary sources and tertiary sources? When you have a choice between different types of sources, say between asking your friend what time a concert starts and looking it up on the Internet, which do you usually choose and why?**

Sources can be categorized as primary, secondary, or tertiary, based on the type of information an author uses—and the distance between the author and that information. A primary source is a record of information encountered firsthand, such as original photographs, interviews, correspondence, or historical documents. For example, if you read a letter written by a slave, that letter would be considered a primary source. However, if you read the letter in an anthology that also includes historical interpretations about the letters, then that book would be considered a secondary source. The categories of primary, secondary, and tertiary are not always clear-cut. Sometimes, something that would be a primary source in one circumstance would be a secondary source in another. For example, if Liz interviews Amy, the interview is a primary source for the researcher Liz; however, if Liz publishes this interview, and our editor Ellen reads the interview, it is a secondary source for Ellen.

We advise you to keep these distinctions in mind, but not to get too caught up in categorizing sources precisely in these terms. That said, here are a few rules of thumb to keep in mind:

1. A **primary source** is an original artifact, like a journal entry or photograph. If you were conducting research on the author Virginia Woolf, you might use one of her journal entries to get a sense of how her personal experiences shaped the novels she wrote.

2. A **secondary source** is written about an original artifact and often includes interpretation or analysis. If you were conducting research on Virginia Woolf, you might read a biography of her to get a sense of how her life intersected with historical events and to get a sense of the overall themes of her life.

3. A **tertiary source** is based on multiple secondary sources and presents uncontested information about a topic. In your hypothetical Virginia Woolf project, you might consult an encyclopedia of famous women to get a quick sense of the achievements Woolf is most famous for.

## Primary Sources

In a primary text, a writer reports directly what he or she has witnessed, experienced, or created. For example, a piece of original music can be considered a primary source. Composers of primary sources rarely create their compositions to analyze, interpret, or evaluate data. If you are doing scientific research and encounter a rare plant specimen in the field, that plant specimen would be considered a primary source. If you are doing research on the Civil War and you find a map of a battlefield, that map would be considered a primary source. A place where you can find such a primary source is at the Library of Congress site, particularly in the American Memory collection, where the map of Gettysburg shown on page 312 and other Civil War maps are housed.

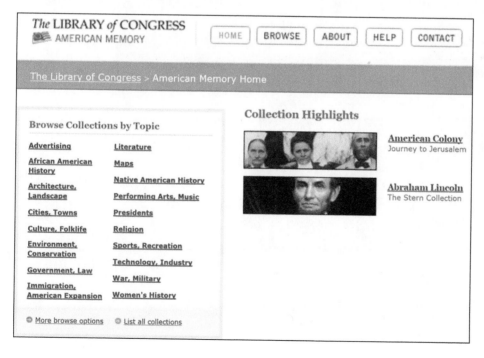

◀ WEB SITE FOR PRIMARY SOURCES **The Library of Congress** is an authoritative public archive of primary sources. The map on page 312 is from the LOC American Memory collection. *Library of Congress.*

## Secondary Sources

In a secondary source, a writer looks at a primary source—and offers an analysis, interpretation, or evaluation of that source. For example, a critique of a song (a primary source) is a secondary source. A critique of Lady Gaga's album *Born This Way* found in *Rolling Stone* magazine would be considered a secondary source; a YouTube video of Lady Gaga performing a song from *Born This Way* would be considered a primary source. If you were researching George Washington and found the biography *His Excellency: George Washington* by Joseph J. Ellis, that book would be considered a secondary source, while the George Washington Papers, original documents collected by the Library of Congress, are a primary source. (For more original documents, see the Manuscript Division at the Library of Congress.)

▲ SECONDARY SOURCE: BOOK
**Joseph J. Ellis,** *His Excellency: George Washington. Copyright © 2004 by Alfred A. Knopf, a division of Random House, Inc. from His Excellency: George Washington by Joseph J. Ellis. Used by permission of Alfred A. Knopf a division of Random House, Inc. Any third party use of this material, outside of this publication, is prohibited.*

## Tertiary Sources

Authors of tertiary texts synthesize, critique, and/or analyze secondary sources without adding new information. Essentially, authors of tertiary (or thirdhand) sources compile primary and/or secondary sources. They tend to present a generalized view of a given subject. For example, a music encyclopedia that mentions the critique (secondary source) of a piece of music (primary source) would be considered a tertiary source. *Wikipedia* is considered a tertiary source because it essentially summarizes information found in secondary sources.

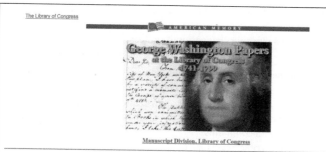

The complete George Washington Papers collection from the Manuscript Division at the Library of Congress consists of approximately 65,000 documents. This is the largest collection of original Washington documents in the world. Document types in the collection as a whole include correspondence, letterbooks, commonplace books, diaries, journals, financial account books, military records, reports, a Washington from 1741 through 1799. The collection is organized into nine Series or groupings. Commonplace books, c travel journals, document his youth and early adulthood as a Virginia county surveyor and as colonel of the militia durin War. Washington's election as delegate to the First and Second Continental Congresses and his command of the America Revolutionary war are well documented as well as his two presidential administrations from 1789 through 1797. Becaus Washington's interests, activities, and correspondents, which include ordinary citizens as well as celebrated figures, his p for almost every aspect of colonial and early American history. In its online presentation, the George Washington Papers approximately 152,000 images. This project is funded by Reuters America, Inc. and the Reuters Foundation.

◄ PRIMARY SOURCE: DOCUMENTS
**The Library of Congress.** The George Washington Papers. *Library of Congress.*

◄ PRIMARY SOURCE:
MAP **The Library of Congress.**
"Field of Gettysburg." American Memory collection.
*The Library of Congress.*

◄ TERTIARY SOURCE: WIKI SOFTWARE ENCYCLOPEDIA
**Wikipedia.** *The Wikipedia trademark is licensed under CC BY-SA 3.0. (Author User: Paul Stansifer, User: Nohat, Philip Metschan.)*

## When Should I Draw on a Primary Source? When Might a Secondary or Tertiary Source Be Best?

The kind of source you turn to depends on your purposes as a researcher and writer:

» When you want to get an overall sense of a topic or find uncontested factual information, look for a **tertiary source**.

» When you want original artifacts without the interpretation or analysis of others, look for a **primary source**.

» In most other cases, when you want to know how others have made sense of or interpreted primary sources, you should look for **secondary sources**.

Imagine you are conducting research about graphic novels and their presentation of female characters. Following are some sources you might turn to. They are organized into general and specialized academic categories. They are further divided by whether a given source is primary, secondary, or tertiary.

CHART ▶
**Types of sources: primary, secondary, and tertiary,** for a project on graphic novels and female characters. As you begin your research of any topic, keep in mind the variety of sources out there, aimed at different audiences, and composed for different purposes. Which are right for you?

| | General sources | Specialized academic sources |
|---|---|---|
| **PRIMARY SOURCES** | • An interview with a graphic novelist that appears in the entertainment section of the newspaper<br>• A graphic novel<br>• A blog entry written by a graphic novelist about the creation of graphic novel characters<br>• A movie poster for a film adaptation of a graphic novel | • An interview with a graphic novelist that appears in a peer-reviewed journal (an academic journal containing research by scholars in the field, reviewed by an editorial board of peers, such as other academic experts)<br>• A professor's lecture about graphic novels in a literature course |
| **SECONDARY SOURCES** | • A book about the history of graphic novels geared toward a general audience<br>• A blog entry by a fan of graphic novels that summarizes and comments on several different graphic novels | • A scholarly article about a graphic novel<br>• A scholarly article that offers a feminist critique of graphic novels |
| **TERTIARY SOURCES** | • An encyclopedia entry about graphic novels<br>• A review of a film adaptation of a graphic novel<br>• A specialized encyclopedia of comic books and graphic novels | • A review of literature in a scholarly book on graphic novels<br>• An annotated bibliography of articles about graphic novels |

## How Do I Preview a Source Critically?

Previewing your sources before committing to them is worth the effort. Ask yourself the following questions to identify what you might expect from a particular source, and whether you will want to use it in your research.

# 1. What Is the Overall Rhetorical Situation?

That is, what is the context of the source? Who wrote this piece, why, for whom, and how? And how does this impact the value of this text as a potential source?

Following is an example that we'll refer to throughout this section. It's an editorial published at Bloomberg.com.

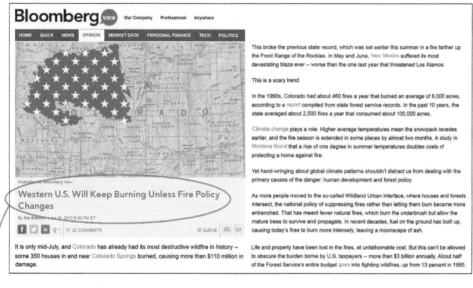

◀ EDITORIAL,
EXCERPTED
**Bloomberg.com.**
An opinion piece by
the editorial board
of Bloomberg has a
specific purpose and
is written for a specific
audience. These
factors are important
to consider when you
are choosing sources.

## What's the Rhetorical Situation?

Bloomberg Editors, "Western U.S. Will Keep Burning Unless Fire Policy Changes"

To get a sense of the rhetorical situation of this Bloomberg editorial—or any potential source—ask and answer some basic questions:

▶ **Who wrote this piece?** The editorial board at Bloomberg, an influential news organization focused on business and finance and with clout in both of these areas.

▶ **Why?** The Bloomberg editors wanted to address the disastrous Colorado fires of the summer of 2012. Their purpose was to persuade readers that the government could adopt a course of action that could prevent future fires—and also save taxpayers money.

▶ **For whom?** Bloomberg's audience includes general readers with Internet access interested in business news and a "business take" on issues—both in Colorado and across the country—as well as business and government leaders who could do something about the problem.

▶ **How?** The editors collaborated to come up with their collective view on government policies regarding fires in the Rockies. They published their editorial in the opinion section of their Web site. The editorial includes hyperlinks to related materials, and there are options for commenting and linking out to social networking.

As you look at sources, think about the rhetorical context of each by paying attention to the authors and their purposes, their target audiences and how they appeal to them, and the modes and media that they use for delivering their messages.

**Purpose**    First, ask yourself: Who is the author of this piece? What are his or her reasons for writing? What assumptions does the author make? How does all of this fit in with what I'm looking for? Keep in mind:

» *What is the author's background?* This information will give you a sense of the author's credibility (ethos) and his or her perspective on the topic at hand. Begin by reading any biographical information provided and see if there are links to any other writing the author has done on this topic. For example, an article from a collection published by the surgeon general about the causes of heart disease is very likely to be more dependable than an article written by someone who is not a doctor. The authors of the editorial about fire policy (p. 315) are the members of Bloomberg's editorial board. Bloomberg is a well-respected news group focused on money and the marketplace, part of what makes this source a trustworthy one.

» *Is the author seeking to persuade?* Report information? Tell a story? All of the above? How does this fit with the type of information you're looking for? Begin by examining the title and then skim the piece with a critical eye.

» *What are the author's biases?* While you're skimming, keep an eye out for assumptions built into the text. For example, an article by Facebook founder Mark Zuckerberg on the value of social networking will be biased in favor of social networking, while an article written by a more neutral, objective author not employed in the social networking business may be less biased. While both sources may have value, you need to keep in mind the authors' viewpoints and how they fit with what you want to say. The Bloomberg editorial (p. 315) represents the viewpoints of editors whose priorities are business growth and other financial concerns rather than the environment and other aspects of fire policy.

**Audience**    Ask yourself: Where did I find this text? Was it published in a popular magazine? A specialized academic journal? At a particular Web site? If so, who is the main audience for that magazine, journal, or Web site?

» *Am I part of the author's primary audience?* Based on the text's origin and a quick read of its contents, is the author aiming at a general readership or a narrower, more specialized audience? Evaluate the piece in terms of whether you find it readable, challenging, or perhaps oversimplified or condescending. Ask yourself: How much subject knowledge does the author assume readers have? For example, an engineer writing for a technical journal will assume readers are also engineers or specialists in related fields. That engineer is not writing to a

Have you ever discovered something about a writer that made you question his or her reliability? Have you ever been unsure about a writer's trustworthiness and then made a discovery that changed your mind?

general reader. As for the editors at Bloomberg (p. 315), they write for business-people, not environmentalists, so their take on fire policy is likely going to mesh better with the concerns of the business community than those of tree huggers.

» *Am I* not *part of the author's primary audience?* Don't dismiss a source just because you're not part of the author's primary audience. There may be something to learn from the piece. Let's say you're researching mining safety violations and settlements, and you locate a brochure created by a mining company. The target audience for the brochure is the local community—including relatives of people killed in a recent disaster at the mine. Perhaps the brochure oversimplifies the situation and denies responsibility, or perhaps it offers an apology and reparations. In either case, understanding an author's rhetorical situation (in this case, a company trying to appeal to employees and families) is valuable to you as a researcher.

**Rhetorical appeals**   In general, what strategies does the author use to build his or her case and connect with readers?

» *Does the author use humor?* Again, examine the title and skim the composition. If the author uses humor, does it work to strengthen the piece? How well does a humorous piece fit in with your topic and research?

» *Does the author use ethos, logos, and pathos to connect with readers?* How much authority does the author convey in the writing? Is the writing logical? To what extent does it appeal to your emotions? For example, you might realize as you analyze an author's appeal to pathos that his or her argument is not logical. At that point (unless you want a piece that is not logical, perhaps so you can critique it), you might decide not to use the source. It's a good sign when authors of a source incorporate statistical data, as the Bloomberg editors do (see p. 315), for example, to build a logical case that current fire policy must change. In the case of the Bloomberg editorial, the numerical data particularly appeals to their business and government audience.

**Modes & media**

» *Modes* In what mode was the source produced—written, audio, video, or something else? How does the composer's choice of mode contribute to the composition? What assumptions do you have about the mode? For example, it's fair to assume that hearing an audio essay, which features the composer's voice, is a more intimate experience than reading an article online. By considering mode you're more aware of how the author appeals to his or her audience. For example, a documentary film can have more of a dramatic impact on viewers than a researched article on readers because viewers use multiple senses to experience a film.

Do you think that some modes are more reliable than others? For example, do you assume that printed sources are more authoritative than stories you hear on the radio? Why or why not?

» *Media* In what medium is the source delivered—print, digital, or something else? What does the composer's choice of medium tell you about his or her assumptions about the audience? For example, digital sources are used primarily by audiences with access to computers or smartphones. Think, too, about the relationship between medium and the currency of information. A composer who publishes online can make revisions to the piece, adding links to newer articles on the topic at hand. For example, the Bloomberg editorial (p. 315) is digital, with written and visual components. The digital nature allows for the composers to update hyperlinks throughout the editorial, connecting readers with the latest writing on the topic.

## 2. What Is the Genre of the Piece?

What are you looking at? What kind of composition is it? What qualities is this genre known for? What makes this text a potentially workable source, or not?

Following is an example that we'll refer to throughout this section. It's a photo essay published at *Time* magazine's Web site. The photos are by Danny Wilcox Frazier of Redux photography, and the text was written by editors at *Time*.

PHOTO ESSAY ▶
**Time.** This photo essay, "In Boise, Housing Struggles to Emerge From Its Malaise," includes photos by Danny Wilcox Frazier of Redux, and captions by *Time* editors. As you consider sources, think about the genre of those sources (see the box on p. 319). *Photo essay: Danny Wilcox Frazier / Redux Pictures. Time branding: © 2009. Time Inc. Reprinted/Translated from TIME.COM and published with permission of Time Inc. Reproduction in any manner in any language in whole or in part without written permission is prohibited. TIME and the TIME logo are trademarks of Time Inc. Used under license.*

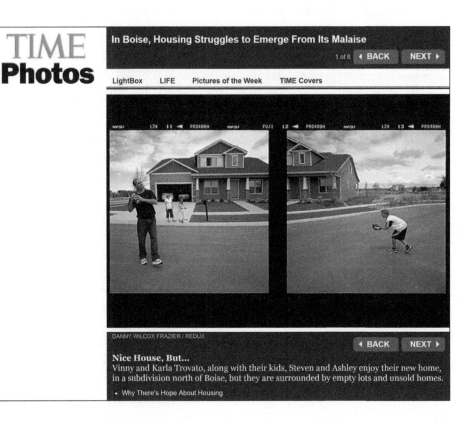

## What's the Genre?

*Time* and Danny Wilcox Frazier/Redux, "In Boise, Housing Struggles to Emerge From Its Malaise"

When you look at a potential source, you want to understand its rhetorical situation (see the Bloomberg editorial on p. 315)—its authorship, purpose, audience, etc.

You also want a sense of the genre that the composer chose—will it work for you?—as well as the style, design, and other sources drawn on. Ask and answer the following questions:

▶ **What am I looking at?** The image on page 318 is from a photo essay published online, created by *Time* editors and a photographer.

▶ **What qualities is this genre known for?** Photo essayists combine images and words to tell a story and/or to make an argument. Here, the editors at *Time* show the impact of an economic crisis—and hoped-for recovery—on a community. The title, "In Boise, Housing Struggles to Emerge From Its Malaise," suggests the argument being made.

▶ **What makes this text a potentially workable source, or not?** The authorship of this photo essay and its publication in a respected magazine make it a promising source. Also promising is that the journalists who composed the piece also conducted interviews with residents. The genre makes it useful to a researcher looking for a persuasive visual/textual argument based in primary research.

**Elements of the genre**   Ask yourself: What do I know about the genre? What can I expect or assume about it? Keep in mind:

» *What is the scope of the information?* Different genres present different amounts and degrees of information: An encyclopedia entry provides an overview of information, while a peer-reviewed journal article provides in-depth treatment.

» *How reliable is the information?* Some genres are known for their reliability and objectivity, others less so. For example, in terms of factual accuracy, a peer-reviewed journal article is probably more reliable than a political ad. (See also Chapter 1, "Understanding Genres.")

» *What is the connection between genre and purpose?* There is a relationship between an author's purpose and his or her choice of genre. For example, an author writing a blog probably wants to inform and/or persuade others. On the other hand, the author of an encyclopedia entry seeks to provide uncontested knowledge, while the creator of a TV ad is definitely out to convince viewers to buy something. Previewing a source in terms of its genre gives you a set of expectations to consider before you decide whether to read the source more closely. (See also Chapter 1, "Understanding Genres.") For example, the authors of the photo essay (see p. 318) chose that genre for a reason. The *Time* editors and photographer Danny Wilcox Frazier, who collaborated on the photo essay, chose to focus on the human side of the housing crisis in Boise. Consider how differently the business-oriented Bloomberg editorial board might have dealt with the same issue, perhaps writing an opinion piece on the financial aspects of the crisis rather than on how people deal with losing their homes.

**Style**   When evaluating a source, pay attention to the style of the author. Ask yourself:

» *How does the author use language?* As you skim, pay attention to the writer's word choice and vocabulary level. To what extent do they contribute to (or undermine) the author's ethos? How formal or informal is the language? Does the writer use slang? If so, keep in mind that slang is not an indicator of unreliability, just as formal language is not an indicator of reliability.

» *What is the author's tone? How does he or she use voice?* Describe the author's presence in the text. How does he or she use stylistic techniques to create a memorable voice and tone? For example, if you want to learn about the day-to-day impact of Asperger's syndrome, you may be drawn to a first-person text (or video, etc.) created by someone who is being treated for Asperger's and who can explain it from an intimate point of view. For any source, pay attention to tone—some authors may be off-putting, while an author with an engaging voice and tone might get you to read a piece that you weren't initially sure about.

» *How well does the author's style work with the chosen genre?* Think of the author's style in the context of the genre the author composed in. For example, if the author has written an editorial, ask yourself: Is the style generally in keeping with other editorials? For example, is it direct and persuasive?

» *What special techniques does the author use? How much detail does he or she provide?* Does the author use literary techniques, such as dialogue, setting, and metaphor? How do these techniques work to get and keep your attention? And how specific does the author get in terms of detail? Paying attention to these factors will assist you in deciding whether to commit to the source; in the best cases, other authors provide examples of techniques that you can adapt in your own writing. Consider the *Time*/Frazier photo essay as a source (p. 318). The editors don't go into much detail in the textual part of the essay, but the photos they chose highlight the personal connections people have with their homes.

**Design**   All compositions—from the lowliest e-mail to the biggest-budget film—are designed. Ask yourself: Is the source I'm looking at presented in a way that draws me in?

» *How are text and images laid out?* How does the author use spatial arrangement to guide your reading? How does formatting, such as use of capital letters, bold, or special fonts, direct your attention or shape your understanding of the source's organization? Is color used to highlight information? As with style, you might notice how an author uses design elements to communicate with a reader and decide to try some of the same techniques yourself. Designs that you find annoying or gimmicky may turn you off to a source, and the opposite may happen too: Clever design that resonates with you can draw you in.

» *How are sound and other nontext/nonimage elements arranged?* How does the composer use sound to guide your listening? How does the composer use sound to evoke emotion? How do these elements direct your attention toward or away from aspects of the piece? Note, for example, how in the *Time*/Frazier photo essay (p. 318), the photos stand out against the black background.

**Sources**    When you preview a text, learn what you can about its author's research methods, and therefore the text's validity. Ask yourself:

» *How did the author gather and analyze data?* For example, if you're looking at an article that draws its data from surveys of large groups, you expect to encounter a lot of statistics and charts that compile the data. You'd also hope that the data is dependable. For example, the *Time* editors who created the photo essay on the housing situation in Idaho visited the location and conducted interviews, gathering information firsthand.

» *What types of sources did the author draw on?* Pay attention to where the author obtained the information on which the piece is based. Also, keep in mind the type of information you're looking for. For example, if you want facts on a specific topic and the source you're looking at is anecdotal or only relies on the author's experiences rather than on scientific research, you might decide the source won't be of use to you after all.

» *Did the author document sources?* Are sources listed in a bibliography or Works Cited list? Within the text, are specific details about sources given, such as page numbers and dates of publication for written sources? For example, in the *Time*/Frazier photo essay (p. 318), the writers refer to the names of the homeowners in the text of the piece.

» *Did the author not conduct research?* Not all authors conduct outside research, especially when they compose in particular genres such as the memoir. In the case of the memoir, the source that informs the piece is the author himself or herself—it's based on his or her own experiences.

What is the price of drawing on unreliable sources? Have you ever lost faith in an author because of the sources he or she used? What were the sources? What made them seem unreliable?

# PREVIEWING A SOURCE

## Emily Kahn: Women in Comic Books Project

▲ STUDENT AUTHOR
**Emily Kahn.**
*iStockphoto.*

Let's follow a student, Emily Kahn, as she previews a possible source. Emily is interested in comics and graphic novels, and she plans to write an academic argument about the portrayal of women in these works. She locates a promising-looking article on the topic of women in graphic works in *Lightspeed: Science Fiction & Fantasy*, a weekly online magazine for fans of sci-fi and fantasy literature. The article, "The Objectification of Women in Comic Books," is by a writer named Jehanzeb Dar.

Before Emily reads the article in depth or adds it to her working bibliography, she will preview it. This means she'll dig around to better understand the context of the article. Keeping in mind the factors outlined above, Emily will set out to learn basic information about the publisher and author of the article—in addition to the author's purpose, audience, choice of genre, and more.

---

☞ **Attention, researchers! A word about previewing.**

When you find a source, do basic detective work before you commit to it. Start by getting to know its publisher and author. Ask yourself:

1. Where did the piece appear? Was it published by a scholarly journal? A well-known news outlet? An obscure but solid-looking blog? To what extent does the publisher have a specific point of view or agenda (e.g., *The Weekly Standard* states that it is a conservative publication)? How will this perspective fit in (or compare/contrast) with my project?

2. Who is the author? Someone I've heard of? Someone I don't know, but who seems to be a good writer?

---

### 1. What Is *Lightspeed* Magazine?

Emily first considers who publishes the magazine in which the article appears. She asks herself:

» What type of magazine is this?
» Who publishes it?
» What is the quality of the work presented there?
» Who is the main audience?
» Are the articles in the magazine peer-reviewed? Scholarly?

On the "About" page, she reads a note from the publisher:

## ABOUT

*Lightspeed* is an online science fiction and fantasy magazine. In its pages, you will find science fiction: from near-future, sociological soft SF, to far-future, star-spanning hard SF—and fantasy: from epic fantasy, sword-and-sorcery, and contemporary urban tales, to magical realism, science-fantasy, and folktales. No subject is off-limits, and we encourage our writers to take chances with their fiction and push the envelope.

*Lightspeed* was a finalist for the 2011 & 2012 Hugo Awards, and stories from Lightspeed have been nominated for the Hugo Award, the Nebula Award, and the Theodore Sturgeon Award.

Edited by bestselling anthologist John Joseph Adams, every month *Lightspeed* brings you a mix of originals and reprints, and featuring a variety of authors—from the bestsellers and award-winners you already know to the best new voices you haven't heard of yet. When you read *Lightspeed*, it is our hope that you'll see where science fiction and fantasy comes from, where it is now, and where it's going.

◀ MAGAZINE *Lightspeed,* "About" page. Emily begins her initial research, locating an article, "The Objectification of Women in Comic Books," in an online magazine for sci-fi fans, titled *Lightspeed*. She goes to the "About" page to learn more about the publication and the people behind it. *John Joseph Adams.*

For Emily, the fact that *Lightspeed* has been nominated for a number of awards and that the editor seems to be knowledgeable are important selling points. While at first glance *Lightspeed* might look like a fanzine, she sees when she browses the contents that the nonfiction pieces published there seem sophisticated in terms of subject matter, cultural analysis, and the use of sources and Works Cited lists. *Lightspeed* may be more scholarly than she'd originally thought, though it's very readable for a general audience. She's not sure what to assume about it, so she reads on.

MAGAZINE ▶
***Lightspeed.*** Emily peruses the homepage for the magazine to get a sense of its focus and audience. *John Joseph Adams.*

## 2. Who Are the Editors & Staff Members at *Lightspeed* Magazine?

Emily scrolls down to the masthead to find out more about the magazine's editorial staff.

She asks herself:

» What can I learn about who runs the magazine?

» Who is the publisher or main editor? What are his or her credentials? Is this an independent company, or is a parent company in charge?

» Who are the other editors and regular contributors to the magazine? What else have they written, and for what publications?

» Are the editors and contributors scholars? Critics? Fans of the genres of science and fantasy fiction? Authors themselves?

▲ STUDENT AUTHOR
**Emily Kahn.**
*iStockphoto.*

Emily is curious about the publisher and editor-in-chief, John Joseph Adams, and sees that he has won several awards as an anthologist and also is affiliated with Wired.com. She notices that *Lightspeed*'s monthly sponsor is Orbit Books, an imprint of Hachette, which publishes books by authors she has read, so that adds to the magazine's credibility. Reading down the masthead, she sees that many editors are published authors themselves who also write critical articles for other magazines devoted to fantasy, science fiction, horror, culture, and comics. Emily is pleasantly surprised that the editors of *Lightspeed* are more than enthusiastic consumers of science fiction and fantasy: They are experts as well. From the information Emily reads on the "About," "Our Staff," and "Our Sponsor" pages, she finds that *Lightspeed* magazine may be an appropriate source for her paper.

◄ MAGAZINE **Lightspeed,** excerpt from the masthead on the "Our Staff" page. Emily browses *Lightspeed*'s staff page to learn about who puts the magazine together. *John Joseph Adams.*

## Our Staff

### John Joseph Adams
Publisher/Editor-in-Chief

John Joseph Adams, in addition to serving as publisher and editor of *Lightspeed* (and its sister magazine, *Nightmare*), is the bestselling editor of many anthologies, such as *The Mad Scientist's Guide to World Domination, Oz Reimagined, Epic: Legends of Fantasy, Other Worlds Than These, Armored, Under the Moons of Mars, Brave New Worlds, Wastelands, The Living Dead, The Living Dead 2, By Blood We Live, Federations, The Improbable Adventures of Sherlock Holmes,* and *The Way of the Wizard.* He has been nominated for six Hugo Awards and four World Fantasy Awards, and he has been called "the reigning king of the anthology world" by Barnes & Noble.com. John is also the co-host of Wired.com's *The Geek's Guide to the Galaxy* podcast. Find him on Twitter @JohnJosephAdams.

### Robert Barton Bland
Assistant Publisher

Robert Barton Bland dabbles in writing, independent film, and, when struck by fancy, will even patronize the arts. He subsidized and helped found his sister's start-up dance company, Company Stefanie Batten Bland, currently a Baryshnikov Arts/Jerome Robbins New Fellow. Rob also produced the touring and creation of "Chapters an Evening of Repertory," which toured at Symphony Space in New York City, Saratoga Arts Festival, and in 2010 at Ris Orangis in France. In film, Rob is a two-time CINE Eagle Award winner for the independent shorts, "On Time" and "Writer's Block," and is currently executive producing a feature length independent film, *79 Parts,* directed by Ari Taub. Rob is also an alum of Jeanne Cavelos's Odyssey Workshop (2001), and he is currently pecking away at an urban fantasy novel, *Divinity Bind.*

### Rich Horton
Reprint Editor

Rich Horton is a Software Engineer living in the St. Louis area, working for a major Aerospace corporation. His job sometimes has a science fictional side, but he'd go to jail if he told you why. He also writes a monthly column for *Locus* Magazine, and columns and reviews for *Black Gate, SF Site,* and other publications. He edits *The Year's Best Science Fiction & Fantasy* series of anthologies for Prime Books, as well as such other anthologies as *War and Space: Recent Combat* and *Superheroes.*

### Jack Kincaid
Podcast Host

Jack Kincaid is best known as the creator and producer of the cyberpunk audio drama series, Edict Zero – FIS. He is a speculative fiction writer with a handful of short stories published and many novels waiting in the wings. One novel, *Hoad's Grim,* he released as a podcast in 2008-2009. He is also a diverse voice actor whose work can be heard in audio dramas on the web and in podcasts such as *The Geek's Guide to the Galaxy,* among other places. His background includes theatre, A/V production, music, games, sound design, and early machinima. Find him on Twitter at @jackkincaid9.

### Jim Freund
Podcast Editor

Jim Freund has been involved in producing radio programs of and about literary sf/f since 1967, when he began working at New York City's WBAI-FM at age 13. Jim has been sole host of the radio program, *Hour of the Wolf,* since 1974. Over the years, he has produced many radio dramas and lost track long ago of how many interviews and readings he has conducted. His work has been twice nominated for and was once a winner of the Major Armstrong Award for Excellence in Radio Production. Jim is currently Producer and Executive Curator of The New York Review of Science Fiction

### Karen Jones
Art Director

Karen Jones is a freelance User Interface Designer based in Brooklyn, New York. Her creative pursuits include photography, vector-based art, and character design for video games. When she isn't working in Photoshop or Illustrator or looking for artists on Cool Vibe and Deviant Art, she's being chased by zombies on the Xbox 360, reading about the art and architecture of the ancient world, or traveling. Follow her on Twitter at @karenJUX.

### Christie Yant
Assistant Editor

Christie Yant has published fiction in the magazines *Beneath Ceaseless Skies, Crossed Genres, Daily Science Fiction, Fireside, Shimmer,* has been featured on io9 and Wired.com, and has been included in the anthologies *The Way of the Wizard, Armored,* and *The Year's Best Science Fiction & Fantasy, 2011 Edition.* In the past, she has served as a book reviewer for Audible.com, and she occasionally narrates for StarShipSofa and blogs at Inkpunks.com, a website for aspiring and newly-pro writers. She lives in a former Temperance colony on the central coast of California, where she sometimes gets to watch rocket launches with her husband and her two amazing daughters. Learn more at Inkhaven.net.

MAGAZINE ▶
***Lightspeed,*** "Our Sponsor" page. Emily discovers that the magazine is backed by various print publisher sponsors. *John Joseph Adams.*

## Our Sponsor

*Lightspeed's* sponsor this month is <u>Orbit Books</u>:

Orbit US is the Science Fiction and Fantasy imprint at Hachette Book Group USA. Our authors include Joe Abercrombie, Iain M. Banks, Gail Carriger, Lilith Saintcrow and Brent Weeks. They publish a wide range of fiction from both established and debut authors.

Orbit also publishes digital short stories from their authors. The stories are available at all major ebook retailers —currently in the US and Canada, and further afield in the very near future. You can find their short fiction program at www.orbitshortfiction.com.

## 3. Who Is Jehanzeb, the Author of the Article?

Emily sees that *Lightspeed* attributes the article to a writer named Jehanzeb, for whom no last name is given. She asks herself:

» How can I discover the last name of the author, so that I can learn more about this writer?

» Is there a biography somewhere? Maybe a link to a blog or personal Web site?

» What else has this author written—whether on this topic or others? And where has his work been published?

» How much credibility does the author convey?

Emily first needs to discover Jehanzeb's full name. She notices a brief biography at the end of the article, which links to Jehanzeb's blog, where the article was first published. She also sees that *Lightspeed* has published three other articles by Jehanzeb on the topic of women in comics. To learn more, Emily follows the link to Jehanzeb's *Broken Mystic* blog, where he posts poems, personal writing, and articles. There she links to

AUTHOR PHOTO & BIO ▶
**Jehanzeb Dar.**
A photo from Jehanzeb's blog and a brief biographical note that appears with his article in *Lightspeed.* Emily begins to find out more about Dar, the author of the article she's interested in. *Photo: Jehanzeb Dar. Bio: John Joseph Adams.*

*<u>Jehanzeb</u> is a film student who writes about Islam, Feminism, Politics, and Media. This piece was originally published on his <u>blog</u>.*

**Tagged as:** comics

## Related Posts

○ <u>A Critique of Muslim Women in Comics -- AK Comics' Jalia and Aya</u>

○ <u>A Critique of Muslim Women in Comics -- The 99</u>

○ <u>Female, Muslim, and Mutant</u>

◀ PHOTO & BIO
**Jehanzeb Dar,** blog, *Muslim Reverie.* Emily discovers that Dar has an Internet presence; he's the author of a blog, and has been quoted in an Associated Press article (see below). *Jehanzeb Dar.*

a second blog, called *Muslim Reverie*, where Jehanzeb posts about "politics, current events, feminism, and media literacy." Here Emily discovers that his last name is Dar. She notices e-mail links at both blogs, so she can contact him directly. She thinks she might do that if she decides to use his article as a source in her research.

Now that Emily knows Jehanzeb's full name, she does a quick Google search to learn more about him. She wonders: Has Jehanzeb Dar published elsewhere—besides *Lightspeed* magazine and his blog? To what extent is he considered an expert on comics? A critic? She's interested to discover that Jehanzeb was interviewed by the Associated Press about the film *Prince of Persia.* In the AP article, which also appeared in media outlets including MSNBC's *Today, The Huffington Post, The Washington Times,* and *Bloomberg Businessweek,* among others, Jehanzeb argues that the role played by Jake Gyllenhaal (a white actor) should have gone to an actor of Middle Eastern descent. Dar also posted on his blog about the topic (see "This Prince Is Not Persian"). He is noted in different sources as a blogger, filmmaker, video gamer, and critic.

◀ ARTICLE EXCERPT
**Associated Press / Deepti Hajela,** excerpt from "Critics: 'Airbender' & 'Prince' Were 'Whitewashed,'" in which Jehanzeb Dar is quoted. *The YGS Group.*

By tracking down information through the bio that appeared with the article, through Jehanzeb's blogs, and through a Google search, Emily has turned up some rich information. As her mental picture of Jehanzeb gets clearer—as a writer, and as a thinker and critic who takes part in larger, public conversations about the presentation of race in popular culture—she becomes more interested in his article on women in comics as a source for her paper.

## 4. What Type of Article Is This? Will It Work for My Topic?

Now that Emily has a better sense of *Lightspeed* magazine and the writer Jehanzeb Dar, she's ready to do a closer reading of the article itself. Below is Dar's article, along with Emily's notes in the margins—you can see how she identifies her assumptions and also begins to read the piece closely and critically. At this point, she is still deciding on whether to use this source. Once she's done some annotating, she's ready to make her final call.

---

 **Attention, readers! A little history on this article.**

Jehanzeb Dar's article on women in graphic works was originally published at *Lightspeed* magazine (formerly *Fantasy* magazine). The piece included here is an updated version of the essay that Dar sent us for publication in this book. How did he revise his work? Why not read both versions of the article to find out? (Go to fantasy-magazine.com and search by author and title.)

---

## Guided Process: How to Preview a Source

## Emily Kahn (Student)

### *Women in Comic Books Project: Previewing Jehanzeb Dar*

As she reads, Emily asks herself the following questions:

▲ STUDENT AUTHOR
**Emily Kahn.**
*iStockphoto.*

» What is Dar's main purpose? And how does this fit in with my research questions?

» Who is his primary audience? Am I part of it? How does he connect with readers through rhetorical appeals?

» What genre is this piece? Based on what I know about the genre, what assumptions can I make?

» What is Dar's writing style? How do his techniques, voice, and tone affect me as a reader? How much detail does he use?

» Does the design of the article support what Dar seeks to achieve?

» What sources does he draw on? Does he document them? What type of sources are they—and how reliable are they?

*(The following article appears by permission of Jehanzeb Dar. The* Lightspeed *branding appears by permission of John Joseph Adams.)*

ORBIT BOOKS PRESENTS...

LIGHTSPEED
SCIENCE FICTION & FANTASY

© Armand Baltazar

HOME   ABOUT ▾   FICTION ▾   NONFICTION ▾   PODCASTS ▾   EBOOKS/SUBSCRIBE ▾   NEWSLETTER ▾   ⦿ RSS

# The Objectification of Women in Comic Books

*by* JEHANZEB

During World War II, a handsome American intelligence officer, Colonel Steve Trevor, crash-lands his plane on a mysterious island inhabited by the beautiful Amazons of Greek mythology. This new world is known as "Paradise Island" (what else would an island populated by Amazonian women be called, right?) and changes the course of human destiny. A princess by the name of Diana attends Trevor's wounds and subsequently falls in love with him. When she learns about the U.S. war against the Nazis, she dons a costume of America's red, white, and blue, and departs for the "Man's World." She becomes Wonder Woman—"beautiful as Aphrodite, wise as Athena, stronger than Hercules, and swifter than Mercury." She can fly like Superman and hurl heavy objects like the Hulk, and if you refuse to tell her the truth, she'll crack out her golden lasso and tie you up (especially if you're a heterosexual man).

At first glance, she may look like an empowered, kick-butt, feminist superheroine amidst a realm dominated by white heterosexual male superheroes. But is Wonder Woman really empowered? Is she really a symbol of feminism in comic books? Is her message really all about defending sisterhood, freedom, and democracy?

A historical overview is necessary to examine the role women have played in mainstream comic books as well as how intersecting dynamics of race and gender have impacted the way women are presented.

*Continues next page*

---

**Emily's notes on Dar's essay**

**What genre is this?**

Definitely an article/essay. The title indicates the author is making an argument about sexism in comics. I know it's a researched argument because there is a references/Works Cited page at the end.

**What can I assume about this genre?**

I assume Dar will make claims (and maybe counterarguments) and support them with evidence from outside sources.

**What is the author's style?**

His style is serious and scholarly, but the tone is kind of entertaining—he uses terms such as "kick-butt." He also uses lots of detail.

**How does the author use design?**

I like the subheadings. They divide the article into sections on different portrayals of women in comics.

## Emily's notes on Dar's essay

**How does the author work with sources?**

He cites sources in the text and in a References list. Looks like APA format.

Sources look to be from experts on comics and feminist and cultural critics. He also draws on comics themselves.

**Who is the author?**

Dar is a writer concerned with comics and critical of the portrayal of women in them. He also writes about issues related to race and popular culture.

**What is the author's purpose?**

The title says to me that Dar wants to persuade readers that women are objectified in comic books. As I read further, I see that he argues that even strong female characters are created to be alluring.

*(Continued on p. 331.)*

## 1. The Damsel in Distress

Originally, the only women that appeared in mainstream American comic books were white women, though they played very small roles. In the late 1930s, superpowered heroes like Superman and Captain Marvel dominated the stage while women scarcely had any presence. If women made appearances, they were depicted as dependent and "damsels in distress"—victims (typically of male violence) needing to be rescued by the male protagonist (who typically exerts more violence over the male villain). The "damsel in distress" is not only a prize that needs to be won by either the male villain or hero, but also an object that measures the masculinity of the male characters. For example, Superman's "masculinity is defined by what it is not, namely 'feminine,' and by all its associated traits—hard *not* soft, strong *not* weak, reserved *not* emotional, active *not* passive" (Brown, 2001, p. 168). The manner in which women service masculinity is apparent in the first issue of *Superman*, where news reporter and future love interest Lois Lane is kidnapped by criminals and eventually saved by Superman. A romantic relationship is not developed between the two characters and nothing is learned about who Lois is—she is only a weak "feminine" body reinforcing Superman's strong "masculinity" and "savior" role. Superman simply rescues her from villains, flies her to safety, and then flies away. Such one-dimensional portrayals were evident in other ways women were depicted: as the "girl-Friday . . . seductive vamp, or perhaps, the long-suffering girlfriend" (Lavin, 1998, p. 93). The stereotypical gender roles were quite obvious: men alone are capable of succeeding independently and being courageous, while women are dependent and weak beauties relegated to the background. These early attitudes toward women in comic books are quite suggestive of common sexist-defined role patterns where women are thought to be less intelligent than men and only have a place in the house as a caretaker and/or source of emotional support. As New York cartoonist Jules Feiffer states, "The ideal of masculine strength, whether Gary Cooper's, Lil Abner's, or Superman's, was for one to be so virile and handsome, to be in such a position of strength, that he need never go near girls. Except to help them" (1965).

## 2. Women as Sex Objects

The role of women changed dramatically during World War II when patriotic characters emerged and surprisingly attracted the interest of new readers, who were both men and women. Arguably, the most noteworthy female character was Wonder Woman. As mentioned above, she possesses enormous superhuman strength, has the ability to fly, and can overcome any obstacle that comes her way. Even more interesting is how her love interest, Colonel Trevor, is constantly being rescued by her, as if he is the male version of the aforementioned Lois Lane. Rather than the male rescuing the female in every episode, it is reversed in the Wonder Woman comics. In the following years, other strong superheroine characters surfaced like Miss America—the female version of Captain America—Mary Marvel, Supergirl, She-Hulk, and many others. They carried the symbolic message that "girls could do anything boys could do, and often better, especially if they stuck together" (Robbins, 2002).

However, despite these new portrayals of strong and powerful female characters like Wonder Woman, something else was occurring: they were being depicted as sex objects. As stated by Michael Lavin: "Powerful super-heroines like DC's Wonder Woman or Marvel's She-Hulk may easily overcome the most overwhelming threats and obstacles, but they are invariably depicted as alluring objects of desire, wearing the scantiest of costumes." The images of women with large bust sizes, hourglass figures, bare legs, and half-naked appearances became enormously popular after the success of Wonder Woman. Believe it or not, comic books were filled with so many sexual images of women that they were known as "headlight comic books" (crudely referring to the female anatomy). Comic book historian Ron Goulart writes: "In the days before the advent of *Playboy* and *Penthouse*, comic books offered one way

*Continues next page*

Emily's notes on Dar's essay

Looks like this is a feminist critique of comics. He also includes a section on the future of comics, so he's looking forward too.

**Who is the author writing for?**

For the editors and readers of *Lightspeed* magazine; the audience is mainly people who are experts on comics and interested in critical commentary about comics.

**How does the author use appeals?**

Dar appears to make his points using logic; he establishes his ethos/intelligence/expertise and uses sources. In this article he doesn't appeal to readers' emotions as a strategy.

to girl watch" (quoted in Lavin, p. 93). A prime example of "headlight comics" was in Bill Ward's *Torchy*, a series that ran from 1946 to 1950. The comic books contained dull and uninteresting storylines where the scriptwriters were merely making an excuse to draw Torchy as a tall, bare-legged blonde, who walked around in her underwear.

The escalating amount of sex and violence in comic books eventually led to complaints, particularly by psychologist Fredric Wertham who held a symposium in 1948 on the "Psychopathology of Comic Books." He also wrote a book, *Seduction of the Innocent*, which correlated a connection between "juvenile delinquency and comic book reading" (Lavin, 1998, p. 95). As a result, the Comics Code Authority established a written code that set the guidelines for comic book publishing. During this time, the comic book industry took a remarkable new turn where the constant objectification of women was seized. The brief period where comic books were geared more toward teenage girls wouldn't last long, as superheroes reemerged in the late 1960s, along with their scantily clad superheroines and damsels in distress. Women were drawn in the same stereotypical fashion, but this time, the artists took it one step further on the skimpy scale. Consider the White Queen, a female villain who appeared in the *X-Men* comics during the 1980s. She was "the stuff of male sexual fantasy: a push-up bustier, panties, and high-heel boots, all in white" (Lavin, 1998, p. 94).

Today, women are becoming more and more sexualized. As described by Jones and Jacobs (1995, p. 341):

> Females, perpetually bending over, arching their backs, and heaving their anti-gravity breasts into readers' faces, defied all laws of physics . . . the Victoria's Secret catalogue became the Bible of every super-hero artist, an endless source of stilted poses ripe for swiping by boys who wanted their fantasies of women far removed from any human reality.

One study conducted by Jessica H. Zellers shows an examination of how women are depicted in eighteen comic books. She finds that "of the suggestively clad, partially clad, or naked individuals . . . about three times as many were women (296) than men (107)." From the comic book sample where there were 1,768 male characters and 786 female characters, only 6 percent of all males were suggestively clad, partially clad, or naked; while of all the females, 38 percent were suggestively clad, partially clad, or naked. Additionally, of all males, 2 percent were naked, while of all females, 24 percent were naked. Zellers writes: "It is incredible that almost one out of every four females was, at some point, depicted in the nude" (2005, p. 34).

### 3. "Women of Color" as "Exotic Others"

Often in the analysis of women in comic books, nonwhite women, or women of color, are marginalized or given no mention at all. Without discussing the way women of color are depicted in mainstream American comic books, the analysis remains centered on white women and ignores the manner in which sexism and racism intersect. It would be a mistake to assume that "all women" suffer from the same mistreatment or objectification in comic books. As feminist bell hooks explains:

> A central tenet of modern feminist thought has been the assertion that "all women are oppressed." This assertion implies that women share a common lot, that factors like class, race, religion, sexual preference, etc. do not create a diversity of experience that determines the extent to which sexism will be an oppressive force in the lives of individual women. (1984, p. 5)

During the early history of comic books, which is often referred to as the Golden Age (late 1930s to early 1950s), people of color rarely appeared as superheroes. Lothar, Prince of the Seven Sons, was the first black character to appear in a comic strip titled *Mandrake the Magician*. Lothar was an "illiterate strongman dressed in animal skins" and catered to stereotypical images of "poverty and servitude" (Hogan, 2004, para. 3). A young black male superhero was featured in the 1940s war comic *Young Allies*, but was "nothing more than a minstrel stereotype in a zoot suit, who supplied comic relief"

*Continues next page*

Emily Kahn, *Women in Comic Books Project*

(Lendrum, 2005, p. 365). Such demeaning caricatures of black men in comic books paralleled the blackface performances in minstrel shows and American cartoons, which featured white actors and cartoon characters, including Mickey Mouse, wearing black makeup to create stereotypical depictions of African Americans. By the civil rights movement in the 1960s, significant changes had been made and new black characters emerged. However, the changes didn't guarantee a departure from stereotypes.

While black male superheroes, such as Black Panther, Luke Cage, Black Lightning, and Black Goliath, made their debuts in the 1960s and 1970s, they were presented as hypermasculine bodies (also note that three of the four black characters mentioned have their race emphasized in their names). That is, they were drawn with larger muscles than their white counterparts, were portrayed as more violent, and reinforced racial stereotypes of black men being "overly masculine" (Lendrum, 2005, p. 365). When black superheroines were introduced in the 1970s, particularly with the appearance of Storm, a mutant who has the ability to control the weather, their bodies were subjected to both sexist and racist stereotypes. In Storm's origin story, for example, she is recruited by X-Men leader Professor X, who finds her being worshipped as a rain goddess by a tribe in Africa. Storm is depicted as mythical and topless, although her long, flowing white hair conveniently covers her breasts. Not only is Storm depicted as a sex object, but she is also exoticized as a *racialized* sex object. As Jeffrey A. Brown, author of *Dangerous Curves: Action Heroines, Gender, Fetishism, and Popular Culture* (2011, p. 170), explains:

> In particular, women of color are consistently marketed and consumed as more bodily, more sexual, and more mysterious than their Caucasian counterparts. In short, ethnically identified women are routinely overwritten by cultural stereotypes and expectations of exotic Otherness, and all the sexual fantasies that implies.

While Storm adds diversity and challenges whiteness in the comic book genre, she also perpetuates the Otherness of women of color. In other words, due to her blackness, not only must she be a character from "over there," but she must also embody popular stereotypes and expectations white writers have about the continent of Africa. One can find a similar pattern when observing the Afghan Muslim super-heroine named Sooraya Qadir, or Dust, who made her 2002 debut in *X-Men*. Although she is intended to be a "positive" representation of Muslims in comic books, her character reinforces Orientalist stereo-types, that is, inaccurate presentations of "the East," particularly the Middle East, in order to reinforce "cultural superiority" of western civilization. Her face and body are fully veiled, though that didn't stop the artists from showing off her curvy figure.

She also needs to be rescued by a white man, namely Wolverine, from misogynist Afghan men who try to take off her clothes and molest her. When Wolverine brings Dust to the X-Men headquarters, she repeatedly says "*toorab*," the Arabic word for "dust." According to Wolverine, "It's all she says."

Dust is not only an "exoticized beauty" who speaks (one word) in a "foreign language" and hides her voluptuous figure behind a black veil, but also a vehicle for a disturbing imperialist narrative. For instance, if one considers how Wolverine slaughters a pile of Afghan militants and saves Dust from sexual molestation, one can see how Wolverine represents a western military intervention to "liberate" the "oppressed Muslim woman." In other words, Wolverine's violent presence in Afghanistan is justified because Dust needs rescuing from Afghan Muslim men (because Orientalism teaches us Islam is misogy-nistic). This narrative demonstrates how the woman of color, per-ceived as being "victimized" by her own people, becomes an object of imperial heteropatriarchal possession because her body, like her land, is violable and obtainable for Western masculinist power. Similarly, in Western politics and war propaganda, the struggle of Afghan women against sexist oppression is used to justify U.S. war and occupation

*Continues next page*

Emily Kahn, *Women in Comic Books Project*      335

in Afghanistan, despite the fact that bombs and bullets kill Afghan women, men, and children (Smith, 2005, p. 7).

It is worth noting that more superheroines of color are appearing in contemporary comic books, specifically in those produced by the two major comic publishers, DC and Marvel. Brown (2011, p. 168) lists a significant number:

> Latina characters Arana, White Tiger, Fire, and Tarantula; the African American or African heroines Storm, Vixen, Onyx, Steel 2.0, Thunder, Lady Hawk, Misty Knight; the Asian Psylocke, Colleen Wing, Katana, and the most recent Batgirl, the Native North American Rainmaker, Dawnstar, and the most recent Shaman. . . .

These characters have undoubtedly enriched comic books with immense diversity, but only a quick glance at their names is needed to see how they're accompanied by racial stereotypes. Sexual objectification of women of color is accentuated as they are seen as "exotic" and "physically different, but in an exciting way." As Brown (2011, p. 176) states: "While white superheroines are clearly fetishized as sexual ideals as well, the inscription of hypersexuality coupled with ethnicity perpetuates specific cultural stereotypes of exotic Otherness."

## 4. Exploitation and Sexism

Although some comic book artists argue that drawing women voluptuously and provocatively is a symbol of their strength and power, there are other points that can be emphasized to argue that women are being exploited. Consider the creator of Wonder Woman: a psychologist named William Moulton Marston (pen name: Charles Moulton) who also invented the lie detector. Revealing Marston's intentions and goals on the character of Wonder Woman sheds light upon new attitudes toward women in the world of graphic novels. The fact that Wonder Woman comes from a woman-only "Paradise Island" is enough to suggest heterosexual male fantasy, but Marston also states, "Give [men] an alluring woman stronger than themselves to submit to, and they'll be proud to become her willing slaves." Though Wonder Woman is not subordinate to or weaker than her surrounding male characters in terms of strength and powers, she is being exoticized and idolized by her male creator. Her weapon is a golden lasso, which critics have called an erotic symbol of sexual control since she uses it to make her adversaries obey her commands. Marston has been criticized for his bondage fixations—a recurring theme of Wonder Women tying up both men and women. This theme was so prevalent that the editor of DC comics, Sheldon Mayer, was uncomfortable with it and tried to tone it down (but was unsuccessful). In one 1948 story of Wonder Woman, there are no fewer than seventy-five panels of Wonder Woman tying up men or women in ropes.

One may also find sexist undertones in how many other female characters have abilities and superpowers ranging from being skilled in mundane arts like gymnastics and mind control (Maher, 2005, para. 11). Women of color like the aforementioned Dust have powers that align with dull and unimaginative racial stereotypes. That is, since Dust is from Afghanistan, which is presented as a dusty landscape, she has the ability to manipulate, you guessed it, dust! Sarah Rainmaker, of Apache descent, has the ability to control the weather and, yep, make it rain! White female characters like Madame Mirage, White Queen, and Malice have the ability to use mind control to manipulate their opponents, mostly men! White Queen specifically uses her powers of mind control to manipulate and deceive men in order to gain wealth and power (Lavin, 1998, p. 94). The voluptuous Catwoman uses her beauty to manipulate Batman, Poison Ivy uses her seductive and deadly love potions to gain what she wants, and Malice is able to control the emotional centers of the brain. Hmm, what's next? A female character who marries a rich old man only to have him killed off just to inherit the wealth and property? Wait, they already have a character like that: White Rabbit from the Spider-Man comics!

*Continues next page*

Emily Kahn, *Women in Comic Books Project*

Sexist representations of women can be found in the work of Frank Miller, one of the most popular and successful comic book writers/artists, who is also notorious for his racist (see his *300* series) and sexist undertones. The misogyny in his comic books is too obvious to be missed. Elektra, for example, is a troubled female assassin and antiheroine. Miller named her after the Greek mythological character of the same name and, as in the myth, Elektra's character develops a sexual attraction to her father (which is the symptom of the Electra complex in neo-Freudian psychology). Early in her life, her Electra complex is strengthened when her father rapes her, but then she is told that it never really happened. "It was only a fantasy . . . and she wanted it to happen. Her belief in her desire for the father grows, but her father dies before she can resolve the Electra complex" (Baughman, 1990, p. 28). One can't help but ask, "What purpose does Elektra's Electra complex serve?"

Frank Miller has also subjected other female characters to subordinate positions, such as Ava Lord in his series *Sin City*. Ava Lord says to a male character: "You're right about me! I'm nothing but a selfish slut who threw away the only man she ever loved . . . I'm such a fool. Such a selfish stupid slut" (Maher, 2005, para. 13). Another character he sexualizes is Vicki Vale in his *All Star Batman and Robin the Boy Wonder* comics. She is drawn in her pink bras and panties while thinking about her upcoming date with Bruce Wayne (a.k.a. Batman). On one panel, she is sucking her finger suggestively, and on the bottom panel, there is a shameless close-up of her buttocks. Below is an excerpt from Frank Miller's script for artist Jim Lee. It speaks for itself:

> OK, Jim, I'm shameless. Let's go with an ASS SHOT. Panties detailed. Balloons from above. She's walking, restless as always. We can't take our eyes off her. Especially since she's got one fine ass.

As analyzed by a feminist comic book reader, Vicki Vale's character is there to "reassure the readership of their hetero-masculinity." She is quintessentially "watched by male watchers: the writer/director (Frank), his artist, and the presumed male audience that buys the book" (Rubinstein, para. 7).

### 5. The Heterosexual Male Gaze

One could argue that what is at work here is the concept of the "male gaze." This feminist theory was first introduced in the essay "Visual Pleasure and Narrative Cinema" by film theorist Laura Mulvey in 1975. Male gaze is described as "a symptom of power asymmetry" that "projects its fantasy onto the female figure." A defining characteristic of male gaze is how the heterosexual male lets the camera "linger on the curves of the female body." The male gaze "denies women agency, relegating them to the status of objects" (p. 7). When applied to comic books, what we see presented about women is through the gaze of the male. The women are presented as men would want to see them. Similarly, the same images are presented to women as something they should aspire to be if they want to be with a man. In other words, the power and control that characters like Wonder Woman have may be perceived as a woman's control or power over a man, but it is in fact fake control. The male writers can take it away at will. Consider the following "adjustments" made by male writers on the storylines of female characters: "Batwoman is killed, Batgirl is paralyzed, Mirage is raped, while Black Canary is tortured, made infertile, and de-powered!" (Maher, 2005, para. 14). In other words, femininity has no control at all, as long as male writers and artists persist with these depictions and attitudes.

However, the concept of the male gaze needs to be expanded upon in order to recognize the white heterosexual male gaze that is at work. When women of color are objectified, they are seen in the way white heterosexual men want to see them: as exotic, hypersexualized Others. A 2005 Marvel comics series titled *Daughters of the Dragon: Samurai Bullets* starred the black superheroine Misty Knight and her Asian partner Colleen Wing. Misty falls victim to "hypersexualized characterization," which begins early in the series when "her naked body is glimpsed in the shower over the course of two full pages"

*Continues next page*

(Brown, 2011, p. 178). After losing a half-naked fight with a white female villain, Misty has rough sex with Iron Fist to "blow off some steam." Brown elaborates:

> Though the act is not depicted (thanks primarily to comics code restrictions), the aftermath is shown and it is clear the encounter was aggressive—headboards and lamps are broken—and as Misty dresses Danny [Iron Fist] lies spent in the broken bed, declaring "I think I need an I.V. drip and some pancakes." This scene has no bearing on the story except to mark Misty's assertive and animalistic hyper-sexuality. Rarely, if ever, do white superheroines hook up for random sexual encounters just to "blow off some steam."

Dust also serves as an example of how a Muslim woman is typically perceived in mainstream western media: veiled, oppressed, shy, and mysterious. Through the lens of the heterosexual male gaze, she is veiled and oppressed, but also "sexy," as is illustrated by her skin-tight *abaya*, or outer garment.

I found countless images of female characters in extremely provocative poses: bending over, arching their heads back, tossing their hair, fighting in the rain, and so on. Even the popular characters like Wonder Woman, Storm, Supergirl, and Jean Grey were not spared.

### 6. What Is the Future for Women in Comic Books?

According to the article "Why Don't 'Black Books' Sell?" by Alan Donald, the comic book industry and readership is dominated by young white men (2003, para. 6). Comics writer-artist Terry Brooks observes that most attendees at comic book conventions are white men. In addition to the racial homogeny, fans are "treated to the sight of several scantily clad professional models dressed in the costumes of popular comic book babes." The models are hired by comics companies to promote upcoming publications, and "for a small fee, any fan can immortalize the fantasy by having his picture taken with one of the role-playing women" (Lavin, 1998, p. 96).

This is not to say women and people of color don't read comic books. There certainly are some who do, but one may also argue that the sexism and racism contribute to the lower number of women readers, particularly women of color. According to comic book artist Trina Robbins:

> Women just don't go into comic-book stores. . . . A woman gets as far as the door, and after the cardboard life-size cut-out of a babe with giant breasts in a little thong bikini and spike-heel boots, the next thing that hits her is the smell. It smells like unwashed teenage boys, and it has this real porn-store atmosphere.

While one may argue that Robbins is generalizing about the nonpresence of women in comic books, she raises an important point about the atmosphere comic book stores create. The images on the covers of comic books featuring Wonder Woman, Catwoman, and other scantily clad superheroines (or random women dangling from the necks of their male saviors) are comparable to the sexualized images featured on the covers of "men's magazines" like *Maxim* and *Playboy*.

The increasing popularity of comic books has influenced other entertainment industries, especially Hollywood. Comic books are being adapted into movies more than ever before. Consider films like *The Dark Knight*, *X-Men*, *Iron Man*, and the Spider-Man films. These films are not only successful, but critically acclaimed as well. Now consider the protagonists of these films: predominantly white men. Has there been a Wonder Woman film in recent years? There have been two comic book films in the past decade with a female protagonist: *Catwoman* and *Elektra*. However, these films were critical and financial failures at the box office. Catwoman is portrayed as a shy black woman who transforms into a hypersexual, animalistic vigilante, while Elektra does battle in a midriff and has an onscreen kiss with another woman (I wonder how heterosexual male fans would react if Batman kissed another man?). Not only are the films taken less seri-

*Continues next page*

Emily Kahn, *Women in Comic Books Project*          341

ously than the aforementioned comic book movies, but they also seem to be poor excuses to watch Halle Berry and Jennifer Garner fight crime in skintight and revealing costumes.

If there were a Wonder Woman movie, would she have the same fate as Catwoman and Elektra? Considering that Wolverine earned his own spin-off film, would we see a movie about Storm? If so, would the filmmakers depict these superheroines as complex and three-dimensional characters with dilemmas and inner struggles? The X-Men include powerful female characters who can move objects with their minds, control the weather, and run through walls, among other things, but the male characters take center stage. Also, if we look at characters like Supergirl, Batgirl, and Spider-Girl, we notice what they all have in common. That is, they would not have existed if it were not for the original male characters: Superman, Batman, and Spider-Man, respectively. Superman tells Supergirl that he will take care of her like a "big brother," but if Supergirl is the cousin of Superman, then why in the world would she need to be looked after? This is an example of how male dependency is prevalent in comic books, both implicitly and explicitly.

Sexist undertones and stereotypical images are getting worse and increasingly sleazier. Comic books have a unique blend of complex narratives and visual art, which makes them a very popular and appealing form of art, but they also reinforce stereotypes about women—stereotypes about the "ideal" feminine body image: large breasts, thin waists, toned buttocks, long legs, and so on. These "ideals" are misleading because they are setting a standard for beauty in women, and considering the growing popularity of the superhero genre in Hollywood films, more viewers are being attracted to comic books.

We need new interpretations of female comic book characters. Wardrobes have been reinterpreted in the *X-Men* films directed by Bryan Singer; instead of wearing tight leather or spandex, the characters are wearing less provocative clothing (see Anna Paquin's Rogue). However, if we focused only on clothing, we would be overlooking the way in which women are relegated to marginalized and/or stereotypical roles. In *X-Men: First Class*, the character Angel is a woman of color with superhuman powers, but she is depicted as a stripper. I mention this not to degrade real women who work in the profession, but rather to highlight the pattern in which women of color are consistently hypersexualized in media. Furthermore, Angel decides to betray Professor Xavier's human-friendly mutants by joining the more militant and antihuman mutants led by Magneto. Instead of seeing these stereotypes about gender and race reproduced in comic books and their film adaptations, we need to see more realistic, diverse, and complex female characters—characters that we can not only relate to, but also learn from.

Some admirable efforts have been produced by comic book writer Chris Claremont, who introduced "a string of independent, strong-willed, and generally admirable heroines" in the mid '70s (Lavin, 1998, p. 97). Fourteen-year-old Kitty Pryde (or Shadowcat) of the X-Men is an excellent example of a multilayered female character. She is a teenager who suffers from anxiety, peer pressure, and loneliness, and she has a longing to be treated as an adult. In addition to being a well-developed character, she is not drawn unrealistically with large breasts like Wonder Woman. Another positive female character, Jubilee, is also from the *X-Men* series.

As more female writers and artists make contributions to the industry, male writers and artists will need to be inspired to work against sexism, the objectification of women, and the sexualization of women of color. The more sexualized images and stereotypical roles of women in comic books persist and are left unchallenged, the more sexist ideals for beauty will be reinforced and the less we will see of inspiring superheroines—of all racial backgrounds—truly taking a stand for truth, justice, and liberty.

*Continues next page*

Emily Kahn, *Women in Comic Books Project*

## References

Baughman, L. (1990). A psychoanalytic reading of a female comic book hero: *Elektra: Assassin*. *Women and Language, 13*, 27–30.

Brown, J. A. (2001). *Black superheroes, Milestone comics, and their fans*. Jackson: University Press of Mississippi. 168.

Brown, J. A. (2011). *Dangerous curves: Action heroines, gender, fetishism, and popular culture*. Jackson: University Press of Mississippi. 168, 170, 176, 178.

Donald, A., et al. (2003, September 9). The panel: Why don't 'black books' sell?" *Silver Bullet Comic Books*. Retrieved from http://www.silverbulletcomicbooks.com/panel/1063121223602.htm

Feiffer, J. (1965). *The great comic book heroes*. New York: Dial Press. 21.

Gorman, M. (2003). *Getting graphic! Using graphic novels to promote literacy with preteens and teens*. Worthington, Ohio: Linworth Publishing.

Hendrix, G. (2007, December 11). Out for justice. *The New York Sun*.

Hogan, E. (2004, February 5). Afros, icons, and spandex: A brief history of the African American superhero. *Open Your Mouth*. Retrieved from http://www.comicbookresources.com/?page=article&id=14623

hooks, b. (1984). *Feminist theory: From margin to center*. Cambridge, MA: South End Press. 5.

Jones, G., & Jacobs, W. (2005). *The comic book heroes* (rev. ed.). Rocklin, CA: Prima Publishing.

Lavin, M. (1998). Women in comic books. *Serials Review, 24*, 93–100.

Lendrum, R. (2005). The super black macho, one baaad mutha: Black superhero masculinity in 1970s mainstream comic books. *Extrapolation, 46*, 360–372.

Maher, K. (2005, June 2). Comic contempt. *The London Times*. Retrieved from http://www.thetimes.co.uk/tto/arts/film/article2429806.ece

Mulvey, L. (1975). Visual pleasure and narrative cinema. *Screen, 16*(3), 6–18.

Robbins, T. (2002, September). Gender differences in comics. *Image & Narrative*. Retrieved from http://www.imageandnarrative.be /inarchive/gender/trinarobbins.htm

Robbins, T. Women in comics: An introductory guide. Retrieved from http://readingwithpictures.org/wp-content/uploads /2008/03/women.pdf

Rubinstein, A. [Tekanji]. (2006, August 26). FAQ: What is the male gaze? Retrieved from http://finallyfeminism101 .wordpress.com/2007/08/26/faq-what-is-the-"male-gaze"

Smith, A. (2005). *Conquest: Sexual violence and American Indian genocide*. Cambridge, MA: South End Press. 7.

Zellers, J. H. (2005). *Naked ladies and macho men: A feminist content analysis of a burgeoning graphic novels collection* (Unpublished master's thesis). University of North Carolina, Chapel Hill, NC. 34.

## 5. Should I Add This Source to My Working Bibliography?

Emily is now satisfied that the author of the article is knowledgeable and that the article itself is interesting, readable, and potentially quite useful for her research project. She decides to add it to her working bibliography. She will return to the piece again later. Emily's next step is to create a research plan. (See pp. 364–65 for information on research plans.)

# EVALUATING A SOURCE

Evaluating a source is much like previewing a source (see pp. 322–28), only with more depth and attention to specifics. Once you've decided that a source is a potential "keeper," it's time to do a closer reading of it and decide whether it fits in with your research plan. Your main questions include:

» Is this a trustworthy source—do the author and publication convey an ethos of credibility?

» Will it work for my assignment—and further my purpose?

## Calvin Sweet: Hurricane Katrina Project

In the following pages, we will follow student Calvin Sweet as he looks at three different sources related to his topic, Hurricane Katrina. These sources, which appear on pages 354–63, are:

» **Madison Gray**, "The Press, Race and Katrina," an argument/editorial from *Time* magazine online.

» **Lincoln Shlensky**, "Hurricane Katrina, Race and Class: Part I," an argument/editorial from Shlensky's blog, titled *Aulula*.

» **Ed Gordon and Allison Keyes**, "Katrina Coverage Exposes Race, Class Fault Lines," a news report with analysis from National Public Radio (NPR), *News & Notes* program.

▲ STUDENT AUTHOR
**Calvin Sweet.**
*Shutterstock.*

You'll read these sources along with Calvin in the next few pages. For now, here is information on each author, and the context in which his work appeared.

**Madison Gray, "The Press, Race and Katrina"**   Madison Gray, a journalist and the Home Page Producer for *Time*, makes choices about the content that appears daily at Time.com. On his LinkedIn page, he describes himself as a "writer, online editor, breaking news monitor, and critical thinker." Gray was educated at Central Michigan University and his experience includes work with AOL Black Voices and the Knight Digital Media Center. He writes in his biography for *Time*: "Looking at my years in this craft, you could call me jack-of-all trades, but I'm really a student. Beginning in my hometown of Detroit, first writing [for] business, then doing radio, transitioning to a major daily, and finally finding my way to the East Coast to find a place in Internet news, the surprises keep on coming." Madison Gray wrote his editorial about Hurricane Katrina in 2006, almost one year after the storm. In it,

◄ AUTHOR PHOTO
**Madison Gray.** On his Twitter page, Madison Gray comments on his career to date: "Two decades, three continents, no apologies. I deliver news like Thelonius, baby: straight, no chaser." Gray's experience contributes to his ethos as a trustworthy source. *Kenneth B. Goldberg.*

Gray calls attention to his views on how journalists handled the reporting of Katrina, especially in terms of race. Gray's editorial appears on page 354.

**Lincoln Shlensky, "Hurricane Katrina, Race and Class: Part I"**   Dr. Lincoln Shlensky, author of the blog *Aulula*, is an assistant professor of English at the University of Victoria. During Hurricane Katrina, Shlensky was an assistant professor of English at the University of Alabama in Mobile. As a resident of Mobile, he was directly affected by Katrina. In his blog entry titled "Hurricane Katrina, Race and Class: Part I," he discusses his perspective on Katrina in relation to how the press covered the event. An excerpt from Shlensky's blog entry appears on page 358.

Home    Related Sites ▾    Student Resources ▾    University of Victoria ▾    Dr. Lincoln Z. Shlensky ▾

**Lincoln Z. Shlensky, PhD**
**Assistant Professor**
**Department of English**
**University of Victoria**

**Lincoln Z. Shlensky** is an assistant professor of English at the University of Victoria, where he specializes in cultural and media studies, with a focus on the postcolonial Caribbean, Jewish and diaspora studies, and film.

**Employment**

Assistant Professor. Department of English, University of Victoria, Victoria, British Columbia. July 2006-present.

Assistant Professor. Department of English, University of South Alabama, Mobile, Alabama. August 2003-July 2006.

**Education**

Ph.D., Comparative Literature (English, French, Hebrew)
  University of California, Berkeley                           2003
M.A., Comparative Literature (English, French)
  University of California, Berkeley                           1991
B.A., *magna cum laude*, Semiotics (Honors), Brown University   1987

◀ AUTHOR CURRICULUM VITAE **Lincoln Shlensky.** This CV from Shlensky's Web site (shlensky.com) indicates that, like Gray, he may be an authoritative source. *By permission of Lincoln Z. Shlensky. Photo by Caren Zilber-Shlensky. Web site by Jason Francisco.*

**Ed Gordon and Allison Keyes, "Katrina Coverage Exposes Race, Class Fault Lines"**   Ed Gordon is the host and executive producer of *Conversations with Ed Gordon*, a nationally-syndicated program, and former host of NPR's *News & Notes*. Gordon, known for his interviews with President Obama and pop culture celebrities, has contributed to CBS's *60 Minutes II*, NBC's *Today Show* and *Dateline*, and a roundtable talk show on BET called *Weekly with Ed Gordon*. Allison

**AUTHOR HOMEPAGE.** ▶
**Allison Keyes.**
Biography and photo
at National Public
Radio (npr.org). © 2015
National Public Radio,
Inc. "Allison Keyes,
NPR Biography" is used
with the permission of
NPR. Any unauthorized
duplication is strictly
prohibited.

**AUTHOR PHOTO.** ▶
**Ed Gordon.**
Photo by Johnny Nunez/
WireImage/Getty
Images.

Keyes is a broadcast journalist who covers national news for NPR and contributes to *Morning Edition*, *All Things Considered*, and *Weekend Edition Sunday*. Keyes, who is well-known for her accounts of the terrorist attacks of New York, has reported for several news outlets and produced segments for ABC's *Good Morning America* and *World News Tonight*. A member of the National Association of Black Journalists, Keyes has commented that her work on NPR's *News & Notes* allowed her to focus on national news affecting communities of color.

Gordon and Keyes's news report and analysis of the media coverage of Hurricane Katrina was featured on NPR's *News & Notes* program on September 13, 2005 (the hurricane made landfall in New Orleans on August 29). In this piece, Gordon (host of the program) and Keyes (reporter and commentator of the story) examine ways that race and class may have affected the media's reporting and analysis of the storm and its victims. An excerpt from their news story appears on page 361.

Before we read these sources on Hurricane Katrina in depth, we'll identify some guidelines for evaluating sources.

## How Do I Evaluate a Source? How Is This Different from Previewing?

While some of this overlaps with advice on previewing sources, we are asking you to do a more in-depth analysis of texts than you did earlier in the chapter. To evaluate whether a source is strong enough to draw upon for your own writing, ask yourself the questions posed in the following section.

**1. Is this source relevant to my project?**   First, determine whether the source you're looking at is related to and useful for your project and research question(s).

Ask yourself: Does the information in the source generate additional research questions related to my original question—does it get me deeper into my research? Does the source contribute to my knowledge on the topic—did I learn something new about the subject? In other words, does the author simply rehash what others have said, or does he or she say something new—or provide an alternative perspective? If the author simply duplicates knowledge, then the source is probably not a good choice for your project.

**2. What is the author's level of credibility?**   When evaluating a source, you need to figure out how trustworthy the author is. Ask yourself:

» *What can I find out by Googling the author?* Learn about the author's education, degrees held, and any institutional, organizational, or professional affiliations. Find out whether the author is mentioned in other sources on the topic, and to what extent he or she is considered to be an "expert" on the subject by other experts in the field. Research other works by the author: One indicator of expertise is whether someone has published numerous times on the subject. However, don't discount the author's credibility just because this is the author's first piece on the subject—the author could be a rising scholar in the field.

» *What if I can't figure out who the individual author is?* If there is no obvious author, look at the reliability of the organization sponsoring the Web site. For example, if the site is the American Diabetes Association, you can assume that the information presented is researched and reliable because it is an organization that publishes researched articles on diabetes. Additionally, this organization funds research. On its Web site, the association states, "We provide objective and credible information."

No matter how much you might agree with the viewpoint conveyed in a source or how much you might like the way the author has presented information, establishing the author's credibility is absolutely necessary if you are to use this source in your research. If you cannot trust the author, then you should not use the source.

**3. What is the author's purpose? To persuade? Inform? Tell a story? Some combination?**   Identify the author's purpose by reading the source critically and carefully. As you read, ask yourself the following questions to determine the author's objectives:

» What is the author's thesis? Does the thesis make an argument?

» Is the author trying to get me to agree with an opinion?

» Is the author presenting facts and information to teach me about the subject?

» Does the author use a narrative structure (include characters, conflict, setting)?

Once you have determined the purpose, ask yourself whether the author's purpose fits with your research question(s). A persuasive source can provide infor-

Have you ever Googled someone? If so, how did what you discovered affect your view of that person? If you've ever Googled yourself, how accurate was the information you found? What type of person did the information portray?

mation that you can use to support or refute your argument. Informative and narrative sources may provide background for you or lend a personal perspective to your subject. For example, student Calvin Sweet's sources (see p. 346) are three works in which authors seek to inform and persuade readers about Hurricane Katrina. One of these texts, Madison Gray's "The Press, Race and Katrina" (p. 354), presents an argument critiquing the way the press handled the reporting of Katrina in relationship to race. Calvin knows this because as he reads the article, he notes that the author discusses and provides specific examples from the media. He also circles explicit related statements such as, "many journalists who monitored the coverage felt in hindsight that African Americans caught in Katrina's wake were misrepresented in the press."

When determining an author's purpose, remember that genre might be able to give you a clue. For example, if the source is an editorial, you can assume that the author's purpose is to persuade you; however, the author might also be telling a story to support that opinion. You need to read the source carefully to fully know the author's purpose.

Ultimately, by knowing the author's purpose you can determine whether the source is a good fit for your research topic. If your goal is to persuade your reader, then a source that provides useful evidence is a good fit. If the author's purpose is to tell a story and none of the information helps you advance your own claim, then you shouldn't use that source.

**4. Who is the author's target audience? How does the author use rhetorical appeals to reach that audience?** When you preview a source, you determine the author's audience (see "Previewing a Source," p. 322). In order to determine the audience, ask yourself the following questions:

» Does the place of publication offer clues about audience? (For example, an editorial in *Bloomberg Businessweek* is clearly aimed at a business audience.)

» Does the author use a formal or informal tone?

» What level of detail is presented in the piece?

» Does the author include information that assumes previous knowledge?

» Does the author use jargon or vocabulary used by experts?

When Calvin reads Shlensky's blog entry about Katrina (p. 358), he notices that the author uses informal language, such as "I'm doing okay." This tells Calvin that Shlensky's primary audience is people concerned about how Hurricane Katrina affected him.

Once you've determined the audience for the text, take a look at how the author appeals to that audience. Is the author establishing a sense of credibility that speaks to particular readers? Is the author using an emotional appeal to connect with the audience? Calvin notices that Shlensky begins his blog with an emotional appeal to those who know him, discussing the long lines for gas he experiences and his concern for those who live closer to where the hurricane hit.

Besides identifying the audience and analyzing rhetorical appeals, you also need to examine the evidence the author provides and determine whether it is appropriate for his or her intended audience. Pay attention, too, to how the author keeps readers' perspectives in mind, so that they will continue to read the piece. For example, when Calvin reads the NPR news report and analysis by Gordon and Keyes, he sees that they begin with a claim about disparities, a claim that they support with an example (the survivors in the Super Dome). This alerts audiences that the piece will draw on specific evidence.

Knowing whether a source is written for a general audience or experts in the field helps you determine how appropriate the source is for research. For example, you may want to choose more specialized sources, written for a specific audience, if you're looking for detail and research so you can dig deeper into your topic inquiry. Or, if you want to make an argument—supported by research and data—about the impact of global warming on animals, you might turn to the journal *Nature* (written for a specialized audience), rather than *USA Today* (written for a general audience).

**5. What is the source's genre? Does the author make the most of its conventions?**   Let's say you're considering using a news and opinion blog as a source. As you evaluate it, look at a few other examples to see how other bloggers typically convey information—and the types of conventions they tend to adhere to. How does your potential source compare with other blogs? Does your blogger take advantage of the conventions of the genre? For example, does he clearly identify himself as the author? Does he embed hyperlinks to additional details or sources? Does he invite feedback? If not, you might want to consider using a different source. When an author chooses to ignore the traditional conventions of a genre, he may also ignore other things, such as using reliable evidence to support opinions.

**6. How does the author use evidence—and how reliable is that evidence?** As you evaluate a source, pay close attention to how the author supports his claims and arguments. Look at:

» *Sufficient support: Does the author use enough evidence?* If not, that's a problem. A skilled persuasive writer will back up each claim with an appropriate example. Read the source and (1) make a note every time the author makes a claim, and (2) also note whether the claim is supported. Notice also whether the evidence is vague and general, or specific and detailed. For example, Madison Gray, the author of one of Calvin Sweet's sources on Hurricane Katrina, race, and the media, writes:

Do you read any blogs regularly? If so, think of two or three that you particularly enjoy. What do they have in common in terms of how the bloggers present information? Do they share design elements, such as headings and lists? Are there things that are done better on one blog than on the others?

### CLAIM

"In fact, many journalists who monitored the coverage felt in hindsight that African Americans caught in Katrina's wake were misrepresented in the press."

Gray follows that claim with evidence—a quote from one person—that shows that at least one person believed there was misrepresentation. However, he doesn't sufficiently support his statement that "many journalists" felt that way. He could have made a stronger case by drawing on, say, a study of many journalists, or providing multiple quotes from journalists, for example.

### INADEQUATE EVIDENCE

"I don't think African Americans were portrayed in the best light," said Camille Jackson, a staff writer for the Southern Poverty Law Center's Tolerance.org Web site. "It came out just how uncomfortable the media is when it comes to race, with the exception of a few."

---

### ☞ Attention, researchers! A note about evidence.

Wondering what we mean by "evidence"? Evidence is facts, examples, and source citations that authors use to illustrate and support each point they make in their compositions. Skilled authors use evidence to develop their arguments as well as their ethos. The type of evidence authors choose reflects upon them; for example, citing a celebrity gossip magazine as evidence suggests shallowness, while citing the *Wall Street Journal* suggests professionalism.

When you're evaluating a source, look at how the author uses evidence: Think of the evidence as the foundation upon which the argument is built. A shoddy foundation can cause even the most beautiful building to crumble.

---

» *Timeliness: Is the source and evidence current?* In most cases, you'll want to draw on sources that are as recent as possible. For example, if you are researching current trends in social media and how they affect elections, you would want the most up-to-date information. With this same topic, you might also choose to draw on perspectives from the past in order to compare how things might have changed. In either case, be sure to check the dates of your sources and when they were last updated, especially when you research online.

Timeliness mattered to Calvin Sweet when he conducted research on Hurricane Katrina. He knew he wanted a contemporary account of the hurricane, told by someone who had survived it. He wanted reporting based on actual events that occurred at the moment of the storm—so he looked for sources published on or around the storm date. He was excited to find Lincoln Z. Shlensky's blog entry, "Hurricane Katrina, Race and Class: Part I," dated September 2, 2005, just a few days after the August 29, 2005, landfall of the hurricane as well as the NPR report dated September 13, 2005.

If Calvin had wanted a source focused on the longer-term aftermath of the storm—perhaps a yearlong study on the impact of the hurricane on people's lives—he'd probably have searched for sources written in 2006 or later. Such a source would likely draw on research conducted over time; the author could report the information provided in a study, or perhaps reflect on the situation, drawing on the study's data as supporting evidence for his claims. Depending on how you plan to use a source, its timeliness could make a difference. If you are looking for a contemporary account of an incident, then obviously a reflection written ten years later would not be appropriate.

**7. Does the author cite sources?**   As you evaluate a source, ask yourself: Does the author give credit to others? Does he mention the work of others in the text itself—perhaps with hyperlinks or a list of credits? How easily can I tell where the author obtained his or her information? If you can't tell what sources the author drew on, it's possible that the information isn't well researched or can't be supported.

Citation conventions—and by this we mean the format in which an author identifies his sources—can vary across genres. Before you can judge whether an author has cited sources properly, you need to be aware of the documentation conventions for the genre you are looking at. For example:

» Authors of newspaper articles usually cite sources in the body of the article itself, by using quotations and naming people and publications they've drawn on.

» Authors of blogs usually cite sources by providing hyperlinks to them, assuming the sources are online sources. You can see this in the two blog entries on Katrina featured in this chapter.

» Authors of peer-reviewed journal articles usually use strict source-citing conventions; for example, *The American Journal of Family Therapy*, a peer-reviewed journal on family behavioral health, requires authors to cite sources in accordance with the *Publication Manual of the American Psychological Association*. (See Chapter 7 for information on APA documentation style.) Considering that professional counselors rely on information in *The American Journal of Family Therapy* to inform their professional practice and research, it makes sense that source citation would be taken very seriously by the editors.

The Internet has made it possible to invent new genres quickly and easily. For example, just a short time ago, a "tweet" did not exist, but now the genre is incredibly popular. How do you think creators and users of these new genres decide how to cite their sources? What factors might contribute to their decisions?

Once you know something about the citation conventions of a genre, ask yourself: Does the author of the source I'm evaluating cite sources the way he should? For example, a journalist who doesn't mention any sources in an article or editorial should raise eyebrows—but a blogger who uses hyperlinks (rather than an academic style such as APA) should not. In a reliable text, an author makes it clear where he or she drew from the material of others. The author provides this information in the format that is common to that genre. If the source you're looking at falls short on this score, you may want to look for a different one.

# Guided Process: How to Evaluate Sources

▲ STUDENT AUTHOR
PHOTO
**Calvin Sweet.**
*Shutterstock.*

## Calvin Sweet (Student)

### *Hurricane Katrina Project: Evaluating 3 Sources*

Let's circle back to Calvin Sweet, who has identified a research question—and three sources that he's thinking of using.

RESEARCH QUESTION

How did the press treat race and class in their coverage of Hurricane Katrina and what are the consequences of that treatment?

Using the guidelines on pages 348–53, Calvin now evaluates his sources. His notes in the margins of each source show his thinking. He begins with Madison Gray's editorial for *Time*. (For biographical information on Madison Gray, see p. 346.) *(Article & Time branding: © 2009. Time Inc. Reprinted/Translated from TIME.COM and published with permission of Time Inc. Reproduction in any manner in any language in whole or in part without written permission is prohibited. TIME and the TIME logo are trademarks of Time Inc. Used under license.)*

**Calvin's notes on Gray's argument**

Relevant to my topic?

Yes. I want to look at media coverage of Katrina, as it relates to race and class. Madison Gray's critique of the storm coverage relates directly to my topic.

Credible author?

Yes. Gray writes for *Time*, so I trust he's a reliable journalist. He's also reported for the AP, *The New York Times,* and the *Detroit News;* he's a member of the New York Association of Black Journalists.

---

## TIME

VIEWPOINT

# The Press, Race and Katrina
## Madison Gray

Home    NewsFeed    U.S.    Politics    World    Business    Tech    Health    Science    Entertainment    Style    Opinion    Photos

If you watched any television, listened to any radio, picked up a newspaper or visited a news Web site in the days that followed Hurricane Katrina last year, you probably were witness to the result of dozens of on-the-spot editorial decisions made by news managers around the country.

As much as we may have wanted to avoid the issue in those first confusing days, because New Orleans was 67% African American prior to the storm, race played a significant role in criticisms of government, both local and federal, humanitarian aid and not surprisingly, the media. Fortunately, the fourth estate has its own self-policing mechanisms and is much faster than government and other industries at evaluating and scrutinizing itself. But it is only in recent years that the media has taken a look at how it relates to the country's racial divisions, and Katrina provided an opportunity to do just that.

Keith Woods, faculty dean of the Poynter Institute, a St. Petersburg, Florida–based journalism training organization, said many

# TIME

mistakes were made by the media, but in bringing attention to the crisis, the press got it right.

"The media brought a palpable sense of outrage with the coverage from the very beginning," said Woods. "If you looked at NPR, CNN, and scattered sightings of the networks and newspapers, where they did well was to recognize the size of the story and the need to stay with it."

But where race comes in is more difficult, he told me. Where journalism failed is not in any lack of emphasis on how disproportionately blacks were affected, but in how "too many people were making the surface observation that there were lots of blacks affected without spending the time parsing the facts that would make it meaningful or informative."

In fact, many journalists who monitored the coverage felt in hindsight that African Americans caught in Katrina's wake were misrepresented in the press.

"I don't think African Americans were portrayed in the best light," said Camille Jackson, a staff writer for the Southern Poverty Law Center's Tolerance.org Web site. "It came out just how uncomfortable the media is when it comes to race, with the exception of a few."

Jackson authored a series of articles for the Web site that spoke to media outlets referring to victims as "hoodlums," "animals" and "thugs." But she said it comes from cultural insensitivity in the media, which led to false news reports and eventually to a curtailing of emergency response.

She warned that the important lesson to be learned is "to be an honest journalist, to tell the whole story, and be aware of your

*Continues next page*

## Calvin's notes on Gray's argument

I did a search for Gray on Google and found his 2008 article on Rodney King that won a journalism award. Race definitely factors into some of his articles.

### Author's purpose?

Gray wants to persuade readers that "African Americans caught in Katrina's wake were misrepresented in the press." He also wants to inform about how journalists dealt with race in reporting the storm.

### Audience?

Gray is writing for *Time* readers, especially African Americans who experienced Katrina and whose stories were not properly reflected in the press. His readers are also probably interested in journalism and concerned about media bias. Gray relies on ethos to appeal to readers' concerns.

Calvin's notes on Gray's argument

**Identifiable genre/ mode/media?**

This magazine article is an editorial: Gray's column is titled "Viewpoint." Its mode is written and it is published online.

Essentially, Gray's article is an argument. He presents his case in short paragraphs and works in sources and quotes: This technique is common to editorials and other journalistic writing.

**Reliable evidence?**

Gray's sources include a journalism dean, a journalist, and other media experts; he also refers to a congressional report. That all seems solid.

Gray writes: "many journalists who monitored the coverage felt in hindsight that African Americans caught in Katrina's wake were misrepresented in the press."

*(Continued on p. 357.)*

## TIME

Home    NewsFeed    U.S.    Politics    World    Business    Tech    Health    Science    Entertainment    Style    Opinion    Photos

own personal biases. I know it's scary, but we're going to have to start talking about race so that we can get at the fear."

Buttressing criticisms of the press response to Katrina was a bipartisan Congressional report released in February that outright accuses the media of making a bad situation worse. It does not specify race in its pages, but its accusations implicate press reports that it says contributed to the confusion.

The report from the bipartisan House committee investigated preparations for and responses to Katrina and found that media reports of gunshots fired at rescue helicopters, rapes and murders in the Superdome, and mass rioting in the streets were unsubstantiated at best, and many were simply false. "It's clear accurate reporting was among Katrina's many victims," the report says. "If anyone rioted, it was the media."

But Margaret Engel, managing editor of the Newseum, an Arlington, Virginia–based interactive news museum, said there are more important things to consider, like images that seemingly cast a divide between black and white survivors. Two in particular were now-infamous captions placed with Agence France-Presse and Associated Press photos. The AFP photo caption described two whites as "finding" food, while the AP caption described a black youth as "looting" a store.

"That to me is much more troubling than reporters quoting cops who didn't really know," said Engel. "I think you'll find that some of the stories on that day of looting were wildly overstated. It's not good that the press reported that, but it is a footnote to the overall coverage which riveted the nation over the lack of response." She added: "I think for Congress to cast the media response as rumor-mongering is to miss the forest for the trees."

# TIME

Home NewsFeed U.S. Politics World Business Tech Health Science Entertainment Style Opinion Photos

Despite the varied points of view, two things are clear. First, mistakes were made. As Woods pointed out, there has never been a how-to book on covering a disaster that nearly wipes out a whole city. Secondly, and most importantly, if African Americans in New Orleans are to be fairly served, the story must be told. "Now that the initial event has passed, the problem is maintaining people's attention," said Richard Prince, chairman of the National Association of Black Journalists' Media Monitoring Committee. "People are desperate for media attention because they fear the country will forget them. While a lot of reporters have covered the follow-up, it has not been compelling enough."

Prince said that the way to learn from what happened is for journalists to continually go to the Gulf Coast Region and find new stories, which are abundant. "They call it one of the worst natural disasters in the history of the country. So many people have a story to tell; somehow those stories have to be told."

**Calvin's notes on Gray's argument**

He supports this claim by mentioning one specific journalist. Are there others he could mention to back this statement more strongly?

**Sources cited?**

Gray attributes his information to sources when he quotes people and names them in the body of the editorial.

He also provides hyperlinks so readers can get more information. For example, I clicked on the Keith Woods link and it took me to the Poynter Institute, where Woods was faculty dean (until 2010 when he joined NPR).

After reading through the informative and persuasive piece in *Time*, Calvin decided he wanted a more personal lens into the issues of the press and its reporting of Katrina. He found Lincoln Shlensky's blog containing writing about his views related to press coverage of Katrina. Additionally, he found that Shlensky provided the argumentative take on the situation that he was looking for. (For more biographical information on Lincoln Shlensky, see p. 347). *(The following blog post is reprinted here by permission of Lincoln Z. Shlensky.)*

Calvin Sweet, *Hurricane Katrina Project*     **357**

**Calvin's notes on Shlensky's argument**

**Relevant to my topic?**

Yes. Shlensky focuses on issues of race and how they affected the media's response to the disaster. This will be a valuable source for my research.

**Credible author?**

Yes. Shlensky is a college professor, and I trust that his research and sources are valid. His area of specialty is Caribbean literature (he holds a PhD), and according to his CV, he's presented numerous times on this subject, looking at issues of race in relationship to literature.

Because he's regularly subject to the peer review of fellow academics, I'd imagine Shlensky is careful with how he states things. Also, as an educator, he may look at his loss during Katrina through a more analytical than emotional lens.

# AULULA

A LYTTELL POTTE

## LINCOLN Z. SHLENSKY

## Hurricane Katrina, Race and Class: Part I

I have been in Pensacola, Florida, since late Tuesday because my house in Mobile still is without electricity. I'm doing okay here, but I look forward to getting back home as soon as electricity is restored. The University is supposed to reopen on September 6th, but that may change, depending on conditions. Yesterday and today the gas stations here in Pensacola were mainly without gas, and I waited in a long line at the one station that (only briefly) had gas to offer. It's scary to see people begin to panic when basic commodities are in short supply; I can only imagine to what degree such a sense of panic must be magnified nearer to the epicenter, where essential necessities such as water, food, and sanitation are in severe shortage.

From my vantage—geographically and emotionally near the disaster, but safely buffered from its worst deprivations—much of the press coverage has not adequately dealt with the most difficult social issues that mark this still unfolding catastrophe. It is difficult to avoid concluding that one important cause of the slow response to the debacle has to do with the fact that most of the people who are caught up in it are poor and black. Here in Pensacola I keep hearing blame expressed towards the victims: "they should have heeded the call to evacuate." Even the FEMA chief said as much in a news conference today. So where, I must ask, were the buses he should have provided to take them away before Katrina hit? Where were the troops to supervise evacuation? Where were the emergency shelters and health services? People who ought to know better do not seem to understand or acknowledge the enormous differential in available resources—access to transportation, money, information, social services,

# AULULA

etc.—that forms the background to this human catastrophe. Terms such as "looting" are tossed about in the press and on TV with no class or race analysis at all. In recent news reports, there is an emerging discussion of the *political* background to the calamity: the Bush administration's curtailment of federal funding for levee repair in order to pay for the war in Iraq, rampant commercial housing development on environmentally protected wetlands, financial evisceration of FEMA, and so on. But there's been little or no discussion of the economic background that makes New Orleans a kind of "Third World" nation unto itself, with fearsomely deteriorated housing projects, extraordinarily high crime and murder rates, and one of the worst public education systems in the country.

Major newspaper editors and TV producers have prepared very few reports about issues of race in this disaster, and those reports that have appeared so far seem to me deeply insufficient in their analysis of endemic class and race problems. I've been communicating with a national magazine reporter friend of mine since Tuesday night about the issues of race and class in this catastrophe; here's my email comment on this topic from earlier today:

CNN addressed the race question today on TV, but only to ask softball questions of Jesse Jackson, who to his discredit didn't exhibit even a modicum of the anger of one Louisiana black political leader, who said: "While the Administration has spoken of 'shock and awe' in the war on terror, the response to this disaster has been 'shockingly awful.'"

The *Washington Post* also ran a puff piece that doesn't ask any of the relevant questions, such as whether the Administration's response would have been faster if these were white people suffering the agonies of a slow motion disaster. Here's the link to the *Post*'s piece.

Michael Moore also had this to say in a letter to President Bush circulated today:

*Continues next page*

## Calvin's notes on Shlensky's argument

**Author's purpose?**

Shlensky writes his post to persuade readers that "much of the press coverage has not adequately dealt with the most difficult social issues that mark this still unfolding catastrophe . . . [because] most of the people who are caught up in it are poor and black."

**Audience?**

Shlensky writes to those critical of the media. He appeals to his audience with ethos (using quotes and evidence from media coverage) and pathos, hoping his audience gets angry enough to demand attention to the issues of race.

## Calvin's notes on Shlensky's argument

**Identifiable genre/ mode/medium?**

Shlensky mixes information and opinion. He uses blog conventions such as hyperlinks, comments, and an archive of his previous posts.

**Reliable evidence?**

There is a good amount of evidence and it's varied, including firsthand observations and references to a news report and Michael Moore's letter to President Bush. The entry is timely (he wrote it within days of Katrina making landfall).

**Sources cited?**

Shlensky attributes quotes and information throughout. He also uses hyperlinks to take you to the full source, such as when he discusses the *Washington Post* article.

# AULULA

No, Mr. Bush, you just stay the course. It's not your fault that 30 percent of New Orleans lives in poverty or that tens of thousands had no transportation to get out of town. C'mon, they're black! I mean, it's not like this happened to Kennebunkport. Can you imagine leaving white people on their roofs for five days? Don't make me laugh! Race has nothing—NOTHING—to do with this!

(See Michael Moore's full letter here.)

A member of the Congressional Black Caucus had to remind reporters today to stop referring to those displaced by the flooding with the blanket term "refugees" (recalling, of course, the waves of Haitian or Central American or Southeast Asian refugees who sought shelter in the United States): these people are citizens, she said, deserving of the full protections guaranteed to all Americans.

The federal government promised on Wednesday that those receiving food stamps could get their full allotment at the beginning of September, rather than the usual piecemeal distribution throughout the month. How very generous. What these people need is relief money and access to services now—even the 50,000 or so exhausted and traumatized people whose images we've seen at the N.O. Superdome and at the Civic Center are just a few of the far larger number of those residents of the region displaced by the hurricane, many of whom live from monthly paycheck to paycheck. It will be months at the very least before these people can return home; their jobs may be gone for good. The mayor of New Orleans was actually caught off camera crying in frustration today at the slow pace of the federal response.

If there is a hopeful side to this tragedy, it is perhaps that Hurricane Katrina's damage and efforts to relieve those displaced by the storm may spark a wider national discussion about the ongoing and unaddressed issues of race and economic disparity in America. If that doesn't happen, I fear that there will be even further

## AULULA

deterioration in the living conditions and economic predicament of those left destitute and homeless by Katrina—a situation in which our own government's years of neglect must be included as a crucial contributing factor. We must not let such a deterioration of conditions for those hardest hit by Katrina occur.

What happens next, when tens or hundreds of thousands of Americans require long-term recovery help, will be an important barometer of our society's ability to heal itself.

After realizing that Shlensky's blog contained a lot of evidence to support the writer's opinion, Calvin decided that a news report might give him an additional perspective on Hurricane Katrina. Even though NPR journalists Ed Gordon and Allison Keyes were not reporting from New Orleans and do not identify themselves as being directly affected by the hurricane, their examination of how the media covered Katrina raises questions that will help Calvin dig deeper into his research. (For biographical information on Gordon and Keyes, see p. 348.) *© National Public Radio, Inc. The NPR news report titled "Katrina Coverage Exposes Race, Class Fault Lines" was originally broadcast on NPR's News & Notes program on September 13, 2005 and is used here with the permission of NPR. Any unauthorized duplication is strictly prohibited. (Audio is available at npr.org/templates/story/story.php?storyId=4844457.)*

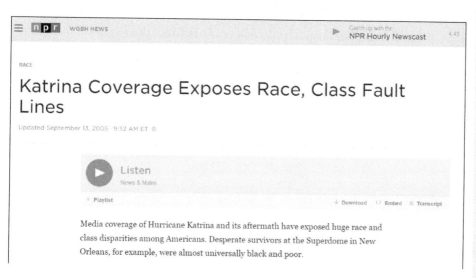

**Calvin's notes on Gordon and Keyes's analysis**

Relevant to my topic?
Yes. I'm intrigued by the journalists' choice of public figures (Wolf Blitzer, Barbara Bush, Kanye West, etc.), editing in audio clips of comments on the disaster and the media coverage of it. In the transcript of the story, Keyes makes

*(Continued on p. 362.)*

*Continues next page*

very specific points and backs each one with evidence. This piece adds an angle that is different from the other two sources.

**Credible authors?**

Like Madison Gray, Gordon (*News & Notes* program host) and Keyes (reporter and commentator) are respected journalists with experience in reporting news and providing analysis. (See the authors' bios.) Also, National Public Radio (NPR) is a news source where reporters are held to high standards. (See npr.org/about.)

**Authors' purpose?**

Gordon and Keyes want to inform listeners about how the media covered the storm and its victims. They also want to persuade listeners to examine the tragedy of Katrina and to take a critical look at how race and class may have affected the national response to the disaster.

**Audience?**

The audience for NPR's *News &*

# Katrina Coverage Exposes Race, Class Fault Lines

🖹 Transcript

SHARE

ED GORDON, host:

From NPR News, this is NEWS & NOTES. I'm Ed Gordon.

Images of the evacuees from Hurricane Katrina, overwhelmingly poor and disproportionately black, have dominated news coverage in the weeks since the storm slammed into the Gulf Coast. NPR's Allison Keyes begins our examination of the way race and social class may have influenced reporting and analysis of the catastrophe.

ALLISON KEYES reporting:

Reporters and anchors, even veterans like CNN's Wolf Blitzer, were stunned by what they saw in the days after the storm hit.

Mr. WOLF BLITZER (CNN): So many of these people, almost all of them that we see are so poor, and they are so black, and this is going to raise lots of questions for people who are watching this story unfold.

KEYES: On his first visit, President Bush told reporters that he looked forward to sitting on the porch of Mississippi Senator Trent Lott's new house after it was rebuilt. Critics blasted former first lady Barbara Bush for this comment about the evacuees staying at Houston's Astrodome on the radio program "Marketplace."

(Soundbite of "Marketplace")

Mrs. BARBARA BUSH (Former First Lady): So many of the people in the arena here, you know, were underprivileged anyway. This is working very well for them.

KEYES: During a telethon to support Hurricane Katrina victims, rapper Kanye West voiced what seems, at least anecdotally, to be the opinion of many African-Americans.

(Soundbite of telethon)

Mr. KANYE WEST (Rapper): I hate the way they portray us in the media.

KEYES: He also said...

(Soundbite of telethon)

Mr. WEST: George Bush doesn't care about black people.

Mr. WEST: George Bush doesn't care about black people.

KEYES: Many people spent the first five days after the storm watching the 24-hour cable channels. They saw Americans, mostly black, wading or swimming through neck-deep water, carrying food, water and clothes. Some carried televisions. On one hand, USC critical studies Professor Todd Boyd says the media helped draw attention to the dire straits victims faced, but on the other, he says, some of the images were problematic.

# Katrina Coverage Exposes Race, Class Fault Lines

Professor TODD BOYD (USC): When you look at, you know, just the large number of displaced black people there were, that was a certain image. And then when you start to show images of looting, that, of course, plays into some very old stereotypes in society and, I think, sort of confirms for a lot of people what they believe already.

KEYES: Boyd also says race affects everyone's perception of this coverage.

Prof. BOYD: If you're black, you know, race factors into everything that happens to you. If you're not, then, you know, maybe it seems strange. Maybe you think, `Oh, this doesn't have anything to do with it,' but it does. It has to do with race. It also has to do with class.

KEYES: Boyd says coverage of this hurricane has exposed a class of people who live in this country under Third World conditions, and Americans don't want to accept that. Nationally syndicated columnist Clarence Page of the Chicago Tribune says the invisible poor haven't taken center stage for years. He calls this coverage the first big racial eruption in the media since the O.J. Simpson trial 10 years ago.

Mr. CLARENCE PAGE (Chicago Tribune): We saw a story that already contained enough elements to be a big media story suddenly became this whole allegory about modern America and how we deal with our own divisions around race and class.

KEYES: Boyd says coverage of this hurricane has exposed a class of people who live in this country under Third World conditions, and Americans don't want to accept that. Nationally syndicated columnist Clarence Page of the Chicago Tribune says the invisible poor haven't taken center stage for years. He calls this coverage the first big racial eruption in the media since the O.J. Simpson trial 10 years ago.

Mr. CLARENCE PAGE (Chicago Tribune): We saw a story that already contained enough elements to be a big media story suddenly became this whole allegory about modern America and how we deal with our own divisions around race and class.

KEYES: Gregory Kane, a self-described black conservative who writes for The Baltimore Sun and BlackAmericaWeb.com, says he believes some black leaders were playing the race card more than the media. He cites the controversy over use of the word `refugee.'

Mr. GREGORY KANE (The Baltimore Sun; BlackAmericaWeb.com): Some people saw something racial in that. Well, first of all, the definitions I looked up indicate that it just means someone who seeks refuge, and I assume that means everybody who is trying to get the heck out of New Orleans.

KEYES: Kane doesn't believe the media coverage itself was racist. On the local channels in Baltimore, he says he saw looters of all colors, but Kane says the underlying issues that cause this problem do deal with race and class.

Mr. KANE: There are a lot of black folks in New Orleans who are poor, but that's because the poor are disproportionately black. But what you have here is a class issue that apparently some decision was made that we're not going to get the poor folks out of New Orleans.

KEYES: The Tribune's Page says he hopes this disaster and its coverage lead to some

*Continues next page*

Calvin Sweet, *Hurricane Katrina Project*    363

---

## Calvin's notes on Gordon and Keyes's analysis

*Notes* program includes a general, popular audience interested in national news and public radio journalism. The program, as Keyes suggests in her NPR biography, is particularly focused on news and events that affect people of color.

### Identifiable genre/mode/medium?

Yes. This is a radio news report. The audio content features voices and sound clips from events. The content is also available as a print transcript. It is broadcast by radio and through the Internet and is available to anyone with access to these technologies.

### Reliable evidence?

Yes, the journalists cite evidence to support each point. Evidence includes clips of other speakers with various points of view. I'm also confident that this is reliable because NPR holds rigorous standards and I assume someone fact-checks their content.

# Katrina Coverage Exposes Race, Class Fault Lines

serious conversation about how we close some of the gaps. But, he adds, he's too old and pessimistic to think that will happen. Allison Keyes, NPR News.

SHARE

## Calvin Sweet (Student)

### Hurricane Katrina Project: Research Plan

Following his evaluation of the works of Gray, Shlensky, and Gordon and Keyes, Calvin maps his research out in a little more detail.

**Research Assignment: Research Plan**

Calvin Sweet
Professor Elizabeth Kleinfeld
English 102
February 1, 20—
Research Plan: Hurricane Katrina Project

1. Your research question.

   My research question is twofold: How did the press treat race and class in their coverage of Katrina, and what are the consequences of that treatment?

2. Your goals.

   My starting point was to find out how the press covered Katrina. I want to be a journalist, and I remember my cousin who interned at a newspaper in 2007 saying that the writers at that paper were still talking about how "slanted" the Katrina coverage was. One of my goals is to discover what the Katrina coverage was. In the research I've done so far, it looks like some people think the coverage treated both race and class unfairly. If my research continues to support this view, I'll argue that press coverage didn't adequately take race and class into account and that there were serious consequences because of that. I believe my research would be considered inductive, because I truly haven't made up my mind and even these thoughts I have now are completely based on the three sources I've read. The next source I read could make me see things differently.

3. Types of sources.

I will continue reading blogs about Katrina. I think reading about people who experienced it gives me an understanding of what actually happened and how race and class mattered in what happened. I also need to read the press coverage and analysis, which I have just begun with the *Time* article and NPR story. In fact, analyzing the press coverage itself will be a major part of my research. I can do *EBSCOhost* searches to find articles. To make my argument that there are consequences because of the coverage, I need to follow up on things like Shlensky's idea that this could all lead to more discussion of race and class. For example, I need to find out if there have been more discussions of race and class, maybe by comparing how many articles a particular newspaper published on race and class issues in the two years before and the two years after Katrina. I will also watch Spike Lee's documentary *When the Levees Broke*. My assumption is that it will be like all of Lee's other films, in which race and class are examined.

For primary sources, I will look for YouTube videos by Katrina survivors to see how they portray race and class. I will also interview Professor Hughes in the African American studies department to see if she can share any insights with me.

4. Your timeline.

- Find and read more blogs: March 20-31

- Schedule interview with Professor Kleinfeld: April 1

- Write interview questions: April 5

- Conduct interview: April 7

- Watch Spike Lee film on Netflix: April 8-10

- Find and read press coverage: April 11-25

- Draft: April 25-May 6

- Revise: May 7-14

- Edit: May 14

- Submit: May 15

# 7 INTEGRATING & DOCUMENTING SOURCES

VIDEO STILL ▶
**Stephen Colbert,** during taping of *The Colbert Report.* Comedy and news programs can be interesting research sources. See MLA documentation for this source on page 402. *AP Photo/Joseph Kaczmarek.*

In this chapter, we focus on two things: (1) how to integrate sources, and (2) how to cite and document sources using two popular documentation styles. First, we'll show you how to incorporate sources into your own compositions, through quotations, paraphrases, and summaries (pp. 369–87). As you'll discover, there are reasons for choosing one method over the others, or combining methods, depending on your purposes. We'll follow the processes of student writers as they work with their sources (see Guided Processes in this chapter). We will also take a look at the issue of plagiarism. Composers who plagiarize use a source unethically, for example, by using an idea or language from a source without giving credit to that source with an attribution, parenthetical citation, and bibliographical entry. Plagiarism is not always a deliberate act; it can simply be the result of sloppiness. Whether it's intentional or not, plagiarism is a serious offense in any academic setting. However, if you follow the advice in this chapter (especially on pp. 387–92), you can be confident of your integrity and ethos as an author.

In the second part of the chapter, we will show you how to cite sources within the text of your own compositions, and how to document them in lists at the end of your paper. Because the documentation styles of the Modern Language Association (MLA) and American Psychological Association (APA) are the ones most typically used in the humanities and social sciences, we've provided detailed coverage of both (MLA, pp. 395–414; APA, pp. 415–35). There are other popular styles—such as *Chicago* style, used by some of the humanities disciplines, and the American Medical Association (AMA) style, used by health and medical fields. If you are using those styles, we refer you to chicagomanualofstyle.org and amamanualofstyle.com.

For an Index of Sources & Contexts for material referenced in this chapter, see the e-Pages at **bedfordstmartins.com /bookofgenres.**

# INTEGRATING SOURCES INTO YOUR WRITING

When we talk about integrating sources, we mean a host of different and related activities. We mean using source material in our own compositions, perhaps to provide context for our ideas or evidence for our claims. We also mean showing how the source material we've used relates to other source material—does it agree with other sources? Does it contradict other sources? Does it provide a perspective missing in other sources? And finally, we mean citing our sources to credit outside sources throughout the text of our papers and documenting them in a Works Cited list (MLA) or References list (APA) so that interested readers can track the sources down for themselves.

# Using a Parenthetical Citation or Signal Phrase

Here are examples of how Emily Kahn (the student introduced in Chapter 6) integrated an article into a paper she wrote. She found the article, "The Objectification of Women in Comic Books" by Jehanzeb Dar, online in the fantasy magazine, *Lightspeed*.

In this first example, Emily presents Dar's name in what's called a parenthetical citation. Parenthetical citations must include the author's last name and the page number from the source that the material is taken from. Because Dar's article is from an online magazine, there are no page numbers to list.

EMILY'S IN-TEXT CITATION (MLA style—names author in parentheses)
The writer argues that the comic book industry may begin to attract female readers and readers of color if comics authors reject sexism and racism. He concludes: "As more female writers and artists make contributions to the industry, male writers and artists will need to be inspired to work against sexism, the objectification of women, and the sexualization of women of color" (Dar 000).

author's last name ——— if there is a page number, it goes here

Alternatively, Emily could have cited Dar's article as follows, by naming him in a signal phrase.

EMILY'S IN-TEXT CITATION (MLA style—names author in a signal phrase)
author named in signal phrase

Jehanzeb Dar argues that if the comic book industry wants to attract female readers, then comic book authors need to reject sexism and racism. He concludes: "As more female writers and artists make contributions to the industry, male writers and artists will need to be inspired to work against sexism, the objectification of women, and the sexualization of women of color" (00-00).

were this a print article, with page numbers, the page or pages referred to would go here

At the end of her paper, Emily provides a bibliographic entry for her references to Dar's article.

EMILY'S WORKS CITED ENTRY (MLA style)
author name: last, first        title of article        title of magazine

Dar, Jehanzeb. "The Objectification of Women in Comic Books." *Lightspeed*,

publisher        publication date        article URL

John Joseph Adams, Aug. 2008, www.fantasy-magazine.com/non-fiction/

articles/the-objectification-of-women-in-graphic-novels/.

Using the MLA style of documentation, Emily:

» Cites Dar's article in the text of her paper, using an in-text citation that includes his name (no page number available)

» Documents Dar's article with a corresponding entry in her Works Cited list

» Avoids plagiarism, by citing Dar's article in *both* the text of her paper *and* her Works Cited list

## Overview: Quoting, Paraphrasing, & Summarizing

**Quoting**   In the example on page 368, Emily quotes directly from Dar's article. To signify to her readers that she is using Dar's exact words, she surrounds his words with quotation marks:

**EMILY'S DIRECT QUOTATION FROM THE SOURCE (Dar)**
He concludes: "As more female writers and artists make contributions to the industry, male writers and artists will need to be inspired to work against sexism, the objectification of women, and the sexualization of women of color" (Dar).

Emily chooses to include a quotation in order to state the specifics of Dar's argument. The quotation also serves to back up her first sentence, in which she summarizes Dar's main argument.

**Paraphrasing**   Elsewhere in her paper, Emily paraphrases Dar's argument. To paraphrase, a writer takes the ideas of a source and puts them into his or her own words. A paraphrase rewords without significantly condensing a specific passage.

**ORIGINAL PASSAGE FROM SOURCE (Dar)**
The role of women changed dramatically during World War II when patriotic characters emerged and surprisingly attracted the interest of new readers, who were both men and women. Arguably, the most noteworthy female character was Wonder Woman.

**EMILY'S PARAPHRASE**
According to Dar, Wonder Woman was the most interesting character to come out of the comics of the World War II era.

Note that Emily rephrases Dar's sentences and condenses them into one. She also attributes the entire idea to Dar by naming him in a signal phrase: "According to Dar . . ." If the article were in print, she would also include a parenthetical note at the end with the page number on which the idea was mentioned.

As you can see in the examples above, Emily always gives credit to Dar when she refers to his ideas, even if she changes his words, as in a summary or paraphrase.

☞ **Attention, writers! A little summary goes a long way.**

Although summarizing an entire work is occasionally the way to go, we recommend that you do this sparingly.

Choose summary to step back and give a "big picture" view to your readers, or to provide context.

In general, focus on specific points and passages of your sources; draw on these through quotations, paraphrases, or a combination of these. Support your arguments with specifics from your sources and your paper will be richer, more detailed, and ultimately, more persuasive.

Integrating sources smoothly into your own writing allows you to maintain control over the authorial voice that your readers hear. For example, although the examples above show Emily referring to Dar's ideas, it is clear that she, not Dar, is the author of her paper. Dar's voice never overtakes Emily's. While she draws on the source through quotations, paraphrases, and summary, she does so smoothly. Like Emily, you'll need to decide how and when to use these methods of drawing on sources. You'll also need to decide whether you're going to cite them through signal phrases, such as "According to Dar," or through parenthetical citations, such as "(Dar 000)." And if your instructor has not requested that you use a particular documentation style, you'll need to decide which format to use: MLA, APA, or another method of documentation.

**Summarizing**     In the example on page 368, Emily summarizes the main point of Dar's entire article in her first sentence:

**EMILY'S SUMMARY OF ENTIRE SOURCE**
Jehanzeb Dar argues that if the comic book industry wants to attract female readers, then comic book authors need to reject sexism and racism.

Emily manages to summarize in one sentence a point Dar makes in nine paragraphs. A summary condenses material significantly and focuses only on the point made, not the details that support or illustrate the point. Emily wants to reference Dar's central argument, so summary makes sense.

## Quoting

### What Does It Mean to Quote from a Source?

When you quote from a source, you provide a passage from that text—in the author's exact language. The best time to quote from a text is when the language from a passage contributes in a crucial way to the argument you are making.

When you quote from a passage, you should:

**Use the exact words from the original without alteration**     If you do need to alter the words for the sake of agreement of verb tense, use brackets to indicate what you've altered. To shorten a passage, use ellipses.

**ORIGINAL PASSAGE FROM SOURCE**
"Sexist undertones and stereotypical images are getting worse and increasingly sleazier."

**EMILY'S ALTERED QUOTE (changes shown in brackets)**
Dar points out that "[s]exist undertones and stereotypical images [have gotten] worse and increasingly sleaz[y]."

**Surround the quoted passage with quotation marks**   An exception is long quotes, which should be indented in a block. A long quote, per MLA, is more than four lines long; in APA style, it is more than forty words long.

**Give credit to the author of the source being quoted**   An attribution phrase, such as "Dar points out that," gives credit and cues readers to hear someone else's voice for a moment or two. Conventions for crediting sources differ. As with summaries and paraphrases, you may need to provide a parenthetical citation and/or a bibliographic entry if that is appropriate for the genre you are composing in.

Quote from other authors to present their specific language for good reasons; for example, if a passage supports (or refutes) the point you're making.

Let's look at an example. Suppose a student named Omar Sadi is writing about the possible connection between extreme weather and global warming. One of his sources is *Yale Environment 360*, published by Yale University and its School of Forestry and Environmental Studies. In that journal, Omar finds an article that gathers the views of eight climate experts.

☞ **Attention, writers! A caution against quoting too much.**

Remember that every time you quote an author, you are, in effect, turning over the microphone to someone else. So when should you let someone else take the microphone? Perhaps if the author makes a point in language so vivid it deserves a moment in the spotlight. Or if the author's language or phrasing is particularly precise or interesting or humorous. Our point is this: Quote mindfully. Don't use quotations just because you think it will be too much work to paraphrase. Whether you choose to quote, paraphrase, or summarize from a source, be sure to credit it in the text of your paper and list it in your Works Cited (MLA) or References (APA) list.

# Forum: Is Extreme Weather Linked to Global Warming?

*In the past year, the world has seen a large number of extreme weather events, from the Russian heat wave last summer, to the severe flooding in Pakistan, to the recent tornadoes in the U.S. In a Yale Environment 360 forum, a panel of experts weighs in on whether the wild weather may be tied to increasing global temperatures.*

That global air and ocean temperatures are rising, and that human activity is largely to blame, is no longer a subject of debate among the vast majority of the world's climate scientists. But there is no such consensus when talk turns to another important question: Is climate change already causing more extreme weather events, including worsening downpours and flooding, intensifying heat waves, and more powerful hurricanes?

*Yale Environment 360* asked eight leading climate experts whether they think there is growing evidence that human-caused global warming is contributing to an increased incidence of extreme weather — and to cite specific recent examples in their answers. Their responses varied, with some contending that rising temperatures already are creating more tempestuous weather and others saying that more extreme weather may be likely but that not enough data yet exists to discern a trend in that direction. Scientists in both camps said two physical phenomena — warmer air holds more moisture, and higher temperatures exacerbate naturally occurring heat waves — would almost by definition mean more extremes. But some argued that the growing human toll from hurricanes, tornadoes, floods, and heat waves is primarily related to burgeoning human population and the related degradation of the environment.

**Gabriele C. Hegerl, professor of climate system science at the University of Edinburgh.**
Not all extreme events are expected to increase or even change. For example, there is quite a bit of evidence that greenhouse gas increases have contributed to recent widespread changes in the frequency of extreme temperatures, but this encompasses both decreases in the number of cold days and nights and increases in the number of warm nights. The widespread recent warming, which for global and continental mean data has been found to be likely due largely to human influences, leads to a changing probability of extreme temperatures. However, there are also cases where the tail of the temperature distribution is changing differently from the mean. Warming can lead to more severe drought in regions and seasons where precipitation decreases or remains largely unchanged, while evaporation increases due to warmer temperatures. Furthermore, the warming atmosphere has been shown to become moister. This probably explains the statistically significant shift towards more extreme precipitation events worldwide, which cannot be explained by climate variability and is best explained by human influences.

**Roger A. Pielke Jr., professor of environmental studies at the University of Colorado.**
The IPCC [Intergovernmental Panel on Climate Change] defines "climate change" as a change in the statistics of weather occurring over 30 years or longer and persisting for decades. Thus, the detection of a change in climate requires long-term records. To suggest that particular extreme weather events are evidence of climate change is not just wrong, but wrongheaded — every bit as much as the claims made during a particularly cold and snowy winter (or even several in a row) that such events somehow disprove climate change. Weather is not climate and short-term climate variability is not climate change.

◀ ARTICLE
*Yale Environment 360,* Yale University's online magazine. The article "Forum: Is Extreme Weather Linked to Global Warming?" presents the views of climate scientists, including Gabriele C. Hegerl and Roger A. Pielke Jr. *Yale Environment 360.*

He decides that the experts' perspectives and voices will support his main argument, and he chooses to quote from the source as follows.

### OMAR'S EFFECTIVE QUOTING

In a recent forum published by *Yale Environment 360*, a panel of experts addressed the question: Is extreme weather linked to global warming? Like many of the panelists, University of Colorado professor Roger A. Pielke Jr. said that because the Intergovernmental Panel on Climate Change defines climate change as a persistent change of weather that takes place over the course of thirty years or more, the question posed cannot be answered now. Instead, Pielke says, we need long-term studies and records to scientifically support a connection. He argues:

> To suggest that particular extreme weather events are evidence of climate change is not just wrong, but wrongheaded. . . . Weather is not climate and short-term climate variability is not climate change.

*quotation from a source*

So how do scientists explain the extreme weather of recent years? And what are the best ways of evaluating the impact of global warming on the weather? . . .

## When Should I Quote from a Source?

A great time to quote from a source is when the ideas or language of the original is so striking that you can't truly capture them in a paraphrase or summary. For example, 9/11 hero Todd Beamer's words "let's roll" could be paraphrased as "we should act now," but such a paraphrase lacks the energy and emotion of the original. It would be best to quote Beamer. Here are some other instances when you might quote rather than paraphrase or summarize:

**Quote from a source when the author or speaker is an expert in a given field**   For example, the passage quoted from the *Yale Environment 360* article (p. 371) clearly provides the essence of one expert's views on a question that is central to student writer Omar's purpose. Quoting the exact words of an expert can carry weight, add credibility, and help support your argument.

**Quote from a source when a paraphrase or summary would alter the author's meaning**   For example, this might be the case when your source is a legal document, as in the following:

### STUDENT'S QUOTATION FROM A LEGAL DOCUMENT

In the Supreme Court's historical ruling on school segregation, Chief Justice Earl Warren offered the court's final opinion in *Brown v. Board of Education*, ruling for the plaintiffs:

> We conclude that in the field of public education the doctrine of "separate but equal" has no place. Separate educational facilities are inherently unequal. Therefore, we hold that the plaintiffs and others similarly situated for whom the actions have been brought are, by reason of the segregation complained of, deprived of the equal protection of the laws guaranteed by the Fourteenth Amendment.

*quotation from a source*

It was this ruling that changed . . .

Note: Because the quoted passage is long, it is "blocked" rather than run in with the text; there are no quotation marks in this case.

**Quote from a source when a paraphrase or summary would not capture the essence of the author's clear and memorable words and tone**   For example, supermodel Linda Evangelista once famously said, "We don't wake up for less than $10,000 a day." If you were to paraphrase this, you would lose the tone and spirit of her comment.

**Quote from a text if your purpose is to analyze that text**   For example, if you were writing an analysis of a work of literature, you would include in your paper specific passages to discuss. Let's say you want to comment on mystery writer Agatha Christie's use of an omniscient narrator and want to give an example from her writing to illustrate your point. You might write something like this:

> STUDENT'S QUOTATION OF A PASSAGE FOR ANALYSIS
> In *Secret Adversary*, Christie uses her narrator to convey a quick analysis of a character's true nature:
>> Although she was accustomed to take the lead, and to pride herself on her quick-wittedness, in reality she had relied upon Tommy more than she realized at the time. There was something so eminently sober and clear-headed about him, his common sense and soundness of vision were so unvarying, that without him Tuppence felt much like a rudderless ship (88).     *quotation from a source*
>
> The narrator's commentary on Tommy, conveyed through Tuppence's point of view, serves to . . .

## How Do I Quote from a Source?

To quote a source, do the following:

» Integrate the quote into your prose by providing a context for the quotation. In other words, don't simply plop the quote into the prose, expecting your reader to understand how it fits within the material that precedes and follows it.

» Signal the reader that a quote is coming. This is usually best done by using the author's name (Kleinfeld discusses ". . .").

» If the quote is shorter than four lines, integrate it into your sentences. If the quote is longer than four lines, use a blocked quote format.

## Guided Process: How to Quote from a Source

### Paul Pierre (Student)

*Nonviolent Protest Project: Quoting Gandhi*

▲ STUDENT AUTHOR
**Paul Pierre.**

Let's look at the process of student Paul Pierre. He's researching nonviolent protest and has come across some speeches by Mohandas K. Gandhi (commonly known as Mahatma Gandhi), the philosophical leader of the early twentieth-century independence movement in India. Gandhi became famous for using only nonviolent protest strategies.

Paul decides to read some of Gandhi's writings and speeches, and to summarize and paraphrase them within his own writing. However, when he reads "The Doctrine of the Sword," in which Gandhi defines nonviolence, Paul decides that Gandhi's original words are powerful and that he should quote them directly.

Paul located the text of this 1920 article by Gandhi at the Web site of a research foundation dedicated to the author. Gandhi's article was originally published in his weekly journal, *Young India. (Web site artwork, Courtesy of Gandhi Book Centre, mkgandhi.org.)*

Comprehensive Site By Gandhian Institute Bombay Sarvodaya Mandal & Gandhi Research Foundation

**Mahatma Gandhi's**
*writings, philosophy, audio, video & photographs*

### The Doctrine Of The Sword

### By M. K. Gandhi

In this age of the rule of brute force, it is almost impossible for anyone to believe that anyone else could possibly reject the law of final supremacy of brute force. . . .

I do believe that where there is only a choice between cowardice and violence I would advise violence. Thus when my eldest son asked me what he should have done, had he been present when I was almost fatally assaulted in 1908, whether he should have run away and seen me killed or whether he should have used his physical force which he could and wanted to use, and defended me, I told him that it was his duty to defend me even by using violence. . . .

I am not a visionary. I claim to be a practical idealist. The religion of nonviolence is not meant merely for the Rishis and saints. It is meant for the common people as well. Nonviolence is the law of our species as

**Paul's notes on Gandhi's article**

**1.** *I read the whole article* and chose the passage I thought was most significant to my argument about nonviolence.

**2.** *I thought about how this source works with my other sources.* In my research, I've looked into how well-known political figures define *nonviolence.* Gandhi, probably the best known of these figures, offers a perspective that I think is crucial to present.

**3.** *I tried paraphrasing Gandhi's words.* Here's what I came up with:

**MY PARAPHRASE**
Gandhi named in signal phrase, so no parenthetical citation needed
For Gandhi, nonviolence was a type of active defiance.

I don't think it works. My paraphrase is a lot less powerful than Gandhi's original words.

Comprehensive Site By Gandhian Institute Bombay Sarvodaya Mandal & Gandhi Research Foundation

**Mahatma Gandhi's**
*writings, philosophy, audio, video & photographs*

violence is the law of the brute. The spirit lies dormant in the brute and he knows no law but that of physical might. The dignity of man requires obedience to a higher law to the strength of the spirit.

I have therefore ventured to place before India the ancient law of self sacrifice. For Satyagrah and its offshoots, non-cooperation and civil resistance are nothing but new names for the law of suffering. The Rishis, who discovered the law of nonviolence in the midst of nonviolence, were greater geniuses than Newton. They were themselves greater warriors than Wellington. Having themselves known the use of arms, they realized their uselessness, and taught a weary world that its salvation lay not through violence, but through nonviolence.

Nonviolence in its dynamic condition means conscious suffering. It does not mean meek submission to the will of the evil-doer, but it means the putting of one's whole soul against the will of the tyrant. Working under this law of being, it is possible for a single individual to defy the whole might of an unjust empire to save his honor, his religion, his soul and lay the foundation for the empire's fall or its regeneration.

And so I am not pleading for India to practice nonviolence because it is weak. I want her to practice nonviolence being conscious of her strength and power. . . .

---

**Paul's notes on Gandhi's article**

**4.** *I decided to quote Gandhi directly. Here's what I wrote and included in my final audio essay:*

**MY QUOTATION**
Gandhi named in signal phrase, so no parenthetical citation needed

Gandhi was adamant that nonviolence is different from being passive, explaining, "Nonviolence in its dynamic condition means conscious suffering. It does not mean meek submission to the will of the evil-doer, but it means the putting of one's whole soul against the will of the tyrant."

**5.** *I cited the Gandhi article as a source in my Works Cited list.* Even though I created an audio essay about nonviolent protest, my instructor asked me to formally cite all my sources. I submitted (with my audio essay) an Artist's Statement in which I documented all my research according to MLA style. Here's the entry that corresponds with my in-text citation of the Gandhi article.

**MY WORKS CITED ENTRY (MLA STYLE)**
author name:         title of short work
last, first          from a Web site

Gandhi, M. K. "The Doctrine of the Sword."
                    title of site
1920. *Mahatma Gandhi Complete*
                    publisher
*Information Web Site*, Bombay
Sarvodaya Mandal and Gandhi
                    URL
Research, www.mkgandhi.org/
nonviolence/D_sword.htm.
                    date of access
Accessed 15 Sept. 2013.

---

Paul is satisfied that quoting is best in this case. Why? Because Gandhi's words are distinctive and indicate a tone and sensibility that would be lost in a summary or paraphrase.

## Paraphrasing

### What Does It Mean to Paraphrase a Source?

When you paraphrase a source, you basically restate what you've read from a text or a part of a text. Like when you summarize a source, you capture the author's main idea—usually the main idea behind an entire book or movie, for example—in your own words (for more on summary, see p. 384). However, when you *paraphrase* a source, you capture *all* of the author's ideas in your own words—including details and supporting evidence. Typically you won't paraphrase an entire source; instead you'll probably paraphrase a passage or a sentence or two.

Paraphrasing is handy when you want to share specifics but don't want to use the author's exact original wording. While quoting can be a good option (pp. 370–73), there are times when you want the voice to be all your own. There are still other times when an author's tone is not a good fit for your purpose and audience; in these cases, use paraphrase to present that author's perspective smoothly.

A paraphrase should:

» Provide not only the big-picture message of a source, but also the details that the author uses to support his or her argument.

» Be in your own words and voice, with the same level of formality and vocabulary as the rest of your piece.

» Change both the words and the order of the ideas presented in the original.

» Usually end up being close to the same length as the original.

» Give credit to the author of the source being paraphrased. If you are using MLA or APA conventions, be sure to credit your source with an in-text citation and correlating entry for the Works Cited or References list.

Let's look at an example. Shelby Prince, a student writing about therapeutic uses of music (p. 377), found a blog called *The Contrapuntist*, where she read a post by Miguel Cano, titled "How Music Saved My Life, and Why Music Education Should Be Taken More Seriously." She wanted to integrate Cano's experience into her writing without shifting over to his voice. She decided to paraphrase.

ORIGINAL PASSAGE FROM SOURCE
That sad instrument became my life; it became my outlet to express my frustration with teenage life. I took it everywhere, practiced everywhere and played for everyone. Like every other 15-year-old, my dream was to become a rock star. I wanted to be like my guitar heroes Alex Skolnick (from Testament), and Marty Friedman (formerly from Megadeth). Eventually, I became introduced to classical guitar music.

---

☞ **Attention, writers! How to paraphrase fairly.**

When you paraphrase a passage from a source, make sure that the details you paraphrase are consistent with the "big picture" of your source; for example, if a source's author is positive overall about an experimental drug treatment, it would be unfair to paraphrase only the few negative details provided. However, it would be okay to mention the negative details, provided that you offer them in the context of the author's main (pro-treatment) argument.

---

HOME   ABOUT ME   ADVERTISING & DISCLOSURE

## The Contrapuntist

Culture Through | A Musical Lens

### How Music Saved My Life, and Why Music Education Should Be Taken More Seriously

*by CONTRAPUNTIST*
*In MUSIC EDUCATION*

A few days ago I came across a story reported by Reuters that Venezuelan President Hugo Chavez public music programs have taken 300,000 kids out of slums in a country with some of the "highest murder rates in the world." I reminisced about how music saved my life. I grew up in a middle class home with a family that made decent income, but the city was plagued with gang activity and poverty when I lived there.

At the end of my freshman year of high school, my grandfather brought me my first nylon/classical guitar from Paracho, Mexico. It was a mediocre instrument, good for a beginner. In fact, if I tried to play it now, it's so warped that after hitting a few notes it would sound like Arnold Schoenberg meets Henry Cowell, while attempting to play J. S. Bach. Sad! That sad instrument became my life; it became my outlet to express my frustration with teenage life. I took it everywhere, practiced everywhere and played for everyone. Like every other 15-year-old, my dream was to become a rock star. I wanted to be like my guitar heroes Alex Skolnick (from Testament), and Marty Friedman (formerly from Megadeth). Eventually, I became introduced to classical guitar music.

---

**SHELBY'S PARAPHRASE**

Before classical guitar music entered his life, the blogger fantasized about becoming a rock star like Alex Skolnick or Marty Friedman, and became almost physically attached to the guitar. That guitar enabled him to cope with his teenage angst (Cano).

parenthetical citation names source

▲ BLOG POST
**Miguel Cano, "How Music Saved My Life."** This excerpt can be found at the *Contrapuntist* blog. *Miguel Cano.*

## When Should I Paraphrase a Source?

Consider paraphrasing in the following situations:

**When you don't want to quote an author directly**   You may decide not to quote because you don't want too many competing voices in your piece. In this case, you could paraphrase the sentences from your source, keeping your voice dominant. (See "When Should I Quote from a Source?" on p. 372.)

**When *your* audience is very different from your source author's audience** For example, the source you are using may have been written for a specialized or technical audience, and the language might not be suitable for your readers. That is the case in the first example on page 378. A student is writing for an audience of nonexperts about various approaches to treating people convicted of crimes. However, one of her sources is very technical; it was written for criminologists and who are familiar with legal terminology. This is an excellent opportunity to paraphrase. The following passage is from an article titled "A Comparative Recidivism Analysis of Releasees from Private and Public Prisons," by Lonn Lanza-Kaduce, Karen F. Parker, and Charles W. Thomas, from the journal *Crime & Delinquency.*

ORIGINAL PASSAGE

Recidivism was operationalized in alternative ways. FDOC records on arrest histories, sentencing, and the movement of inmates in and out of prison were the sources of the data, which were used to develop five different indicators of recidivism.

STUDENT'S PARAPHRASE

authors named in signal phrase; no parenthetical citation needed

Lanza-Kaduce, Parker, and Thomas examined the Florida Department of Correction's records, looking for signs that a prison releasee had returned to prison, such as a record of the releasee's being arrested again or sentenced to another prison term.

**You want your writing to flow with your own ideas and words; you want your tone to dominate**   Paraphrasing allows you to convey all of your source's information, but in your own consistent words and style. For example, imagine you are writing a blog entry in a very informal, snappy tone, and you want to paraphrase the very formal speech Queen Elizabeth II gave in Dublin in 2011.

ORIGINAL PASSAGE

Indeed, so much of this visit reminds us of the complexity of our history, its many layers and traditions, but also the importance of forbearance and conciliation. Of being able to bow to the past, but not be bound by it.

STUDENT'S PARAPHRASE (with humorous intent)

author named in signal phrase; no parenthetical citation needed

The Queen remarked that you gotta remember the past, baby, but you can't let it hold you back. Our relationship's had problems, she told the Irish, but that don't mean it's gotta end.

Note: This paraphrase style can work for nonacademic genres; however, for formal research papers, we do not recommend this technique.

For an entertaining look at the opposite situation—a writer paraphrasing extremely informal writing to make it more formal—check out the Twitter feed for Queen's English 50c, in which the writer (Andrew O'Neill, a British comedian) translates the rapper 50 Cent's tweets into "proper English."

## How Do I Paraphrase a Source?

When you want to paraphrase a source, do the following:

**Read (or view or listen to) the passage**

**Put the source away and write down the passage from memory**   This ensures that you are articulating the ideas in your own words.

**Restate the sentence or passage in your own words—while maintaining the sense of the author's original words**   The following paraphrase retains the meaning of the original passage (from an article by Edison Elementary, "HG/HGT Education") while transforming it into a totally different voice and structure.

ORIGINAL PASSAGE

Giftedness is a collection of certain characteristics that have been displayed by remarkable adults and children past and present. Among the gifted there is great diversity; they are not a homogeneous group.

STUDENT'S PARAPHRASE   author named in signal phrase; no parenthetical citation needed

According to educators at Edison Elementary, gifted adults or children are unique individuals who exhibit traits that make them stand out from their peers.

Think of paraphrasing as rephrasing. When you paraphrase, you do more than swap out key words with similar words. Below is an example of an unsuccessful paraphrase created through an inadvisable technique called "patch writing." When people patch write, they simply switch out key words and replace them with synonyms. The result is clunky at best.

The shaded words in the original (again, from the "HG/HGT Education" article by Edison Elementary) are the words the writer replaced with synonyms in the patch-written version.

ORIGINAL PASSAGE

Giftedness is a collection of certain characteristics that have been displayed by remarkable adults and children past and present.

STUDENT'S UNSUCCESSFUL PARAPHRASE (what NOT to do)

According to educators at Edison Elementary, specialness is a group of particular traits that have been shown by extraordinary people of all ages throughout time.

Notice how the patch-written version is not all that different from the original passage—only now it lacks style and voice. The writer chose to switch out words, for example, replacing *collection* with *group*. He also did not change the sentence structure or word order, and kept many of the smaller words (articles and prepositions) as they were in the original. The writer would have done better to use the original quote.

**Compare your sentence(s) to the original, making sure that you have altered the language and style enough so that the words are your own**

**Compare your sentence(s) to the original, making sure that you haven't altered the meaning or intent of the author**   Keep in mind that there are some words that you cannot change without changing the meaning of the author's content. Proper nouns and numbers, for example, should not be changed.

**Always, always, always attribute your paraphrase to its source**   Use the style that is appropriate to the genre you're composing in. For academic genres, see MLA and APA guidelines on pages 395–435.

▲ STUDENT AUTHOR
**Paul Pierre.**

# Guided Process: How to Paraphrase a Source ▼

## Paul Pierre (Student)

### *Nonviolent Protest Project:* Paraphrasing Julia Bacha

Paul, who is writing about nonviolent protest, finds a presentation by documentary filmmaker Julia Bacha. In it, Bacha argues that nonviolent protest is ignored by the media and tells a story about nonviolent protest in a Palestinian town, a story she portrays in her documentary *Budrus*. Following is a step-by-step look at how Paul paraphrased from this source. Images presented on pages 381–83 are stills from Bacha's documentary film. *(Julia Bacha's presentation and images appear courtesy of Just Vision Media.)*

---

## JUST VISION

HOME   ABOUT US   FILMS   VISIONARIES   RESOURCES   GET INVOLVED   EVENTS   NEWS   STORE   DONATE

JULIA BACHA   (Director, Producer, 2009)    العربية   עברית

## Budrus

**TRANSCRIPT:** I'm a filmmaker. For the last 8 years, I have dedicated my life to documenting the work of Israelis and Palestinians who are trying to end the conflict using peaceful means. When I travel with my work across Europe and the United States, one question always comes up: Where is the Palestinian Gandhi? Why aren't Palestinians using nonviolent resistance?

The challenge I face when I hear this question is that often I have just returned from the Middle East where I spent my time filming dozens of Palestinians who are using nonviolence to defend their lands and water resources from Israeli soldiers and settlers. These leaders are trying to forge a massive national nonviolent movement to end the occupation and build peace in the region. Yet, most of you have probably never heard about them. This divide between what's happening on the ground and perceptions abroad is one of the key reasons why we don't have yet a Palestinian peaceful resistance movement that has been successful.

I'm [going to] talk about the power of attention, the power of your attention, and the emergence and de-

---

### Paul's notes on Bacha's presentation

1. *I watched Bacha's entire presentation.* Then I watched it again. One section of what Bacha said really stood out for me—where she talks about a specific nonviolent protest in Budrus. I think I might want to use some of this in my audio essay. I watched that section of her talk a few times.

2. *Next, I read the transcript.* The entire text of Bacha's talk is available online. I focused especially on the passage that includes the Budrus story.

3. *I put the transcript aside, and paraphrased the passage from memory.* Here is what I came up with:

#### MY DRAFT PARAPHRASE (of Bacha)
Violent and nonviolent protesters are similar in that to be effective, they need an audience to respond to them. When the media fails to cover nonviolent protest, they deprive nonviolent protestors of an audience (Bacha).

> parenthetical citation
> names author of source

## JUST VISION

HOME   ABOUT US   FILMS   VISIONARIES   RESOURCES   GET INVOLVED   EVENTS   NEWS   STORE   DONATE

JULIA BACHA   (Director, Producer, 2009)   العربية   עברית

velopment of nonviolent movements in the West Bank, Gaza and elsewhere—but . . . my case study is going to be Palestine. I believe that what's mostly missing for nonviolence to grow is not for Palestinians to start adopting nonviolence, but for us to start paying attention to those who already are. Allow me to illustrate this point by taking you to this village called Budrus.

About seven years ago, they faced extinction, because Israel announced it would build a separation barrier, and part of this barrier would be built on top of the village. They would lose 40 percent of their land and be surrounded, so they would lose free access to the rest of the West Bank. Through inspired local leadership, they launched a peaceful resistance campaign to stop that from happening.

Let me show you some brief clips, so you have a sense for what that actually looked like on the ground.

FROM THE DOCUMENTARY *BUDRUS:*
*Palestinian Woman*: We were told the wall would separate Palestine from Israel. Here in Budrus, we realized the wall would steal our land.

*Israeli Man:* The fence has, in fact, created a solution to terror.

*Man:* Today you're invited to a peaceful march. You are joined by dozens of your Israeli brothers and sisters.

*Continues next page*

*4. I reread the passage in the transcript and evaluated my draft paraphrase. I thought I could have done a better job in paraphrasing/restating what Bacha had to say.*

*5. I revised and finalized my paraphrase. I thought the wording of my draft paraphrase was not different enough from Bacha's original text, especially in voice and structure. Here's how I revised to correct those problems:*

**MY IN-TEXT CITATION (paraphrase of Bacha)**
Bacha named in signal phrase, so no parenthetical citation needed

Julia Bacha points out that all protesters—including nonviolent ones—need an audience in order to matter. It's a problem that violent protests are the ones we read about, the ones that get attention. When the media fails to cover nonviolent protest, she argues, they deprive peaceful protesters of an audience and of the potential to make a difference.

*6. I cited Bacha as a source in my Works Cited list. Although audio essays don't usually include a Works Cited list, my instructor asked me to submit one with my Artist's Statement. This caused me some strife because the MLA style for documenting digital sources is confusing to me. However, after consulting a handbook, I cited my source as follows:*

**MY WORKS CITED ENTRY (MLA style)**
title of short work
author name   from Web site   site title
Bacha, Julia. "Budrus." *Just Vision,*
publication
date            URL
Aug. 2011, www.justvision.org/
optional
descriptive label
budrus. Film clip.

*Israeli Activist:* Nothing scares the army more than non-violent opposition.

*Woman:* We saw the men trying to push the soldiers, but none of them could do that. But I think the girls could do it.

**JUST VISION**

JULIA BACHA   (Director, Producer, 2009)      العربية   עברית

*Fatah Party Member:* We must empty our minds of traditional thinking.

*Hamas Party Member:* We were in complete harmony, and we wanted to spread it to all of Palestine.

*Chanting:* One united nation. Fatah, Hamas and the *Popular* Front!

*News Anchor:* The clashes over the fence continue.

They were allowed to use any force necessary

*Reporter:* Israeli border police were sent to disperse the crowd. They were allowed to use any force necessary.

(Gunshots)

*Man:* These are live bullets. It's like Fallujah. Shooting everywhere.

*Israeli Activist:* I was sure we were all going to die. But there were others around me who weren't even cowering.

*Israeli Soldier:* A nonviolent protest is not going to stop the [unclear].

*Protester:* This is a peaceful march. There is no need to use violence.

*Chanting:* We can do it! We can do it! We can do it!

In the paraphrase above (and in his summary on p. 387), Paul strips out references to Palestinians and Israelis. He believes Bacha's idea is relevant to conflicts outside of the Middle East, so he captures Bacha's comparison of violent and nonviolent protest but omits the details of the parties involved.

## Summarizing

### What Does It Mean to Summarize a Source?

When you summarize a source, you pare the whole thing down to its essence. You eliminate all specific details and give your reader the main point of what the source's author is saying. For example, you might summarize a source in the text of a paper you are writing when you want to investigate or compare the main ideas behind several different sources.

When you summarize, you should:

» Capture the ideas of the source's author.

» Be considerably shorter than the original work. For example, if you are summarizing a two-page article, your summary might be only a paragraph or less. (In the example on p. 370, a student writer summarizes twenty-one paragraphs in just one sentence.)

» Write in your own words—not the words of the source's author.

» Give credit to the author of the source summarized. Depending on the genre you compose in, the conventions for crediting sources differ. (In the example below, the student uses a signal phrase to name her source author.)

Let's return to Shelby, the student who is writing about therapeutic uses of music. She finds an article in the blog section of *The Huffington Post* by opera singer Susanne Mentzer, titled "The Catharsis of Song."

Shelby decides she wants to include the opera singer's perspective in her paper, but she wants to do so broadly and briefly, in her Introduction, to draw in her readers. Following are the first few paragraphs from Mentzer's post—as well as Shelby's summary of the post (which she read in its entirety at the *Huffington Post* blog).

> **SHELBY'S SUMMARY OF AN ENTIRE ARTICLE**
> Opera singer Susanne Mentzer has used singing to alleviate both her own stress and tension and the stress and tension of others.

### When Should I Summarize a Source?

As a researcher and writer, you might choose to summarize a source when you want to capture the main ideas of a source without going into details. As in the example of Shelby's summary above, the details of Mentzer's experiences, such as crying during rehearsal, are irrelevant to Shelby's point about the therapeutic nature of music; what matters to Shelby is that Mentzer, a professional singer, has experienced the therapeutic aspects of music in several different contexts.

 **Attention, researchers! Summarizing versus paraphrasing.**

When you summarize a passage from a source, you pick up on *the main points* the author is making and describe them in your own words. When you paraphrase, on the other hand, you do provide a type of summary—but one in which you restate/rephrase the author's words (not just the main points). Summarizing and paraphrasing are both subjective actions, and require you to retain the spirit of the author's meaning and ideas, even if you use them to contrast with your own.

## Susanne Mentzer
*Opera singer*

### The Catharsis of Song

Posted: 09/08/11 07:42 PM ET

The human singing voice has the power to release deep emotions. Many know of sounds that give us goosebumps. From the point of view of one who makes sounds, I refer to it as my primal scream therapy. The wonderfulness of singing can be the primal, super-human sound that pours out of one's body. It can also be humbling.

It is thought that hearing is the last sense to leave us when we die. Over the past year, I sang both my parents into the next world. In the ICU, for my mother, an amateur singer who was particularly proud of me, I think I sang my entire repertoire of hymns and arias, toned down to a low dynamic. At one point she awakened with a smile and said, in the slow, whispered voice of one who could barely breathe, "You were singing!" I am not sure if Dad heard me in his last hours, but I would like to think so. It was a privilege that I would not trade for the world.

Even in my career I have had my own cathartic release of emotion. I once sang a matinee opera performance in Bonn, Germany, after having just put my 10-month old son and his father into a taxi to the airport to fly to the States. It was excruciatingly painful to let my child go but I was contractually obligated to stay. I went to the theater, sang my guts out, and became a blubbering idiot during curtain calls. (Fortunately, it was a dramatic role, the Composer in Strauss's Ariadne auf Naxos.) My colleagues mentioned that I was really "on" that show and that I gave so much emotion. Only then did I share what I was really crying about.

Here's another example. Let's say your project is on skateboarding, and you want to draw on an NPR story by Sarah Reynolds titled "Fingerboarding: Skateboarding without 'Fear Factor.'" The audio article is four minutes long. Rather than detailing the whole recording, you decide you only care about fingerboarding and how popular it's become. This is a perfect situation for summarizing. Of course, you'd credit Sarah Reynolds in your text and Works Cited or References list.

## How Do I Summarize a Source?

To summarize a source, do the following:

» Read (or view or listen to) the source.

» Put the source away and write down the main ideas from memory. This ensures that you are articulating the ideas in your own words.

» Look over the main ideas you wrote down and organize them. For example, begin with a general statement and then move on to the supporting ideas.

» Also, make sure you're simply capturing the main ideas and arguments of the source's author, and not adding any of your own opinions.

» Go back and reread or re-listen to or review the original source. Compare it to what you've written to make sure you haven't distorted any of the points. Make sure you also haven't left out any of the central points.

Attribute your summary to its source. Do this not only in the text of your paper but in your Works Cited or References list as well.

▲ ORIGINAL SOURCE
**Susanne Mentzer, "The Catharsis of Song."** This article was published at *The Blog,* which is hosted by *The Huffington Post.* Shown here are just the first few paragraphs. © 9/8/11 *Huffington Post.* All rights reserved. Used by permission and protected by the Copyright Laws of the United States. The printing, copying, redistribution, or retransmission of this Content without express written permission is prohibited.

▲ **STUDENT AUTHOR**
**Paul Pierre.**

## Guided Process: How to Summarize a Source

### Paul Pierre (Student)

*Nonviolent Protest Project: Summarizing Julia Bacha*

Paul, who earlier in this chapter paraphrased a passage from a talk by Julia Bacha, decides that he wants to summarize a different passage. Following are the steps he took. *(Julia Bacha's presentation and images appear courtesy of Just Vision Media.)*

---

### JUST VISION

HOME   ABOUT US   FILMS   VISIONARIES   RESOURCES   GET INVOLVED   EVENTS   NEWS   STORE   DONATE

العربية   עברית

JULIA BACHA   (Director, Producer, 2009)

## Budrus

**TRANSCRIPT:** When I first heard about the story of Budrus, I was surprised that the international media had failed to cover the extraordinary set of events that happened seven years ago, in 2003. What was even more surprising was the fact that Budrus was successful. The residents, after 10 months of peaceful resistance, convinced the Israeli government to move the route of the barrier off their lands and to the green line, which is the internationally recognized boundary between Israel and the Palestinian Territories. The resistance in Budrus has since spread to villages across the West Bank and to Palestinian neighborhoods in Jerusalem. Yet the media remains mostly silent on these stories. This silence carries profound consequences for the likelihood that nonviolence can grow, or even survive, in Palestine.

Violent resistance and nonviolent resistance share one very important thing in common; they are both a form of theater seeking an audience to their cause. If violent

---

### Paul's notes on Bacha's presentation

**1.** *I revisited Bacha's talk,* and was struck by a passage in which she gives a viewpoint on Palestine and nonviolent resistance. I decided to include that material, in some way, in my audio essay.

**2.** *I reread the transcript,* focusing on the section on Palestine and nonviolent resistance. I decided that it might be best to summarize Bacha's argument.

**3.** *I drafted a summary of the passage.* To do this, I put the transcript away, and tried to provide an overview of what Bacha said in this part of her talk. Here is what I wrote:

#### MY DRAFT SUMMARY (of Bacha's passage)
Bacha named in signal phrase, so no parenthetical citation needed

Bacha says that residents of the Palestinian town of Budrus were able to successfully protest against the Israeli building of a fence using nonviolent strategies; however, the news reports of the conflict all focused on a few incidents that involved violence.

**4.** *Next, I re-viewed Bacha's talk.* I wanted to make sure I had accurately captured her point. Satisfied that I had, I put the summary away for the night.

**5.** *I revised my summary of Bacha's point.* The next day, when I reread my

---

## JUST VISION

HOME   ABOUT US   FILMS   VISIONARIES   RESOURCES   GET INVOLVED   EVENTS   NEWS   STORE   DONATE

JULIA BACHA   (Director, Producer, 200   العربية   עברית

actors are the only ones constantly getting front-page covers and attracting international attention to the Palestinian issue, it becomes very hard for nonviolent leaders to make the case to their communities that civil disobedience is a viable option in addressing their plight.

### Paul's notes on Bacha's presentation

summary, I decided to cut back on some details of what Bacha had to say. Specifically, I opted not to mention that the Palestinians protested against Israel. For my audio essay, I wanted to stay focused on my main argument—that the media doesn't give enough attention to nonviolent protest—and didn't want to sidetrack my audience with the politics surrounding the protest itself. With this in mind, I revised as follows:

### MY REVISED SUMMARY (of Bacha's passage)

Bacha describes and shows clips of protests in the Middle East that were completely nonviolent. This is in stark contrast to the media reports of the conflict, which failed to mention the nonviolent protests and focused on a handful of violent skirmishes.

**6.** *Next, I included my summary of Bacha's point in my audio essay. I drew on Bacha's words to support my argument that nonviolent protest is more powerful than violent protest.*

**7.** *I cited Bacha's talk as a source in my Works Cited list.*

### MY WORKS CITED ENTRY (MLA style)

title of short work

author name   from Web site   ┌─site title

Bacha, Julia. "Budrus." *Just Vision*,

publication
date                              URL

Aug. 2011, www.justvision.org/

optional
descriptive label

budrus. Film transcript.

## Avoiding Plagiarism

Plagiarism is misrepresenting the ideas or words of others as your own. It includes submitting papers you didn't write, failing to adequately cite sources, and copying small bits and pieces from sources into your own work without properly documenting them. Plagiarism is unethical and committing an act of plagiarism can have serious consequences on your grade, your academic career, and your karma. Your school probably has a statement on academic integrity, defining penalties for acts of academic dishonesty. Be sure to familiarize yourself with the academic integrity policy at your school.

## Comparing Passages from a Source

Some plagiarism is unintentional. Writers may read several sources that express similar ideas and only cite one of these sources. Or writers may forget which source they got an idea from and not cite any source at all. Another all-too-common type of unintentional plagiarism occurs when a writer tries to paraphrase a source but doesn't significantly change the original source's language. Here are a couple of examples:

**Original passage**  From a podcast by Adam Hinterthuer, found online at *Scientific American*:

> Want to live a happier life? Try surrounding yourself with happy friends or at least find friends with happy friends. A study published online December 4th in the *British Medical Journal* says happiness can quickly go viral within your social network.

**Passage plagiarized**  The writer misrepresents the source; the source's author, Hinterthuer, is cited, but the writer has gotten the content wrong. Hinterthuer mentions only one study—not "a lot":

> There is a lot of research indicating that happiness is contagious. Simply surrounding yourself with happy friends can make you a happier person (Hinterthuer).

**Passage plagiarized**  In this case, the writer needs to provide an in-text citation. He/she has not shown that this information was obtained from the source, Hinterthuer:

> Recent research indicates that happiness is contagious. Simply surrounding yourself with happy friends can make you a happier person.

**Passage correctly presented with an in-text citation**

SUMMARY WITH MLA IN-TEXT CITATION
Recent research indicates that happiness is contagious. Simply surrounding yourself with happy friends can make you a happier person (Hinterthuer).

WORKS CITED ENTRY
Hinterthuer, Adam. "Happiness Is Contagious." *Scientific American*, 5 Dec. 2008, www.scientificamerican.com/podcast/episode.cfm?id=happiness-is -contagious-08-12-05. MP3 file.

SUMMARY WITH APA IN-TEXT CITATION
Recent research indicated that happiness is contagious. Simply surrounding yourself with happy friends can make you a happier person (Hinterthuer, 2008).

REFERENCES LIST ENTRY

Hinterthuer, Adam. "Happiness is contagious." *Scientific American*. MP3 audio file. http://www.scientificamerican.com/podcast/episode.cfm?id=happiness-is -contagious-08-12-05.

It's important to realize that whether plagiarism is intentional or unintentional, it is a violation of academic ethics and most schools' codes of conduct. If in doubt about whether to cite a source, cite it. This will prevent you from unintentionally plagiarizing. (For more on avoiding plagiarism, see below.)

---

## CHECKLIST Getting Help and Avoiding Plagiarism

☐ **Visit your writing center.** If you don't know how to properly summarize or paraphrase a source, consult your instructor or a writing-center tutor for help. It's never a good idea to plagiarize and then plan to apologize if caught. If you're not sure if you're using source material in a way that constitutes plagiarism, get help: Take your draft to your instructor or a tutor and explain what you're having trouble with. As long as you haven't yet turned in the paper, you haven't done anything wrong.

☐ **Use detection software.** If your school subscribes to a plagiarism-detection program like turnitin.com, you can submit a draft of your writing to the program and it will generate a report that indicates what percentage of the draft is from other sources. The report will alert you to places where you've used sources without properly citing them.

☐ **Manage your time.** Allow yourself enough time to complete your writing assignment. Sometimes students accidentally plagiarize because they don't give themselves time to properly double-check all their citations.

☐ **When in doubt, cite that source.** Remember, too, that using an image, audio clip, or video is just like quoting words from someone. These texts need to be cited just as any other source would be.

---

## How to Avoid Plagiarism during Your Research & Composing Process

There are certain crucial moments when researchers and writers can make mistakes that can lead to plagiarism. Please be especially careful at these points:

**When taking notes as you conduct research** Get in the habit of recording the source's bibliographic information and using quotation marks anytime you use the exact words of a source, even if you use just a few words from the source. For example, you might write in your notes:

> Source: *Our Stressful Lives* site, http://www.ourstressfullives.com/pets-and-stress-relief.html
> *About the source*: This site is authored by a "Certified Stress Management Coach," Jill Rheaume, who has also published a stress management workbook. She offers a variety of tips for stress management. I found the following article from the "Pets and Stress Relief: Other Benefits" section of the site, mainly from paragraph 9.

**Notes:** Rheaume writes (in paragraph 3) that pets "make great listeners" and help reduce stress in many other ways. In paragraph 9 she writes: "Pets also increase the 'love chemical' oxytocin in our brains. In addition, they can also increase our serotonin, known as the 'happiness chemical.' Both of these things can help to reduce or even prevent stress and prove that our pets can increase our feelings of happiness and help to improve our moods."

▼ WEB SITE
**Jill Rheaume,**
*Our Stressful Lives.*
By permission of Jill
Rheaume, Owner/Editor
of OurStressfulLives.com.

Alternatively, you might want to create a screen capture of each source (or otherwise save the original content), so you can refer back to the original as you write.

Our Stressful Lives
Helping you live a less stressful life.℠

HOME   WHAT'S NEW   SUBMISSIONS   PRODUCTS

## About Me

Welcome to OurStressfulLives.com!

My name is Jill Rheaume and I live in Kansas, USA. Thank you for visiting my website and taking the time to get to know a bit about me and why I created this site.

For me, stress was always something that I struggled with. I enjoyed writing and journaling and that helped relieve some of my stress... but that by itself just wasn't good enough.

Then, in late 2007, I met a man who became my "life guru". He taught me that stress is not insurmountable and he gave me practical tools to manage my stress so that I could begin living a happier and healthier life.

I consider myself and my life a constant work in progress and one of the things I've learned along the way is that proper stress management is not only necessary, it is also my passion.

I have spent a lot of time researching and trying different techniques to better manage the day-to-day stress in my life and now that I've mastered my own stress, as a Stress Management Coach, my goal is to help you do the same.

Jill R.

## Pets and Stress Relief

Pets and Stress Relief: How Your Pet Can Help You Relieve Your Stress

It's a proven fact that the pets that we love so much do actually help to relieve our stress... something that many pet owners probably already suspected.

I am personally a huge animal lover and so this is a particular topic that I am very excited to share with you.

### Companionship

Our pets are great companions. They can help us avoid feelings of loneliness and are often our confidants... they make great listeners. And unless you've trained your pet to talk (as you can with some birds) they don't give back talk or argue.

## Gaining the Health Benefits of Pets

Health Benefits of Pets

As an animal lover and pet owner, it seems quite obvious to me that my pets make me "feel better". They certainly cheer me up when I'm down, give me comfort when I'm sad or scared, and make me laugh when I least expect it. So I wondered... what are the health benefits of having a pet?

### Stress Relief

Any pet owner can probably tell you a funny story about something their "little baby" did. Animals have a way of being quite humorous and laughter is a great way to relieve stress! But in addition to laughter, they can create feelings of calm and love through the natural increase of a chemical called Oxytocin "the love hormone".

They can help to increase the amount of physical activity we receive and decrease our blood pressure. All of which can help relieve stress.

**When quoting as you draft**   Always put quotation marks around the words you're using from the source. (In this case, there are quotation marks within quotation marks.)

MLA QUOTATION (no in-text cite needed because author is named)
Rheaume writes: "Pets also increase the 'love chemical' oxytocin in our brains."

WORKS CITED ENTRY

Rheaume, Jill. "Pets and Stress Relief: Other Benefits." *Our Stressful Lives,*
www.ourstressfullives.com/pets-and-stress-relief.html. Accessed 20 Aug. 2013.

APA IN-TEXT CITATION

Rheaume wrote: "Pets also increase the 'love chemical' oxytocin in our brains."

REFERENCES LIST ENTRY

Rheaume, Jill. "Pets and stress relief: Other benefits." OurStressfulLives.com. Retrieved from http://www.ourstressfullives.com/pets-and-stress-relief.html.

**When paraphrasing as you draft**   Always credit the source you're paraphrasing. If you aren't sure if you've adequately rephrased the source's idea in your
own words, ask a friend, classmate, or writing-center tutor to compare the original
passage with your paraphrase. One trick to use when paraphrasing is to read the
passage you want to paraphrase and then put the source out of sight and rewrite
the idea in your own words. When you do this, you minimize the chance of accidentally using the words of the original. A paraphrase of the above content from Jill
Rheaume's site follows. Note that even though we're not using Rheaume's exact
words, we still provide the in-text citation.

PARAPHRASE WITH MLA IN-TEXT CITATION

Pets can make us healthier by raising the levels of oxytocin and serotonin in our brains
(Rheaume).

WORKS CITED ENTRY

Rheaume, Jill. "Pets and Stress Relief: Other Benefits." *Our Stressful Lives,*
www.ourstressfullives.com/pets-and-stress-relief.html. Accessed 20 Aug. 2013.

PARAPHRASE WITH APA IN-TEXT CITATION

Pets can make us healthier by raising the levels of oxytocin and serotonin in our brains
(Rheaume).

REFERENCES LIST ENTRY

Rheaume, Jill. "Pets and stress relief: Other benefits." OurStressfulLives.com. Retrieved from http://www.ourstressfullives.com/pets-and-stress-relief.html.

**When summarizing as you draft**   You can use the same strategies for summarizing that you use for paraphrasing.

SUMMARY IN MLA STYLE (no in-text citation needed because author is named)

Stress management coach Jill Rheaume writes that interactions with our pets can
make us happier and more loving by altering levels of certain chemicals in the brain.

WORKS CITED ENTRY

Rheaume, Jill. "Pets and Stress Relief: Other Benefits." *Our Stressful Lives,*
www.ourstressfullives.com/pets-and-stress-relief.html. Accessed 20 Aug. 2013.

SUMMARY WITH APA IN-TEXT CITATION

Stress management coach Jill Rheaume wrote that interactions with our pets can make us happier and more loving by altering levels of certain chemicals in the brain (2008-2012, para. 9).

REFERENCES LIST ENTRY

Rheaume, Jill. "Pets and stress relief: Other benefits." OurStressfulLives.com. Retrieved from http://www.ourstressfullives.com/pets-and-stress-relief.html.

**When drafting—without referring to notes**   Don't trust your memory! Writers sometimes don't cite sources in their drafts, thinking they'll go back later and add citations. This is a dangerous practice because if you run out of time and end up not adding those citations, you've plagiarized. *Always cite your sources*, even in a rough draft.

**When integrating sources**   When in doubt as to whether or not you should cite a source, cite it. It's always better to give too much credit with source citations than to give insufficient credit. You may wonder, for example, if a piece of information counts as "general knowledge," and therefore doesn't need to be cited. If you're not sure if it counts as "general knowledge," go ahead and cite a source.

## How to Avoid Plagiarism When Using Online Sources

As tempting as it is to copy and paste chunks of online sources into your notes or drafts, minimize this practice because it greatly increases your chances of accidentally plagiarizing. Get in the habit of putting quotation marks around every direct quote. If you paraphrase or summarize, copy the original text into a document and indicate clearly—with color coding, highlighting, labeling, or some other device—that it is the original content from your source, and then work on your composition in a separate document. Another strategy is to create screen captures of each online source, always accompanied by the URL that will lead you back to that content.

## How to Avoid Plagiarism When Composing a Multigenre/Multimodal Project

All the above guidelines apply to multigenre/multimodal projects: Cite your sources in drafts, give credit generously, and be meticulous about using quotation marks around quoted material in your notes. Even if you are composing in a genre or mode that doesn't use the MLA or APA format for citations, you still need to credit your sources in ways that are appropriate to the genre or mode of your composition. Additionally, your instructor may want you to submit a Works Cited list or an Author's or Artist's Statement that includes MLA or APA citations. (See Chapter 1, p. 35, for example.)

# DOCUMENTING SOURCES:
# A GUIDE TO MLA & APA STYLES

Documenting (or citing) a source means giving credit to the authors of any texts—including images, video, sound, or any other composition—that inform your writing, whether you're writing a research paper or creating other types of research-based compositions.

When you document sources, you show your audience where you got your information. You also develop your ethos as an author by showing that you've used reliable source material. Failing to give credit to your sources is a form of dishonesty and is considered plagiarism (pp. 387–92); it leads readers to conclude that all of the ideas and facts that you state come from your own independent thinking or research.

Whether you quote, paraphrase, or summarize from a source, you need to cite it. (For more on quoting, see pp. 370–75; for paraphrasing, see pp. 376–83; for summarizing, see pp. 384–87.)

As composers, when we cite sources, we do so using specific documentation styles. The documentation style you will use depends on the audience you're writing for: Are you writing for an academic audience, your peers, or a general/popular audience? Another factor is the subject matter you're writing about—and the discipline associated with that subject. For example, are your target readers associated with the humanities, social sciences, or sciences? The style you choose also depends on the genre you're composing in (e.g., whether you're writing a straight-up research paper or something else). Following are some guidelines for choosing a documentation style.

---

☞ **Attention, researchers! Why don't musicians document their sources when they sample music?**

Many hip-hop musicians use sampling (taking a part of a song) when they create their songs. For example, Nas's song "Can't Forget About You" includes a sample from Nat King Cole's classic "Unforgettable." Not only does the sample figure in the song, but clearly Nas's title was inspired by Nat King Cole. He doesn't provide formal documentation because it is a convention within the music industry that some sampling is deemed appropriate. This, however, is subject to legal interpretation if the original composer wants to challenge the originality of the composition. To avoid potential legal issues, most musicians will obtain permission prior to including samples in their own compositions—and include some kind of credit in the liner notes. If there *are* liner notes.

Composers of other genres often draw upon other sources; however, because of the conventions of the genres they're working in, they might not use formal academic documentation. Such genres include obituaries, memoirs, sets of instructions, and poems.

---

# How to Choose a Documentation Style

**Are you writing a research paper for a specific academic discipline?**

» For papers for an English course or other humanities course or peer-reviewed journal, you will almost always use the documentation style of the Modern Language Association (MLA; mla.org). However, in some English courses that focus on writing in or across disciplines, you might use the documentation style that is associated with your major area of study.

» For papers for a social science course or peer-reviewed journal, you will probably use the format of the American Psychological Association (APA; apastyle.org).

» For papers for a history course or peer-reviewed journal, you will likely use *Chicago* style, based on *The Chicago Manual of Style* (chicagomanualofstyle.org).

» For papers for a science course or peer-reviewed journal, you will probably use the style specified by the Council of Science Editors in *Scientific Style and Format: The CSE Manual for Authors, Editors, and Publishers* (councilscienceeditors.org).

**Are you composing a photo essay, ad, or documentary, or in some other alternative genre? And are your subject and audience based in the humanities, social sciences, or sciences?**   While MLA tends to be the default documentation style of the English composition course, and is likely the format your instructor may require, you might have the option of deciding for yourself which documentation style would be best for your composition and chosen subject. For example, if your topic involves criminal justice or gender studies, you could make a case for using APA style. And if you are creating a lab report or doctor's notes, you might use the CSE documentation style.

Most of our students submit MLA-style Works Cited lists with their compositions, though some, depending on their chosen genres, subjects, and major areas of study, use APA, *Chicago*, or CSE. If you plan to use one of these styles, you might want to discuss it with your instructor first, and make a case for why that style would be best.

**Are you composing an Author's Statement to accompany your genre composition?**   If you are creating an Author's Statement to accompany your composition (whether it's a research paper or alternative genre project), we recommend the MLA style of documentation, unless you've made a case for using APA, *Chicago*, or CSE. (For more on the Author's Statement—the reflective piece that can be submitted with any genre composition—see pp. 233–46.)

While there are several documentation styles for you to choose from, the following sections of this chapter provide basic guidance for using MLA and APA styles, as these are the styles you are most likely to use in conjunction with this textbook.

# MLA Style

The MLA style of documentation is presented in the *MLA Handbook*, 8th ed. (MLA, 2016). It is commonly used in English courses and other courses in the humanities. This style has been around a long time, but it has evolved to take into account the many types of sources we work with today.

The MLA style of documentation has two main components:

1. In-text citations

2. List of Works Cited (a.k.a. Works Cited list)

**The in-text citation**   Each time you cite a source in your paper—whether through a signal phrase or a parenthetical reference—you cue readers to a corresponding entry in your Works Cited list. When you include an in-text citation, you:

» Name the author of your source (or title if author is not provided)

» Provide a page number for that source (if there is one)

» Make sure you have a corresponding entry in your Works Cited list

**The list of Works Cited**   In your Works Cited list, at the end of your paper, you:

» Provide publication information about each source (for Web sources that don't provide publication dates, provide an "Accessed" date)

» Alphabetize your sources by authors' last names (or by title if an author is not provided)

» Include a URL for each online source (for more on this, see the box on p. 402)

Following is an example of an in-text citation along with its corresponding entry in the Works Cited list.

IN-TEXT CITATION
"Parents with this philosophy know there may be things their daughter hides from them, but they don't take it as a personal insult or an indication that their relationship with their daughter is weak" (Wiseman 54).

author —— exact page that quotation is from

WORKS CITED ENTRY

author:
last name, first name     title of book     publisher     publication year     page number

Wiseman, Rosalind. *Queen Bees and Wannabes*. Three Rivers Press, 2002, p. 54.

**In-text citations: General guidelines**    There are two main ways to handle an in-text citation: by using a signal phrase or a parenthetical reference (or some combination).

SIGNAL PHRASE (author named in phrase)

author

Wiseman suggests that "parents with this philosophy know there may be things their daughter hides from them, but they don't take it as a personal insult or an indication that their relationship with their daughter is weak" (54).

exact page that quotation is from

PARENTHETICAL REFERENCE (author cited in parentheses)

"Parents with this philosophy know there may be things their daughter hides from them, but they don't take it as a personal insult or an indication that their relationship with their daughter is weak" (Wiseman 54).

author      exact page that quotation is from

**Works Cited entries: General guidelines**    For each in-text citation in your paper, you need to provide a corresponding entry in your Works Cited list. The following guidelines provide the basic format for the MLA Works Cited entry.

» Name the author by last name, followed by first name.

author     book title     publisher     year     page range     descriptive label (optional, for clarity)

King, Stephen. *Full Dark, No Stars*. Pocket Books, 2011, pp. 1-12. Kindle.*

» For works by three or more authors or editors, list the name that appears first on the cover or title page, followed by "et al." (See also page 401, entry 5.) Note that for university presses you should use the abbreviation "UP."

lead author or editor:
last name, first name, then et al.     spell out "editors"     book title

Bearman, Peter, et al., editors. *After Tobacco: What Would Happen If Americans*

publisher     publication year     page range

*Stopped Smoking?* Columbia UP, 2011, pp. 30-36.

---

*Provide a page range if your source is an e-book with numbered pages.

» Present the titles of long works—books or entire Web sites—in italics.

author — book title — publisher from title page (or copyright page) — publication year — page range

Burroughs, Augusten. *Running with Scissors: A Memoir.* Picador, 2002, pp. 113-17.

author — Web site title — publisher

Sullivan, Andrew. *The Dish: Biased & Balanced.* The Daily Beast, andrewsullivan

URL — in the absence of a publication date, provide an access date

.thedailybeast.com/. Accessed 8 Sept. 2013.

» Present the titles of short works—articles or other short pieces from books or periodicals—in quotation marks.

author — article title — periodical title — publication date — page range

Parker, James. "Notes from the Underworld." *The Atlantic,* May 2011, pp. 38-41.

author — article title — periodical and site title — publication date

Acosta, Judith. "Do Guns Make the Man?" *The Huffington Post,* 21 July 2011,

URL

www.huffingtonpost.com/judith-acosta/do-guns-make-the-man_b_901918.html.

» Present titles with initial capital letters—except in the case of articles (*a, the,* etc.), prepositions (*to, from, with,* etc.), or coordinating conjunctions (*and, but, or, for,* etc.), unless these words come first or last.

author — book title — publisher — publication year — page range

Hemingway, Ernest. *To Have and Have Not.* Scribner's, 1937, pp. 1-4.

author — book title — publisher from title page (or copyright page) — publication year — page range — descriptive label (optional, for clarity)

Grafton, Sue. *V Is for Vengeance.* G. P. Putnam's Sons, 2011, pp. 12-13. Kindle.

» For print works, include the publisher's name as it appears on the title page. If no publisher is given on the title page, then see the copyright page.

author — book title — publisher — publication year — page range

Lahiri, Jhumpa. *Unaccustomed Earth.* Bloomsbury Publishing, 2008, pp. 52-56.

» For both print and online works, provide the date that the piece was published. For online sources, if no publication date is provided, include the date you accessed the source. For online sources, provide the URL at the end of the entry (omitting https://).

author — article title — publication title — publisher

Sumners, Christina. "Animal Acumen: Elephantine Intelligence." *NOVA*, PBS,

publication date — URL

26 Aug. 2011, www.pbs.org/wgbh/nova/insidenova/2011/08/elephants.html.

» When needed to clarify a source, you can include a descriptive label. MLA makes this practice optional. Whatever you decide, be consistent.

author — book title

Gates, Henry Louis, Jr. *Life upon These Shores: Looking at African American History:*

publisher — publication year — page range — descriptive label

*1513-2008.* Alfred A. Knopf, 2011, pp. 112-14. Kindle.

developer — title — publisher — publication year — optional descriptive label

Bungie. *Halo: Combat Evolved.* Microsoft Studios, 15 Nov. 2001. Video game.

Organize your Works Cited list alphabetically. For entries of more than one line, indent additional lines five spaces (this is called hanging indentation).

Works Cited

Acosta, Judith. "Do Guns Make the Man?" *The Huffington Post*, 21 July 2011, www.huffingtonpost.com/judith-acosta/do-guns-make-the -man_b_901918.html.

Bearman, Peter, et al., editors. *After Tobacco: What Would Happen If Americans Stopped Smoking?* Columbia UP, 2011, pp. 30-36.

Bungie. *Halo: Combat Evolved*. Microsoft Studios, 15 Nov. 2001. Video game.

Burroughs, Augusten. *Running with Scissors: A Memoir.* Picador, 2002, pp. 113-17.

Gates, Henry Louis, Jr. *Life upon These Shores: Looking at African American History: 1513-2008*. Alfred A. Knopf, 2011, pp. 112-14. Kindle.

Grafton, Sue. *V Is for Vengeance*. G. P. Putnam's and Sons, 2011, pp. 12-13. Kindle.

Hemingway, Ernest. *To Have and Have Not.* Scribner's, 1937, pp. 1-4.

King, Stephen. *Full Dark, No Stars.* Pocket Books, 2011, pp. 1-12. Kindle.

Lahiri, Jhumpa. *Unaccustomed Earth*. Bloomsbury Publishing, 2008, pp. 52-56.

Parker, James. "Notes from the Underworld." *The Atlantic*, May 2011, pp. 38-41.

Sullivan, Andrew. *The Dish: Biased & Balanced. The Daily Beast*, andrewsullivan .thedailybeast.com/. Accessed 8 Sept. 2013.

Sumners, Christina. "Animal Acumen: Elephantine Intelligence." *NOVA*, PBS, 26 Aug. 2011, www.pbs.org/wgbh/nova/insidenova/2011/08/elephants.html.

# MLA Models

## Models for Basic Situations

**1. Author is named in a signal phrase** When citing a source in the text of your paper, you need to name your author. You can do this in a signal phrase or in a parenthetical reference (along with the source's page number) following your citation. It's simplest to name the author in a signal phrase and keep the parenthetical reference brief. The following citation refers to material from Jonathan Safran Foer's book *Eating Animals* (Little, Brown and Company, 2009).

IN-TEXT CITATION
Jonathan Safran Foer argues that we can't trust language. "When it comes to eating animals," he writes, "words are as often used to misdirect and camouflage as they are to communicate" (45).

WORKS CITED ENTRY
Foer, Jonathan Safran. *Eating Animals*. Little, Brown and Company, 2009,
    pp. 1-86.

**2. Author is named in parentheses** If you decide not to name your author in a signal phrase, then name the author in your parenthetical reference along with the page number; don't use any punctuation between the name and page number.

IN-TEXT CITATION
Others argue that in addition to distrusting factory farming, we should also distrust the words associated with it, such as "natural" and "free range" (Foer 45).

WORKS CITED ENTRY
Foer, Jonathan Safran. *Eating Animals*. Little, Brown and Company, 2009,
    pp. 1-86.

**3. Individual author name is not provided** If you cannot locate an author name for your source, use the title. Provide the complete title of the text (or video, etc.) in a signal phrase—or give a shortened version of the title in the parenthetical reference. (Note: If the author is an organization, see example 6 on p. 403.) Following are sample citations for an article titled "Best Places to Live: 2012" that appears on CNN's *Money Magazine* site.

IN-TEXT CITATION (title in signal phrase; no page number available)
According to a recent *Money Magazine* article, "Best Places to Live: 2012," Carmel, Indiana, is the winner of all American small towns in terms of housing, finances, and overall quality of life.

OR (shortened title in parentheses; no page number available)
Carmel, Indiana, was recently determined to be the best American small town to live in ("Best Places").

"Best Places to Live: 2012." *Money Magazine*, CNN, Sept. 2012, money.cnn
.com/magazines/moneymag/best-places/2012/snapshots/PL1810342
.html?iid=spl100.

**4. Author identified by screen name only**   Some online sources identify an
author, but not by a traditional first and last name. For example, the author of an
eHow article is simply identified as an "eHow Contributor."

IN-TEXT CITATION (no page number available)

Another piece of career-building advice is to ask for extra training and to research and
learn more about your industry (eHow Contributor).

WORKS CITED ENTRY

eHow Contributor. "How to Get Along with the Boss." Demand Media, 4 Nov. 2010,
ehow.com/how_2057947_get-along-boss.html.

◀ ARTICLE
**eHow.com,** "How to
Get Along With the
Boss." *Article reprinted
with permission from
eHow.com.*

**5. More than one author**   Some sources have multiple authors. If your source has
*two authors*, include both of their names. Following is a reference to *The Worst-Case
Scenario Survival Handbook: Life*, a book by Joshua Piven and David Borgenicht
(San Francisco: Chronicle Books, 2006).

IN-TEXT CITATION (two authors)

To escape a stampede of giraffes, the best plan of action is to dive or wade into the
nearest body of water. Giraffes tend to avoid water unless they are thirsty (Piven and
Borgenicht 185).

WORKS CITED ENTRY

Piven, Joshua, and David Borgenicht. *The Worst-Case Scenario Survival Handbook:
Life*. Chronicle Books, 2006, p. 185.

*For three or more authors*, use the phrase "et al." (short for the Latin phrase *et alia*,
which means "and others"). Following is a reference to an article published in

*Nutrition Journal* titled "A Survey of Energy Drink Consumption Patterns among College Students." It was written by Brenda M. Malinauskas, Victor G. Aeby, Reginald F. Overton, Tracy Carpenter-Aeby, and Kimberly Barber-Heidal.

IN-TEXT CITATION (four or more authors; no page number available)

According to a 2007 study, college students consume Red Bull and other energy drinks when they feel sleep-deprived (67%), need an energy boost (65%), drink alcohol (54%), study or complete a major project (50%), drive long distances (45%), and have hangovers (17%) (Malinauskas et al.).

WORKS CITED ENTRY

Malinauskas, Brenda M., et al. "A Survey of Energy Drink Consumption Patterns Among College Students." *Nutrition Journal*, vol. 6, no. 5, 2007, www.nutritionj.com/content/6/1/35.

---

👉 **Attention, researchers using MLA! Does your source have no page numbers?**

Many digital sources do not have page numbers. When using these sources, do your best to meet MLA's requirements:

Provide the author, title, publisher/publication title, date of publication, and if no publication date is given, provide your access date. Also, please note: While MLA does not require you to provide descriptive labels such as "photograph," "chart," "map," "cartoon," "episode," etc., you can choose to do so if you think this would be helpful to your readers.

The Works Cited entry for an episode of *The Colbert Report* that you found online could look like this:

WORKS CITED ENTRY (for online clip)

    host         episode title       name of show/series    publisher

Colbert, Stephen, host. "Let Them Buy Cake." *The Colbert Report*, Comedy Central,

        episode date            URL

13 Dec. 2011, www.colbertnation.com/the-colbert-report-videos/404252/

                                optional descriptive label

december-13-2011/the-word---let-them-buy-cake. Episode.

The Works Cited entry for a film you saw in a theater could look like this:

WORKS CITED ENTRY (for movie)

     director         movie title        major performers

Nolan, Christopher, director. *The Dark Knight Rises*. Performances by Christian Bale, Tom

                        release

                  publisher   date   optional descriptive label

Hardy, and Anne Hathaway, Warner Bros., 2012. Film.

▲ VIDEO STILL
**Stephen Colbert,** during taping of *The Colbert Report* at the University of Pennsylvania, April 4, 2008. *AP Photo/Joseph Kaczmarek.*

**6. Author is an organization**  Follow the same basic format as for sources with any other type of author.

IN-TEXT CITATION (no page number available)
Mental health is a human and civil rights issue (Mental Health America).

WORKS CITED ENTRY
Mental Health America. "Position Statement 21: Rights of Persons with Mental Health and Substance Use Conditions." *Mental Health America*, www.nmha.org/go/position-statements/21. Accessed 30 Sept. 2013.

**7. No page numbers**  Many online sources (unless the source is a PDF) have no page numbers. The box on page 402 and examples 3 and 4 (pp. 400–01) show how to handle entries for sources without page numbers.

Another example: a video by *South Park* creators Trey Parker and Matt Stone, which animates a lecture by the philosopher Alan Watts, was found on YouTube.

IN-TEXT CITATION
The animated version of Watts's main arguments about life, music, and how success is measured creates a layered experience for viewers (Parker and Stone).

WORKS CITED ENTRY
Parker, Trey, and Matt Stone. "Life and Music." *YouTube*, 18 June 2007, www.youtube.com/watch?v=ERbvKrH-GC4.

**8. Source used more than once in a paragraph**  If you refer to a source multiple times in one paragraph, you can provide the author's name(s) just once, as long as it's clear it's still the same source. For example, see the citation for the article titled "Panic Disorder" from *The Journal of the American Medical Association*. The authors are Janet M. Torpy, Alison E. Burke, and Robert M. Golub.

IN-TEXT CITATION
According to research published in *The Journal of the American Medical Association*, not everyone who has a panic attack gets diagnosed with panic disorder (Torpy et al.). Still, as the article makes clear, many Americans suffer from mental health issues.

WORKS CITED ENTRY
Torpy, Janet M., et al. "Panic Disorder." *Journal of the American Medical Association*, vol. 305, no. 12, 2011, pp. 20-30, jama.jamanetwork.com/article.aspx?articleid=646264.

## Models for Specific Types of Sources

**9. Book**   For more in-text citation models for books, see examples 1, 2, and 5 (pp. 400 and 401). The following is from *Unbearable Lightness: A Story of Loss and Gain* by Portia de Rossi.

IN-TEXT CITATION
In Hollywood, where thinness is demanded at any cost but is extolled as the product of health and fitness, those who strive for perfection have to lie. As one actress puts it: "How could I possibly explain my weight maintenance when it was attributed to starving and bingeing?" (de Rossi 90).

WORKS CITED ENTRY
de Rossi, Portia. *Unbearable Lightness: A Story of Loss and Gain*. Atria Books,
     2010, p. 90.

**10. Article or essay**   The following model shows how to cite an article from an online periodical. In February 2012, *National Geographic* published an article by Tom O'Neill titled "Lady with a Secret."

IN-TEXT CITATION (article from online magazine)
A chalk-and-ink drawing, titled *La Bella Principessa*, may be the work of Leonardo da Vinci (O'Neill).

WORKS CITED ENTRY
O'Neill, Tom. "Lady with a Secret." *National Geographic*, Feb. 2012, ngm
     .nationalgeographic.com/2012/02/lost-da-vinci/o-neill-text.

The following model shows how to cite an article from a database.

IN-TEXT CITATION (article from a database)
Some images have the power to "spur a revolution" (Childs).

WORKS CITED ENTRY
Childs, Arcynta Ali. "The Power of Imagery in Advancing Civil Rights." *Smithsonian*,
     Oct. 2011, pp. 40-41. *OmniFile Full Text Select*, web.b.ebscohost.com.ezproxy
     .bpl.org/.

**11. Source quoted in another source**   The following models show how to cite a source that is quoted in another source. "Is Anybody Out There?" by Phil Plait was published by *Discover* magazine (in its November 2010 issue). Plait's article features several quotations from four major astronomers. To cite one of those quotations, use the phrase "qtd. in" to indicate that you did not read the quoted source itself, but rather found the quoted material in another source.

According to Gibor Basri, professor of astronomy at Berkeley, proof of whether "anybody's out there" may come down to a radio signal. "There are about 60 radio telescopes scanning the skies for these signals right now," he says. "That would be the definitive answer to the search for life: If you get an intelligent signal, then you know for sure" (qtd. in Plait).

WORKS CITED ENTRY

Plait, Phil. "Is Anybody Out There?" *Discover*, Kalmbach Publishing, Nov. 2010, discovermagazine.com/2010/nov/25-is-anybody-out-there/article_view ?b_start:int=0&-C=.

**12. Encyclopedia or dictionary entry—or wiki entry**   In your signal phrase or parenthetical reference, provide the word or phrase that you looked up in the dictionary or encyclopedia. If the work or entry has an author, provide that also. For the following example, there is no author provided by *Encyclopaedia Britannica*. Also, because the source (*Encyclopaedia Britannica*) and publisher (Encyclopaedia Britannica, Inc.) are essentially the same, MLA does not require that the publisher name be included in the Works Cited list.

IN-TEXT CITATION (for online encyclopedia)

The phrase "carpe diem," which traces back to an ancient Roman poet, means to seize or "pluck the day" ("Carpe diem").

WORKS CITED ENTRY

"Carpe diem." *Encyclopaedia Britannica*, www.britannica.com/EBchecked/ topic/96702/carpe-diem. Accessed 30 Sept. 2013.

## ENCYCLOPÆDIA BRITANNICA
ADVOCACY FOR ANIMALS | BLOG | HELP | SCHOOL & LIBRARY PRODUCTS | SHOP

### carpe diem

Introduction      Related      Contributors & Bibliography

**carpe diem,** ( Latin: "pluck the day") phrase used by the Roman poet Horace to express the idea that one should enjoy life while one can. The sentiment has been expressed in many literatures, especially in 16th- and 17th-century English poetry. Two of the best-known examples are Robert Herrick's "To the Virgins, to Make Much of Time" and Andrew Marvell's "To His Coy Mistress."

◀ ENCYCLOPEDIA ENTRY
**"Carpe diem"** from *Encyclopaedia Britannica Online*. See MLA documentation for this source on page 406. *Reprinted with permission from Encyclopaedia Britannica, © 2012 by Encyclopaedia Britannica, Inc.*

IN-TEXT CITATION (for online source)

The wombat is in danger because of destruction to its habitat; meanwhile, a project by a Swiss mining company is experimenting with relocating some of these animals from their native region in Australia to a new colony elsewhere in the country ("Wombat").

WORKS CITED ENTRY

"Wombat." *Wikipedia*, en.wikipedia.org/wiki/Wombat. Accessed 1 Sept. 2013.

---

👉 **Attention, *Wikipedia* lovers!**

Check with your instructor about using *Wikipedia* as a source. It is a public wiki that can be edited by anyone. Tip: *Wikipedia* can be a great place to start your research, especially because the "Reference," "Further reading," and "External links" sections can often lead you to excellent and reliable sources to use in your research project. For example, the "Wombat" entry provides links to Australian governmental information, BBC articles, and books authored by wombat experts. See also *Wikipedia*'s entry "Researching with Wikipedia" (or go to wikipedia.org and type in "Researching with Wikipedia").

---

**13. Entire Web site** In the rare instance that you will want to cite an entire Web site—rather than a specific portion of it, such as an article—use the following model. (For information on citing a short work from a Web site, see example 14 below.) MLA requires that you provide a Web site's author. Note that an author can be an organization such as a library or museum. If no author is provided, begin your Works Cited entry with the title of the site.

### Web site with no author

IN-TEXT CITATION

It is possible for an Internet radio station, drawing from a database and using your preferences for artists, songs, and genres, to personalize your experience, playing only the music you want to hear (Pandora).

Web site title

WORKS CITED ENTRY

*Pandora*. Music Genome Project and Pandora Media Inc., www.pandora.com/. Accessed 2 Sept. 2013.

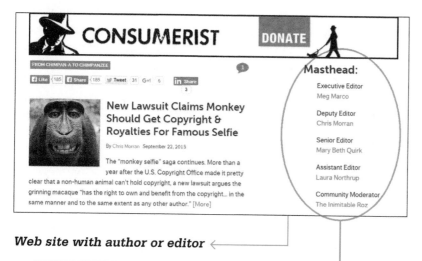

◀ WEB SITE
***The Consumerist.***
*Copyright © 2015 by Consumers Union of U.S., Inc., d/b/a Consumer Reports, a nonprofit organization in Yonkers, NY 10703-1057. Reprinted with permission from the September 23, 2015 posting on Consumerist.com for educational purposes only. (consumerist.com)*

### Web site with author or editor

IN-TEXT CITATION

One consumer-focused site gives an unflinching critique of big business, addressing the question: What is the worst company in America? (Marco et al.)

Web site editors

WORKS CITED ENTRY

Marco, Meg, et al., editors. *The Consumerist*, consumerist.com/. Accessed 30 Sept. 2013.

**14. Short work from a Web site** Most of what you cite from the Internet can be categorized as a "short work from a Web site." A short work is any text (of any type and medium) that is not book length or that appears as an internal page or section of a Web site. A short work can be an article, report, poem, song, video, and so on.

### Short work with no author

To avoid deep vein thrombosis during air travel, it can help to wear loose clothing and to stroll through the cabin once every hour ("Healthy Travel").

title of short work from a Web site

"Healthy Travel Tips." *Delta*, www.delta.com/traveling_checkin/travel_tips/health/index.jsp. Accessed 30 Sept. 2013.

### Short work with an author

A new genetically engineered salmon produced by a biotech firm will not be labeled as such, according to standards set by the Food and Drug Administration (Bittman).

author

Bittman, Mark. "Why Aren't GMO Foods Labeled?" *Opinionator*, 15 Feb. 2011, opinionator.blogs.nytimes.com/2011/02/15/why-arent-g-m-o-foods-labeled/.

**15. Video, movie, or TV show**   In general, cite these sources as you would a short work from a Web site (see example 14). When citing a movie or any work that includes a director, begin with the title and then identify the director, as shown below. NOTE: Although MLA style does not require it, keep in mind that you can add a descriptive label to your Works Cited entry if you think that would be helpful to your readers. For example, you can add words to indicate a source's type, such as "episode," "advertisement," "cartoon," "pamphlet," "photograph," "painting," and so on.

The opening scene of one episode of *Family Guy* is all about consumption: Peter can't resist the cookie dough batter, while Stewie is tempted by the Abercrombie catalog (MacFarlane).

director

MacFarlane, Seth, director. "The Big Bang Theory." *Family Guy*, Fox, 8 May 2011, hulu.com/watch/237564/family-guy-the-big-bang-theory. Episode.

**16. Video game, online game, or software**   To cite an entire video game, follow the format for an entire Web site (see example 13). For a clip from a video game, follow the format for a short work from a Web site. As noted in example 15, you can include descriptive labels such as *game*, *software*, and so on.

### Entire video game

The goal of one popular game is to plow, plant, and harvest on "your own" virtual land (FarmVille 2).

video game title

*FarmVille 2*. Zynga, 2012, FarmVille.com. Game.

### Clip from video game

Players can build their enterprises by acquiring such animals as the arctic fox and the armadillo ("My Mastery").

title of video game clip

"My Mastery." *FarmVille 2*. Zynga, 2012, FarmVille.com. Game clip.

clip title

**17. Visuals (photos, maps, charts, posters)**    Cite these as you would a short work from a Web site (see example 14) or other, longer work. Include the following, if available: author's or artist's name, title of the work, name of publication, and date of publication. You also have the option to note the type of the composition that your source is, for example, "photograph," "map," "chart," or "poster."

The image is a reminder that among those evicted by the Chicago Housing Authority are families with small children (Reblando).

photographer

Reblando, Jason. "Jessica Moore's Son Maurice Booker (left), 5, with a Friend."
    *The New York Times*, 3 Sept. 2011, www.nytimes.com/2011/09/04/us/
    04cncfirststrike.html?_r=1. Photograph.

**18. Comic strip/graphic work**    Think of comic strips as short works—from longer works such as Web sites, magazines, and so on—and cite them as you would a short work or article from a Web site (see example 14), online journal, book, or other source. As an option, you can include the label "cartoon" or "comic strip" at

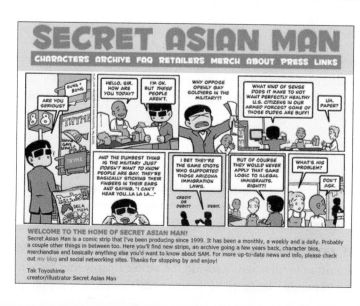

◀ COMIC STRIP
**Tak Toyoshima,**
"Why Oppose Openly Gay Soldiers in the Military?" From *Secret Asian Man*.
*Tak Toyoshima creator/ illustrator* Secret Asian Man.

the end of your Works Cited entry if you think that would benefit your readers. For graphic novels (fiction) or memoirs (nonfiction), follow the format that you would for a book. In some cases, the author is also the illustrator; when that is not the case, be sure to include the name of the illustrator, preceded by the phrase "Illustrated by" (see example below).

### Comic strip

IN-TEXT CITATION

The comic offers social commentary on issues such as racism, immigration, gay rights, the military, and consumption (Toyoshima).
author/artist

WORKS CITED ENTRY

Toyoshima, Tak. "Why Oppose Openly Gay Soldiers in the Military?" *Secret Asian Man*, 22 Aug. 2010, www.secretasianman.com/home.htm. Comic strip.

### Excerpt from a graphic memoir (author is also illustrator)

IN-TEXT CITATION

In 1980, a year after Iran's Islamic Revolution, she and her female classmates were obliged to wear a veil to school (Satrapi 3).
author/artist

WORKS CITED ENTRY

Satrapi, Marjane. *Persepolis*. Pantheon Books, 2004, pp. 1-8. Graphic memoir.

### Excerpt from a graphic novel (with an author and an illustrator)

IN-TEXT CITATION

The story opens with a journal entry that makes clear the character's obsessions with gore, filth, and death, not to mention Communists and intellectuals (Moore 1).
author

WORKS CITED ENTRY          artist

Moore, Alan. *Watchmen*. Illustrated by Dave Gibbons, DC Comics, 2008, pp. 1-32. Graphic novel.

**19. Advertisement**   To cite an ad, give the name the product being advertised. Following are the in-text citation and Works Cited entry for an ad for Dove Visible Care Body Wash, found at the company Web site. For the in-text citation, provide a shortened version of the product name.

IN-TEXT CITATION

A recent ad campaign for body wash claims to renew and soften skin, promising "visible results in just one week" (Dove Visible).
ad title (shortened)

WORKS CITED ENTRY

Dove Visible Care Body Wash. *Dove*. Unilever, www.dovecloseup.com/default .aspx#home. Accessed 30 Sept. 2013. Advertisement.

**20. Personal e-mail, text message, letter, or interview**   To cite an e-mail message (that you've written or received), provide the writer's name and the subject line. Next, provide the words "Received by" followed by the name of the recipient and the date the message was received. It is optional to include the descriptive label "E-mail" at the end. For a text message you've received, provide the writer's name followed by "Received by the author," followed by the date the text was received. For a letter you've received, provide the author's name and the phrase "Received by the author," followed by the date it was received. To cite an interview that you've conducted, provide the interviewee's name and "Interview by the author" followed by the date.

### E-mail *(received)*

IN-TEXT CITATION
Once customers search for a flight, hotel, or car, the organization e-mails periodic pricing updates, which can lead to a better deal for the consumer (Hotwire).

author of e-mail

WORKS CITED ENTRY
Hotwire. "Another Way to Save on Portsmouth Hotels." Received by the author, 15 Sept. 2013. E-mail.

### Text Message *(received)*

IN-TEXT CITATION
At the rally, a student was pepper-sprayed (Tamura).

author of text message

WORKS CITED ENTRY
Tamura, Annika. Received by the author, 1 Oct. 2011. Text message.

### Letter *(received)*

IN-TEXT CITATION
I received an unsettling report of suspicious activity involving my personal credit information (Experian).

author of letter

WORKS CITED ENTRY
Experian National Consumer Assistance Center. Received by the author, 15 Jan. 2013. Letter.

### Interview *(conducted)*

IN-TEXT CITATION
The world-traveling journalist admitted that while she might have wanted to stay home on her couch eating Ben and Jerry's Chunky Monkey, she did not have the time: Moscow, Afghanistan, and Cairo awaited (Amanpour).

person interviewed

WORKS CITED ENTRY
Amanpour, Christiane. Interview with the author, 21 Feb. 2013.

**21. Blog post or social media posting**   Cite as you would a short work from a Web site (see example 14); if the entry has no title, create a brief title based on the first line of the entry. For Twitter posts, however, MLA requires the full text of the tweet, presented without changes, in place of the title.

**Monica Brady-Myerov**

The sun is up on Whitey Bulger's former hideout. I'm surprised at how modest and almost shabby it is, compared to what he could have afforded!

IN-TEXT CITATION

One journalist who covered the James "Whitey" Bulger story was surprised by the shabbiness of the mob fugitive's Santa Monica apartment (Brady-Myerov).

                author

WORKS CITED ENTRY

Brady-Myerov, Monica. "Whitey Bulger's former hideout." *Facebook*, 24 June 2011,
    www.facebook.com/bradymyerov.

**22. Audio recording or podcast from the Web**    Cite audio recordings or podcasts that you've accessed online in the same way you would a short work from a Web site (see example 14).

### *Podcast*

IN-TEXT CITATION

It's holiday time, and an unemployed writer takes a job as a Macy's Christmas elf
("Sedaris Returns").

    podcast title

WORKS CITED ENTRY

"Sedaris Returns as Crumpet the Elf on NPR." *Morning Edition*, 24 Dec. 2004,
    www.npr.org/templates/story/ story.php?storyId=4243755. Podcast.

### *Song*

IN-TEXT CITATION

The artist performs her iconic song in "Single Ladies (Put a Ring on It)" as her alter ego,
Sasha Fierce (Knowles).

WORKS CITED ENTRY

Knowles, Beyoncé. "Single Ladies (Put a Ring on It)." *I Am . . . Sasha Fierce*, Columbia,
    2008, itunes.apple.com/us/album/i-am...-sasha-fierce/id296016891. Song.

**23. Phone app**    Cite a phone app as you would a Web site; or if you're referring to part of the app, cite it as you would a short work from a Web site (see example 14). It is optional to include the descriptive label "Phone app."

IN-TEXT CITATION

The creators of the app pitch it as a "one-stop GPS outdoor recreation app," with maps created for the screen—maps that are not simply shrunken versions of outdated USGS maps (AccuTerra).

      app title

*AccuTerra*. Version 3.1 for iPhone. Intermap Technologies, *iTunes*, 13 July 2011,
     itunes.apple.com/us/app/accuterra-unlimited-maps-gps/id355787609?mt=8.
     Phone app.

**24. Government or business document**   For a government document, provide the author, title, and date. If there is no author, provide the name of the government agency (and department, if any). Follow the rules for a short work from a longer work (e.g., a book, journal, or Web site). For a historical document, such as the one included below, provide the title in italics.

### Government document

He wrote: "[A]ll persons held as slaves within any State or designated part of a State, the people whereof shall then be in rebellion against the United States, shall be then, thenceforward, and forever free" (Lincoln).
                                                                              author

Lincoln, Abraham. *Emancipation Proclamation*. 1 Jan. 1863. The Library of Congress,
     www.loc.gov/pictures/item/97507511/resource/cph.3b53030/?sid=40c1ec586dad
     774d8a08ebfbf8cdff07. Accessed 30 Sept. 2013.

### Business document *(annual report)*

Even a major corporation such as Microsoft has felt the sting of the global recession (Ballmer).
     author

Ballmer, Steven A. "Microsoft Corporation: Annual Report 2012." Microsoft, 10 Oct.
     2012, www.microsoft.com/investor/reports/ar12/index.html.

**25. Literary work (novel, poem, fairy tale, etc.)**   Provide the author, title, publisher, and date. For Web sources, provide a URL. For e-books, it is optional to include a descriptive label, for example "Kindle" or "Nook," to identify for readers the brand platform.

### Novel

McCarthy, Cormac. *All the Pretty Horses*. Alfred A. Knopf, 1992.

### Novel

McCarthy, Cormac. *All the Pretty Horses*. Vintage International, 11 Aug. 2010. Kindle.

### Poem

WORKS CITED ENTRY

Crane, Hart. "At Melville's Tomb." *Poetry Out Loud*, www.poetryoutloud.org/
poem/172021. Accessed 11 Apr. 2013.

**26. Selection from an anthology or textbook**   Begin with the selection author and title, followed by the anthology or textbook title, editors, publisher, year,
and page range.

IN-TEXT CITATION

The cost of fruits and vegetables versus the cost of meat and dairy has a lot to do
with government subsidies (The Physicians Committee).

author of selection (shortened)

WORKS CITED ENTRY       ┌── author of selection

The Physicians Committee for Responsible Medicine. "Why Does a Salad Cost More
Than a Big Mac?" *Bedford Book of Genres: A Guide*, edited by Amy Braziller
and Elizabeth Kleinfeld, Bedford/St. Martin's, 2013, p. 121.

*information on
textbook where
selection appears*

**27. Object/artifact (cereal box, etc.)**   If you find an object or artifact online, cite
it as a short work from a Web site (see example 14). As an option, you can include
a descriptive label for the item in your Works Cited entry.

IN-TEXT CITATION

Children might be drawn to the sunny yellow box, but parents likely focus on the red
heart and the soft claim about lowering cholesterol (Cheerios).

name of object

▲ OBJECT
**Cheerios box.**
*iStockphoto.*

**Object** *(found online)*

WORKS CITED ENTRY

"Cheerios." General Mills, www.cheerios.com/Products/Cheerios. Accessed 30 Sept.
2013. Cereal box.

**Object** *(found in physical world)*

WORKS CITED ENTRY

"Cheerios." General Mills. Cereal box.

# APA Style

The APA style of documentation is the style presented in the *Publication Manual of the American Psychological Association*, 6th ed. (Washington: APA, 2010). It is commonly used in the behavioral and social science disciplines, which include courses in psychology and in sociology, and some English and cultural studies courses.

The APA style of documentation has two main components:

1. In-text citations

2. List of References

**The in-text citation** Your in-text citations refer your readers to your list. Each time you cite a source in your paper—whether through a signal phrase or a parenthetical reference—you cue readers to a corresponding entry in your References list. When you include an in-text citation, you:

» Name the author of your source

» Provide the source's year of publication—and (if it's a print source) a corresponding page number

» Make sure you have a corresponding entry (for each in-text citation) in your References list

**The References list** In your References list, at the end of your paper, you:

» Provide publication information about each source

» Alphabetize your sources by authors' last names (or by title if an author is not provided)

The following example shows an in-text citation along with its corresponding entry in the References list.

IN-TEXT CITATION

As students who visit our writing centers are working with

                  author    ┌ publication year

multimodal compositions (Sheridan, 2010), it makes sense to open up our idea of what it means to help with the entire composing processes (p. 3).

               └exact page where information is from

**Attention, researchers! A note about APA & tense.**

When you use a signal phrase to discuss a source, you must introduce the source by using the past or present perfect tenses. For example: "Lady Gaga (2013) said," or "Lady Gaga (2013) has argued." For more examples, see the APA in-text citation models provided in this chapter (pp. 419–35).

Note that MLA dictates a different approach, and requires you to use the present tense: for example: "Lady Gaga (2013) says," or "Lady Gaga (2013) argues." See pages 400–414 for MLA models.

author — publication year — title of chapter — editors

Sheridan, D. M. (2010). Writing centers and the multimodal turn. In D. M. Sheridan &

title of book

J. A. Inman (Eds.), *Multiliteracy centers: Writing center work, new media, and multimodal rhetoric* (pp. 1-22). Cresskill, NJ: Hampton Press.

page range of chapter — place of publication — publisher

**In-text citations: General guidelines**   There are two main ways to handle an in-text citation: by using a signal phrase or a parenthetical reference (or some combination).

SIGNAL PHRASE (author named in phrase)

authors — publication year

Kingsolver, Kingsolver, and Hopp (2007) explained to readers that they "had come to the farmland to eat deliberately" (p. 23).

exact page that quotation is from

PARENTHETICAL REFERENCE (author named in parentheses)

In discussing psychiatric illnesses, the author argued, "Psychiatry has found a way to medicalize all human behavior and offer a pharmaceutical intervention for everything" (Plante, 2012, para. 3).

author — publication year — for this online source, no page number is available, but source has paragraph numbers

**References entries: General guidelines**   Provide a corresponding entry in your References list for each in-text citation in your paper. The following guidelines provide the basic format for the APA References list entry.

» Give the author's last name, followed by initials for all first and middle names. Provide additional authors' names with each last name followed by initials for first and middle names.

author: last name + initial(s) — publication year — title of book

Ben-Shahar, T. (2007). *Happier: Learn the secrets to daily joy and lasting fulfillment.*

place of publication — publisher — page range

New York, NY: McGraw-Hill, 20-32.

authors: last name + initial(s) — publication year — title of article

Watkins, P. C., Woodward, K., Stone, T., & Kolts, R. L. (2003). Gratitude and happiness:

title of article

Development of a measure of gratitude, and relationships with subjective well-being.

title of journal — volume — page range

*Social Behavior and Personality*, *31*, 131-151.

» Present the titles of long works—books or entire Web sites—in italics. Capitalize the first word of the title; other words in the title (except proper nouns) are lowercased. If there is a subtitle, capitalize the first word of the subtitle.

author: last
name + initial(s)   publication
year                                  title of book

Deutsch, D. (2011). *The beginning of infinity: Explanations that transform the world.*

place of publication   publisher   page range

New York, NY: Viking Penguin, 112-133.

» Present the titles of short works from books or Web sites without quotation marks or italics. Capitalize the first word of the title; other words are lowercased (though be sure to retain the capitalization of proper nouns). If there is a subtitle, capitalize the first word of the subtitle. IMPORTANT: For all online sources, include the URL. Although APA suggests you provide the URL for the source's homepage, we recommend that you provide the exact URL for the specific article or other work you're referring to. For example, the article cited below is from Salon.com. The URL takes readers to the page for the article itself, not Salon's homepage.

author: last
name + initial(s)   publication year,
month, day                title of article                    title of magazine

Mustich, E. (2011, June 15). Can students be disciplined for online speech? *Salon*

paragraph range                                      article URL

(paras. 1-6). Retrieved from http://news.salon.com/2011/06/15/students
_online_speech/singleton

» For print works, present the city and state of publication, and spell out the entire name of the publisher.

author: last
name + initial(s)   publication
year                                  title of book

Lieber, L. (2008). *The Einstein theory of relativity: A trip to the fourth dimension.*

place of publication   publisher   page range

Philadelphia, PA: Paul Dry Books, 17-24.

» For both print and online works, provide the date that the piece was published. For online sources, provide the URL, but not the access date—unless there is a chance the content of the source may change.

author: last
name + initial(s)   publication
year                                  title of book

Clark, D. P. (2010). *Germs, genes, and civilization: How epidemics shaped who we are*

place of publication                publisher            page range

*today.* Upper Saddle River, NJ: Pearson Education, Inc., 19-23.

author: last name + initial(s)  publication year, month, day  title of photo essay

Lewis, T. (2012, August 13). Slimy but cute: 10 newly discovered amphibians

descriptive label  title of magazine  photo essay URL

[Photo essay]. *Wired*. Retrieved from http://www.wired.com/wiredscience/2012 /08/new-amphibian-species/

» If your source is a work that would benefit from clarification, provide that term in brackets. (See models for these on pp. 430–33.)

author  publication year, month, day  title of newspaper editorial

*The Denver Post* Editorial Board. (2012, January 20). School trans fat ban not needed

descriptive label  title of newspaper  editorial URL

[Editorial]. *The Denver Post*. Retrieved from http://www.denverpost.com /opinion/ci_19778812

Organize your References list alphabetically. For entries of more than one line, indent additional lines five spaces (this is called hanging indentation).

### References

Ben-Shahar, T. (2007). *Happier: Learn the secrets to daily joy and lasting fulfillment*. New York, NY: McGraw-Hill, 1-12.

Clark, D. P. (2010). *Germs, genes, and civilization: How epidemics shaped who we are today*. Upper Saddle River, NJ: Pearson Educational, Inc., 19-23.

*The Denver Post* Editorial Board. (2012, January 20). School trans fat ban not needed [Editorial]. *The Denver Post*. Retrieved from http:// www.denverpost.com/opinion/ci_19778812

Deutsch, D. (2011). *The beginning of infinity: Explanations that transform the world*. New York, NY: Viking Penguin, 112-133.

Kingsolver, B., Kingsolver, C., & Hopp, S. L. (2007). *Animal, vegetable, miracle: A year of food life*. New York, NY: HarperCollins, 23.

Lewis, T. (2012, August 13). Slimy but cute: 10 newly discovered amphibians [Photo essay]. Wired. Retrieved from http://www.wired.com /wiredscience/2012/08/new-amphibian-species/

Lieber, L. (2008). *The Einstein theory of relativity: A trip to the fourth dimension*. Philadelphia, PA: Paul Dry Books, 17-24.

Mustich, E. (2011, June 15). Can students be disciplined for online speech? *Salon* (paras.1-6). Retrieved from http://news.salon.com/2011/06/15 /students_online_speech/singleton

Plante, T. (2012, February 1). The psychopathology of everything [Editorial Weblog post]. *Do the right thing: Spirit, science, and health. Psychology Today*, para. 3. Retrieved from http://www.psychologytoday.com /blog/do-the-right-thing/201202/the-psychopathology-everything

Sheridan, D. M. (2010). Writing centers and the multimodal turn. In D. M. Sheridan & J. A. Inman (Eds.), *Multiliteracy centers: Writing center work, new media, and multimodal rhetoric* (pp. 1-22). Cresskill, NJ: Hampton Press.

Watkins, P. C., Woodward, K., Stone, T., & Kolts, R. L. (2003). Gratitude and happiness: Development of a measure of gratitude, and relationships with subjective well-being. *Social Behavior and Personality, 31,* 131-151.

# APA Models

## Models for Basic Situations

**1. Author is named in a signal phrase**   When citing a source, name your author in a signal phrase—that is, name the author in the body of your text, and provide the source publication year and page number in parentheses. Or use a parenthetical reference—as shown in the example below—and provide everything in parentheses: the author's last name, the source publication year, and page number.

The simplest, cleanest method is to name the author in a signal phrase and keep the parenthetical reference brief:

IN-TEXT CITATION
David Myers (2011) identified shifts in the study of human behavior. He wrote: "I find myself fascinated by today's psychology, with its studies of the neuroscience of our moods and memories, the reach of our adaptive unconscious, and the shaping power of the social and cultural context" (p. 4).

REFERENCES LIST ENTRY
Myers, D. (2011). *Psychology* (10th ed.). New York, NY: Worth Publishers, 1-4.

**2. Author is named in parentheses**   If you don't name your author in a signal phrase, then do so in your parenthetical reference along with the publication year and page number; use commas between the name, year, and page number.

IN-TEXT CITATION
Part of what has made the study of psychology so interesting is the current focus on neuroscience, the adaptive unconscious, and social and cultural factors (Myers, 2011, p. 4).

REFERENCES LIST ENTRY
Myers, D. (2011). *Psychology* (10th ed.). New York, NY: Worth. 1-4.

**3. Individual author name is not provided**   In the rare case that you cannot locate an author name for your source, use the title (or the first word or two of the title) in parentheses. (Note: If the author is an organization, see example 6.)

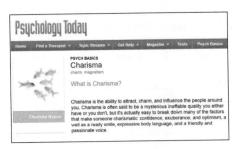

Following are sample citations for a brief article titled "Psych Basics: Charisma" that appears on *Psychology Today*'s site.

IN-TEXT CITATION (title in signal phrase; no page number available)
According to a current *Psychology Today* article, "Psych Basics: Charisma" (2012), charming and influencing others requires "confidence, exuberance, and optimism" (para. 1).

OR (shortened title in parentheses; no page number available)
Charisma is said to be a quality that you either have or you don't ("Charisma," 2012, para. 1).

REFERENCES LIST ENTRY
Psych basics: Charisma. (2012). *Psychology Today*, para. 1. Retrieved from http://www.psychologytoday.com/basics/charisma

ALTERNATIVE APPROACH: If you consider the publisher, *Psychology Today*, as the author, here is how the in-text citation and References list entry would work:

IN-TEXT CITATION (organization treated as author)
There are physical aspects to charisma, as well: smiling, using body language, and speaking with a friendly voice (*Psychology Today*, 2012, para. 1).

REFERENCES LIST ENTRY
*Psychology Today*. (2012). Psych basics: Charisma. *Psychology Today*, para. 1. Retrieved from http://www.psychologytoday.com/basics/charisma

**4. Author identified by screen name only**   Some online sources identify an author, but not by a traditional first and last name. For example, the author of an eHow article is simply identified as an "eHow Contributor."

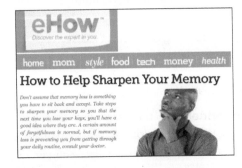

Among the suggestions for improving memory were doing crossword puzzles, reading, and playing word games (eHow Contributor, 2011).

REFERENCES LIST ENTRY
eHow Contributor. (2011, September 6). How to sharpen your memory. *eHow*. Retrieved from http://www.ehow.com/how_5594193_sharpen-memory.html

**5. More than one author**   Some sources have multiple authors. In general, you will list only up to five names in your in-text citations; for your References list, you can list up to seven authors, using an "&" just before the final name. Below is a reference to *The Worst-Case Scenario Survival Handbook: Work*, a book by Joshua Piven and David Borgenicht (San Francisco: Chronicle Books, 2003).

IN-TEXT CITATION (two authors)
To avoid taking a nightmare job, the authors recommended that applicants should schedule a morning interview and observe the mood of workers as they arrive: slouching, pouting, or looking dejected are all signs of low morale (Piven & Borgenicht, 2003, p. 16).

REFERENCES LIST ENTRY
Piven, J., & Borgenicht, D. (2003). *The worst-case scenario survival handbook: Work*. San Francisco, CA: Chronicle Books, 1-32.

*For three to five authors*, identify all authors the first time you use the source in text; afterward, use only the first author's name and the phrase "et al." (short for the Latin phrase *et alia*, which means "and others"). Note: The article cited in the example below is from a database; many databases provide a DOI number for use in your References list entry. If there is no DOI, then use the phrase "Retrieved from" followed by the URL.

IN-TEXT CITATION (three to five authors)
A recent study found a boost in girl power in India, thanks to affirmative action laws that gave women leadership roles in their village councils. In terms of career goals, the gender gap for teen girls in the villages with women leaders closed by 32% (Beaman, Duflo, Pande, & Topalova, 2012, pp. 582-586).

LATER CITATIONS
(Beaman et al., 2012, pp. 582-586)

REFERENCES LIST ENTRY (article retrieved from database with DOI)
Beaman, L., Duflo, E., Pande, R., & Topalova, P. (2012, January 12). Female leadership raises aspirations and educational attainment for girls: A policy experiment in India. *Science, 335*, 582-586. doi:10.1126/science.1212382

REFERENCES LIST ENTRY (article from publisher site, abstract or summary only)
Beaman, L., Duflo, E., Pande, R., & Topalova, P. (2012, January 12). Female leadership raises aspirations and educational attainment for girls: A policy experiment in India [Abstract]. *Science, 335*, 582-586. Retrieved from http://www.sciencemag.org/content/335/6068/582.abstract

*For six or more authors*, for your in-text citations, name the first author listed, followed by "et al." In your References list entry, list up to seven authors. If there are more than seven authors, list the first six followed by three ellipsis dots and the last author's name. Following is a reference to an article published in the British journal *Animal Behaviour* titled "Firefly Flashing and Jumping Spider Predation." It was written by Skye M. Long, Sara Lewis, Leo Jean-Louis, George Ramos, Jamie Richmond, and Elizabeth M. Jako.

IN-TEXT CITATION (six or more authors)
Sadly for fireflies, flashing does more than entice mates; it can attract predators, including two species of attacking spiders (Long et al., 2012, pp. 81-86).

REFERENCES LIST ENTRY (up to seven authors)
Long, S. M., Lewis, S., Jean-Louis, L., Ramos, G., Richmond, J., & Jako, E. M. (2012). Firefly flashing and jumping spider predation. *Animal Behaviour, 83,* 81-86. doi:10.1016/j.anbehav.2011.10.008

**6. Author is an organization**    Follow the same basic format as for sources with any other type of author.

ARTICLE ▶
**American Civil Liberties Union,**
"Protecting Civil Liberties In The Digital Age." *American Civil Liberties Union, aclu.org.*

IN-TEXT CITATION
The American Civil Liberties Union argued that since 9/11, our civil liberties have "undergone constant erosion" thanks to expanded powers of government security agencies (ACLU, 2012, para. 1).

OR

Since 9/11, Americans' civil liberties, especially in the digital realm, have been under attack by security agencies such as the NSA and FBI (American Civil Liberties Union [ACLU], 2012, para. 1).

LATER CITATIONS
(ACLU, 2012)

REFERENCES LIST ENTRY
American Civil Liberties Union. (2012). Protecting civil liberties in the digital age, paras. 1-3. Retrieved from http://www.aclu.org/protecting-civil-liberties-digital-age

**7. No page numbers**   Most print sources have numbered pages, but unless your online source is provided as a PDF file, it probably will not include page numbers. Examples 3 and 6 show in-text citations for sources that have no page numbers; in those cases we provided paragraph numbers. Here is another example of an online source that lacks page numbers: a video by Erik Qualman, which presents statistics on social media, was found on YouTube.

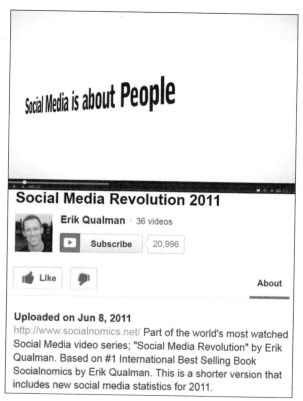

◀ VIDEO
**Erik Qualman,**
"Social Media is about People," from You-Tube. *Erik Qualman.*

IN-TEXT CITATION

Erik Qualman's (2011) video provided a fast-paced barrage of statistics showing the rapid growth of social media.

REFERENCES LIST ENTRY

Qualman, E. [Screen name: Socialnomics09] (2011, June 8). Social media revolution 2011 [Video file]. Retrieved from http://www.youtube.com/watch?v=3SuNx0UrnEo

**8. Source used more than once in a paragraph**    Let's say that you give the author's name in a signal phrase in the text of your paper (and the publication date and page number in parentheses). To refer to that same source later in the same paragraph, simply provide the page number (or paragraph number).

### For a print source

The example below refers to an article by Rob Sheffield about *Mad Men*; it appeared in the print edition of *Rolling Stone* on March 29, 2012.

IN-TEXT CITATION

Sheffield (2012) wrote that Draper built his career by "hustling in the dirty world of American dreams" (p. 36). I've always assumed that, unlike the rest of us, Don Draper, the cool ad man, is immune to the beautiful lies he sells. But as the writers further developed the character, he has become more impulsive, a man looking for Disney happiness and fresh starts. What's clear is this: "[T]his guy believes in Hollywood happy endings" (p. 36).

REFERENCES LIST ENTRY

Sheffield, R. (2012, March 29). More desperate than mad. *Rolling Stone* (1153), p. 36.

### For an online source

The example below refers to an article by Miriam Coleman about Madonna's 2012 Super Bowl performance; it was published at *Rolling Stone's* Web site on February 5, 2012. Note that while there are no page numbers for this source, we have provided paragraph numbers.

IN-TEXT CITATION

Miriam Coleman (2012) detailed how Madonna was "ushered in on a golden chariot pulled by a phalanx of centurions" for the first part of her Super Bowl performance (para. 1). As a high priestess of popular culture, Madonna understands fanfare and branding, not to mention big entrances and exits: "In the final moment of the show, gold beams projected up into the sky as Madonna disappeared from the stage in a massive plume of smoke" (para. 3).

REFERENCES LIST ENTRY

Coleman, M. (2012, February 5). Madonna's glittering Super Bowl spectacle. *Rolling Stone*, paras. 1-3. Retrieved from http://www.rollingstone.com/music/news /madonnas-glittering-super-bowl-spectacle-20120205

**Attention, researchers using APA! Does your source have no page numbers?**

For most online sources (anything that's not a PDF), you will not be able to provide page numbers. However, for online articles and other text-based digital sources, you can provide paragraph numbers. Paragraph numbers help your readers see exactly where you drew from a source.

For sources you cannot provide paragraph numbers for—videos, audio recordings, and many other types of digital media—we recommend that you do your best to provide whatever information will guide your audience to a particular moment in that video or audio recording. You can provide a time range, for example.

Let's look again at the Qualman video presented as part of example 7 (p. 423). Here is how you might cite a particular moment from that source.

◀ VIDEO
**Erik Qualman,** "Social Media is about People" from YouTube. *Erik Qualman.*

IN-TEXT CITATION

According to Erik Qualman's (2011) video on the role of social media, "If Facebook were a country it'd be the world's 3rd largest" (0:42-0:44).

Let's say that elsewhere in your paper you refer to other moments of the video, which is two minutes and thirty-five seconds long. This is what a very precise References list entry would look like.

REFERENCES LIST ENTRY

Qualman, E. (2011, June 8). Social media revolution 2011 [Video file]. Retrieved from http://www.youtube.com/watch?v=3SuNx0UrnEo (0:01-2:35)

## Models for Specific Types of Sources

**9. Book**  For more in-text citation models for books, see examples 1, 2, and 5. The following is from *Just Kids* by Patti Smith.

☞ **Attention, researchers! Citing entire works is a rarity.**

When working with sources, 99.9 percent of the time you refer to specific passages and pages from a source—and include them in both your in-text citation and the corresponding References list entry. In the *extremely* rare instance that you need to summarize an entire work (as shown in the example below), you do not need to provide specific page numbers. Unless you are creating an annotated bibliography (p. 299), we do not recommend that you make a practice of summarizing entire sources.

→ IN-TEXT CITATION (that summarizes entire work)

In her memoir, Patti Smith (2010) described numerous adventures with the artist Robert Mapplethorpe, highlighting stories from when they lived in the Chelsea Hotel.

REFERENCES LIST ENTRY

Smith, P. (2010). *Just kids*. New York, NY: HarperCollins.

IN-TEXT CITATION (that quotes from a specific passage)

Smith (2010) writes: "My mother gave me *The Fabulous Life of Diego Rivera* for my sixteenth birthday. I was transported by the scope of his murals, descriptions of his travels and tribulations, his loves and labor" (p. 12).

REFERENCES LIST ENTRY

Smith, P. (2010). *Just kids*. New York, NY: HarperCollins, 1-12.

IN-TEXT CITATION (that paraphrases a specific passage)

She was quite taken by a sixteenth birthday gift from her mother: *The Fabulous Life of Diego Rivera* (Smith, 2010, p. 12).

REFERENCES LIST ENTRY

Smith, P. (2010). *Just kids*. New York, NY: HarperCollins, 1-12.

**10. Article or essay**    The following models show how to cite online and print articles. In February 2012, a magazine called *5280: The Denver Magazine* published an article by Josh Dean—"The Australian Shepherd Is From"—in two forms: online and in print.

IN-TEXT CITATION (article from an online magazine)

According to Dean (2012), "[D]ogs that appeared to be Aussies were doing their jobs all over the West, but no one seemed interested in documenting their provenance" (para. 1).

REFERENCES LIST ENTRY

Dean, J. (2012, February). The Australian shepherd is from [Electronic version]. *5280: The Denver Magazine*, paras. 1-38. Retrieved from http://www.5280.com /magazine/2012/02/australian-shepherd

IN-TEXT CITATION (article from a print magazine)

In his article, Dean (2012) argued that although the Australian shepherd "isn't Colorado's official state dog . . . it really should be" (p. 75).

REFERENCES LIST ENTRY

Dean, J. (2012, February). The Australian shepherd is from. *5280: The Denver Magazine*, 70-75, 110-118.

**11. Source quoted in another source**    The following models show how to cite a source that is quoted in another source, whether online or print. "Is Anybody Out There?" by Phil Plait was published by *Discover* magazine in two different forms—in a print edition (in its November 2010 issue) and online at discovermagazine.com (on January 27, 2011). Plait's article features several quotations from four major astronomers. To cite one of those quotations, you need to use the phrase "as cited in" to indicate that you did not read the quoted source itself, but rather found the quoted material in another source.

IN-TEXT CITATION (article from an online magazine)

According to Gibor Basri, professor of astronomy at Berkeley, proof of whether "anybody's out there" may come down to a radio signal. "There are about 60 radio telescopes scanning the skies for these signals right now," he said. "That would be the definitive answer to the search for life: If you get an intelligent signal, then you know for sure" (as cited in Plait).

REFERENCES LIST ENTRY

Plait, P. (2011, January). "Is anybody out there?" *Discover* (paras. 1-3). Retrieved from http://discovermagazine.com/2010/nov/25-is-anybody-out-there/article_view?b_start:int=0&-C=.

IN-TEXT CITATION (article from a print magazine)

According to Gibor Basri, professor of astronomy at Berkeley, proof of whether "anybody's out there" may come down to a radio signal. "There are about 60 radio telescopes scanning the skies for these signals right now," he says. "That would be the definitive answer to the search for life: If you get an intelligent signal, then you know for sure" (as cited in Plait, 2010).

REFERENCES LIST ENTRY

Plait, P. (2010, November). Is anybody out there? *Discover*, 49-51.

**12. Encyclopedia or dictionary entry—or wiki entry**    When the author or authors of an entry are named, follow the format that you would for an article (see example 10). When no author is named, use the name of the publisher or publication—or begin the citation with the title of the entry. If there is a publication date, provide it. If not, then indicate that there is no date by using "n.d." in parentheses following the author's name.

IN-TEXT CITATION (for online dictionary)

According to *Merriam-Webster* (2012), psychoanalysis is used to "treat emotional disorders." 　　　　— publisher name

REFERENCES LIST ENTRY

*Merriam-Webster*. (2012). Psychoanalysis. Retrieved from http://www.merriam-webster.com/dictionary/psychoanalysis

Unlike *Merriam-Webster*, *Wikipedia* is a multiple-authored wiki: This means that the authors and the content itself change all the time. Following is a model for citing a *Wikipedia* entry. We've included a "Retrieved from" date, because any *Wikipedia* entry cited today may be quite different by tomorrow.

IN-TEXT CITATION (for a wiki)
Racial segregation (2012), according to *Wikipedia*, is defined as "the separation of humans into racial groups in daily life" (para. 1).

REFERENCES LIST ENTRY
Wikipedia. (2012, February 6). Racial Segregation. Retrieved February 8, 2012, from http://en.wikipedia.org/wiki/Racial_segregation (para.1)

---

 **Attention, Wikipedia lovers!**

Check with your instructor about using *Wikipedia* as a source. It is a public wiki that can be edited by anyone. Tip: *Wikipedia* can be a great place to start your research, especially because the "Reference," "Further Reading," and "External Links" sections can often lead you to excellent and reliable sources to use in your research project. For example, the "Racial segregation" entry provides links to *The Washington Post*, *The American Historical Review*, and books authored by experts on apartheid. You can also go to wikipedia.org and type in "Researching with Wikipedia."

---

**13. Entire Web site**  In the extremely rare instance that you will want to cite an entire Web site—rather than a specific portion of it, such as an article—use the following model. (For information on citing a short work from a Web site, see example 14 below.) APA requires that for Web sources, you provide the name of the organization that authored the page, the publication date (use "n.d." if there is none), the name of the site, and the URL.

Note: All Web sites have an author—or at least a hosting organization. If an individual person or persons are not named as authors, then consider the organization that hosts or publishes the site to be the author. Similarly, if you find an article at MSNBC.com that does not list an individual author, then you should consider MSNBC.com as the author of that article.

### Web site with an organization as author

IN-TEXT CITATION  _Web site sponsor/publisher_
Fastweb (2012) divided its scholarship links into categories including "Art Scholarships," "Hispanic Scholarships," and "Scholarships for College Freshmen."

REFERENCES LIST ENTRY
Fastweb. (2012). Retrieved from http://www.fastweb.com

**14. Short work from a Web site**  Most of what you cite from the Internet can be categorized as a "short work from a Web site." A short work is any text (of any type and medium) that is not book length or that appears as an internal page or section of a Web site. A short work can be an article, report, poem, song, video, and so on. In some cases, you will include a descriptive label (see example 15 on p. 430).

### Short work with an organization as author

IN-TEXT CITATION  _Web site sponsor/publisher_
The WebMD entry "Anxiety Disorders" (2009) defined various types of disorders, such as panic disorder and social anxiety disorder.

REFERENCES LIST ENTRY
WebMD (2009). Anxiety disorders. Retrieved from http://www.webmd.com/anxiety
-panic/guide/mental-health-anxiety-disorders

### Short work with an individual author

IN-TEXT CITATION
All is not necessarily lost in a relationship if someone cheats. Sometimes, according to Clark-Flory (2012), infidelity might bring couples closer and "[open] new lines of communication" (para. 1).

REFERENCES LIST ENTRY
Clark-Flory, T. (2012, January 23). When infidelity heals. _Salon_. Retrieved from http://
life.salon.com/2012/01/23/when_infidelity_heals/singleton/

**15. Video, movie, or TV show**   In general, if you find these sources online, cite them as you would a short work from a Web site (see also example 14). Include an identifying label in brackets: "Television series episode," "Film," and so on.

IN-TEXT CITATION
During the *Big Bang Theory* episode "The Friendship Connection," the character Wolowitz spent time trying to choose an astronaut nickname (Lorre, Kaplan, & Reynolds, 2012).

REFERENCES LIST ENTRY (for a TV episode)
Lorre, C., Kaplan, E., & Reynolds, J. (Writers), & Cendrowski, M. (Director). (2012, February 2). The friendship connection [Television series episode]. In Lorre, C., Prady, B., & Molaro, S. (Producers), *Big bang theory*. New York, NY: CBS.

REFERENCES LIST ENTRY (for a different episode, online)
Lorre, C., Kaplan, E., & Reynolds, J. (Writers), & Cendrowski, M. (Director). (2012, January 19). The recombination hypothesis [Television series episode]. In Lorre, C., Prady, B., & Molaro, S. (Producers), *Big bang theory*. Retrieved from http://www.cbs.com/shows/big_bang_theory/video/2188321432/the-big-bang-theory-the-recombination-hypothesis

**16. Video game, online game, or software**   To cite an entire video game, follow the format for an entire Web site and include a description—"Video game," "Online game," or "Computer software"—in brackets. For a clip from a video game, follow the format for a short work from a Web site (see example 14).

### Entire video game

IN-TEXT CITATION
The goal of one popular game was to plow, plant, and harvest on "your own" virtual land (Zynga, 2009).
video game publisher

REFERENCES LIST ENTRY
Zynga. (2009). *FarmVille* 2 [Online game]. Zynga. Retrieved October 13, 2012 from http://www.farmville.com/

### Clip from video game

IN-TEXT CITATION
Players can build their enterprises by acquiring such animals as the arctic fox and the armadillo (Zynga, 2009).
video game publisher

REFERENCES LIST ENTRY
Zynga. (2009). My mastery. [Online game clip]. *FarmVille 2*. Zynga. Retrieved February 13, 2012 from http://www.farmville.com/

**17. Visuals (photos, maps, charts, posters)**   Cite these works as you would a short work from a Web site (see example 14), or other longer work. Include the following, if available: author's or artist's name, date of composition, title of the work, and publication's name. Also note the medium of the composition—"Photograph," "Map," "Chart," "Poster," and so on—in brackets.

IN-TEXT CITATION

Most visitors spend time in the capital city of Kuala Lumpur, located in the southwestern part of the country (Lonely Planet, 2012).
*author of map*

REFERENCES LIST ENTRY

Lonely Planet. (2012). Malaysia [Map]. Retrieved from http://www.lonelyplanet.com/maps /asia/malaysia/

**18. Comic strip/graphic work**   Think of comic strips as short works—from longer works such as Web sites, magazines, and so on—and cite them as you would a short work or article from a Web site, online journal, book, or other source. Include the description—"Cartoon" or "Comic strip"—in brackets. For graphic novels (fiction) or memoirs (nonfiction), follow the format that you would for a book. In some cases, the author is also the illustrator; when that is not the case, in parentheses after the title, indicate the illustrator's name followed by the word "illustrator."

### *Comic strip*

IN-TEXT CITATION   *author/artist*

Thomas's (2012) comic strip offered a commentary on the mentality of social media users.

REFERENCES LIST ENTRY

Thomas, C. (2012, February 5). Watch your head [Comic strip]. *The Washington Post Writer's Group*. Retrieved from http://www.cartoonistgroup.com/properties /wpwg.php?id=106&today=2012-02-05

### *Excerpt from a graphic memoir* (author is also illustrator)

IN-TEXT CITATION   *author/artist*

In her graphic memoir, Crumb (2007, pp. 1-7) chronicled her life journey from New York to the south of France.

REFERENCES LIST ENTRY

Crumb, A. K. (2007). *Need more love: A graphic memoir*. London, United Kingdom: MQ Publications, 1-7.

### *Excerpt from a graphic novel* (with an author and an illustrator)

IN-TEXT CITATION   *author*

Powell (2008) retold the classic story of Little Red Riding Hood in graphic novel form.

REFERENCES LIST ENTRY   *artist*

Powell, M. (2008). *Red Riding Hood: The graphic novel*. (Victor Rivas, illustrator.) North Mankato, MN: Stone Arch Books, 1-4.

**19. Advertisement**   To cite an ad, name the product being advertised, along with the word "Advertisement" in brackets. Following are the in-text citation and

References list entry for an ad created by the BBDO advertising firm for FedEx Kinko's. We found it at the Ads of the World Web site (which is not a publication).

IN-TEXT CITATION        author of ad

One ad for FedEx Kinko's featured a larger-than-life highlighter (BBDO, 2007).

REFERENCES LIST ENTRY

BBDO advertising firm. (2007, March). FedEx Kinko's Giant Highlighter [Advertisement]. Retrieved from http://adsoftheworld.com/media/ambient /fedex_kinko_giant_highlighter?size=_original

**20. Personal e-mail, letter, or interview**    Even though APA does not require you to list e-mails, personal interviews, letters, memos, or other personal communications in your References list, we recommend you do so for the sake of clarity. To cite an item in the text of your paper, include the author's first and middle initials (if known) and last name and the term "personal communication" (regardless of whether it was an interview, letter, or e-mail), and then the full date of the communication. In your References list, you can indicate in brackets the medium of the item, such as "E-mail."

### E-mail *(received)*

IN-TEXT CITATION

Metro State's first Undergraduate Research Conference was scheduled to take place in April (P. Ansburg, personal communication, February 9, 2012).

author of e-mail

REFERENCES LIST ENTRY

Ansburg, P. (2012, February 9). First annual metro state undergraduate research conference [E-mail].

### Interview *(conducted)*

IN-TEXT CITATION        person interviewed

I spoke to one tutor who described a method known as "glossing" (P. Calzia, personal communication, May 2, 2011).

REFERENCES LIST ENTRY

Calzia, P. (2011, May 2). Writing center discussion [Interview by E. Kleinfeld].

**21. Blog post or social media posting**    Cite postings as you would any short work from a Web site (see example 14). In your References list entry, add in brackets a brief description of the item: "Web log," "Facebook post," "Twitter post," and so on. Note: APA requires that you use the term "Web log." As with example 4, use the author's screen name if that is all that is provided.

IN-TEXT CITATION

      author

Marino (2012) used social media to convey some of the items on his bucket list.

REFERENCES LIST ENTRY

Marino, B. (2012). Bucket list [Facebook post]. Retrieved from http://www.facebook.com
    /billy.marino1

**22. Audio recording or podcast**    Cite podcasts that you've accessed online in the same way you would cite a short work from a Web site (see example 14). Audio recordings should be cited similarly to works of art, regardless of whether they are downloaded from the Web or not.

### Podcast from Web

IN-TEXT CITATION

Conan (2012) introduced listeners to historian Noah Andre Trudeau and described Trudeau's mission to collect artifacts from President Lincoln's presidency.

REFERENCES LIST ENTRY

Conan, N. (2012, February 9). Historian seeks artifacts from Lincoln's last days [Audio podcast]. Retrieved from National Public Radio Web site: http://www.npr.org
    /programs/talk-of-the-nation/

### Song from the Web *(via iTunes)*

IN-TEXT CITATION

Ritter's (2010) song "The Curse" played with the ideas of love at first sight and coming back from the dead.

REFERENCES LIST ENTRY

Ritter, J. (2010). The curse [Song]. On *So Runs the World Away*. Brea, CA: Pytheas Recordings. Retrieved from http://itunes.apple.com/us/album/change-of-time
    /id362130747?i=362130766&ign-mpt=uo%3D4

**23. Phone app**    Cite a phone app as you would an advertisement, but include "Phone app" in brackets. Use the date of the most recent iteration of the phone app as the publication date. Put the developer's or publisher's name where you would put an author for a print source.

IN-TEXT CITATION

The social media app called MassUp was created to help bicyclists gather in large groups (Bedno, 2010).
    app publisher

REFERENCES LIST ENTRY

Bedno, A. (2010, November 17). MassUp [Phone app.]. Retrieved from http://www
    .apple.com/webapps/sports/massup.html

**24. Government or business document**    For a government document, provide the author, government organization and department, title, and date, as well as publication information. If there is no author, provide the name of the government agency (and department, if any).

### Government document

One of the top concerns of organizers of farmers' markets was the availability of parking for customers (Ragland & Tropp, 2006, pp. 6-10).

authors

Ragland, E., & Tropp, D. U.S. Department of Agriculture, Agricultural Marketing

title of document

Service. (2006). *USDA national farmers market managers survey.* Washington, DC: U.S. Department of Agriculture, 6-10.

### Business document *(annual report)*

The company that makes Clif Bars had in place a plan that allowed employees to purchase stock in the company (Pham & Hammond, 2010).

authors

title of document

Pham, T., & Hammond, E. (Eds.). Clif Bar & Company (2010). All aspirations: Clif Bar & Company annual report [PDF file]. Retrieved from http://www.clifbar.com /uploads/default/ClifBar_AA2010.pdf

**25. Literary work (novel, poem, fairy tale, etc.)**   Provide the author, date, title, publisher's city, and publisher. For a selection (such as an essay) within a longer work (such as a collection of essays), provide the selection title before the full title.

One technique the author used was simile. For example, she described "bundled dough mounds" as being "as white and round as babies" (McCoy, 2012, p. 1).

### Novel *(print)*

McCoy, S. (2012). *The baker's daughter: A novel.* New York, NY: The Crown Publishing Group, 1-232.

### Novel *(e-book)*

McCoy, S. (2012). *The baker's daughter: A novel* [Kindle version]. Retrieved from http:// www.amazon.com/The-Bakers-Daughter-Novel-ebook/dp/B004W3IEI6

**26. Selection from an anthology or textbook**   Include the selection author, publication date, and selection title, followed by the anthology editors, anthology title, page range of selection, publisher's city, and publisher.

The cost of fruits and vegetables versus the cost of meat and dairy has had a lot to do with government subsidies (The Physicians Committee, 2012).

author of selection (shortened)

*author of selection*

The Physicians Committee for Responsible Medicine. (2012). Why does a salad cost
more than a Big Mac? [Chart]. In A. Braziller & E. Kleinfeld (Eds.), *Bedford book
of genres: A guide* (p. 121). Boston, MA: Bedford/St. Martin's.

*information on textbook where selection appears*

**27. Object/artifact (cereal box, etc.)**   If you find an object or artifact online, cite
it as a short work from a Web site, but include a description of the item in brackets.
If you find such a source in the physical world, cite it as a work with an author and
include a descriptor in brackets.

IN-TEXT CITATION
The box is a cheerful sunny yellow meant to attract children, but parents likely focus
on the red heart and the soft claim about lowering cholesterol (General Mills, 2012).

*author is an organization*

**Object** *(found online)*

REFERENCES LIST ENTRY
General Mills. (n.d.). Cheerios [Cereal box]. Retrieved from http://www.cheerios.com
/Products/Cheerios

**Object** *(found in physical world)*

REFERENCES LIST ENTRY
General Mills. (n.d.). Cheerios [Cereal box].

▲ OBJECT
**Cheerios box.**
*iStockphoto.*

# 8

# COMPOSING IN GENRES

**CONTENTS**

**FILM STILL** ▶
Hugh Jackman as
Wolverine, from
*X-Men*: a source
for student Gwen
Ganow's superhero
project. *Everett
Collection.*

By now you are familiar with a variety of genres (introduced in Chapters 1–4) and the choices writers and artists make. You've experienced a range of rhetorical situations and seen how composers work with genres. You've learned how to identify sources and draw on them to develop your ideas—from basic topic to research question to research plan (Chapters 5–7).

You've built your foundation. Now it's time to choose your genre—and create your own composition. To help you with this process, we've provided a model. In this chapter, we'll follow Gwen Ganow, one of Amy's former students, as she drafts, chooses her genre, revises, finishes, and polishes a film review and an accompanying Author's Statement.

As you'll see, choosing a genre and drafting are related activities that sometimes overlap. Sometimes you need to start drafting before you can decide on a genre, or vice versa.

In this chapter, we'll guide you through the following processes, along with Gwen, as she moves from exploratory draft to finished genre composition and accompanying Author's Statement. *(Gwen Ganow's superhero project presented in Chapters 8 through 10 appears by permission of Gwen Dalynn Ganow.)*

▲ STUDENT AUTHOR PHOTO **Gwen Ganow,** Amy's student at Red Rocks Community College. *This image appears throughout chapter by permission of Gwen Dalynn Ganow.*

# ROUGH DRAFTING

At this stage, you know your topic. You've formed a research question and gathered sources, and have a general idea of what you want to say. (For help with topics and research questions, see Chapter 5.) You may have decided on your genre, but don't worry if you haven't. Perhaps you know you want to persuade your audience about the importance of spaying and neutering pets, but aren't sure whether you'll create an editorial, a collage, or an ad, for example. Regardless, you'll want to get your ideas out of your head and down on paper (or up on your computer screen).

## Advice for Rough Drafting

As you begin your rough/exploratory draft, remember that it is just for you. No one else ever needs to see it. Think of your first draft not as an organized, perfect piece of writing with a clear purpose, but as a messy opportunity for creativity and experimentation.

Don't worry about a thesis, or about being logical or eloquent. Instead, focus on quantity rather than quality. That's right: quantity not quality. Think of words in the first draft as raw materials. You want as much raw material to work with as possible. Imagine an artist beginning a painting. Would she have only the exact amount of paint she needs to create her piece? What if she changes her mind

☞ **Attention, composers! Wondering how to begin?**

As you think about what form your composition will take, ask yourself the following:

- What do I want to accomplish? Who is my primary audience, and how will I connect with my audience?

- What genre will work best for my rhetorical situation and be most persuasive?

- What genre(s) am I already an expert in? Which are the most challenging? Which work best with my schedule?

For an Index of Sources & Contexts for material referenced in this chapter; see the e-Pages at **bedfordstmartins.com /bookofgenres.**

midway through the painting and wants to use more yellow than red? Wouldn't it make sense for her to begin with extra paint in each color to allow her the flexibility to modify her ideas? Writing and other kinds of composing are similar. Beginning with more words than you need gives you more options. Here are some pointers for getting your first draft written:

1. Set a timer for thirty minutes and force yourself to write for the entire time, not stopping for anything. That means no stopping to reread and correct or to refer to sources or models, and definitely no stopping to check Facebook.

2. Don't stop to correct or edit what is on the page.

3. Write until you have five thousand words or you run out of time.

Don't worry about grammar, punctuation, spelling, transitions, topic sentences, organization, titles, and so on. Don't even worry about genre or what the finished piece will look or sound like. Once you have your thoughts down, you can think logically about your purpose, audience, and the points you want to convey.

At this stage, if you're putting pressure on yourself to write flawless, beautiful prose, remind yourself of the term *rough draft*—with *rough* being defined as coarse, rugged, crude, unrefined, graceless, unfinished, tentative, imperfect, or approximate. Take a little more pressure off by thinking of Anne Lamott's phrase "shitty first draft." Everybody, including published authors, writes them.

Let's take a look at one student's drafting process. When Gwen Ganow took a composition class with Amy at Red Rocks Community College, she composed an argument about superheroes and social attitudes, starting with this question:

**RESEARCH QUESTION**
**To what extent do superheroes reflect real-world values and attitudes?**

She then moved from that question to an exploratory rough draft.

▲ STUDENT AUTHOR PHOTO **Gwen Ganow.**

## Guided Reading: A Rough Draft

### Gwen Ganow (Student)

### *Superhero Project: Rough Draft*

Gwen began with some exploratory drafting to solidify what she wanted to say about superhero comics and social attitudes.

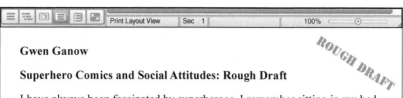

**Gwen Ganow**

**Superhero Comics and Social Attitudes: Rough Draft**

I have always been fascinated by superheroes. I remember sitting in my bedroom in second grade looking at some comic books. You might say I was sort of obsessed with them as time went on. I had posters that I would sit in bed and stare at. In a way, they were my first love.

Man, those superheroes—very, very cool. I loved the power they had.

Power things: challenges and obstacles—evil men trying to destroy someone—usually evil men, seldom women. The superhero protects the innocent people.

Seems that the city was always the setting—can't remember a superhero in the suburbs—why are they set in the city?

Regardless of challenges, the superhero wins. Why can't they die? What would that mean? Losing hope, maybe. Okay, that's a downer. I need them to win.

They always seemed like giant protectors and a way for me to escape. I remember that I didn't really have a favorite superhero at the time, but rather loved them for their concept. At night I would find myself reading even after lights out, wanting to see how the superhero would save the day.

Prejudice or intolerance—superheroes are often seen as different in a bad way. It causes social problems for them. They worry that their loved ones will be hurt—like Spider-Man and Mary Jane. The superhero is actually a victim of injustice. Many become superheroes because of injustice in their life, like Batman's parents being murdered.

I think of superheroes sometimes as the champions fighting discrimination. They take out the evil powers. I'm thinking I'd like to explore some of how they do that. Do they fight racial injustice? Are there other forms of intolerance?

Other areas of intolerance in life: racism, sexism, prejudice against GLBT community?

---

**What characterizes a rough draft?**

**THE GENRE'S CONVENTIONS**

**Elements of the genre**

A rough draft is characterized by free-form thought and questions. It is really a brainstorming tool to discover what you've learned from research, what you think of your topic, and what you might want to say about it.

*(Continued on p. 440.)*

**What is the author, Gwen Ganow, doing?**

**GWEN'S RHETORICAL SITUATION**

**Purpose**

In this early draft, Gwen explores possible angles for her project. She thinks about how she might pursue her research question: "To what extent do superheroes reflect real-world values and attitudes?"

*(Continued on p. 440.)*

## THE GENRE'S CONVENTIONS

### Style

Gwen is not worried about style, grammar, or how the draft reads. It's not meant to be perfect. Her writing is very casual, as if she's writing in a journal to herself.

### Design

A rough draft is not designed. It's typically a Microsoft Word document.

### Sources

Gwen does not discuss sources in this draft, but she could have, depending on how far along she was in her research process.

## GWEN'S RHETORICAL SITUATION

She allows herself to be unfocused as she starts with her fascination with superheroes. After doing this low-stakes drafting she realizes that she wants to cover how superheroes fight intolerance.

### Audience

At this point, Gwen is writing for herself and her instructor, Amy. They'll go over this draft together to try to pin down a direction. Gwen will later identify a specific outside-of-the-classroom audience.

### Rhetorical appeals

Gwen is not concerned right now about ethos, logos, and pathos. She's in exploration mode.

### Modes & media

Gwen e-mailed this Word document to her instructor.

After writing her first draft, Gwen talked with Amy about directions she might take with her topic. Together they decided that Gwen should look back at her initial research, specifically the sources dealing with the history of comics.

CHECKLIST **Getting Started on a Rough Draft?** Keep the following questions in mind.

### Exploration

- ☐ **What do I already know about my topic?** What intrigues me about this topic? What questions do I still have about it?
- ☐ **Based on my research so far, what arguments am I familiar with about this topic?** Are there some that resonate for me more than others? Do I have an opinion on this topic?
- ☐ **Is there a way to narrow my topic** by time, place, demographics, or something else? For example, if I write about gun control, do I focus on guns on college campuses (narrow by place) or the growth of shooting ranges geared toward women (narrow by demographics)?

### Rhetorical Situation

- ☐ **What is my purpose?** What do I want to say—and how do I want to say it? Do I want to tell a story? Inform? Persuade? Some combination?
- ☐ **Who am I composing for?** Is my primary audience mainly the other students in this course? My instructor? Anyone with access to the course space or blog? Or to the campus newspaper or Web site? Who makes up my secondary audience? Am I writing for a broader, more public audience too? For others on campus? For anyone with an Internet connection?
- ☐ **How will I connect with my audience?** How will I establish my authority as a composer (ethos) so that my readers will trust me? What is the most logical way for me to present what I have to say? To what extent will I want to appeal to my audience's emotions? For example, if I want to persuade people to take a certain action, how will I cultivate their enthusiasm?

# REREADING & ANNOTATING SOURCES

We believe that critical reading is a crucial part of the composing process. By critical reading, we mean more than simply moving your eyes across a page of text. When you read critically, you read with an eye for detail, noticing not just *what* another author or artist says but *how* she says it. For example, imagine you are reading an article in *The Onion* that you think is hilarious. As you read, you relate to the content and subject, but you might also zoom in on what the author does to make the piece so funny: maybe using a lot of exaggeration and sarcasm, as well as clever details. You might then try using exaggeration and sarcasm in a piece you are writing, to heighten the humor.

Earlier in this book, we focused on reading a variety of genres (Chapters 1–4), on reading to explore topics and creating a research plan (Chapter 5), and on previewing, evaluating, and choosing sources (Chapter 6). When you read as part of your composing process, we recommend the following steps.

## Steps for Rereading & Annotating Sources

**Step 1. Preview each source.** If you've already done this earlier in your process, do it again to refresh your memory. (For a more thorough explanation, see "How Do I Preview a Source Critically?" on pp. 314–21.) Ask yourself the following:

» Who is the author of this text (remember, a text can be written words, video, an audio podcast, or something else)? What, if anything, do I know about him or her? Are any details or credentials provided?

» What can I figure out from the title? A title will usually hint at an author's topic and purpose. Consider two titles: "How to Conserve Water at Home" and "Political Factors Affecting Nationwide Water Conservation Efforts." Both pieces are obviously about saving water, but the titles make clear that the authors wrote for different purposes and audiences. The first piece is most likely aimed at homeowners and is probably very straightforward; the second piece sounds more technical and may have been written for scientists, a government agency, or some other specialized audience.

» What can I determine about this piece based on where it was published or appeared?

**Step 2. Mark up each source.** This means writing notes on the piece you are reading (or if the piece is not text-based—say you're working with video—using the annotating tools at your disposal). Annotating is different from highlighting. Highlighting allows you to remind yourself of what you found interesting or important as you read, but it doesn't allow you to record why you found things interesting or important. Annotating is more active; it gives you the chance to record your critical thoughts as you read more closely. It also keeps you engaged with the text, as it allows you to "talk back" to it.

We advise that you follow steps 3–7 as you annotate, incorporating these points into your notes.

**Step 3. Identify each author's purpose & main points.**   What is the author's purpose? How clear is it? Can you put it in your own words? This is a good way to check your own understanding of what you're reading. If you can summarize what you've read in your own words—that is, without quoting the piece you've read—then you probably understand it. By the same token, if you can't summarize it in your own words, chances are you don't fully grasp what you've read and you should reread more carefully.

**Step 4. Identify each author's audience.**   Who do you think is the composer's primary audience? What makes you think so? Can you tell who the author's secondary audiences might be? How does the author address his or her audience? What kind of relationship does the author try to create with the audience? For example, if the author writes in the first person and addresses the audience as "you," that creates a sense of intimacy. How do you feel toward the author and why?

**Step 5. Analyze each author's use of sources, evidence, & rhetorical appeals.**   Notice whether the piece presents statistics, anecdotes, personal experiences, or other types of evidence to support its points. Also note whether the piece is using ethos, pathos, or logos. As you notice these things, keep in mind that if you are positively affected by the use of evidence and rhetorical appeals in the piece, you might want to try the same techniques in your own writing.

**Step 6. Pay some attention to the genre and the conventions that are evident.**   Keep your eyes open for how genre conventions help you identify the genre. Begin thinking about how you could incorporate the conventions into your own genre piece. Which features and conventions get your attention and guide you through the piece? For example, do images give you a clearer picture of statistics that would otherwise confuse you?

**Step 7. Notice each author's style & techniques.**   Be aware of how the writing affects you, and notice techniques you might want to try yourself. Whenever you see an author doing something particularly effective or interesting—say, integrating dialogue or introducing an image or presenting an argument—note how the author does it so that you can try it yourself.

CHECKLIST **Analyzing Sources & Genres as You Draft?** Keep the following questions in mind.

## The Rhetorical Situation

☐ **Purpose.** What seems to be the author's purpose? How is that purpose made clear? How is that purpose achieved? How could I use similar techniques to establish my purpose in the piece I'm drafting?

☐ **Audience.** Who seems to be the targeted audience for the piece? How is that made clear? How are vocabulary, examples and details, organization, and other elements geared toward the targeted reader? How could I use similar techniques to engage my audience?

☐ **Rhetorical appeals.** How does the author use rhetorical appeals to connect with the audience? How could I use similar appeals in my own piece?

☐ **Modes & media.** How does the author's choice of mode and medium affect my level of engagement with the piece? For example, if the piece is a video, does the background music keep me interested or distract me? Can I use the author's choices about mode and medium as models for my own choices? Or as cautionary tales?

## The Genre's Conventions

☐ **Elements of the genre.** How does the author use the elements of the genre to guide me through the piece? If I am composing in the same genre, how can I use the elements of the genre to guide readers through the piece?

☐ **Style.** How do the word choices, sentence structures, use of literary devices (like metaphor), and other stylistic techniques used by the author get me engaged in the piece? How can I use similar stylistic techniques to keep my readers engaged?

☐ **Design.** How has the author used design elements, such as color, images, and font, to emphasize the purpose and main point? How could I use similar design elements to convey my purpose and main point?

☐ **Sources.** What kinds of sources does the author refer to? How are these sources cited? How does the author make it clear when source material has been consulted? How can I use the author's strategies with sources as a model (or anti-model) for what I want to do?

## Guided Process: How to Reread & Annotate a Source

### Gwen Ganow (Student)

### *Superhero Project: An Annotated Source*

▲ STUDENT AUTHOR
PHOTO **Gwen
Ganow.**

Gwen decided to return to her sources, which included Dwight Decker's essay "Fredric Wertham: Anti-Comics Crusader Who Turned Advocate" (see p. 445), Brandford Wright's book *Comic Book Nation*, and various comic books by Alex Ross. She focused on the Dwight Decker essay, which she had found through a simple Google search on the history of comics. She especially liked how the author of the piece approached comics as a subject worthy of serious study. She also liked the author's tone and thought she might want to use a similar tone in her own writing. In this way, Gwen read this piece as both a source of information and a source of inspiration for *how* to write about her topic.

Gwen found Dwight Decker's article at *The Art Bin*, a magazine published by Karl-Erik Tallmo of Slowfox Press and archived at the press's blog. Decker notes at the end of his article: "This is a re-written version of an article that appeared in the magazine *Amazing Heroes* in 1987. Also available in Swedish. © Dwight Decker, 1987, 1997." *Amazing Heroes* (1981–1992, published by Fantagraphics Books) was a magazine about comics for comic book fans.

Also included with Decker's article is the following biography:

"Born 1952, Dwight R. Decker has been an active comics fan since 1967. By day he is a technical writer in the electronics industry, and by night he works as a freelance comics translator for publishers in the United States and Europe. [Decker] publishes his own fanzine, *Torch*, [and is] presently living in Phoenix, Arizona."

*("Fredric Wertham—Anti-Comics Crusader Who Turned Advocate" by Dwight R. Decker is reprinted here by permission of the author, © Dwight R. Decker.)*

# Fredric Wertham – Anti-Comics Crusader Who Turned Advocate

by Dwight Decker

Illustration:
Asa Harvard

In the late 1940s and early 1950s, a distinguished psychiatrist named Dr. Fredric Wertham made a name for himself in the United States by leading a crusade against violent comic books. His 1954 book exposing the comic-book industry, *Seduction of the Innocent*, is still remembered in American comics fandom as a wildly exaggerated and overwrought polemic and has gone on to become a collector's item in its own right. Even the comic books mentioned in the text or used as source illustrations have also become collector's items because of their association with him and the book. Facing a public relations nightmare and hearings by the U.S. Senate subcommittee on juvenile delinquency, fearful publishers either went out of business or banded together to form a Comics Code Authority that would censor comic books before some outside body did it for them.

American comics fans have no cause to love Dr. Wertham. They remember him as the man who attacked comics with his hysterical book, helped kill EC Comics (the one publisher doing anything like adult-level material), and brought on the Comics Code that reduced American comics to a childish mentality. Many fans have associated Dr. Wertham with Senator Joseph McCarthy, well-known for his anti-Communist crusade at about the same time, and legends circulate of Dr. Wertham accusing comic books of being a Communist plot or some such.

**"Seduction of the Innocent—the influence of comic books on today's youth."** On the book's inner flap you could read: **"90,000,000 comic books are read each month. You think they are mostly about floppy-eared bunnies, attractive little mice and chipmunks? Go take a look."**

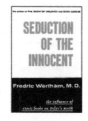

SEDUCTION
OF THE
INNOCENT

Fredric Wertham, M. D.

*the influence of
comic books on today's youth*

The actual story is somewhat different, and much more complicated. As an indicator of the general trend of Dr. Wertham's thinking, consider these three quotes from his various books:

> I have known many adults who have treasured throughout their lives some of the books they read as children. I have never come across any adult or adolescent who had outgrown comic-book reading who would ever dream of keeping any of these "books" for any sentimental or other reason. —*Seduction of the Innocent* (1954)

> When *Seduction of the Innocent* appeared in the middle fifties, it started a grass-roots social reaction. . . . A change occurred. Murder in comic books decreased, and so did the number of crime-comic-book publishers. Within a few years after the publication of *Seduction of the Innocent*, twenty-four out of twenty-nine crime-comic-book publishers went out of business. But it was only a partial victory. We now meet some of the child

*Continues next page*

Gwen's notes on
Decker's article

I see from his bio that the author, Dwight Decker, is a freelance comic translator.

The title suggests a focus on one man, with the purpose of showing how Wertham changed his stance on the value of comics.

Decker's purpose seems to be to inform readers about the complex life of a man who rejected and then embraced comics. The article also seems to be a commentary on the value of comics, to some extent.

At the end of the piece, Decker notes that the article originally appeared in *Amazing Heroes*. I Googled "Amazing Heroes" and found out it's a defunct magazine for comic book fans. So Decker was writing to an audience who knew something about comics. It doesn't seem to be an analytical journal, per se, but this piece seems rather scholarly to me.

comic-book readers as parents of the "battered child" or in similar roles. Moreover, very many of the old comic books are still around at reduced prices. —*A Sign for Cain* (1966)

Comic-book collecting which started as a nice nostalgic hobby is in some danger of becoming an overpriced, overcommercialized transaction. —*The World of Fanzines* (1974)

A man probably has a right to change his mind over the course of twenty years, but did Dr. Wertham really change his? How did a prominent psychiatrist and author get mixed up with comic books in the first place?

**Fredric Wertham, 1895–1981.**

According to his obituary in the *New York Times* (December 1, 1981), Fredric Wertham was born in Munich, Germany, in 1895. He studied at Kings College in London and at the Universities of Munich and Erlangen, and received his MD from the University of Würzburg in 1921. He did post-graduate study in London, Vienna, and Paris, and correspondence with Sigmund Freud led him to take up psychiatry as his life's work. He settled in the United States in 1922, becoming a citizen in 1927.

Wertham's subsequent career was impressive. He held the posts of senior psychiatrist for the New York City Department of Hospitals and director of the mental hygiene clinics at Bellevue Hospital and later Queens General Hospital. He was also director of the Lafargue Clinic in Harlem, a mental hygiene clinic for the poor in a mostly black section of New York City. His article for the *American Journal of Psychotherapy*, "Psychological Effects of School Segregation," was submitted to the United States Supreme Court as an important piece of evidence in the legal case that led to the 1954 ruling that declared racial segregation in schools to be unconstitutional.

Where Dr. Wertham made his name was as a consulting psychiatrist for the court system. The psychiatric clinic he directed for the New York City court was probably the first clinic in the United States in which all convicted felons received a psychiatric examination. His recommendations led to the modernization of facilities and methodology at many mental and criminal holding institutions.

Dr. Wertham was also an author. His first book was *The Brain as an Organ* (1934), a straightforward scientific work. *Dark Legend,* however, was a psychological case history of a seventeen-year-old boy who murdered his mother, written for a more general audience and with literary allusions. The reviews were mostly favorable, though an MD referred to "slips and inconsistencies which definitely mar the book as a scientific study." Criticisms of sloppy writing would dog every book Wertham wrote. His 1949 book, *Show of Violence,* is a general study of murder in which he discusses some of the major murder cases he was involved with as either a court witness or a consultant.

Parents and educators had been complaining about comic books for years. As early as December, 1940, when comic books were still in their infancy, the *National Education Association Journal* ran an article discussing "An Antidote to the Comic Magazine Poison." Dr. Wertham ran into comic books in the course of his work with juvenile offenders, and noting that many of the delinquents read them avidly, concluded that they were important environmental factors leading the kids to crime and violence. He presented his case in an article published in the May 29, 1947, issue of the *Saturday Review of Literature,* and after that he was off and running in his crusade against violent comic books. Over the next seven years, he would give lectures, write articles, and testify as an expert witness before legislative committees investigating the comic-book menace, culminating in the publication of his book *Seduction of the Innocent* in 1954.

Latterday American comics fans, who look back at the anti-comics crusade with fear and loathing, and fret nervously over whether it might happen again, tend to ignore the point that comics publishers of the early '50s virtually cut their own throats. While Dr. Wertham overstated his case to a sometimes ludicrous degree, he didn't have to: comics really were as crude, violent, and tasteless as he claimed, as any parent or legislator could easily confirm. With the postwar eclipse of costume heroes, comic books moved into increasingly violent and graphic crime and horror. Parents and legislators were worried enough about children seeing pictures of endless murders and mutilations and severed body parts in comics that were anything but fuzzy bunny books; then a distinguished psychiatrist came along and told them exactly what they had suspected all along—yes, children who read crime comic books became hardened to violence, and even accepted it as a useful problem-solving device. Comic books taught children to be cruel, sexually warped, dishonest, and contemptuous of soft virtues like pity or love. Comic books were still relatively mild in 1947 when Dr. Wertham began his crusade, but some publishers lost all restraint into the 1950s, running increasingly violent and gory stories that only confirmed everything he said.

This researched argument originally appeared in *The Art Bin*, an early online magazine, now archived by its publisher, Karl-Erik Tallmo.

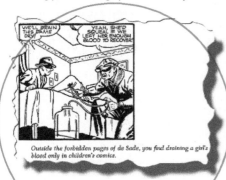

*Outside the forbidden pages of de Sade, you find draining a girl's blood only in children's comics.*

**One of Dr. Wertham's samples from the book, with his own caption.**

*Seduction of the Innocent* is a remarkable book. Like most of Dr. Wertham's publications, it is short on proof of its assertions and long on polemics, anecdotes related without any sources cited, and literary quotations or allusions crowbarred into the text. Several generations of comics fans have had a chance to discover the book and react to it now, and everything you've heard about it is probably true. Dr. Wertham does accuse Superman of being a fascist, Batman and Robin of being a homosexual fantasy of a man and a boy living together, and Wonder Woman of being just plain kinky (judging from the early years of that strip, with all the downright astonishing emphasis on bondage and submission, I'd have to say he called that one pretty well). He does make the claim that comic-book drawings contain "pictures within pictures" for "those who know how to look," his Exhibit A being the shading of a man's shoulder muscles that supposedly evoke a woman's naked torso when squinted at right. Dr. Wertham does badly misinterpret a few stories, notably an EC one in which some overly patriotic citizens beat a man to death for not saluting the flag, only to discover at the end that he was blind and couldn't see it; Wertham claimed that the story *favored* rough treatment of insufficiently patriotic individuals, somehow missing the point of a fairly heavyhanded story.

This researched argument, in effect, is posted on a blog, but does not reflect the typical conventions such as hyperlinks and comments, for example. This may be because it was published in the early days of the Internet, before blog conventions were what they are now.

I like the use of text and images— and also Decker's personable but authoritative style. He isn't simply an excited comics fan; he seems like a scholar and takes comics seriously. He persuades me that comics are a worthy topic of study and that I could write about them seriously myself.

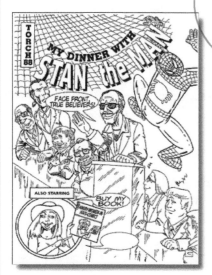

**Mr. Decker's own fanzine *Torch*.**
*By permission of Douglas Jones.*

**NOTE: Several paragraphs are intentionally omitted. Decker's final paragraphs appear below. —Eds.**

*Continues next page*

Dr. Wertham's account in the introductory chapter [of his book *The World of Fanzines*] of how he got involved with fanzines is interesting, as he doesn't mention *Seduction of the Innocent* or his anti-comic book work in the '50s. The unknowing reader is left with the impression that Wertham is simply a public figure known for his "writings or talks on such subjects as mass media, youth problems, or violence," and fanzine editors sent him their publications just to communicate pleasantly with the nice gentleman in response. Wertham gives no hint of his personal position in the world of fanzines as a near-legendary bogeyman, regarded by many of their editors and contributors as incarnate evil walking the earth.

He seemed to only reluctantly acknowledge comic books and science fiction as the source of fanzines and fandom, and gave a couple of the most skewed capsule histories of the genres I've ever seen, concentrating on their anti-war and non-violent aspects. In discussing the comics fanzines' emphasis on superheroes, he offered the remark that "the creative imagination of fanzine writers and artists, especially the younger ones, tends in the direction of heroes, maybe in that lies a message for our unheroic age." This is more than a little remarkable coming from the man who in *Seduction* classified superheroes as a bizarre variant of "crime comics" and thought Superman in particular was a fascist avatar. Mostly, he glosses over the comic-book connection of comics fandom, treating it puzzledly or condescendingly when he can't avoid it, and seems to proceed on the premise that fandom just spontaneously organized itself as a communications vehicle for teenagers, with comic books only an incidental, even accidental aspect of it all. As usual, Dr. Wertham concentrates on violence and is delighted to report that there isn't any in the world of fanzines.

*The World of Fanzines* is a masterpiece of scholarship gone off the track. It's the only book you'll find about its subject in most libraries even though the author never quite understood what he was writing about. He never said as much—he couldn't admit it for the sake of professional pride, perhaps—but *The World of Fanzines* contradicts everything Dr. Wertham wrote about comic books and their readers in his previous books.

In the end, he decided, we'd turned out pretty much all right.

# CHOOSING A GENRE TO COMPOSE IN

After reviewing your sources and creating a rough, exploratory draft, you should have a better sense of what you want to say about your topic. Your next decision is to choose a genre. You may find the checklist on page 450 helpful.

## Steps for Choosing a Genre to Compose In

**Step 1. Revisit your topic & research question.** Remember that rough draft? Since you've done more reading and analyzed a variety of genres, what's changed for you? How might that affect your focus?

**Step 2. Focus on your purpose.** Look over your initial draft and highlight some of the main ideas you want to explore. Make a list of four or five of them. Next, choose the idea that energizes you the most, the one that you will be most excited to write about. Then, decide on the primary purpose of the piece you are composing.

**Step 3. Really think about your audience.**   Consider your audience. Keep in mind that aspects of your topic that are obvious to you may not be obvious to your audience.

**Step 4. Strategize on how you'll use rhetorical appeals.**   Start thinking about how to appeal to your audience's senses of ethos, logos, and pathos. Many composers begin with only a general sense of how they will use rhetorical appeals, but while drafting realize which appeals will be most effective.

**Step 5. Consider your mode & medium.**   Once you have narrowed the scope of your purpose and audience, think about whether you want to work with text, visuals, video, audio, or some combination. Consider the advantages of each, as well as your skills and the tools available to you. If you have access to a multimodal composing lab on campus, you may be more interested in experimenting with sound and images than if you have to teach yourself how to use sound- and image-editing software.

**Step 6. Narrow your choices down to three possible genres.**   Now that you have your purpose and audience, and are developing a sense of how you'll work with text and other media, put together a short list of potential genres you want to consider composing in. At this point, it can be helpful to look at the particular conventions of the genres you are considering.

**Step 7. Look at examples of the three genres you're interested in.**   There are many features to consider when looking at genre:

» **Is point of view important for your purpose and audience?**   Determining the point of view for your genre piece helps you narrow your genre selection. If you need your piece to be first person so that it includes your perspective, then make sure you choose a genre that accommodates this point of view.

» **What type of connection do you want to establish with your audience?**   If you want to remain at a critical distance from your audience in order to establish a more authoritative voice, you might choose a genre that emphasizes ethos in its rhetorical appeal. If you want to make a closer connection with your audience, perhaps appealing to their emotions regarding the topic, then you might choose a genre that emphasizes pathos.

» **What tone do you want to use in order to achieve your purpose?**   Some writers, especially those composing a scientific report, for example, adopt a formal tone, one that perhaps incorporates jargon from the field that will be familiar to his or her readers. If you want your piece to have that level of formality, make sure to choose a genre that utilizes formality. On the other hand, if you desire to convey your message using a more informal tone, look for genres whose style is marked by a less formal tone.

**Step 8. Zero in on how you'll use your sources.**   Finally, you'll need to think about how you will use sources in your piece—and how the genre you're considering typically deals with sources. You may realize that you need to do more research or simply reread the sources you've gathered more carefully. You'll also want to look at samples of the genre you're thinking of working in. Keep this in mind: Genre decisions at this point are still tentative; as you draft, you may stumble upon a completely different genre idea that fits your purpose, audience, and other aspects of your rhetorical situation. Keep an open mind as you draft. Remember that the drafting process is a process of discovery.

---

**CHECKLIST** **Choosing a Genre?** Keep the following questions in mind.

### The Rhetorical Situation

- ☐ **Purpose.** What is my purpose? Which genres are best for what I want to do? If I want to persuade, should I consider creating an advertisement? An editorial? Something else?

- ☐ **Audience.** How familiar is my audience with my topic? What assumptions might my audience make about my topic? What expectations will my audience have about my piece?

- ☐ **Rhetorical appeals.** How will I connect with my audience? For example, if I create an ad or an editorial, how will I work within that genre to be as compelling and convincing as possible?

- ☐ **Modes & media.** What is the best mode for saying what I want to say? If I rely on text only, will anything be lost? And what medium would be best?

### The Genre's Conventions

- ☐ **Elements of the genres.** What are my favorite genres? Which ones do I know the most about? Which ones do I want to try out? Which ones can I get help with? Among the sources I've drawn on in my research, which ones stood out? What are their genres? What features make a particular genre what it is? How would I use (or not use) those features?

- ☐ **Style.** What are my strengths as a writer/composer? What tone will be most appropriate for my composition, considering the genre I choose to use? For example, if I create an ad, can I be funny? What kind of vocabulary would I use? How much detail would be appropriate?

- ☐ **Design.** Once I choose the genre for my composition, how will it look (or sound)? Will I use a conventional design, or perhaps tailor a standard layout or structure to my own purposes?

- ☐ **Sources.** What do I already know about my topic? What sources have I gathered? Which ones will work best as sources for my composition, and why? To what extent will I need to draw on my sources? Will I need to quote from them? Document them?

---

# Guided Process: How to Choose a Genre to Compose In ▼

## Gwen Ganow (Student)

### *Superhero Project: Brainstorm to Refine Topic & Purpose*

In the following pages, Gwen Ganow decides which genre she'd like to compose in. She does so by:

1. Brainstorming about her topic and rhetorical situation
2. Looking at three examples of persuasive genres: an ad, a researched argument, and a film review
3. Deciding how she wants to use sources—and which genre will work best overall. In this section, Gwen moves from brainstorming about a possible genre to compose in—to making a final choice about which genre will be best for her project. (Spoiler alert: It's a film review.)

▲ STUDENT AUTHOR
PHOTO **Gwen
Ganow.**

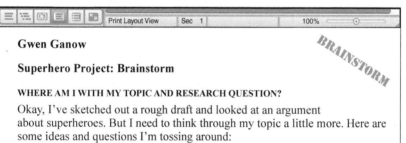

Gwen Ganow

**Superhero Project: Brainstorm**

BRAINSTORM

**WHERE AM I WITH MY TOPIC AND RESEARCH QUESTION?**

Okay, I've sketched out a rough draft and looked at an argument about superheroes. But I need to think through my topic a little more. Here are some ideas and questions I'm tossing around:

- Now that I've read some more, I may focus totally on superheroes, rather than comics as a whole. Good idea?
- Most comics have superheroes. Why? Also, they are kind of underdogs with power. What does that have to do with the real world?
- Superheroes are sort of in the real world—but also in a kind of magical world where they always persevere. Why this duality?
- Superheroes use their power to protect others. Why do they care so much? And why do fans seem to need superheroes to win?
- Superheroes mainly fight injustice. Superheroes are themselves almost always victims of injustice.
    - I like the injustice angle, which gets back to my idea of writing about a social issue. Not sure what I'll say, but I may present an argument about superheroes, power, and social inequality.

**WHAT IS MY PURPOSE?**

I need to decide what I want to say. Also, how and why. What do I want to present to my audience about superheroes? Do I want to:

*Continues next page*

### Gwen's notes on her project

My early research question about comics and social attitude—"To what extent do superheroes reflect real-world values and attitudes?"—is too broad.

Will revise to something like: How/why are superheroes victims of injustice? What does that have to do with their fight against injustice?

**Ganow, *Superhero Project: Brainstorm,* Continued**

**Gwen's notes on
her project**

What I really want
to do is present
some type of per-
suasive argument
about superheroes.

| ☰ ☷ ▣ ▤ ▤ ▣ | Print Layout View | Sec 1 | 100% ⊙ |

### Tell a story?

I could tell a story about a superhero fighting some evil. The story would show some societal intolerance, maybe racism, and it would show how the superhero struggles but ultimately wins. But that's not really a fresh concept. Also, what would be the advantage of telling a story? Would I create a work of fiction with a moral or lesson—or a narrative essay? I'm not sure that's right for my topic.

### Report information?

I might present information about how a superhero fights injustice. Instead of telling a story, I would give concrete information so that my reader sees how the superhero ultimately promotes tolerance. How do superheroes promote tolerance? If I took on that question, I'd need to provide information. I'd also offer analysis through my perspective. More like arguing a case. Hmm.

### Persuade?

I could try to convince people that we need superheroes in the world to fight intolerance. I might use my idea of how we need hope and how superheroes give us that hope. Also, what are superheroes—and why do we need them? So I'd be defining superheroes, but also creating a persuasive argument. The question now is, how? Would an advertisement be a good idea, or some other persuasive genre?

### WHO IS MY AUDIENCE?
### Okay, who do I want my target readers/viewers to be?

Mainly, people who enjoy comics. Probably they read them as children and teens because they loved the stories and heroes. Also, my classmates and in-structor. Beyond the people in my course, I'd like to aim at a primary audience of people who are really into comics—who know something about them and their history. A kind of expert audience.

I know I want to
make a case about
superheroes. I see
my primary audi-
ence as comic and
superhero fans like
me. I see my sec-
ondary audience
as people who may
have less interest
in superheroes.

So I have a mix of potential readers—my primary, expert audience of comics fans—and people in my classroom who may have varying levels of knowledge and interest in the topic.

### What do they know about superheroes?

My primary audience already knows something about superheroes. They aren't necessarily as obsessed as I am, but they have a certain passion about the topic. They do have some level of specialized knowledge, which means I'll have to craft my argument in ways to hook in uninterested people—but also speak to my core readers (appreciative fans).

### What expectations will they have?

As comic book lovers/experts, my target audience will expect me to be well-informed about superheroes. If I'm going to persuade them of something, I'll need to draw on evidence and details from comics to support my points. Whatever genre I choose for my composition, something visual and narrative will appeal to this audience.

*Ganow, **Superhero Project: Brainstorm,** Continued*

**Gwen's notes on her project**

**What assumptions might they already hold about superheroes?**
For most comic readers, superheroes save the day. They represent good battling evil (or vice versa) and usually do a lot of rescuing (or sabotage). At least these are my own assumptions as a comics expert.

**HOW WILL I USE RHETORICAL APPEALS?**
**Ethos**
I think of ethos as having to do with authority. As an author, if I want to persuade my audience, it's going to be crucial to convince them that my information and argument are credible—and that I am qualified (or authorized) to make the argument. I've grown up with comics and have a good base of knowledge; I'll establish that in my composition. That will help me with my ethos.

I'll be making an argument, so it makes sense to emphasize ethos (my own authority as a comics fan) and logos (logic) to reach my audience. Also pathos—my primary audience has an emotional relationship with comics.

**Logos**
I associate logos with logic. I'll need to build a logical case for my audience. How to do this will become clearer once I choose a genre, I think. But I'll need to be methodical and organized. Depending on the form my composition takes, I'll have to find ways to present and support my argument clearly. Thinking back to some of my sources, I like how Dwight Decker does that in his researched essay. Maybe reread?

**Pathos**
Emotions. Hmm. I'm not totally sure how I'll work with pathos. But part of what makes me care about superheroes is my emotional connection to them as people who care—who put themselves "in harm's way," as they say, to help and rescue others. I hadn't thought of tapping into emotions in my piece, but it might come in handy, especially if I emphasize superheroes as righters of wrongs and fighters of injustice. I also may want to use humor as a persuasive strategy.

**WHAT MODES AND MEDIA WILL I WORK WITH?**
Even though I don't know what genre I'll compose in, I should probably think of the media I'm most comfortable with. That might impact my choice of genre. Okay, so will my composition be:

**Visual? Textual?**
My composition will probably have more text than visuals. My comics-fan audience may expect visuals, but I'm more comfortable working in text—and presenting arguments that way. Also, I'll be drawing on sources. How would I do that in a nontextual medium? Though it might be fun to branch out into working with images.

I think I'll use both words and images—but mainly words. I'd like my sources to be apparent, especially to online readers. I'd also like to be able to integrate/embed media such as video.

I'm a good writer, but I feel less comfortable as an artist. Maybe I can use existing images from comics in my work to support my points. (Many of my sources are visual.) Or maybe it doesn't matter that creating visuals isn't my strong suit. Should I experiment?

*Continues next page*

**Ganow, *Superhero Project: Brainstorm,* Continued**

**Gwen's notes on her project**

I want to be persuasive—what genres will help me convince my audience of comics lovers of my views on superheroes? Given my skills and timeframe, I'd consider three possibilities: an ad, a researched argument (which I could morph into a presentation), or a film review.

**Sound? Motion (video or animation)? Other digital delivery?**
I probably won't use sound, but I would consider using video clips from superhero films or animated works. I'd need to use existing content because I don't have expertise in creating this stuff myself. Also, I have a limited time frame. In a future iteration of this project, I might use other media. I might even collaborate with someone who knows how to work with video.

If I create a written text for a digital environment, I can embed links. That might be an easy way to bring in my sources. I'd like to build into my work some existing clips from films and animations.

**WHAT ARE SOME PERSUASIVE GENRES? WHICH ONE SHOULD I CHOOSE?**
Here are the genres I'm familiar with that are associated with persuading. Which option do I like best?

**Ad?**
I like that I could mix visuals with text if I made an ad. Where would I publish this ad? It would need to be somewhere that comic book fans would see it. Not sure where that would be. I also like the idea of making a commercial. Sounds fun. An ad is very obviously persuasive. This could work for me, though it wouldn't showcase my sources. But I could include them in an Artist's Statement. If my ad is image centered, then I will be creating a type of visual argument. That may be a good way to reach comic book lovers.

**Editorial?**
I could easily write an editorial, and maybe include some images. But I've done a lot of research, and I'd really like to show off my sources. How might this work? Most editorials are pretty short, and I'm not sure how much space I'll need to make my case. Yeah, I don't think a traditional newspaper-type editorial will work, given that I want to use images. But maybe a researched argument?

**Researched argument?**
This may be a better option than an editorial. I've done research and want to draw on that. If I choose this genre, I won't have to worry about length problems and could easily include visuals to make my case. I'm now thinking I could present this online in a magazine, journal, or blog. I see researched arguments and presentations as related genres. Could work. This genre would give me a framework for arguing about superheroes, and I could include related/supporting images and clips.

**Collage or other visual argument—such as a comic?**
It would be cool to create a persuasive comic, but I'd want help with the images and don't have a lot of time. While I love the idea of creating some kind of visual argument—I think my best bet is to work existing visuals into my composition in a meaningful way.

**Presentation?**
I can see myself translating a researched argument into a presentation at some point.

*Ganow, **Superhero Project: Brainstorm,** Continued*

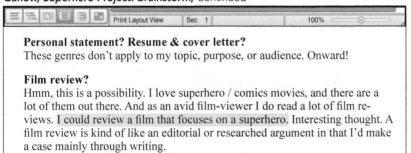

**Personal statement? Resume & cover letter?**
These genres don't apply to my topic, purpose, or audience. Onward!

**Film review?**
Hmm, this is a possibility. I love superhero / comics movies, and there are a lot of them out there. And as an avid film-viewer I do read a lot of film reviews. I could review a film that focuses on a superhero. Interesting thought. A film review is kind of like an editorial or researched argument in that I'd make a case mainly through writing.

For more on **rhetorical appeals,** see Chapter 1, page 11.

For more on **argument and persuasion,** see Chapter 4, "Persuasive Genres."

# Gwen Ganow (Student)

## *Superhero Project: 3 Annotated Persuasive Genres*

Now that Gwen has narrowed her choice of genre down to three types—an ad, a researched argument, and a film review—she looks at an example of each:

» AD: **Douglas & Gordon,** "He Was No Ordinary Estate Agent," from the Douglas & Gordon Web site

» RESEARCHED ARGUMENT: **Shannon Cochran,** "The Cold Shoulder: Saving Super-heroines from Comic-book Violence," from *Bitch* magazine online

» FILM REVIEW: **A. O. Scott,** "*Iron Man*: Heavy Suit, Light Touches," from *The New York Times* online

She annotates these sources, reading them not only for information about her topic, but also to find out more about the genres and their conventions. For example, how did the composers of these works incorporate sources?

As she reads these sources closely, she asks herself: Which of these persuasive genres—an ad, researched argument, or film review—should I ultimately choose for my composition?

Gwen analyzes and annotates each piece according to the author's/artist's rhetorical situation and use of genre conventions.

How do I know
this is **an ad**?
And do I want
to create
one?

THE GENRE'S
CONVENTIONS

**Gwen's notes
on Douglas &
Gordon ad**

**Elements of the
genre**
I like this ad's
simplicity. The
real estate agent
superhero is vivid
and colorful. The
name of the agency
is easy to find; the
brand is reinforced
by the logo on the
hero's chest and
beside the company
name.

**Style**
Not much text—
mainly the head-
line—and what's
there is conversa-
tional. Effective.

**Design**
The image plays
on pop culture.
The ad creators
mimic comic books
with the speech
bubble and text
boxes.

**Sources**
The ad makers
draw on the image
of Superman. But
they don't have to
cite this source.
That's handy.

*Text of ad:*
He was no ordinary estate agent.
With over 45 years experience in property and a team of more
than 150 well trained, enthusiastic everyday superheroes, D&G is
dedicated to providing you with an extraordinary service. We're
here to fight for truth, justice and the best deal on your property.
*Ad reprinted here by courtesy of Douglas & Gordon.*

What are the
ad's composers,
**Douglas &
Gordon**,
doing?

THE RHETORICAL
SITUATION

**Gwen's notes
on Douglas &
Gordon ad**

**Purpose**
Douglas & Gordon
want to persuade
viewers that their
agents can save the
day. If I created an
ad, what would my
argument be?

**Audience**
This ad is aimed at
people buying or
selling real estate.
I've identified my
main audience as
comic book lovers.
But where would
I place an ad so it
reaches my audi-
ence?

**Rhetorical appeals**
The ad creators
appeal to pathos/
emotion through
the message that
their agents can
rescue you. They
appeal to ethos
through the com-
pany branding.

**Modes & media**
This ad is online,
but could easily
translate to a print
magazine, for ex-
ample. I like that.

Next, Gwen looks at an example of a researched argument, asking herself: Would I want to compose in this genre? *(Shannon Cochran's article is reprinted here courtesy of* Bitch Magazine.*)*

**How do I know this is a researched argument?** Do I want to write one?

THE GENRE'S CONVENTIONS

**Gwen's notes on Cochran's article**

Elements of the genre
In a researched argument, the writer makes a case by presenting claims and backing them up with evidence and sources. Here, Shannon Cochran, who wrote this piece for the feminist magazine *Bitch*, refers to her sources clearly and in keeping with how sources are treated in magazine articles (e.g., not MLA or APA). She makes it easy to tell what's from a source—e.g., in the first paragraph, she clearly attributes a quotation from DC director Dan DiDio. She also synthesizes different sources together.

# bitchmedia

## The Cold Shoulder · Shannon Cochran

**Saving Superheroines from Comic-book Violence**

There's a new Bat in Gotham City. Like Bruce Wayne, she's a rich socialite by day and a black-clad vigilante at night. And, also like Bruce Wayne, in both incarnations she's apt to sweep the ladies off their feet. Kate Kane, the new, revamped Batwoman, isn't the first lesbian character to debut in the DC Comics universe, but she might have the highest profile. Last June, DC Executive Director Dan DiDio issued a press release saying the move was intended "to get a better cross-section of our readership and the world."

But the new Caped Crusader may find Gotham City a hostile work environment. Many of the series' previous female characters met with unfortunate fates. An earlier Batwoman was murdered, a female Robin was tortured to death with a power drill, one Batgirl was shot by the Joker, and another one was turned to villainy. In fact, it's so common for female superheroes to be killed in gruesome ways, comic-book fans have a term for it: "women in refrigerators." The phrase was coined in 1999 by comic-book writer Gail Simone, whose many credits include a stint on the Superman title *Action Comics* as well as current authorship of the *Birds of Prey* series.

The women-in-refrigerators syndrome got its name from a 1994 *Green Lantern* story arc, in which the titular hero's girlfriend is strangled and later discovered in a fridge. In an e-mail interview, Simone explains: "I and some male friends started making a list of the characters that had been killed, mutilated, or depowered (also a telling trend, as the more powerful a female character was, the more likely it was that she would lose those powers). It was shockingly long, and almost no one in the already small pool of valid superheroines escaped the wave of gynocentric violence."

*Continues next page*

**What is the composer, Shannon Cochran, doing?**

THE RHETORICAL SITUATION

**Gwen's notes on Cochran's article**

Purpose
Cochran argues that female superheroes should not be victimized in comic books. I like how she clearly states her argument. That's something I would do if I were to write a researched argument.

Audience
Cochran is writing for feminists who are into comics. Her audience is kind of like mine—readers with a perspective on comics and social issues.

**Gwen's notes on
Cochran's article**

**Style**
She writes in the
third person, and
sometimes in the
first person, here
and there. Her
tone is a little for-
mal, especially in
places where she
draws on sources.
I like that she
treats the subject
seriously, but in a
lively way.

**Design**
Cochran designed
this piece for
easy reading—it's
organized into
blocked para-
graphs—with visu-
als placed in the
foreground. I like
that, but I think
the author could
have used more
visuals and made
more of what digi-
tal media offers.

# bitch media

But so what? Don't superheroes die all the time in comic books, regardless of their biology? Sure, but as Simone says: "First, there's [always been] a larger selection of male characters, so a handful killed made barely a ripple. Second, they didn't seem to be killed in the same way—they tended to die heroically, to go down fight-ing. Whereas in many cases, the superLADIES were simply found on the kitchen table already carved up." Furthermore, she points out, most of the men recovered with lightning speed. Take Batman and Batgirl: "Both had their backs broken [Batman broke his in a dramatic Batcave confrontation with the villain Bane; Batgirl broke hers when she was ambushed in her home and shot in the spine by the Joker, never given a chance to fight]. Less than a year later, Batman was fine. Batgirl—now named Oracle—was in a wheelchair and remained so for many years."

Alan Moore, the writer responsible for the story arc that led to Batgirl's shattered spine, provides some insight into the editorial perspective behind the decision. As he told the industry magazine *Wizard*: "I asked DC if they had any problem with me crippling Barbara Gordon—who was Batgirl at the time—and if I remember, I spoke to Len Wein, who was our editor on the project, and he said, 'Hold on to the phone, I'm just going to walk down the hall and I'm going to ask [former DC Executive Editorial Director] Dick Giordano if it's alright,' and there was a brief period where I was put on hold and then, as I remember it, Len got back onto the phone and said, 'Yeah, okay, cripple the bitch.'"

Moore later regretted the story arc that retired Batgirl, stating in several interviews that he felt the decision was shallow and ill-conceived. However, Barbara Gordon was far from the only victim of the women-in-refrigerators syndrome. The list Simone created in 1999 included more than 90 female characters, among them Aquagirl, Hawkwoman, Elasti-Girl, Nova, Lady Flash, and at least two different Supergirls. In the eight years since, few of the list's characters have returned to life or regained their powers.

Simone also contacted other comic creators, both male and female, asking for their reactions to the list. Her letters were cir-culated on message boards and fan sites, provoking widespread debate and discussion in the comic-book world. Simone and her compatriots decided to create a Web site detailing the women-in-refrigerators phenomenon (now archived at http://unheardtaunts .com/wir/). The site includes Simone's original list, along with a number of the responses it sparked.

For female fans like myself, Simone had pinpointed a problem we felt keenly but had not been able to articulate. "WiR syndrome" was the terminology we needed to make our discontent with the indus-try's sexism coherent, and Simone's list was the ammunition behind

**Gwen's notes on
Cochran's article**

**Rhetorical appeals**
Cochran builds
her ethos with her
research sources.
She also appeals
to readers' pathos,
e.g., through her
choice of visuals,
which convey both
sex and violence;
her images are
meant to tap into
readers' emotions
and get a reaction.
Like her, I'd use
my research to
convey my author-
ity; I'm now more
convinced of the
value of visuals
and pathos in per-
suading readers.

# bitchmedia

our arguments. And it seemed that her observations impacted the industry. "For whatever reason," Simone notes, "the next generation of writers paid a great deal more attention to making fun, entertaining, kick-ass superheroines." Notable examples include characters like Mark Andreyko's Manhunter at DC, or over at Marvel, Brian Michael Bendis's Jessica Jones, Tamora Pierce's White Tiger, and Dan Slott and Juan Bobillo's She-Hulk (thankfully reinvented as much more than a green slice of cheesecake). According to Simone, these characters have generated more female fans.

But many female fans are still angry over treatment of past characters. Although Stephanie Brown might not be well known to casual fans of the Batman mythos, readers of DC's Batman titles knew her for 12 years as Spoiler, a young and impulsive vigilante with a sunny optimism that made her an endearing foil to Batman's endlessly brooding ways. Robin's girlfriend for many years, Stephanie eventually filled out Robin's tights herself when the former Boy Wonder resigned his post. Shortly after, in 2004, Stephanie met her grisly end by the aforementioned power-drill torture by the supervillain Black Mask. The sequence spanned multiple issues and featured graphic artwork that blatantly sexualized the teenage heroine during her bondage and torture. An action figure of Black Mask, complete with power drill, was subsequently issued. No action figure of the Girl Wonder was ever made.

It felt like comics were backsliding badly. Before Stephanie Brown took over for Robin, I'd gone years without reading a *Batman* comic. It was a cover picture of Stephanie in action under the brassy logo "Robin: Girl Wonder" that had reinvigorated my interest. Soon I was buying four *Batman*-related titles every month and splurging for the occasional *Teen Titans* crossover. Stephanie's brutal death felt like a kick in the gut. I'd been a rube to fall for a promise that DC never intended to keep.

And I wasn't the only one angry about it. Mary Borsellino, a graduate student in cultural studies at Melbourne University, posted a rant on her blog that articulated her "rage and disgust" at Stephanie's treatment. Within two hours, her post had gathered about a hundred comments from like-minded fans.

"I felt like this was a sign," Borsellino wrote in an e-mail exchange, "that this was something that needed to be sustained. So I registered Girl-Wonder.org that evening."

Project Girl Wonder was initially dedicated to protesting the treatment of Stephanie Brown, but quickly took on a life of its own. While Stephanie remains the site's official symbol, Girl-Wonder.org's mission has expanded into a campaign demanding better treatment for *all* women in comics. As the site proclaims: "Batman and other

*Continues next page*

**bitch**media

superhero stories are the modern age's fables, and if we don't stop the spread of this rot now they will be irrevocably corrupted by it. Stephanie Brown is a symbol of the need for change. And we're going to see that the change begins." The site attracted more than 100,000 visitors in its first couple months, with hundreds of registered users filling the message boards. In the years since, Girl-Wonder.org has organized a letter-writing campaign, distributed literature about the WiR problem to conventions and local comic stores, and sparked a new wave of debate within the industry.

For Borsellino, the Girl Wonder campaign is fueled not only by depictions in the comics, but also by the apparent disdain shown by industry editors toward their female audience. In an e-mail interview, Borsellino wrote: "Less than a week [after Stephanie's death], [DiDio] started shooting his mouth off in an interview, and described Stephanie's death-by-torture as having a 'major impact' on the lives of heroes." This statement bothered Borsellino because it was untrue (Stephanie's death didn't seem to impact male superheroes) and because of what it implied. "It completely failed to acknowledge that anybody could possibly have the girl as their hero. No, the girls are the ones who die and thereby make the boys, the real heroes, sad. It's pathetic." DiDio provoked another wave of outrage when, in response to a question from a fan at a comics convention, he allegedly intimated that Stephanie Brown deserved her torture and death because she had failed to obey Batman's orders to stay out of the fight with Black Mask.

Simone believes the anger against DiDio may be misdirected: "I'm not against shock and repulsion as story elements at all, in fact. I think comics that are slightly lurid are wonderfully compelling, and my own work regularly contains things that are simply inappropriate for anyone, thank God. And thankfully, Dan is dead serious about more diversity in both the characters and creators. It's not just more good female characters we need—it's more good gay characters, more good Asian characters, more good African-American characters, and on and on."

But the reality isn't so rosy. A former industry employee who maintains a blog at occasionalsuperheroine.blogspot.com recently removed all of her previous posts and replaced them with a twelve-part "Goodbye to Comics," in which she referenced the sexual harassment that had been a daily part of her job until she was driven to resign.

DiDio and other industry honchos might make the right noises about increasing diversity and female audiences, but even in death, Stephanie Brown has been treated unfairly. While another fallen Robin (Jason Todd, now resurrected as Red Hood) was honored with a permanent memorial in the Batcave, no sign of Stephanie's service has been installed. According to Coordinating Editor Jann

# bitchmedia

Jones, no plans for a memorial are in the works. For the boys: glorious deaths and dramatic returns. For the girls: punishment, torture, and forgotten fates.

Meanwhile, Girl-Wonder.org has expanded to include three regular columnists who keep tabs on the ongoing portrayals of female superheroes in the mainstream and alternative comics; they also recommend comics featuring strong female characters. Academic papers with titles like "The Secret Origins of Jessica Jones: Multiplicity, Irony and a Feminist Perspective on Brian Michael Bendis's *Alias*" or "Wonder Woman: Lesbian or Dyke? Paradise Island as a Woman's Community" are archived on the site. Two independent Web comics are hosted by Girl-Wonder.org, and Borsellino says she'd like to see the support for creators expand: "Someday I'd love to generate the funds to get more female creators to conventions, so their work can be seen by editors, and to perhaps have a Girl-Wonder.org publishing imprint to get titles into stores, even if only in small numbers."

The future will belong to those creators. "We are making strides at DC," Simone affirms. "I write a book with an Asian lead [*The All-New Atom*], another with a nearly all-female cast [*Birds of Prey*], another with a cast of senior citizens [(*Welcome to*) *Tranquility*], and another with an openly lesbian couple, among others. That would have been almost unimaginable a few years back. We've got a lot to do, but I'm very optimistic and excited to be part of it."

Borsellino is also looking forward to a brighter future for female characters and fans, but she thinks that groups like hers will be necessary to keep the industry in line. "I want Girl-Wonder.org to stand like a watchdog. We're working on forging contacts with media groups, so that the next time DC or Marvel try to do something as sickening as [the arc in which Stephanie Brown was murdered], they'll have to consider that there's this group of very noisy, very angry feminists watching their every move and hitting their speed-dial as they do it."

Both Simone and Borsellino are optimistic about DC's new Batwoman. "I think it could be an amazing book," Simone says. But Borsellino notes that her presence has come with a price. "To get Kate Kane, we lost Cass Cain, Stephanie Brown, and Leslie Thompkins entirely [the latter, though not killed, was exiled to Africa]. Barbara Gordon and Helena Bertinelli were permanently relocated to Metropolis. Onyx has vanished without any follow-up. So that's six female characters—one Asian, one poor, one elderly, one disabled, one Italian, and one black—traded off the team in order to get one rich, white, young, pretty, gay woman."

Hopefully, Batwoman will be strong and capable enough to navigate the streets of Gotham City on her own. But it can't hurt that there's a legion of real-life Girl Wonders to watch her back. We've lost enough of our heroines already.

Gwen Ganow, *3 Annotated Persuasive Genres*

Gwen then looks at an example of a film review. *(A. O. Scott's review reprinted here from The New York Times, May 2, 2008. © 2008 The New York Times. All rights reserved.)*

**THE GENRE'S CONVENTIONS**

**Gwen's notes on Scott's review**

**Elements of the genre**

In a film review, a writer presents an argument about a movie and backs that up by drawing on moments from the film, and even from film history. Here, Scott's lead paragraph gets readers' attention and identifies the genre of the film. In his review Scott makes clear what he thinks of the film.

**Style**

Scott writes in the third person. His tone is mostly formal but is sometimes informal, e.g., his use of exclamation points and phrases including: "Yeah, that guy." He even addresses the reader as "you." I like that informality a lot.

## The New York Times

## Movies
# Heavy Suit, Light Touches

By A. O. SCOTT

MOVIE REVIEW | 'IRON MAN'
**Iron Man (2008)**

Zade Rosenthal/Paramount Pictures

Iron Man, based on the Marvel comic and with Robert Downey Jr. as the title character, opens on Friday nationwide. Jon Favreau directed.

The world at the moment does not suffer from a shortage of super-heroes. And yet in some ways the glut of anti-evil crusaders with cool costumes and troubled souls takes the pressure off of *Iron Man*, which clanks into theaters today ahead of Hellboy, Batman, and the Incredible Hulk. This summer those guys are all in sequels or redos, so *Iron Man* (a Marvel property not to be confused with the Man of Steel, who belongs to DC and who's taking a break this year) has the advantage of novelty in addition to a seasonal head start.

And *Iron Man*, directed by Jon Favreau (*Elf*, *Zathura*), has the advantage of being an unusually good superhero picture. Or at least—since it certainly has its problems—a superhero movie that's good in unusual ways. The film benefits from a script (credited to Mark Fergus, Hawk Ostby, Art Marcum, and Matt Holloway) that generally chooses clever dialogue over manufactured catchphrases and lumbering exposition, and also from a crackerjack cast that accepts the filmmakers' invitation to do some real acting rather than just flex and glower and shriek for a paycheck.

There's some of that too, of course. The hero must flex and furrow his brow; the bad guy must glower and scheme; the girl must

**THE RHETORICAL SITUATION**

**Gwen's notes on Scott's review**

**Purpose**

Scott wants to persuade readers that *Iron Man* is a film to see. He shows readers that it's a "superhero movie that's good in unusual ways." I like that his purpose is extremely clear and that he draws on moments in the film to support his claims.

**Audience**

As a film critic for *The New York Times*, Scott writes for anyone generally interested in movies. In this case, his audience also consists of people familiar with the Marvel comic, people who like Robert Downey Jr., and people who like imagined worlds. My audience is similar: They are fans of comics and people who like superheroes.

# The New York Times

shriek and fret. There should also be a skeptical but supportive friend. Those are the rules of the genre, as unbreakable as the pseudoscientific principles that explain everything (An arc reactor! Of course!) and the Law of the Bald Villain. In *Iron Man* it all plays out more or less as expected, from the trial-and-error building of the costume to the climactic showdown, with lots of flying, chasing and noisemaking in between. (I note that there is one sharp, subversive surprise right at the very end.)

What is less expected is that Mr. Favreau, somewhat in the manner of those sly studio-era craftsmen who kept their artistry close to the vest so the bosses wouldn't confiscate it, wears the genre paradigm as a light cloak rather than a suit of iron. Instead of the tedious, moralizing, pop-Freudian origin story we often get in the first installments of comic-book-franchise movies—childhood trauma; identity crisis; longing for justice versus thirst for revenge; wake me up when the explosions start—*Iron Man* plunges us immediately into a world that crackles with character and incident.

It is not quite the real world, but it's a bit closer than Gotham or Metropolis. We catch up with Tony Stark in dusty Afghanistan, where he is enjoying a Scotch on the rocks in the back of an armored American military vehicle. Tony is a media celebrity, a former M.I.T. whiz kid and the scion of a family whose company makes and sells high-tech weaponry. He's also a bon vivant and an incorrigible playboy. On paper the character is completely preposterous, but since Tony is played by Robert Downey Jr., he's almost immediately as authentic and familiar—as much fun, as much trouble—as your ex-boyfriend or your old college roommate. Yeah, that guy.

Tony's skeptical friend (see above) is Rhodey, an Air Force officer played with good-humored sidekick weariness by Terrence Howard. The girl is one Pepper Potts (Gwyneth Paltrow, also in evident good humor), Tony's smitten, ultracompetent assistant. His partner and sort-of mentor in Stark Enterprises is Obadiah Stane, played by Jeff Bridges with wit and exuberance and—spoiler alert!—a shaved head.

These are all first-rate actors, and Mr. Downey's antic energy and emotional unpredictability bring out their agility and resourcefulness. Within the big, crowded movements of this pop symphony is a series of brilliant duets that sometimes seem to have the swing and spontaneity of jazz improvisation: Mr. Downey and Ms. Paltrow on the dance floor; Mr. Downey and Mr. Howard drinking sake on an airplane; Mr. Downey and Shaun Toub working on blueprints in a cave; Mr. Downey and Mr. Bridges sparring over a box of pizza.

Those moments are what you are likely to remember. The plot is serviceable, which is to say that it's placed at the service of the

*Continues next page*

# The New York Times

actors (and the special-effects artists), who deftly toss it around and sometimes forget it's there. One important twist seems glaringly arbitrary and unmotivated, but this lapse may represent an act of carefree sabotage rather than carelessness. You know this ostensibly shocking revelation is coming, and the writers know you know it's coming, so why worry too much about whether it makes sense? Similarly, the patina of geopolitical relevance is worn thin and eventually discarded, and Tony's crisis of conscience when he discovers what his weapons are being used for is more of a narrative convenience than a real moral theme.

All of which is to say that *Iron Man*, in spite of the heavy encumbrances Tony must wear when he turns into the title character, is distinguished by light touches and grace notes. The hardware is impressive, don't get me wrong, but at these prices it had better be. If you're throwing around a hundred million dollars and you have Batman and the Hulk on your tail, you had better be sure that the arc reactors are in good working order and that the gold-titanium alloy suit gleams like new and flies like a bird.

And everything works pretty well. But even dazzling, computer-aided visual effects, these days, are not so special. And who doesn't have superpowers? Actually, Iron Man doesn't; his heroism is all handicraft, elbow grease and applied intelligence. Those things account for the best parts of *Iron Man* as well.

*Iron Man* is rated PG-13 (Parents strongly cautioned). It has a lot of action violence, none of it especially graphic or gruesome. Also, Iron Man has sex, and not with the suit on. But not completely naked either.

**Opens on Friday nationwide.**

Directed by Jon Favreau; written by Mark Fergus, Hawk Ostby, Art Marcum and Matt Holloway based on the character created by Stan Lee, Larry Lieber, Don Heck and Jack Kirby; director of photography, Matthew Libatique; edited by Dan Lebental; music by Ramin Djawadi; production designer, J. Michael Riva; visual effects by John Nelson; produced by Avi Arad and Kevin Feige; released by Paramount Pictures and Marvel Entertainment. Running time: 2 hours 6 minutes.

With: Robert Downey Jr. (Tony Stark), Terrence Howard (Rhodey), Jeff Bridges (Obadiah Stane), Shaun Toub (Yinsen) and Gwyneth Paltrow (Pepper Potts).

# Gwen Ganow (Student)

## *Notes on Final Genre Choice*

Now that Gwen has decided she wants to write a film review, she needs to think about that genre in terms of how she'll pull in sources and work with evidence. She does some more brainstorming to think this through.

She wants to figure out how she might work in the research she's done, and what kind of evidence she'll need to draw on to convince readers to agree with her evaluation of whatever film she will review.

| ☰ ☷ ◫ ☰ ▤ ▥ | Print Layout View | Sec 1 | 100% ⊙ |

*NOTES*

**Gwen Ganow**

**Genre Choice: Film Review**

I like the idea of composing an ad or a researched argument, but I think that a film review is a genre that my target audience can connect with. Why? Because superheroes are a big part of pop culture and tons of films feature them. I assume that, like me, my comic- and superhero-loving audience sees these films and reads reviews of them.

How will I draw on sources in my genre composition?

Okay, I'm going to write a film review. Now what?

- **What film will I review?** It has to be one about superheroes. Should I choose something contemporary? Or a classic? And once I choose, should I read others' reviews of that film or will those sources just distract me?
- **How will I work with research I've done? What more do I need to find out about?** Once I know what film I'll review, I will need to learn about other works the director, writer, and producer have been involved in. Maybe the actors too. Also, how can I draw on research I've already done? I'm thinking that one of my sources in particular—a book I've read titled *Who Needs a Superhero?* by H. Michael Brewer—could come in handy, in addition to the film itself, which is my main source.
- **What do I know about film reviews?** I may need to do more reading on the film review as a genre. What makes a film review successful? Maybe I should look at more examples. I'll reread the section in Chapter 4 on film reviews and take a closer look at the Roger Ebert example. He's a known and respected reviewer.
- **Do I need to know more about how comics fans think of superhero movies?** Especially when a story is moved from the page to the screen? I might need to do some primary research on this. Maybe I should interview some comics fans.

**Gwen's notes on her genre choice**

The film review is a genre I know, and a great venue for presenting an argument about superheroes.

I need to choose a superhero film to review. But which one?

I need to read more film reviews—especially those by Roger Ebert.

I need to look back at my other sources—and maybe interview people from my potential audience.

# COMPOSING YOUR GENRE PIECE

Remember that "shitty first draft" we mentioned at the beginning of this chapter? Let's circle back to that. It might not look much like an editorial or an investigative journalism piece or whatever genre you've chosen. That's okay. But now that you've followed Gwen to this point, you may have more ideas about what you want to do—and why and how. Hopefully you have a more solid sense of your own rhetorical situation and have focused in on a genre that you want to compose in.

When you do return to your draft, try this: Review the conventions of the genre you've chosen, and start nudging your rough draft into the shape of your chosen genre. For example, if you're writing an editorial, you'll want a pithy first paragraph that makes the issue you're discussing and your position on it clear. If you're composing an ad, step back and think about how visuals could work with your text.

## Steps for Composing

You have your topic, your basic ideas, and the genre figured out. Now it's time to start composing in the genre.

**Step 1. Write a solid draft.**  Review the exploratory rough draft you created earlier in this process and begin fleshing it out so it has a beginning, middle, and end, or whatever elements are appropriate for your chosen genre. It should include, at least in rough form, the main points you want to make, and include some examples or evidence you'll use to support your points.

☞ **Attention, composers! Wondering about media?**

What medium will best suit your genre and rhetorical situation? Will you reach your audiences best through a print or physical medium—or in a digital environment? If you're composing online, will you use audio? How about video or animation? What medium will your primary audience respond to best?

Working from this draft, follow the steps below to evaluate and revise it.

**Step 2. Evaluate your use of sources & evidence.**  Look at a really good example of the genre you're working in—and compare it to yours. How does that author support claims with evidence? Draw on sources? What kind of evidence will your audience expect and respond to? Will anecdotes and personal stories be convincing to your audience, or will they be more convinced by statistics and references to peer-reviewed studies?

Note: Refer to the sample of your genre as you complete steps 3–7.

**Step 3. Confirm the scope of information to provide.**  How much coverage of the topic is appropriate for the genre you've selected? Examine the sample of the genre you're comparing your draft to. Does it present an overview of the subject? What is the level of detail?

**Step 4. Consider your use of style.**  Think about voice, tone, language, and point of view. Is the genre you're composing in characterized by the use of first or third person? How explicit and present will your voice and experience be in the piece? Look at the example you're comparing your piece to. Does that composer use an objective, authoritative tone, or a personal, subjective tone, or something else?

**Step 5. Look at how you use rhetorical appeals.** Look at your draft and the sample genre piece you're consulting. To what extent does the other author use ethos, pathos, and/or logos? How effective is his/her approach, and what might you want to adapt for your own work?

**Step 6. Look at your organization.** How have you organized your content? Is this the best way, considering who your audience is and what you're trying to achieve? Is it logical? Persuasive? Does the sample you're consulting have anything to offer you in terms of a model for improving your work?

**Step 7. Consider your mix of words & images.** This is also a moment to think about design and medium. Are you being as effective as you could be? Again, consult your example.

**Step 8. Make a list of what you want to work on when you revise.** Base your list on what you've determined in steps 2–7.

**Step 9. Revise your draft based on your revision list.** After you've revised, reread your work and make notes to address things you want to improve for the next draft.

**Step 10. Revise a little more.** Get your work in the best shape you can in the time you have.

---

☞ **Attention, composers! A word on design.**

What are the design features of the genre you're composing in? How will you use design? Consider:

*Layout.* In your genre, how are elements typically arranged spatially? How are visuals presented? How will your layout help readers/viewers quickly orient themselves?

*Color.* How can you use color to guide your audience's attention? What colors are often associated with your genre? For example, many ads are designed with bright colors.

*Chunking & fonts (if you're working with text).* Will it be best to present information in short paragraphs organized under headings? Or are you going to do something else? How can a font help you achieve your purpose and reach your audience? What fonts are associated with your genre? For example, Times New Roman works in newspapers; sans serif fonts work well in a digital environment.

*Context.* Is the design you have in mind appropriate, considering when and where and how your audience will encounter the piece?

---

## Guided Process:
## How to Compose a Genre Piece

### Gwen Ganow (Student)

### *Superhero Project: Film Review Draft 1*

Gwen has a clear sense of her genre—as well as her rhetorical situation. She now gets down to writing. In the following section, she writes a first draft of her film review. She then spends time evaluating it—reading it against a published film review—to see how she might improve her own. In this process, she reviews her work for how well she deals with purpose, audience, and other rhetorical concerns, as well as how well she works in the genre of the film review itself. After this process, she revises her work, creating a second and third draft.

**Gwen's notes on
her film review**

I decided to review
the film *X-Men*—
it's a significant
film in the super-
hero genre that my
audience will be
familiar with. This
is my first attempt
at a draft.

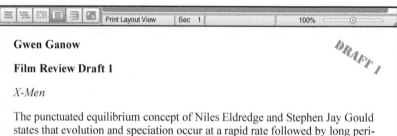

Gwen Ganow

**Film Review Draft 1**

*X-Men*

The punctuated equilibrium concept of Niles Eldredge and Stephen Jay Gould states that evolution and speciation occur at a rapid rate followed by long periods of stasis. The film *X-Men* explores how a modern American society would react to its own punctuated equilibrium in which a new, superhuman species rises and suddenly integrates with "normal" humans. Through the events and emotions of the movie *X-Men*, our past and current social issues of prejudice and intolerance as an American society become exposed.

*X-Men* opens with a powerful image of prejudice and intolerance, a Nazi concentration camp. While unloading a new trainload of Jews, Nazi soldiers rip a young boy from the arms of his parents. He sits in the rain crying and watches helplessly as his parents are herded off to other buildings. His yellow Star of David, his label of difference, is the only color against the dismal backdrop of rain, mud, and hate. The young boy survives his Nazi captors and grows up to be a mutant with the power to move and control metal.

The movie leaves the scene of war and enters the chambers of Congress where a Senate committee hearing is taking place. Magneto attends this committee hearing of the Senate because he is curious about what the American government is doing about the so-called "mutant problem" in the United States. Senator Kelly, a staunch supporter of the Mutant Registration Act, is debated by Dr. Jean Grey (a mutant herself). Jean Grey argues against the Mutant Registration Act and says, "Mutants who have revealed themselves publicly have been met with fear, hostility, and violence." To this, Senator Kelly responds with the questions, "Are they dangerous? Do you want your children in school with mutants? Do you want your children to be taught by mutant teachers?"

**Ganow,** *Film Review Draft 1,* Continued

To shield the younger generation from the violence created by the words of intolerance spoken by Senator Kelly, Charles Xavier (a mutant with powerful psychic abilities) creates Xavier's School for Gifted Youngsters and makes it a place for young mutants who have recently discovered that they are very different from their peers and have run away from home. Here he offers these young men and women a place of refuge and sense of inclusiveness. This is a safe environment where they can be taught how to control their developing minds and powers by some of Xavier's finest past students like Storm, Cyclops, and Jean Grey, who become mentors to a new generation of young mutants, afraid of the world around them. Charles Xavier never gives up hope that humanity will come to realize the error of their judgment. He teaches his students that intolerance should not be returned with even more intolerance.

Magneto's view of humanity is radically different from the views of Charles Xavier. Magneto sees nothing wrong with trying to solve the plight of mutants by using violence and fear against humans. He devises a plan using his own powers combined with a radiation-generating machine to change non-mutants into mutants. By doing this, he feels that vengeance will be carried out by putting would-be persecutors into the lives of the people they sought to persecute and chooses Senator Kelly as his first test subject. Magneto tells the senator, "Humankind has always feared what it doesn't understand. You have nothing to fear from God and nothing to fear from me. Not anymore."

The fear, intolerance, and violence toward mutants that is conveyed in *X-Men* closely ties in with the fear, intolerance, and violence endured by the GLBT community today. Sometimes, the reality of the comic book universe resembles our own reality more than we would like to admit. The movie *X-Men* questions whether we as Americans really believe in freedom for all or whether we really mean freedom for some.

# Gwen Ganow

## *Superhero Project: Evaluation of Film Review Draft 1*

Next, Gwen evaluates her film review by comparing it to an excellent example of the genre: A. O. Scott's review *"Iron Man:* Heavy Suit, Light Touches," which she looked at earlier. She evaluates Scott's use of evidence and sources, his scope and use of rhetorical appeals, and his organization and use of visuals. Then she applies this lens to her own review. (*A. O. Scott's review reprinted here from* The New York Times, *May 2, 2008.* © 2008 The New York Times. *All rights reserved.*)

## Gwen's notes on Scott's review

### Scott's use of evidence & sources

Scott contextualizes *Iron Man* with other movies of the same genre. He also refers to the director, his other films, and the scriptwriters.

He gives lots of plot details but never gives the story away. He supports each claim with brief snippets from the plot. E.g., when he talks about the "brilliant duets" (paragraph 7), he backs that up with evidence from specific scenes.

### Scott's scope

Scott's scope is in line with his purpose: to evaluate the film overall—to make an argument in favor of it. He chooses key details about characters and from specific scenes to support his claims and overall case.

He summarizes quite a bit: He offers just a snapshot of the plot by providing setting, character descriptions, and parts of the story.

---

## The New York Times

# Movies

## Heavy Suit, Light Touches

By A. O. SCOTT

MOVIE REVIEW | 'IRON MAN'
**Iron Man (2008)**

Iron Man, based on the Marvel comic and with Robert Downey Jr. as the title character, opens on Friday nationwide. Jon Favreau directed.

The world at the moment does not suffer from a shortage of superheroes. And yet in some ways the glut of anti-evil crusaders with cool costumes and troubled souls takes the pressure off of *Iron Man*, which clanks into theaters today ahead of Hellboy, Batman, and the Incredible Hulk. This summer those guys are all in sequels or redos, so *Iron Man* (a Marvel property not to be confused with the Man of Steel, who belongs to DC and who's taking a break this year) has the advantage of novelty in addition to a seasonal head start.

---

Print Layout View    Sec 1    100%

*DRAFT 1*

**Gwen Ganow**

**Film Review Draft 1**

*X-Men*

The punctuated equilibrium concept of Niles Eldredge and Stephen Jay Gould states that evolution and speciation occur at a rapid rate followed by long periods of stasis. The film *X-Men* explores how a modern American society would react to its own punctuated equilibrium in which a new, superhuman species rises and suddenly integrates with "normal" humans. Through the events and emotions of the movie *X-Men*, our past and current social issues of prejudice and intolerance as an American society become exposed.

---

## Gwen's notes on her own review

### My use of evidence & sources

In my own review, I contextualize *X-Men* in terms of the theory of "punctuated equilibrium" (and cite Eldredge and Gould as my source).

I support my claims about the "powerful image of prejudice and intolerance" (paragraph 2) with plot details and specifics from a scene.

Like Scott, the evidence I use to support my argument includes details from the plot and other aspects of the film and its creators.

### My scope

I go into way more detail than Scott does, maybe because I am retelling the plot chronologically. Is this a problem? Do I need to pull back from some of my details to give more summary? Should I choose my details more carefully?

**Ganow,** *Film Review Draft 1,* *Continued*

## Gwen's notes on Scott's review

Scott makes broad statements when he delivers snappy and fun one-liners. E.g., in his line "The hero must flex and furrow his brow," Scott makes a generalization about action movies.

### Scott's style

I like Scott's writing style. It's almost as if I can hear him speaking, especially in lines such as: "The hero must flex and furrow his brow; the bad guy must glower and scheme; the girl must shriek and fret."

He chooses each word carefully and keeps his language varied and interesting. E.g., he uses a variety of terms (*film*, *picture*) to refer to the movie.

Scott writes in the third person, but I like how he sometimes invites the reader in by using the word *we*.

*X-Men* opens with a powerful image of prejudice and intolerance, a Nazi concentration camp. While unloading a new trainload of Jews, Nazi soldiers rip a young boy from the arms of his parents. He sits in the rain crying and watches helplessly as his parents are herded off to other buildings. His yellow Star of David, his label of difference, is the only color against the dismal backdrop of rain, mud, and hate. The young boy survives his Nazi captors and grows up to be a mutant with the power to move and control metal.

The movie leaves the scene of war and enters the chambers of Congress where a Senate committee hearing is taking place. Magneto attends this committee hearing of the Senate because he is curious about what the American government is doing about the so-called "mutant problem" in the United States. Senator Kelly, a staunch supporter of the Mutant Registration Act, is debated by Dr. Jean Grey (a mutant herself). Jean Grey argues against the Mutant Registration Act and says, "Mutants who have revealed themselves publicly have been met with fear, hostility, and violence." To this, Senator Kelly responds with the questions, "Are they dangerous? Do you want your children in school with mutants? Do you want your children to be taught by mutant teachers?"

To shield the younger generation from the violence created by the words of intolerance spoken by Senator Kelly, Charles Xavier (a mutant with powerful psychic abilities) creates Xavier's School for Gifted Youngsters and makes it a place for young mutants who have recently discovered that they are very different from their peers and have run away from home. Here he offers these young men and women a place of refuge and sense of inclusiveness. This is a safe environment where they can be taught how to control their developing minds and powers by some of Xavier's finest past students like Storm, Cyclops, and Jean Grey, who become mentors to a new generation of young mutants, afraid of the world around them. Charles Xavier never gives up hope that humanity will come to realize the error of their judgment. He teaches his students that intolerance should not be returned with even more intolerance.

## Gwen's notes on her own review

### My style

I'm not sure my voice comes through enough in my review. I think I sound knowledgeable, but I'm not so sure how present I am in the writing in terms of voice, personality, or humor.

My review does not seem as personal or subjective as Scott's. I think my perspective is more objective. Is that a strong point? Or a problem?

### My use of rhetorical appeals

I want to establish myself as a kind of expert on superheroes and film. I like how Dwight Decker established his ethos in his researched essay. I'm modeling my language on his. Is it right for a film review? I'm not sure how well I've conveyed my ethos. I also need to persuade my audience, so I need to appeal to pathos.

## Gwen's notes on Scott's review

### Scott's use of rhetorical appeals

Scott builds his ethos by drawing on evidence and by crediting the film's creators. He also makes it clear that he is very qualified to write about superhero action flicks.

He also appeals to readers through pathos. He entices readers to go see *Iron Man* through his language and tone.

### Scott's organization

Scott begins with general comments about superheroes and the popularity of superhero movies before he moves onto *Iron Man*.

Next, he situates the film within its genre, hinting at his opinion of the movie. He outlines some of his expectations.

He makes claims that he supports with details of the plot and characters; he closes with a final evaluation of the film.

### Scott's use of visuals

He includes a few visuals. The large still featuring Robert Downey Jr., who plays the lead, is pretty striking. There is also a small picture further into the review.

## Gwen's notes on her own review

### My organization

I move through the plot, giving readers a general sense of the story.

I don't discuss the film in terms of a broader context. Should I? I'm also not sure I present my argument clearly enough. I think I need to be more direct.

### My use of visuals

I haven't yet incorporated any images/film stills into my review, but I need to. Which characters/key scenes do I want to show? Why?

### What to focus on when I revise

Revise/reorganize the review so it isn't just a chronological plot summary. Will be challenging. Maybe I should think about the main points I want to make, and then choose supporting details from the plot as needed, much as Scott does.

Establish a clearer sense of voice. Also, should I worry about the shift from third to first person? How much personality can I inject into my review?

Make sure I'm giving a clear evaluation of the film. I need my argument about the film to be stronger. Is it worth seeing? Why or why not? Also, I want readers to see the dilemma of the hero as related to that of the GLBT community.

Do more to establish ethos and appeal to readers' emotions.

Pay more attention to language. For example, don't just use the word *movie* throughout.

Incorporate visuals—also maybe embed video.

# Gwen Ganow (Student)

## *Superhero Project: Film Review Draft 2*

Gwen returns now to her draft and begins to rework it, based on her evaluation of it, her comparison of it to the A. O. Scott review, and her list of what to focus on when she revises.

**Gwen Ganow**

**Film Review Draft 2**

*X-Men:* Mutants R Us

As a "hard-core" comic book fan, I always considered the 2000 *X-Men* film the epitome of a true comic book movie. What sets the *X-Men* apart from other comic book films is that the story behind the X-Men is not overshadowed by special effects. In *X-Men*, equilibrium is punctured; humans face a sudden and dramatic evolutionary change, one that results in the existence of "mutants." The mutants are humans with superhuman powers, who look human enough to integrate invisibly into society. The movie explores how American society might react to the existence of these mutants, exposing our past and current social issues of prejudice and intolerance. Bryan Singer, best known for 1995's *The Usual Suspects*, directs from the screenplay written by David Hayter.

Created by Stan Lee and Jack Kirby in 1963, X-Men are children of parents who were exposed to atmospheric radiation and became genetically altered. The mutant kids are outsiders in the world, and are envied and feared by "normal" humans. The alienation of the X-Men is similar to that of other groups of people who have experienced prejudice, like African Americans, Jews, Japanese, and homosexuals. Singer makes this parallel explicit with the opening scene.

*X-Men* opens with a powerful image of prejudice and intolerance, a Nazi concentration camp. While unloading a new trainload of Jews, Nazi soldiers rip a young boy from the arms of his parents. He sits in the rain crying and watches helplessly as his parents are herded off to other buildings. His yellow Star of David is the only color against the dismal backdrop of rain, mud, and hate. The young boy survives his Nazi captors and grows up to be a mutant known as Magneto with the power to move and control metal.

The movie leaves the scene of war and enters the chambers of Congress where a Senate committee hearing is taking place on the Mutant Registration Act, which would require mutants to register with the government and list their special abilities, making it impossible for them to blend in unnoticed with the rest of society. Magneto, played by Ian McKellen, attends this committee hearing because he is curious about what the American government is doing about the so-called "mutant problem." Senator Kelly, played by Bruce Davison, a staunch supporter of the Mutant Registration Act, is debated by Dr. Jean Grey, a mutant herself, played by Famke Janssen. Kelly supports the Mutant

*Continues next page*

### Gwen's comments on her film review

Overall, I've done a better job evaluating the film and making an argument about it. It's clear what I think of the movie and why.

This draft is more interesting and readable. I've done more to appeal to my audience of superhero/comic lovers. For example, my first sentence and paragraph are aimed at drawing them in.

My writing still seems stiff in places. I want to make the style and tone a little more casual; also, I want to tighten up the wording and do more to make this flow.

**Ganow,** *Film Review Draft 2,* *Continued*

Print Layout View    Sec 1    100%

Registration Act, believing that mutants are a danger to "normal" humans and should be locked away, while Grey argues that forcing mutants to register would create the potential for them to be treated as freaks.

The performers share good chemistry, with Hugh Jackman's Wolverine's and James Marsden's Cyclops's one-upmanship bringing humor to their scenes. Patrick Stewart's Charles Xavier seems both fatherly and professorial, and Anna Paquin as Rogue does a fine job conveying fear about her future as a mutant and lovesickness over Wolverine. Rebecca Romijn makes an impression in a role that relies more on physical presence than lines.

In *X-Men*, responses to prejudice by the victims of prejudice are explored through the actions of two important mutants, both leaders of mutant groups. Charles Xavier, a mutant with powerful psychic abilities, creates a school for the gifted for young runaway mutants. Here he offers these young men and women a place of refuge and a sense of inclusiveness. This is a safe environment where they can be taught how to control their developing minds and powers by some of Xavier's finest past students like Storm, Cyclops, and Jean Grey, who become mentors to a new generation of young mutants, afraid of the world around them. Xavier's "turn the other cheek" philosophy links him to the Jesus Christ of the Christian culture. The fact that Charles Xavier provides a safe house for people rejected by humanity also links him to our real-life organizations like NAACP, GLBT (gay, lesbian, bisexual, and transgender) resource centers, and some of our churches.

The other leader is Magneto, who fronts the Brotherhood of Mutants. Magneto's perspective on humanity stems from his experiences as a young boy at a WWII concentration camp, which was captured in the film's opening scene. This experience left Magneto distrustful of humanity and convinced that mutants are bound to suffer the same fate met by the inmates of the Nazi death camps. To preserve the survival of his mutant species, Magneto declares war on humankind. Magneto's view of humanity is radically different from the views of Charles Xavier. Magneto sees nothing wrong with trying to solve the plight of mutants by using violence and fear against humans.

Although the film is worth seeing for the performances and direction alone, the special effects, while relatively low-key for a superhero movie, are stunning. Magneto's spinning contraption, the fight scenes, and Storm's weather conjuring add to the fun. Finally, while there is seldom a clear right and wrong in real life, Singer's film makes it easy for us to take the right side. The heroes of the film are clearly Professor Xavier's X-Men. In this way, Singer allows us to imagine the consequences of violence and anger, as shown by Magneto's band of mutants, and ultimately root for Xavier's more tolerant gang.

# Gwen Ganow (Student)

## Superhero Project: Film Review Final

Gwen revises some more: this time with plenty of attention to design, images, and embedded links. She also polishes her writing, and continues to evaluate her choice of mode and medium, with thoughts of future iterations of her project. Below is an excerpt from her final review.

**Gwen Ganow**

**Film Review Final**

*FINAL*

*X-Men*: Mutants R Us

As a "hard-core" comic book fan, I always considered the 2000 *X-Men* film the epitome of a true comic book movie. What sets the *X-Men* apart from other comic book films is that the story behind the X-Men is not overshadowed by special effects. In *X-Men*, it's the story that matters. In the world of this film, the equilibrium of existence has been punctured; humans face a sudden and dramatic evolutionary change, one that results in the existence of "mutants." The mutants are humans with superhuman powers, who look human enough to integrate invisibly into society. The movie explores how American society might react to the existence of these mutants, exposing our past and current social issues of prejudice and intolerance.

Bryan Singer, best known for 1995's *The Usual Suspects*, directs from the screenplay written by David Hayter. . . .

The performers share good chemistry, with Hugh Jackman's Wolverine's and James Marsden's Cyclops's one-upmanship bringing humor to their scenes. Patrick Stewart's Charles Xavier seems both fatherly and professorial, and Anna Paquin as Rogue does a fine job.

Hugh ▶
Jackman as
Wolverine,
from *X-Men*
(2000).
*Everett
Collection.*

### Gwen's notes on her film review

My writing is a little smoother now and flows better.

I've decided that I want to deliver my film review digitally. I'm taking advantage of digital tools, including embedded links. E.g., I've added a link to the film trailer at Amazon, which illustrates the points I make in paragraph 1, and included another link to the director's bio at IMDb. I like the digital format, too, because I can give readers the option to comment on my work and to share it on social media.

As for future versions of this material, I'd consider an audio podcast. Podcasts give a clear sense of the writer's voice, views, and personality, something I'm striving for.

# COMPOSING AN ACCOMPANYING AUTHOR'S OR ARTIST'S STATEMENT

What is an Author's or Artist's Statement? It's a piece of reflective and persuasive writing in which you explain the choices you made in a separate composition. Artists, filmmakers, novelists, and other composers commonly write statements of the intentions, processes, and inspirations behind a particular work or body of work. In this case, we're talking specifically about the Statement that you can write to accompany the genre piece you've created.

## Advice for Composing Your Statement

Your Statement is a critical analysis of what you did and why, how successful you think you were, what you might have done differently, and any plans you may have for further revision—or even of repurposing the project for something else. If your genre piece is not ultimately as successful as you'd hoped, consider the Statement a chance to explore what didn't work and what you might do differently next time. The Statement is an opportunity to explain to your audience (particularly your peer and instructor audience) such specifics as why you chose your genre, what your rhetorical purposes were, how you wanted to affect your audience, and how your research informed your composition.

If your instructor asks you to write such an accompanying Statement, approach the drafting of it just as you would for any persuasive writing that brings in sources. Refer to the pieces you worked with along the way when composing your genre piece: Draw on any brainstorm lists, notes, and revisions of drafts. This will help you reconstruct your process and remember the choices you've made. Just as with any other composition, you'll want to get reader feedback and revise. (For more on Author's and Artist's Statements, see pp. 237–46. For more on revision, see Chapter 9.)

Following are instructions that we give our students for creating their Statements. Note: This is the assignment that Gwen will respond to on pages 478–79.

---

**ENG 101, Professor Braziller**

**Assignment: Compose an Author's or Artist's Statement**

For this course, every genre piece you create must be accompanied by an Artist's or Author's Statement. In that document, please explain:

- **The rhetorical choices you made as you composed your genre piece.**
  Define your purpose, audience, and how you wished to affect your audience.

---

Please also cover your use of rhetorical appeals, and the mode and medium you chose to work in.

- **How you worked within (or broke out of) genre conventions.**
  Discuss the elements that define the genre most typically, and how you responded to those in your composition. Discuss your style (written and other), your use of design, and how you drew on sources. In fact, as you write, please draw on sources and cite them in the text of your paper and in a list at the end.

**Note:** Your Statement should be documented in MLA or APA style. Within the text of your Statement, please draw on specific sources that informed your composition. Include *both* in-text citations and a list of Works Cited or References at the end of your Statement. Remember, you're reflecting on your process—and persuading your readers that you made thoughtful choices. Maybe your choices weren't all perfect, but that's okay. This is your chance to explain your intentions.

**Use these questions to guide your Statement.**

Rhetorical choices

- What was your purpose? For example, did you set out to tell a story, report information, or present a persuasive argument? Or some combination? How well do you think you achieved your purpose? What, if anything, might you have done differently?

- Who was your intended primary audience? Secondary audience? Why? Characterize the people in each group. What are their assumptions and expectations about your topic? How did you speak to these audiences? What message did you want them to take away from your composition? For example, did you want them to take a specific action?

- Did you use one or more of the rhetorical appeals (ethos, logos, pathos), and how effective were you in reaching your audience through the appeals?

- How and why did you choose the mode and medium you decided on? What are the advantages to these choices? How might you alter your choices in future iterations of the project?

Genre conventions

- Why did you choose the genre you did? What elements of the genre interested you most? How did you use or subvert the conventions of the genre?

- What choices did you make in terms of style (including organization, language, voice, and tone)? What did you consider in making these choices?

- Evaluate your design. Why did you choose to work with text, images, video, and audio (and any other elements) as you did? How effective do you think you were? What might you have done differently if you had had more time?

- What sources did you draw on for this piece? How did you decide which sources were right for you? How did you integrate them into your composition? Did you cite them according to the conventions of your genre?

# Guided Process: How to Compose an Author's Statement ▼

## Gwen Ganow (Student)

### Superhero Project: Author's Statement Draft 1

Following is Gwen's first draft of her Statement to accompany her film review.

**Gwen's notes
on her Author's
Statement**

**My purpose**
Do I convey clearly
and persuasively
enough why I
chose to write a
film review? Not
sure. Also, should I
comment more on
process? And what
might I have done
differently or better?

**My audience**
Have I succeeded
in explaining my
choices to readers?

**My use of rhetorical
appeals**
I focused on using
pathos and logos.
Have I emphasized
one over the other?
Is that a good idea?

**My choice of and
use of modes &
media**
I should talk more
directly about
modes and media.
I'll ask my instruc-
tor about this.

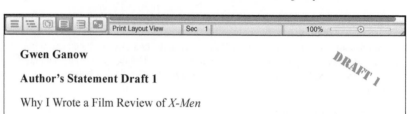

Gwen Ganow

**Author's Statement Draft 1**

Why I Wrote a Film Review of *X-Men*

There are two reasons I chose to write a film review. As a "hard-core" comic book fan, I always considered *X-Men* (Singer) as a good example of what a true comic book movie should be. What sets the movie apart from other comic book movies is that the story behind *X-Men* is not overshadowed by special effects. The second reason I chose to do a film review was to show another perspective on how comic books are interrelated with our modern culture. Superheroes, heroes, antiheroes, and villains don't just come to us through the pop culture pages of a comic book. They have also expanded their influence to include the American silver screen. The stories of these comic book characters are now told by our Hollywood actors and actresses.

Created by Stan Lee and Jack Kirby in 1963, the X-Men are the children of humans who were exposed to atmospheric radiation and became genetically altered. These children are born with "differences" and become outsiders in a world that considers them mutants. Even though they do not show any outward signs of difference, their extrahuman powers evoke the envy and fear of ordinary people (Brewer 134). We can link the alienation of the X-Men to groups of people who have gone through their own form of prejudice in real life. African Americans, Jews, Japanese, and homosexuals have all endured the pain of living in an American society that is quick to respond in fear to someone who may be different from the norm.

In *X-Men*, solutions to the problems of prejudice are explored through the actions of two important mutants. Both of these men are leaders, one being the leader of the X-Men, the other the leader of the Brotherhood of Mutants. Charles Xavier creates a school for the gifted for young ostracized mutants. He teaches his mutant students to use their powers to benefit humanity, even if that same humanity hated and distrusted them (Brewer 142). Xavier's "turn the other cheek" philosophy links him to the Jesus Christ of Christian culture. The fact that Xavier provides a safe house for people rejected by humanity also links him to our real life organizations like NAACP, GLBT resource centers, and some of our churches.

Magneto's perspective on humanity stems from his experiences as a young boy at a WWII concentration camp. This experience left Magneto distrustful of humanity, and he is convinced that mutants are bound to suffer the same

**Ganow, *Author's Statement Draft 1*,** *Continued*

fate met by the inmates of the Nazi death camps (Brewer 143). To preserve the survival of his mutant species, Magneto declares war on humankind. We can link the thoughts and actions of Magneto to our own real-world thoughts and actions. We, as humans, have always wanted to put our persecutors into the shoes and lives of the persecuted. If we were given the technology to right the wrongs against us, would we create a machine similar to Magneto's? As humans, why are we quick to return violence with more violence?

Overall, I wanted my readers to see my passion for the subject. I wanted to persuade them, using pathos, to understand that you could read the film as a larger statement on the intolerance GLBT people often face. One of the ways I achieved this was by relying on logos, helping my readers follow the film logically, using strategies employed in other film reviews, such as giving snippets of the plot and using some of the plot summary to highlight the film's strength.

I studied several film reviews to help me figure out how to best create my review. One of the things that was missing from my initial draft was placing the film in a broader context. Thus, in my revision I began the review by discussing my relationship to comics (even if briefly) and then moved on to the film itself. I also incorporated the theory of punctuated equilibrium to help establish my ethos; I know about the theory because of my zoology/biology major. Another thing I wanted to make sure to achieve in the film review was a clear evaluation of the film. My earlier draft did not really make this clear; it primarily consisted of a retelling of some of the plot. In the revision I made sure to include this, not only in the close of the review but with some word choices in the review, such as "powerful image," "good chemistry," and "fine job."

When comic book fans or superhero film fans finish reading my review, I hope that they will see that *X-Men* is definitely an appealing film. More importantly, though, I want my audience to realize that lessons about ourselves can be learned through the story of the X-Men. By witnessing and learning from the actions of a misguided mutant like Magneto, humankind can learn how to be more understanding and tolerant—like Charles Xavier.

Works Cited

Brewer, H. Michael. *Who Needs a Superhero? Finding Virtue, Vice, and What's Holy in the Comics*. Baker Books, 2004, pp. 134-44.
Singer, Bryan, director. *X-Men*. Performances by Hugh Jackman, Ian McKellen, and Patrick Stewart, Marvel Studios, 2000. Film.

---

**Gwen's notes on her Author's Statement**

My use of sources
My instructor has asked me to use MLA-style citation in this Statement. I've supported my claims with evidence, but need to double-check my in-text citations in the next draft.

Should I include images in my Statement, too? Would that help me make my case?

After reading Gwen's Statement and considering her purposes, do you think she made a good choice of genre? Why or why not? Has she observed all the conventions of film reviews? Has she ignored any? What are the effects of her choices?

If you were Gwen, what would be your main goals in revising this draft Statement?

---

From this point, Gwen will discuss the draft with her classmates and instructor, and get ready to revise her Statement. For more on the next steps (and to see where Gwen goes from here), see Chapter 9, "Revising & Remixing Your Work."

# 9 REVISING & REMIXING YOUR WORK

## CONTENTS

POWERPOINT SLIDE ▶
**Gwen Ganow,** Remix
of film
review project.
*Slide: Gwen Dalynn
Ganow. X-Men poster:
Everett Collection.*

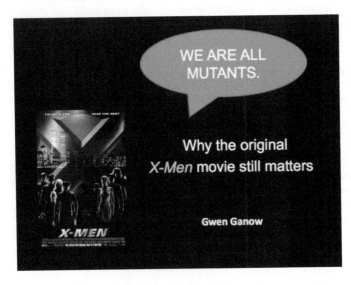

While feedback can help during any stage of your composing process, once you have a solid draft of your work, it's an ideal time to get some advice on how to make it even better. In this chapter, we pick up where we left off with Gwen Ganow (remember her from Chapter 8?). She's finished her genre piece—a film review of the movie *X-Men*—and has a first draft of her accompanying Author's Statement, which still needs work. In the first part of this chapter, she revises two drafts and polishes her final Statement, working with her own ideas and those she gets from peer review.

For an Index of Sources & Contexts for material referenced in this chapter, see the e-Pages at **bedfordstmartins .com/bookofgenres.**

Later, Gwen decides she wants to remix her genre project: to repurpose her film review and create something entirely new. Later in this chapter, we provide guidelines for remixing any genre project—that is, advice for how to work with your topic, research, and any composing you've already done, to make something totally different.

# REVISING YOUR WORK

Why revise, you ask? Because your first draft is geared toward getting your ideas out of your head and onto the page. Some people call this a writer-based draft. A writer-based draft usually has gaps in development and logic. The purpose and sense of audience are usually unclear. They become clear through revision, and as you move toward a more audience-focused composition.

## Revising Based on Your Own Observations

Gwen has a solid first draft of her Author's Statement to accompany her film review. Now she wants some input from others—from her instructor and classmates—on how to revise her Statement so it's more analytical and persuasive. As noted in

▲ STUDENT AUTHOR PHOTO
**Gwen Ganow.** *Gwen Dalynn Ganow.*

◀ DRAFT AUTHOR'S STATEMENT & FILM REVIEW **Gwen Ganow.** (Gwen's film review appears in Chapter 8.) *Gwen Dalynn Ganow.*

Chapter 8, her Statement is, arguably, more important than the film review she wrote. Gwen's Author's Statement gives her an opportunity to explain the choices she made in addressing her rhetorical situation and working with her genre. But it's also a document in which she can reflect on and learn from her own process.

When you create an Author's or Artist's Statement, you develop skills that will transfer into other settings. You learn to reflect critically on your own work—so that you can improve on it. This is a skill, a habit, even, that you (and all of us) can use in other coursework and outside of school—in future professions or when creating for any audience.

Need another reason why reflecting on your genre project (and revising your Author's or Artist's Statement) is a good idea? Here's an example. In art school, students hardly ever create the "perfect" painting or sculpture or installation in one course or semester. Often, they'll sketch, paint drafts, or create models that they'll use later, as maps or inspiration when they can flesh out their vision for the composition in a different or fuller way. Drafting, thinking critically, and revising go a long way in making great authors and artists truly great. Why not be great?

## Revising Based on Peer Review

Let's say that, like Gwen, you've created your genre piece and/or your Author's or Artist's Statement. You've done some revising, and you feel that you've done the best you can. Maybe you can no longer review the content objectively, because you've been working on it for a while. Asking others for feedback on your draft is an excellent way to find out how well you've met your purposes or reached your audience. Readers/viewers/listeners will experience your composition with fresh eyes and ears. They can help you figure out where you need to make connections more explicit, where you need to develop examples, and where the draft could be restructured, among other things.

Respondents to your work can be classmates, a teacher, a tutor, friends, parents, or coworkers. Ideally your respondents are from your intended primary audience. These individuals are most likely to give you solid advice on how well you're doing in terms of your rhetorical situation and chosen genre. The respondents you choose, even if they're not part of your primary audience, should be those whose opinions you value, people whom you can trust to respond constructively. They should be able to articulate clearly their reactions to your draft.

Ask for responses at any point in your composing process. For example, at the beginning, when you're brainstorming, you can ask others to talk with you about your ideas and approach to your topic. Once you have a rough draft or a first solid draft, you can ask others to respond to your focus, development, voice, and organization.

☞ **Attention, authors & artists! Who should respond to your drafts?**

Friends, family, and roommates may not be familiar with your topic, but they can tell you whether your argument is logical, for example, or whether your introductory paragraph is clear. They can point out spots in the draft where they got confused, or found inconsistencies, or wanted more explanation or evidence.

That said, responses from your classmates, writing center tutor, or instructor, or from others in your target audience, are probably going to be most helpful. We recommend that you ask at least one person from your intended primary audience to respond to your draft.

Once you have completed your first or second draft, ask respondents to give you feedback on how clearly you convey your purpose, how well you're reaching your audience, and what you might do better or differently. Respondents can also help you see counterarguments and other perspectives at this stage. Near the end of your composing process, ask respondents to take a finer focus: Ask whether your transitions between ideas are consistent, and whether you need to do any fine-tuning in regard to working in your genre, for example.

To get feedback that will be helpful, ask yourself: What do I want to know from my respondents? What would be most helpful to know at this stage? Here are some questions you might ask respondents:

» Would you take a look at my paper (or watch my video, or listen to my podcast, etc.) and tell me what you think? As someone who isn't (or is) familiar with my topic, how well do you think I am conveying my ideas? How persuasive do you find the writing? I'm looking for "big picture" comments right now.

» I'm really struggling with adding specific details (or some other issue). Can you read my draft and point out some places where I could add more detail?

» Other respondents have found some parts of my composition confusing (or identified some other specific problem). Could you take a look at this and let me know if you're sometimes confused, and at what point you start to feel that way?

Gathering responses doesn't mean you'll implement every change that your respondents suggest. You may ultimately decide not to make a particular recommended change, perhaps because you disagree with the suggestion or think the reader misunderstood your purpose. But even if you disagree with a reader comment, consider why the reader made it. And if more than one person makes the same recommendation, you might want to consider it more seriously.

---

CHECKLIST **Questions to Ask People Responding to Your Draft.**

Wherever you are in your composing process, it can be helpful to get feedback. Here are some more questions you might want to ask your respondents.

☐ **What kind of genre does this piece appear to be? How can you tell?**
Possible follow-up questions:
  ☐ Can you suggest some ways to make it read more like an encyclopedia entry/photo essay/blog/other genre piece?
  ☐ Can you suggest any areas that are not consistent with the genre?

☐ **What would you say is the purpose of this document? How can you tell?**
Possible follow-up questions:
  ☐ Can you suggest some ways to make the purpose of the piece clearer?
  ☐ Can you point to some places where the purpose is not consistent?

☐ **How would you characterize the rhetorical appeals the genre piece uses?**
Possible follow-up questions:

    ☐ Can you suggest ways to make the appeal to my audience more defined?

    ☐ Can you suggest some ways to emphasize ethos so that my reader accepts the piece's credibility?

    ☐ Can you suggest some ways to emphasize pathos so that my reader understands the emotion behind the piece?

☐ **How would you characterize the writing style of this document?**
Possible follow-up questions:

    ☐ Can you point to some places where that style is particularly apparent?

    ☐ Can you point to some places where that style is not apparent?

    ☐ Can you point to some places where the style is inconsistent?

    ☐ Can you suggest some ways to make the style more consistent with that of an encyclopedia entry/photo essay/blog/other genre piece?

☐ **How would you characterize the tone of this document?**
Possible follow-up questions:

    ☐ Can you point to some places where that tone is particularly apparent?

    ☐ Can you point to some places where that tone is not apparent?

    ☐ Can you point to some places where the tone is inconsistent?

    ☐ Can you suggest some ways to make the tone more consistent with that of an encyclopedia entry/photo essay/blog/other genre piece?

☐ **How would you characterize the voice in this document?**
Possible follow-up questions:

    ☐ Can you point to some places where that voice is particularly strong?

    ☐ Can you point to some places where that voice is not as strong?

    ☐ Can you point to some places where the voice is inconsistent?

    ☐ Can you suggest some ways to make the voice more consistent with that of an encyclopedia entry/photo essay/blog/other genre piece?

☐ **How do the design elements direct your attention?**
Possible follow-up questions:

    ☐ Can you suggest some ways I might better use design to help me get into my topic?

    ☐ Can you suggest some ways to emphasize the visual elements?

    ☐ Can you suggest some ways to help the text have more impact on the reader?

    ☐ Can you suggest some ways design elements might clarify for readers that this is an encyclopedia entry/photo essay/blog/other genre piece?

☐ **How can you tell that research has informed the piece?**
Possible follow-up questions:

    ☐ Can you suggest some ways I might make the piece appear more credible?

    ☐ Can you suggest some areas where I might make the research connection more explicit?

    ☐ Can you suggest some topics I might research to help me achieve my purpose?

## Guided Process: Integrating Peer Feedback: Draft to Finished Composition ▼

## Gwen Ganow (Student)

### *Superhero Project: Author's Statement*
### *Draft 1—with Peer Review*

Let's circle back to Gwen Ganow and her draft of the Author's Statement that will accompany her film review.

**Draft 1**   Gwen asks her respondents—a few of her classmates—the following questions about her Author's Statement:

» Have I made my purpose in writing a film review clear?

» Have I clearly communicated the ways I used rhetorical appeals to reach my audience?

» Is my tone reflective and persuasive enough for an Author's Statement?

Her readers report back that they want more information about how Gwen thinks she demonstrated her passion for the subject. They also suggest that she clearly connect her research and what she incorporated into her review, to make her Statement more reflective and persuasive. Finally, one respondent recommends that Gwen rethink the organization of the second half of her Statement.

Gwen Ganow

Author's Statement Draft 1

DRAFT 1

Why I Wrote a Film Review of *X-Men*

There are two reasons I chose to write a film review. As a "hard-core" comic book fan, I always considered *X-Men* (Singer) as a good example of what a true comic book movie should be. What sets the movie apart from other comic book movies is that the story behind *X-Men* is not overshadowed by special effects. The second reason I chose to do a film review was to show another perspective on how comic books are interrelated with our modern culture. Superheroes, heroes, antiheroes, and villains don't just come to us through the pop culture pages of a comic book. They have also expanded their influence to include the American silver screen. The stories of these comic book characters are now told by our Hollywood actors and actresses.

Created by Stan Lee and Jack Kirby in 1963, the X-Men are the children of humans who were exposed to atmospheric radiation and became genetically

*Continues next page*

Ganow, *Author's Statement Draft 1*, Continued

altered. These children are born with "differences" and become outsiders in a world that considers them mutants. Even though they do not show any outward signs of difference, their extrahuman powers evoke the envy and fear of ordinary people (Brewer 134). We can link the alienation of the X-Men to groups of people who have gone through their own form of prejudice in real life. African Americans, Jews, Japanese, and homosexuals have all endured the pain of living in an American society that is quick to respond in fear to someone who may be different from the norm.

In *X-Men*, solutions to the problems of prejudice are explored through the actions of two important mutants. Both of these men are leaders, one being the leader of the X-Men, the other the leader of the Brotherhood of Mutants. Charles Xavier creates a school for the gifted for young ostracized mutants. He teaches his mutant students to use their powers to benefit humanity, even if that same humanity hated and distrusted them (Brewer 142). Xavier's "turn the other cheek" philosophy links him to the Jesus Christ of Christian culture. The fact that Xavier provides a safe house for people rejected by humanity also links him to our real life organizations like NAACP, GLBT resource centers, and some of our churches.

Magneto's perspective on humanity stems from his experiences as a young boy at a WWII concentration camp. This experience left Magneto distrustful of humanity, and he is convinced that mutants are bound to suffer the same fate met by the inmates of the Nazi death camps (Brewer 143). To preserve the survival of his mutant species, Magneto declares war on humankind. We can link the thoughts and actions of Magneto to our own real-world thoughts and actions. We, as humans, have always wanted to put our persecutors into the shoes and lives of the persecuted. If we were given the technology to right the wrongs against us, would we create a machine similar to Magneto's? As humans, why are we quick to return violence with more violence?

Overall, I wanted my readers to see my passion for the subject. I wanted to persuade them, using pathos, to understand that you could read the film as a larger statement on the intolerance GLBT people often face. One of the ways I achieved this was by relying on logos, helping my readers follow the film logically, using strategies employed in other film reviews, such as giving snippets of the plot and using some of the plot summary to highlight the film's strength.

I studied several film reviews to help me figure out how to best create my review. One of the things that was missing from my initial draft was placing the film in a broader context. Thus, in my revision I began the review by discussing my relationship to comics (even if briefly) and then moved on to the film itself. I also incorporated the theory of punctuated equilibrium to help establish my ethos; I know about the theory because of my zoology/biology major. Another thing I wanted to make sure to achieve in the film review was a clear evaluation of the film. My earlier draft did not really make this clear; it primarily consisted of a retelling of some of the plot. In the revision I made sure to include this, not only in the close of the review but with some word choices in the review, such as "powerful image," "good chemistry," and "fine job."

**Ganow, *Author's Statement Draft 1*,** *Continued*

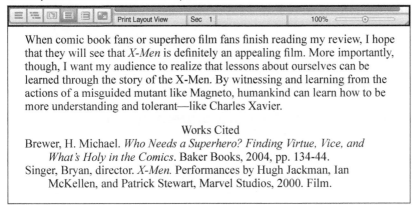

When comic book fans or superhero film fans finish reading my review, I hope that they will see that *X-Men* is definitely an appealing film. More importantly, though, I want my audience to realize that lessons about ourselves can be learned through the story of the X-Men. By witnessing and learning from the actions of a misguided mutant like Magneto, humankind can learn how to be more understanding and tolerant—like Charles Xavier.

Works Cited

Brewer, H. Michael. *Who Needs a Superhero? Finding Virtue, Vice, and What's Holy in the Comics*. Baker Books, 2004, pp. 134-44.

Singer, Bryan, director. *X-Men*. Performances by Hugh Jackman, Ian McKellen, and Patrick Stewart, Marvel Studios, 2000. Film.

With these factors in mind, Gwen created a list of what to focus on in her next draft.

# Gwen Ganow (Student)

## *Superhero Project: Author's Statement Revision List*

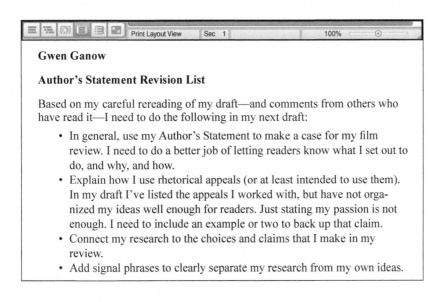

**Gwen Ganow**

**Author's Statement Revision List**

Based on my careful rereading of my draft—and comments from others who have read it—I need to do the following in my next draft:

- In general, use my Author's Statement to make a case for my film review. I need to do a better job of letting readers know what I set out to do, and why, and how.
- Explain how I use rhetorical appeals (or at least intended to use them). In my draft I've listed the appeals I worked with, but have not organized my ideas well enough for readers. Just stating my passion is not enough. I need to include an example or two to back up that claim.
- Connect my research to the choices and claims that I make in my review.
- Add signal phrases to clearly separate my research from my own ideas.

Gwen then implemented these revisions in the following draft. The blue text in the body of the Statement indicates places where Gwen reworked her Statement.

## Gwen Ganow (Student)

### Superhero Project: Author's Statement
### Draft 2

**Gwen's notes on draft 2 of her Author's Statement**

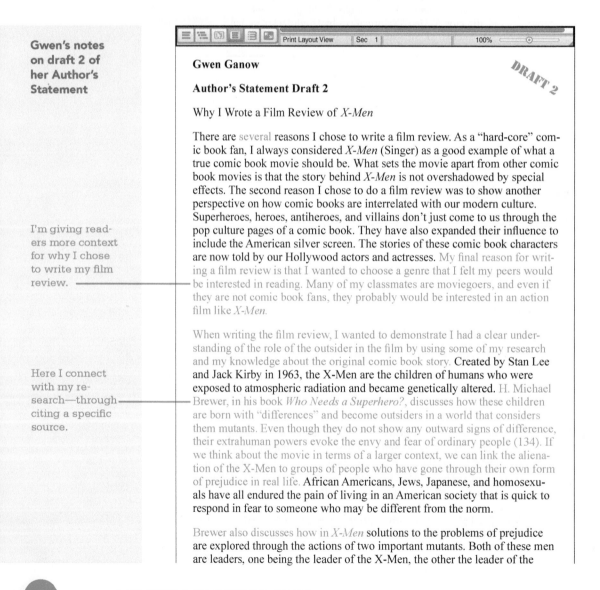

Gwen Ganow

**Author's Statement Draft 2**

Why I Wrote a Film Review of *X-Men*

There are several reasons I chose to write a film review. As a "hard-core" comic book fan, I always considered *X-Men* (Singer) as a good example of what a true comic book movie should be. What sets the movie apart from other comic book movies is that the story behind *X-Men* is not overshadowed by special effects. The second reason I chose to do a film review was to show another perspective on how comic books are interrelated with our modern culture. Superheroes, heroes, antiheroes, and villains don't just come to us through the pop culture pages of a comic book. They have also expanded their influence to include the American silver screen. The stories of these comic book characters are now told by our Hollywood actors and actresses. My final reason for writing a film review is that I wanted to choose a genre that I felt my peers would be interested in reading. Many of my classmates are moviegoers, and even if they are not comic book fans, they probably would be interested in an action film like *X-Men*.

When writing the film review, I wanted to demonstrate I had a clear understanding of the role of the outsider in the film by using some of my research and my knowledge about the original comic book story. Created by Stan Lee and Jack Kirby in 1963, the X-Men are the children of humans who were exposed to atmospheric radiation and became genetically altered. H. Michael Brewer, in his book *Who Needs a Superhero?*, discusses how these children are born with "differences" and become outsiders in a world that considers them mutants. Even though they do not show any outward signs of difference, their extrahuman powers evoke the envy and fear of ordinary people (134). If we think about the movie in terms of a larger context, we can link the alienation of the X-Men to groups of people who have gone through their own form of prejudice in real life. African Americans, Jews, Japanese, and homosexuals have all endured the pain of living in an American society that is quick to respond in fear to someone who may be different from the norm.

Brewer also discusses how in *X-Men* solutions to the problems of prejudice are explored through the actions of two important mutants. Both of these men are leaders, one being the leader of the X-Men, the other the leader of the

**I'm giving readers more context for why I chose to write my film review.**

**Here I connect with my research—through citing a specific source.**

Ganow, *Author's Statement Draft 2,* Continued

**Gwen's notes on draft 2 of her Author's Statement**

Brotherhood of Mutants. Charles Xavier creates a school for the gifted for young ostracized mutants. He teaches his mutant students to use their powers to benefit humanity, even if that same humanity hated and distrusted them (142). Xavier's "turn the other cheek" philosophy links him to the Jesus Christ of Christian culture. The fact that Xavier provides a safe house for people rejected by humanity also links him to our real life organizations like NAACP, GLBT resource centers, and some of our churches.

In his book, Brewer also focuses on how Magneto's perspective on humanity stems from his experiences as a young boy at a WWII concentration camp. This experience left Magneto distrustful of humanity, and he is convinced that mutants are bound to suffer the same fate met by the inmates of the Nazi death camps (143). To preserve the survival of his mutant species, Magneto declares war on humankind. We can link the thoughts and actions of Magneto to our own real-world thoughts and actions. We, as humans, have always wanted to put our persecutors into the shoes and lives of the persecuted. If we were given the technology to right the wrongs against us, would we create a machine similar to Magneto's? As humans, why are we quick to return violence with more violence?

> I've worked in signal phrases to make my research more apparent and to make my Statement more readable.

Overall, I wanted my readers to see my passion for the subject. One of the ways I did this was by opening with the fact that I am a "hard-core" comic book fan. Besides demonstrating my passion, I wanted to persuade my readers, by using pathos, to understand that you could read the film as a larger statement on the intolerance GLBT people often face. One of the ways I achieved this was by relying on logos, helping my readers follow the film logically, using strategies employed in other film reviews, such as giving snippets of the plot and using some of the plot summary to highlight the film's strength. While both pathos and logos are important for reaching my audience, I realized that if I did not establish my ethos, people would not care about what I had to say. By incorporating the theory of punctuated equilibrium, which I know about because of my zoology/biology major, and connecting it to the film, I help readers view me as a knowledgeable and informed writer.

> I've made it clearer how I set out to use ethos, pathos, and logos, and backed that up with details.

I studied several film reviews to help me figure out how to best create my review. One of the things that was missing from my initial draft was placing the film in a broader context. Thus, in my revision I began the review by discussing my relationship to comics (even if briefly) and then moved on to the film itself. Another thing I wanted to make sure to achieve in the film review was a clear evaluation of the film. My earlier draft did not really make this clear; it primarily consisted of a retelling of some of the plot. In the revision I made sure to include this, not only in the close of the review but with some word choices in the review, such as "powerful image," "good chemistry," and "fine job."

When comic book fans or superhero film fans finish reading my review, I hope that they will see that *X-Men* is definitely an appealing film. More importantly, though, I want my audience to realize that lessons about ourselves can be learned through the story of the X-Men. By witnessing and learning from the actions of a misguided mutant like Magneto, humankind can learn how to be more understanding and tolerant—like Charles Xavier.

*Continues next page*

**Ganow, *Author's Statement Draft 2*,** *Continued*

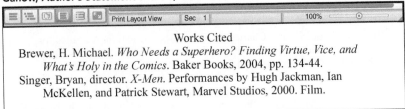

Works Cited

Brewer, H. Michael. *Who Needs a Superhero? Finding Virtue, Vice, and What's Holy in the Comics*. Baker Books, 2004, pp. 134-44.

Singer, Bryan, director. *X-Men*. Performances by Hugh Jackman, Ian McKellen, and Patrick Stewart, Marvel Studios, 2000. Film.

At this point, Gwen asks her respondents to read the above draft with the following questions in mind:

» Is my tone persuasive enough?

» Have I said enough about the film reviews I studied as models?

» What is the single most important revision I can make to strengthen my Author's Statement?

Respondents suggest that Gwen:

» Improve her persuasiveness by looking carefully at the word choices in her Author's Statement

» Make more-specific comments about the film reviews she used as models for her own review

» Refer to more than one outside source

Gwen agrees with the first two suggestions, but feels that adding more sources is not necessary to achieve her purpose. With this feedback and her own ideas in mind, Gwen creates a quick revision list before moving on to her final draft.

# Gwen Ganow (Student)

## *Superhero Project: Author's Statement Revision List*

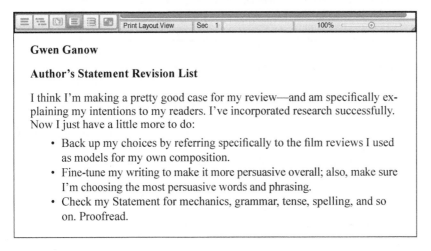

> **Gwen Ganow**
>
> **Author's Statement Revision List**
>
> I think I'm making a pretty good case for my review—and am specifically explaining my intentions to my readers. I've incorporated research successfully. Now I just have a little more to do:
>
> - Back up my choices by referring specifically to the film reviews I used as models for my own composition.
> - Fine-tune my writing to make it more persuasive overall; also, make sure I'm choosing the most persuasive words and phrasing.
> - Check my Statement for mechanics, grammar, tense, spelling, and so on. Proofread.

With these points in mind, Gwen revises her Statement a final time. The document below (created in Microsoft Word) shows Gwen's edits as tracked changes.

# Gwen Ganow (Student)

## *Superhero Project: Author's Statement Final (shows edits)*

> **Gwen Ganow**
>
> **Author's Statement FINAL (shows edits)**
>
> Why I Wrote a Film Review of *X-Men*
>
> Why did I choose to write a film review—and to write one about *X-Men*? I have several reasons. ~~There are several reasons I chose to write a film review.~~ As First, as a "hard-core" comic book fan, I've always considered *X-Men* (Singer) ~~as~~ to be a good example of what a true comic book movie should be. ~~What sets the movie apart from other comic book movies is that the story behind X-Men is not overshadowed by special effects.~~ *X-Men*, the film, inspired me to write a review because of what sets it apart from other comic book films: the *X-Men* story itself. The filmmaker clearly understood this, and did not clutter the story with over-the-top special effects. **The second reason I chose to** ~~do~~

*Continues next page*

*Ganow, Author's Statement: Final (shows edits), Continued*

Print Layout View — Sec 1 — 100%

write a film review is a little broader: I wanted to comment on ~~was to show another perspective on~~ how comic books are ~~interrelated~~ intertwined with ~~our~~ modern popular culture. Superheroes, heroes, antiheroes, and villains don't just come to us through ~~the pop culture pages of a~~ comic books anymore. They ~~have also~~ come to us through Hollywood, brought to life ~~expanded their influence to include the American silver screen. A~~ by the actors and actresses who portray the characters and stories of America's favorite superheroes. ~~The stories of these comic book characters are now told by our Hollywood actors and actresses.~~ My final reason for choosing to write a film review, rather than a researched journal article, for example, is that I wanted to choose a genre that I ~~felt~~ knew my peers would relate to. ~~be interested in reading.~~ Many of my classmates are moviegoers and readers of reviews: ~~, and e~~Even if they are not comic book fans, they are likely to ~~probably would~~ be interested in an action film like *X-Men*, and therefore in a review of the film.

~~When writing the~~ In my ~~film~~ review, I wanted to demonstrate ~~I had~~ a clear understanding of the role of the outsider in *X-Men*. ~~the film.~~ To do this, I drew on ~~by using some of my~~ research and my own knowledge ~~about~~ of the original *X-Men* comic book story. Created by Stan Lee and Jack Kirby in 1963, the X-Men are the children of humans who were exposed to atmospheric radiation and became genetically altered. H. Michael Brewer, in his book *Who Needs a Superhero?*, discusses how these children are born with "differences" and become outsiders in a world that considers them mutants. Even though they do not show any outward signs of difference, their extrahuman powers evoke the envy and fear of ordinary people (134). If we think about the movie in terms of a larger context, we can link the alienation of the X-Men to groups of people who have gone through their own form of prejudice in real life. African Americans, Jews, Japanese, and ~~homosexuals~~ gay men and lesbians have ~~all~~ endured the pain of living in an American society that is quick to respond in fear to someone who may be different from the norm.

Brewer also discusses how in *X-Men* authors Lee and Kirby explore solutions to the problems of prejudice ~~are explored~~ through ~~the actions of~~ two important mutants: Charles Xavier and Magneto. Both of these characters ~~men~~ are leaders: Xavier ~~, one being the leader of~~ leads the X-Men, while Magneto ~~the other the leader of~~ leads the Brotherhood of Mutants. ~~Charles~~ Xavier creates a school for the gifted for young ~~ostracized~~ outcast mutants:~~,~~ where he ~~He~~ teaches ~~his mutant students~~ them to use their powers to benefit humanity, even if that same humanity hate~~d~~s and distrust~~ed~~s them (142). Xavier's "turn the other cheek" philosophy links him to the Jesus Christ of Christian culture. The fact that Xavier provides a safe house for people rejected by humanity also links him to our real-life organizations ~~like~~ such as the NAACP, GLBT resource centers, and some of our churches.

In his book, Brewer also focuses on how Magneto's perspective on humanity stems from his experiences as a young boy at a WWII concentration camp. ~~This experience~~ Life in the camp left Magneto distrustful and despairing of humanity, and ~~he is~~ convinced that mutants are bound to suffer the same fate as Jews imprisoned and murdered in ~~met by the inmates of the~~ Nazi death camps (143). To preserve the survival of his mutant species, Magneto declares war on humankind. ~~We can link~~ I see Magneto's ~~the thoughts and actions~~ distrust and violence as related to contemporary life and the collective urge to "right wrongs," gain

**Ganow, *Author's Statement: Final* (shows edits),** *Continued*

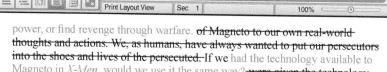

power, or find revenge through warfare. ~~of Magneto to our own real-world thoughts and actions. We, as humans, have always wanted to put our persecutors into the shoes and lives of the persecuted.~~ If we had the technology available to Magneto in *X-Men*, would we use it the same way? ~~were given the technology to right the wrongs against us, would we create a machine similar to Magneto's? As humans, why are we quick to~~ Would we return violence with more violence?

In my review, I consciously worked with rhetorical appeals. Overall, I wanted my readers to see my passion for my topic—toward superheroes, society, and the film *X-Men*. ~~the subject.~~ I worked to establish ethos ~~One of the ways I did this was opening with the fact that I am~~ by letting readers know I am a ~~"hard-core"~~ serious comic book fan and think of myself as somewhat of an expert on the genre. Besides demonstrating my passion, I wanted to persuade my readers; ~~by using pathos,~~ by appealing to emotion to persuade them to ~~understand that you could~~ read the film as a larger statement—a statement on the intolerance that "outsiders," specifically GLBT people, often face. I supported my argument logically, with ~~One of the ways I achieved this was by relying on logos, helping my readers follow the film logically,~~ key points from the plot, ~~using~~ and used strategies I learned from other film reviewers, such as using summary and highlighting particular moments in a film. ~~employed in other film reviews, such as giving snippets of the plot and using some of the plot summary to highlight the film's strength.~~ While both pathos and logos ~~are~~ were important for reaching my audience, I realized that if I did not establish my ethos, people would not care about what I had to say. For example, I ~~By~~ incorporat~~ing~~ed the theory of punctuated equilibrium that I learned about in my studies as a ~~, which I know about because of my~~ zoology/biology major, and used that as a lens for reading ~~and connecting it to~~ the film~~;~~. I believe this perspective, and the fact that I am a longtime and avid comics reader, helped my audience see ~~I help readers view~~ me as a knowledgeable and informed writer.

I studied several film reviews to help me figure out how to best create my own review. ~~One of the things~~ Something that I did not do in ~~was missing from~~ my initial draft was to place ~~placing~~ the film in a broader context. ~~Thus, in my revision~~ In my next draft, I began with a brief discussion of ~~the review by discussing~~ my relationship to comics ~~(even if briefly)~~ and then moved on to the film itself. Another thing I focused on in revisions was ~~wanted~~ to make sure ~~to achieve in the film review was~~ I gave a clear opinion ~~a clear evaluation~~ of the film. I did not do this in ~~My~~ my earlier draft, ~~did not really make this clear; it primarily consisted of a~~ which was also too focused on retelling ~~of some of~~ the plot~~:~~—and not focused enough on evaluating it. In my revised review, ~~the revision~~ I made sure to be more straightforward in my opinion, and to choose words that supported my observations clearly. I sharpened up my language to make it more persuasive and precise, using phrases ~~include this, not only in the close of the review but with some word choices in the review,~~ such as "powerful image," and "good chemistry," ~~and "fine job."~~

When comic book fans or superhero film fans ~~finish reading~~ read my review, I want them to ~~hope that they will~~ see that *X-Men* is ~~definitely an appealing~~ a film worth seeing—and one that offers insight into human experience. ~~More importantly, though,~~ I want my audience to realize that—through the story of the

*Continues next page*

Ganow, *Author's Statement: Final (shows edits), Continued*

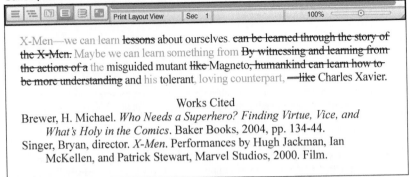

X-Men—we can learn ~~lessons~~ about ourselves. ~~can be learned through the story of the X-Men.~~ Maybe we can learn something from ~~By witnessing and learning from the actions of a~~ the misguided mutant ~~like~~ Magneto, ~~humankind can learn how to be more understanding~~ and his tolerant, ~~loving counterpart,~~ ~~—like~~ Charles Xavier.

### Works Cited

Brewer, H. Michael. *Who Needs a Superhero? Finding Virtue, Vice, and What's Holy in the Comics*. Baker Books, 2004, pp. 134-44.

Singer, Bryan, director. *X-Men*. Performances by Hugh Jackman, Ian McKellen, and Patrick Stewart, Marvel Studios, 2000. Film.

The following document shows Gwen's work with her edits accepted.

## Gwen Ganow (Student)

### Superhero Project: Author's Statement
### Final (edits incorporated)

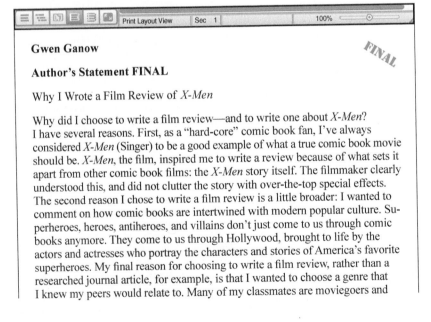

Gwen Ganow

**Author's Statement FINAL**

FINAL

Why I Wrote a Film Review of *X-Men*

Why did I choose to write a film review—and to write one about *X-Men*? I have several reasons. First, as a "hard-core" comic book fan, I've always considered *X-Men* (Singer) to be a good example of what a true comic book movie should be. *X-Men*, the film, inspired me to write a review because of what sets it apart from other comic book films: the *X-Men* story itself. The filmmaker clearly understood this, and did not clutter the story with over-the-top special effects. The second reason I chose to write a film review is a little broader: I wanted to comment on how comic books are intertwined with modern popular culture. Superheroes, heroes, antiheroes, and villains don't just come to us through comic books anymore. They come to us through Hollywood, brought to life by the actors and actresses who portray the characters and stories of America's favorite superheroes. My final reason for choosing to write a film review, rather than a researched journal article, for example, is that I wanted to choose a genre that I knew my peers would relate to. Many of my classmates are moviegoers and

**Ganow, *Author's Statement: Final*,** *Continued*

readers of reviews: Even if they are not comic book fans, they are likely to be interested in an action film like *X-Men*, and therefore in a review of the film.

In my review, I wanted to demonstrate a clear understanding of the role of the outsider in *X-Men*. To do this, I drew on research and my own knowledge of the original *X-Men* comic book story. Created by Stan Lee and Jack Kirby in 1963, the *X-Men* are the children of humans who were exposed to atmospheric radiation and became genetically altered. H. Michael Brewer, in his book *Who Needs a Superhero?*, discusses how these children are born with "differences" and become outsiders in a world that considers them mutants. Even though they do not show any outward signs of difference, their extrahuman powers evoke the envy and fear of ordinary people (134). If we think about the movie in terms of a larger context, we can link the alienation of the X-Men to groups of people who have gone through their own form of prejudice in real life. African Americans, Jews, Japanese, and gay men and lesbians have endured the pain of living in an American society that is quick to respond in fear to someone who may be different from the norm.

Brewer also discusses how in *X-Men* authors Lee and Kirby explore solutions to the problem of prejudice through two important mutants: Charles Xavier and Magneto. Both of these characters are leaders; Xavier leads the X-Men, while Magneto leads the Brotherhood of Mutants. Xavier creates a school for the gifted for young outcast mutants, where he teaches them to use their powers to benefit humanity, even if that same humanity hates and distrusts them (142). Xavier's "turn the other cheek" philosophy links him to the Jesus Christ of Christian culture. The fact that Xavier provides a safe house for people rejected by humanity also links him to our real-life organizations such as the NAACP, GLBT resource centers, and some of our churches.

In his book, Brewer also focuses on how Magneto's perspective on humanity stems from his experiences as a young boy at a WWII concentration camp. Life in the camp left Magneto distrustful and despairing of humanity, and convinced that mutants are bound to suffer the same fate as Jews imprisoned and murdered in Nazi death camps (143). To preserve the survival of his mutant species, Magneto declares war on humankind. I see Magneto's distrust and violence as related to contemporary life and the collective urge to "right wrongs," gain power, or find revenge through warfare. If we had the technology available to Magneto in *X-Men*, would we use it the same way? Would we return violence with more violence?

In my review, I consciously worked with rhetorical appeals. Overall, I wanted my readers to see my passion for my topic—toward superheroes, society, and the film *X-Men*. I worked to establish ethos by letting readers know I am a serious comic book fan and think of myself as somewhat of an expert on the genre. Besides demonstrating my passion, I wanted to persuade my readers by using pathos, by appealing to emotion to persuade them to read the film as a larger statement—a statement on the intolerance that "outsiders," specifically GLBT people, often face. I supported my argument logically, with key points from the plot, and used strategies I learned from other film reviewers, such as using summary and highlighting particular moments in a film. While both pathos and

*Continues next page*

☞ **Attention, authors & artists! A word on using technology for peer review.**

If you are drafting your composition in a Microsoft Word or Apache OpenOffice document, there are features that allow you to track your changes so others can edit and add comments on your draft electronically. This might be handy if you can't arrange to meet with a reader in person. E-mail your draft to a reader, or share it in a space such as Google Drive (drive.google.com) or DropBox (dropbox .com).

**Ganow, *Author's Statement: Final*, *Continued***

Print Layout View    Sec  1    100%

logos were important for reaching my audience, I realized that if I did not establish my ethos, people would not care about what I had to say. For example,
I incorporated the theory of punctuated equilibrium that I learned about in my
studies as a zoology/biology major, and used that as a lens for reading the film.
I believe this perspective, and the fact that I am a longtime and avid comics
reader, helped my audience see me as a knowledgeable and informed writer.

I studied several film reviews to help me figure out how to best create my own
review. Something that I did not do in my initial draft was to place the film
in a broader context. In my next draft, I began with a brief discussion of my
relationship to comics and then moved on to the film itself. Another thing I
focused on in revisions was to make sure I gave a clear opinion of the film. I
did not do this in my earlier draft, which was also too focused on retelling the
plot—and not focused enough on evaluating it. In my revised review, I made
sure to be more straightforward in my opinion, and to choose words that supported my observations clearly. I sharpened up my language to make it more
persuasive and precise, using phrases such as "powerful image" and "good
chemistry."

When comic book fans or superhero film fans read my review, I want them
to see that *X-Men* is a film worth seeing—and one that offers insight into human experience. I want my audience to realize that—through the story of the
X-Men—we can learn about ourselves. Maybe we can learn something from
the misguided mutant Magneto and his tolerant, loving counterpart, Charles
Xavier.

Works Cited

Brewer, H. Michael. *Who Needs a Superhero? Finding Virtue, Vice, and
    What's Holy in the Comics.* Baker Books, 2004, pp. 134-44.
Singer, Bryan, director. *X-Men.* Performances by Hugh Jackman, Ian
    McKellen, and Patrick Stewart, Marvel Studios, 2000. Film.

# REMIXING YOUR WORK INTO DIFFERENT GENRES

Sometimes we ask our students to remix their finished genre piece into a different genre. For example, Gwen, who composed a film review on superheroes and justice, thought at one point that she'd create a presentation, animation, or advertisement. Remixing her film review would be an opportunity to work in a different genre on a topic she had already researched and written about—and to think about the different ways of reaching an audience that other genres allow.

## Guided Process: Remixing a Genre Project

### Gwen Ganow (Student)

*Remix of Film Review*
*PowerPoint: "We Are All Mutants"*

Gwen wants to shape her film review into something new. When our students create remixes, we ask them to think their projects through as shown in the following assignment.

---

**ENG 101, Professor Braziller**

**Assignment: Remix Your Genre Project**

**What is a remix?** When you remix an object or composition, you repurpose it. For example, Martha Stewart might repurpose flowerpots to be utensil holders in her kitchen. Originally intended for outdoor use to hold soil and plants, the pots will need to be overhauled for indoor kitchen use. Stewart would probably wash them, apply a nontoxic sealant, and paint them or decorate them in some way. The finished product—the utensil holder that was formerly a flowerpot—is a remix.

**How will you create a remix?** Your assignment is to remix one of the genre pieces you've already composed. You will repurpose your creation for a different context. This may involve changing the purpose, audience, and/or message of your original piece. You should not have to do significant new research for your remix. Your energy should go toward revising your original material to fit into a new mode and/or genre appropriate to your new context.

For example, you might remix an editorial you wrote about school funding into a short YouTube video. The editorial was originally geared toward politicians or taxpayers, but you now imagine an audience of college students. Thus, you need to make the editorial interesting and palatable to college students. You also need to take into account the conventions of the new genre.

You might also consider taking parts from several of your genre pieces and weaving them together into a new work. Quilters do this when they take scraps of fabric from outgrown clothing and sew them together into a new item: a quilt.

---

Gwen repurposes her film review to create a PowerPoint presentation that begins with a top 10 list (inspired by the "Top Ten" lists feature of the *Late Show with David Letterman*). In this case, her purpose is to persuade an audience of fans who watched the film when it came out in the year 2000, to watch it again. She chooses the genre of the top 10 list because it gives her the opportunity to use humor to persuade. Her plan is to share her list with friends and fans on social media sites, and to ask them to contribute their own lists of reasons for watching the *X-Men* movie again.

Following are her first three slides.

POWERPOINT SLIDE ▶
**Gwen Ganow,** Remix
of film review.
*Slides: Gwen Dalynn
Ganow. X-Men poster:
Everett Collection.*

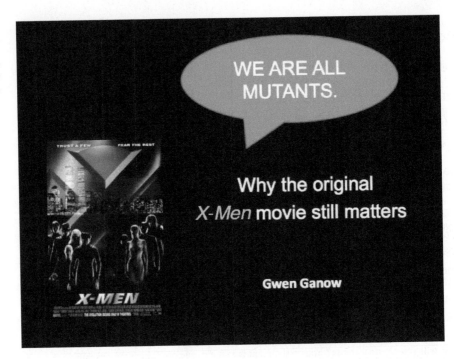

◄ POWERPOINT SLIDES
**Gwen Ganow,** "We
Are All Mutants."
*Gwen Dalynn Ganow.*

Top **10** reasons to watch
the original *X-Men* movie again

10. The year 2000 was a wicked long time ago.

9. Hugh Jackman cage-fight scenes.

8. Pre-*True Blood* Anna Paquin. Halle Berry. Lycra.

7. Need refresher on details of Mutant Registration Act.

6. Xavier School for Gifted Youngsters is way cooler than Hogwarts.

Top **10** reasons to watch
the original *X-Men* movie again

5. That scene where Jackman flips the fork-fingered bird.

4. Far too long since a Holocaust survivor with magnetic-field-control superpowers tried for world domination.

3. "Trust a few and fear the rest" starting to sound like a good idea.

2. Humans (except for Patrick Stewart) still totally overrated.

1. You are *such* a geek.

CHECKLIST **Remixing a genre piece?** Keep the following questions in mind.

| WHAT'S MY RHETORICAL SITUATION? | WHAT GENRE CONVENTIONS MATTER? |
|---|---|

☐ **Purpose.** What is the purpose of my new, remixed composition? How can I make that purpose clear?

☐ **Audience.** Who is the targeted audience for my remix? How can I take my new audience's expectations, values, and concerns into account? What kind of vocabulary, examples and details, organization, and other elements should I use to appeal to my new audience?

☐ **Rhetorical appeals.** How can I use rhetorical appeals to connect with my new audience?

☐ **Modes & media.** What mode and medium will be most likely to engage my new audience?

☐ **Elements of the genre.** How can I use the elements of my new genre to guide my new audience's experience?

☐ **Style.** How can I use word choice, sentence structure, literary devices (like metaphor), and other stylistic techniques to keep my new audience engaged?

☐ **Design.** How can I use design elements, such as color, images, and font, to emphasize my purpose and main point?

☐ **Sources.** What kinds of sources should I use to convince my new audience of my point? How should I cite these sources appropriately in my new genre?

# 10 ASSEMBLING A MULTIGENRE PROJECT

**CONTENTS**

MULTIGENRE PROJECT ▶
**Neil Carr,**
"Video Games and
Violence."
*Neil Carr.*

What is a multigenre project? It's a collection of three or more genre compositions, built around a single topic. A multigenre project is an opportunity to experiment. It also gives you the chance to practice in a variety of rhetorical situations, forms of composition, and types of media.

Let's look at an example. You've conducted research on the topic of, say, the significance of the bond between people and dogs. Through the course of your research, brainstorming, and drafting, you decide that you want to make the case that dogs were essential to the rise of civilization (persuasive). You also want to present a history of the relationship between humans and canines (informative), and perhaps even tell a story of a particular relationship (narrative). You are strong in a variety of genres and media (better at some than others). Your audience is one of general readers; that is, it's an unspecialized audience, but one with some interest in dogs and humanity. A multigenre project for your topic could include a few of these genres and media options:

» INFORMATIVE. An **annotated timeline** tracing human-canine interactions from ancient times to the present.

» PERSUASIVE. A brief TED talk–style video **presentation** on how and why dogs were critical to human civilization.

» NARRATIVE. A **story** of how dogs and humans relate now.

» PERSUASIVE. A **photo essay** or **slide show** that demonstrates how dogs benefit humans by reducing stress.

» INFORMATIVE. An **annotated map** locating where humans first settled and domesticated dogs.

» NARRATIVE. An **interview** with a dog behaviorist, a therapy dog trainer, or a psychologist who uses dogs to treat humans.

» PERSUASIVE. An **Author's or Artist's Statement** that brings everything together.

Alternatively, maybe you want to put together a collection of genre pieces that are entirely persuasive. Why not? There are a lot of interesting options. In this chapter, we want to introduce you to possibilities. Elsewhere in this book, we provide advice on how to compose in specific genres; here we're going to show you how, once you've composed your individual genre pieces, you can put them together into a coherent whole. We also provide you with sample projects by student authors and artists Neil Carr, Gwen Ganow, and Dawson Swan.

For another example of a **multigenre project,** see Kristen LaCroix's work in Chapter 1.

# THE POSSIBILITIES OF THE MULTIGENRE PROJECT

Just like any research endeavor, a genre project allows you to join a conversation about a particular subject or issue. Whether you research and compose a single genre piece or multiple related pieces, you address a research question, make clear arguments, and draw on sources, all while keeping a strong sense of purpose and audience. Unlike more traditional academic projects, genre projects let you break away from (or embrace, if you prefer) the usual forms such as the research paper. Multigenre projects go a step beyond: They open up unlimited channels and formats for you to convey your points. Nothing is out of bounds. Think handmade objects, videos, blogs, animations, photo essays, collages, and other visual arguments. Further, genre projects, and multigenre projects in particular, offer you the chance to connect with audiences beyond the classroom.

## Your Rhetorical Situation

When you begin thinking about creating a multigenre project, consider the following:

**Furthering your purpose**    You can do this by assembling a coherent collection. Think of each genre piece as a chapter that contributes to a whole. You will unify the pieces by building in relationships among them by choosing a sequence and package (more on this on pp. 504–506)—and by composing an Introduction that pulls everything together. For multigenre projects, we recommend that you compose a separate Author's or Artist's Statement for each of your individual genre pieces, and use the Introduction to discuss how the pieces work together. However, it also works to create one Author's or Artist's Statement for the entire project. Check with your instructor about specific preferences. (For more on Author's and Artist's Statements, see Chapter 4, pp. 231–44.)

**Reaching your audience**    You might do this by providing different *perspectives*. As you decide on the genres to compose in, think about whether you want to convey multiple perspectives on your topic through each piece. For example, if you are presenting an argument, you could address a different point of view in each composition.

**Using rhetorical appeals to your advantage**    Imagine how you might use each genre piece to make your case through different rhetorical appeals. Maybe in one genre you emphasize ethos; in another, logos; and in another, pathos. Or maybe you want to organize your project around a single rhetorical appeal.

**Choosing modes and media**   Think about using a mix of modes and media throughout your pieces so that your audience has different ways to connect with your message. Some of the best projects we've seen are a combination of textual, visual, and audio compositions.

## The Conventions of the Multigenre Project

For advice, examples, and guidelines for composing in individual genres, see Chapters 1–4.

Every multigenre project will be different—a culmination of one author's choices about which genres to mix together, which perspectives to represent, which voices or tones to incorporate. There are no "conventions" for a multigenre work beyond the use of multiple genres to convey ideas to an audience. Typically, we ask student composers of multigenre projects to provide an Introduction, a separate Author's or Artist's Statement for each individual piece, or a single statement in which they reflect on each of their genre pieces. The Statement(s) should include Works Cited lists.

## THE STEPS TO ASSEMBLING A MULTIGENRE PROJECT

For help with **Author's and Artist's Statements,** see Chapter 4, pages 237–46, and Chapter 8, pages 476–79.

**1. Introduce your project and provide context**   Write a one- to two-page Introduction that gives your audience an overview of your topic, your scope, and what sparked your interest in your topic. Provide a brief explanation for your rationale for the sequence of your genre pieces (more on that below). You can provide more details— and cite and document your research—in your Author's or Artist's Statement(s), which is typically longer than the Introduction and includes a list of References or Works Cited. Alternatively, you can combine your Introduction and Statement into one document, as some of our students have done.

Your Introduction should also provide any context that your audience will need to fully understand your project and individual genre pieces. This means you may need to provide a brief history of your topic, the people who are key to its larger discussion, and the main controversies surrounding it.

**2. Sequence your genre pieces**   Do this in a way that will make sense to your audience. Each piece should prepare your audience for the one that follows it. Sequencing helps orient your audience, and it also helps you methodically achieve your purpose. Here are some scenarios:

» If your goal is to convince your audience to take action on a specific problem, begin with a composition that highlights that problem, and end with a piece that offers a possible solution and/or makes a direct call to action. An alternative approach could be to begin with a visual piece that shows what could happen if no one took action to solve the problem.

» If your purpose is to compare or contrast specific views on your topic, you might arrange your pieces to highlight differences and similarities.

» If one of your goals is to tell a story, sequence your pieces into a narrative structure (consider a beginning, middle, and end), and bring out narrative elements such as character and conflict.

» If you want to emphasize a particular rhetorical appeal, think about how the order of your genre pieces could do that. For example, to emphasize pathos, you could begin and end with the pieces that will evoke the most emotion in your audience. Alternatively, if establishing your ethos is more important, you might begin with a piece that establishes your expertise and credibility, such as a researched journal article.

**3. Title your project**    Your title should reflect your topic and your "take" on your topic. Create a title that will spark the interest of your target audience, a title that is memorable and provocative. The title should reflect your project's message but can go beyond simply stating it. Consider how the tone and word choice of the title will build expectations in readers' minds about what the project will or will not do.

Here are some titles our students have come up with:

» Dawson Swan's project on nature and mental health: "The Threat of Nature Deficit Disorder" (p. 514)

» Gwen Ganow's project on how the concept of superheroes intersects with "real life": "When Worlds Collide: Why Superheroes Matter" (p. 511)

» Scarlet Moody's project on Rwanda radio: "The Rwandan Genocide and Radio-Television's Libre des Milles Collines"

» Emma Jones's project on Alzheimer's disease: "The Road of Life"

**4. Create an Author's or Artist's Statement**    Use your Statement to discuss your research, explain your rhetorical choices, and evaluate your project overall. (See Chapter 4, pp. 231–44, and Chapter 8, pp. 476–79, for advice and examples.) We encourage our students to write a Statement for each genre piece, and provide an Introduction or project-wide Statement to unify their work.

**5. Package your project creatively**    While a standard research paper is generally packaged quite simply, with a cover page or perhaps in a folder, a multigenre project can be packaged more imaginatively. As with every other aspect of your project, your package and delivery will impact your audience and indicate your tone and angle on your subject. For example, a multigenre project packaged in a

---

☞ **Attention, authors & artists! Need some ideas for genres?**

Working on a multigenre project? Great. There are lots of genres to choose from. Here are just a few (they can be delivered in digital, print, and/or 3-D physical media): researched arguments, editorials, articles, user manuals, brochures, encyclopedia articles, obituaries, exposés, editorials, letters to the editor, interviews, book reviews, essays, surveys, business letters, poems, personal letters, short stories, scripts, journal entries, memoirs, advice columns, political speeches, eulogies, tabloid articles, restaurant menus, top 10 lists, resumes, directions, syllabi, Web pages, photographs, collages, photo essays, charts, graphs, advertisements, comics, cartoons, posters, movie posters, skit performances, paintings, sketches, musical scores, musical performances, sculptures, audio essays, film clips, and scrapbook pages.

miniature black coffin indicates somberness, while a project presented in a minia-ture pink-polka-dotted coffin suggests a humorous and ironic approach.

Here are some ways students have packaged their projects in the past:

» A project on globalization: All the components were rolled up inside a mailing tube covered with stamps and postal marks from around the world.

» A project on the drinking age: All the genre pieces were presented in a wire wine bottle carrier.

» A project on education: The title page was designed to look like the cover of a teacher's grade book, and all the pieces inside had pale blue columns on the borders (like grade books have).

Which of the project titles on page 505 most pique your interest? Why? What does each title suggest about the scope and focus of the project?

**CHECKLIST** Assembling a Multigenre Project? Keep the following questions in mind.

Wherever you are in your composing process, it can be helpful to get feedback. Here are some more questions you might want to ask your respondents.

### THE RHETORICAL SITUATION

☐ **Purpose.** What is the overall purpose of my project? What are the purposes of my individual genre pieces? What is the effect of reading/viewing each piece in isolation versus reading/viewing each piece as a group? When all are experienced together, how is the effect different from reading/viewing each piece in isolation? How can I sequence or package my pieces to best achieve my overarching purpose? What title will signal my overall purpose to my readers?

☐ **Audience.** How does my Introduction and Author's/Artist's Statement work to draw my audience in? If I aim to persuade my audience, how does the sequencing encourage readers/viewers to accept my point of view? What kind of packaging will capture the attention of my audience?

☐ **Rhetorical appeals.** How do my individual genre compositions, Author's/Artist's Statements, and Introduction, taken together, establish my credibility (ethos)? Is there a clear logical aspect to

the project (logos)? Is there something that will resonate emotionally (pathos) with readers? Given my audience, should I emphasize one appeal over another, perhaps highlighting it in my Introduction? Given my purpose, can I use sequencing to begin and end my project with a particular appeal?

☐ **Modes & media.** Have I used a mix of modes and media throughout my pieces so that my audience has different ways to connect with my message? Have I balanced one mode/medium with others so that the project overall isn't text-heavy or too visual?

### THE GENRE'S CONVENTIONS

There are no conventions for multigenre projects. However, there are conventions for individual genres. See Chapters 1–4 for advice and examples.

# EXAMPLES OF MULTIGENRE PROJECTS

Let's take a look at some student projects. We've annotated these to highlight the components of each project and how the student assembled them into a whole. We've also indicated how our students handled their rhetorical choices (regarding purpose, audience, rhetorical appeals, and modes and media) and the possibilities of the multigenre project (elements, style, design, and use of sources).

## Guided Reading: A Multigenre Project

### Neil Carr (Student)

*Video Games and Violence: Who Should We Blame When Kids Are Violent?*

One multigenre project will look very different from another. Here is student author Neil Carr's multigenre project on video games and violence.

*(Project reprinted by permission of Neil Carr.)*

◀ STUDENT AUTHOR PHOTO
**Neil Carr.**
*Courtesy Neil Carr.*

**What are the parts? How do they work together?**

MULTIGENRE PIECES

**Neil's project consists of:**

An informative and persuasive **researched essay** on studies of video games and violence (p. 508).

A narrative and persuasive **audio diary** of a truancy officer (see recorder).

*(Continued on p. 508.)*

**What is the author/artist, Neil Carr, doing?**

NEIL'S RHETORICAL SITUATION

**Purpose**

Neil wants to persuade his audience that video games and their makers should not be blamed for the violent real-life behavior of some players.

**Audience**

Neil identifies his primary audience as general readers who do not have specialized knowledge of video games. He's aiming at regular citizens/taxpayers. He sequences his compositions so that his audience will get a sense of the humanity of gamers themselves, as well as the escape aspects of gaming, before he moves on to more detailed research findings.

**Rhetorical appeals**

Neil's choice to compose both a film script and an audio diary—both narrative and persuasive genres—indicates that appealing to pathos and ethos is important to him.

## MULTIGENRE PIECES

A narrative and persuasive **film script** of the story of two boys, one who plays video games and one who doesn't, comparing their tendencies toward violence.

The **film** (on DVD).

**To unify his project, Neil provides:**

An **Introduction** with contextual information.

An **Author's Statement** in which he discusses his research, explains his rhetorical choices, and evaluates his project as a whole.

**Packaging** for his print pieces—a binder with an illustrated cover—and a recorder that contains his audio piece.

## NEIL'S RHETORICAL SITUATION

### Modes & media

Neil chooses film and audio to engage his audience in a narrative, persuasive, and entertaining way. However, he opts to present his own views and research findings on the topic in a traditional research paper.

### Multigenre conventions

There are no conventions for multigenre projects. However, there are conventions for individual genres. See Chapters 1–4 for examples.

Let's look at the audio diary from Neil's multigenre project.

**What makes
this an audio
diary?**

**What is the
author/artist,
Neil Carr,
doing?**

**THE GENRE'S
CONVENTIONS**

**NEIL'S RHETORICAL
SITUATION**

### Elements of the genre

A diary entry is a first-person narrative in which the writer records thoughts and observations.

### Style

A diary entry is very casual; it often reads/ sounds like a person's speaking voice. In this case, Neil has adapted some literary narrative elements, and has written this piece almost like dialogue or even a short scene from a play.

### Design

In this case, Neil has provided a transcript of the audio diary. He has formatted it as a Word document; it looks like an essay.

---

**Neil Carr**

**Audio Diary of a Truancy Officer (transcript)**

March 31, 2013. This is truancy officer Mike Rendar, and this is the first entry of my audio diary. I've never done one of these before, but I decided to start because I've been put on a new duty—a pretty strange one. See, as a truancy officer, I usually patrol looking for kids trying to ditch their classes. When I find them, I ticket them—or rather, their parents—and get them to where they need to be. Well, I got called in by Sergeant Purser yesterday, on my day off, so he could tell me about my new assignment.

It seems that some kid named Thomas Miller was expelled from school yesterday for fighting. I guess with everything that's been going on lately . . . the school shootings and violence and all . . . Higher-ups must think the kid is gonna hurt someone.

I looked into the kid's profile, and I can see what they mean, but I just don't think it's gonna happen. Call it a hunch. [sigh] Oh, well. I'll begin my observation today . . . Here we go.

I spent all day yesterday watching this kid . . . nothing. He lives in a crappy little apartment with his dad. They live on the bottom floor, so I can go peek in the window sometime. At first, I waited in my car because the shades were all closed. Finally, the kid's dad opened the shades and left about 7:30 AM. Probably for work.

Once Dad left, I looked in to see what was going on. Nothing. Kid was probably sleeping. A couple hours later, I checked again. Kid was playing some video game. I checked again an hour later—same story. An hour later—no change.

That was when I realized this whole damn thing is political. The chief just doesn't want to get caught with his pants down . . . who can blame him. Anyway, the most exciting thing the kid did all day was switch from playing the video game to surfing the Net. I couldn't see what Web sites he was going to. Coulda been buying knitting needles . . . or looking up a recipe for a bomb.

April 1, 2013. It's morning again and I'm sitting in my car outside the kid's apartment . . . again. I've had way too much time to think just sitting here. I'm starting to wonder if what I'm doing is even legal. Course, even if it isn't, I wouldn't bring it up with Sergeant Purser. Up until now, I've enjoyed my job and I'd like to keep it. Besides, there's probably some new amendment to the Patriot Act.

*Continues next page*

---

### Purpose

Neil channels the voice of a truancy officer to make a point about video gamers. This piece fits in with the broader purpose of his multigenre project: to persuade others that video games and their producers should not be blamed for the violent behavior of some gamers.

### Audience

Neil's audience includes his classmates, his instructor, and a general audience.

If this had been a "real" audio diary by Officer Rendar, the audience could have been the court, if he'd been asked to submit his observations.

**Carr, *Audio Diary (transcript),* Continued**

THE GENRE'S
CONVENTIONS

## Sources

Typically the source for a diary entry is the writer's own experience. In this case, however, Neil is channeling a truancy officer's voice and experience. He has also based this on his research on how gamers respond to video games, and what video games may or may not have to do with violence.

NEIL'S RHETORICAL SITUATION

## Rhetorical appeals

Neil clearly appeals to ethos by choosing a truancy officer to be the speaker in this creative audio diary. The officer has authority and knowledge of teen behavior. Neil also appeals to pathos by presenting the officer as a sympathetic character; he also uses humor.

## Modes & media

Neil created an audio diary, which could just as easily have been a video diary. Either can be delivered in a digital environment. When he submitted his project, he included this paper transcript of the recording.

---

`≡ ≡ 🖾 🖽 ≣ 🖾   Print Layout View   Sec  1        100% ═══○══`

But this kid never leaves the damn house. I wanna go invite him out to Denny's . . . McDonald's, 7-Eleven, anything! Who doesn't leave their house?

It's the end of the day. Another day this kid hasn't moved. Seems to be having fun with his games, though. At least one of us is having a good time. He went online again today. I hope the kid is getting a girlfriend or something. [chuckle]

I wonder if his dad even knows he's been expelled. Wouldn't surprise me if he didn't . . . They never talk to each other.

April 2, 2013. I think I got too many of my personal thoughts in this thing yesterday. I guess I forgot I may have to turn this over to a court someday. Hopefully not. Problem is, it might be the only thing keeping me sane on this job. Hmm, either way I gotta try and keep it more professional today.

I just checked on the Miller kid . . . like I do every hour. He's back at it, playing his game. His father left approximately forty-five minutes ago. I'm going to go approach the window and see what I can see.

Ah geez . . . I went up to the window, and I was being as sneaky as a person can be in daylight, but I think the kid might've seen me . . . [pause] Hmmm, you know, I didn't think about this before, but if he sees me . . . [chuckle] I won't have to do this crappy duty anymore. I'll lie low out here for a while, maybe he didn't notice me after all.

[laughing] Wow, now that was surprising. The kid walks out his door, looks me straight in the eye, and hocks a loogie from his patio to the hood of my car. Man, that kid has got range! Since he didn't pull a gun and blow me away, I doubt the kid's actually gonna hurt anyone. Still, he's got some nerve to go spitting on a cop car.

Anyway, my cover is blown so I'm heading back to Purser's office now . . . He'll probably rip me a new one, but that's better than working this job. What a waste. Rendar out.

---

**Gwen Ganow (Student)**

*When Worlds Collide:*
*Why Superheroes Matter*

In her multigenre project, "When Worlds Collide: Why Superheroes Matter," Gwen Ganow represents a variety of genres and media, as her table of contents shows (see p. 512). (To learn more about Gwen's project, see Chapters 8 and 9.) *(Project reprinted by permission of Gwen Dalynn Ganow.)*

▲ STUDENT AUTHOR PHOTO
**Gwen Ganow.**

# *When Worlds Collide:*
# *Why Superheroes Matter*

Gwen Ganow
**Project Contents**

---

**What are the parts? How do they work together?**

**MULTIGENRE PIECES**

**Gwen's project consists of:**

A persuasive **researched argument** essay that examines the power of superheroes (item 2).

*(Continued on p. 512.)*

**What is the author/artist, Gwen Ganow, doing?**

**GWEN'S RHETORICAL SITUATION**

**Purpose**

Gwen's overall purpose is to persuade her audience that superheroes can help convey hope and strength to marginalized people who experience intolerance.

## MULTIGENRE PIECES

An informative and narrative **collage** that combines a number of paintings of comic book superheroes, original comic book artwork, and quotations from the comic books (item 3).

A narrative and persuasive **journal entry** written from the perspective of a young boy who reads comic books during the 1950s (item 4).

An informative **brochure** about a support group for gay superheroes and their allies (item 5).

A persuasive **film review** of the movie *X-Men* (item 6).

A persuasive **Power-Point presentation** on the movie *X-Men*, featuring a **top 10 list** (item 7).

A narrative **memoir** in which Gwen explores her experience with comic books with her mother, who is also a comic book fan (item 8).

**To unify her project, Gwen provides:**

An **Introduction** that offers context. In it, she explains her research and rhetorical choices, and evaluates her project (item 1).

**Packaging.** Gwen puts her project together in a Word document that she can e-mail to her instructor. This format suits her project because some of her genre pieces—such as her film review and PowerPoint—include embedded links to film clips and other media.

## GWEN'S RHETORICAL SITUATION

### Audience

Gwen's primary audience is made up of comic book readers; her choice for sequencing the genre pieces reflects her desire for readers to be immersed in the world of the superhero right away.

### Rhetorical appeals

Gwen's choice to compose a film review, researched argument, and brochure indicates that appeals based on ethos and logos are most important to her. However, she also conveys pathos, especially in her journal entry, memoir, and film review.

### Modes & media

Gwen decides on a mix of text and visuals in her project to help readers visualize, relate to, and interpret the world of the superhero.

### Multigenre conventions

There are no conventions for multigenre projects. However, there are conventions for individual genres. See Chapters 1–4 for examples.

## What makes this a **persuasive brochure**?

### THE GENRE'S CONVENTIONS

### Elements of the genre

Brochures are usually used to inform and/or persuade an audience, which is the case here. They are usually brief, to the point, and visual.

### Style

Gwen uses a casual but persuasive tone, and plays with the concept of the superhero to move readers/viewers to action.

### Design

She works in two columns to present her content. In column 1 she chooses gay pride flags instead of bullets to telegraph the message behind the brochure. In column 2 she presents her eye-catching images and centers the invitation to the meeting.

### Sources

Gwen draws on the sources she has used in her research. See her Works Cited list in Chapter 9 (p. 487).

---

Let's examine the brochure from Gwen's multigenre project.

**Superhero GSA Brochure**
**Gay/Straight Alliance: Be a Superhero**

 Sometimes you are Superman, and sometimes you are just Clark Kent, but your gay identity should never be hidden within yourself.

 If your parents love you even though you're an alien/mutant/superhero, they'll still love you even if you're gay.

 All gay superheroes need a Fortress of Solitude. One can be found in your GLBT (Gay, Lesbian, Bisexual, and Transgender) resource center.

 Superheroes fight for what is right. This includes the coexistence of all religions, all skin colors, and all sexual orientations.

 Sticks and stones will not break your steel bones.

 Secrets hurt everyone, even superheroes.

 Bigotry and hatred can be just as deadly as kryptonite. Always stand up for yourself, and let strength and hope guide your path.

 You're not alone. Superheroes have to struggle and fight for what they believe in.

 Captain America fights for freedom, democracy, and the American way. He desires these things for ALL Americans.

© Haze, 2006, <http://images.search.yahoo.com>.

**Hear ye! Hear ye!**
The GSA of Metropolis would like to invite all gay and straight superheroes to its first meeting of the year. Come as you are with an open heart and an open mind for a "brown bag" discussion on marriage in the twenty-first century. Through support for each other, we can lead the way for humanity.
The GSA meeting will be held at the time and place stated below:

GSA Headquarters
5655 W. Kent Ave.
Metropolis
Special Guest Speaker, Captain America
5-7 p.m.
Capes and refreshments will be provided.

---

## What is the author/artist, **Gwen Ganow**, doing?

### GWEN'S RHETORICAL SITUATION

### Purpose

In this brochure, Gwen makes a case for gay marriage, arguing for tolerance and presenting an invitation to a GSA (Gay/Straight Alliance) meeting. The brochure relates to her project on superheroes, "otherness," and acceptance.

### Audience

The audience for this piece is specifically gay teens, but Gwen also makes it relevant for her wider audience of comics/superhero fans as well as her classmates and instructor.

### Rhetorical appeals

Gwen uses mainly pathos in this piece, both in her list (e.g., "Secrets hurt" and "You're not alone") and by choosing festive images of kissing couples.

### Modes & media

This piece can be used as a physical flyer or shared on digital media (in which case it can include links to the GSA, for example).

## Guided Reading:
A Multigenre Project ▼

### Dawson Swan (Student)

## *The Threat of Nature Deficit Disorder*

**What are the parts? How do they work together?**

In his multigenre project, Dawson Swan works with a variety of genres and media, as the image below shows. *(Project reprinted by permission of Dawson Swan.)*

▲ STUDENT AUTHOR PHOTO **Dawson Swan.**

**MULTIGENRE PIECES**

**Dawson's project consists of:**
A persuasive **poster** (staked into a chunk of real dirt and grass, complete with a dandelion).

**What is the author/artist, Dawson Swan, doing?**

**DAWSON'S RHETORICAL SITUATION**

**Purpose**
Dawson's overall purpose is to persuade his audience that nature deficit disorder is real and that it should be taken seriously by parents, educators, and doctors.

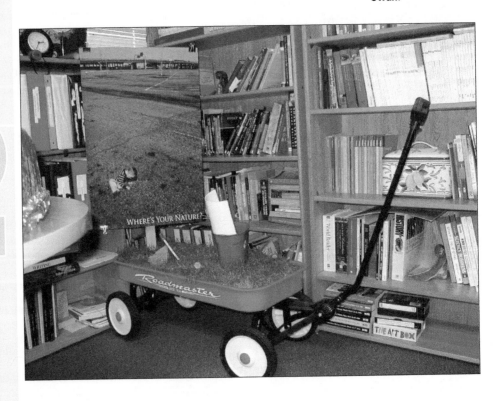

## MULTIGENRE PIECES

A **compilation CD**, leaning against a rock, of songs about nature, accompanied by liner notes that identify each song and the message it sends about nature.

A research-based **magazine article**, rolled up and "planted" in a green flowerpot.

**To unify his project, Dawson provides:**

An **Introduction** that prepares his audience to experience his project and serves as his Author's/Artist's Statement. In it, he explains his research and rhetorical choices and evaluates his project (item 1).

**Packaging** consisting of a Roadmaster wagon, which represents childhood play and nature.

## DAWSON'S RHETORICAL SITUATION

### Audience

Dawson's primary audience is educated adults; his choice for packaging the components reflects his view that exposure to nature is important for all children.

### Rhetorical appeals

Dawson's choice of the poster with a small child, the music CD, and the wagon used as packaging indicate that appeals to pathos are most important to him.

### Modes & media

Dawson's project includes print (the magazine article), audio (the CD), and visual pieces (the poster, the artwork with the CD, and the packaging).

### Multigenre conventions

There are no conventions for multigenre projects. However, there are conventions for individual genres. See Chapters 1–4 for examples.

Dawson Swan, *The Threat of Nature Deficit Disorder*

Let's take a closer look at Dawson's Introduction to his multigenre project.

What makes this an **Introduction** to a multigenre project?

### THE GENRE'S CONVENTIONS

#### Elements of the genre

Dawson begins by acknowledging that many people will initially view his topic as a joke; this helps him build rapport with his readers. He gives an overview of the different pieces in the project and prepares readers for what to expect.

#### Style

Dawson writes in a formal tone, which develops his ethos as someone who takes this issue seriously.

#### Design

The design of Dawson's Introduction is minimal; he formats his Introduction into paragraphs for easy reading.

Print Layout View    Sec  1                              100%

**Dawson Swan**

**Introduction**

**The Threat of Nature Deficit Disorder**

"Things are not like they used to be." I've heard this said many times in reference to technology, nature, parenting, music, and the world in general. That phrase will always be true because change is inevitable, but there is one change that is occurring unnoticed today that I believe requires our urgent attention. This change has resulted in a condition that has recently been identified as nature deficit disorder (NDD). Richard Louv introduced this condition in his book *Last Child in the Woods: Saving Our Children from Nature-Deficit Disorder*. Most people have never heard of this "disease," and when they do hear about it, their initial reaction is that it is a joke, just a clever play on words. Unfortunately NDD and the misery it causes are very real (pp. 22-24).

In today's society, it seems we no longer have time to relax, to take a walk outside and smell the roses. Instead, we are bombarded by tight schedules, economic pressures, and chronic stress. The former secretary of education Richard Riley was quoted as saying, "The top ten jobs that will be in demand in 2010 didn't exist in 2004. Students are being prepared for jobs that don't exist, using technologies that haven't been invented, to solve problems that we don't know about yet" (qtd. in Fisch). This shows how incredibly overwhelming it can be to simply live in our culture and to plan for the future, let alone find time to be outside.

Due to continually advancing technology, globalization is becoming a reality. The quantity of data created every day is increasing exponentially. Toddlers are learning to use technology scientists wouldn't have dreamed of thirty years ago. As a result, it is becoming vitally important to train our children about technology. Fortunately the young generations are easily able to learn to use technology, but there is always much more to be learned as technology continues to advance. The increasing need for technological "geeks" is drawing more and more of us into cyberspace and shoving nature off into a corner.

Ironically, going "green" is becoming increasingly popular. Our culture is reveling in new ways to better the environment and preserve nature, but it is seriously missing the point because the culture, particularly pop culture, has little firsthand knowledge of nature. We would rather stay inside and watch the hit TV show *Planet Earth* on our massive high-definition TVs than take a walk outside. Instead of climbing a mountain or sitting on our porch watching the sunset, we would rather sit in front of a computer monitor and look at beautiful photographs of exotic places. This misguided relationship with nature has created a synthetic

What is the author/artist, **Dawson Swan**, doing?

### DAWSON'S RHETORICAL SITUATION

#### Purpose

Dawson introduces his topic and argues for its importance.

#### Audience

The audience for this piece is people who don't understand the gravity of nature deficit disorder, so Dawson takes a serious tone.

#### Rhetorical appeals

Dawson appeals to logos when he explains his genre choices and the order in which he wants them viewed/ read and why.

**Swan,** *Nature Deficit Disorder,* Continued

THE GENRE'S
CONVENTIONS

**Sources**

Dawson incorpo-
rates three outside
sources: two books
and a video that
went viral in 2007
about how the
world is changing.
He uses the MLA
style of documenta-
tion, which requires
parenthetical in-text
citations that are, in
turn, included in a
Works Cited list on
page 518. (See also
MLA coverage in
Chapter 7.)

environment and a secondhand relationship with the earth—an
environment that is convenient and controlled. While those who
have generated this environment are supposedly pursuing the
natural, they have only created a vague reflection of the real
thing. Our culture is sadly lacking in an understanding of the true
meaning of "natural."

Now you may ask, "Why should I care? I get enough nature
from the Discovery Channel and an occasional ski trip." Well,
look at it this way. The generation that is currently approaching,
or is already in, the child-rearing stage is the largest generation
ever (Tapscott 20). The men and women of this generation are
going to begin having children, and the decisions they make
about how they raise their children will have a monumental
impact on the future.

The logical next question you may ask is, "Is NDD a real
threat?" Yes it is, and its effects can be devastating: obesity,
ADD, emotional disorders, high blood pressure, and chronic pain
that kids develop decades before they should. These conditions
have always been there, but now they are disturbingly prevalent.

This project serves a couple of purposes: First, I want to inform
people of NDD, and if they already know about it, I want to
increase their knowledge and alert them to how urgent it is to take
action. Second, I hope that this project gives inspiration to fight
NDD. It can be as easy as walking outside, looking up at the stars,
or smelling the fragrance of a wildflower in the night air.

I planned each part of the project to fit into a different category
of media so I could communicate to more people. My first piece
is a poster that can be displayed nearly anywhere, and it quickly
draws people in—far more than an essay or a brochure can. A
poster evokes emotion and thoughts of childhoods spent playing
outside. This sets them up for my second piece.

The second and third pieces actually merge into a CD album,
which can reach people on multiple levels. The artwork for the
album is made up of photographs I have taken of nature during
the last couple of years. These pictures grab the attention of the
viewer and create a relaxing and thought-provoking environment
for them to take part in as they experience the second half of
the album—the music and lyrics (I searched through hundreds
of songs to find specific songs about nature). I wrote an
Introduction to the album that describes the purpose of each
piece and its message.

My fourth piece is a magazine article. It could appear in
parenting magazines because my primary audience is people

DAWSON'S
RHETORICAL
SITUATION

**Modes & media**

The mode and me-
dium were dictated
by the assignment,
which specified that
the Introduction be
a print-based essay.
Dawson felt that
visuals did not need
to be part of the
Introduction because
the project itself was
so eye-catching. So
he used text exclu-
sively to explain his
decisions.

*Continues next page*

Dawson Swan, *The Threat of Nature Deficit Disorder*

**Swan,** *Nature Deficit Disorder,* Continued

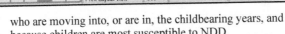

who are moving into, or are in, the childbearing years, and because children are most susceptible to NDD.

I have concluded that these pieces fit together best in a conference setting where the poster in a booth would initially draw people. Then they would see the CD. It could be considered a fund-raiser for my topic or maybe just a sampler. After leafing through the pages of artwork and listening to the music, people would want to know what it's all about, and they could read the magazine article. The article brings everything home and explains NDD in depth. Between these four pieces, a variety of media are used to grab people's attention, engaging both their minds and hearts. NDD is a compelling subject that affects everyone. Although a presentation of the simple facts of NDD would be enough to win people over, the potential of engaging them emotionally just as nature herself does, is fulfilled through photographs, poetry, and music.

Works Cited

Fisch, Karl. "Did You Know 2.0?" *YouTube*, www.youtube.com/watch?v=pMcfrLYDm2U&feature=related. Accessed 13 Oct. 2012.

Louv, Richard. *Last Child in the Woods: Saving Our Children from Nature-Deficit Disorder.* Algonquin, 2005, pp. 22-24.

Tapscott, Don. *Growing Up Digital: The Rise of the Net Generation.* McGraw-Hill, 1998, p. 20.

Who does Dawson seem to be writing his Introduction to? How can you tell? How would you describe the voice he uses? How well does he prepare you for experiencing his project?

# Index of Genres

---

🖻 For e-Pages content, visit **bedfordstmartins.com/bookofgenres.**

# Index of Themes

For e-Pages content, visit **bedfordstmartins.com/bookofgenres**.

🄴 For e-Pages content, visit **bedfordstmartins.com/bookofgenres**.

🖻 For e-Pages content, visit **bedfordstmartins.com/bookofgenres.**

🖥 For e-Pages content, visit **bedfordstmartins.com/bookofgenres**.

🖸 For e-Pages content, visit **bedfordstmartins.com/bookofgenres**.

🖻 For e-Pages content, visit **bedfordstmartins.com/bookofgenres.**

🖳 For e-Pages content, visit **bedfordstmartins.com/bookofgenres**.

## Journalism

## Literacy & Language

## Literature & Creative Nonfiction

🄴 For e-Pages content, visit **bedfordstmartins.com/bookofgenres**.

🖸 For e-Pages content, visit **bedfordstmartins.com/bookofgenres.**

▣ For e-Pages content, visit **bedfordstmartins.com/bookofgenres.**

🄴 For e-Pages content, visit **bedfordstmartins.com/bookofgenres**.

# Index

🖾 For e-Pages content, visit **bedfordstmartins.com/bookofgenres.**

🖥 For e-Pages content, visit **bedfordstmartins.com/bookofgenres.**

🖿 For e-Pages content, visit **bedfordstmartins.com/bookofgenres.**

[e] For e-Pages content, visit **bedfordstmartins.com/bookofgenres**.

[e] For e-Pages content, visit **bedfordstmartins.com/bookofgenres**.

🖥 For e-Pages content, visit **bedfordstmartins.com/bookofgenres.**

🖻 For e-Pages content, visit **bedfordstmartins.com/bookofgenres**.

🔲 For e-Pages content, visit **bedfordstmartins.com/bookofgenres.**

🖥 For e-Pages content, visit **bedfordstmartins.com/bookofgenres**.

🖳 For e-Pages content, visit **bedfordstmartins.com/bookofgenres.**

🅔 For e-Pages content, visit **bedfordstmartins.com/bookofgenres**.

🖳 For e-Pages content, visit **bedfordstmartins.com/bookofgenres.**

🖳 For e-Pages content, visit **bedfordstmartins.com/bookofgenres.**

For e-Pages content, visit **bedfordstmartins.com/bookofgenres.**

**Missing something?** To access the online material that accompanies this text, visit **bedfordstmartins.com/bookofgenres**. Students who do not buy a new book can purchase access at this site.

# Inside the Bedford Integrated Media for *The Bedford Book of Genres*

## Guided Readings

These texts, annotated by the authors of this book, highlight the rhetorical situations and genre-related choices that composers make. Each is introduced with guidelines for analysis and followed by questions and checklists for drafting.

**FAIRY TALE** Charles Perrault, *Little Red Riding Hood*

**SHORT STORY** Annie Proulx, *55 Miles to the Gas Pump*

**DRAMATIC FILM** George A. Romero & John A. Russo, *From Night of the Living Dead*

**MAP** Chris Peterson, *BurgerMap: Alaska, Kriner's Diner*

**DOCUMENTARY FILM** Doug Pray, *From Scratch*

**BUSINESS MEMO** Ellen Thibault, *Video Project*

**PRESENTATION** Sunni Brown, *The Doodle Revolution*

**PERSONAL STATEMENT** "Stay-at-Home Dad"/TopLawSchools .com, *Personal Statement for Penn Law School*

**COVER LETTER & RESUME** Julia Nollen, *Application for Marketing Assistant Job*

**FILM REVIEW** Roger Ebert, *Ratatouille: Waiter, There's a Rat in My Soup*

## Thematic Readings

These texts highlight the relationships between themes and genres, and serve as sources and models for student work.

### American Identity

**EDITORIAL** Matthew Yglesias, *The Myth of Majority-Minority America*

**SOCIAL HISTORY** Ted Merwin, *What Makes the Jewish Deli Quintessentially American*

**POSTER/AD CAMPAIGN** Homeless Coalition of Hillsborough County, *Not Who You Expected? Shameya, Age 18; Jeff, Age 44*

### Subculture Identity

**WIKI ENTRY/INSTRUCTIONS** eHow, *How to Become a Geek*

**INTERVIEW** Deborah Solomon, *Patti Smith: She Is a Punk Rocker*

### Bodies 101

**POEM** Walt Whitman, *From "I Sing the Body Electric"*

**INSTRUCTIONS** American Heart Association & University of Washington School of Medicine, *Cardiopulmonary Resuscitation (CPR)*

**MEDICAL HISTORY** Dr. John G. Sotos, *The Health and Medical History of President Ronald Reagan*

### Cigarettes, Drugs, & Alcohol

**SPOOF AD** *Adbusters* Magazine, *Joe Chemo*

**PORTFOLIO OF ADS** Stanford School of Medicine (curators), *Vintage Cigarette Ads*

**MAP & CHART** John Hoffman & Susan Froemke, *Addiction Is a National Concern; Drugs and Alcohol at a Glance*

### Pollution & Activism

**ARTICLE** Leyla Kokmen, *Environmental Justice for All*

**SPEECH** Barack Obama, *The BP Oil Spill*

**COMPLAINT LETTER** Credo Action, *Tell the Bureau of Land Management: Ban Fracking on Federal Lands*

### Plastics, Recycling, & Wildlife

**OBJECT/AD** Surfrider Foundation, *Catch of the Day: Plastic Surprise*

**AD** Oceana, *Love Flipper and His Friends?*

**BROCHURE** Casella Resource Solutions, *Zero-Sort: How Recycling Gets Done*

**COMIC & PIE CHART** Environmental Protection Agency, *From Adventures of the Garbage Gremlin; Municipal Solid Waste Chart*

### Mythical Heroes

**SLIDE PRESENTATION** Bryan M. Davis, *Archetypes and the Hero's Journey*

**MAP** Prestwick House Maps, *The Journey of Odysseus*

**INTERVIEW** Joseph Campbell, *The Hero's Adventure*

**ARGUMENT/BLOG POST** Lex at *FANgirl*, *The Heroine's Journey: How Campbell's Model Doesn't Fit*

### Killers: Serial & Accused

**RESEARCHED REPORT** Federal Bureau of Investigation, *Common Myths and Misconceptions Regarding Serial Murder*

**ARGUMENT** David Von Drehle, *It's All about Him*

**MURDER INDICTMENT** Commonwealth of Massachusetts, *Lizzie Borden*